DEMOCRATIC GOVERNANCE

A NEW PARADIGM FOR DEVELOPMENT?

NOTICE TO THE READER

The analyses and conclusions offered in this book are the responsibility of their authors alone. They do not collectively commit the authors. They do not necessarily reflect the views held by the French Ministry for Foreign and European Affairs (MFEA).

Ministry of Foreign and European Affairs

Democratic Governance

A New Paradigm for Development?

Séverine Bellina, Hervé Magro and Violaine de Villemeur
(Eds)

Translated by Katy Albiston, Anna Harrison, Julie de Rouville,
Trista Selous, Eugénie Stephenson, Christine Tipper, Alison Tippetts,
David Vaughn, Nicky Wallace under the managment
of Françoise Pinteaux-Jones for Allied Translators.

HURST & COMPANY, LONDON

First published in the United Kingdom by
C. Hurst & Co. (Publishers) Ltd.,
41 Great Russell Street, London WC1B 3PL
© Editions Karthala, 2009
All rights reserved.
Printed in India

A catalogue data record for this volume is available
from the British Library.

ISBNs

978-1-84904-018-1 *casebound*
978-1-84904-019-8 *paperback*

www.hurstpub.co.uk

This book is published in collaboration with
the French Ministry of Foreign and European Affairs.

CONTENTS

6 CONTENTS

III
RULE OF LAW, DEMOCRACY AND HUMAN RIGHTS:
THE CORNERSTONES OF DEMOCRATIC GOVERNANCE

IV
GOVERNANCE AND TERRITORIES

V
DEVELOPMENT POLICIES
AND DEMOCRATIC GOVERNANCE

VI
WHICH DEVELOPMENT COOPERATION TOOLS
FOR DEMOCRATIC GOVERNANCE?

Acknowledgements

« On ne ramasse pas une pierre avec un seul doigt. »
Proverbe malien.

"You don't pick up a stone with just one finger"
Malian Proverb

This book is a collective work. We wish to express our gratitude to the authors without whose commitment this project could not have come into being. We thank them for their trust, for the quality of the exchanges we had with them and for the quality of their contribution. We also owe thanks and acknowledgements to our colleagues at the Democratic Governance Unit for their support, careful proofreading and observations. Our special thanks go to Élisabeth Dau for her dedicated support.

Foreword

This book aims to enrich the debate on governance and its impact on our way of thinking and acting. It concerns all those interested in the issue of governance, and more broadly, all those who wish to contribute to sustainable human development in all its dimensions: economic, social, political and cultural.

It also concerns those interested in the legitimacy, efficiency and role of institutions; in how they are representative and in their interaction with society; and it concerns those interested in public policy design and implementation aimed at conflict prevention. And finally, it concerns all those interested in the efficiency and the consequences of their own actions.

Late in 2006, following a review of development policies initiated by the French Ministry of Foreign and European Affairs and its partners, France adopted a democratic governance strategy. This approach converges with the "Governance in the European Consensus on Development. Towards a harmonised approach within the European Union", also adopted in 2006. These documents represent a major shift in the recent evolution of the governance debate.

In order to deepen and to continue this reflection, this book proposes a debate that avoids "one size fits all" solutions and is based on the following questions:

- How do we assess the impact of governance on development? To what extent does the democratic governance approach go beyond the managerial model? Can we reconcile governance with democracy models imposed from outside?
- How can multilevel governance be achieved?
- What are the functional tools of democratic governance? Is democratic governance compatible with the conditions of aid? Should we bypass the so-called failed states, thus making them weaker?

This book brings together multiple points of view. We must thank all the authors who agreed to take part in this publication, and have thereby contributed to this interdisciplinary and intercultural dialogue.

Violaine DE VILLEMEUR,
Head of the Democratic Governance Unit
Ministry of Foreign and European Affairs

Introduction

Séverine BELLINA
(Translated from the French)

For the past two decades governance has, in general terms, become one of the most commonly used terms in the field of international relations and more specifically in that of cooperation and development. For many specialists, it has even entered the category of "mots-valises", buzzwords, dogma, etc. that dominate the debates and drive the actions in the field of development. While some analyses remind us that a term can lose in significance what it gains in propagation, it turns out that the possible and varied uses of such words are what enriches them (Sauquet and Vielajus, 2008) and, practically speaking, are as important as the fluid and diverse meanings they represent. Steering a course between the world of experts and that of academics, between conveying innovative analyses and simply chiming in the liberal "idiom", governance remains a notion that has multiple definitions, an unfinished concept (Hermet and Kazancigil, 2005). It has nonetheless become an inescapable paradigm for the politics of development, and as is highlighted in this document (notably by J.M. Severino and Olivier Ray, M. Delmas-Marty, H. Salama), a vehicle towards framing a new international law.

There is therefore no reason why the diversity of disciplinary and cultural outlooks should not be at the heart of a debate that is so central to the world of development and to the international community. The Ministry of Foreign and European Affairs has therefore chosen to adopt towards governance, a formula the French Agency for Development had used in 2007 in order to explore the notion of fragile States and organizations[1]. Taking the form of multi-actor analytical exchanges, it

---

1. J.M. Châtaigner et H. Magro (dir.), États et sociétés fragiles. Entre conflits, reconstruction et développement, Paris, Karthala, 2007.

promoted the addition of francophone and French perspectives to an international debate in which a great deal of Anglo-Saxon literature abounds. The objective was to propose an original vision, capable if necessary to go beyond conventional or generally developed terminology and issues in the realm of development and international arenas. From these cross perspectives emerged, along with other considerations, a contribution to "a fecund questioning of the concept itself by broadening the issue of fragility beyond that of the State, to organisations and actors", freeing the analysis from "its stigmatising connotation" (M. Diallo, 2008).

This work pursues and enlarges on this attempt towards the development of a debate and a questioning of the concept of governance through multi-actor, interdisciplinary and intercultural dialogue, in order to, it is hoped, diversify and enrich the current thinking on this issue.

Let us immediately state that such an endeavour is not an easy task – first of all because of a very specific French and francophone context. For many French-speaking actors, it is apparently averred that governance is an Anglo-Saxon notion that has emerged from the world of enterprise (corporate governance). In consequence, it is not without some mistrust, if not outright resistance, that this concept of governance has been received.

There is also the international context. For, while the response of francophone actors pointed to an unconscious cultural position, it also represented, perhaps predominantly for some, an unease regarding the notion of good governance. In this dogmatic incarnation it promptly gets implemented as a tool for institutional reform aimed at making globalisation more efficient. This understanding has, more often than not, remained anchored in the collective imaginary, and today the use of the concept of governance is still regularly assimilated in people's minds to this particular acception, channelling the debate around just a few themes (transparency, fight against corruption, etc.). Fortunately, here again, for the past few years, this thinking has evolved and a more open debate regarding governance has begun.

A concept in need of clarification

However this debate has not, so far, led to much clarification of confusions engendered by the specificity of each term, each approach, or each actor. As a result, a vagueness envelopes a notion most often considered as a "catch all", and which even specialists find unwieldy, whereas a strong innovative tendency is emerging that questions not only governance in aid recipient countries, but also the governance of this aid itself. Moreover, far beyond development, these are challenges common to humanity as a whole that are now put into perspective by governance: local realities/universality, economic growth/social equity, etc. And, as governance questions power and the relations between the states and their societies, an intercultural dialogue is emerging (notably between French and English speakers) leading to exchange and even a rare convergence on the role of the State and that of societies in the institutionalisation of power.

One of the initial obstacles to be dealt with is the diversity of vocabularies which is used by a multiplicity of actors. We note an undifferentiated usage of terms with definitions that are nonetheless very specific and cover different issues: development, economic development, sustainable development, sustainable human development; governance, good governance, democratic governance and democracy, etc. Even the most renowned experts cannot always avoid this stumbling block, not least international instances in which one might assume that the definition of commonly used terms would be the object of a precise consensus.

The origin and history of the word governance give a first example of these differences. They are rarely presented in the same way, and vary according to the actor, each emphasising one or other aspect of its history. Certainly the time in which the genesis of governance was systematically reduced to the private sector and corporate governance has passed. And, however you look at it, the ancient origin of the concept of governance is now underlined. While it is possible to trace the term back to the verb kubeirn, used by Plato in "The Republic", which refers to the notion of piloting a ship, the term may have first appeared in France in the twelfth century, and referred to the running of bailiwicks. However, generally, it is as a synonym of the word government that its more or less distant origin is established. In this sense, we also find the term, in the thirteenth century, in English, in Spanish and in Portuguese. In the French language, it was later to become a term of law (in 1478), to be used in the larger sense, "the charge of governance" (1679). The term made its comeback in contemporary terminology with the English word governance, taking on the meaning of management.

In fact, it is this latter reference that often remains, subconsciously, assimilated to the origin of the notion of governance. Moreover, this particular acception of the term corporate governance, as early as the nineteen thirties, remained for a very long time presented as the very origin of the term. This narrow interpretation was ferried by functionalist and utilitarian Anglo-American trends of thought. It was essentially developed by enterprise experts and financial and political organisations, and legitimised by some elements of academic research. It instilled a normative dimension to the notion of governance that was henceforth disseminated as an instrument of institutional reform aimed at efficiency within a pragmatic and technocratic conception of social relations. From the local (notably urban in the seventies) to the global (with the Commission on Global Governance in 1995 and the notion of multi-level governance at the European level), governance emerged in international language as a dominant expression, and soon after as a doctrine: good governance (in French bonne gouvernance).

Thus governance was firstly developed as a means of reforming institutions with a view to efficiency in developing countries. This tendency is very much influenced by international organisations, which, as of the nineteen nineties, under the influence of the Bretton Woods Institutions, quickly joined by other cooperation actors, got "good governance" built up as dogma in their development policies. Very soon after that, it became a condition of their efficiency and justified the transposition to the administrative sector of management methods borrowed from the private sector. It had become a real method for the treatment of social, economic and political problems and for State reforms, aimed at creating favourable conditions for market mechanisms.

Policies emerging as part of the "Washington consensus" included a public management system distinct from the State-controlled system, lead to a reduction in the role of the State in modernisation and development (the crisis of the welfare state in OECD countries and the end of the modernising State in developing countries) and were a vehicle for structural adjustment plan policies. From the second part of the 1990's, these policies were showing their limitations, notably in terms of efficiency, of impact in the fight against poverty, of ownership and essentially of social implications. A re-thinking of aid efficiency was then undertaken, rehabilitating public action.

This evolution made it possible to consider the institutional and political aspects of development. For development partners, it translated, as early as 1997, in the publication of the World Bank report The State in a Changing World; the importance of the State in governance and development, was thus affirmed. It was comforted by the New-Institutional Economics trend (D. North). Political economy since then has taken a growing place in the analyses and the elaboration of development policies. The role of institutions in general, be they formal or informal, and of the State in particular, in the production of growth and economic development, had been rehabilitated. The questioning has thus shifted toward factors that generate trust between actors and that allow the reduction of uncertainty in economic, social and political relations.

For development cooperation, the response was to be found in the operational machinery, or tool kit, copied from existing institutions in developed countries. This machinery would be "good governance":

respect for individual rights, secure contracts, efficient administrations, and democratic political institutions. This "good governance" is presented as a universal solution designed to generate the confidence necessary to economic growth. Formulated as a series of technical measures, if appropriated by developing countries, this tool brings forth their economic development. With this perspective in mind, the characteristics attributed to "good governance" are those of efficiency (budgetary rigor, market orientated policies, the rolling back of the State and privatisation) and of democracy (transparency, equity, justice, promotion of the rule of law, civil and socio-economic rights and decentralisation). The fight against corruption constitutes the central focus of "good governance". Based on this initial conception, "good governance" implies: the rule of law; good administration; the responsibility of government; openness; the participation of non-governmental actors, notably private enterprise and civil society.

This "good governance" approach has kept evolving in order better to take the historical and political contexts into consideration. The consequences of a weak – or indeed non-existent – ownership of the development programs, including "good governance", have in this way been exposed. As a result, the importance, not only of the content of economic policies but also of the manner in which they are elaborated and implemented and therefore of participative processes was recognised at international level among development practitioners. In this context, a consensus has emerged, within the donor community, on the core governance principles.

This resulted in repeated commitment by the international community in favour of governance (Millennium Summit and Millennium Declaration – 2000, Monterrey Conference – 2002, NEPAD, G 8 Meeting in Kananaskis – 2002, etc.). Little by little, the connection between "good governance" and the fight against poverty was reaffirmed and aid governance was questioned. It was assumed that the respect of principles common to development inducing governance would prevent abuses in the exercise of public power, limit public authorities' arbitrariness and create stable conditions conducive to economic development and the well-being of citizens. The objective was to reinforce the capabilities of governments and administrations to observe and put into place the principles that would advance the adhesion and participation of all actors in the policies concerning them. As reiterated in the framework of the Paris Declaration in March 2005 on aid effectiveness, ownership, alignment and harmonisation, constitute the three prerequisite principles to improving the efficiency of aid.

A debate in progress

The last few years have seen the multiplication of governance strategies meant to be innovative. France thus adopted in 2006 a specific strategy intended to feed its cooperation policies[2]. Most of its European partners have followed suit. However, it is the adoption of "Governance in the European consensus on Development – Toward a harmonised approach within the European Union" in 2006[3] that constitutes a fundamental step in the debate on governance, and more particularly in exceeding the managerial approach; the integrated approach, the political dimension and the different levels of governance (from local to global) are henceforth included in governance projects. Dialogue, context driven pragmatism and local capacities development have replaced the promotion of a uniform model. The normative and prescriptive dimensions of governance are balanced by the rediscovery of its analytical strength. It emerges as an approach allowing a better understanding of the legitimate exercise of power in a given society and therefore the elaboration by societies themselves of their own governance modalities, according to the challenges they must face within the framework of international agreements. For development policies, this translates into a reversal of perspective, at least in theory; the logic of needs replaces that of supply. Semantics change: the notion of partnerships, dialogue, legitimacy, process and long-term appear more systematically in governance discourse and programs. "Good governance" is rethought in the framework of democratic governance. Initially conveyed by the United Nations Development Program (UNDP) since 1997, it is now enriched and has become a new frame of reference for development policies. This demonstrates less a duality between "good governance" and democratic governance than the evolution of the field towards a greater integration and disciplinary openness, based on acquisitions and lessons learned through experience.

The reestablishment of the political aspect of governance de facto summons its analytical aspect, hence the applicability of the conceptual and disciplinary tools beyond the economic field. But this evolution, stimulating though it be, must now translate into the practices of development, and this is far from being the case. Moreover, whether practitioners or academics (some even speak of distance), many feel today the need to clarify the field of governance, and possibly to rethink it

---

2. Governance strategy for French cooperation, also available in English and Spanish, Dec.2006. http://www.diplomatie.gouv.fr/fr/actions-france_830/gouvernance_1053/index.html.
3. COM (2006) 421 final.
http://eur-lex.europa.eu/LexUriServ/LexUriServ.do?uri=COM:2006:0421:FIN:EN:PDF

altogether. Governance, according to them, is at a "crossroads" (J. Bossuyt, 2008). They advise rethinking the dominant practices that have been developed around governance for the past two decades (A. Olukoshi, 2008) and to devise a new generation of governance projects (M. Fogaça de Medeiros, F. Ngaruko and S. Sacko, 2008). However, the literature, whether scientific or institutional, does not seem yet to provide a diversity of views allowing us to exit prevalent thinking on the subject, nor even to help us understand and translate current dynamics into public policies.

A thought in the making

It therefore seemed important to try to involve numerous actors in order to allow an outline of the diversity of this debate to emerge. The number and the quality of respondents to our call are a testament to the interest this theme represents in the debate on development. We obviously leave it to readers to draw their conclusions from the various articles included in this collective publication. However, it is interesting to note that while its authors were solicited on the basis of the overall problematics, the plan continued to evolve until the last minute. Moreover, beyond the wealth of ideas, what has emerged, beyond our expectations, are very strong transversal axes. These axes do not only concern the governance of the Other, meaning countries receiving aid, but also worldwide governance. They are valid on all continents. Resulting from the analysis of the lessons drawn from the first generation of development policies in the field of governance, and even more of the hard facts in their diversity and complexity, they brought out the following driving ideas:[4]

1. The necessity to go beyond a technicist approach – and prescriptive and dogmatic utilisations – of governance and its evaluation, has been confirmed. Almost all the articles in the present work refer to it. Some of them assert it more directly, such as A. Olukoshi's article, which invites us to "the abandon of the notion of governance as it is so frequently used – the a-historical, all-purpose and unidimensional view", translated into technical terms, or M. Sauquet and M. Vielajus, who suggest "a distancing from governance as a simple institutional toolkit, copied from Western

---

4. These driving ideas are presented here with references to articles (by author) bearing the most directly upon the concerned themes. To qualify as driving concepts, the theme blocs have been identified on grounds of recurrence, indeed their surfeit, in a number of articles in this work.

democratic models". C. Oman and C. Arndt notably remind us of the limits of quantitative logic in the elaboration of governance indicators.

2. The economic prism does not allow for a full grasp of all the aspects and implications of governance. J. Rojas Elgueta and P. Calame show that, from Latin America to Asia, economic growth and development are no doubt fundamental but not sufficient: the question of legitimate democratic governance is at the heart of the debate. C. Santiso points to the importance of the analysis of power and political legitimacy when it comes to financial governance. So it behoves to take into account all aspects of governance (political, economic, social, cultural, etc.) covering, according to Ph. Darmuzey, "all the activities of a society" and he adds: "The notion of 'democratic governance' clearly expresses the dynamic and evolutionary, multidimensional and political character of governance".

3. It is now generally accepted that analyses need to include the political dimension of governance. For, as N. Meisel and J. Ould Aoudia assert, "development processes, particularly governance reforms, pertain to mechanisms that are inherently political and endogenous to societies" for they belong to the political realm. Accordingly, D. Darbon shows that the political analysis of the interface between the State, power and societies supplements a purely managerial analysis. The embededdeness of State and society is the principle of power legitimacy. This is indeed what is at stake in the legality-legitimacy dialectic, whose exclusively Western content is being called into question (S. Mappa). Indeed, governance emerges as a method of analysis and comprehension of the exercise of power, of collective action and of the management of conflicts inherent to all societies. Governance reflects the decisional process within all social groupings (the State, business, collectivities, associations, the family unit, etc.) and at all levels (from local to global). Political decision calls on the intervention of multiple actors, with diverse kinds of legitimacy, alongside the State. Collective action is founded in shared objectives. Conflict management is supported by the opposing parties' agreement on procedural rules to preside over political contests.

4. Governance and democracy must not be confused, as A. Olukoshi reminds us, even if the ideal form of governance is democratic in content. Indeed, governance questions legitimacy beyond elections and the notion of representation. "Democratic" governance therefore does not refer to the institutional finality of governance but underlines its nature as a process of association to decision-making (J. Elgueta Rojas) springing from a legitimate State (J.M. Chataîgner). Democratic governance must be legitimate, insist H. Pereira Rosa and O. Sy. Institutions are rooted in the

social fabric, as demonstrated by S. Rumin, S. Bellina and H. Magro.

5. From this standpoint, "institutional development", the mainstay of numerous policies and projects for development, also aims, beyond technology, to reinforce the sociological anchorage of institutions and the institutionalisation of power, so that institutional engineering can become the driver of political pluralism, which embodies social plurality (M. Leclerc-Olive). The reinforcement of institutional and human capabilities is therefore at the heart of governance policies. The object is to reinforce local capabilities and define programs for the reinforcement of institutional capacities, based on the specific political context and historical background involved (A. Kokeniya, C. Garrity and S. Pradhan). The fact is that democratic governance "does not create results, it paves the way" (J.M. Chataîgner) – and this, via the creation of space for interactions between the actors (among which the public institution).

6. The necessity for multi-actor or inter-actor dynamics, within the framework of spaces of dialogue based on networks as well as on the capitalisation of knowledge and experiences, is developed at length. Such frameworks permit to devise negotiated public policies, to operate from the local to the global, to institutionalise power through the definition of collective projects and of general interest. This is a major axis in the implementation of governance in sectoral policies and public/private partnership approaches (J. Elgueta Rojas) in terms of effective delivery of public service or fair delivery of basic services. This requires of the State that, central and decentralised, it be the guarantor of the general interest, establishing the articulations and reciprocal responsibilities of the actors in the framework of national policies (P. Victoria). It is also the entire logic that presides over the new dynamics of governance (G. Houngbo; M.A. Savané; J.P. Vidon; O. Loubière and M. Roy, P. Laye).

7. Concerns over the legitimacy and efficacy of power, in the context of globalisation and participative public action, lead to privileging a territorial approach of governance: seeking for a given problem, the most relevant regulatory space and adjusting the perimeter of public policies to the populations' progression and needs. The territory, C. Lopes reminds us, is the intersection of the local with the global. It is the "connection points for the distinct interests and the power struggles between political, economic and social actors belonging to multiple tiers".

8. Local governance, anchored in local territory, constitutes the privileged space for governance actors mobilization; it represents a life space, where citizenship is learned, and different interests and different legitimacy sources confronted, where numerous (notably informal)

economical and inter-ethnic dynamics cohabit. Public management decentralization, based on local democratic governance, facilitates the refoundation of the State through the emergence of "citizenship founded on a new social contract" (J.P. Elong Mbassi), through a redefinition of public action that favours new relationship models between public authorities and society (J. Fogaça de Medeiros).

9. It is within the interactions between the different levels of governance that each is reinforced. The double dynamics of local governance and regional integration affirmation is at the heart of the political refoundation of the State process (J.P. Elong Mbassi). These are also the issues concerning complementarity between local and national economic governance and integration in the worldwide economy studied by F. Yatta, or the question of urban governance in the context of globalisation exposed by C. Goldblum and A. Osmont.

10. Development cooperation should therefore carry out what J. Bossuyt rates a "Copernican revolution". The author pleads in favour of "a paradigm shift in the thinking on governance support". International development actors are affirmed as full-fledged political actors in recipient countries. Democratic governance directly questions, J.M. Chataîgner writes, "our approach to partnership and in fine the role that development institutions grant more or less generously to their country partners: co-financer, project manager, project owner, evaluator, beneficiary, client, forced consumer or even beggar".

11. Naturally, this approach reopens the debate on conditionality versus incentive, on dialogue versus sanctions. This questioning is particularly sensitive in the European Union's new approach, which clearly favours incentive politics (Ph. Darmuzey).

12. And finally, rethinking aid governance actually brings us to question "international collective action" for, as stated by J.M. Severino and O. Ray, "public development assistance solidifies the aspiration for better global governance". The definition of public good and rule of law at global level (M. Delmas-Marty) represents thus a major stake in improving global governance. While there are many obstacles, notably concerning the definition of public good, the dynamic of global public goods confirms that the challenges brought on by governance are common ones (environment, water, pandemics, democracy, security, etc.) and require appropriate global governance.

So that this publication turns out in the end as the weaving together of emerging thinking, with diverse voices covering different experiences and sensibilities but that end up converging, even though it might seem presumptuous to speak of an interdisciplinary and intercultural new trend of thought.

Of course, this publication has no pretension to being exhaustive and even less to the definition of absolute truths. It is less a descriptive approach (thus many "traditional" aspects of governance are not directly dealt with herein) than an analytical exercise, opening avenues of comprehension, considerations and propositions. "Is comprehension not the purpose itself?"(G. Pambou Tchivounda, 1982). This analysis is called to open, as concretely as possible, on practical applications in the field of governance, as well as on the elaboration, by the international community, of development policies and tools adapted to governance challenges, this being based on realities.

With this in mind, the publication is divided into six parts. The first gives an overview of governance issues on the various continents and of global governance. The next three parts focus on the identification, in a new light, the analysis and the articulation of democratic governance key axes (legitimacy, power, institutions, Rule of Law, Human Rights, democracy and territories). On the strength of the analysis of the stakes and key axes previously identified, the two final parts focus on proposing elements of discussion and concrete paths to rethinking development policies and the redeployment of development cooperation tools in a manner consistent with the new paradigm brought on by democratic governance.

***

The first part casts a critical eye on current governance issues and modes on each continent, raising questions regarding aid governance, whose impact on global governance is also analysed in the last article of this part. These cross perspectives bring out paths that will be explored further along in the work, in order to expand on the critical analysis of certain observations or else to develop proposals. It was particularly important to set the backdrop by restating the facts and the socio-cultural, historical, economic and political anchorage to each specific context. This part consists of five articles.

In the first, Henrique Pereira Rosa shares with us the reflections inspired by his experience as Head of State in Guinea-Bissau. He explains how the responsibilities of recipient country governments and those of donors are connected in order to construct efficient partnerships for human development. The author underlines the importance of legitimate democratic governance. It is not synonymous with formal democratisation. Yet, it is at this level that the support of donors intervenes, although the efficiency of the reform of governance cannot be reduced to governmental technocracy. It rests essentially on the reinforcement of citizenship. This is indeed what is at stake in the reinforcement of the State, notably in countries in crisis, where it remains the leading actor in governance reform, in citizenship reinforcement, as well as the efficient utilisation of international funding and of development. In the second article, Ousmane Sy reminds us of the specificities of the governance crisis in Africa in relation to that of the world, and emphasises the stakes of African governance: public administration (management) and its present variants. He shows that paths do exist, in relation to the decentralisation of public administration, towards the refoundation of the African State and more globally towards legitimate democratic governance adapted to the specificities of the societies concerned. It follows that the respect of universal principles of governance is less a question of applying a standard, pre-established model (such as the one suggested by cooperation agencies, notably for "good governance") than a response specific to each context. Pierre Calame, in a third article, posits that Asian governance, particularly in its Chinese form, calls into question, if need be, the normative governance model advocated by international institutions. Not only is Asian governance not a counter-example of this model, but, what is more, it constitutes an example never before seen of economic efficiency and development. However, the analysis of the Chinese example, using the five general principles of governance elaborated by the author leads to look, beyond the framework of economical development, to questions concerning sustainability and human development. Efficiency becomes relative and global governance, and the particular role of Europe, is brought to the fore. In the fifth article, Jaime Rojas Elgueta introduces us to the Latin American experience. Governance issues are crystallised around the social inequality that accompanies economic growth, making this region of the world a "real economic and social paradox". The inefficiency of development aid policies is underlined. Governance is at the heart of political action in the region, with as a cornerstone the participation of citizens, of the private sector (with a key role played by small and mid-size enterprises) and other actors. The importance of local and municipal governance, as well as the partnership with Europe, are stressed. Chiming in with these analyses, the article written by Jean-Michel Severino and Olivier Ray discusses the leading role of public development assistance, in the construction of a global public policy, enabling a response to the common stakes of global governance. Like a prism, the former shows us the possible fields of reinforced global governance, the "structural difficulties" of "collective international action" whose hard core resides in the common apprehension of the "common good". The question of how to define it and the difficulties encountered to that end prove clearly that the differences in perception and practice, here again, are concretely anchored in histories, socio-cultural practices, values and "political mythologies" that are different – indeed perhaps incompatible – between the Western nations on the one hand, and the remaining combined nations on the other.

These socio-cultural and historical anchorages of governance processes are what create its eminently political nature (in the generic sense) and forge the legitimacy of political power, which the second part of the work explores in order to emphasise the key underlying dimensions of democratic governance. In five articles focusing on the questions of legitimacy, power and institution, the authors assert that political power is not frozen or cut loose from its cultural and social soil, and State capacity (political regulation) even less so.

Michel Sauquet and Martin Vielajus open this part by showing that all the richness of the concept of governance resides in its approach, as a set of processes that allow the instauration of economic, social and political regulations truly suited to a society's realities. This perspective leads to a disengagement from normative and prescriptive frames of references. It presses for the reform of policies of development centred on the legitimacy and the deep-rootedness of power, the role of non-state actors and that of the local level and its dovetailing with other sectors of governance. To that end, it is the reality of political dynamics and structures of each society, including Western ones, that should be analysed. This is also the conclusion reached by Sophia Mappa, who invites us to consider, the time of this second article, the notions of legality and legitimacy; the author reminds us that they remain steeped in the theory and practice of European and Western political power. So, supposing these notions were reinstated at the heart of governance and the policies of development questioned through this prism wouldn't that, very coherently, lead us to outgrow the current frame of reference based upon Western values? State, power and society cannot be considered autonomously. Their non-imbededness is actually characteristic of the fragility of political power, of the State and of the societies that it is supposed to regulate. Dominique Darbon demonstrates, in a third article, that governance offers a reading of State, power and society relations/imbededness, which was originally managerial and has also become political. This helps understand reality and the complexities of social and political functioning. The author takes on this analysis with the notion of projected States and societies, in which the imbededness between political power and societies becomes the very principle of democratic governance and of the refounding/reconstruction of State and society. These practices of Nation Building, State Building and refounding of the State are precisely what Michèle Leclerc-Olive analyses in her article. She pleads in favour of policies for refounding the State on legitimacy and a strictly political basis. Institutional engineering then becomes the vector of political pluralism embodying social plurality and no longer that of technicist and instrumental views of democracy. Neither does it bend to the cultural refounding frame of reference with its risks of ethnic and religious fragmentation. Massaër Diallo, in the sixth and last article in this chapter, comes to similar conclusions on the role of democratic governance and the end of the crisis. The sustainability of this crisis exit, that must involve the prevention of its recurrence – if not its occurrence in the first place, requires us to always consider the existing correlations between history, sociology, and states' fragilities and conflicts. This must be taken into account, and enable a better contextualisation of the intervention and response to crises, notably in the prevailing multilateral framework, liable, the author points out, to yield other benefits.

Legitimate governance is therefore intimately bound in its cultural grounding and an appreciation of the historicity of societies on the one hand, and in the respect of common or universal principles such as Human Rights, democracy and the rule of law, on the other. These two vectors of governance legitimacy are not contradictory. Quite the reverse, they are part of a dialogical dynamic that must prevent any backsliding in terms of cultural relativism or universality as the instrument of a dominant culture. Democratic governance sets the diversity/universality dialectic in a perspective that goes beyond the simple technical or normative frames of reference attached to the modern international supra-State order.

The framework for this debate is set up by Adebayo Olukoshi, who calls for the abandonment of dominant prescriptive practices in the field of governance. For, he states, while the "ideal form" of governance is democratic, governance and democracy are nonetheless not synonymous. The legitimacy of power constitutes a precondition to democratic governance that cannot therefore be in any way reduced to a purely technocratic concept, but must, on the contrary, be rehabilitated as a permanent dynamic, integrating power relations and historical paths with what that implies of non-linearity and true grounding of democracy and legitimacy in the long term. In the second article of this part, Ibrahim Salama shows that the Human Rights/governance dialectic requires transcending syncretic tendencies and breaching some taboos. In fact, the integration of Human Rights in governance challenges international law and rests on the indivisibility and the universality of Human Rights. It notably leads to the fulfilment of a right to development and to "demystifying" the idea of cultural particularities in order to draw out all positive potential and not fall into relativism. It is also in reference to international law and global governance that Mireille Delmas-Marty analyses the relationship between governance and the rule of law. The growing affirmation of the concept of rule of law at national level unavoidably challenges the international level and the respect by international society of principles of law beyond inter and supra State laws. It is through a hybridization of governance methodology and the rule of law, that is to say, in the coordination of relations between the actors and the sub/ordination of powers, that the author proposes to create "the legal monster" intended to frame global governance. The last two articles of this part cast the axes of democracy, civil rights and rule of law under the light of financial governance. Carlos Santiso focuses on the importance at national level, of the role of parliaments and budgetary democracy that highlights, according to this author, one of the challenges of democratic governance in developing countries and emerging economies: The balance of power between the executive and the legislative. Hence, regarding budgetary matters, grasping the relationships between the prerogatives of government and parliamentary sovereignty warrants an analysis of power games as well as formal and informal arrangements. This opens new avenues in terms of institutional reform and the roles of parliaments towards reinforcing budgetary democracy. These reform axes also apply – this time at international level – to the management of public finance in greater transparency and democratic governance. This is what emerges from the analysis of the Extractive Industries Transparency Initiative (EITI), which Jean-Pierre Vidon, Olivier Loubière and Michel Roy present in the last article of this part. The EITI puts forward a multi-actors approach and an integrated process for fighting corruption. This is not only about fighting against the poor management of natural resources, but also about fending off this source of fragility and conflict relying on the consolidation of democratic governance.

The preceding chapters have led us from the local to the global, reminding us that governance, while profoundly anchored in territories, results from a permanent dovetailing between the two. The affirmation of democratic governance is corollary to that of the territorial dimension of governance. The fourth part focuses on this issue. Global governance, regional integration, local governance and territory(ies) of governance are indeed requisite as the strategic dimensions of governance.

The first article by Carlos Lopes presents all the stakes that hinge on local governance to enable countries to take on the challenge of development, of globalisation and to successfully fight against poverty. The territory is established as the space for the creation of solutions that are adapted to the complexity of mutations in a "glocalised" world around the "reinforcement of local capacities in favour of participative and multi-partners development initiatives, based on South-South networks of knowledge transfer". Jean-Pierre Elong Mbassi reminds us in his article that the legitimacy of the State in Africa is now part of a dual movement: that of decentralisation and of regional integration. While both are party to and part of refounding the State, difficulties remain, and fears about the risks of State fragmentation continue. And yet, the decentralisation of public management is giving more power to local authorities and non-State actors. Also, it advances the emergence of "citizenship based upon a new social contract", adapted to the societies' socio-political reality. In a third article, Mahaman Tidjani Alou analyses the territorial dimension of decentralisation and the implication of the redefinition of relations between the State and the local level. Two paths are suggested by the author: decentralisation as a policy of territorial production and as a dynamic of territorial construction; the former would address the role and the latter the formal structuring of the State. Speaking of the particular challenge of urban governance in the context of globalisation, Charles Goldblum and Annik Osmont explain in their article a difficult paradox; the integration of cities into the world economy is at times incompatible with participative local democracy. In a fifth article, François Yatta sets the parameters of local economic governance in Africa, as its necessary complementarity with national economic governance. Moreover, the author underlines the trends that allow these aspects to reinforce each other. It is an integrated approach of local governance based on participation and fairness that Jose Fogaça de Medeiros presents, through local solidarity governance programs. The object is to redefine public action at the local level around principles of plurality, dialogue and consensus, by privileging new relationship modes between public authorities and society. The Porto Alegre experience demonstrates that such dynamics are conducive to mutual trust between stakeholders. Participation rests on the existence of spaces for dialogue and on the possibility of exchanges between actors. For Pierre Laye, this is precisely what is at stake in urban mediation, for which he suggests an analysis and paths for institutionalisation in the last article of this part.

In the fifth part, the authors analyse development policies, subject them to criticism and frame proposals to transform them in a democratic governance perspective. The nature of programs, the institutional change, the evolution of partners in development's political arrangements, as well as aid governance are put into perspective.

In this area, as shown by Jean Bossuyt in the first article, beyond the complexity inherent to the promotion of governance, donors' approaches also require attention. The author calls for a change in their work ethic. Governance actually represents a veritable "Copernican revolution" in international aid, which, from fundamentally financial and technical, is becoming political. This implies a change in paradigm, with aid agencies assuming their roles as political actors. Accordingly, most partners in development review their institutional and political procedures following the example of the European Commission, whose article examines the evolution of policies and tools of implementation. Again, based upon the European experience, Philippe Darmuzey presents the innovations and transformations brought on by the adoption, in 2006, of the European consensus on governance, which places democratic governance at the heart of the European Union's external action. Suggesting a pragmatic and broadened approach to governance, the consensus aims at establishing a veritable incentive partnership with recipient countries. The need to follow recipes yielding a universal State model in order to be accepted by the international community is a thing of the past – so the author asserts – to be replaced by shared responsibility and long-term commitment in the respect of ownership. European aid encourages partner countries to engage in reforms intending notably to reinforce the legitimacy of power and thus a stable State, accepted by all, and advancing democracy. In the article that follows, the UNDP's Bureau for Development Policy reminds us that good governance, for human development and the achievement of Millennium Development Goals, is democratic governance. To the UNDP, governance of a democratic nature is based upon the participation of everyone in the elaboration of decisions that concern them, on the one hand, and upon States that are "reactive" (capable of efficiently responding to the demands of citizens) and responsible (accountable, transparent, etc.) on the other. The methodology and axes prioritised by UNDP action for democratic governance (participation, ability to govern in a reactive and responsible manner and the respect of accepted international norms and principles concerning civil human rights, gender equality and the fight against corruption) are presented here. In the fourth article, Anupama Dokeniya, Colum Garrity and Sanjay Pradhan state that the new strategy promoting governance and the fight against corruption as detailed by the World Bank (2007) insists on the institutions' positive impact on long-term growth and on the reduction of poverty. The World Bank's action discards the application of any single formula, aiming at reinforcing, and not substituting, local capacities, at creating country programs according to the initial political context and according to long-term historical processes that determine the terms and limits of institutional reforms. It is about reinforcing governance demand and developing the multi-partner networks and partnerships based on mutual responsibility and clarity in monitoring, in order to improve governance and favour real development and efficient service delivery. As for Séverine Bellina and Hervé Magro, they revisit the State-governance dialectic. With governance, the role of the State is affirmed, whereas between "good governance" and democratic governance, diagnosis and proposed actions vary. Revisiting the approaches developed in order to analyse the State in Africa, the authors remind us that the questions of legitimacy and institutionalisation of power, and therefore public action, are at the heart of governance challenges. The approaches based on the reference to a unique model, the transfer of norms and techniques, far from consolidating them and advancing the refoundation of the State, render it fragile. The necessarily endogenous nature of development processes is also at the core of Nicolas Meisel and Jacques Ould Aoudia's contribution, in which they advocate re-examining the institutions' economic analyses, and the role development policies assign to them. Approaching the question through the lens of political economy, the authors restate the institutional core of development processes, before they achieve a political expression. It is also the role of the State that is being discussed in the part written by Pierre Victoria. Setting forth the viewpoint of the private sector and sectoral policies, such as, crucially, those concerning water, the author shows that the efficiency of development actions and the achievement of the Millennium Development Goals in this realm are less a question of techniques and finances than of governance. A State, guarantor of the general interest in the framework of national public policies, ensuring the articulation of responsibilities between stakeholders (national/local and private operators), is the best assurance of a public/private partnership based on trust and guaranteeing the population the efficient delivery of public services and sustainable human development. Soumana Sako and Floribert Ngaruko conclude this part advocating a second generation of governance reforms. The evolution of development policies toward the affirmation of the importance of human, organisational and institutional capacities; participation and deep-rootedness as intrinsic qualities of public policies; and sustainable human development have been the basis for the affirmation of governance as a development approach for the past two decades. However, this is not enough to create a sufficiently developed approach of governance, capable of mitigating the contradictions and existing divergences in the implementation of governance. The fact is that beyond political pretences governance remains operationalised according to the partners'specific agendas, as a means of pressure nay of conditionality – with unconvincing results.

The sixth and final part is dedicated to the identification, presentation and analysis of development cooperation tools adapted to democratic governance. The five articles in this part identify the dynamics necessary to the strategic support of democratic governance, on the basis of which to elaborate or rethink the new generation of cooperation tools.

In the first article, Jean-Marc Châtaigner, referring to the much talked about toolkits designed for the implementation of policies and development projects, underlines the current paradox and the necessary transformations for those wishing to develop the instruments of democratic governance. Democratic governance, with its double dimension (approach and systems), reorders, indeed reverses, development cooperation practices and aid governance, since the role of partner countries becomes central to it. The objectives and the very nature of aid tools change; the point is now to enable societies to develop their own governance modalities. Thus the timeliness (of programs and of results), the very quality of donors intervention (inclusive, networked) and the nature of evaluation (according to the context and ongoing processes) are at stake. Gilbert Houngbo illustrates, in a second article, the pressing necessity to reinforce innovative tools to support a new approach of governance that allows Africa to go beyond the structural deficits in this area and achieve the Millennium development goals. The key initiatives mentioned by the author are at the heart of a readjustment in UNDP support to governance programs in Africa. Centred on partnership and riding on local dynamics (inherent to populations and national policies), they aim, through the process of debate, at creating the means of reinventing governance and reinforcing democracy. Citizenship and the capacities of the States are called for in democratic governance in Africa. Serge Rumin explains, using the example of transitional justice, that the strengthening of institutional capacities can no longer be based, as is generally the case in current programs, upon a functionalist approach of institutions that neglects the fundamental aspect that is their social origins. It is therefore on cohesion and social regulation that the objective on strengthening institutional capacities should focus. Supporting tools must therefore allow exchanges, links and interaction between institutions and societies. The aggravated context of disconnection between institutions and societies, which is characteristic in situations of fragility, confirms this analysis, which is valid for all programs and instruments for institutional capacities development towards democratic governance. In the fourth article, Christiane Arndt and Charles Oman show us the limits of the governance indicators as well as the necessary precautions to take in order to avoid "problematic" or "mistaken" utilisations of these indicators, especially when the question of deciding to invest or determine the quality of governance in a country arises. The limits of these tools reside in their quantitative logic, and it is in becoming more specific and especially more transparent that they can be improved. As an innovative evaluation tool and a unique process of governance, the African Peer Review Mechanism – or APRM – is described by Marie-Angélique Savané in the fifth article in this part. While the APRM is now recognised as the most innovative democratic governance tool in Africa on a continental scale, the author reminds us that both its operation and the governance process it represents have yet to become properly appreciated. Expanding the APRM's success and efficiency depends on a better knowledge and comprehension of its key axes and of the stakes involved in order to allow for its critique and subsequent improvement leading to a greater appropriation by the African actors themselves.

I

CROSS PERSPECTIVES ON GOVERNANCE

1

Governance Reform and International Cooperation for Development

The Point of View of a Former Head of State

Henrique PEREIRA ROSA
(Translated from the Portuguese)

A partnership founded on shared responsibility between recipient and donor countries

Today the question of governance and its reform counts among the recurring concerns of international organisations, the political community, the world of research and observers of modern public administration. It is also central in the field of social communication, the object of questioning by citizens as well as civil society.

For the states that are partners in development, involved in activities of cooperation and solidarity, the reform and effectiveness of governance in recipient countries has become an inescapable and at times even decisive factor.

Obviously, it is not reasonable for resources allocated to cooperation in developing countries to be used incorrectly by the governments of recipient countries, who receive this aid in the name of the people that they represent, people suffering from the lack of infrastructure and basic services, people experiencing particularly low indicators of human development, people subject to serious poverty, even hunger and misery. As one observer noted, "in spite of the increase in the resources allocated to solidarity, results are few"! Nevertheless, attributing total responsibility for the success or failure of an enterprise – that is by definition always bilateral or multilateral – to a single party in the partnership would be an oversimplification that is prejudicial to the analysis of the problem. But regardless, it appears that in partnerships for development cooperation, the "success stories" – they do exist – are, as a rule, only present in cases where they were guided or guaranteed by a good governance. Governance reform is veritably a decisive factor in the success or failure of aid policy.

Developed countries also have lessons to learn, errors to correct, tools that need improving and new models to invent. Guy Verhofstadt, until recently prime minister of the Kingdom of Belgium, asserted in an open letter:

> "In developing countries up to 70% of the population make their living from agriculture. In the rich North, the figure is seldom more than 5%. Billions of people depend on agriculture for survival, and yet the OECD countries still levy import duties averaging 40% on agricultural products. [...] Subsidies, which at one time helped Europe to eliminate its own food shortage, are today driving farmers in developing countries off their land. Every year, Europe pays out €120 million in development aid to South Africa. But every year South Africa loses a similar amount of potential export income due to the dumping of European sugar on its market. We Europeans fight poverty with one hand, but stop it from disappearing with the other. We alleviate poverty, but we perpetuate it at the same time."

It is not our place to comment upon the assertions of this European statesman and politician who speaks neither in our name, nor addresses his words to us, the public actors of poor developing countries. He is speaking "from the inside", from the developed world, bringing to light the contradiction between discourse and reality. However, I believe his declaration demonstrates that the responsibilities of donors, as well as those of recipients, come together in this enterprise of solidarity and cooperation for development.

Thus, the problem posed is complex. On one hand is the necessity for international cooperation to be able to count on governance reform in countries receiving aid, in order to enhance the value in the field of the resources being provided. And on the other hand is the question of knowing how to reconcile the flow of aid with the real needs for development poor countries continue to experience. Will our institutions turn out to be truly prepared – with the will, dependability, and above all, sufficient capability – to make good use of the resources of international aid?

It seems that as soon as the practices of governments confronted with the aid they receive is evoked in the context of governance and its reform, everyone's first thought is the risk of corruption. Certainly, governance reform entails a merciless fight against corruption, corruption which weakens and perverts the meaning of cooperation, but it is not enough.

"Democratic governance. A new paradigm for development", involving government, the democratic order and development as the objective of public intervention, seems to be a sufficiently wide-ranging expression to stimulate debate. In order to explore this perspective, its potentials and its limits, I share the opinion of those who consider it pertinent to conduct an exchange of points of view, experiences and expectations. We must take into account the necessity of improving the already-existing tools of cooperation that have proved their worth, without abandoning the search for new paths that would allow more positive interaction, enlarging the horizons of cooperation with new development objectives.

Aid for development and legitimate democratic governance: beyond democratic conditionality

During the Cold War, ideological criteria seemed the determining factor in deciding which programmes to adopt for cooperation between industrialised and developing states. From this cooperation, strongly branded at the time by the ideological definitions of "friend" or "enemy" in the geopolitical (as well as geo-economic) competition then under way, rich countries asserted that their development assistance was a means for extending their influence, creating alliances and reinforcing their political position in the countries where their programmes were applied.

After the fall of the Berlin Wall, which thankfully put an end to the Cold War, what followed were more than small changes – the world's political structure itself was drastically altered. With the symbol of the fall of the Berlin Wall, a new groundswell of political democratisation asserted itself in the countries most lacking international aid. This surge was also evoked in French President François Mitterrand's striking speech at La Baule, in June 1990.

I do not think I risk being mistaken if I claim that the idea of basing the effort of development on the paradigm of democratic governance can be traced to this post-Cold War wave of democratisation. Since then it has become obvious it would be difficult or even impossible to conceive of a "well understood" process of development which did not encompass a fully verified and confirmed process of participatory democracy.

Little by little, development assistance from developed countries has been subjected to the condition that countries who are candidates for receiving public aid must demonstrate the "right" democratic behaviour. This tendency has been translated into the allocation of resources to supporting democratic processes, protecting liberty and favouring change that can lead to the strengthening of democracy. One would almost have you believe that it was enough to bring together the criteria of democracy – free and fair elections, efficient democratic institutions, respect for Human Rights, etc. – in order for countries to gain access to the resources indispensable to their progress. The quality of legitimate democratic governance was little mentioned. The belief that an "invisible hand" necessarily led to making the best choices, or at least choices that were the lesser evil (as in the theory of the "perfect market"), obscured dangers that were not, properly speaking, those of the democratic model, but rather of its perversion.

Internal efficiency of governance reform: consolidating citizenship

Governance reform can only be assessed in relationship to its results, and therefore in relationship to its efficiency. For both sides of the partnership that forms the basis for cooperation, governance reform is a requirement that clearly concerns not only the country receiving aid. In fact, any cooperation hoping to have a positive effect cannot withstand bad governance of the resources that are put at the disposition of recipient countries. So the question is one of internal effectiveness, which cannot be reduced to government technocracy.

Democratic governance calls for the reinforcement of citizenship. Without this reinforcement of citizenship – by way of citizens' responsible exercise of their rights and duties – the fundamental conditions for a democratisation of governance have not been assembled. Everywhere citizenship doesn't count, either because of the passivity or disinterest of citizens, or because it is in the interest of the state to not encourage it, policies fail to achieve their fixed objectives, corruption poisons public institutions, and there is no validation of governmental acts nor evaluation of the results of policies. Impunity triumphs and development is once again delayed.

Consequently, governance reform goes hand in hand with the reinforcement of citizenship and cannot be understood as merely the product of government officials. And yet, reinforcement of citizenship is not always considered a part of relationships for cooperation, which often pursue an intergovernmental agenda. And if it finally does play a part, it appears only in the specific context of encouragement and support for formal democratic processes.

Perhaps I am wrong to underline the importance of the reinforcement of citizenship, instead of broaching subjects generally considered more gripping, such as the Lomé (Togo) and Cotonou (Bénin) Conventions, the Millennium Development Goals (MDG), the Europe-Africa Summit, or still further the actions of the World Bank and other important factors that come into play in the fight against poverty.

I want to underline that my experience as a public official and politician in my country did not only consist in the exercise of governmental responsibilities. I came from the business world, a world I haven't abandoned. I have also been strongly engaged in social questions, taking part in varied and always-rewarding pursuits in my country's civil society. This led to my compatriots deciding to grant me their confidence. This is the path – as a social actor struggling to reinforce citizenship, the guarantee of the emergence of democracy – which led me to exercising the honourable responsibilities of President of the Republic of my country.

As President, having exercised my functions during a period of transition troubled by political unrest, with the still visible after-effects of a political and military conflict that had destroyed lives and property, as well as disappointing the generous expectations of my compatriots, I was confronted with the harsh reality – the resources of international aid which had been entrusted to our governments since independence were being wasted. I witnessed the collapse of political order, I observed the cost of bad governance, I was confronted with the disorientation of the political class and the deterioration of public institutions, ultimately leading to a state crisis.

But in the awakening of citizenship, in the surge of my country's civil society, I discovered the indispensable energies for a new start, an age of hope – in peace, cooperation, solidarity and development. This experience set into motion my examination of the central role citizenship plays in governance. Because finally, what do the state, public services and cooperation policy serve for, if they do not result in enriching citizenship and society?

Governance reform: an act of governing

The fight against corruption, the reinforcement of citizenship, and the strengthening of the democratic order are the necessary conditions governments must fulfil if they hope to work for the development of their countries and people, accompanied by the support of international partners.

In this perspective, the question of the state can not be avoided, especially in situations of recurrent crisis, where the presence of the state is imperative.

One can not speak of governance reform without evoking the state, without calling for its intervention in its own role, in the best sense of the term: democratic role of law; Social state; State for science and knowledge; developmentalist/ developmental state, etc. This is why, regardless of all the vicissitudes, the state remains the cornerstone to the question of governance reform.

All the problems start here. We need the state to encourage citizenship, we need the state to create an enable climate in order to not reduce the effectiveness of governance we need the state to optimise the resources provided by cooperation and international solidarity. But what kind of state are we talking about?

In Europe, it seems that European citizens are already "tired" of states that are economically interventionist, actively pursuing the goal of favouring the development of their own country. The state is a victim of its own success. As one researcher told us:

> "The role of the state moved from a laissez-faire period in the 18th century to a period of intervention and intrusion in the economy in the 20th century. The 1980s called into question the status quo concerning the role of the state, tending to diminish its role in economic and social life. A state reduced and diminished."

The situation is not the same in developing countries. The state, at least in my country, has never known a history paved with success. Even before its stabilisation, it was already under the crossfire of neoliberal critics from abroad. Because of our country's economic weakness, it is heavily dependent on variations in the external economic situation, as well as on the economic schools of thought that theorise about them. The changes in our circumstances ended up by imposing neoliberal therapies on us, whose effects have still not been completely assessed.

Economically backwards, with the stock markets characteristic of pre-capitalist subsistence economies and with an emerging private sector and a (post-colonial) state order that is still young, our countries often display the situations of blockage that are characteristic of the absence of a strong state and of a private sector endowed with a real economic and financial capacity. Nevertheless, it is upon these two vacillating pillars, a fragile political order (the state) and a weak (market) economy (without forgetting the insufficient level of schooling that often characterises our societies), that we attempt to construct our democratic order, as well as that which is its expression, democratic governance.

It comes as no surprise that democracy has been marred by populist excesses that sometimes have ethnic or even racist overtones. The breakdown of the state is not just an exaggeration made by intellectuals.

Democratic experiences, at least in some African countries, have attracted the world's attention precisely because they have disappointed many of the hopes they had aroused. As if it were enough to organise regular elections in order for democratic governance to automatically follow.

Because our democratic convictions are quite strong, it is difficult for us to bring a critical eye to the harsh reality of certain democratic processes that end up aggravating the problems they should have resolved – from the splintering of national unity to corruption and the loss of institutional legitimacy, often dominated by populist motivations. But one cannot wish for a "return" to the pre-democratic model of a strong state. That is not an option.

The major risk – unfortunately a very real risk – is that we begin to reinforce the momentum for a return to the past, a return to tribalism, be it of democratic appearance, with its terrible logic of exclusion. That can only result in the impoverishment of society and the weakening of institutions. Africa has clearly experienced examples of democratic detours provoked by bad governments, bad reversals in situation, ethnical and tribal radicalisation, etc. Are these only growing pains? Perhaps. Or is it the crisis of democratic growth that is superimposed upon the crisis of the state itself?

In any case, the question posed above, "how can we reconcile cooperation and development?", leads to another, "how can we assure that our democratic processes do not merely generate governance that is democratic in appearance only (the formal exercise of democracy by the authorities), but instead leads to democratic governance possessing the capacity to favour development?" What must we do in order for the effectiveness of governance reform to tend more and more towards democratic governance?

In order to truly answer this question it is necessary to ask ourselves what reform of the state – which must be defined as an administration with real powers, actively present throughout the entire national territory, something which still does not exist today in certain African countries – must be considered indispensable or sufficient as premise for the application of governance reform? Who will keep a watchful eye on the state to avoid that, if the current crisis continues or worsens, governance reform will not be transformed into something that is virtual, lacking any practical consequences?

Shouldn't the re-establishment of the state and its institutions be written into the international assistance agenda, as a prerequisite condition – at least in certain countries, such as mine, Guinea-Bissau – in order to consider "democratic governance" as "a new paradigm for development"?

As specified in my introductory statement – governance reform based on democratic governance and development assistance through international cooperation are of great importance. Nevertheless, it will also be necessary to broach the problem of financing the aid – the resources – that developed countries direct towards poor countries. But we won't spend more time here on that matter. Developed countries know better than we do where and how to mobilise international resources in order to increase official development assistance (ODA).

In the past, we enthusiastically welcomed the prospect of the Tobin tax, championed by Nobel laureate James Tobin, based on the idea of taxing currency exchanges to step up the level of aid. Commentators claim it is difficult to apply because of its inherent risks for the currency markets, risks that were not fully assessed by its inventor. Similarly, the proposition by George Soros to resort to Special Drawing Rights to increase international aid and support development efforts in poor countries gave rise to widespread hopes. Hopes that were reinforced by the political commitment that presided over defining the Millennium Development Goals.

But reality lies in the fact that the debate concerning governance reform casts a very important part of the responsibility on developing countries. No flow of financing to developing countries produces the desired effects when governments are corrupt or do not know what they wish for in terms of their development. Donors do not want to run risks. The transfer of public resources to developing countries, by the intermediary of cooperation, requires as prerequisite a democratic government and the will and capacity of the government to foster development.

Invoking or displaying poverty are not enough to earn the right to receive financing from international cooperation, or to receive development aid in addition to humanitarian aid. We must provide proof that we wish to escape poverty by the intermediary of a governance that is lucid, transparent and resolutely engaged on the path of development and of extreme poverty alleviation.

I will conclude by returning to Guy Verhofstadt's pertinent remarks – if the countries of the Organisation for Economic Cooperation and Development (OECD), who are major donors, do not change their policy, then "they will alleviate poverty" by the intermediary of cooperation but "they will perpetuate it at the same time" – by way of their commerce, their subsidies, their protectionism, "by driving farmers in developing countries off their land". That is how protectionist trade can undermine the best efforts of development cooperation.

2

Governance

A Global Question that Calls for Specific Responses in Africa

Ousmane Sy
(Translated from the French)

Global governance is in crisis

Despite the dismantling of the Eastern Bloc and the end of the Cold War, centres of tension are multiplying across the planet. Poverty has become endemic and is deepening in the so-called developing countries. Nor does this impoverishment spare certain categories of the population in wealthy countries. The liberalism constructed upon the principle of pre-eminence of the market as the only instrument for social regulation has apparently triumphed. Society is defenceless when confronted with the deterioration of its human and natural environments. On every continent, a minority monopolises available resources and is growing richer, to the detriment of a majority sinking into the tribulations of poverty. In general, the gap between rich and poor countries increases more and more everyday. Consequently, to avert social crisis, "poor" countries open their doors, allowing the young to leave in search of a better future. On the other side, for the same reasons, "rich" countries close their borders to protect their privileges. And nevertheless, in this situation of two worlds looking daggers at each other, we can also see that humanity has never before accumulated as much of the wealth and knowledge that could allow it to find solutions, founded on solidarity and responsibility, for all the problems confronting it. And yet the continents and the states that make them up seem to be advancing by great bounds towards crisis and confrontation. On a global level this is being reinforced because the mechanisms of regulation have become obsolete in regards to the evolution of individuals, communities and societies. The establishment of new mechanisms is far from simple. This explains the crisis at the global level of governance.

Africa has its specificities in this global crisis

In this situation of global governance in crisis, Africa, despite the impression it gives of apparently standing stuck in place, is experiencing strong political, economic and sociocultural evolution. In recent years, under the joint pressure of its people and of donor organisations, all the nations on the African continent have committed themselves to the process of liberalisation of their economies, the building of pluralistic democracies, and the decentralisation of the administration of public affairs. Many sectors that were under state control have been opened to actors of the private sector, both national and international. A profusion of political parties and civil organisations have been founded and are attempting to assert themselves as regulators of the process of transformation of their societies. In virtually every country, decentralised public institutions have been established, after reforms that enabled the transfer of responsibilities and resources towards local and regional levels. On the interstate level, several initiatives for political and economic integration are under way, even if they are still far from adequately taking into consideration the existing complementarity between nations and the age-old economic exchange relationships that predate the borders inherited from colonisation.

But all these transformations are still unable to reverse strong trends whose persistence endangers the stability of weakening states, thus compromising any possibility of progress in development on the continent. In Africa, more than anywhere else, poverty has tended to become more generalised over the last two decades. According to the Food and Agriculture Organisation of the United Nations (FAO), 186 million Africans are threatened by severe food shortages. On the average, 45-50% of sub-Saharan Africans live below the poverty level.

Conflicts are becoming generalised within the borders of countries, pouring waves of refugees and displaced persons onto the roads, filling improvised refugee camps, and as a result, aggravating the precariousness experienced by the population. In countries not touched by conflicts, access to basic public services (education, health, water and a healthy environment) remain a challenge that is far from being met – to the point that the capability of Africa to meet the Millennium Development Goals is in doubt. This situation results in the growing marginalisation of the continent on the international scene, where public opinion no longer hesitates to openly question the relevance of continuing aid to Africa.

The economic crisis and the conflicts concerning eroding resources (because of a growing population that is increasingly urban) pave the way for the resurgence of ethnic demands. The insecurity, both human and material, that this situation perpetuates over the futures of men, women, and above all, young people – who prefer to seek their safety outside the continent – further destroys a social fabric already undermined by the assault of modernity.

And yet Africa has no shortage of the assets that can serve its development. Among them, its youth (more than half of the continent's population is in fact under fifteen), the immensity of its natural resources, its cultural potential and finally, the African Diaspora, an economically enterprising presence active across the globe. African youth are open to the world and seized by a great thirst for change.

Concerning natural resources (mineral, forest, animal), Africa abounds in them. But to quote the Congolese proverb, the continent resembles "a honey pot without a lid, victim to every fly".[1] Paradox that Stephen Smith evokes in comparing the situation on the African continent to the Japanese archipelago, "Japan is poor and the Japanese are rich, but Africa is rich and the Africans are poor".

In this context of paradox that inspires only disillusionment and despair for the majority of African people, and above all for the youngest, states seem helpless to assume their responsibility for organising the delivery of public services and regulating public spaces. The weakness of public administrations and their persistent incapacity to mobilise the resources of their country and use them judiciously for the good of their people have ended up depriving public institutions of any credibility.

This situation of crisis, aggravated by the absence of a credible alternative, facilitates the ascension to power of individuals who "fear neither God nor man", in other words, who refuse to subject themselves to any ethical rule. Civil war breaking out nearly everywhere, the inadequacy of the models of representative democracy under construction, and finally, the supervision exercised over national authorities by the "international community" by way of aid and international agreements, all end up undermining the credibility of the continent's government leadership. The persistence – and even the exacerbation – of all these

---

1. A wise man from the North Kivu region of the Democratic Republic of the Congo (Pole Institute – November 2005).

phenomena of bad governance, after almost five decades of independence, reveal a profound crisis in public action that is Africa's specificity in this world in crisis.

This specificity first reveals the limitations of the framework and models of public administration under development

Established on the territories of former colonies after independence, the new states aspire to a national identity. But it is not recognised or is simply rejected by the identities inherited from history or pre-colonial geography. Even with the passing of time, these states have simply been incapable of building a common destiny for development. One reason is that these legal and territorial national entities, the inviolability of whose borders was reaffirmed at the founding of the Organisation of African Unity (OAU) in Addis Ababa in 1963, never made sense in the eyes of the vast majority of African people, even if they have adapted to them. Most of the continent's wars take place in countries where the state, with its legal and institutional norms, finds it difficult to live with the plurality of communities and nationalities. This weak historical legitimacy is compounded by their poor capacity for mobilising populations and their resources. The administrative models constructed at independence have prolonged the habits and attitudes of colonial administrations. Brutality and clientelism remain the only relationship between the public administrations of the new states and their citizens.

With the establishment of mistrust, rural and urban communities have developed various attitudes towards the national state, which remains a foreign body. The transplant has not taken.

On one hand, assistance from the state is solicited because it is necessary to squeeze out maximum benefits for oneself and one's own. The state in return finds it extremely difficult to demand any return for the services expected of it. Consequently it ends up adopting a demagogic and paternalistic attitude. International donors follow suit. The illusion of the deliverance of public services at no cost has taken hold, since the money comes from the donors, and it's enough just to keep them happy.

On the other hand, the national state and the fruit of its fragmentation remain the pet hate that communities fear. An entire arsenal of strategies has been put into place to protect oneself and everything that is important to oneself from the tyrants and assault rifles that incarnate the state. The state then takes on the colour of a predator functioning only by force and whose only vocation is to humiliate its victims. The example of village chiefs is rather symbolic of this ambiguous relationship between communities and the post-colonial state. In several Malian villages I know, there are two types of village chiefs. The true chief – authentic and legitimate and whom the entire village greatly respects – is not declared to the state because it is necessary to protect him from humiliation and harassment. In his place, village notables offer a substitute who is referred to as the "Administrative Village Chief". This fictitious chief is very often young and considered clever and tough. He is appointed by the village to act as liaison with the administration. In return he benefits from the village's gratitude and a few small advantages. This attitude of the community symbolises all the ambiguities, misunderstandings and discrepancies that are still the reality between post-colonial states and their people. This distance between institutions and the community seems to me the most resonant characteristic of the crisis of the state and of public administration in Africa.

The models of democracy being built in Africa are carriers of exclusion, and therefore of conflict and instability, because they end up marginalising the majority of people from public administration. These models – founded on the pre-eminence of legality, on legitimacy, and on the system of "winner-loser" voting – only perpetuate the existing gap between state institutions and local communities. The initiatives and precaution surrounding the preparation and monitoring of elections are based exclusively on the demand for respect of regulations and the rule of law. National and independent electoral commissions and the numerous observers only concern themselves with respect for legal texts. No measure nor any national or international authority verifies nor speaks up about the legitimacy of the result that comes from the urns after the vote.

Generalisation of the system of winner (majority) and loser (minority) is experienced as exclusion, to which the only remaining response is to refuse to play a game where there is no longer any place for the minority. In the worst cases, the losers – because they no longer have their place, and so are not recognised or acknowledged – take up arms to defend their cause. The confrontations and instability borne from these processes – which at best produce leaders of fragile legitimacy, and at worst produce excluded people who take up arms, "the war lords" – sink the country and the entire continent into the precariousness and material and intellectual misery that can lead only to chaos. The benevolent support and speeches of the "international community" can do nothing as long as the old paradigms remain.

Africans must find strategies enabling new forms of governance adapted to the specificities of their societies

In this approach which must necessarily lead to the refoundation of the post-colonial state, governance appears as the core issue around which policies of decentralisation and regional integration will define different levels of government and their modes of interaction. It is the responsibility of Africans to lucidly consider the futures of their societies, to decide the challenges to undertake, to propose and put into place strategies enabling change. The initiatives presently under way in the domains of decentralisation and regional and African integration must be the principle levers for change, enabling a reversal of the current processes.

African societies, while responding to the challenge of their integration with the rest of the world, must first anchor themselves in their own points of reference in order to invent governance models that are legitimate and credible, indispensable to all democratic governance. Unfortunately, the current models are reduced to a list of universal recipes that all developing countries must respect in order to gain the favour of the "international community". The concept of "good governance" as it is advocated for Africa is reductionist in regards to the real issues confronting development in Africa.

In order for it to be legitimate, and therefore accepted, governance must conform to the following principles: the responsibility of leaders, transparency and intelligibility for the people concerning public decision making, the possibility to anticipate a common future and therefore envisage its long term progression, and finally the capacity to anticipate, if not regulate, the conflicts linked to all evolution. But the core body of these principles, the manner of organising and verifying their effectiveness, can not be made according to a standardised model. The questions posed by forging democratic governance in relationship to the respect of these principles are admittedly common to all societies, but the nature of the responses must necessarily be specific.

These principles must form the basis for reflection that will underlie necessary governance reform in Africa. This analysis is based on the fact that underdevelopment in Africa is due – beyond bad public administration – to the inadequacy of the options and practices of governance that are promoted in relationship with the expectations of African societies and of the international community, and that any strategy for escaping the crisis can only be constructed by way of a veritable process refoundation of the state in Africa.

Far from any reflex of withdrawal, this perspective repositions the debate concerning the place of Africa in the world on the right path. Because the multiple identities we all assume in today's world make each African in his village or neighbourhood into a local citizen who must put down roots in the culture of his territory, and yet also remain the citizen of a country, of a continent, and a citizen of the world. And so all these levels must be linked if we wish to give meaning to redefining governance. This refoundation also requires that Africans take a new look at their own societies to once again find the meaning and values that guide human activities, basing them on reality and experience and not on dogma developed by international institutions.

Public administration decentralisation must be at the heart of any democratic governance strategies

The political preoccupations underlying the decentralisation reform that is taking place in African countries are just as old as those that were the motivation for the attainment of national independence. In fact, all the leaders or political groups, from independence to the present, that at one time or another have had to make the important choices about the running of a country have consistently expressed the will to move towards the decentralisation of public administration for the construction of new independent states.[2] The reasons for this constant evocation of decentralisation by politicians can be found in the history of the formation of the old African nations.

All African cultures share respect for diversity and take it into account in the development of norms for the management of the relationships between individuals, groups and communities. This principle of building unity while respecting diversity forms part of the important paradigms that were the basis for the process of decentralisation. Before being a technique of public administration, decentralisation is above all a frame of mind, and therefore a culture of public administration.

But decentralisation, in contrast with the way it is perceived, is not only about installing local government and its administrative bodies. The latter must become drivers of development, with elected officials having the capacity to join together in partnership with other local actors, as much for the deepening of local democracy as for the stimulation of local economies. But in most cases these economies are largely informal. The

---

2. Almost all the Constitutions of the first independent republics refer to local and/or regional levels of government administered by elected bodies.

actors of the sector have often made the choice of turning to the informal economy because the central administrations have no response to their questions. All the same, in most countries it employs and nourishes more people than any other sector, permitting the alleviation of social crises, thus of political crises as well. The informal sector possesses the greatest potential for the development of local economies. It is therefore the responsibility of local administrations to join together in partnerships with the actors of the informal economy, assuring they contribute to the building of a solid national economy. This is one of the costs of development.

One of the most crucial challenges of the process of decentralisation in Africa also consists in the harmonious cohabitation of so called new and traditional forms of legitimacy. The latter in fact "occupy" local territory where they remain solidly established. The bodies elected by universal suffrage in new decentralised local and regional government have been set up using the model of representative democracy – the challenge is to adapt this choice to the realities of our societies.

It is still common to observe today that the legitimacy of traditional chiefs remains superior, and therefore better assumed, than that resulting from universal suffrage. The new modern forms of legitimacy do not at all weaken the strength of traditional forms, which are conferred by history, blood, pacts and ancient reciprocities. I believe that one form of legitimacy does not threaten another, they must co-exist. But it is important to define norms for this cohabitation. The great challenge for African societies is to remain anchored in their traditions while at the same time opening to modernity, since the stability of democratic governance risks being compromised by ignoring or not taking into consideration long standing sociocultural realities. Decentralisation also possesses the advantage of opening debate and giving a better image of governance. In fact, it correctly brings the debate back on topic, to the necessary balance to be constructed between society and the institutions entrusted with governing it.

In a context where "good governance" has been reduced to a few concepts (democratic elections, the fight against corruption, the transparency of public administration – all admittedly important, but insufficient in themselves), will we find no acceptable response to the visible indifference of Africans – both the simple citizens as well as political leaders – concerning the public good and the public interest (of which the state must become the repository and the symbol), except altering that universally-held image of the state. It is equally futile to claim to respond to the question of the fragile legitimacy of present-day leaders without fully understanding the conception of power and of the relationships to power. In other words, the question of governance is much more holistic than the manner with which it has been tackled until now.

From this point of view, decentralisation must be considered as the first of two stages of the "reform rocket of the state"[3]. It must enable the post-colonial African state to rebuild its legitimacy from the bottom up. The real and honest exercise of their responsibilities by elected local authorities, and the allotment of public resources – as well as their verifiable administration by these same authorities – will reinforce their legitimacy. Indirectly this will also lead to giving root to institutional construction in the day-to-day experience of the people. This pre-eminence of the local level must nevertheless not be disengaged from also pursuing workable interaction between the varied legitimacies – traditional and elected – that cohabit at this level, in accordance with the principle of "active subsidiarity" dear to Pierre Calame. Moreover, putting the needs of local actors into direct contact with the public decision-making that should be present to respond to it is a guarantee of effective policy. On one side, we create the possibility of a stronger implication by these actors in public administration. On the other, we also introduce more flexibility in the responses of public decision makers, and a power of verification by the citizens over the deciders.

Finally, through decentralisation, the state shares its responsibilities in the conception and supervision of territorial development with the decentralised authorities – one may therefore hope for a truly shared production of development across the territory. Such synergy is a guarantee of the long-sought-for effectiveness of development, of a more rational and balanced partnership with the international cooperation actors, and of relief to the pressure on central government institutions. It is at the price of the establishment of these horizontal networks that we can compensate for the insufficiencies of the strictly vertical approaches of present-day public administration in Africa.

In conclusion, I will say that decentralisation, regardless of all the anxiety and questions it evokes in Africa, is neither the destruction of the state nor its abdication facing its responsibilities. On the contrary, decentralisation is the path that will enable African states to promote a balanced and harmonious development of their territories, to improve the mobilisation of all their capacity and human experience towards democratisation processes under way, and finally, to create bases for new financial resources through the stimulation of local economies, real foundation for a stable national economy and renewed governance.

---

3. The second being regional integration.

Bibliography

Alliance pour refonder la gouvernance en Afrique, (2005). Changeons l'Afrique, 15 propositions pour commencer gouvernance en Afrique, "Compte rendu du forum sur la gouvernance en Afrique".

Alliance pour refonder la gouvernance en Afrique, (2005). Pour une gouvernance légitime "Une contribution au débat sur la gouvernance en Afrique", Forum sur la gouvernance, Gouvernance en Afrique, Addis Abeba, cahier n° 2007-03, November 2005.

Alliance pour refonder la gouvernance en Afrique, (2007). Profils de gouvernance "un diagnostic de la gouvernance en Afrique à partir des expériences concrètes d'acteurs", Gouvernance en Afrique, cahier n° 2007-02.

World Bank, (1998). Finding.

Calame, P. (2003). La démocratie en miettes, Paris, Charles Léopold Mayer.

Commission de L'Union Africaine and Alliance pour refonder la gouvernance en Afrique (2006). Compte rendu du Forum sur la gouvernance en Afrique, February 2006.

FAO, (2004). The State of Food Insecurity in the World.

Institut de Recherche et de débat sur la Gouvernance and Alliance pour refonder la gouvernance en Afrique, (2007). Entre tradition et modernité : quelle gouvernance pour l'Afrique, Actes du colloque de Bamako.

Smith S., (2003). Négrologie, pourquoi l'Afrique meurt, Calmann Levy.

3

Governance

The Asian Counterexample?

Pierre CALAME
(Translated from the French)

Did you say counterexample?

According to the normative model advocated by international institutions, and in particular the World Bank under Wolfowitz, "good governance" is a precondition to economic development. The absence of corruption equals good governance; democracy equals poverty reduction. China doesn't fit this norm, so they've invented the "Asian counterexample". The ancient Greeks, believing the sun and stars turned around the earth, described the resisting planets as "wandering stars". It took the arrival of Copernicus to discover that the counterexample called into question the model itself. Today China doesn't fit in. The only way out is to change the model.

Let's start by examining the facts, sticking to data produced by international institutions

In the 2008 World Bank's world development report, "Agriculture for Development", was a chart concerning the evolution of poverty in the world between 1993 and 2002 [see following page].

DEMOCRATIC GOVERNANCE

Figure 1. The number of poor rose in South Asia
and in Sub-Saharan Africa between 1993 and 2002.
($1-a-day poverty line)

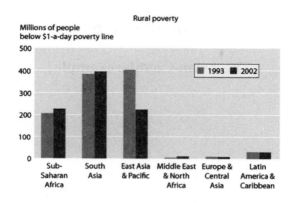

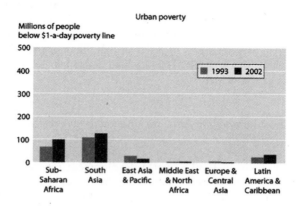

Source: Ravaillon, Chan and Sangraula (2007).

Only the Eastern and Pacific Asia zone (to speak clearly, China) experienced a decline in poverty, both rural and urban. In another report, the World Bank underlined that two thirds of the decline in poverty in the world took place in China. How is it possible to deduce that democracy is the source of poverty reduction? Is "good governance" at least a source of economic development? In the report published by Nicolas Meisel (French Development Agency) and Jacques Ould Aoudia (Treasury Directorate and Economic Policy-France), titled "Is 'Good Governance' a Good Development Strategy?", they underline that two countries stand out, China, with an average annual growth of 8.9%, and Vietnam, with annual growth of 5.5%. The other significant example, if I put aside small countries such as Mozambique, Uganda and Botswana, is India, with its 4% annual growth rate. The world's economic growth today comes from these countries. Everything else is pure fiction?

What is the dominant discourse based on?

After the fall of the Berlin Wall, imposing the "Neoliberal" model became convenient. In the late 1980s, we were already speaking of the "Asian miracle" (Asia necessarily eluding the general rule!). It was already obvious that there was no development without a strong state, capable of "governing the market"[1]. But this evidence didn't conform with the "Washington consensus" that confused a strong state with a parasitic state. The logic of international institutions, in order to support evidence so obviously opposed to the facts, turns to three techniques: swamp the reader with selectively-collected figures; eliminate any weighting of different criteria; force history to bear out biased assumptions.

Regarding the first, quoting the World Bank:

> "These indicators are based on several hundred individual variables measuring perceptions of governance, drawn from thirty-seven separate data sources constructed by thirty-one different organisations."

But who are these organisations? More than half of them are tied to large businesses and development banks. The "governance" indicators are closely related to the indicators produced by rating agencies to inform investors concerning investment risks. The efficiency of public action is reduced to knowing if a given country is ready to host big foreign companies. The virtually mono-cultural character of these institutions

---

1. Judet, P. (2005). Le tiers monde n'est pas dans l'impasse, Paris, Charles Léopold Mayer.

needs to be noted. All of them, with the exception of the European Investment Bank, are based in the United States or financed by USAID (United States Agency for International Development). Among them, Freedom House makes it clear that their "Board of Trustees is composed of people united in the view that American leadership in international affairs is essential to the causes of international affairs and democracy". Heritage Foundation, for its part, intends "to formulate and promote conservative public policies".

The World Bank puts major and minor corruption both in the same basket. And yet in many countries, doesn't "petty" corruption fall under the World Bank's own recomendations of "full coverage" for the costs of service done? In poor countries, civil servants complement their salaries by the generalisation of petty corruption. Regarding major corruption, the World Bank makes no distinction between that which doesn't prevent productive investment, and that which diverts it.

The second sleight of hand consists in incorporating heterogeneous data or data of significantly different size, such as for example the emission of greenhouse gases and sulphur content in the atmosphere. Or again, as in the two charts shown, rendering China and Zimbabwe as two similar points on a chart – without taking their population into account.

Finally, this literature seeks to convince by resorting to historical shortcuts. The crisis of 1929 having contributed to the emergence of fascism and then to the war, it becomes ever so tempting to deduce that "democracies don't make war" and that the disappearance of democracy is the cause of the war! In passing, we forget that the war effort pulled the US out of the stagnation the crisis of 1929-1933 had plunged it into. After the war, American assistance to Western Europe permitted the development of democratic regimes (except when it was necessary to support dictatorships in Greece, Spain and Portugal) and the virtuous circle was established – innovation creates growth, growth and the relatively equitable redistribution of its fruit assures a lasting peace. From this very exceptional conjunction in time and place of democracy, economic development and peace, we'd like to deduce that these three processes follow and reinforce one another in every instance. In many cases that isn't so – in Chile it was Pinochet's economic success that created the conditions for a return to democracy by reinforcing the middle class. The same thing happened in South Korea. In China, the phenomenal success of development under the authoritarian system of government shook up social relationships by creating a large middle class and a new class of business people. Today these new social actors, concerned with perpetuating their newly acquired positions, are opening to the world, favouring the establishment of a state of law and driven by democratic aspirations that the state must come to terms with one day. In all three of these cases, economic growth led to democracy and not the opposite.

The ingredients of Chinese economic development

In reality it is not democracy that is necessary to economic development, but rather stability. Multinational companies invest not in democratic countries, but instead in countries where there is an unshakeable will for development, strong and (more or less voluntarily) accepted government, and where the state has the capacity to "coordinate civil servants and fulfil their expectations" (Nicolas Meisel and Jacques Ould Aoudia). Let us see how these factors, as I have set them out, are demonstrated in China.

Openness and avenging history

The present-day history of China descends directly from the humiliation suffered in the 19th century because of its backwardness in the fields of science and technology. With the Opium Wars, for the first time China, which saw itself as the centre of civilisation, was defeated both militarily and culturally by Western powers. The defeat in 1895 by Japan amplified the trauma. "The child dared to tread on its mother's head" can still be heard today. Translation: China brought civilisation to Japan, which in return attacked it unmercifully in the thirties.

Everything that follows ensues from this trauma.

It was necessary at all costs for China to appropriate the victor's scientific and technological advantages in order to again accede to its natural station. Beginning at the end of the nineteenth century a strategy of openness for China began to be outlined, somewhat resembling Japan during the Meiji period, in order to seek out wherever necessary the innovations that could be useful for China's recovery. This attitude remains clearly visible today, our Chinese partners remaining ever watchful for whatever they may derive from the foreign experience that is most useful – from their point of view.

Drivers of development such as these reinforce the real legitimacy of a government, today run by the Communist Party, which in turn has taken charge of this project of openness and of avenging history. Even if this government is neither democratic nor particularly well-liked.

I've often heard my Chinese counterparts say, "with the Qing Dynasty and Maoism we learned the price of isolation. We want to open to the world. But exclusively in order to favour development." In French I call this "ouvermeture", or "closopenness" if you will – it is like a living organism, cultivating the ability to seek nourishment everywhere on the outside, but then digesting it for its own profit.

Pragmatism and organisational capacity, long term vision and human factors

When Deng Xiaoping launched the openness in 1978, he used the metaphor of crossing a river by stepping from stone to stone, carefully using the toe to first test each step. This efficient pragmatism often strikes me in my conversations with Chinese counterparts. No scruples, and above all no complexes, about using solutions from elsewhere. If it proves effective for China, continue, if not, try something else.

Their capacity to create, in a mere twenty years, port and urban infrastructures such as Shenzhen near Hong Kong or Pudong near Shanghai, attest to their tremendous capacity for planning and investment. Even if I personally find Shenzhen to be a city without a soul, one can not but notice it represents an alliance between considerable technical capacity and tremendous faith in the future.

This pragmatism and conviction didn't ensue from a sudden illumination by Deng Xiaoping to simply pursue the opposite course from Mao. They correspond to the conjunction of historical and cultural factors that after the terrible upheavals of the sixties enabled society to set itself back in motion – the compactness of the elite, the reorientation of forces towards the economy, the mobilisation of cultural symbols and the importance granted to knowledge, the mobilisation of the domestic population as well as the Diaspora, the saving capacity, the ability to synthesise tradition and modernity – all of these elements combine into a Chinese version of "The Glorious Thirties".

Compactness of the elite

In October 2007 we organised an important China-Europe forum for dialogue between the two societies. I was struck on that occasion by the ease of transversal contacts, notably among different generations. In 1977-78, Chinese universities modified their recruitment after the long digression of the cultural revolution. Applications to take the extremely selective university entrance examinations came from young people who had just completed their secondary education. But also from – across a half-dozen different age brackets – all the brilliant students who had been sent off to the fields, factories or mines during the cultural revolution. I noticed that all these surviving schoolmates had maintained contact with each other, and as contemporaries to the entire adventure of Chinese economic development, today they can be found in numerous posts of responsibility, in universities, businesses or the public administration of cities.

Reorientation of energy towards economic development and the good use of nepotism

For the academics and people in places of responsibility whose careers stopped in 1989, the way out was either to emigrate or to choose, as in the France of Louis Philippe, the economic outlet. As everyone knows, if one wants to take on political responsibilities in China, one doesn't engage in political debate, one obtains the Party card and works one's way up the ranks. This isn't terribly attractive, but the interpenetration of the Party and the State, as well as the business world today, means that most of those that engage in the Party do so the same way one would decide to embrace a career in the civil service in France. The most obvious result is the mass of talent engaged in economic activity – perhaps for lack of the possibility to do something more satisfying on an existential plane, but it comes to the same.

China epitomises a country of networking. A recent study shows that 90% of the new class of the economically powerful is composed of the offspring of party dignitaries. That study was rapidly removed from circulation. It might have demoralised young people who believe in meritocracy. Rapid enrichment, to the best of my knowledge, is almost always based on collusion between entrepreneurs and local political power, between the economic sector and the Party. One can – and must – see this from a perspective of injustice, and in correlation, from the point of view of corruption. But let's unemotionally examine, from the perspective of economic efficiency, the manner that both in China and Russia the nomenklatura have taken possession of the levers of the market economy. Russia, advised by the Chicago Boys, ventured into a pretence of democracy and a hasty privatisation that led to a capitalism of unearned income based on raw materials. The result was that from 1990 to 2004 the gross domestic product per capita in Russia diminished by an average of 0.6% per year. In the same period, as we have seen, China augmented the same figure by 8.9%. Predators in Russia, the new holders of economic power were productive for China.

All reflection concerning good governance converges to agree that the capacity for cooperation by actors of different types is one of the keys. This is obvious in economic development. It is also true for human development in general. But let's remain exclusively in the field of economic development. In Japan, the MITI was at the heart of post-war reconstruction. In China, the reinvestment of political and family networks enabled the creation of relatively stable configurations and above all a considerable reduction of transaction costs. Mentioning that is obviously not politically correct, but it is a reality.

Mobilisation of cultural symbols and the importance of knowledge

In the wake of Max Weber, there has been a lot of rambling on about cultural factors. No people experience real development unless it is constructed from its own culturally core. Until the fifties, Confucianism was considered as a cultural insurmontable obstacle to development. But with the Singapore success story, it was redefined as a source of efficiency. Today China returns it to a place of honour. It will be interesting to evaluate Confucianism's real influence as an undercurrent favouring loyalty, respect for hierarchy, and the spirit of sacrifice, all favourable to rapid development.

Born of Mandarin tradition, faith in knowledge and the desire for social advancement explain parents' exceptional investment in the scholastic destiny of their children. The ideal is obviously to attend one of the ten elite universities. For the majority of young people, unable to overcome the trial of extremely difficult entrance examinations, various solutions are available – the private universities that are today flourishing in China, or what comes to the same, fee-based public universities, overseas studies, or second-class universities, in that order. Today Europe counts 180,000 Chinese students, individuals who were unable to attend the best Chinese universities or pay for a private university whose monthly fees far exceeds the average income of most parents.

Mobilisation of the domestic population and of the Diaspora

I have met many Chinese couples where both the man and the woman are engaged in professional activities and the child is entrusted to grandparents, even if they live quite far away. Family solidarity offset the disengagement of the state's social services. Also at the service of China's recovery project, one must take into account the role of the Diaspora, which spares no pains with its aid, including the contribution of the technical tools it has gained command of in the best foreign universities. Just as when one tries to understand the feeble development of open-source software in China, we are answered with a smile, "for us all software is free". This kind of thinking can even be found among the members of the opposition to the present government who are expatriates, the ones I know feel a duty to contribute to this historical recovery of China.

Saving capacity

A savings rate amounting to 40% of the Gross National Product is maintained in China. Two different mechanisms play their part.

The first is the state's ability to withhold wealth at the source, as was the case during the Maoist period. At the time of the economic upturn, money was progressively distributed, but it remained socially and politically easy enough to continue to retain a large withholding at the source.

The second mechanism is paradoxically linked to the weak rate of remuneration of monetary savings, the need to constitute savings for a rainy day, the need to offset weaknesses in the retirement and social protection systems, and to the cost of education. In China one can find young people who are the only wage-earner for both their parents, as well as four grandparents and a few great-grandparents. This is one of the factors pushing individuals to invest in the real estate.

Capacity to synthesise tradition and modernity

An anecdote throws a little light on this point. One of my friends from Shanghai was given responsibility for setting up a mechanism for urban management responding to the thousands of ordinary problems: bursting water pipes, makeshift roadside installations, illicitly dumped rubbish, etc. He conceived a very effective system, adopting the traditional idea of neighbourhood watchmen responsible for a small turf they keep an eye on at times. Already present under Maoism, but probably even more ancient, these neighbourhood watchmen were recruited among the unemployed, and furnished with a state-of-the-art terminal allowing them to transmit information to technical and administrative services. It once took days before action could be taken, today it takes hours.

Gradualness in the integration of excess labour and in the spread of development

At the time of its economic takeoff, China found itself confronted with a duality between the developed coastal regions, founded on the principle of a high level of capitalism, and the rural Western regions where the economic level was not superior to Africa. Adopting a strategy of gradual diffusion, it began by bringing sectors of coastal China and its population into industries for global production (clothing, automotive, capital goods, electronic goods, etc.), then gradually bringing them up towards economic sectors of strong added value – the design and management of high-order services.

China's main problem was to control the rhythm of growth and its stages. It did so by strongly drawing upon the foreign companies that today still involve more than 50% of Chinese exports. China has never doubted its capacity, at the right moment, to recuperate the fruit of technology transfers. It is appreciably successful today, and hopes to soon also do as well with international commerce. In this process, the most complex management problem is in the gradual transfer of the workforce – facilitated by the authoritarian nature of the government – first towards free trade zones such as Shenzhen, and then rapidly towards large and dynamic economic regions such as Shanghai and Guangdong.

What Europe did in managing its progressive urbanisation and in integrating workers from the countryside and the immigrant workforce, China did by allowing a massively over-populated rural workforce to come to the big cities. In Shanghai they speak of five million "undocumented people" working and often sleeping on the work sites. They are second class citizens, comparable to North African and Portuguese immigrants during France's Glorious Thirty – the shantytowns around Paris didn't disappear until the seventies. But it would be an optical illusion to compare the Chinese process with a country like France, or even with Europe as a whole. It more resembles the couple formed by both Europe and Africa – Chinese internal migration being comparable to African immigration towards Europe, with its millions of undocumented people.

As already-developed regions attempt to rise into the domains of greater added value destined for international production, development spreads out in the direction of inland China and Vietnam.

One of the characteristics of this manner of managing development is its brutality. Protest demonstrations and rioting increased drastically, principally on the occasion of land and real estate problems, but without transforming themselves into a wider movement. For example, the way China was able to reabsorb 80 million workers from unproductive socialist enterprises, by bluntly putting them out of work, transforming what was supposedly the elite of the proletariat into people reduced to seeking subsistence all without a revolution comparable with the cultural revolution, was admittedly something totally stupefying for us.

Decentralisation of economic initiative

Harbin University, which is dedicated to space technology, designed and managed for its own greater profit a gigantic superstore installed in former underground atomic shelters. The story behind the story is that the minister of defence and the space industry, tired of hearing the university president ask for funding, told him "we'll give you these underground facilities that are no longer used. Figure out how to use them to make money". And what's more, in many universities, the most important person – with the exception of the general secretary of the party – is the vice-president in charge of doing business to fill the university's treasury.

I am far from familiar with every city in China, but based on the evidence, their capacity for initiative in the economic field is considerable. I was invited in 2001 to give a presentation before the conference of Chinese mayors, speaking after the Vice-Prime Minister at the time, Wen Jiabao, who has since become Prime Minister. His speech was surprising. Far from encouraging local elected officials to take initiatives in the economic sphere, he very sharply reprimanded them by saying, in substance:

> "Each one of you is engaged in projects each more Pharaonic than the next, everyone wants a higher tower or a bigger shopping centre than his neighbour (making one think of the competition between towns in the twelfth century for who would have the highest and largest cathedral), but with all that, you're headed straight to economic ruin, or to environmental catastrophe, and certainly both."

These words weren't intended for foreign journalists in order to demonstrate how much China cares about the environment. It was well and truly for domestic use and illustrated that the real control that the central government exercises over local processes is... how can we put it... far from perfect. But it also shows an important decentralisation of capacities and the will to take advantage of local resources.

Chinese economic development and the theory of governance

Perhaps what follows will seem too optimistic. But on the contrary, I believe it's necessary to take into consideration all these elements from the perspective of the theory of governance, demonstrating the advantages of this frenzied economic development. Beyond the enormous differences in form and context, the art of societies to manage themselves answers five great fundamental principles:

– the legitimacy and the cultural integration of the exercise of power: the society recognises itself in the manner it is run and recognises the capability of those who run it to do so,

– democracy, citizenship and ethics: the different members of society find themselves implicated in controlling the collective future and assume a balance of rights and responsibilities,

– the efficiency and competence of administrative systems,

– cooperation of different types of actors in the production of the common good; they identify themselves in a shared ethic that is the basis of "living together",

– the interaction of different levels of governance.

Let's briefly re-examine what preceded in the light of these principles.

Legitimacy and cultural integration

Today's Chinese leadership enjoys a certain legitimacy as long as they show themselves capable of incarnating the project of avenging history and assure the gradual access of the entire population to general well-being. It is a form of barter: you accept my authority, I'll assure you prosperity.

A work recently published under the direction of Mireille Delmas-Marty and Pierre-Etienne Will[2] thoroughly examines the regulatory systems that were likely to have foreshadowed the first signs of democracy in imperial China. While not a specialist myself, I am tempted to see similarities between the ancient rises in popular protest, admonitions to the emperor and the administration of the social order, with the readjustments we see in contemporary China, including the courage of domestic dissidents who are counted as august elders in Chinese history.

For more than a century, the well-educated have asked, "how can we be both modern and Chinese?" The insistence of leaders to re-label as Chinese anything borrowed from the occident may provoke smiles. After "Chinese Marxism", Hu Jintao promoted "Chinese Democracy" – under the direction of the Party. Mere propaganda? For myself, I believe that each society must make the effort of reinventing in each period of time a mode of administration with which it can identify, even while importing and assimilating external contributions.

---

2. Delmas-Marty, M. and Will, P.-E. (2007). La Chine et la démocratie, Paris, Éditions Fayard.

The openness advocated by Deng Xiao Ping proceeded in that spirit – in order to launch reform, it was necessary to stop speaking in slogans and to dare to think for oneself without fearing reality – notably concerning the situation in other countries. Who could have thought that in a country traumatised by costly Maoist digressions, such an enterprise of "liberation of the mind" could be possible? Who could have foreseen, regardless of the dramatic episode of Tian An Men, that the authorities would so rapidly gain control of development tools? Adherence to Deng's pragmatic approach corresponded all too well to the aspirations of a large sector of the population that wanted to escape poverty, put an end to adventurism and empty formulas, and guard against the fragmentation of the country.

China takes its time to "digest" contributions from the outside, whether they be technological or approaches to directing society. It ceaselessly publishes works by foreign thinkers. There is no risk of it renouncing a past of which it is all too proud.

Democracy, citizenship and ethics

In this respect, we are far from Western style democracy. Nevertheless, debates about the future of society, contradictions about the present model of development or the place of China in the world find an echo in the media, in the Party, with intellectuals and in gatherings of experts.

The media is closely watched by the powers that be. But we observe cracks such as Phoenix, the Hong Kong-based private television network that is watched everywhere, the press group South China Morning Post, under Party control but singularly independent, and specialised journals that are reserved for a more intellectual audience, but that exhibit an incontestable liberty of tone. Is the censorship stronger than that of Maxwell or Murdoch? Lets allow the reader to decide.

The Communist Party, 72 million members, reflects from within the contradictions that come to life in a society shaken by vertiginous economic expansion. Its aptitude to manage the risks, integrate the capitalists, and maintain a grip on the regional feudalism that insistently repeatedly escapes its control, presupposes more than the ability to stay in power by repression alone. Its immense difference from the institutional forms of our democratic societies, living under the light of the media, has little to do with the machinery the Party employs. But that doesn't prevent it from being sensitive to movements in public opinion (notably via Internet) and to demonstrate a level of adaptability without equal among the (rare) communist parties in power.

Finally there are the experts, academics and academicians. They participate more directly in the choices effected by the government than in France, and the reports of the Academy of Sciences I have been able to consult are of very high quality and candour. A Japanese-style process of gradual construction of consensus also seems to me to be at work in China. I wonder if a comparison between the present-day operation of the European Commission, that gradually builds consensus from the dialogue between member states and the intervention of lobbies, doesn't present analogies with the Chinese decision-making process.

The difficult point is ethics. Are the Chinese agreed today on the common values of "living together"? The project of avenging history is not enough. It may even unleash nationalistic failings – more-or-less instrumentalised by the authorities – representing a potential for danger that is not merely anecdotic. I've mentioned the confusion and erosion of points of reference. In conversations with young Chinese, their first-line attitude is a form of materialistic cynicism. They're afraid of "being taken in again" with ideology, that anything that is not of materialistic interest or related to prestige is suspect. But a society cannot be lastingly founded on cynicism.

Efficiency and competence of the administrative system

In relationship with urban growth, we've already seen the capacity of the Chinese state to coordinate civil servants and fulfil their expectations. Are these capacities, so visible in the field, adapted to the needs of Chinese society in the coming period? I'm markedly less sure.

China will need to confront problems of a new complexity. It knows and wants to prepare itself, but in order to do so a change in its administrative system is necessary. One can easily see this in the domains of water or the environment – a more systematic approach will be necessary and the Chinese administration, as far as I can see, has a hard time finding new bearings. That said, the problem is not specifically Chinese, but worldwide.

Shared production of the public good

Among the most prominent new business leaders figure children of the leaders of the heroic generation. Raised in affluence, they have often seen their elders suffer brutal reversals in fortune. In the same way, many of the "new rich" who were not lucky enough to benefit from their parents' network have themselves known poverty. Certain of them engage in actions for the public good, creating foundations, restoring monasteries, constructing schools, organising scholarship programs for poor children, etc. Social cohesion might well crumble in the coming years if the extremely wealthy no longer justify themselves by an active participation in China's recovery. Much will depend upon the ability of leaders to invent new schema for cooperation between different types of actors.

Interaction of levels of governance

In the West still reigns the illusion that each level of governance has its own jurisdiction. In China, local government, with the exception of poor rural districts, disposes of considerable fiscal resources granting them an important autonomy in the economic domain. Furthermore, their size is much more suited to developing a strategy of development. Instead the question is of the central government's capability of imposing on local government the reorientation of the model of development that everyone, the governed, experts and public opinion, all demand. The challenge will be the reconstruction of points of convergence of interests and interaction between central and local power, if the beautiful slogan "harmonious society" is to become something more than a pious hope.

Will the economic efficiency of Chinese governance enable sustainable human development?

Chinese governance displays, as soon as we move away from the strict question of economic development, very numerous flaws that in the more or less close future may lead to tragedy. "Finally", exclaims the reader, "we are leaving behind the fairy tale!" But no. It was necessary to start by explaining how for the first time in history a group of more than a billion people could conduct, for thirty years, development of this extent. But it still remains that in the light of the UNDP's Human Development Index, or the New Economic Foundation's "Well-being Manifesto", it is reasonable to call into question the progress of development of China – as well as that in most Western countries for that matter!

Numerous Chinese say themselves that China simultaneously suffers from the problems of underdeveloped countries – great poverty, low levels of public services, a very deteriorated natural environment, strong corruption – as well as the problems of overdeveloped countries, pollution, obesity, fragmentation of the family, children living in virtual worlds, etc.

On the economic level, the costs of the ingredients of production – land, capital, natural resources, energy, labour – are too low to encourage a constant effort of efficiency. On this level, the absence of any counter-power to the Chinese Communist Party will have important consequences in the future. The extremely rapid destruction of natural resources, sacrificed by a strategy of development by local government as well as by a short-sighted view of the benefits of scientific and technological developments, is alarming.

One of the questions posed in the Internet forum of the People's Daily [people.com.cn] where I often take part, struck me, "in Europe do the poor also hate the rich?" The Chinese government, in making economic development its absolute priority, has "broken the iron rice bowl", certainly concerning poverty – but also a minimum level of security assured for everyone. Can this new form of social pact, rebuilt around a project of avenging history and a tremendous will to "make it", resist the extravagant arrogance of a second generation of wealth, notably issued from the Party? Perhaps yes – as long as they remain enterprising and continue creating wealth.

In my discussions with them, young Chinese people all share pride in a China once again recognised as a world power that matters. But the over-ideologisation of the Maoist period and the difficulty of gaining a critical perspective on the past have finally created, in reaction against ideology, an intimidating loss of references – creating an oscillation between radical materialistic cynicism and the search for fundamental reasons for living.

Tian An Men, the Cultural Revolution, the Anti-Rightist Movement, the Great Leap Forward, none of these major events in contemporary Chinese history is allowed to become the object of scientific analysis, any more than it can give rise to a veritable public debate restituting history in all of its complexity. As long as the Party refuses this examination, real understanding of the present will escape the population. Some young people may even be tempted by an idealised rereading of Mao Zedong's China, where virtue and solidarity reigned for one and all.

In my exchanges with Chinese friends, I have often come to feel as if I am in a Greek tragedy where the heroes find themselves driven towards death by a story they take part in, unable to resist. But then again, isn't China just the extreme manifestation of our feeling in the West of heading towards the destruction of humanity, actors of our own trajectory towards ruin, opposing it with nothing but vague incantations about durable development?

The second China-Europe forum, in October 2007, was the occasion for a dialogue unique in its genre between Chinese society and European society [www.china-europa-forum.net]. Forty-six socio-professional and thematic workshops, bringing together a total of 300 Chinese and 550

Europeans, enabled progress in dialogue concerning every aspect of the evolution of our two societies. The conclusion is limpid. Overall, we are facing four common challenges – the radical reorientation of our models of development; the construction of ethics and identity bridging our historical roots and the challenges of the future; the necessity of together constructing world governance on the scale of our interdependencies; a revolution of governance enabling, in China as in Europe, the management of questions of a new complexity, simultaneously local and global, demanding we take into consideration the relationship between the issues and between the actors, entailing new ways of associating citizens with the major choices upon which our common future depends, founding a new social contract based upon the balance of rights and responsibilities.

Still too often, China sees itself in a course of catching up with the West. Moreover this is the argument most frequently advanced when someone from the outside points out the environmental damage resulting from development, the waste of raw materials and of persons, unrestrained capitalism, etc. – "yes, but we're only at the beginning, you Westerners did the same – now that you are rich, you can pay attention to the environment." But these are, if I may venture to say so, defensive arguments, arguments intended for foreigners. The doubt is much deeper in China. The leaders know full well that in the next stage it will be necessary to invent new forms of governance and that China is taking part in the conceptual and institutional invention of the twenty-first century. For the moment, China remains curious about everything that comes from the exterior – as long as it isn't a question of accepting lessons on good governance from a West that has happily pillaged the planet's resources. Having put the conventional thinking of the World Bank and other international institutions failingly to the test, and strong with its newly-found power, China is in a position to speak out for itself, without complex, concerning the definition of the rules for the coming new world. The road is wide for profound reflection among equals!

4

Governance for Equality
in Latin America

Jaime Rojas ELGUETA

"A country does not have to be considered ready for democracy,
it has to become fit through democracy."
Amartya SEN

Growth and economic inequality

In the imagination of Europeans, Latin America has always been a place in the middle of nowhere. A place where it is possible to use one's imagination, where one can give free play to associations, where to transform one's frustrated hopes or, in the negative case, a place of punishment and expiation. It is said, for example, that Darwin asked two men in Mendoza (Argentina):

> "Why are you not working? One of them replied, seriously, that the days were too long and the other one that he was too poor. The abundance of horses and food does not make people feel like working"[1].

This paternalistic point of view, which differs from Darwin's usually innovative view, is still firmly innate in the thinking of most of Latin America's elites. The image of Latin America as a place of punishment and atonement is, instead, reflected in Thomas Mann's Buddenbrooks family which sends the less brilliant son to Valparaiso and Daniel Defoe who, after his economic collapse, sends Robinson Crusoe to the island of Juan Fernandez.

---

1. Darwin, C. (2004). Viaggio di un naturalista intorno al mondo, Turin, Einaudi Editore.

Perhaps it is time to look at Latin America, as ex-President Lagos of Chile says, though not as an assiduous student, but rather as a creative one[2]. Without sticking too much to lessons learned, one may find proper solutions in a context of strong contrasts in light and shadows. In fact, for attentive observers, Latin America is positioned on the international scene as a real economic and social paradox[3].

The region presents numerous serious social problems such as ethnic discrimination in schools, a marked tendency towards family disintegration, a wave of rising youth crime and high unemployment rates. Development policies for reducing poverty have proven to be, in general, ineffective.

The region has reached more than 90% primary school enrolment, but as a result of poverty, family disarray (which is greatly affected by poverty) and widespread child labour, only 40% of children finish secondary school. Among the 20% of the poorer population this percentage is much lower: only 12%. 88% of poor students drop out before finishing elementary or secondary school[4]. The latest data available for 2005 (Economic Commission for Latin America, CEPAL), indicate that 39.8% and 15.4% of the population exist in a situation of poverty or extreme poverty, respectively. Thus, around 209 million people live in poverty and 81 million in conditions of indigence. The region beats the world record for inequality: half of the wealth is concentrated in 10% of the population (as opposed to 30% in industrialized countries). When compared with other countries, it is possible to notice that the gap between the richest 10% and the poorest 10% is 14 to 1 in Italy and 17 to 1 in the United States; while it is 54 to 1 in Brazil, 59 to 1 in Colombia, and 63 to 1 in Guatemala. For 8 of 10 Latin Americans, the levels of inequality today are "unfair" or "very unfair" (Latinobarómetro, 2007). It should also be noted

---

2. Lagos Escobar, R. (2007). "Chile: creatividad para el desarrollo", Letras Libres, Year VI, No 72.

3. The population of South America amounted, in 2005, to 542 million people of whom 58% are concentrated in just two countries, Brazil and Mexico. The population is expected to reach 628 million in 2015 of which 81% will live in cities. The region is made up of various sub-regional blocs: Mexico, Central America (Costa Rica, El Salvador, Guatemala, Honduras, Nicaragua, Panama), South America, which includes the Andean Community (Colombia, Ecuador, Bolivia, Peru) on one side, and Chile and the Mercosur (Argentina, Brazil, Paraguay, Venezuela, Uruguay) on the other. Latin America has been immersed, since the 60s, in an integration process of sub-regional integration, which has recently been accompanied by the proliferation of free trade agreements between countries that have played a decisive role in trade, contributing to economic growth and the development of the region.

4. Kliksberg, B. (2007). "Como avanzar la participación en América Latina, el continente más desigual. Anotaciones estratégicas", CLAD's Journal Reforma y Democracia, No 37.

that precariousness and social exclusion very often affect the indigenous people and ethnic minorities.

The tax burden in Latin America is less than half of that of the European Union and of developed countries in general. Consequently, the resources available for public policies are limited. In addition, the tax system is sharply regressive. More than half of the tax revenues come from excise taxes, only a fifth from taxes on income and wealth, and the remainder comes from the social security. This system clearly contributes to increasing inequality.

These disparities impede social mobility, and cause a sense of discouragement and powerlessness. This condition is reflected by the level of participation in decision-making. Socio-economic weakness means lack of information and education, of access to influential networks, of contacts, which results in poverty and asymmetries of power, which reinforces socio-economic asymmetries, and vice versa.

It should, however, be noted that in 2006, the economic growth of the region was as high as 5.6%. CEPAL anticipates a GDP growth rate of 5.0% for 2007 and 4.5% for 2008. If forecasts are confirmed, after six years of consecutive growth (2003-2008), the per capita GDP in the region will have reached an accumulative increase of 20.6%, which is equivalent to an annual average increase of over 4%. Despite such growth rates, the region is still the most unfair on the planet where the distribution of wealth is concerned.

Incidences of poverty and employment have, however, registered slight improvements, which lead CEPAL to talk of a "cautious optimism about the near future".

Governance and social cohesion

The economic growth of recent years has been accompanied by an exceptional political context: an unprecedented wave of elections between November 2005 and December 2006 involved 12 of the 20 Latin American countries. This phenomenon produced a very high level of mobilization of citizens and an electoral agenda which was focused on the topics of inequality and discrimination[5].

A common feature in the 12 elections was the fact that most candidates promised to promote increased citizen involvement and made a great

---

5. Rojas Elgueta, J. (2006). Afterword "Cinque scenari per il futuro", Atlante LUISS 2006, Rome, Luiss University Press.

effort to include this issue in their speeches and proposals for government programmes.

Actually, this trend had already started some time ago as is reflected by the fact that institutional crises of the past decade were resolved through constitutional decisions and that 14 presidents were removed from power because of their poor performance, without military intervention.

Citizens' pressure for increased involvement grows by the day. This is reflected in opinion polls, which show that authoritarianism or lack of communication are immediately received in a negative manner, and in massive protests if governments' promises are not maintained, or when requirements are not being attended to.

This characterization of the region puts the issue of governance at the heart of the political agenda. Latin America presents a mixed picture, as we have seen, where the light of hope appears in the increase in life expectancy, the reduction in illiteracy, extensive primary education, the decreasing rates of fertility and the progressive incorporation of women into the labour market, alternating with shadows remaining with the persistence of poverty and the growth of the informal economy, thereby aggravating the general conditions of good governance[6].

In this chapter, governance is referred to as a joint decision-making process that involves public and private organizations, businesses, individual citizens and international organizations[7]74. While in Europe social cohesion is more closely related to a sense of belonging, political participation, social integration and development as a way to remove barriers to freedom, as Amartya Sen says[8], it is an important element for the implementation of governance in Latin America.

In Latin America, the objective of achieving social cohesion is directly related to the possibilities of overcoming social inequality. This is because there is a pressing need to address persistent problems which, despite some progress reached in recent years, continue to exist: high rates of poverty and destitution, extreme inequality, and various forms of social

---

6. It may be interesting to keep in mind that a distinction is made in Latin America between "governance" and "good governance". According to the Spanish Royal Academy, Governance is "the art or manner of governing whose objective is to achieve a sustainable economic, social and institutional development, promoting a healthy balance between the State, the civil society and the market economy". Good governance, instead, is defined as "the ability of a social system to face challenges and seize opportunities in positive terms, to meet the expectations and needs of its members according to a system of formal and informal rules and procedures within which its members formulate their expectations and strategies" (UNDP, 2004; UN-CEPAL, 2007).

7. Bresser Preira, L. C. (2006). "El modelo estructural de gobernanza pública", Clad's journal Reforma y Democracia, No 36.

8. Sen, A. (2000). "Desarrollo y libertad", Editorial, Planeta.

discrimination[9]. According to CEPAL, social cohesion in Latin America refers not only to mechanisms in place for inclusion and exclusion in society, but also to how these can influence the perceptions and attitudes of the individuals in a society or community.

Social cohesion is the key to governance in Latin America to help confront inequality. Today, as the ex-President of BID, Enrique Iglesias, affirms, "public policies" is no longer a "bad phrase to pronounce"[10]. Moreover, the various States increasingly ask to get involved in solving problems and at the same time do not abandon the market economy, which is considered as the most desirable one (Latinbarometro, 2007).

The emergence of new policies and experiences in this area indicates that governance is an effective way to combat inequality through the increasing participation of citizens, businesses and other actors. This is why, in the following section, focus is placed on two areas of experience of governance: municipal policies and the participation of civic organizations in local development, and public policy support to businesses, in particular to the micro, small and medium enterprises (MSMEs). We also take into account some of the European experiences in order to explore, at the end, possible new alliances between Latin America and Europe.

Experiences of municipal governance

The *Consensus Pucon*[11] declares the importance of governance for social cohesion:

> "Taking into consideration that the objective of any public policy is the welfare of the people, we need to strengthen the capacities of public institutions in order to meet the demands for citizens' integration and belonging. To this end, it is necessary to promote criteria to universalize the diversity and the complexity of these requirements, as well as to enhance the quality of governance to make it a real instrument in the service of social cohesion".

---

9. For further information (2007) "Cohesión social y gobernabilidad en América Latina", "Corporación Escenarios", discussion paper for the 8° Biarritz Forum, held on October 8th and 9th, Santiago del Chile.

10. For further information: XVII Ibero-American Summit, held on November 8th and 9th, 2007, Santiago del Chile.

11. For further information (2007) "IX Conferencia Iberoamericana de Ministros de Administración Publica y Reforma del Estado", May 31st and June 1st, Pucon, Chile.

Various cities in Europe and Latin America are developing a proper concept of social cohesion, connected to the reality of belonging and the political and social climate. The term social cohesion is therefore not univocal, but an empirical concept. Beyond the meaning that a city attributes to social cohesion, the success factor is governance, i.e. the way the development process of cohesion is managed.

To better express this concept, reference is made to five experiences that are regarded as great successes for their sustainability over time. These five experiences have, indeed, attracted the attention of international organizations, and are considered as true laboratories of social participation. Three of these experiences take place in Latin America, the other two in Europe.

For Latin America: Porto Alegre (Brazil), a municipality with a participatory budget; Villa El Salvador (Perù), a municipality which is experimenting with a process of self-management; Rosario (Argentina), an excellent example of good governance.

For Europe: the case of citizens' clubs and societies which collaborate with the Municipality of Hospitalet (Spain), and the system of membership and collective participation of the Municipality of Amsterdam (Netherlands)[12].

The experience of Rosario (Argentina, 1 million inhabitants) began in the 90s, in a particular context which was characterized by serious problems of unemployment, poverty, social exclusion, and acute social tensions. The new municipal government, led by a minority party, launched a project in a direction that was completely different from policies undertaken at a national level. Rather than starting a privatization process, the new local government initiated a profound reform in order to make municipalities become organizations oriented towards active social inclusion, efficient, with a high level of professionalism, and fully interconnected with the public through multiple forms of popular participation. Today, Rosario is an example of an inclusive and participatory city.[13]

The experience of Porto Alegre (Brazil, 1.3 million inhabitants) started in 1989. This city also had a number of serious social problems to

12. Rojas Elgueta, J. (2007) "Ciudadanía y participación. Los casos de l'Hospitalet y de Amsterdam", CD-ROM "Lecciones y experiencias del Programa URB-AL. La contribución de las políticas locales y regionales a la cohesión social y territorial", European Commission, Rosario.

13. The project "Feria de Gobernabilidad Local para América Latina" of the United Nations Development Program identified Rosario in 2003 as one of the most well managed cities of Latin America according to a wide set of indicators. For further information: (2006) "Experiencia Rosario. Políticas para la gobernabilidad", UNDP, Rosario.

begin with: a significant portion of the population, in fact, was living in "favelas", and very critical of the administration which was regarded as inefficient and corrupt. The new municipal government, therefore, decided to launch a pioneering experiment aimed at creating a new relationship between the Municipality and the local civil society through the massive participation of its citizens in making decisions about the destination of economic resources and public investments. By promoting the idea among citizens that each single person can really influence public decision-making, this experience has been universally recognized as a milestone in the field of urban management[14].

Villa El Salvador (Peru, 350.000 inhabitants) is one of the most recent municipalities of Lima, founded as a result of the rapid growth of its population. Villa El Salvador has the typical features of the desert zones of the Peruvian coast and is characterized by its high degree of social organization: today, there are over 3,000 associations actively operating in a highly evolved process of local community development. Villa el Salvador has a particular form of social organization that makes citizens' groups the focus of local public management[15].

Half the population of Hospitalet de Llobregat (Catalonia, Spain, 260.000 inhabitants) are either immigrants or their descendants; 65% of immigrants are Latin American. The city, through its Strategic Plan and the civic association system (a phenomenon to which the local institutions also contribute), seeks to increase the economic well-being and social welfare of its citizens. The values that inspire the public policies are equality, environmental improvement, solidarity and the increase of the partnership in line with the Municipality's concept of active citizenship.

Amsterdam (Netherlands, 739.000 inhabitants) is the city in Europe with the highest percentage of ethnic minorities: there are 170 different ethnic groups, representing 48% of the total population. This city demonstrates that it is possible to transform cultural diversity into an engine for social development, where every individual has the opportunity

---

14. Habitat II of the UNO listed this experience among the 42 best examples of urban management in the world, and the Urban Management Program of the UNO in Latin America described it as one of the 22 best practices of public management. For further information: Kliksberg, B. (2007) "Como avanzar la participación en América Latina, el continente más desigual? Anotaciones estratégicas", Clad' Journal Reforma y Democracia, No 37.

15. The industrial park of this city, for example, is the result of the progressive organization of small entrepreneurs scattered everywhere in the slums and, at first, very poorly networked. For further information: Michel Azcueda (2007) "La experiencia de Villa El Salvador – Perù", CD-ROM "Lecciones y experiencias del Programa URB-AL. La contribución de las políticas locales y regionales a la cohesión social y territorial", European Commission, Rosario.

to develop his or her own talents to become what s/he wants to be. This idea is associated with the slogan "People make Amsterdam".

What are the conditions of governance of these experiences?

• Deep knowledge of the city, of its potential, of the people's interests, of social relationships within the community and the relationship with the outside world, of human and material resources, the culture and traditions, as well as the recent and past history (citizen's biography). It is important that the knowledge of the local reality is constantly being updated, so that information concerning the development of the local community is complete and shared among all its members.

• Image and goals that are closely related to the identity of the city. The process of defining the objective to be pursued should not be bureaucratic, but participatory and felt by the population. The objective has to be built gradually, becoming more and more "visible" both, for members of the community, and also for those from elsewhere.

• Attainable and tangible targets, shared by the population, which citizens can recognize as their own. Achieving one objective creates the basis for achieving another, more difficult one. It is essential to unify the individual interests with the collective ones, as it helps to increase the level of efficiency and to strengthen citizens' identity and that of the community as a whole.

• Representative organisations. It is necessary that the resident population, the different social sectors, people of different ages, gender and background, form representative organizations in order to ensure individual and collective participation.

• Horizontal management of the process of "citizen's participation". The five cities cited above did not adopt a paternalistic attitude towards the most socially disadvantaged groups. On the contrary, they consider the citizens' diversity as a keystone. All five cities have found a specific way to accomplish social cohesion, involving the citizens in the process of policy management.

• Counting on the resources that are available. It is necessary to develop a plan which starts from what is effectively available at the moment, basing it on a realistic potential for growth.

• Disseminating information to achieve enhanced transparency. Information is a precondition for a transparent public administration.

What can we learn from these experiences?

There are no models for social cohesion, just as there is no unique solution. Models do not exist because the definition of public policies is a process that arises from the particular identity of a city. Moreover, there isn't a unique single solution, because each process develops over time and requires permanent transformation; moveover each process is different.

Increasing the value of the micro, small and medium enterprises (MSMEs): a common objective

The deepening economic gap in Latin American which has led to social exclusion confirms the need for economic and employment policies that are aimed at equal development. This approach is important in relation to the objectives of the new economic agenda in Latin America, whose goals are: competitiveness, promotion of international trade, more infrastructures, and the creation of social networks. These goals are closely interrelated and highlight the need for filling the gaps between territories within one and the same country and between territories of different countries[16].

Though the phenomenon of regional development is primarily associated with economic aspects, it also has political, cultural and social dimensions. For this reason, the design of regional development policies is based on a multilevel approach to governance, which, in the view of the Organization for Economic Cooperation Development (OECD), should be twofold: vertical (connections between national, regional, and municipal levels) and horizontal (interaction between homologue entities and regions).

The vision of citizenship in Latin America is overcoming numerous difficulties that derive from the ultra-orthodox economic thinking which was prevalent in the past two decades. The idea of doing without the State, minimizing its role and entrusting everything to the market, is changing in favour of a new idea which is based on the partnership between an able and socially sensitive State, socially responsible

---

16. Rojas Elgueta, J. y M. Burgarella, "El valor de las Mipymes en el futuro de la cooperación económica Europa - América Latina", European Commission, conference "Supporting MSMEs in Latin America. Experiences and perspectives of the Al-Invest Programme", November, 21st-23rd, 2007, Bologna.

enterprises and a fully mobilized civil society. A paradigm of regional development is emerging which places the improvement and increase of "equal economic competitiveness" at the centre of its activities. It redesigns the relationship between business and territory: the territory becomes the strategic environment in which to compete, and companies start perceiving the need to act according to criteria of equity in favour of a balanced regional development. New policies and instruments for institutional intervention are being inaugurated and space is opening up for new social and economic actors that had previously been considered marginal.

Positively influencing people's productive opportunities has an important impact on social cohesion, because it reinforces the sense of belonging, i.e. makes people consider themselves both, as agents and beneficiaries of the development process.

Micro, small and medium enterprises (MSMEs) are key players in regional development. They are socially and economically important, in Europe as well as in Latin America. In the EU, they account for 99% of all enterprises, some 65 million jobs and provide a significant contribution to entrepreneurship and innovation (European Media & Marketing Survey – EMS 2006). In Latin America, their importance is equally significant, although quite variable depending on the country, and essentially depending on the influence of the "formal" micro enterprises.

In Latin America, public policies in favour of local economic development increasingly focus on micro enterprises and their social, political and economic role. The economic weight and relevance of the employment of micro enterprises are closely connected to their strong links with the territory. Contrary to the past, the present challenge is that the small and micro enterprises become relevant economic actors in local development. This challenge has become a common objective of decision makers in many Latin American countries.

The best indicator of the (economic and social) value attributed to the MSMEs as actors in the field of governance and territorial cohesion, is the proliferation of institutions, structures and tools established to provide support to clusters of MSMEs and to territorial innovation. This is also reflected by the fact that in most parts of Latin America, MSME-supporting policies are dealt with by those holding the rank of Minister or Deputy Minister.

A growing number of public and private institutions are experimenting with initiatives to stimulate cooperation between companies. An example of a long-term policy to develop business competitiveness and partnership between enterprises is the policy launched by the Chilean National Council for Innovation and Competitiveness, designed for the forthcoming 15 years (National Council for Innovation and Competitiveness, Chile,

2007). Another example is Mexico where national policies tend to reinforce the support for territorial development and internationalization of business associations, considering these two aspects as two sides of the same coin (OECD, 2004).

Partly thanks to the cooperation with Europe, local development in Latin America has in recent years generated the development of a number of concepts, of new public institutions and laws aimed at economic promotion: business incubators, local development agencies, business service centres, etc. This kind of experience helps increase awareness of the importance of promoting business associativity to develop business competitiveness.

The evolution from a simple action plan (aimed at promoting punctual support for the creation of individual enterprises) towards a more complex one (which stimulates medium-term transformation processes that are oriented towards groups of enterprises) is a trend that characterizes many programs and policies.

This trend indicates that governance is also important for integration between policies, apart from the integration of the actors. Local economic development is not opposed to internationalization of production, and the latter is no longer a separate sphere of social development. Competitiveness is pursued with greater vigour if smaller enterprises are associated with those who share common values such as high product quality as a unique result of a combination of local production factors, respect for decent working conditions and for the environment.

Some relevant aspects for the future

To develop a vision for the future, the following aspects need to be kept in mind:
• A clear and strong idea of identity is the element that sustains governance. Identity is recognizable through the analysis of biographies: biographies are not only about individuals, but also about organizations and cities. Each city has its own origin which defines its character. Civic identity develops through partnerships. It allows for the participation of individuals in organizations which are able to formulate their own needs. In the context of governance, policies must be consistent with the idea of a collective identity. The concept seems simple in itself. The challenge, which is not easy to solve, is to convert an idea into intention, and to convert an intention into action. The solution may be facilitated through an enhanced emphasis on process: the process of translation from

ideas to intentions and from intention to subsequent action. Therefore, the exercise of governance is nothing more than the management of a specific process characterized by the interaction between individuals and between organizations with a strong identity. The style of management of this process can be quite different: directive (vertical) or dialogical (horizontal). The latter is characterized by leadership which guides and supports the process, making it more visible and less codified. It is also typical for the governance experiences described above which indicate a direction for the future.

• Latin America is the region of the world which shows the highest affinity with Europe. The sustainability of social, territorial, environmental and relational development is increasingly important for business development. Sustainability is increasingly considered to be the success factor for competitiveness. Therefore, policies no longer tend to be an antithesis to social and territorial development. In other words, in Latin America and Europe enterprises require a favourable environment in order to be competitive. Moreover, the strategic dimension of competitiveness and innovation develops through partnership (business association). Opportunities for a growth in competitiveness are presently higher than they were in the past. For the future, a new strategic alliance for collaboration and cooperation can be vitalized, whose basis can be found in the statements of the summits of Guadalajara (2004) and Vienna (2006)[17].

• As stated at the beginning of this chapter, Europe has always regarded Latin America as a virtual subject rather than a real one that it can engage with in common long-term strategies. A possible way to change this view is to pay attention to some common requirements for socio-economic development in the international context: to value the small and medium businesses in order to promote sustainable and egalitarian development. Economic cooperation between the territories of the two continents can develop this value. The objective could be, somehow, the same, even if the reasons and the point of growth achieved in the two continents are different. It seems that today's Europe and Latin America face, however, the same problem: the first asks itself "How to compete in the international scenario, where other economies are growing more and faster?", and the second asks "How to define and implement policies that enhance equity?" Therefore, the big question for both, Latin America and Europe is "How to compete ethically against unfair competition?"

---

17. For information: EC (2007), Regional paper for Latin America 2007-2013, E/2007/1417, Brussels.

One of the working hypothesis for the future may be the building of strategic territorial alliances between European and Latin American clusters of enterprises to jointly tackle the global marketplace[18]. The overriding demand of the smaller enterprises, though not only of these, is to restore the competitiveness of the product. Size is not a factor which compromises the ability of small businesses to position themselves in international markets. The fundamental factors for competitiveness are quality and product innovation: innovation of traditional products, of processes and organizations so as to encourage the talents and capacities of individuals. The central theme is, therefore, global governance. The key relationships are between local stakeholders (public and private) and between these and national and local governments. The relationship between local and national governments can be strengthened, in particular, thanks to the common aspects of identity between the two continents – aspects that in the last few decades have been somewhat underestimated.

---

18. The definitions of "aggregations of enterprises" are many and varied. There are several concepts of combination of enterprises, which not necessarily have to do with the production chain (clusters, industrial district). From our point of view, the important thing is that, despite the specific meaning of "aggregation", we refer to the common objective of the business collaboration between enterprises.

5

Global governance

The Illusory Quest for the Leviathan?

Jean-Michel SEVERINO and Olivier RAY
(Translated from the French)

«Le plus grand problème pour l'espèce humaine,
celui que la nature la force à résoudre, est de parvenir
à une société civile administrant universellement le droit.»[1]

"Why, by interweaving our destiny with that of any part of Europe,
entangle our peace and prosperity in the toils of European ambition,
rival-ship, interest, humour, or caprice? It is our true policy to steer
clear of permanent alliances with any portion of the foreign world,
so far [...] as we are now at liberty to do it."[2]

Solidarity and global regulations: public policy in response to the challenges of globalisation

Every human community is built on mechanisms for coordination, arbitration and decision. If these systems of governance remain largely imperfect in numerous countries across the planet, those of the international community pose problems even more vast. And yet it is not for lack of being confronted with urgent challenges. The need for solidarity and global regulation are becoming more pressing day by day.

---

1. 'The greatest problem for the human species, whose solution nature compels it to seek, is to achieve a universal civil society administered in accord with the law.' Kant, E. (1794). The Idea for a Universal History from a Cosmopolitan Point of View.
2. Washington, G. (1796). Farewell Address.

First, the need for solidarity. Globalisation, a phase of rapid intensification of cross-border interactions, is not new. Neither is poverty. But never has the clash between poverty and wealth been as intense as today. Each year, while the global Gross Domestic Product (GDP) progresses four or five points, four million additional people suffer from malnutrition – the indisputable mark of misery. The persistence of illnesses that we know how to treat also brings into question our humanist principles – two million inhabitants of the South continue to die from paludism every year, a sign of the limits of global solidarity. Even as econometricians wonder about the correlations between globalisation and inequalities, the perception of inequities in a globalised news media is undeniably increasing. A mixture of objective inequality and the growing perception of injustice, this "planetary gap between haves and have-nots", pushes communities to turn in on themselves in isolationism and exacerbates political tension. Every year it pushes millions of people onto the painful path of exile. The challenges that it incarnates, in the North as in the South, thus call out for the emergence of international social policy enabling the redistribution of some of the gains of globalisation and supporting integration of the most fragile economies into the global economic system[3].

Next, the need for regulation. Perhaps even more than global social questions, the endangerment of the public good on a global level affecting that which we depend upon to live – health, environment – is alarming. Even if the latest wave of H5N1 caused no more than a few hundred deaths across the planet, even if Ebola is today contained, even if the Chikungunya alpha-virus has still not killed, what will happen with the next epizootic diseases? The AIDS epidemic has shown us. Viruses know no border, the emergence of new planetary pandemics renders the creation of true global health policies necessary. Scientific research these last ten years doesn't allow the least doubt that the rate of global warming and the deterioration of the environment is such that over the coming century it may menace the very existence of part of humanity. Confronted with an environmental crisis that goes beyond the competence of individual nations, only global-wide environmental policy will enable creation of the necessary change.

---

3. Cf. Naudet, J.-D., Severino, J.-M. and Charnoz, O. (2007). 'Aide internationale : vers une justice sociale globale', Esprit.

Development aid, figure of the aspirations and failings of global governance

Combining the redistributive mandate of global social action with the regulatory mandate necessary for the protection of global public property, development assistance can be conceived, here in the beginning of the 21st century, as the embryo of such a planetary public policy for the management of North-South relations concerning globalisation. It indeed addresses itself to the regions at the heart of the identified challenges. Because of the socio-economic weaknesses affecting their rapidly growing populations, the countries of the South are often the first victims of global deregulation, whether they are climatic, sanitary or economic. But these countries are also actors that are largely implicated themselves – consider the massive deforestation in Indonesia or the health risks linked to the weakness of veterinary systems in many African countries. Because of this fact, as well as because of the precious natural patrimony they house, these countries are necessarily at the heart of the sustainable solutions that the international community must bring to these planetary challenges.

And yet even if global governance can be considered in the context of this emerging global political policy, we still have good reasons to worry. From summit to conference, we're forced to acknowledge that the innumerable attempts at dialogue and mutual agreement end with results lacking any proportion with the scale of the problems they are intended to treat. Effectively, regardless of all the signs of urgency, the implementation of financing for global solidarity continues to stumble over difficulties of organisation, coherence, mobilisation of the actors, divisions and "stowaways", that undermine its effectiveness on the only scale that matters, global. The precise and largely agreed-upon definition of global public "evils" (poverty, insecurity, illness or climatic disturbances), the expert quantification of the means that must be mobilised to treat them, and the often sophisticated tools needed for their treatment all come up against the incessant challenges of all collective action.

Negotiations on climate change are a telling example. We now know with a high degree of precision the dangers we are exposed to (rising sea levels, drought and famine, deregulation of ecosystems, loss of biodiversity, etc.), their locations as well as their probable time lines. Collectively, we master tools (technical, financial, regulatory, etc.) that are more and more effective in the fight against greenhouse gases. We also know the annual cost that would be implicated in their reduction to acceptable levels, in the adaptation of our environment to climate change and in insuring against the damage they provoke – roughly 1.5% of global GNP, which is to say one point less than arms spending. In spite of that, today in 2008 the international community still lacks the unified mechanism for collective action that we nevertheless know we must create.

Reform of the United Nations, a persistent news story in the international press for decades, offers striking resemblances: even though everyone agrees on the diagnostic of the present problems (insufficient representation of emerging powers, duplication of organisations and internal incoherencies, etc.) and that we can identify the necessary ingredients for a veritable reform of the United Nations, the historical summit that was supposed to produce an ambitious renovation of the system in 2005 fizzled out without a whimper – tainted by a succession of political compromises.

Global health policy also suffers from related symptoms. The ambitious objectives announced to drum rolls each year in the treatment of AIDS, paludism or tuberculosis are rarely reached. Even if this can seldom be attributed to a lack of means: World Health Organisation (WHO), United Nations Children's Fund (UNICEF), United Nations Population Fund (UNPFA), Joint United Nations Program on HIV/AIDS (UNAIDS), NGO (Non-governmental organisations (NGO), foundations, bilateral development agencies, The Global Fund To Fight AIDS, Tuberculosis and Malaria, International Drug Purchase Facility to improve access to treatment against HIV/AIDS, tuberculosis and malaria (UNITAID), pharmaceutical laboratories, etc. – the splintering of global health policy among the multitude of institutions responsible for it and the whole host of mechanisms for its financing bring about a revolting loss of efficiency in the treatment of the diseases that continue to overwhelm the populations of the South. Experts estimate that 2.5 billion dollars a year would be enough to prevent and treat paludism. But while the resources are largely available, the incoherencies between actors regarding strategy, the ceaseless processes of negotiation over the policies to put into place, and the competition to obtain financing result in these efforts falling far short of their potential.

Genealogy of the common good: the origins of collective action

How can we explain the persistent dysfunctioning of these international public policies, of which the necessity is nevertheless recognised by all and the problems largely well-documented? Admittedly, in addition to the constraints of all collective action are the obstacles of language, culture and national susceptibilities. Anyone who has worked in an international organisation cannot be unaware of these constraints. But it is not enough to explain the permanent tribulations of mechanisms for global governance. In reality they can be linked to a more fundamental factor, the absence of a concept of "common good" at a global level. Even while humanity has in fact never before been so united by the series of menaces weighing down on its shoulders, in practice the general interest of the international community continues to be strictly defined as the sum of the particular interests of the member states that compose it. And yet as a famous French political scientist wrote, "the addition of the self-interest of individuals will never add up to the general interest"[4].

In our societies, this concept arose from royal proclamation. The "common good" issued from individual interests was largely constituted by violence, as the monarchies succeeded in crushing feudalism, religious authorities and particularisms of all sorts. "I am the State", Louis XIV is supposed to have exclaimed – the common good is incarnated in the monarchy, who personifies the nation. The revolutionaries, seizing power from the monarchy, had only to democratise this powerful concept, inherited from an absolutist system. By confiding sovereignty to the people via parliament and the electoral ritual, they enabled it to become a part of the definition of common good. But, by preoccupation for efficiency in the administration of the state, the republic cheerfully persisted in crushing individual interests in the service of a "general interest", presented as more legitimate.

But on a global scale, no authoritarian form existed before the common good. The "international community" is a quite particular community, in that it more resembles the State of Nature described by Hobbes (characterised by the absence of central authority, and therefore by anarchy and violence) than the Social Contract as it was conceived of by Jean-Jacques Rousseau. The mechanism for definition of the common good, prerequisite for political action, here resembles a process of permanent bargaining, where integrated and coherent public policy can be led only in the case of lasting agreement between the whole of the concerned parties – some 192 nations, a series of private actors and a battery of international organisations. We find ourselves at the heart of the problem in international negotiation concerning the climate, trade or Human Rights: In the absence of the Leviathan, we live in a profoundly unstable system, with its fragile consensus perpetually called into question.

---

4. Burdeau, G. Traité de Sciences Politiques.

Taking example from the genesis of our own political systems, we Europeans deplore the absence of a "planetary social contract" – or we deplore its limited scope, if we define international law as a rough version of it. In all logic, we affirm that global governance, in order to advance, requires reinforcement of the central authority of the international system and the emergence of common values. In a profoundly Kantian view of history, we believe this will yield greater efficiency, coherence, and ultimately, peace. Therefore our project for global governance consists more or less in gradually instituting a network of organisations, associated with the United Nations, modelled on the classical state (the General Assembly of the United Nations representing a form of "world parliament", the International Court of Justice and the International Criminal Court "a world system of justice", the Security Council a "world government", the Secretary General of the United Nations a "world president", etc.), supported by a certain consensus of international public opinion concerning their legitimacy. We have only to turn our regard to Brussels in order to persuade ourselves. The European Union, born from the desire to influence the course of the fratricidal history of Europe, is nothing but the gradual constitution of a social contract on a multinational regional level thanks to the establishment of organisations charged with incarnating it. And the improbable success of the European utopia dreamed up by Schumann and Monet can be explained by the fact that each European state is fundamentally the heir of this Rousseauian tradition of the construction of a general interest by way of the state. While it is neither illegitimate nor unreasonable to aspire to reproduce this political experience on a planetary scale, it is important to become aware that this aspiration is not universally shared. Our vision of global governance, fundamentally developed from the concept of common good, is the product of a collective memory that is ours alone. It comes into conflict with that of peoples and nations heir to their differing histories.

The lot reserved to the report "Delivering as One' commissioned by the Secretary General of the United Nations, Kofi Annan, for the improvement and coherence of the UN system, illustrate this discrepancy. The High-level Panel on United Nations System-wide Coherence, of which I was a member, was given responsibility for recommending a corpus of reforms that would enable to render more effective the workings of the United Nations, notably in the areas of development, humanitarian assistance and the environment. Beginning with the diagnosis that global governance of these planetary challenges suffered from harmful splintering (overlapping organisations and the incoherency of recommended policies, resulting in the operational ineffectiveness of the entire UN system), our recommendations went in the direction of a greater integration of organisations and financing, with the establishment of a clearer chain of command, oriented towards measurable goals. These ambitious findings were based on a very "organised" vision of global governance, postulating the existence of well-understood general interest in the domains of development and the protection of the environment. Beyond the resistance to change present in all organisations, this methodological bias may explain why this exercise in reform (even if recognised on both sides of the Atlantic as necessary and urgent) has still not resulted in the recommended changes. Building on the apparent consensus concerning the system's patent problems, the report anticipated possible agreement concerning the solutions to apply in the matter of governance. Efficiency would logically follow from greater integration, better organisation and more stable financing of the institutions in charge of elaborating and implementing global public policy.

Re-examining the fault lines: the clash of political mythologies in the West

This episode betrayed the existence of a veritable shock of cultures concerning global governance, resulting in profound mutual incomprehension in the domain of coordination. These fundamental differences, which express themselves most vigorously in trans-Atlantic relations, question the supposed unity of point of view of a largely phantasmagoric "West". The manner Europeans have campaigned for the establishment of planetary public institutions in recent decades shows that we have insufficiently taken into account the fundamental conceptual differences regarding common good on a global level. In effect, the world's greatest power does not share the institution-oriented vision of international relations that is ours. Refusing to postulate the existence of any given general interest on an international level (where would it come from?), Americans conceive of global governance as a system of free competition between different actors – public or private – who establish cautious bilateral contracts. It consists, as it were, in a vast market endowed with a minimum of exogenous rules, leaving free reign between institutions and ways of doing things. Moreover, Americans envision cooperation by way of a multilateral system as nothing but one of the options to resolving a given problem. Their power allows them the liberty to pursue a policy labelled "forum-shopping" – the American government temporarily invests itself in organisations susceptible of serving their policy, while weakening others. And simultaneously reserving the right to act unilaterally at any time. A regrettable tendency for those who conceive of these institutions as the foundation stone of global governance.

In reality it corresponds to a vision of political efficiency quite different from our own. While we see the institutional jungle of the United Nations, where different agencies servicing the same policies find themselves in competition with one another, as one of the causes of its inefficiency, the Americans perceive this same organisation as an excessively centralised bureaucracy, a stickler for regulations. Where we esteem that more planning and coordination are necessary, they advocate decentralisation. Where we judge that efficient public policy requires continuous funding, they believe that the permanent search for resources is one of the levers of effective management. According to the American conception of international relations, improvement in the efficiency of the United Nations will come with its gradual evolution towards a system of weak organisations, all in competition with one another, where in order to survive, the different actors (who have no reason to exist except their demonstrable efficiency), must convince donors of the validity of their action. In the image of Schumpeter's "creative destruction", the disappearance of the least efficient actors thus enables the conservation of the system's health and vigour. Once this competition between actors is assured, the frontiers of competences between the institutions (another element of the "Delivering as One" report) are of little importance according to this analysis, the most efficient finding themselves awarded new missions. That this system ends up creating incoherencies in the field is not the primary concern of Americans, because their vision is not, in the final analysis, that of a coherent and structured international scene. As in any efficient market, what is important is that the client (the donor) is satisfied with the service provided. Consequently it is not shocking that the "common good", promoted by organisations in charge of defending it, largely agree with the interests of their financiers. John Bolton, the influential and quite outspoken neoconservative, vigorously defended this vision of the UN system during his mandate as United States ambassador to the United Nations – shocking in passing more than one African diplomat.

A telling example of this conception of the "common good" as the result of the interaction between individual interests rather than from political organisation is the role played on the international scene by the great American philanthropists. Encouraged by big fiscal gifts accorded by the federal government, Bill Gates and other fabulously wealthy benefactors act internationally with a strike force well superior to that of important development organisations. The Bill and Melinda Gates Foundation today is worth close to seventy billion dollars (the equivalent of the Gross Domestic Product of Bangladesh or Vietnam), spending three billion dollars a year, including a substantial part in international agriculture, health and education programmes. Overseas donations by American foundations exceed three billion dollars annually – which is to say more than France spends on development aid by way of multilateral organisations, the European Development Fund, the World Bank, or the UN. In this way the United States manages to tighten its grip on an important part of the international agenda by way of its great fortunes. In fact, these private foundations have become, by way of the capital they mobilise, veritable actors influencing the agenda, "agenda-setters", in the world of development. Ted Turner, American billionaire who has set himself the objective of keeping a watchful eye on the correct payment of American contributions to the UN budget, has contributed more than a billion dollars – since founding his "United Nations Foundation" in 1998 – to humanitarian projects led by the UN – substituting himself de facto for the American government, which in turn assumes an important fiscal price (donations to philanthropic foundations being exempt from taxation in the United States) in order that private actors develop a so-called action of general interest on the international plane. Contrary to what is often said about the figures of official development assistance (that represents less than 0.2% of their GDP), American activity on the international scene is not necessarily less generous than that of Europe, but radically different in its tools, actors and philosophy. This accumulation of individual actions gives free reign to various community actions of solidarity, beginning with those of religious communities, more and more active in Africa and the Middle East. Despite the progressive emergence on European soil of private foundations and the energy of charitable NGOs, such a privatisation of international action seems inconceivable on this side of the Atlantic. In the European political system, public action is traditionally financed by taxes, by intermediary of the state, and exercised by force of law. The legitimacy of governmental policy is judged well superior to that of a Mister Turner, Gates or Soros, for whom no one has voted and therefore no citizen would be able to influence their actions. Nevertheless, on the other coast of the Atlantic their legitimacy is real and indisputable, their economic success serving as the ultimate proof of their value. That which we deplore as the communitisation of American foreign politics (take for example the role of evangelist lobbies in Washington, which carry important weight in choices about American aid), the Americans see as a symbol of their profoundly democratic nature.

In the same way our political culture of the social contract influences our conception of global governance, factors profoundly rooted in American identity are at the origin of this fragmenting and divisive vision of collective international action. "Americans do not embrace ideology because America is an ideology" writes Siobhan McEvoy-Levy[5]; this ideology is determinant for understanding America. In effect, how can we explain the American refusal to define common good on a global level, by means of global institutions, in the image of how we see the European Community organisations at the European level? According to the "American myth", founding story from which Americans draw their identity and their political culture, the archetypal American is an individual (a devout and courageous head of the household) at the conquest of the hostile western frontier. In contrast to Europeans, he knows no previously constituted government capable of defining or defending any idea of "general interest" at all. Moreover, the pilgrims who landed on the coast of the new world in the 17th century, whom American mythology continues to consider as the veritable ancestors of the American people, were precisely religious communities fleeing European countries who bloodily repressed their minorities. The idea that in this new world the state could continue to impose its conception of common good to the detriment of individual interests was properly inconceivable. What's more, the Americans rapidly made this clear to the British crown.

The first pilgrims fleeing that violent, corrupt and miscreant Europe to forge their own destiny gave meaning to their flight by attributing a messianic calling to it, "For we must consider that we shall be as a City upon a hill. The eyes of all people are upon us".[6] It would have therefore been properly inconceivable for their heirs to compromise this dearly-paid liberty by linking themselves, by the intermediary of restrictive treaties, to their former henchmen. From the Carter Doctrine to the project for the greater Middle East, this sense of American mission, "the manifest destiny", remains keen. The supremacy of American ideals (whether they concern human rights, democracy or freedom of enterprise) therefore can not be inflicted with the compromises implied by restrictive international treaties with less virtuous states. After all, before it was incarnated by the European Union, the old continent was the battleground of religious war, Napoleonic crusades, the First World War and Nazism. The isolationism that long defined American foreign policy, and the profound hostility to anything resembling world government, finds its roots in the genesis itself of the American nation and in the self-definition of American society.

The differences in American and European approaches to climate change illustrate this shock of cultures that puts a damper on all progress in global governance. The refusal of the United States to sign the

5. Cf. McEvoy-Levy, S. (2001). American Exceptionalism and U.S. Foreign Policy: Public Diplomacy at the End of the Cold War. Macmillan.

6. Winthrop, J. (1630). Governor of the Massachusetts Bay Colony, address, 'A Modell of Christian Charity'.

Kyoto Protocol and the over cautiousness of American negotiators in Bali in December 2007 clearly attests to the profound hostility to any engagement that constrains the afore-mentioned American sovereignty. But they are also symbolic of the unfailing faith – without any European equivalent – in the capacity of technological progress to save us from the catastrophic consequences of climate change. This faith in the future and in progress, particularly well-anchored in American political culture, is characteristic of the world's foremost nation of immigrants. The millions of Europeans who travelled to American coasts in the 19th century, the Mexicans who cross the Rio Grande or the Asians who land by thousands every year to tempt their chance on the West Coast share this same American dream and are transformed by this same certainty in a better life tomorrow. It is not surprising that while Europeans develop a set of complex regulations, establish a common market for carbon exchange and establish diverse institutions to combat climate change (are these not the tools that sealed European construction's success?), the Americans place their faith in technological innovation. But consequently neither is it surprising that a new system of global governance of the environment proves to be so difficult to attain.

Identity processes: unbreachable gulf for global governance?

Why have we delved so far back into the past to find the American and European origins of global governance? Because their deep roots in our respective processes of self-definition teach us there is little chance for their radical or rapid evolution. And yet we live today in an international system lacking in all central authority. In this, the situation is closer to the American vision of global governance, centred on the concept of the market. Defence of the status quo being by definition much easier than establishment of a planetary social contract based on reinforced and legitimate institutions, the perpetuation of the system we know today is the most probable hypothesis for the coming decades. The international community will continue to find partial consensus where there are converging interests, to the detriment of the coherence of the whole system – and therefore to the detriment of its effectiveness.

Must we resign ourselves to this chaos? Is it vain to combat for policies of regulation and world-wide solidarity as we conceive them? Certainly not. But this analysis must give form to our strategy for action in these ambitious projects. Two errors are to be prescribed if we wish to advance on the path of more organised and effective global governance.

The first error, nevertheless common among Europeans, is to start from the principle that every rational actor shares the same vision of common good, to which global governance must tend. The truth is that we are not all products of the same history, and that we have developed quite different manners to envisage common good. The second error is to think that our conception of effectiveness and common good is superior to that of Americans, who "don't understand anything". Because the shock of cultures we have described is above all a shock of modes of rationality. The profound ineffectiveness of the mechanisms for global governance experienced today can be explained, not in the inherent ineffectiveness of one or the other of these visions of global governance, but in the fundamental incompatibility between two ways of thinking.

All the same, we have good reasons to believe in a stronger vision of general interest and in an elaborate organisation of relations between states.

The first is the immensity and the gravity of the dangers we are facing. It is not particularly original to assert that the interdependence between peoples will grow in this time of globalisation. Neither is it useful to draw up a catalogue of the calamities we are exposed to because of the growth of planetary inequality, global warming or emerging diseases. It is enough to recognise that for the first time in human history, these challenges menace not only the international community as a whole, but also its most privileged subjects. And "the imagination works harder in darkness than it does in the light"[7]. The tragedy of Hurricane Katrina in New Orleans demonstrated that rising sea levels and the intensification of natural disasters no longer affects only faraway under-developed peoples, rendering the cost of idleness more visible and the necessity of regulation more obvious. As for the global social question, it menaces the very opening of the international system, as the losers of globalisation, undermined by their sense of identity, take refuge in constrictive communitisations. In the absence of global approaches to solidarity and regulation, globalisation thus digs its own grave.

The second reason, which is superimposed upon the first, is the emergence on the forefront of the international scene of countries whose history and political culture are more compatible with organised solutions to global governance. For example, the African continent will total more than one fifth of world population in the next forty years; the world will therefore be more attentive to African nations' strong attachment to using the United Nations system for treating the problems facing Africa. In the next fifty years, the anticipated increase in the Chinese GDP will hurl it into a percentage of the world's GDP never before experienced

---

7. Kant, E. The end of all things.

in history – the 21st century will not be American, but Asian. Tomorrow, we will discuss global policy first with the Chinese. And thousands of years ago, when our ancestors were members of dispersed tribes, Chinese civilisation had already constructed a strong imperial central power, that the communist party has extended to this very day. Even more than ours, their society has acquired a structured vision, based on common good. Will an Asian hegemony reveal itself as more responsible than the precedent? Today, that is difficult to assert. We can nevertheless wager that the emergence from now until then of an international system that is more multi-polar, a space for complex negotiation between Asian, African, American and European powers, will offer a more favourable environment for the construction of global institutions.

What multilateral policy for a world of complexity and possibility?

Must we Europeans patiently wait for the coming of such a multi-polar and structured world? Even if none of us will live long enough to see it, we can start establishing its foundations today. To this end, we should concentrate our efforts in four directions.

Despite the resonance of exceptionalism in American society and its determinate influence upon the foreign policy of the world's foremost power (the neoconservatism that has invested the White House for the last eight years is its most unilateral expression), founding differences exist between political currents in the United States, that moreover seldom embrace the lines of bipartisan divisions. So we must be attentive to the nuances of American society and take advantage of its diversity, in order to know how to seize upon the opportunities for cooperation that will inevitably arise. Issues such as climate change or the combat against AIDS can furnish opportunities for working, along side numerous American actors, for the construction of the stable and effective systems we need.

In Europe we continue to largely conceive of emerging countries as adversaries. Obsessed by the competition that they represent for our employment, vexed by the growing share of global wealth they represent, surprised by the audacity with which they dare make use of their burgeoning power, we fail to perceive the long term benefits their emergence represents. India, China, South Africa and Brazil effectively have become inescapable actors in the multilateral game. Symbolic of this change in the times, Beijing announced at the end of 2007 its first payment as contributor to the International Development Association, the section of the World Bank in charge of donations to the poorest countries. It is first with these emerging countries that we will build the future; let's find forums favourable to respectful and frank dialogue.

France and its European partners must put their financing in phase with their multilateral viewpoint. It's a question of being coherent, but also of being effective. Even if our financing of the international multilateral system is generous, it is essentially directed towards Europe and the organisations of Bretton Woods – the World Bank and the International Monetary Fund. Only two per cent of Official Development Assistance passes through the United Nations. In order to advance in the direction of better global governance, we must raise our means to the level of the ambitions we place in the UN, and exercise deeper influence there. Despite all its present insufficiencies, it is from the UN system that will germinate the global governance we so need.

Finally, we must pursue the building of a stronger Europe, more in line with its neighbours. Its marginalisation in the Middle East peace process and the vicissitudes in its African policy are the proof – the European Union has much to do in order for its own foreign policy to gain coherence, effectiveness and visibility. This is the only way it can constitute an intermediary level of global governance, and succeed in mobilising its African partners in the multilateral approach.

Yes, the global house is burning. But humanity is not looking away. Short-sighted, it watches the blaze through multiform lenses, perceiving differently its origin, trajectory and ravages. At the centre of this vast inferno, searching for the arsonist is vain. Mutual accusations of egoism, futile. Finding out how to harmonise our vision, converging our understanding of the world, using dialogue as well as the balance of power – fully aware we will end up with essentially imperfect results – from now on this is where the urgency must be found in the slow evolution of global governance. It will demand patient work in respect for our different cultures, where we must renounce our complexes of superiority in order to accept living together in a world of complexity and possibility.

II

POWERS, INSTITUTIONS, LEGITIMACY:
AT THE HEART OF DEMOCRATIC GOVERNANCE

6

Legitimacies, Actors and Territories

Rooting Governance in the Diversity of Cultures

Michel SAUQUET and Martin VIELAJUS
(Translated from the French)

Today, in the field of international cooperation, the most diverse currents of thought seek their answers in the concept of "governance". So that it has come to embrace a great many, sometimes conflicting, meanings and levels of understanding, and has for some ten years been at the core of much of the debates conducted in national and international institutions for cooperation and development. Some see in the word governance little more than the manifestation of the latest semantic "trend", almost devoid of substance and best ignored. The way we look at it, the case for discarding terms abused by the political discourse, de-legitimised out of hand as buzzwords, to replace them by more specific, less tainted ones can prove counter-productive. This instrumentalisation of a term belonging to the international political vocabulary by actors with vastly different profiles and agendas is its main asset. The breadth of meanings attached to the word governance effectively calls into question the aptness of the Western political model, its language, its mindset to take on board the full implications of socio-political dynamics and structures at work in other regions of the world. It is incidentally one mission of the Institute for Research and Debate on Governance (IRG) to make visible and to analyse the significance of this diversity.

Helping frame a fresh definition of governance in the context of development invites scrutiny of the political and an in-depth questioning of the very workings of the cooperation process. Here is the opportunity to cast a critical eye at a number of North-South logics partly in hock to the colonial past.

The way the concept is understood appears to generate two trends, which highlight in our view the fundamental cleavage at the heart of this debate.

The first trend consists in thinking governance as an institutional toolbox, crudely drawn from democratic models operating in Europe or North America. This toolbox is characterised first and foremost by a range of norms (administrative management, rule of Law, electoral process, etc.) the application of which is mainly assessed by external donors. The diverse elements of this approach will frequently be found together under the heading of "good governance". This desire to assess each country's political and institutional frameworks is, of course, one of the key outcomes of the critical analysis conducted collectively by the donor community on aid efficiency, starting with research by Burnside and Dollar (1997) in particular. However, the international institutions' wish to exert some control over Southern countries' political process and its adjustment to the Western model is not exactly new. For instance the practice of electoral observation goes back to 1919 and the Treaty of Versailles. In 1948, it became the United Nations' classical instrument as, at a government's invitation, they may ensure the supervision of national elections. From the seventies onwards, other intergovernmental[1] or non-governmental international[2] outfits assisted, or indeed replaced the United Nations in this role.

Faced with this rather prescriptive understanding of the so-called "good governance" model, a number of critical voices rose over the past ten years to call into question the "universal" nature of the western political toolbox and to criticise the actual modalities of transfer of one good governance system towards countries whose history and social dynamics are very different from those in the North. This critical approach, which is much in evidence in the recent analyses of the French Ministry for Foreign and European Affairs, and particularly within the Democratic Governance Unit, marks a shift in the understanding of Governance. No longer the mere description of a collection of existing institutions, administrations and assorted levels of operation it becomes more broadly, the processes permitting the implementation of economic, social and political regulations.

---

1. Main regional or international organisations running electoral observation missions: The United Nations, the OSCE (Organisation for Security and Cooperation in Europe), The African Union, the OAS (Organization of American States), ASEAN (Association of Southeast Asian Nations).

2. Main international NGOs organising electoral observation missions: The Carter Foundation, the NDI (National Democratic Institute, the IRI (International Republican Institute).

Thus broadened, this approach fits pretty closely with the distinction N. Meisel and J. Ould Aouida established, in their "Institutional Profiles"[3] initiative, between institutional functions, which can generally be recognised as universal and timeless (like generating trust, maintaining law and order in society...), and institutional arrangements (or institutional forms) which take different shapes according to countries, according to their level of development, their history, etc. Indeed, the danger of the approach driven by the "good governance" ideal rests with too frequently homing in on the presence of specific institutional arrangements while sidelining the cultural, social, economic realities of the countries aid is aimed at. To be sure, the vast diversity of histories and backgrounds does not preclude the presence of common problems: existing authority(ies)'s legitimacy and deep-rootedness; sound operation of public institutions and loss of trust in the State; status of non-state actors in the co-production of common good; the real governance status of the local level, etc. But the way the diverse actors seek to resolve these problems and the way they can do so from one culture to the next are often radically different.

As a result, the way the quality of governance in these countries is today assessed by the international institutions frequently fails to recognise the realities and aspirations of the said countries as well as the very interest of the donor countries since it does nothing to bolster the efficiency of their aid. A more rounded knowledge of African, Latino-American, Chinese developments – ideally better taken into account – by organisations from the so-called Northern countries thus appears to us an important component of what could be a new vision of international cooperation.

The IRG has had, through its research partnerships and international forums, ample opportunity over recent years to consider the diversity of institutional arrangements in Africa, China or South America whilst at the same time being able to bring out the constancy of those common concerns, those functions, more or less universal, that run through the full range of societies. We propose to take a closer look at three of them: the legitimacy of power, the role of non-state actors and the articulations between governance levels – and to explore the breadth of answers proposed by particular cultures and political contexts.

---

3. N. Meisel, J. Ould Aoudia, Is "good governance" a good development strategy? internal working paper.

The plurality of sources of power legitimacy
Knowing it, adjusting it

Cooperation policies cannot afford to ignore the extent of institutional tensions, indeed of political schizophrenia at work today in many Southern countries. They are, understandably, keen to work with the institutions set in the legal framework of the partner countries, but today, analyses abound on the relationship between legality and legitimacy. Whilst it would be simplistic systematically to oppose these two strands, it would be similarly naïve to equate power legitimacy with the existing actors and institution's compliance with legality. This legality, even though it arises from a democratic elaboration process, remains bound in formal and technical rules and it may, in due course, no longer correspond to the principles that shaped it. As against this, legitimacy is first and foremost rooted in the cultural and social context. Beyond or alongside legal rules, it measures, as Dominique Darbon[4] observes: "the leader's capacity to impose himself socially as such, to make sure that his legal status is associated with acceptance by the people so that they obey, but above all that they accept and desire to do so because it corresponds to their beliefs about power." If the citizens do not, or no longer, recognise themselves in the way they are ruled, if the power is not, or no longer, rooted in its local or national history, culture, modernity, then it is bound to lose some of its legitimacy hence its efficiency.

In some regions of Africa, Andean America and Central Asia, the IRG is currently striving to analyse and gain a better grasp of this tension, to gather ideas, experiences and proposals aimed at reducing it. It particularly seeks to pinpoint and question the main legitimating processes, whether they result in legal dispositions or not: Western style democratic electoral process; traditional processes for the selection of leaders; conflict resolution processes; processes to create or restore trust in the State.

First, democratic elections: In the course of the symposium "Between Tradition and Modernity: African Governance for Tomorrow[5]", A Malian academic, Bintou Sanankoua, sighting the practical difficulties of electoral consultation in Western Africa stressed the need "to reinforce democracy by making it understandable to the people". This kind of observation, pretty widespread on the African continent does not elicit the same operational conclusions and even the African actors vastly diverge

---

4. IRG, (2007). Between Tradition and Modernity: African Governance for Tomorrow. Conference proceedings, Bamako 23-25 January 2007.
    5. ibid.

in their opinion on this point. Most recognise the need for an educational input and the adjustment of the technical electoral instruments then turn to international specialists and observers to organise elections in optimal conditions. But others, and their stance is less broadly known, see there a duty to question in-depth a system which they consider completely unrelated to their culture. A system, they say, where the say of an eighteen-year-old has as much weight as that of an elder just does not make sense – anymore than a majority rule whereby the polls return winners and losers in a culture where the political and social system is historically founded in consensus. Indeed, the democratic foundations of multipartism, upon which elections rest is hardly a familiar notion. The upshot of all this is the poor participation in the electoral process which seriously undermines its legitimacy. A Malian academic observed wryly during the same symposium:

> "Political parties are formed on the basis of alliances of interests – and sometimes with no government programme other than procuring their sponsors with a share of the national wealth. The ordinary populace get nothing out of it and become averse to playing in the hands of opportunists of any colour or shade. No wonder then that, on Election Day, the citizens steer clear of the polling stations. The rare people who carry out their 'civic duty' are very frequently motivated by objectives quite foreign to patriotism such as support for a relation who, it is hoped, will remember them if he wins..."

Must democratic elections be accordingly considered unredeemably unsuited to Southern countries? Not many would go this far. Nevertheless it is becoming patently clear that they need appropriating in order to impact, beyond the purely technical exercise, on the people's minds and representations. Most importantly, it is clear that they cannot be counted the only source of power legitimacy. Articulation with traditional models of legitimacy is the essence.

Second type of legitimating process: the "traditional" leader selection model. There exists a de facto traditional chiefdom which still holds sway in African towns and villages and which French colonial administrators (like Apartheid operators in South Africa) had strategically exploited to their own advantage. Understandably wishing to break with the past, for the best part of half a century, French cooperation and development policies have ignored its presence. But today, the "governance" approach recommends taking into account this political, cultural and sociological reality, not with a view to manipulate but on the contrary in the name of pragmatism and the quest for synergies in the exercise of powers. It may be rather rare to find traditional authorities sanctioned with an official status at national level, but that takes nothing away from their active engagement with the nuts and bolts of local life (for instance, from the Andes to Austral Africa, in cooperatives or farmers' associations).

However, this approach requires a number of precautions, for the concept of tradition is not immune to ambiguity or manipulations of all kinds. Engaged in a re-think of governance in Africa, our partners at the Bamako Symposium sought to retrieve the values and attainments of the pre-colonial tradition concerning political regulation and leader selection models. They did get back to a range of still valid governance principles, notably in the field of conflict resolution but they also discerned risks of idealisation, selective re-writing of history, blanket assimilation of the tradition with all that does not fit in with Western modernity. They no less asserted the necessity to seek complementarity between local powers' inner workings and structures, the outcomes of their own history and the rules required by constitutional dispositions. This calls for exploring the possibilities of a legal pluralism able to accommodate, say in the case of land rights or family law, the coexistence of customary law with so-called modern law. "Participative" constitutional processes can be envisaged, similar to those pioneered in South Africa, which integrated several levels of traditional authorities within its legal provisions or to the constituting processes in Ecuador and Bolivia, countries where traditional Andean regulation models still prevail. The IRG has sought to follow closely these processes whereby, by means of "consultation tables", minority representatives and traditional powers sit together with elected representatives to bring proposals before the Constituent Assembly.

Third legitimating process observable in many African and Latino-American countries: the process (be it pacific or otherwise, bondable or otherwise) of conflict resolution. As it turns out, in these countries the groups that overcame a dictatorship or the oppression of colonial domination have built up through fighting and years of resistance or militancy a legitimacy often underpinned by the charisma of leaders who did not necessarily require poll returns to win. If elections occur after they took power, they often are a foregone conclusion and, even when several parties compete, they reinforce the overwhelming weight of the "liberation" party or the party born of the fight against dictatorship. The most conspicuous case is of course that of the African National Congress (ANC) in South Africa. Standing if necessary against other legitimacies, a historic and ideological one can hold on to its support for a very long time, aided in no small measure by leaders who, when campaigning, make much of their past sacrifice and struggle.

Cooperation outfits must also bear in mind this legitimating process by political struggle in the context of countries where the conflicts are not resolved. In this respect, Colombia (where the IRG now has an antenna) presents particularly complex challenges in terms of legitimacy. Our partner Ingrid Bolivar[6] of the Universidad de Los Andes shows in particular that several forms of legitimacy coexist: "institutionalised legitimacies" falling under the democratic and legal institutions and the "armed actors' legitimacies" arising from the political regulation modes imposed by paramilitary or guerilla fighters in some regions of the country.

Last legitimating factor liable to be taken into account by cooperation policies based on the new "governance" approach: a State's aptitude to fulfil its role and to create trust. Many users of the word "governance" are wont to think that the future will see civil society and private enterprise take on a large part of the functions of a parasitic state unable to fulfil its public service mission in satisfactory conditions. We do not subscribe to this: there is good cause to think on the contrary that for the multi-actor dynamics of governance to operate, both actors must be sturdy, efficient and trustworthy.

The question of trust in the State as governance instrument is one of the IRG's current research threads[7], which asks three basic questions. First, what decides the degree of trust the citizens have in the State: efficiency in the provision of public services? Transparency? The relevance of a government's programme and action set against the facts on the ground? The greater or lesser proximity between citizens and authorities and the place afforded dialogue and participation? Second, how is trust measured, with what indicators? Third what are the conditions to the restoration of trust in the State and who can re-establish it? Why, the State of course, by reforming its methods with a view to gain in efficiency, relevance, responsibility but also the whole public affairs education system[8], the citizens themselves[9] and finally external players such as Northern countries' cooperation and development services or the international institutions. According to the greater or lesser recognition these institutions grant the beneficiary countries' government, they can have a decisive influence on its public credibility. If the "governance" approach in cooperation policies shows more interest than in the past in partner countries' civil societies, this, as we are about to see, does not presuppose a corresponding retreat of the public actors.

---

6. 2006", Colombia, nota de análisis, on line on the IRG site http://www.institutgouvernance.org.

7. In the framework of an international cooperation with the Ash Institute at Harvard's John F. Kennedy School of Government and The University of Warwick, UK.

8. The IRG is currently setting up, in partnership with IDHEAP, the Swiss Graduate School of Public Administration and several other partner universities an "Observatory of Public Affairs Training (OFAP)" with a web site, shortly to be made accessible to the public via the IRG site www.institut-gouvernance.org.

9. Viz the campaigns conducted in 2005-2006 by youth organisations in the suburbs of France's largest cities towards greater participation in electoral consultations.

The multiplicity of civil society configurations and their ambiguous role in the promotion of democratic governance

One of the defining features of the "governance" approach in development policies is the so-called multi-actor slant to the devising of public affairs management; the point is specifically to grant a new position to non-state actors such as civil society organisations (NGOs, social movements, trade-unions...) and business. However prior identification of these non-state actors' profile and the definition of their role alongside public authorities represent major challenges the minute the "democratic governance" model attempts forays beyond the Western trodden path. Let us take a closer look at these challenges on the basis of the promotion policies aimed at Southern "civil societies".

First question: why back civil societies? Two entirely separate answers confront each other, which have never been quite disentangled even though they drive very different civil society support models.

Like as many Trojan horses, civil society organisations can first be considered as instruments forcing open partner countries' political arenas. Indeed, many international donors have thus allocated a large part of their "democratic governance" funding to such organisations. The basic assumption is of a civil society inherently conducive to democratisation. Thus the European Commission:

> "Close cooperation with and promotion of civil society is essential to ensure the widest possible participation of all sectors of society to provide the conditions for [...] strengthening the democratic fabric of society."[10]

Civil society then takes on the mantle of "protest" leading to the loosening up of undemocratic regimes. This makes it heir to a very specific history started notably with the onset of the late eighties' East European liberation movements, and extended to a number of authoritarian regimes in sub-Saharan Africa and Latin America. According to the report drawn by Freedom House in 2005[11], the resistance activity of civil society organisations can be considered key to the democratic transition of fifty out of the sixty-seven countries where it took place over the past few years.

---

10. European Commission, Communication from the Commission to the Council and the European Parliament - The European Community's Development Policy /* COM/2000/0212 final */, 26/04/2000, Brussels.

11. Freedom House, How Freedom is Won: From Civic Resistance to Durable Democracy, Special Report, May 2005.

And yet the donors' "civil society option" does not just work on these political premises. Civil society organisations are also seen as the socio-economic safety net necessary to prop up the structural adjustments that weaken the State's redistributive role. For structural adjustment programmes come in most Southern countries with a shift leading the State to delegate a number of its responsibilities to civil society actors. What was the administration's preserve is open to them, in particular in the realm of public works and the management of collective infrastructures. Thus Egypt, a trailblazer in terms of associative sector growth, instigated at the end of the eighties a complete rehaul of its health system in partnership with the World Bank and the IMF, whereby the State is released from a large share of its expenses in the field. Indeed the World Bank, hardly involved in the health sector until the eighties, opened with its Financing Health Services in Developing Countries. An Agenda for Reform[12] report a sweeping campaign towards liberalising this sector. Within a few years a multilateral cooperation programme was set up bringing together The World Bank, USAID (United States Agency for International Development) and the European Union alongside the Egyptian government in a project for the reform of the country's health system. This reform programme premiered the implementation of a model of direct relationship between the international instances involved and the health-focused NGOs operating at the local level in Egypt. To the government's reluctance in foregoing its intermediary role between its local NGOs and the international community, the latter opposes the crucial impact civil society organisations have on grass-root communities frequently excluded from public social services.

The trend, endorsed by many financial backers is to couple these two movements of, on the one hand the promotion of democratic governance and on the other the socio-economic compromise that necessarily comes with structural adjustment policy. The main argument for this coupling is that furthering democracy is not just the preserve of advocacy organisations but that it also falls to many organisations providing social services. Those frequently offer means to curb State activities in the sectors in which they operate. The more a network of sector specific associations is dense and active, the more it can structure and supervise State action – and the more it can mobilise an opposition capable of challenging its excesses. More broadly, through their very role as public service providers, civil society organisations may emerge as new forums enabling the citizens to become more involved in public life.

---

12. World Bank, Financing Health Services in Developing Countries. An Agenda for Reform, 1987.

However, identifying the most relevant actors and, more importantly, the most legitimate in the social field – those capable of bringing to the people suitable services and local responses may have precious little to do with their "democratic" credentials. Either because these actors are broadly controlled by the State and thus ill equipped to loosen the political stranglehold: The few major Chinese "GONGOs" (Government orientated NGOs) operating in the field of social services provisions offer, as the IRG was able to observe through its study of the far ranging "Project Hope", an essential contribution to China's overall socio-economic balance[13]. Or because their ambitions do not meet objectives of democratic governance: in the Islamo-Arab world, the social services provision networks are often closely associated to religious actors, mostly moderate but sometimes radical, those local operators cannot be by-passed and enjoy a strong legitimacy in their countries. Pushing the analysis to a perhaps provoking extreme, Hezbollah and Hamas may to some extent be considered as networks coordinating the provision of services to the populations, with, among others, the undoubted aim to ensure at local level the legitimacy of their terrorist action. The social action of a welter of NGOs well established in suburbs largely ignored by State services thus ensures a strong popular legitimacy to networks whose contribution to the reinforcement of democratic governance may quite clearly be called into question...

So, in the context of development policies, the profile of a civil society conducive to the promotion of democratic governance must be considered in a different way, based on civil society's functions much more than on its institutional format. Classically, the Western approach to civil society rests on a requisite depersonalisation of social relationships, a de facto rejection of the slightest hint of kinship or any other form of traditional solidarity in its genesis. It discards a whole component of local solidarity networks that bridges the gap between individuals and authorities, and counts for a facet of democratisation at the local level. That is why Sabine Freizer[14] suggests the concept of civil society should be broadened defining it, via this very "democratic function", as a set of formal or informal group activities that brings people into contact with each other, creates mutual trust and furthers the discussion of the issues at stake in the public debate. This definition includes traditional community bonds as a driving force of civil society's dynamics.

---

13. IRG, Proceedings of the seminar "The governance of NGOs and their role in co-producing public services", IRG, February 2008.
14. S. Freizer, « Central Asian Fragmented Civil Society – Communal and Neoliberal Forms in Tadjikistan and Uzbekistan », in M. Glasius, D. Lewis et H. Seckinelgin (eds), Exploring Civil Society. Political and Cultural Contexts, Routledge, 2004.

The name of the game, for international cooperation actors, is to succeed in spotting these functions in both types of NGOs: those, recent, more responsive to the international community, more attuned to its philosophy – but so often less legitimate in the field, and those, more traditional networks struggling to translate their actions into the institutional jargon of "democratic governance". Now the facts on the ground often reflect the clumsy juxtaposition of these two types of actors. Bangladesh, a byword for the NGO explosion of recent decades, is a case in point. There, the new civil society does not sit easy with the long-established solidarity models, mainstay of rural communities, the Palli Mangal Samitis, without which no true democratic culture can be brought about.

The rediscovery of the "local": governance's new Eden?

The promotion of a "governance approach" in cooperation policies has finally caught on to the necessity of turning to local institutions and actors. It often translates into the support of decentralisation policies and of reinforcement of local authorities, a trend emphasised today by the action of diasporas, generally directly connected with their home towns and villages.

This year, 2008, the French Ministry for Foreign and European Affairs organises a consultation of cooperation actors operating at the local level in order to draft a "Cooperation Charter in Support of Local Governance". That suggests that returning to the grassroots presents some tricky challenges. Some actors solve these challenges by means of a simple, formal transfer of competence and powers without really addressing the question of the functions and limitations of the local level. Now we think that true democratic governance requires a complete reversal of the way the territory is understood, no longer just as a mere level on which to pin specific and exclusive competences but on the contrary as the founding tier in the construction of public policies.

So, once more, what motivates both in economic and political terms such a resurgence of the local tier?

Centralisation's damaging effects are frequently blamed as restricting economic activity and obstacles to the dialogue between the States' partners in the production of and access to public services. The management of scarce resources being in effect essentially territorialized, a more local approach to its handling is called for which will increase its effectiveness. The local populations' improved access to basic services thus appears to many actors as the most significant indicator of the success of this "territorial transfer". More broadly, promoting local governance is perceived as a partial response to public administration's dysfunction and a way to remove development projects from central bureaucracy's unwieldiness.

Beyond the efficiency argument, the local level represents also and primarily a political response to the crisis in representation that besets a fair number of Southern partners and to the growing distance between the State and the citizen. Decentralisation is indeed seen as the vehicle towards "local democracy" that would advance consultation and public deliberation practices by the citizens and set up a dialogue with actors traditionally remained at the margins of the public arena.

These arguments are met with an obdurate reluctance to acknowledge the true role of the territory and to reinforce it on the part of the partner States but also among cooperation actors in the North.

An online forum recently ran by the UNDP with the support of the IRG who drafted the summary report, pulled together feedback from many decentralisation support programmes coordinated by its national and regional offices. One of the main conclusions was, unsurprisingly, the difficulty cooperation funding – still largely controlled by central government – has in finding its way out of capital cities. To the partner states the local level still too often appears as a drain on aid resources as well as a potential political rival liable to undermine, at the local level, the central tier's legitimacy.

But that resistance to the move towards a genuine "territorial shift" can also be found among Northern actors, busy though they might be promoting local governance. This is due notably to their poor grasp of local issues. Pierre Calame, in his book La Démocratie en miettes[15] bemoans what he calls the "sidelining of the local level" which remains today in people's mind the mere stage of concrete action instead of being the very locus where strategies are developed; which continues to be seen as "the poor man's agora", the bulwark of traditional order rather than an integrative space in our globalised economy, a lever to modernise societies with. So that a yawning gap lays open between a conception of decentralisation as the mere formal transfer of competencies downwards to the local level (mainly seeking to find the administrative tier best suited to each type of competence – employment, education, health – etc.) and the call for a truly "territorial" approach reaching far beyond administrative decentralisation's objectives. There again, the object is to forget the administrative formalities towards local governance and to address the essence of the territory's actual functions.

---

15. P. Calame. (2003). La Démocratie en miettes. Pour une révolution de la gouvernance [Democracy in Tatters]. Paris, Editions Charles Léopold Mayer-Descartes et Cie.

A purely formal devolution of powers towards the local level does not, for instance, ensure a priori the inclusion of marginalized populations into the public space. Local operators frequently confirm on the contrary a consolidation of local elites resulting from a decentralisation process, which enables a minority to highjack the populations' voices, a minority become de facto the authorities' preferred partner. This local democracy deficit is born from the unsuitability of local consultation forums formally set up by central government as part of the decentralisation process and barely appropriated and invested by the local populace. Accordingly, the promotion of local governance requires the setting up or reinforcement of instruments that will give local actors the capability to take on these functions: information interactive tools designed to enable the populations both to access public information and to assess the policies undertaken; training systems targeting the new functions taken up at the local level, etc. Innovative experiments in popular auditing, handbooks for public evaluation, web based civic information are available today and need to be better known and understood to supplement the existing programmes.

Besides, the call for a more territorialized vision of development requires a different approach to local funding. The central governments' lack of political will when faced with the downward transfer of some of their international aid resource is a major challenge. Especially since it must not detract from the necessity to reinforce local resource mobilisation capacities. Indeed, the latter act both towards funding development and towards making local government answerable to their citizenry. A local resource-driven approach is key to preserving young local authorities from total dependency on international aid even as, thanks to that empowering aid, they shake off the control of a barely legitimate state.

In more general terms, the local tier cannot be considered as a mere tool to implement a formalised governance model, externally devised with the risk that it becomes yet another institutional shell unfit to answer the challenges it claims to address. It behoves to start from solid territorial realities, from the specificity of the interactions woven there in order to arrive at the governance approaches best suited to the emergence of suitable and coherent development strategies.

**

It has become clear that these few pages have taken us some way from a purely institutional approach to governance and closer to grasping this concept first and foremost on the basis of territorial reality, at the local level where the populations' full range of needs and drives are expressed. Must we then see the world only through its villages, suburbs or employment basins? Certainly not: the emergence of international networks of local authorities, but also of NGOs, scientists, lawyers, professional associations show that it is the constant to-and-froing between the levels at which societies act and understand themselves and each other that a truly effective governance can be built.

7

Legitimacy and Legality: Words and Realities

Sophia MAPPA
(Translated from the French)

There has been since 2006 a major re-think of development aid policies at the European Commission and in EU member States, including France. Their own assessment of the World Bank's policies that made "good governance" synonymous with fighting corruption, leads them to privilege the inclusion en bloc of socio-political, indeed cultural factors in the concept of "democratic governance"[1]. Aware of the limitations of development aid policies traditionally proposing solutions born of Western experience, they now assert the need for the recipient countries to be at liberty to "(re)found" their states as they wish.

To be sure, the political framework still comes ready-made: their definition of "democratic governance" still includes all the theoretical principles that have historically instituted Western democracies: this regulatory framework which they have signed in the context of international agreements is supposed to commit the signatory states and their societies – even though the facts do not always bear out these engagements. The issue of the legitimacy and legality of state power happens to be part of these commitments. For a long time, European political leaders have believed and been given to understand that these notions were, by way of theory and practice, universal and the necessary foundation of states the world over – or at any rate if they were aid recipients. This being held incontrovertible, the same leaders have been

---

1. Cf. the French ministry of foreign affairs DGCID (General Directorate for International Cooperation and Development), Stratégie gouvernance de la ·coopération française, Paris, December 2006 ; and CTE, Governance in the European Consensus on Development 30.08.2006, COM(2006)421final

brought to book time and again for legitimating and helping unsavoury regimes, and this by public opinions equally convinced of the universality of those values.

Do the new democratic governance policies not aim at resolving this recurrent problem in development cooperation? Does giving local actors a free hand in building their states as they want, do they further their chances of becoming more "legitimate" and more "legal"?

This paper proposes to elucidate the complexities of the question of power legitimacy and legality, with as a starting point a political probing of their effectiveness in Europe and in Africa from a comparative, philosophical and historical angle. It will address the following question: what is the historical underpinning of state power legitimacy and legality in Europe and in Africa and what meaning do these concepts have under present circumstances? What political facts and mutations do they account for and how does this impact on development cooperation?

We shall submit that the theory and praxis of legitimacy and legality are closely tied with the making of modern political power in Europe circa the 17th century. It is a particular socio-historical construct the specificity of which, in comparison to other power constructs lies with its internalisation by European societies. This construct is neither timeless nor universal. Social and political mutations – both are linked – at work since the sixties give legality and legitimacy an actuality and a meaning other than those they had in the "traditional" democratic system. Now these are the democratic principles that inform the democratic governance policies designed for Southern countries in the framework of development cooperation.

In these countries the construction of powers was historically vested with meanings and rationales unacquainted with the meaning of legitimacy and legality, or at any rate assigning to them a meaning different from the one they have in Europe: the specificity of power rested with its externality to the societies which saw it as conferred by forces external to and independent of their will. Democratic governance policies accordingly face a double challenge: on the one hand they must fit in with governance policies devised in Europe for Europe and with the way democracy is understood in this context; on the other hand they must fit in with African socio-political realities. What new deal will steer the new policies clear of the traditional stumbling block whereby the European model, idealised for good measure while not that effective in Europe, gets projected on societies for whom it is not in-built? In our opinion, the legitimacy and legality categories should be rethought along two lines: starting from the mutations experienced in the societies that invented them for one; then, from the experience of other societies, whereas their experience is different.

In order to answer these questions the comparative approach we have adopted will help view the Western "model" in an African light and the African "model" in a Western light, in order better to capture the specificity of both and the way in which they intersect in development cooperation policies. Our second, more philosophical, approach consists in thinking legitimacy and legality in close association with other notions informing power and the analytical categories developed to reflect on it in Europe. This will enable us to bring out the intricacy of the network of social connotations in which they are interlocked, as theory and praxis but also conceptually. Legitimacy and legality hark back to the terminological web that informs both political and social issues: autonomy, freedom, laws and boundaries, reason, national interest, rights, individual, civil society, etc. These notions bear in equal measure on state power and on society. They are rooted in the culture in which they were developed, that is in a set of representations of the world, of values, institutions etc., through which individuals become social beings. There is correlation between the political and social realms. They interlock and partake of an alchemy peculiar to each society and impossible to duplicate elsewhere.

Our third, historical, approach leads to considering change as well as societies' deep-rootedness in their past and thus continuity. The theory and praxis of legitimacy and legality are modern but they are rooted in classical Greek, Roman then Christian problematics. The historical perspective brings home to us the fact that they are not timeless but also that change does not mean rupture. It proceeds from the realities and materials at hand. Democratic governance policies are still using "traditional" democracy theories and concepts whereas, in the governance policies devised for Europe itself, these realities and concepts are reconstructed. In the new configuration, the import has shifted from one sphere to the other and, while old hierarchies endure, they are frequently reversed: the political power is thought of in terms of legitimacy and legality, but loses its primacy over other powers to the economic and, to a lesser degree, the judicial spheres, which are also thought of in those same terms. Is not judicial power today the guarantor of legality?

Because of the historical relations set up between the Western, and more specifically European space, and the African continent, these two socio-cultural areas have been interacting with each other for two centuries while each ran its own historical course. The continuity in their respective histories and in the relationships set up between them from the outset is revealing. Classically the relationship rests, on the Western side, on the projection onto Africa of an idealised Western system and, on the African side on a deep dependency on the West, even in its mental frameworks. Are we today witnessing a historical and relational mutation? Do governance policies allow for mutation?

Given the breadth of the subject we shall not claim to be exhaustive. We are primarily proposing a methodology. In this paper, we will restrict ourselves to outlining some notions on which legitimacy and legality hinge; to the political practices they account for in Europe; and to their mutations under current circumstances (i.e. legitimacy). More broadly we shall refer to the internalisation of power effected by its desacralisation and its autonomy: by the law as mode of government, and by the theory and praxis of boundary setting; by the differenciation between power and the person vested with it, as indeed State power and society; by the action of power on society; by its establishment as the object of collective thought and by the theory of reason as mode of government. We shall set these notions in parallel with the quite different ones presiding over African politics and how it is practiced both at state and society levels: its externality, resulting from its notions of the sacred, of allegiance, of unrestricted power, etc., in order to show, there too, the continuities and shifts of ancient notions into new formulae, notably in the State.

Legitimacy and legality in Europe: words and realities

As Max Weber noted, the West's legal-rational legitimation model has worked because it relied on the Law. Now the import of the Law and its practice are interlocked in a mass of other notions and political and social founding values, not least those of autonomy and freedom, prerequisite to our modern conception of the law.

Unlike African conceptions of power, the Western political system derives from a long drawn out movement starting in ancient Greece with humanity's first experience of autonomisation breaking the tradition of sacralised king-gods. The affirmation of power as instituted by humans, arising from their decision and their action was one of the sources of its legitimacy. This first attempt at autonomy, relinquished during the Middle Ages with its restoration, among other things, of the primacy of the heavenly sphere over the city of men still went through unexpected developments within Christendom. The ancient value of freedom, re-visited by Christian dogma gave us the idea of free will as God's gift to man. Over the centuries, one thing leading to the next, it pervaded European societies' representations and practices to take a radical turn with modernity. This, say in the 17th Century or thereabouts, marked a turning point, a mutation in the continuity with the old order.

A closer historical scrutiny of the processes that brought about that mutation enables us to consider the way change is effected on the basis of the facts in presence. It gives us a measure of the futility of classical development cooperation policies hell-bent on changing the beneficiary countries when pre-determined by the financial backers. For it is possible to track down in each European country the circuitous route of collective choices, of often unconscious shifts of the old into the new, of old notion reversed and pendulum swings, of the intellectual arguments and social balance of power which brought about the singular figure of the modern state. A State many observers, and not least the World Bank, believe universal and almost a-historical.

Modernity's icons have thus been, ever since its advent, autonomous political power and individuals, social constructs that have "freed" human beings from traditional bonds and instituted freedom in the political, social, economic, religious and familial spheres. Political power, set free from divine power, asserts its autonomy from God. The individual, set apart from the group and its hierarchies, asserts his or her freedom of thought, of opinion, of feeling and of action.

It is hardly necessary to recall that, in Europe, Hobbes was first to conceive of this novel State that dared challenge sacred power, in his Leviathan. In France the first political leader to make a good fight of returning God to the heavenly sphere where He belonged was Louis XIV. His famous "l'État, c'est moi" (I am the State) is not just an assertion of his absolute power, as an anachronic reading of history would have it. It is primarily the assertion of his autonomisation in regard to the divine, and his own desacralisation.

Meanwhile, the notions of autonomy and freedom were not restricted to the political sphere alone, as some naive thinkers would have it, in the belief that the only obstacle to democratisation in Africa is the State. They have also informed the institution of the social sphere and brought about a novel trend among humans, driving them to self-institution.

Hegel, among other thinkers, considered his century's values in Europe to be freedom, the individual and his "unlimited value", the creation of a collective power (the State), reason and the law. Because of individual freedom, society is instituted as differentiated and plural, but unified. Acknowledging the singularity of every person led the way to Montesquieu's "recognition of a multitude of singular [though not atomised] beings" who, artificially united in Hobbes' "covenant of every man with every man", gave one person the power to represent them. The legitimacy of the modern state has rested on the consent of individuals who renounced their personal power in its favour because they recognise themselves as its instigators. A society, self-instituted as multiple, has thus instituted a single power, the legitimacy of which is founded in the freedom of the governed. One century later, Rousseau in The Social Contract took a further step towards defining individual freedom and the social contract, prodding the general will towards instituting collective decision: the prerequisite to the respect of conventions decided by human beings was the individual's commitment to himself, in other words, his internalisation of the raison d'être for social institutions. In this framework, general will springs from individual will and this, the sovereign people's general will confers sovereignty and legitimacy to state power. Hegel says much the same when he says that the State reconciles "the objective and the subjective will".

The essence of democratic political power, which followed absolute power and evolved over the centuries, through all too well-known conflicts and regressions, is that it makes itself the object of collective competition and deliberation. In Claude Lefort's fine words, democracy is founded upon the legitimacy of a debate as to what is legitimate and what is illegitimate. This debate is another source of state legitimacy.

In the image of the differentiation within the divine power (One in Three, another transposition of the old into the new), state power is likewise differentiated and plural (judicial, military, administrative powers et al.) but unified and it works for the unity of society. The primacy of the political on the other powers and in particular the military is a case of figure unique in the world to this day. Like in the institution of the social sphere, the power's unity in plurality is consistent with the theory and praxis of the division and separation of the persons and the institutions they represent. Democratic power is posited, in Claude Lefort's memorable formula, as an "empty place".

The individual, consenting through reason to the State's domination allows the sovereignty of the authority and the sovereignty of the people, plurality and unity, individual freedom (thereby divergence and conflict) and general will to coexist. This subtle alchemy between autonomous power and autonomous individual results from the recurring tensions, which, internally debated, have ensured the specificity and the legitimacy of democratic power. If the efforts to export democracy, especially in Africa failed, it is because it met there other alchemies as complex and historical as its own but different.

Limits and law

One of the specificities of the notion of freedom in the West is its correlation with the notion of limit which has historically presided over the definition of power and which partakes of the definition of the law. Individual freedom is defined within the limits set by the law, earthly powers are limited at all levels – from that of a father to that of a head of state. In the image of divine power, which was thought as limited by itself, a modern state's power is both self-limited and limited by rules. It governs by law, to which it is also subjected.

Historically, the specificity of modern law, as compared to other conceptions, e.g. African ones has rested with its desacralisation and its institution as a man-made convention towards living together, free but united. For Hegel, law and freedom were closely linked: "Only that will which obeys law, is free". We find here the implicit idea of the law internalised by individuals and their endorsing its raison d'être. Even for those who, after Hegel, thought that deliberation between all people was an unachievable ideal, obedience to the law was not just a measure of fear but of respect for it: The people's respectful fear is guarantor of collective power, the master indicated in The German Constitution[2].

The law, applied by the State gives it its legality and its legitimacy. One property of the law is that, given as a human institution, it is liable to change through human will. In this way, it is different from the sacralised injunction observable in Africa. But the law as method of government cannot alone guarantee social cohesion. Norms and collective agreements are still needed to set limits to human passions and to govern behaviours. For Durkheim in Suicide, this regulation, which is not always set in law, fixes with relative precision the highest level of comfort each social class may legitimately hope to achieve. It is this "top end" which is codified in Law, this other Western institution steeped in European Roman and Christian history. To be accepted the norm has, yet again, to be endorsed by the people individually. It cannot be imposed by coercion and violence, because the body producing the norm is society, and the norm is directed by shared values, social imaginary significations that each individual negotiates with his own subjectivity. The legitimacy of norms relies on the individual being able to negotiate them, to discuss them with others and to change them.

Power as object of thought

Along the continuum started in ancient Greece then in scholastics, modern power is set as an object for human thought like God or the Prince's power. Unlike most other political systems on earth, modern Western thought focused less on the person of the leader than on the principles of power as an institution: its purpose, the means to achieve it, the need to ensure its permanence, the ethical tensions arising from

---

2. 'Political authority, must be concentrated in one centre (... so long as) popular respect ensures that this centre is secure in itself' in G.W.F. Hegel. Political Writings, Cambridge University Press, 1999.

it. The purposes of preserving human life and the (ideally endless) permanence of the State were deemed inseparable by Hobbes. As a result, the Leviathan's strategy aimed to remove the State (and humanity) from external and, even more so, internal dangers – dangers, that is, inherent to human nature.

Unlike all other states on earth, modern state power makes its action public and subject to external thought. It allows it to be judged. All information concerning it must be available and it must be possible to check it against facts. There is therefore an objective truth to politics which enables the subjects to think in terms of "what they may reasonably desire according to their own interest ... without being held to alliance, friendship or kinship" Philippe de Béthune wrote at the turn of the 17th Century (Gauchet 1994). Not much later, Hobbes will say much the same when asserting that it is the users who determine what power others may have according to their usefulness to the polis.

A broad debate on the State has thus been going on for centuries, which contributed to its being internalised by society as an institution emanating from its own will. The intensity of each society's relation to its state is not uniform. Anglo-Saxon societies are more distant and as a result more given to bringing about a polis. Others, like French society have a visceral relation to it and expect too much protection from it. Whatever the case may be, the internalised state – with its rationale – has been one condition of the effectiveness of government by law and of the pacification of social relations.

Government by reason, is – as is government by law – another specificity and another source of legitimacy. Knowledge of the moral and material situation of the societies governed paved the way both for the development of social sciences and the implementation of sophisticated domination and control devices accepted by the governed. This does not preclude the use of force. Since Machiavelli, the thinking on war, on just war and power's coercive nature is a recurring theme. But as the democratic state seeps deeper into consciousness and in political and social practices, relations between individuals grow more and more pacific.

State and society: political power as third body

Unlike other constructs, state legitimacy in Europe has also relied on a declared differentiation of society. The Christian notion of God and the celestial sphere's otherness from the city of men has translated into the construction of political power as different from society. For thinkers of modernity such as Hegel, the separation of State from society was imperative: the former only asks of the individual what is necessary and keeps institutions down to a minimum in order to preserve the citizens' free will and to allow them considerable scope for action.

The critical analysis of the differences between state and society was joined over the centuries, by champions of the productive society in an unproductive state that does not intervene in economic life while others advocated an active role for the state both in the construction of society and of the market.

A triangular vision (a reworking of the Trinity) prevailed. Western societies are built around three differentiated but unified entities: the state, society and the market. State power has grown into a form hitherto unknown in the history of the world: what Robert Castel judiciously described as a "third body" which regulates society and the market. In this case, the state acts upon society in order to preserve its cohesion but also to transform it. Over the centuries and particularly since the Second World War, an all-powerful state came into being, which gave itself the means to act. It is that role, rather than the "monopoly of legitimate violence" which gave it its legitimacy and made acceptable its domination of society.

These notions, reworked from older notions, or invented over the centuries as required, are thus the specific creations of a specific history. Their signification and their realization mutate in the very societies which invented and implemented them in different ways in Europe and more broadly in the West.

Current evolutions

The mutations experienced in the social, economic and political spheres since the seventies and even more keenly since the eighties are not mere changes within a known paradigm. The democratic system is struck at the heart by, among other things the radicalisation of some of its historical values and by the reversal of its old hierarchies: the radicalisation of the notions of freedoms and individual rights and of utilitarist rationality, along with the reversal of hierarchies whereby economy has taken precedence over politics. We have here an unprecedented internal dynamics, although its germs were apparent to the likes of Durkheim at the turn of the 20th century.

The radicalisation of rights and freedom drives each individual to want ever more regardless of the group and of general interest, once the pillars of state legitimacy. The social field is singularly fragmented. There is no longer the group but groups. By this singular twist, European societies are becoming closer to African societies, traditionally more segmented. The institutions, which embodied the group, are now vested with private, individual and/or corporatist, interests. The state itself is the locus of this disintegration.

The radicalisation of individualism has caused a significant crisis in law enforcement and normativity. Old norms no longer apply and new ones are struggling to emerge that would define new modes of togetherness. The social bond has been weakened and with it the state's capacity for regulation. The question today is to know whether European societies can still be governed.

The otherness of political power and its specificity in respect of society are fading away. The mutations in its third body status now force the State to "count" with a multitude of private actors: businesses, corporatist associations, NGOs, experts and other technocrats. This mega-trend is perceived as a democratisation of power, via "civil society involvement". But whose interests do these different groups serve, and through which procedures? The state is a mirror where, today, democracy rhymes with opacity. In another paradoxical parallel with African countries, the visibility of the leader's person is taking precedent on transparent institutions and policies. Power as an institution is less commonly approached through reason than in the past; mediated through the media, it is the source of the populace's passions and emotions.

Social hierarchies are reversed. Economic imperatives – big earnings, competition, productivity, profitability, efficiency – command individual and state actions, while issues of collective purpose and ethical imperatives are left unanswered. Had not Durkheim drawn attention, in Suicide, to the way economy was breaking free from regulation while politics was being subjected to it? Little could he guess the extent to which his diagnosis would translate into the unchecked unleashing of desires and the almost limitless growth of the market leading to a "constant state of crisis and anomy".

There is no escaping the fact that the democratic imperatives that presided over the drafting of democratic governance policies are being reviewed in Europe in subservience to economic principles. Through different channels, the political loses in Europe some of its specificities as it falls in with more "universal" conceptions, notably populist conceptions focused on personality. The meanings of legitimacy and legality of power are evolving, which does not mean that they are being relinquished. Their re-defined content and realization will depend on the way European societies respond to the crisis sapping the group and the social bond. No doubt the redefinition of the European model will – well, should – be conducted in interaction with the other societies of the world. The prerequisite condition to that end is to eschew the double pitfall of the past. That is, on the one hand, insisting on changing the other while failing to address changes needed closer to home, and on the other hand passing over the complexity of other societies' irreducible specificity. Thinking the necessity (but also the difficulty) of their own change is today an imperative for European – indeed Western – societies which, for centuries, have thought that other societies must adopt their model. Not only is the model suffering growing pains (Gauchet 2007) but the Others are making loud and clear their attachment to their own, and often violently.

Legitimacy and legality in Africa: words without realities

State power in the other societies of the world is rooted in different histories and traditions. None of these societies ever claimed the ancient Greek and Roman inheritance; none has acted in line with this inheritance, in the way Europe did. Analytical categories such as legitimacy and legality are Western legacies. Yet the same concepts account for different realities and modes of government. Like in Europe changes are worked into the socio-historical continuum. For all that a state has been put in place, contrasts endure in the way power is constructed and exercised. A major difference with Europe to this day is the externality of political power and local actors' reluctance to take on responsibilities. Hence, the question of its internal legitimacy cannot be framed in the same way as in the West.

Sacralised power

Like any other of the world's political organisations anterior to the introduction of central government, African communities had instituted some earthly powers – village or tribal chiefs, marabouts, kings, emperors, etc. – in the image of their sacred powers. Indeed earthly powers were thought and understood as deities themselves, bestowed on humans by nature, supernatural forces, God. External to the people and their will, they were vested by the collective imaginary with magic powers. So they made a great show of their omnipotence and capacity to take charge of the material well-being of their subjects and to ensure their protection. Subjected themselves to the sacred powers they replicated, they demanded subordination and fidelity from their subjects.

This subtle imaginary wherein traditional power is sacred, external, both heteronomous and omnipotent was displaced in the new, West driven, set ups in the shape first of the State then of decentralised powers.

However, they experience themselves as possessed with supernatural powers and place their raison d'être not on society's free decision, nor even on the self-will of those vested with it, but on external, divine, supernatural, ethnic forces or, as the case may be, on the West (considered as sacralised power par excellence and to which they yield). Each power owes allegiance to the next power up and each requires its subjects' allegiance, against which they promise unlimited material care and protection.

So that the modern notions of the freedom and autonomy of power and its internalisation by people freely endorsing its raison d'être are foreign to African societies. As Dominique Darbon points out those do not produce rules, norms and methods to manage and regulate the state which they import. If the State in Africa somehow hangs above society, disconnected from it[3], it is not just because it comes from abroad. It is because the local norms that brought it forth privilege its externality to a society that does not see itself as its originator. These same norms – which it would be more appropriate to term collective imaginary – procure it the submission (countermanded by revolt) of the diverse groups co-existing in each country. But they also allow for its injunctions to be circumvented at every turn, for the delusion of omnipotence against a reality of contingency.

State power, and with it, powers evolved on the Western model have no legitimacy, in the Western sense of the term, either in the eyes of society or of those who hold it. When we conducted surveys in the Congo some ten years ago, statesmen were described by their peers as "cunning", "demagogic", "liars", "a pack of wild beasts", "a gangrene". The ideal leader was either the traditional chief or messianic, faith or war figures such as Moses, Che Guevara, André Matswa (Mappa 1998). Today, local representatives we interview in Mauritania and Senegal consider Western-driven powers as deliberately evil, corrupt and arbitrary. Their injunctions are bypassed or obeyed more for fear or in exchange for protection than in support of their judicious rationale (Mappa 2007). Yet the State is not called into question. It is part of the political furniture and is thought irrevocable.

Instead of legitimacy, there is in Africa an ambivalent relation to state power on which the populace places disproportionate hopes and expectations, as though they were traditional powers. Repeatedly disappointed, it turns against the state become scapegoat.

Does it follow that traditional powers are more legitimate? That is the broadly held view in Africa. Seen from outside, the same ambivalence prevails towards them, with the same expectations and the same frustrations.

---

3. See Dominique Darbon's article in this book.

In fact, the notions of the externality of power, the outwards shift of the responsibility for its institution and more broadly the extraversion, allegiance and dependency, the circumventing of injunctions, sacralised though they be, etc. inform the whole social field. In other words, they order social mechanisms and command individual and collective action.

Fragmentation

Another contrast between state-building in Africa and in Europe has to do with the fact that the state is not central. In keeping with the traditional order in which powers were set side by side, even when a royal or imperial power was averred, the postcolonial state has come to replace particular powers – religious, ethnic, territorial – without supplanting them. Unlike in Europe, particular powers have not recognised the primacy of a central power. Coveted by particular chiefs hostile to one another, the State is the stage where the traditional game of scissions and short-lived alliances is played out.

Despite it invoking unity, state power is one agent of societal fragmentation. It may even instigate it through its own connections with particular ethnic groups, religions, territories. The West's expectation, indeed its demand to see the advent in Africa of a legal state, regulating social conflicts is pure projection. The organisation of elections, which in the West bring peace and legitimacy, intensify there the conflicts between chiefs who see the danger to their continued power, and between segments of society, broadly at odds with each other[4].

This way of instituting power is not disputed by political opposition movements. As a rule, the individuals – the chiefs – are called into question but not the concept behind their action, that is power as a social mechanism. Furthermore the juxtaposition of those powers perceived as exogenous, with local powers perceived as "true, authentic and legitimate", which would be a contradiction in terms to Westerners, is not a problem for Africans.

Unlimited power and dispossession

The theory and praxis of power in Africa is rooted in traditions giving the notions of limits, rules, law or even freedom a different meaning to the one they had and still have in Europe. Sacred powers were given as limitless. These powers did not "give" out laws valid for

---

4. 'I was brought up into absolute obedience and ethnic ferocity' says today one of the Rwandan genocide perpetrators (Hatzfeld 2007).

all but prohibitions varying with the pecking order of group members. Unlike in Western law, the prohibitions of revealed law were and still are unchallengeable, given as sacred and immutable. On the whole, the populations did not seek to understand their rationale with a view to observe or oppose them on solid grounds; they obeyed them out of fear, or circumvented them.

The imaginary of untrammelled power can be traced in the construction of the earthly powers. The counterpart of the law is to be found in the prohibitions passed on by tradition. Laws taken from the West have been vested with the traditional meanings of revealed law. In spite of the curbs appearing here and there, the State has, like a head of clan or a patriarch, unlimited power over the persons in the absence of a law working as a third body. Talk of individual freedom stands side by side with the insistence on the individuals' subservience to official will, while freedom of choice becomes synonymous with disobedience and betrayal.

Constraint as a form of government still prevails, elections and elected government not withstanding. Recurring "regressions" of the "democratic mirage" (Akindès, 1996) bear out the difficulty political and economic liberalism has in taking root in African societies where "political liberalisation" often comes with a rise in political criminality. Western pressures for Human Rights are not followed with the anticipated results; they are unheeded, instrumentalized or circumvented by the local powers, which modify the forms of constraint but not its rationale, as B. Hibou observes in the context of Tunisia (2006). Ruling by constraint is accepted by societies that share in this principle and apply it in private practice. Such a shared ethos has to be a source of power legitimacy.

This power is "integrated" in the person who wields it. Institutions imported from the West get fitted to the person of the leader. This subtle alchemy between notions of unbridled freedom and allegiance, integration of power and its personalisation makes for powers which, by Western standards are arbitrary, therefore illegal, be it at state or societal level. These powers hover between constraint and seduction. Now this trend is also perceptible in Europe, where political power appeals more to the "citizens'" emotions than to their thinking ability. How strange the convergence of European democracies with the systems they propose to democratise.

While the action of political power towards social change is a source of its legitimacy in Europe, the African tradition does not share this vision of change and action. The continuity of social order as per the tradition is considered by many Africans as a noble objective and its transformation as desired by public policies imported from the West may not rate everywhere as a priority. Problems, predominantly material in nature, are expected to be resolved without the local actors acting to implement change either on themselves or their environment. This mechanism is consistent with the outwards shifting of responsibility. On the whole, it is expected that problems will be solved from without, through magic forces, by the West. The unexpected turn the reforms proposed by the West take stems from this social mechanism.

Like in Europe, change in Africa grafts itself on the past. The differences between the cultures are substantial and it is unlikely that the Western system can serve as a foundation to cooperation in Africa and more broadly to international cooperation. The questions of legitimacy and legality when addressed from within take a different meaning from the one they have in the West.

By way of conclusion

In some respects, the new democratic governance policies proceed from those that came before them: like in the past, they project on the beneficiary a democratic ideal that is today more than in the past challenged by governance policies devised for Europe. As against that, they could signal Europe's first steps out of her splendid isolation, described by Régis Debray (2007) as a culture so full of its own formulae as to be unable to speak or listen to others. Africa has hitherto been a favoured hunting ground in which to duplicate her policies through the mirror of aid. Foregoing this would be thinking Europe and other societies in their own historicity and specificity. Is it possible to cooperate with different societies as Hubert Vedrine suggests? Is it conceivable to accept as legal and legitimate here what is not so elsewhere, and to be open to others as they are? Is it possible to escape the idea that cooperation means assistance to "the most vulnerable" as Hubert Vedrine goes on to prescribe? Undoubtedly! But this requires a cultural mutation on both sides. For there can be no question that development aid is a relationship which engages the will, or rather the affects of both parties. Perhaps this has already started. Can we not detect in European democratic governance policies some shift, marginal maybe, but no less operating? Let us hope so.

Bibliography

Akindès, F. (1996). Mirage démocratique en Afrique subsaharienne francophone, Codesria.

Castel, R. (1995). Transformation of the Social Question, Transaction Publishers.

Debray, R. (2007). Un mythe contemporain: le dialogue des civilisations, Paris, CNRS éditions.

Gauchet, M. (1994) 'l'État au miroir de la raison d'État : la France et la chrétienté', in Y.-C. Zarka Raison et déraison d'État, Paris, PUF.

Gauchet, M. (2007). L'avènement de la démocratie, I La révolution moderne, II La crise du libéralisme, Paris, Gallimard.

Hibou, B. (2007). La force de l'obéissance, Paris, La Découverte.

Hatzfeld, J. (2007). La stratégie des antilopes, Paris, Seuil.

Lefort, C. (1986). Écrits politiques, Paris, Seuil.

Mappa, S. (1998). Pouvoirs traditionnels et pouvoir d'État en Afrique, Paris, Karthala.

Mappa, S. (2008). Le pouvoir comme objet de pensée, Paris.

Sy, O. 'Governance A global question that calls for specific responses in Africa', in this book.

Védrine, H. (2007). Rapport pour le président de la République sur la France et la mondialisation, Paris, Fayard.

8

State, Power and Society
in the Governance of Projected Societies

Dominique DARBON
(Translated from the French)

Works on the scrutiny and analysis of State, power, society and political organisation in developing countries would fill a library. Why, then, return to these three terms as necessary to grasp the mechanisms of social and political regulation, and international aid as they are difficult to figure out given the multiplicity of their meanings? There are two main reasons for this.

First, their representation and usage in scientific, political and development practice literature have varied a great deal with the ebb and flow of disciplinary debates and ideological tests of strength. The differentiated treatment of these three notions, often taken in isolation, which prevailed from the end of the seventies to the mid-nineties often led to opposing them to each other. A fresh approach privileges anew their interactions and their imbededness, which chart historicized political progress and yield regulation formulae, or what Mosca called "political formulae". In spite of its multiple meanings, a testament to the ideological issues it polarises, the concept of governance focuses on a political analysis actually based on these imbededness and interactions, on the play between autonomy and interdependence which characterises the power relations existing between the State and social organisations (Kjaer et al., 2002). It rests on these three key words, or rather on the gradual and peculiar shifts in their definitions and relationship in terms of managerial prospects. Political regulation – or state capability – is then analysed as the structural interaction and interconnection of leaders with citizens, of agents with structures within networks and management working groups, become the hallmarks of a polity devising policies carried out through politics. This requires a much more complex apprehension of social and political functioning, which cannot be dissociated from the dynamics of social interests and groupings.

Meanwhile, in the poorest developing societies and in fragile environments, these concepts and the outcomes of their interactions and interdependence take a very particular significance bound in their specific historical progress. These states and societies fall into two categories: those whose fragility is cyclical, that is those in which crisis factors do not fundamentally undermine the interconnection between the state-building and society building processes; and those whose fragility is related to a chronic or structural disconnection of these social dynamics and who will be the focus of this study under the heading of "projected societies". Those states and societies experimenting major problems with state building broadly share three fundamental characteristics. First, they are institutionally structured around rules, norms and methods of management and state social and territorial regulations that are mostly not to be found in their local social dynamics at the time of State succession; second they are constantly subjected to variable but common forms of structural, cognitive, financial and organisational dependency leading to the importation or implantation of undertakings, agendas, norms, rules, management and political regulation methods that their internal social dynamics does not accommodate, or only in part and that only some social groupings manage to appropriate according to the norms on which they are founded. Third and last they are shot through with powerful internal dynamics also affected by the dependency syndrome but contributing only fortuitously to the production of official institutional regulation principles. This breeds mismatches, smokescreens and allows room for the subordination of official regulation models, often non-institutionalised, to officious or legally unacceptable, but no less institutionalised, regulation models. The state and the bureaucratic management system, and more broadly, the whole of the official regulation methods are formatted via techniques systematically imported or projected. Those techniques are drawn from the changing experiences of developed societies who have set themselves up as perfect models, rather than from local, everyday social practices absorbing these imports. And yet they do appear to be the specific expression of negotiations the governing and the governed endlessly pursue towards the creation of a political society, hence the coinage of projected societies and states.

So, how is one to analyse the governance of these particular states and societies if not as a catalogue of deviation or deviance given that, by definition, what they represent is nothing but the formal project of what they are intended to be whereas their internal social dynamics can only deliver it in part? How are these states and societies, by definition fragile and low-capacity, to build on established social practices when the terms of reference, governance principles and regulation techniques suggested by international cooperation, are forever modified over time? When they reflect other societies' semantic trends, their "buzzwords" and social issues and not, for the most part, their own internal dynamics, cross-fertilised by external dynamics?

These questions are at the heart of any serious scrutiny of state building. In these particular domains, the notion of governance can only become operative if a) it is explicitly founded in the intimacy of the day to day interaction between our three concepts and b) if the institutionalisation of State social practices gets deeply integrated into the specific historicity of the projected societies. The alternative is to accept that what Peter Berger (1974) termed the Potosi paradigm[1] remains at the heart of development action, or that trusteeship is an option (Krasner 1999).

Dilemmas and dead-ends of social construction by transfer

Which State in poor countries?

Contrary to popular assumptions, the definition of the State, the way it is perceived and the way its missions and functions in society are understood change all the time[2]. These mutations, resulting from dynamics inherent to each society, are strongly directed by the most developed countries who through their moral, economic and political weight and their set-ups for the production of knowledge and analysis (think tanks) propagate their own changes towards other societies and international institutions whose agenda they shape to a great extent (Stone, 1996; Dezalay and Garth, 2002). This cognitive domination of the developed countries via their specialised agencies and societies is not to be criticised when it makes available to the weaker countries the knowledge and know-how that will help them reinforce their capabilities. It becomes questionable when it leads to imposing an agenda, complete with reference systems and techniques, on developing societies whose social dynamics do

---

1. The Potosi paradigm states, using the silver mines workers' suffering as its text, that suffering alone ensures the well-being of future generations.

2. We will here adopt Theda Skocpol's definition "a set of administrative, policing and military organizations headed and more or less well coordinated by an executive authority. Any state first and fundamentally extracts resources from society and deploys these to create and support coercive and administrative organization", which we will progressively weave into the more complex notion of legitimacy. (Skocpol, 1979, Cambridge, p. 29).

not reflect these priorities and whose very limited management capacities will not be able to implement them. (Darbon, 2008; Wunsch, 2000).

Thirty years of reforms and conceptual debate on the State did not yield a linear and unified reframing of the State (on the lines, say of the Westphalian State versus post-Westphalian-Vatelian state model, very trendy until the end of the nineties) but the build-up of expectations pinned on a State whose action methodology and intervention models are looped. So we went from the "benevolent, beneficent and omniscient" development-driving State (1960-1970), to the toxic and development-inhibiting State (1980-1990), to the re-discovery of the relative autonomy of the State by the neo-institutionalists (Skocpol, 1985; DiMaggio and Powell, 1991; Gazibo, 2005). Today, the latter orientations having failed, (World Bank World Development Report, etc.) and in the light of Asian experiences in particular, the not so new concept of developmentalist State is gaining favour, which stresses the need for the State and the social structures and spaces which it claims to control to be embedded (Mkandawire, 2001; Evans, 1995 and 1996). Participative democracy is coming to the fore while the public action approach focused on ongoing state building and society building by means of sectoral and global negotiations is being reinforced (Papadopoulos, 2002; Sabatier, 1999).

The instability in the concept of State and its constant adjustments for close on thirty years has three major impacts.

First, the last 25 years of reform have paradoxically led to a reduction in the material and human intervention capacities of the poorest states. This makes their claim to the monopoly of legitimate violence over the territory and social organizations they are supposed to control the more uncertain.

Next, these mutations have further increased the disenfranchisement of the projected states and societies. Developed or emerging societies take part, via think tanks and other agencies to the conceptualisation effort, and multiply practical and technical experiments through close interaction and interconnection with any number of organized social movements. They evolve reiterative reform processes through which they can socially test new techniques and new governance formulae, and adjust them as they go along. And thus is confirmed the paradox of power, which leads to building states with a very strong enforcement capacity, content to regulate and let the governed groups act, so strong is the osmosis between them. Meanwhile, the major actors of the poorest states and societies, broadly bereft of similar resources, are subjected, at government level, to the transfers of norms, techniques, management methods and other reforms. They cannot organise the experiments and adjustments that would allow them to define the scope of accommodations and derogations requisite for the "society making", to effect embedding. Those societies end up with a strong normative and institutional pluralism and a growing gap between official and unofficial, formal and informal structures, adding to the mounting assortment of techniques, reforms etc. all dead in the water. The management procedures and the workings of the State and its missions are made ever more perplexing for the civil servants like for the populace and lend themselves to all forms of shady dealing, corruption and circumventing strategies. This perpetuates low capacity states, unable to rely on their society to build their strength, for the simple reason that they are not in osmosis with the official management model they propose. The "official state" does not have the benefit of dense, powerful non-state organisations and institutions integrated in official set-ups it runs to relay its policies. By contrast, it is powerfully embedded in very dense institutionalised local social networks that do not operate along "official" governmental lines.

This is how, in the name of "good governance", fragile states with inadequate technical or human capacities adopt very sophisticated management tools they will not be able to operate, to conduct activities they cannot undertake and by means that they do not control.[3] Thus is the State projected (as are society and power), its form and social reality predicted on the basis of what it should do and be, never mind existing local social drives since they are most of the time, at least in the mid-term, conflicting with, indeed opposed to those mutations. The directed technical actions founding these projections may well be legitimate and are frequently based on data-matching (indicators) which Daniel Kaufman, one of the most well-known expert on this topic, considers worthwhile, provided they arise from "thousands" of specific individual answers and rely on a great many other instruments. He does, however warn against their considerable limitations and non-operationality (Kaufmann and Kraay, 2007[4]). This has never stopped those who want to create the new State after techniques and frameworks refined on the basis of the most successful external experience, ready to change formulae as soon as new techniques, even more "successful" come to hand. They merely forget, in their misuse of modelisation, that political states and societies are historical products.

---

3. This brings about Ubuesque situations in which the structures are to all intents and purposes "externalised" or entirely staffed with expats with minimal local managers externally trained and whose career outstrips the national government's framework of esponsibility (e.g. Zambia's Department of Revenue) unless again S. Krasner's trusteeship be an option.

4. This highly critical analysis is to be set against the gloating presentation of the 2006 document, "A Decade of Measuring the Quality of Governance, Governance matters", 2006, notably p. 3. And for a more sophisticated approach to governance, see Hermet, 2005.

Thus the poorest developing countries' "typical" state is characterised by an extreme fragmentation, an assortment of reforms, norms and procedures, technically perfect for the most part but socially unpredictable. On the one hand this assortment is "technically" liable to lead to a better organisation of the state, to more accountability on the part of government agents and leaders and to the empowerment of competing actors (especially non-state ones) as well as a – at least potentially – stronger embedding of public action in the local constructs and negotiation systems. But on the other hand, this thirty year whirligig of incessant reforms, which did not all converge or enjoy much funding, curtails the most fragile states' capacity for action. It deprives them of their means of action (decentralisation, regional integration, adjustments, stream-lining) whilst immunising them against all obligations of transaction or negotiation with their society through the provision of international financial aid and reforms ready-legitimated elsewhere.

And there we have the paradox or dilemmas and contradictions of state-building (Paris and Sisk, 2007). It makes the State, as Grindle has shown (1966), even more destabilized in its capacity to act (administrative capacity), to get its authority and its set of rules accepted (institutional capacity) and to facilitate negotiation (political capacity). The whole effect is to reduce, in the name of local societies' stronger capacity and stronger social dynamism, an already fragile state's capacity to act. This option would be interesting under three conditions: 1) these local societies have at hand trained staff with a sound grasp of the minimal regulation procedures required from a modern state as well as substantial resources, which is not the case; 2) they draw the Western style state model from their own historicity, which even hypothetically is highly improbable; and 3) they are allowed to produce a local regulation system that they control even if it means supporting its modalities (Wunsch, 2000; Darbon, 2002), and this is not happening either. Weakening the state is supposed, via the reinforcement of social structures that do not reflect it, not indeed to enable those to induce or to evolve "bottom-up" the regulation and governance capacity that would make sense to them, but to bring forth a Western style state. Make of it what you will...

These paradoxes show up the impasse to which these conceptions lead which see in the State a purely technical device divorced from political power and society and which refuse to integrate the notion of governance into a democratic dynamics supposing its constant appropriation by the most contradictory social forces also known as civil society.

What of society in the fragile state?

Like the notion of State, that of society has given rise to many studies. References to societies proliferated in the nineties, stressing, in particular in the poorest countries, their great fluidity, expressed in their political dynamism (Balandier, 1979), their "non-capture" (Hyden, 1999), their propensity for the "exit option" (Hirschman, 1970), their aptitude to undermine proposed domination (Bayart et al., 1992), their yield of bonding capital (Putnam, 2002), their creativity (Martin, 1992), their versatility and/or duplicity (Olivier de Sardan et al., 2000). This surge of interest is not without presenting major difficulties: society has become equated to the very specific concept of "civil society". It has been endowed with every quality and set on a collision course with the State presented as its exact opposite. It has been made a homogenous, stable, coherent, trustworthy, honest bloc, beyond the differentiation strategies and above the manoeuvring of those wielding political power. In short, the existence of a civil society has not only been taken as read, it has besides nurtured idealised and illusory representations of the poorest countries' societies.

Now these societies share with their states the burden of fragility and projection. Once again, State and society cannot be thought through independently.

On the one hand the very existence of society raises questions. These projected societies are indeed characterised by their extreme complexity, made more acute by the diversity in the frames of reference – worldviews, zeitgeist which run through them or structure them to the point of making the notion of social citizenship rather elusive. The way projected states are constituted results, most of the time, in the horizontal juxtaposition of social groups whose history and interests are different while they all integrate vertically at e.g. local, state, national, diaspora and global level. This makes for the coexistence of unrelated norms and frames of references; it induces between them unlikely associations and cross-fertilisations and opens the way to "forum shopping" and alternative legitimation. These societies operate on several levels of frames of reference and rules, exhibit a generalised normative, ethical, moral and legal pluralism with ample room for negotiation and interplay (alternative, cumulative) between the frames of references and the cleavages this provides for (Vanderlinden, 1996; Le Roy, 1999). These projected societies are thus essentially complex because they weave into their diversity the capacity to combine cleavages belonging to different scales in space or time while at the same time leaving little room for shifting alliances (Lipset, 1969).

On the other hand, do these groups amount to a civil society[5]? This debate, inexhaustible in the international literature (Howell and Pearce, 2001; Comaroff, 1999: 1-43; Otayek, 2004), remains essential to understanding the nature of the links between the State and society in this type of projected social organisation. In developed countries, State and society are closely embedded, to the point of making up the two sides of the same coin – both autonomous and undividable; neither can exist without the other to such an extent that the social groups become integral actors in the public sphere ("strong publics", Fraser, 1994) and bring forth the political society.

In projected societies and states, this embeddedness, which links autonomy and interdependence, individualism and communality, public and private spheres and their mutual institutionalisation, is less assured. For most people in these social groups, the merging together of the coin's two sides does not happen: the share of local society in the production of national government remains marginal, while governmental influence in "society building" or at least in its administration remains limited, though not inexistent. The odds for opening a public space conciliating private and common interests are very indeed.

And yet "imported" forms of regulation and institutional organisation (including the State), formal and deviant though they might be, are party to the people's history and political culture through all the learning and all the representations they bring about. So that although whole sections of society may appear at first sight on the margins of state and Western modernity far remote from their frames of reference and norms, they no less partake in the cognitive nexus, social practices and networks which closely involve them in their process. This well-known phenomenon (Balandier, 1979; Elias, 1997) makes plain the embeddedness of the State's society with the society "without the State" (Sindjoun, 2002; Darbon, 2007; Albo, 2007) and shows how in the innermost recesses of a failed state, the need for State endures, capable of the most unexpected forms (Tréfon, 2004 and 2007). State and society, or more precisely the state's actors and norms and the actors and norms from the diverse social groups making up local society weave day by day webs of connections and interactions; they keep impacting on and adjusting to each other to contribute to building a local society "as is" and not as it is supposed to be (traditional or projected) (Giddens, 1984). Forms of autonomy and interdependence, of odd combination merging strong individualism (Marie, 1997) and social capital (Putnam, 2002), the portents in short, of a fragile public space are there for all to see.

---

5. Cf. Howell and Pearce, 2001, p. 13-38 for full discussion and two types of definition.

Such are the complex societies which have been given the task to bring forth an embedded state through a relationship of confrontation and negotiation with an official state which they find "given" and whose own institutions and rules work towards re-formatting them. These societies, thus influenced by the official state must evolve a different version of it whilst its own dependence on the outside keeps it "as is". To subscribe to this is to contemplate a governance allowing for society to appropriate imported techniques and procedures, to invalidate them and then come up with new ones. It is to believe in building society in the long term through the complexity of interactions between intelligent actors who fit in with circumstances, confirming thereby the existence of common rules that found their action. This in turn yields in the long term the trust and rules (in Giddens' broadest sense) arising from their needs and the practical knowledge acquired along the way.

What is at stake in state building is the reconnection between the local social groups' social dynamics and the management formulae proposed by the state. This requires the end of the duality whereby an official formal world with next to no impact in terms of effective regulation coexists with a world of illegal, informal adjustments from which actual regulations arise. The idea is to capitalise on locally produced regulation formulae by making them official, starting thereby a selective process towards officialising informal institutionalisation processes.

What power?

The power of the projected states and societies thus hinges on a double bind. Upwards and outwards, it depends on the donors and norm-setters seeking a modicum of broadly artificial – or else very fragile but no less requisite stability. And downwards, it constantly interacts with the local cleavages and social groups on which power rests for social acceptation. That is what makes it a product of the society, and the more respected for imposing rules consented in principle (and not necessarily to the letter) by the social groups whose role it is to dissent and obey.

The stated aim of the international consensus in terms of governance is to produce a democratic power, that is one accountable to the society it runs. All the techniques and recipes called upon to reform the state and re-shape society are supposed to advance the achievement of this goal. Although significant formal progress has been made (Freedom House index) to reinforce the rules of power, the fundamentals have not been addressed, to the extent that some authors speak of "illiberal" democracy (Krasner). The conditions for the mobilisation and constitution of interest groups around common rules, and for the institution of the State often remain hardly compatible with the sound operation of democratic governance, as shown by the proliferation of personalised "political parties", the deterioration of trade unions, the burgeoning of opportunist alliances, the lack of trust, etc. Likewise the concepts of actors strong in their citizen or constituent status, of power understood as a delegation and not an opportunity, of transfers of allegiance and of "citizens" consenting to observe the political order, the very institutionalisation of this order etc. remain in most of those societies at best fragile, at worst just minority pursuits. In projected societies, power hinges on a range of interpretation registers and organisational models on which the elites must play to attract electoral support, at the price of sacrificing ever more to a neopatrimonial power whereby several registers of legitimacy and frames of references interact (Médard, 1991).

Now the development programmes stumble on such cross-breeding (or perversions). Development organisation and financial backers call on pre-determined perceptions of the state-society-power trinity. In other words, there is a constant backsliding from generic definitions very open and allowing many interpretations and variations to the very narrow operational options retained. We move from governance to "good governance", from regulatory models to a few specific regulatory models, from State as organized domination to state as archetypal bureaucratic legal-rational domination[6].

These specific models, these operational conceptions are the more readily imposed as one size fits all frames of reference since they are imposed to/taken on by weak states (though not necessarily fragile) whose capacity for negotiation with donors is at its lowest. Furthermore, their capacity to control and direct efficiently the loose play of de facto renegotiation with interest groups, cleavages and communities making up the whole society is technically very limited for reasons of human and organisational resources over and above the societal specificities highlighted above. The upshot of this is states projected on projected societies, states floating above their societies (suspended states), disconnected states, states that are not imbedded in society. In the – ultimately legitimate and justifiable – name of the greater efficiency of the state or of the reinforcement of society, new norms are being set forth which permit the proliferation of deviant adjustments and exit practices, become perverse and ineffective for want of being developed.

---

6. The first of the six Worldwide Governance Indicator (WGI)'s aggregate indices from the 2006 World Bank Institute deals with "voice and accountability" and therein the way citizens select their government. However, the electoral model is but one mode of selection and may adopt many variations.

Embeddedness as principle of democratic governance

The states' ability effectively to regulate society is partly founded in technical and administrative devices, and in constraint but essentially in intricate relationships of allegiance and embeddedness that bind them together. The stronger the density of interactions and the depth of embeddedness with the governed, the more the state and society appear like moulded into one another (or embedded) and the more governance is efficient and eschews the systematic resort to its enforcement outfits (for all that they are firmly in place). This interplay between the two poles' autonomy and dependence is at the heart of all political sciences' analyses, that is to say of all state building activities.

Governance as a global view

State, power and society are three concepts at the very heart of the governance principle and thus very difficult to interpret given the multiple meanings concentrated on this set of notions (Klingner, 2004). The best and worst definition, the broadest but also the least operational may be drawn from the 2006 World Governance Index. There, one finds governance defined as: "The set of traditions and institutions by which authority in a country is exercised."

This apparently very simple definition actually sums up in a few words the untold complexity of social processes and of all the conflicts and misunderstandings the terms breed. It stresses the import of perceptions; validates the existence of both formal and informal rules; points to the fundamental role of power legitimacy (authority); confirms via the terms of institution and tradition the prerequisite embedding between society and the regulation procedures presiding over its organization; and supposes a high level of trust. In short it quashes any attempt at the purely technical replication of a model or of techniques and only goes to show that the three concepts are interdependent, that they make up distinct facets of the same object and cannot be separated. They spring from each other, thereby constantly adjusting and organizing their internal transformation and embeddedness (Menocal, 2004). The three notions are connected and partake together in the establishment of regulation procedures that are reliable, predictable, controlled and accepted both by the institutions and by the citizens.

Since independence, the trend has been to treat poor countries differently. There, the State was to deliver "landless intensive" development, never mind that it did not have the material, human and political capability for this, and neither was it to rely on a society thought backwards, considered an obstacle and targeted for change. Faced with failure, in the eighties everything had to change: the State, now perceived as the major obstacle to development was weakened and social forces, freely constituted and endowed with all virtues were put in the driving seat. What little State there had been was then destroyed with the result that society organized along lines which do not meet the requirement for creating a state or a liberal style economy for want of a directing authority as Polanyi reminds us.

Governance in projected states requires that two axes be given prominence.

On the one hand a convergence must be furthered between the formal objectives set by the "projection" process and the social trends at work in the societies in order to tie up the state-society link. This convergence is not straightforward, given the number of frames of reference and other interests which course through projected societies, and it will cause normative and ethical conflicts. It is however made easier by the fact that the principles and practices of the projected organization models are now part of these frames of reference (Darbon, 1997). A State cannot be independent from the history of the society it is called to run. It is constantly affected by it – through the staff that runs it to mention but one factor – and can only act because this society has agreed to obey and taken steps to that end. Conversely a society cannot understand itself without taking into account State action and influence as it constantly acts on people's representations, the opportunities they have and the costs and benefits which are the stuff of social interactions, however fragile, projected or failed the state may be (Tréfon, 2004 et 2007; Darbon, 2002; Olivier de Sardan et al., 2000). Society however remote it may be from the reach of the State, its norms, organization modalities and agents cannot be understood without reference to the State which is forever disturbing and controlling the modalities of its change. In this interaction, the power, in societies where state management operates, binds together state and society endeavours.

On the other hand building on experiences becomes a major stake since a society constitutes itself through permanent learning, routines, practical awareness and its actors' mutual adjustments to each others' expectations. Only through building on these acquisitions is any action liable to arrive at common rules. Now, to date, the past thirty years' systematic mid-term changes of reform kits have made it impossible for either the agents of the state or the "citizens" and "constituents" to build on any such experience.

In terms of governance prospects, authority does not boil down to technical or administrative capacity, and the State does not mean a space in which are added together individual actions disconnected from each other. In terms of governance prospects, they both rely on the existence of trust and/or social capital, that is on strong social bonds between all the actors, enabling them to proceed with their individual activity, strong in stable and reliable frames of reference that make social interaction predictable and feasible. A set of ways and means (Giddens, 1987), of institutions devised by the actors and endorsed by them in their everyday activity (making them autonomous) thus provides action frameworks (Goffman, 1974) enabling a set of human groupings to achieve political society in spite of the countless jurisdictions they refer to. It is down to democratic governance to bring about this connection through building on all that has been learnt. And it is also down to a more answerable cooperation, one that would no longer confuse its long-term supreme objectives with the techniques called upon to that end.

Building society on its daily development (the State at Work approach)

In projected states and societies, the way the state is perceived is often as "a given", "non-negotiable" machine, which regulates, rules, manages or predicts the political and social organisation model that should be, without having at its command the capacities required. The constraints of state-building in projected societies are best seen in the relations maintained by low ranking civil servants the so-called "street-level bureaucrats", mostly ill-prepared and doing a routine job with precious little understanding of their mission and a "citizenry" that has not integrated the values of its status. Building fragile states and their governance is thus made tricky by four types of major constraints.

The state can avail itself of so limited material, organisational, financial and human means that it is not in a position to manage the political problems, to include them on the agenda or to open systematic negotiations with interest groups often beset by the same ills.

Society is structurally weak and unable to impose itself by means of political mobilisation or association as a sparring partner to the state machine and power.

Part of the agenda, options and debates is decided by external actors who command the material and financial resources, and the expertise required to implement a particular policy.

The political debate is fractured over a plethora of internal and external actors and possibilities for allegiance shifts (networks) always leaving the "constituents" or "citizens" enough room for manoeuvre to by-pass or avoid the state, so as not to pay the price for their choices, or to extract greater advantages.

The object of "democratic governance" is not to dispute such expectations but to dispute the conditions that yield them, relying in particular on the perspectives gained through public action analysis. Day to day, this leads to privileging specific negotiation and regulation relationships which are set up as and when between the state – or rather some of its instances and representatives – and the relevant sections of society, mobilised in special interest groups around sectoral or spatial policies, and to capitalise on these deliberate practices. The object is to incrementally integrate structuring processes by trial and error or "muddling through" (Lindblom 1959) in the daily fabric of policies and political decisions and to organise the complex regulation of these projected societies. This statisation process (Médard, 1991) brings them to deal, through confrontation-negotiation-transaction with external pressures as well as with the equally confuse and contradictory demands of the diverse interest groups structuring local society. Such local norms for negotiation, mediation, regulation, moderation, combined with pressures from the imported state, yield regulation models enabling State and society to turn their formal statutes into an effective capacity to engage and negotiate, producing rules and trust.

"Democratic governance" aims precisely to leave the production of social regulation's specifics to local actors building into their tactics and strategies the imported norms, while helping form the lasting frameworks that will support them. The concept is demanding as it locks together specific governance-enhancing policies and an agreed upon overall cooperation and development policy, with knowable long term objectives but flexible processes, this is a tall order.

Bibliography

Albo, X. (2007). "Un estado plurinacional y a la vez unitario en Bolivia", Seminario Pulso, La Paz, PIEB.

Balandier, G. (1972). Political Anthropology, New York, Vintage Books.

Bayart, J.-F., C. Toulabor, A.Mbembe (1992). La politique par le bas en Afrique noire, Paris, Karthala.

Berger, P.L. (1974). Pyramids of Sacrifice: Political Ethics and Social Change, New York, Basic books.

Comaroff, J. and J.-L. (1999). Civil Society and the Political Imagination in Africa: Critical Perspectives, Chicago, University of Chicago Press.

Darbon, D. (1997). "Un royaume divisé contre lui-même", in Darbon D. and J. du Bois de Gaudusson (ed.), La création du droit en Afrique,

Paris, Karthala.
Darbon, D. (2003). "Réformer ou reformer les administrations projetées des Afriques ? Entre routine anti-politique et ingénierie politique".
Dezalay, Y. and B.G. Garth, (2002). The internationalization of palace wars: Lawyers, economists, and the contest to transform Latin American states, Chicago, University of Chicago Press.
Dimaggio, P. and W. powell (eds) (1991) The New Institutionalism in Organizational Analysis, Chicago, University of Chicago Press.
Elias, N., M. Schröter (ed.) (2001). The society of individuals, London, Continuum International Publishing Group.
Evans, P. (1995). Embedded Autonomy. States and Industrial Transformation, Princeton, Princeton University Press.
Evans, P. (1996). "Government Action, Social Capital and Development, Reviewing the Evidence of Synergy", World Development, vol. 24, n° 6, p.1119-1132.
Fraser, N. (1994). "Rethinking the Public Sphere: A Contribution to the Critique of Actually Existing Democracy", in Calhoum G. (ed.) (1993) Habermas and the Public Sphere, Cambridge, Cambridge University Press.
Gabizo, M. (2005). Les paradoxes de la démocratisation en Afrique: analyse institutionnelle et stratégique, Montreal, Presses de l'Université de Montréal.
Giddens, A. (1984). The Constitution of the society, Cambridge, Polity Press.
Giddens, A. (1987). Social Theory and Modern Sociology, London, Blackwell.
Goffman, E. (1974). Frame Analysis: An Essay on the Organization of experience, Harvard, Harvard University Press.
Grindle, M.S. (1996). Challenging the state: crisis and innovation in Latin America and Africa, Cambridge, Cambridge University Press.
Hermet, G. (dir.) (2005). La gouvernance, un concept et ses applications, Paris, Karthala.
Hirschman, A.O. (1970). Exit, Voice, and Loyalty: Responses to Decline in Firms, Organizations, and States, Harvard, Harvard University Press.
Howell, J. and J. Pearce (2001). Civil Society and Development, A Critical Exploration, Boulder, Lynne Rienner Publishers.
Hyden, G. (1999). "Governance and the Reconstitution of the Political Order", in Joseph R. (ed.), State, Conflict and Democracy in Africa, Boulder, Lynne Rienner Publishers.
Kaufmann, D. and A. kraay (2007). "On Measuring Governance: Framing Issues for Debate", Draft Issues prepared for the Round Table on Measuring Governance, the World Bank Institute, January 11th.

Kjaer, M., O.H. Hanse, J.P.F. Thomsen (2002). "Conceptualizing State Capacity", DEMSTAR Research Report, n° 6, April.

Klinger, D.E. (2004). "Globalization, Governance, and the Future of Public Administration: Can We Make Sense Out of the Fog of Rhetoric Surrounding the Terminology?" Public Administration Review vol. 64 n° 6, p.737-743.

Krasner, S. (1999). Sovereignty: Organized Hypocrisy, Princeton, Princeton University Press.

Le Roy, E. (1999). Le jeu des lois: une anthropologie dynamique du droit, Paris, LGDJ.

Lindblom, C. (1959). "The Science of Muddling-Through", Public Administration Review, vol. 19, n° 79-88.

Lipset, J.S. (1969). Politics and the Social Science, Oxford, Oxford University Press.

Marie, A. (1997). L'Afrique des individus, Paris, Karthala.

Martin, D.C. (1992). La découverte des cultures politiques, Paris, Presses de la FNSP.

Médard, J.-F. (1991). États d'Afrique noire: formation, mécanismes et crises, Paris, Karthala.

Menocal, A.R. (2004). "And if there Was no State? Critical Reflections on Bates, Polanyi and Evans on the Role of the State in Promoting Development", Third World Quarterly, vol. 25, n° 4, p. 765-777.

Mkandawire, T. (2001). "Thinking About Developmental States in Africa", Cambridge Journal of Economics, 1.

Olivier De Sardan, J.-P. et al. (2000). Les courtiers en développement, Paris, Karthala.

Oomen, T.K. (2004). Nation, Civil Society and Social Movements: Essays in Political Sociology, New Delhi, Sage publications.

Otayek, R. et al. 2004, Les sociétés civiles du Sud: un état des lieux dans trois pays de la ZSP, Paris, MAE, DGCID.

papadopoulos, Y. (2002). "Démocratie, gouvernance et management de l'interdépendance des rapports complexes", in J. Santiso (ed.), À la recherche de la démocratie. Mélanges offerts à G. Hermet, Paris, Karthala.

R. Paris et T.D. Sisk (2007). Managing Contradictions: The Inherent Dilemmas of Postwar Statebuilding, New York, International Peace Academy, IPA Publications.

Putnam, R.D. (2002). Democracies in Flux: The Evolution of Social Capital in Contemporary Society, Oxford, Oxford University Press.

Sabatier, P.A. (1999). Theories of the Policy Process, Boulder, Westview Press.

Sindjoun, L. (2002). L'État ailleurs, entre noyau dur et case vide, Paris, Economica.

Skocpol, T. (1985). "Bringing the State back in, Strategies of analysis in Current Research", in P. Evans et al. Bringing the State back in, Cambridge, Cambridge University Press.

Stone, D. (1996). Capturing the Political Imagination: Think tanks and the Policy Process, London, Frank Cass.

Tréfon, T. (2004). Reinventing Order in the Congo, How People Respond to State Failure in Kinshasa, London, Zed Books.

Tréfon, T. (2007). "Parcours administratifs dans un État en faillite: récits populaires de Lubumbashi (RDC)", Paris, L'Harmattan, coll. Cahiers Africains, n° 74.

Vanderlinden, J. (1996). Anthropologie juridique, Paris, Dalloz.

Weiss, L. (1998). The Myth of the Powerless State: Governing the Economy in a Global Area, Cambridge, Polity Press.

World Bank (2005). "Building Effective States, Forging Engaged Societies": Report of the World Bank Task Force on Capacity Development in Africa.

Wunsch, J.S. (2000). "Refounding the African State and Local Self-Governance: The Neglected Foundation", Journal of Modern African Studies, vol. 38, n° 3, p. 487-509.

9

State-building or Refounding the State?

Theoretical and Political Issues

Michèle LECLERC-OLIVE
(Translated from the French)

In its World Development Report 1997, the World Bank reminds us that State efficiency

> "is vital for the provision of goods and services – and the setting of rules and institutions – that allow markets to flourish and people to lead healthier, happier lives. Without it sustainable development, both economic and social, is impossible. Many said much the same thing fifty years ago, but then they tended to mean that development had to be state-provided. The message of experience since then is rather different: that the state is central to economic and social development, not as a direct provider of growth but as a partner, catalyst and promoter."

For ten years, academics and cooperation agency heads have set analytical frameworks, developed rationales and put forward policies aimed at the (re)construction ("nation-building, state-building") of states deemed "weak", "fragile" or "vulnerable", that they may play the part that is expected of them. At the same time other problems have come into light concerning a necessary state "refounding", notably of African states. This paper proposes to analyse the theoretical and political issues that underpin these new international action programmes directed at the State. What problems do those frames of reference seek to answer? What international action praxis do they advocate? On what conception of the State and its relation to society do they rest? What argumentative style shapes them? This analysis is conducted in the light of empirical research on decentralisations, public services, and the practice of assembly in West Africa. It will also borrow from the political philosophy of public space and democracy.

Analysing international action's frames of reference

The notions of state-building or nation-building used by the "international community[1]" from the early nineties may appear to address the concerns of those who worried at programmes (structural adjustment programmes in particular) underpinned by the conviction that the State must become as lean as possible – and as averse to intervention as possible. But each frame of reference – state-building, nation-building, or refounding – entails a conception of the State and a cooperation or intervention approach it behoves to scrutinise before rejoicing in a happy meeting of minds.

Beforehand, I should like to make an epistemological pause and posit a few preliminary observations on the very notion of frame of reference

> "The frame of reference – I quote the definition given by P. Muller (1990) – is made up with a set of prescriptions which give a political programme its sense through defining choice criteria and target-setting models. The process is both cognitive: it helps to understand reality by limiting its complexity; and prescriptive: it makes it possible to act on reality. Thus, the construction of a frame of reference supposes a dual operation: an exercise in decrypting reality in order to reduce its opacity and an exercise in re-encrypting reality towards a programme of public action".

Thus a descriptive purpose and a programmatic, indeed normative, purpose have been merged blunting the critical analysis of international action's semantics.

A theoretical proposal from Reinhart Koselleck will be particularly useful to untangle the intricacies in the frame of reference concept. The historian introduces the twin concepts of "space of experience" and "horizon of expectancy" as meta-historic categories or indeed more fundamentally as anthropological categories, the crucibles of human action.

---

1. This term is here used loosely; it does not refer to any precise concept.

"Put more concretely, on the one hand, every human being and every human community has a space of experience out of which one acts, in which past things are present or can be remembered, and, on the other, one always acts with reference to specific horizons of expectation" (Koselleck, 2002, p. 111).

R. Koselleck is particularly interested in the gap between the space of experience and the horizon of expectation. To be precise, the author' thesis is that this gap is growing wider:

"The burden of our historical thesis is that in 'Neuzeit' (modern era) the difference between experience and expectation is increasingly enlarged; more precisely, that 'Neuzeit' is only conceived as 'neue Ziet' (new era) from the point at which eager expectations diverge and remove themselves from all previous experience" (Koselleck, 2004, p. 285).

This gap constitutes one condition making it possible to think social change and to act, to avoid repeating the past, in particular in terms of violence and injustice. According to R. Koselleck, the concepts we use to think historical action relate back to a smaller and smaller share of experienced objects.

"This, then, no longer involves concepts that register experience, but rather, concepts that generate experience" (Koselleck, 2004, p. 285).

Contrary to these experience-founding concepts and breaking with the past, the notion of "frame of reference" restores a continuity with the recent past it purports to cast light on. Besides, it does not take into account extended time: its cognitive function stops at the present alone, or the immediate past which leaves no room for the long process of producing memories, experience and history. As for its programmatic dimension, it does not seek to distinguish long-term objectives from the first steps of their implementation. Scrutiny of the semantic progress of the concepts used as frames of reference shows that the charge of meaning they convey before they enter international community-speak gets squeezed out to the point of losing any exploratory potential. For instance from the moment the World Bank introduced the concept of governance as a major policy frame of reference, this term lost for a time one of its major attributes: naming ways to govern in a context where no absolute and unique supremacy could prevail[2].

---

2. This applies particularly to "corporate governance" but also to the usage, back in the sixties, of the term "governance" to analyse the management of academic or municipal institutions.

Thus the state-building frame of reference drew from earlier experiences of state formation a simplistic theory subordinated to its programmatic purpose. Interventionist state-building engineering seeks to rest its feasibility on the grounds that "nearly all states were born of an arbitrary construct and that in the end, the graft worked" (Caplan and Pouligny, 2005). Before becoming a frame of reference for international action, the state-building concept was used in particular by historians developing theories of the State. Thus when John Lonsdale analyses the "colonial moment" in Kenya he distinguishes between state-building, that is "the conscious effort at creating a conscious apparatus of control" and state-formation as "an historical process whose outcome is a largely unconscious and contradictory course of conflicts, negotiations and compromises between diverse groups whose self-serving actions and trade-offs constitute the 'vulgarization' of power " (Lonsdale and Berman, 1992). This conceptual crucible is not requisite only to the analysis of colonial situations. The scrutiny of the endogenous dynamics leading to the organisation and stabilisation of a state show that these processes do not apply only to individual or group action (Braddick, 2000). More broadly, the political order itself cannot be sustained for long by the sole exercise of authority (Lapierre, 1977). The resort to constraint has never been enough to guarantee the institutionalisation of a political order (Darbon, 2007). Scientific application of the state-building concept informs us of its analytical shortfalls and thus warns against the reductionist effects of its use as a mere frame of reference: no public policy should dispense with such historical enquiries – or substitute to them the ready-thought regurgitation of action frames of reference, especially when the object is to contribute to the lasting legitimacy of a political order and state. We shall accordingly keep in mind that the use of these concepts as action frames of reference does not thereby attach to them any descriptive or analytical authority. Such usage must be deconstructed on the strength of concepts enjoying scientific legitimacy.

The analysis of the theoretical and political stakes hanging on these frames of reference calls for three parallel approaches: the one we have just sketched out, that is a review of the semantic route taken by the concepts conscripted into the frame of reference (suppressed meanings cast their own light on the accepted usage); the analysis of the historical and political context of their emergence as action frames of reference; and the links, tensions and oppositions with other, alternative or complementary notions.

Two decisive historical turning points: the end of the Cold War and the 11 September 2001 attacks

Strictly speaking, the evolution of United Nations praxis should be closely followed from its peacekeeping operations to its state-building programmes. We shall be content with a few landmarks (Bendaña, 2004).

The end of the Cold War, culminating with the fall of the Berlin Wall, changed in-depth not only the international scene but also the conceptual frameworks that served to analyse local situations[3] (Samaan, 2006). If, hitherto, the threat could only come from the excessive power of some states, after the fall of the Berlin Wall, many analysts, such as G.B. Helman or S.R. Ratner for instance (1992-1993), now thought international security liable to be endangered by the weakness of some of them and in particular by the existence of some intrastate conflicts. In An Agenda for Peace, his June 1992 report received with much optimism, the Secretary General of the United Nations, Boutros Boutros-Ghali made the "post-conflict peace building" watchword a new priority for the United Nation. However, all failed states do not represent real danger for peace. Neither were all United Nations Member States prepared to support multilateral engagement, on the grounds that the principle of sovereignty forbids intervention in the inner affairs of a state.

Conversely, this sovereignty concept was under critical reappraisal, in the name of "human security" and human rights. The debate on the right of intervention open at the end of the seventies, though it did not lead to the creation of a new right, did nevertheless bring some modifications to the conception of humanitarian law in the name of "duty to protect". In fact, the nineties saw several interventions by Western countries[4] after the Security Council had pronounced them a "threat to international peace and security". It is also during that decade that non-governmental organisations reinforced their base and their legitimacy on the international scene. By the mid-eighties they benefited from an unprecedented support from international cooperation and development aid agencies in order to assist the populations most affected by the structural adjustment plans. By the same token, the international community expected them to flag up the emergence of conflicts liable to threaten international security. Experience had shown (in Sri Lanka,

---

3. Two largely divergent theses mark symbolically and intellectually the start of this new era: The End of History (Fukuyama, 1992) and The Clash of Civilisations (Huntington, 1993).

4. In Iraqi Kurdistan for instance, in 1991. However their cost in civilians lives (e.g. Chechnya) has not earned all conflicts the same international attention.

Angola, Mozambique etc.) that the international set-up had proved unable to take preventative steps for want of "early warning" facilities. Conflicts considered peripheral in Cold War days moved centre stage in a new theory of international security. Thus the humanitarian organisations' line of argument, and that of observers presenting those conflicts as a threat to territorial security (should internal violence spread to other failed states), converged to place the deterioration of states at the heart of the major international agencies' concerns. The 2001 terrorist attacks came to reinforce the threat theory while at the same time discrediting the early warning systems. While in 2000, the neo-conservatives in the Bush team had serious reservations regarding the merits of budgets dedicated to army-led nation-building operations (Samaan, 2006), their point of view had diametrically changed after 9-11.

Originally directed at "failed" or "collapsed" states, the state-building doctrine is today proposed as the paradigmatic frame of reference of an international policy preventatively directed at countries deemed "fragile" or "weak", on the grounds that they are liable to harbour terrorist groups. Shortly after 9-11 a conference organised by the Fund for Peace think-tank extended the list of territories that could represent a threat to world security.

> "Whoever thought that Afghanistan could be a place where terrorism could be bred and organized to attack the United States? This is the most useless, disorganized place. (...) The state had collapsed. A group of people organized themselves and pretended to be a government. (...) What is going to stop terrorists from organizing in Africa?" (quoted by Samaan, 2006).

The policies of institutional engineering – of nation-building or state-building – no longer have much to do today with United Nations peacekeeping missions. In spite of the debates this gives rise to at international level, they now take on missions with full executive, legal and judicial authority (Caplan and Pouligny, 2005: 132). These divest the local instances (when they exist) of an important part of their prerogatives or replace them when they are ineffectual, thus taking the risk of partaking in their de-legitimation or of reinforcing it.

To round off this all too sketchy historical survey, it behoves to recall that in the nineties, the conditionalities imposed by the financial institutions on the beneficiary countries evolved, building in institutional engineering and demands concerning governance. Meanwhile many countries undertook, under pressure from financial backers, or following national conferences, as happened in Africa, some politico-administrative reforms leading to the reinforcement or in a number of cases, to the creation of local authorities. The "decentralisations", in their diversity, amount to reforms likely to re-legitimate a renewed state. But in the eyes of major international cooperation actors, these reforms seem to be gradually losing their reforming potential and the diminishing support awarded them gets channelled into budget support.

Today, armed interventions in the name of the necessary reconstruction of a democratic state – nation-building – as in Iraq, have not corroborated the Bush administration's working hypothesis. The "benevolent hegemony" upheld by the White House government is harshly criticised, notably by Francis Fukuyama, one of the major theorists of state-building (2006). It has therefore become necessary to analyse the doctrinal developments and the rationales underpinning those state-building and nation-building frames of reference.

State-building, nation-building on a sensible scale?

For many researchers, the hope to contribute to the construction of democratic regimes may today be disappointed but it was no less high on the agenda directly after the fall of the Berlin Wall (Chandler, 2006).

By 2004, however, Francis Fukuyama advocated interventions less ambitious than nation-building programmes. According to him only the first phase of these nation-building programmes (narrowly focused on the institutional engineering of state-building) meets Western needs for security. More importantly he maintains that a state's legitimacy (expressed in the multifaceted links it establishes with society) eludes all serious scientific analysis: it consists in a complex alchemy no voluntarist programme could hope to create.

> "[...] only states can be deliberately constructed. if a nation arises from this, it is more a matter of luck than design" (Fukuyama, 2004, p. 99).

State-building could, all told, just amount to a reduced and sensible version of nation-building.

In his latest work (2006), Francis Fukuyama goes further. He now asserts his doubts as to the capacity of any government whatsoever to implement vast programmes of social engineering. This theory, which is at the heart of the neo-conservative doctrine, has, according to him been wrongly dismissed by the Bush administration. Accordingly he invites the White House drastically to reduce its interventions.

This view is not shared by another important actor in the American political debate. The RAND Corporation[5], having published two reports in 2003 and 2005 on the nation-building operations[6] led at the instigation of the United States or under the aegis of the United Nations[7], published in 2007 a guide, The Beginner's Guide to Nation-Building, which provides foreign intervention forces with a handbook of "good practice" towards a nation's reconstruction. In its 2003 report – and its exhaustive inventory of the negative effects brought about by the military intervention in Iraq notwithstanding – the RAND Corporation favoured a continued intervention, the 2007 guide shows no change in this direction. What should be made of this persistence when the nation-building projects have failed to deliver the expected change, indeed have brought about major instabilities[8]?

Beyond the different scope in their ambitions, the two frames of reference have many common features, starting with the resort to military force to back the interventions and the failure to involve the peoples concerned in the institutional engineering system. The very notion of a state's legitimacy, classically measured by the degree of reciprocity developing between a society and its tiers of government becomes subordinated to that of credibility in the eyes of the international community. The civil societies of Southern countries, considered over two decades as credible partners by numerous international cooperation programmes find themselves sidelined in their states' reconstruction process.

Moreover, these doctrines rest on a sequential conception of social change wherein democracy is but a conceivable option, an eventual and fortuitous phase.

"Societies emerging from conflict may be able to wait for democracy, but they need a government immediately to provide law enforcement,

---

5. The RAND Corporation a research centre created in 1946 works very closely with the US army and its publications are at the centre of the US foreign policy debates. The author of The Beginner's Guide to Nation Building, James Dobbins (formerly a diplomat, and special US envoy in most zones of military-humanitarian intervention) runs its International Security and Defense Policy Center (ISDP).

6. The nation-building concept before becoming a frame of reference for international action, referred to the undertakings of freshly independent states, in particular in Africa, where societies were then riven by ethnic and religious conflicts. Education and work were considered major resources towards building nations. To quote but a few examples out of a great many publications: Rivkin, 1969, Jordan and Reninger, 1975, or Francis 1968.

7. For memory, more than 80% of peace operations were set up between 1989 and 2003. The "successful" experiences quoted to justify recent interventions remain the operations undertaken in Germany and Japan directly after the second world war, while there can be no comparison between the contexts (economic globalisation, national economies structures, etc..)

8. It could make sense to consider the transfers of public funding towards private operators these nation-building operations have resulted in; this needs looking into.

education, and public health care [...] The intervening authorities need to choose partners carefully with a view to creating a government and distribution of power that will survive their departure" (RAND, 2007, p. 135).

What is more, the prevailing conception of democracy is reduced to electoral processes alone to select leaders, and ignores modalities of the exercise of power that could contribute to reducing strife between previously conflicting parties.

If the provision of services is to be offered to the populations, they will not take the form of "public" services and have become the preserve of Western NGOs.

> "Because they are frequently more honest, more efficient, and better able to communicate with international donors than are representatives of national or local governments, international NGOs are often the intermediaries of choice to distribute post-conflict assistance. NGOs are more likely to ensure that assistance goes directly to those most in need, not into the pockets of government officials" (RAND, 2007, p. 152-153).

Beyond its procedures, this purely instrumental democracy must first and foremost allow for the defence of private interests, in particular at international community level.

> "If a given international institution does not serve the interests of a democratically constituted nation-state, the latter has the right to limit or to take back its participation in it » (Fukuyama, 2004, p. 111).

The notion of public interest is dismissed on the oft-quoted grounds that a collective preference or priority can only reflect public interest if an institution can guarantee that it is not in fact a private interest. As such a guarantee cannot be ascertained, there is apparently nothing better for us to do than attend to our private interests: regulation, impervious to political intent, will see to their harmonisation. This is not counting with the political philosophies loosely coming under the heading of deliberative democracy and for which the distinction between private interests and general interest loses its key position in structuring historical action. It falls to discussion, "public reasoning", experience-sharing, consultation to define both individual and collective preferences, and political priorities. In this case, it need not be incumbent on an institution (the State or an international agency) to define alone the contents of a policy: what is expected instead is guaranteed deliberation procedures. We have a clash between two plurality policies laying claims to democracy but on the basis of different anthropological premises (Leclerc-Olive, 2003). The conception of "international democracy" as legitimating unilateral operations in the name of self-defence brings up the delicate matter of sovereignty. It may be difficult to narrow it down to its original understanding: the debates on humanitarian interference have seen to its evolution; however, current rationales behind unilateral decision warn against a "two-speed" version of sovereignty. For all that the international community alone has hitherto been allowed to infringe on a state's sovereignty, what practices should emerge at bi-lateral level that would be consistent with deliberative democracy?

Current policies range from claims to unilateral and pre-emptive self-defence to the international community's duty to act. Supposing heavy, nation-building programmes or their lighter, Fukuyama-style, state-building version, those policies rely on diagnoses and political philosophies that are not bereft of alternatives.

The cultural refounding of the State: the horizon of expectation set by the space of experience?

Suggestions are made aimed at reversing the top-down approach that typifies those diverse undertakings towards "weak" states. First the recent past cannot suffice to explain the "weakness" in particular of African states; long-term history is requisite. In many parts of the world, state weakness is associated with the ethnic and religious diversity of the peoples making up their societies. The legitimacy deficit of state institutions (Ekeh, 1975), linked to the want for a genuine anchorage in society justified nation-building as it was originally understood[9]. James S. Wunsch, for instance, suggests banking on the populations' capacity for self-organisation.

> "The slow, bottom-up process by which a true public constitution is built, one which reflects and elaborates generally held values, is built on existing political relationships, and protects social diversity, has never been allowed to develop" (Wunsch, 2000, p. 487).

The author borrows from Tocqueville his conception of municipality – close to community as understood by Dewey: "A community must

---

9. See footnote 6.

always remain a matter of face-to-face intercourse" (Dewey, 1927). Face-to-face intercourse and social pressure work towards the respect of local rules (Wunsch, 2000: 494). The neighbourhood, because of its reduced size is likely to be more homogenous. More importantly, this diagnosis, applied to African states stresses the fact that in those societies, cultural segmentation is more significant than social cleavages (Lijphart, 1977; Michalon, 2003). Wunsch advocates a federal or "consociative" system: this type of political regime, which can be seen in operation in the Netherlands and Switzerland aims to regulate the access to power of communities[10] for which a majority system would be unsuitable. The possible ways to organise are numerous and each country (Austria, Lebanon, Belgium, New Caledonia, etc.) has developed some (at times unstable) devices that rest both on the search for a consensus and on some elaborate dosage in community representation at the different tiers of government. This conception of state refounding thus opts for a strictly bottom-up approach and reckons with an overdetermination of the collective conflicts permeating society via its cultural, ethnic or religious segmentations (and which any democracy is duty-bound to acknowledge, indeed to open to debate).

It is not without interest to note, however, that Wunsch takes his text from classically liberal political philosophies to arrive at his recommendations: He draws his methodology from the Rational Choice theory (Wunsch, 2000: 489) to support this strictly bottom-up approach. But beyond its epistemological grounding, this approach is observably seeking to re-establish the continuity that modernity, if Koselleck is to be believed, has done its level best to breach between a past of prescriptive tradition and identity loyalties and a political future, this in the name of social projects and innovations. Seeking legitimacy in an often idealised and supposedly homogenous past, overlooking what plurality has to offer carries with it the risk of missing out on the potentially liberating capabilities of a truly political space.

Will reforming public authorities help refound the State?

The two strategies discussed here – nation-building (and its "digest" version state-building) and cultural or consociative refounding of the state – hang on opposed conceptions of the role of the international

---

10. Each community offers for instance their own school network and mutualist system taking care of people "from the cradle to the grave".

community. In the first instance the first duty of each state within the international community is to defend its own interests, which may lead it to override Article 1 of the United Nations Charter. In the second, nothing is required from the international community beyond the accompaniment of dynamics internal to a country or a region, without much concern for the current complexity and the history of international relations.

"Consociative" or cultural refounding rests on dynamics that could lead to territorial and social splits, in their quest for a cultural consistency liable to form the base of a governance legitimate in the eyes of the populace. The absence, in J.S. Wunsch's text of any mention of democracy cannot pass unnoticed. At the heart of his analysis lies first and foremost the legitimacy of the political constitution. Whilst T. Michalon proposes to think up a modern state adjusted to African social realities and recent history, this author, along with the nation-building theorists, reduces democracy to its elective component, the ballot. These cultural refounding projects ignore models for the exercise of authority, for the "manufacturing" of a political project, in a context of cultural plurality. How is a legitimate decision arrived at, how do the procedures advance the legitimation of public action beyond ethnic or religious justification? It is this reduction of democracy to the ballot that connotes it as a Western specificity. But any research on what Amartia Sen has termed "public reasoning" practices, or on the practices of assemblies convened to treat common affairs will show that a great many societies have kept in memory such well-tried political devices within their cultures. Thus, for instance, in his book Oman - The Islamic Democratic Tradition, Hussein Ghubash describes a tradition whereby the democratic model rests on Islamic principles of "consensus" and "consultation". Islam holds the believer-citizen responsible for the upholding of an effective political life and democracy. In this political system, the caliph is never there by divine right, he is freely chosen by the community, or at least by "councils". The author sees there an alternative to the Western model of secular democracy. In this thesis, political life and democracy are being studied from looking at the ways things get done, at effective practices. So that, without necessarily subscribing to the author's theses, debates and even dialogues between these practices and other, more up to date ones become possible. It is only an example but it gives an idea of what could be gained by the international community from cross-analyses liable to feed into the devising of cooperation policies.

International community and local governance

So two partly distinct questions overlap each other: that, on the one hand, of governance within countries where the international community intervenes and, on the other hand, of governance within the international community itself, whose "post-Westphalian"[11] (Gantet, 2000) order is still embryonic. The fact is that the international political space needs to be re-thought on the basis of a governance that no longer entails absolute state sovereignty and which relies on everyone to protect the plurality of experiences. What is at stake, at these two levels is the trust in public institutions guaranteeing both plurality and solidarity while holding at bay both state de-legitimation and state sovereignty standing in for arbitrary power.

The best way to open refounding avenues unprejudiced towards societal projects born of the stakeholders seems to lie with keeping up the discussion and exchange of experience leading to the invention of solutions to the problem tradition had hitherto failed to resolve. No doubt a temporary withdrawal into the comfort zone where trust is already established should be allowed. This should further the openness to the other, the stranger, the discussion with an alter who insists on a different identity, a different culture. Political discussion and conflict bring about a shared world, a "form of being-in-the-world born of a political 'acting together'" (Tassin, 2003).

In this respect, the decentralisation reforms – that seem to have faded into insignificance in the face of state and nation-building policies – are potential platforms for experimenting with a political space where anonymity is tamed, and otherness, as well as the right of a former slave or a woman to be heard can become legitimate. The local communities on which cultural refounding projects rely are frequently places where inequalities and discriminations get "assimilated". In the middle ground stand the local authorities where citizens can be in turn actors and spectators, at a safe distance both from the state whose legitimacy needs refounding and of the communal realm from which one must break free to become entitled to speak in public. Here are the possible tiers which are neither mere municipalities tightly controlled by their administration nor narrow neighbourhoods.

"We may, in a city, live side by side with our political opponents, if we are not forced to be cheek by jowl with them at all hours. But how can

---

11. The historical realities classically related to the 1648 Treaty of Westphalia need updating themselves.

it be done, in a small commune, where you are forced to see each other all the time? The political struggle moves to the workshop, the workroom the restroom and life becomes untenable" (Kropotkin, 1976, p. 43).

Such laboratories of active and demanding citizenships may conceivably be compatible with the way to "make" the political project at other institutional levels. Public deliberation, "public reasoning", as democratic governance styles, are ideally suited to informing decision-making at local as well as international level. But it is a public good – the public good par excellence –, which can be proposed but not dictated. It usually requires protection: both fragile and powerful, it is prerequisite to political inventiveness. In the grammar of power, this public good of a special kind has to do with the "power to", the power to act together. As Hannah Arendt points out, this power requires no other justification than itself, unlike the Weberian concept of "power over". Always jostling with the concept of domination, the "power over" can only proceed from superior reason and remains irretrievably associated to strictly dual conceptions of power. The political may be thought in terms of supply and demand, as is sometimes the case within the international community or in theatrical terms when the pragmatic approach to the political project is played out on the political stage. Whatever the case, the notion of governance very fittingly reveals the limitations of the political's binary problematics.

Bibliography

Bendana, A. (2004). "From Peace-Building to State-Building: One Step Forward and Two Steps Backwards ?", Colloque CERI, Paris.

Braddick, M.J. (2000). State Formation in Early Modern England, Cambridge, Cambridge University Press.

Caplan, R. et Pouligny B. (2005). "Histoire et contradictions du state-building", Critique internationale, n° 28, p. 123-138.

Chandler, D. (2006). Empire in Denial. The Politics of State-Building, London, Pluto Press.

Darbon, D. (2007). "L'institutionnalisation de la confiance politique dans les sociétés projetées. Du prêt-à-porter institutionnel à l'ingénierie sociale des formules politiques", 7th global Forum of the United Nations.

Dewey, J. (1927). The Public and its Problems, Swallow Press, Ohio UP / New York, Henry Holt & Company.

Ekeh P.P. (1975). "Colonialism and the Two Publics in Africa: A 158 Theoritical Statement", Comparative Studies in Society and History, vol. 17, n° 1, p. 91-112.

Francis, E.K. (1968). "The Ethnic Factor in Nation-Building", Social Forces, vol. 46, n° 3, p. 338-346.

Fukuyama, F. (1992). The end of History and the Last Man, Glencoe, The Free Press.

Fukuyama, F. (2004). State-Building. Governance and World Order in the 21st Century, New York, Cornell University Press.

Fukuyama, F. (2006). America at the Crossroads. Democracy, Power, and the Neoconservative Legacy, New Haven, Yale University Press.

Fund for Peace Report (2001). "African Prespectives on Military Intervention: Conference Summary", n° 1, December.

Gantet, C. (2000). "Le "tournant westphalien". Anatomie d'une construction historiographique", http://www.ceri-sciencespo.org/ publica/critique/ article/ci09p52-58.pdf.

Ghubash, H. (2006). Oman the islamic democratic tradition, New York, Routledge.

Helman, G.B. and S.R. Ratner (1992-1993). "Saving Failed States", Foreign Policy, n° 89, p. 3-20.

Huntington, S.P. (1993). "The Clash of Civilizations", Foreign Affairs, vol. 72, n° 3, p. 22-49.

Jordan, R.S. and J.P. Renninger (1975). "The New Environment of Nation-Building" The Journal of Modern African Studies, vol. 13, n° 2, p. 187.

Koselleck, R. (1987). "Temps et histoire", Romantisme. Revue de la Société des études romantiques, n° 56, p. 7-12.

Koselleck, R. (2002). The Practice of Conceptual History: Timing History, Spacing Concepts (Cultural Memory in the Present), Stanford, Stanford University Press,

Koselleck, R. (2004). Futures Past. On the Semantics of Historical Times, New York, Columbia University Press.

Kropotkine, P. (1976). Œuvres, Paris, Maspéro (translated by the translator of this paper).

Lapierre, J.W. (1977). Vivre sans État ? Essai sur le pouvoir politique et l'innovation sociale, Paris, Seuil.

Leclerc-Olive, M. (2003). De l'usage de la notion de société civile, PRUD, http://www.isted.com/programmes/prud/synthèses/AtelierA/Leclerc-Olive.pdf.

Lijohart, A. (1977). Democracy in Plural Societies, Yale, Yale University Press.

Lonsdale, J. and B. Berman (1992). Unhappy Valley: Conflict in Kenya and Africa, Oxford, James Currey publishers.

Michalon, P. (2003). Une voie pour l'Afrique: la démocratie "consociative", http://www.mwinda.org/article/michalon.html

Muller, P. (1990). Les politiques publiques, Paris, PUF.

Rand corporation (2003). America's Role in Nation-building from Germany to Iraq, http://www.rand.org/.

Rand corporation (2005). The UN's Role in Nation-building from Congo to Iraq, http://www.rand.org/.

Rand corporation (2007). The Beginner 's Guide to Nation-Building, http://www.rand.org/.

Rivkin, A. (1969). Nation-Building in Africa: Problems and Perspectives, Piscataway, Rutgers University Press.

Salmaan, J.-L. (2006). "De l'effondrement des États au State Building: penser la sécurité internationale depuis 1989", Les Cahiers du RMES, vol. III, n° 1, p. 7-25.

Tassin, E. (2003). Un monde commun. Pour une cosmo-politique des conflits, Paris, Seuil.

Wunsch, J. S. (2000). "Refounding the African State and Local Self-Governance: the Neglected Foundation", The Journal of Modern African Studies, vol. 38, n° 3, p. 487-509.

10

A Sustainable Response to Crises: the Role of Democratic Governance

Lessons Learned from the West African Context

Massaër DIALLO
(Translated from the French)

The notion of crisis describes situations which imply an element of violent conflict[1] of variable scale and intensity. It indicates a conjunction of risks and dangers to peace and security, to stability, and to strategic equilibrium. It relates to an elevated level of tension (which may bring about rupture) in socio-political, strategic, military, diplomatic and/or economic relations. Iraq, Palestine and Lebanon, Darfur and the Ivory Coast represent typical examples of crises.

The accelerated pace of globalisation has a significant impact on crises and their management. The large and medium economic and military powers with the capacity for regional and international intervention increasingly act within a multilateral framework.[2] Thus there is a clear tendency towards multilateralism concerning intervention in the management and/or the resolution of crises. The United Nations, as well as regional organisations and communities, play a pre-eminent role in assigning legitimacy and legality to crisis response.

---

1. Crises can involve more or less acute incidences of violent conflict, such that the term "crisis" is often used in the sense of "armed conflict".

2. This new dynamic of multilateral convergence arises from the globalisation of the stakes (peace and the security of populations are seen as public goods on a global scale) and from a realignment of strategic leadership. Another contributory factor is the emergence of public opinion, both internal and international, which is at once more demanding with respect to the duty to protect peace and less willing to engage unilaterally.

Crisis response is a significant act of governance and, as such, is subject to requirements of accountability, legitimacy and legality, effectiveness and the achievement of results. It depends on a strategy which involves a plan of action. The strategy defines the framework of action, the agenda and how it is to be carried out. Crisis response employs a variety of tools, diplomatic, political, humanitarian, military, economic and/or financial.[3] A lasting solution to crises requires a good knowledge base and an effective approach to their underlying causes.

Socio-political crises and the violent conflicts which are their most acute expression have a causal relationship with the fragility of states and societies. Thus, while it is possible for crises to occur and continue in any country, including the most developed ones, when confronted with terrorism of natural disasters, it is nonetheless clear that socio-political fragility and a weak state constitute major factors in the occurrence of crises and especially of violent conflict.

This article examines the link between fragile states and crises in the context of West Africa, where such a relationship is recognised, from a triple perspective of understanding: political fragility, strategies of response, and the role of multilateralism. It will then look at ways of finding a sustainable response to crises.

Approaches and the problematique of political fragility in Africa

Fragile states and how they arise

Between nine and ten member states[4] of the Economic Community of West African States (ECOWAS), out of a total of fifteen, may be considered in some way or other to be fragile states, taking into account the classification criteria of the Development Assistance Committee (DAC) of the Organisation for Economic Cooperation and Development

---

3. The treatment of the Togo crisis by the European Union is exemplary in this regard; the EU suspended co-operation with the Togolese state after serious incidents in 1993 while at the same time maintaining links to encourage dialogue, democratisation and the development of inclusive governance.

4. Their inclusion is merely indicative and should not be read as a definitive list, but the following states are often cited: Ivory Coast, Gambia, Guinea, Guinea Bissau, Liberia, Mali, Niger, Nigeria, Sierra Leone and Togo. It should be noted that the French position is to take a cautious approach to the notion of fragile states, taking the view that "it is not desirable for France to produce its own list of fragile states in addition to that of other, multilateral, parties" (2007).

(OECD): lack of capacity or inability to deliver basic social services; existence or persistence of violent conflict; whole or partial loss of sovereignty over part of its territory; disturbing or chronic violations of civil, political and/or human rights; endemic corruption; difficulties in guaranteeing the security of its population or in working in partnership for development.

The problematic of the fragile state has produced a lively debate which has provided it with a conceptual basis which is relatively free of the pejorative connotation implied in particular by the term "failed state". A variety of work[5] has contributed to a fertile discussion of the concept itself, broadening the problematique of fragility to that of the state, of societies, and of those engaged in them. The notion of the fragile state moreover enables analysis, and the concept itself, to be freed from the implications of stigma.[6]

Taking into account what we have learned from this analysis and without necessarily subscribing to "the fragility of the notion of the fragile state"[7], should we not go beyond the essentially descriptive logic which is in part a result of a synchronic approach? This approach can identify common characteristics of fragile states, but to tackle this fragility, we must also discern its cause. Every fragile state has a history determined by both its local and regional context. Its weaknesses are a result of and can be revealed by the processes and changes which have impacted on it.

Ivory Coast is a good illustration. This country has in the past been held up as an example of stability, peace and economic success in West Africa. Today it is numbered among the examples of fragile states, fulfilling most of the defining criteria. This fragility is a product of, or at the very least has been exposed by, the conjunction of an internal socio-political process and regional dynamics. Here, as elsewhere in the region, the state has functioned less by virtue of its institutions than through the personal direction of its leader, or "father of the Nation". This role of Chief of State is rooted both in authoritarian constitutional arrangements and in the deliberate invocation of traditional cultural precedents which foreground the role of the chief. The result, increasingly and in a number

---

5. The work of FSG (Fragile States Group) of the Development Assistance Committee (DAC) of the OECD and that published under the direction of J.-M. Châtaigner and H. Magro (2007) have contributed to this conceptualisation.

6. For the CAD – OECD the notion of the fragile state relates to a category of country "where the state lacks either the will or the capacity to engage productively with their citizens to ensure security, safeguard human rights and provide the basic functions for development."

7. See the article entitled "la fragilité de la notion d'État fragile" by Dominique Darbon and Patrick Quantin in Jean-Marc Châtaigner and Hervé Magro, (2007), pp. 477 ff.

of countries, is a situation of quasi state chiefdoms. All that then survives of the State, worthy of recognition and respect, is the power and authority of the chief. Instead of using his power and authority to help build and give credibility to devolved institutions, he competes with them. The fragility and weaknesses of the State produced by this situation only come to light with the advent of a new democratic framework.

Crisis factors in the post-colonial West African state

Two decades from independence, West African states have entered into a phase of change marked by a process of democratisation and the putting into place of structural adjustment policies and economic liberalisation. This constitutes a shock to systems founded on political monolithism based on a "State Party", that is a single party presenting itself officially as the politico-institutional framework of the political régime and providing unique access to the governing elite. This "State Party" claims legitimacy by virtue of its essential role in nation building, avoiding the presumed divisiveness associated with democratic pluralism. This new political phase which began in the years 1980-1990, in reality represents a rupture; it brings about a crisis in the state apparatus long exempted from the need to provide for itself, from responsibility for the operational capacity of its own national defence, and from exercising internal sovereignty. For many countries bilateral cooperation agreements with the former colonial power spare them the need to develop their own capacities. The state, protected externally, takes on relatively few functions, concentrated on security and the perpetuation of political power through elections and plebiscites. The State Party and its charismatic leader remain the centre of gravity at the core of its operation.

The achievement of the Nation State is constrained by the lack of a democratic strategy for integration promoting citizenship that values cultural diversity going beyond ethnicity and which reduces the role of patronage for the elite and for the population at large. Since the 1980s these weaknesses have been exploited by dissidents or rebels. They rely on breaches opened by a three-way democratic deficit, in integration and/ or inclusive governance, and in the distribution of power and resources.

The economic and political liberalisation of the decade 1980-1990 similarly exposes a radical change in the normative bases of legitimacy in post-colonial states. The external requirement for fidelity to an alliance and a bloc has been replaced by references to liberty, liberalisation of the economy, liberal democracy and "good governance".

The regional states concerned, without being simply the product of East/West geo-strategic rivalry, had benefited from protection and/ or politico-diplomatic complaisance which have influenced their own evolution and transformation with regard to internal socio-political dynamics. The end of that era abruptly exposes states which have been symbols of political stability to rapid change. In certain cases democracy is a forceps delivery precipitated by political and social groups which have hitherto been marginalised. Economic and democratic liberalisation impose themselves on an order whose legitimacy derives from an ideology of consensus and unanimity. The impact on the country as a whole has two facets which are at once contradictory and have a complimentary role in bringing these states to a point of crisis:

– a destabilisation in the operation of political regimes produced by the introduction of a multi-party system and pluralist elections which can change the party of government through "sovereign national conferences" functioning as constituencies.

– a proliferation of civil conflicts expressed in some cases as rebellions relating to issues of self determination and/or separatism which demonstrate the crisis of the Nation State.

In certain countries fragility does not rule out performance in security and/or defence matters, especially where political power itself is more or less under threat.[8] Thus fragility may present hypertrophy in its functions in relation to political security and atrophy in those linked to human security and development.[9]

The paradoxical coexistence of this crisis with the advent of political pluralism has negative implications, not only for the process of democratisation, but above all for the process of nation building, already undermined by the recognised weakness of the state.

The last two decades in the history of West Africa have revealed states' weakness, difficulties and/or failure to adapt. They have also shown that radical socio-political changes can provide a catalyst for the state to realign itself or, where this does not happen, to adapt to the democratic and republican values of a newly educated and demanding citizenry. But has not widespread centralism in itself undermined democratic renewal in impeding the development of local democracy

---

8. For example the state of Guinea, surrounded by a "circle of fire" of five bordering countries in conflict, demonstrated a capacity to take the initiative in strategic and defence matters to counter Taylor's NPLF, to put pressure on hostile forces in Liberia and Sierra Leone, and resist incursions by those forces into the forest region of Guinea from 1990 to 2001.

9. In certain countries, such as Guinea-Bissau, hypertrophy can be found, amongst other problems, in the over manning of the military which is rooted in its politico-military history and the difficulties encountered in completing the process of DDR (disarmament, demobilisation and reintegration of combatants).

which might have reinforced nation building? Furthermore, throughout the region the political classes' engagement in democracy seems to have focused narrowly on the acquisition and maintenance of power.

The new generation of conflicts within the state, with a cross-border dimension, play their part in the process of the creation of regions, powers and "micro-sovereignty" which present an alternative to the nation state in crisis. But the fact that actual secession is rarely the aim of these armed conflicts suggests that we may be talking of a historical process, conscious or not, of violent renegotiation on the part of actors who consider themselves, rightly or wrongly, to represent the perceived or real frustration of their communities or territories. In any case, these crises always serve to exacerbate existing weaknesses and engender political and institutional fragility in the affected states.

De-fragilisation and the re-founding of the state

To emerge from political fragility it is essential to find sustainable solutions to these types of conflict by attacking them at their roots. Building democracy and a sense of nation is an important element in this process. In the countries which have succeeded in emerging from crisis, often with the help of the international community (for instance, Liberia and Sierra Leone), the making of a new legitimacy has relied on lessons learned from the experience of exclusion in all its forms. The construction of democracies founded on social and national reunification as well as a genuine separation of powers can engender a new structural equilibrium which may serve as a basis for a sustainable exit from the status of fragile state. Widening participation helps. This must be cemented with greater inclusion for social, political and regional minorities who have been hitherto excluded or marginalised. In this respect the Ouagadougou accords should aid Ivory Coast in emerging from crisis.

"De-fragilisation" of states may be understood as the conclusive (re)building of a new state through the establishment of new inclusive and democratic foundations in which all stake-holders have a share. Its success is dependent on the prevalence of a political will to change throughout the political class, and on the strength of an independent civil society fully involved in the building of democracy and necessarily committed to the establishment of a new social contract. This goes hand in hand with the renewal of political leadership in a region where 75% of the population is under thirty.

The foundations of a sustainable response: legitimacy and prevention

Why respond to crises?

The response to crises, even where they are urgent and recognised as grave, must be both legitimate and legal. This constraint is a significant implication of the increasing predominance of multilateralism. In certain circumstances multilateralism is subject to issues of sovereignty. In some crisis situations this can inhibit rapid action. Such is the case with the projected intervention by the United Nations Organisation (UNO) in Darfur (Sudan). At the beginning of 2008 delays were experienced in the mobilisation of the African Union and UNO hybrid force because the agreement with Sudan was a stumbling block to the deployment, speed of action and operational capacity of the designated troops.

In the current international context there is an ever increasing sensitivity to issues of legitimacy as well as to the impact and consequences of intervention in crises. More than ever these must be well understood and accepted both by the intervening countries and by those in the states and regions where the crisis is occuring.

Whatever the nature of the crisis, diplomatic and political, military, humanitarian or economic, the response can have three features:
– a request[10] or obligation linked to agreements (essentially, bilateral agreements),
– an indirect or direct threat to national interests, international or regional peace,[11]
– a mandate granted in the context of multilateral action.

In the latter two cases Chapter VII of the United Nations Charter forms the legal basis and provides conditions for intervention and/or the implications for the state undertaking the action.

The response to crises is founded partially and increasingly on the necessity, or at the very least the importance, of obtaining a mandate which gives legitimacy to and affirms the requirement for intervention. The duty to interfere as a possible basis for crisis response presents a dilemma: responsibility to protect weighed against issues of sovereignty.

---

10. Where the power in question is responsible for genocide or serious threats to public safety, this may legitimately be from those not acting on behalf of the state. In this context they can request intervention on the basis of the doctrine founded on the responsibility to protect; their demand may be met if their reasons are verified.

11. In this case, response is through a regional or international mechanism. The intervention of NATO in Yugoslavia, of the UN in Kosovo and of ECOWAS in Liberia and in Sierra Leone are illustrations.

Who responds to crises? Those who intervene

The necessity for a better organised international community is highlighted by the increasing challenges to peace and security and the globalisation of risks and threats. A variety of factors contribute to this: the potential conflict of competing economic and financial interests; inequality between military powers and their recovery; the emergence of organised trans-national and trans-regional armed networks which threaten human security, democracy and the development of sustainable peace; a new regional and international overlapping of criminality, terrorism, various kinds of illegal traffic (in arms, persons and drugs), and some armed rebellions.

Neither the UN alone nor individual states (however powerful they are) can deal with these challenges effectively, let alone provide sustainable solutions. Both the lessons learned from the crisis in Iraq and from interventions in Africa make it clear that co-ordination and coherence in crisis response are imperative. The development of multilateralism, while making this easier, makes it all the more necessary.

The UN, the Group of Eight (G8), the DAC-OECD, The European Union, the North Atlantic Treaty Organisation (NATO), the African Union (AU), The Southern Africa Development Community (SADC) and ECOWAS, all have strategies, directives and/or policies which contribute directly or indirectly to the orientation or facilitation of crisis response. The need still remains to de-compartmentalise, to build complementarity and to reinforce the operational effectiveness of the mechanisms for response. What is Africa's place in all this?

In matters of security the pan-African organisations, for instance the AU and certain of its Regional Economic Communities (REC) provide linkage for international action in the response to crises in Sub-Saharan Africa. Of the seventeen crises involving armed forces in 2007 defined as being of a major scale globally, only three took place in Africa. If Africa attracts attention in security matters, it is not simply because of the intensity and/ or the frequency of crises there; it is because of the nature and the breadth of the new risks and threats brought about by state fragility or which may exploit it because the level of debt undermines the continent's capacity to cope. The foremost obstacle to an effective African response is, in effect, socio-political and, above all state fragility. Africa, and, more specifically, West Africa and the Sahel region, represents a weak link because of the number of states concerned. Part of what constitutes a fragile state is the absence of, or weakness in, the capacity of national systems to prevent rebellions and to inhibit and/or deal effectively with criminal activity and the embedding of terrorist organisations.

The region is experiencing a significant demographic surge (with a population increase of 2.5% per annum) in conditions where nearly

50% live below the poverty line. Its structural fragility brings risks of instability in a pressurised geo-strategic context characterised by the possibility of further tension arising from international acquisitiveness for both mining and energy resources.

West Africa can also draw on its potential and on the integration of its refocused capabilities; it can benefit from a new, liberating political energy which springs from embedded and stable democracy, from the governance achieved by re-established states and newly motivated youth. Africa is a fundamental link in international security; it could become more active at a strategic level, aware of its interests and responsibilities. The AU and ECOWAS provide the capacity to participate in the response to regional crises. It has as a resource not only the experience acquired in the management of crises, but also a developing architecture of cohesive security, linked to a preventative strategy open to acting in partnership.

The response to crises must be built on a strategy founded on a shared vision

In spite of contextual diversity and the major operational inequality of the various international and regional actors, they all have a shared vision of a universal need for sustainable peace, and national, regional and international stability and security. Essential to humanitarian, social and economic development, peace and security are also the demands and objectives of defence on a national, as well as on a regional and international scale. Omnipresent, potentially or in reality, terrorism post 9/11 has given impetus to the formation of an international coalition to face the challenge. But are peace and security the only components of the vision which will define strategies for crisis response? Does that vision not also include democracy, the rule of law and respect for human rights? This is a critical question for Africa. Civil society and "think tanks" echo this. Thus, in the context of a reflection on ECOWAS, Anning (2005) speaks of the dilemma in relation to the regimes of the countries which made up the military observer group of ECOWAS (ECOMOG) at the time of its intervention in Liberia: among

> "the leaders involved in the intervention process [featured] dictators..... who, ironically, were trying to 'democratise' Liberia as an inherent part of ECOWAS's mandate."[12]

---

12. Anning, E.K (2005). Security sector reform and democratization in Africa: comparative perspectives. Accra, WANSED, p. 7.

These observations should not however go so far as to conceal the extent of political evolution during the decade 1990/2001, which had its positive repercussions in the Additional Protocol of ECOWAS on Democracy and Good Governance. The rule of law, democracy and the other principles and values implicit in them are manifest in a new political commitment and lie at the heart of references to governance and political life by the fourteen signatories. Their heads of state declare that these new principles, presented as guidelines in matters of governance, proceed from "constitutional convergence" and should as such be applied by law by all of them, once the Protocol is ratified.[13] ECOWAS's mechanism for crisis response is thus founded on a vision of democracy and solidarity which aspires to peace and security for all.

This vision of democratic governance is the indispensable basis, not only for popular legitimation of interventions for peace, but also for coming into line with multilateralist criteria for action.

A coherent and co-ordinated multilateral response founded on shared values

Selective, circumstantial or time-bound, crisis response rests on three pillars: diplomacy, defence, and development. These three pillars may employ a variety of instruments and have four components: politico-diplomatic (mediation or intervention and/or observation), military (intervention, observation, peace-keeping), humanitarian, and economic (through post-conflict development support).[14] In practice crisis response has evolved in two ways which touch on, on the one hand, the foundations and modes of legitimation of intervention, and, on the other hand, participants, forms and levels of action. This evolution can be seen by the decisive role played by regional and global governance[15] in decision

---

13. This is applicable to all since the end of 2005, after its ratification by the required minimum of nine countries.

14. Whatever the category of intervention, co-ordination and coherence must be assured, whether this is unilateral (in which case this applies to different administrative departments), or multilateral. The DAC-OECD is working to improve approaches at the level of administrative coherence, policy co-ordination, harmonisation and the alignment of aid to fragile states. See OECD (2006). Whole government approach to fragile states, DAC guidelines and reference series.

15. The UN plays the central regulatory role and is the ultimate provider of legitimation required for all interventions in crises on a regional and international scale. The European Union is also emerging as a new strategic global player with the diplomatic, political, military (PESC and ESDP), humanitarian (ECHO), and commercial (EDF) capabilities for responding to crises. ECOWAS and the African Union, with their experience and lessons learned in Somalia, Darfur, Liberia and Sierra Leone, may also be ranked as regional players whose actions mark the development of a new trend and thinking in crisis response.

making and management of the response to the political and/or military crises faced by the international community in various parts of the world. Even though the end of bipolarism has not resulted in the reduction of intervention by the United States in the management of major crises, multilateralism is clearly carrying a greater weight,[16] and crisis response depends on international legitimacy and legality. Decision making and intervention are subject to conditions and mechanisms. Intervention is not simply a question of having the power and the means to do so. It is about being able to make a decision to to take action in response to crises, weighed against issues of sovereignty.

Effective response to crises is also about knowing how to prevent them

The responsibility to protect: a doctrine born of bitter lessons learned

Crisis response must develop a preventative capacity which means that the responsibility to protect does not end up as a question of "shutting the stable door after the horse has bolted."

The International Commission on Intervention and State Sovereignty (ICISS)[17] was an initiative of the Canadian government to support the desire expressed by Kofi Annan, Secretary General of the United Nations, to meet the challenge of conceptionalising and operationalising prompt and effective response to humanitarian threats. In effect, crisis response is also linked to the capacity to react in time to offer protection. Multilateral action is constrained by procedures and political considerations which can limit rapid reaction to humanitarian and/or politico-military emergencies resulting from a crisis.[18] Nonetheless mandated or multilateral action remains the avenue most likely to confer legitimacy and legality and that which favours the involvement of other interested parties at a regional and national level.

As far as concerns the capacity for intervention, inequality unquestionably exists between the various categories of actors involved

---

16. As is made clear by the SIPRI Yearbook 2007, of " 60 peace missions....active during the whole or part of 2007, 20 [have been] led by the United Nations, 33 by regional organisations or alliances, 7 by ad hoc coalitions".

17. Its members are mandated to "build a broader understanding of the problem of reconciling intervention for human protection purposes and sovereignty."

18. The spokeman of the ICISS reflected on the implications of blockages in the Security Council where, as had already happened, it is unable or unwilling to play its prescribed role or expressly rejects a proposal to intervene even though humanitarian and human rights issues are clearly at stake (Evans G., (2001), p. 49); it would then be a question of having recourse to an extraordinary meeting of the General Assembly to request approval of military action.

in crises and within each of those categories. Disparities in operational capacity are just as clear between the European Union (EU) and the AU, as between those parts of Europe which are still building up defence and security capacity, and other member states. Levels of development determine response capability in so far as this requires financial,[19] logistical, material, human and technological capacity. But other factors explain why for example NATO can respond more easily than the EU, and why it is even more straightforward to deploy a French force in the name of Europe than to deploy a European force.

Effective crisis response also requires the political and diplomatic capacity to take into account and involve internal players, starting with the protagonists. In this respect the experience of the international community in Ivory Coast constitutes good practice. The international community, under the authority of the United Nations, in this case achieved a united response which linked the global and regional to the national. Those involved at the national level, and above all the two principal protagonists, contributed to the internalisation of the solution by means of the Ougadougou Accord; this represented progress in the formation of and support for an international mechanism for the management of the crisis in Ivory Coast.

Crisis prevention is rooted in a sustainable capacity for anticipation, action and democratic regulation

Prevention requires operational effectiveness and the application of mechanisms for early warning, preventative mediation, but also for deterrence, for observation and for militarily intervention where required. Egalitarian and democratic governance constitutes one of the most important factors in prevention. Weaknesses in this regard remain the basis for most of the crises in this region, despite the progress observed. The reinforcement of preventative capacity clearly must allow for the support and consolidation of:

– the regional security structure of the AU and ECOWAS, especially their early warning system, the Mediation and Security Council and ECOMOG, which should provide the basis for one of the five brigades which should concretise the African Standby Force.[20]

---

19. In 2006, according to figures provided by SIPRI, the total known costs of UN, EU and NATO missions reached a record 5.5 billion dollars.

20. Concerning capacity building, the G8 Africa Action Plan (adopted in 2002 at Kananaskis) should be noted; this anticipated a reinforcement of capacity in Africa for the prevention of crises and for peace keeping by putting in place from 2010 the

– a regional approach and the involvement of national and local actors in the prevention and resolution of crises; regional governance and integration may lessen the impact of state fragility on economic life, security and democracy, to the benefit of citizens. With this approach, if the regional constitutes the bow in the system to be built up, the national should be its string; those countries which have experienced conflicts should above all be involved.

Disarmament, which remains a challenge at national and regional level. Of the fifteen members of ECOWAS, only five have escaped armed conflict and only one of these has never experienced a military coup nor an armed conflict. Eight million small arms and light weapons are circulating in West Africa, and only half of these are held by official forces. Countries emerging from crisis or in a post conflict situation remain vulnerable to a resurgence of these crises because, amongst other reasons, DDR (disarmament, demobilisation and reintegration of combatants), even when carried out relatively well,[21] has not achieved lasting stability among former combatants. Operations have remained compartmentalised by countries faced with a primarily sub-regional process of conflict diffusion. The development of a regional approach to DDR can contribute to meeting these challenges and bring about a community strategy, (both regional and local) in the struggle against the scourge of child soldiers:

– A permanent framework for political dialogue between the various social, political, cultural, economic and institutional actors. Such a framework is indispensable in the rebuilding of state and a sustainable socio-political solution.

– A post conflict policy for state reinforcement or rebuilding of the state which is democratic and inclusive.

African Standby Force of five brigades, one for each Regional Economic Community. The European Union Peace Facility has the same purpose, as has the RECAMP for France and the ACRI/ACOTA for the United States. West Africa hosts the Bamako Centre in Mali and the Kofi Annan Centre in Accra in Ghana. The National Defence College in Abuja in Nigeria will also be established as a training centre as part of this plan of action in order to reinforce civil and military capacity for the prevention of conflicts, the management of crises, and the maintenance of peace.

21. Disarmament, demobilisation and reintegration affected 103,019 combatants in Liberia (at its close on 31 October 2004) and 72,490 combatants in Sierra Leone in October 2005.

Bibliography

Adam, B. (dir.) (2007). Europe Puissance tranquille ? Rôle et identité sur la scène mondiale, Bruxelles, GRIP, Editions Complexe.

Adam, David D. et al. (1999). La nouvelle architecture de sécurité en Europe, Bruxelles; Éditions Complexe.

Adededji, A.G. and I.S. Zabadi (2004). The regional dimension of peace operations into the 21st century; Abuja, National War College.

Adededji, A.G. and I.S. Zabadi (2005). The military and management of internal conflict in Nigeria, Abuja, National War College.

Anning, E.K. (2005). Security sector reform and democratization in Africa: comparative perspectives, Accra, WANSED.

Châtaigner, J.-M. (2005). L'ONU dans la crise en Sierra Leone, Paris; Karthala.

Châtaigner, J.-M. and F. Gaulme (2005). Agir en faveur des acteurs et sociétés fragiles, Paris, AFD.

Châtaigner, J.-M. and H. Magro (ed.) (2007). États et sociétés fragiles; Entre conflits, reconstruction et développement, Paris, Karthala,.

Club du Sahel et de l'Afrique de l'Ouest/ OECD. (2005). La Construction de la paix et de la démocratie en Afrique de l'Ouest, Paris, CSAO/ OECD.

DAC-OECD. (2007). États fragiles : Déclaration d'intention et Principes pour l'engagement international dans les États fragiles et les situations précaires, Paris.

Diallo, M. (2005). Le rapport des Forces de défense at de sécurité au pouvoir politique selon le Protocole additionel de la CEDEAO sur la Démocratie en l'Afrique de l'Ouest et la Bonne gouvernance, Paris, CSAO/OECD.

Evans, G. et al. (2001). The responsibility to protect, Report of the International Commission on Intervention and State Sovereignty (ICISS), Ottawa, CRDI.

Floriquin, N. and E. Berman (dir.) (2006). Armés mais désoeuvrés : Groupes armés, armes légères et sécurité humaine dans la région de la CEDEAO, Bruxelles, GRIP et Small Arms Survey.

Goerens, C. (2007). Sécurité et développement de l'Afrique: une nouvelle approache de l'UE, Cahier de Chailllot no. 99, European Union, Paris, Institut d'études de la sécurité.

Sénat français (2006). La gestion des crises en Africa subsaharienne, Rapport d'information no. 450 fait au nom de la Commission des affaires étrangères, de la défense et des forces armées, session ordinaire2005/2006, Paris, Présidence du sénat, Juillet 2006.

III

RULE OF LAW, DEMOCRACY AND HUMAN RIGHTS:
THE CORNERSTONES
OF DEMOCRATIC GOVERNANCE

11

Demystifying Governance
and Enriching its Democratic Content

Adebayo OLUKOSHI

Governance, as process and system, is an integral part of the historical experience of every society. Africa has not been an exception in this regard. Forged out of a long, often contradictory, always contested trajectory of state formation, dissolution, and recomposition that has been accompanied at different stages by widespread population movements and various phases and types of interaction with the outside world, the continent, inevitably, has grappled with a wide range of core, enduring governance questions that date back to the period from the emergence of the earliest political communities. These questions have contributed, to one degree or another, to the making and character of contemporary state systems, as well as the political cultures underpinning them. The questions have, among others, ranged from the basic rules for the constitution of political communities, the fiscal foundations of the established political order, including policy on taxation, the processes for the absorption of new populations, and the modes of mobilisation of popular consent, to the methods of administration of political territories, the systems of accountability observed by those who occupy positions of leadership, the regimes of political succession that are in place, and the rules for the alternation of power. The questions have also extended to systems of checks-and-balances in the exercise of political power, the articulation of the rights and responsibilities of citizens, and the definition and operationalisation of procedures for inter-generational participation and representation in the polity. In many ways, from the earliest history of African political formations to date, these core governance issues have been recurring decimals on the continent, only being articulated over time in (qualitatively) different local and global contexts by successive generations of actors and actresses (Olukoshi, 1998, 2008).

This essay aims to assess, in an overview manner, the contemporary debate about the African governance experience, doing so in a way which attempts to demystify the concept of governance itself and make the case for the reinforcement of its democratic moorings. The myths that have been consciously and unconsciously constructed around the notion of governance are numerous, and, in the main, originate from a flawed methodological approach which proceeds on the assumption that governance challenges are, for all intents and purposes, the exclusive preserve of the more underdeveloped regions of the world, especially Africa, while the more developed countries, especially in Europe and North America, are deemed to have either mastered or overcome these challenges as to become the singular model against which the progress registered by others must be gauged. As a concept, governance cannot be fully understood independent of democratic theory although care must be taken not to conflate governance with democracy; as practice, it is a domain where democratic forces fight for the expansion of citizen rights and accountability by the public authorities but without prior guarantees on the exact outcomes of the struggles waged. It will be argued in this essay that the recent technocratisation of the concept has not only further fetishised it but also eroded its democratic content. As illustration, the essay will draw on the debate on the independence of the central bank to show the ways in which, in the name of "good" governance, a transnational economic technocracy structured around the international financial institutions (IFIs) has sought to curtail the power of elected officials over entire swathes of fiscal, monetary, trade and industrial policy as to make the experience of democratisation in Africa what Thandika Mkandawire has called a choiceless one (Mkandawire, 1998) that has also failed to yield the dividends that are so essential to the prospects for the reinforcement of democracy, its institutions and processes.

Governance myths reconsidered

Over the years, researchers have grappled with the task of finding appropriate interpretative frames for understanding the dynamics of governance in Africa – and elsewhere in the developing world. Invariably, these efforts have been characterised more by attempts at reading Africa from the lenses of others and less by investments in grasping the complex processes taking place on the continent as contradictory outcomes of context and history that deserve to be understood in their own right – and on their own terms. The first dominant error in much of the conventional discourse on governance revolves, therefore, around the ahistoricism of most of the analyses undertaken. For, taken out of the context of the history of specific societies, the discourse that is produced attempts to provide an understanding of governance in Africa solely or primarily by drawing analogies from the historical experiences of others – especially Europe and the United States – or stylising those experiences into uniform international standards against which attempts are then made to measure the validity of all other records of governance. But, in reality, the governance challenges facing different countries cannot be reduced to one single, all-encompassing narrative that is based on a sanitised, unproblematised and contradiction-free reading of how it was purportedly done in Europe or North America. For, even in Europe and North America, both historically and contemporaneously, the governance experience is uneven, variable, diverse and replete with contradictions.

The stylised standards of governance drawn from a one-sided, unilinear reading of Euro-American or, even more narrowly, Anglo-Saxon experiences, are too frequently packaged in much of the dominant literature and presented as universal norms and principles which every society must strive to attain. This contrived universalism derived from the distinct but narrow historical experiences of one people constitutes the second prevalent error in the dominant governance discourse. Yet, there is only really one thing that is universal about governance, and it is that all societies have their different experiences of it with which they must grapple on a permanent and continuing basis. While there is a case, in theory and in practice, for a sharing of comparative experiences and mutual learning, there is no justifiable reason to take the experience of one set of countries as a model that must be replicated by another irrespective of historical conditions and circumstances. For, in fact, if the governance challenges faced by different societies are the products of their historical circumstances, then it follows that no two experiences can be equated in their material detail, let alone subsumed under a common standard that gives an impression that across the two national boundaries, the components of the governance problematic are exactly one and the same. It also follows that much of the error committed at the level of governance policy formulation is a failure to build on local institutional mechanisms fashioned out of history and expressed in culture, and a preference for importing institutional models that are alien to the local context in many ways, including culturally (Dia, 1996). But, from a historical perspective, no society is tabula rasa in matters of governance and although external influences would always be present to one degree or another, such influences can only become useful where they feed into indigenous institutional mechanisms.

In stylising governance standards, there has, unwittingly, also been a tendency in the dominant discourses on the subject to freeze them into a set of yardsticks that also have the status of a one-size-fits-all. In consequence, rather than the rich texture of diverse experiences that actually exists both historically and contemporaneously and which should underpin it, the theory and practice of governance has become a forlorn quest for uniformity and sameness. By the same token, the failure to recognise adequately the historicity of governance and the struggles that are waged actively around its constitution at any given moment in time has resulted in yet another error of seeking to understand and operationalise the concept in puritanical terms. In fact, no governance system or outcome can be pure insofar as the prevailing system of governance reflects a historic or living balance of power among contending social interests, and, to that extent, is a compromise. And yet, in the treatment of the African experience, few have been able to avoid succumbing to the temptation of deploying a model of governance purity which does not correspond to the historical experience of any other region of the world and which, even in abstract, theoretical terms, does not make too much sense. Such a model of governance purity against which the African experience is measured produces a pre-determined outcome, namely, a perspective on actual experiences of governance that is replete with problems and pathologies, bereft of much sense of cumulative progress and lacking in motion. In so doing, it wrongly reproduces the myth of Africa as a perpetual terrain of unalloyed, perhaps irredeemable "bad" governance. It is standard in the literature to assess the state of governance in any given country in terms either of "good" or "bad" governance. The World Bank which was among the first institutions to use the concept of "good" governance has also led in the effort at defining its core attributes: transparency, rule of law, independent judiciary, property rights, and a free press. In more generalised usage, the notion of "good" governance came to be extended to include corruption (among the elite), the robustness – or lack thereof – of an enabling environment for civil society, and elections which do not meet "internationally- accepted" standards. "Good" governance has been further employed in recent usage to encompass the rights of the populace to quality essential services in a decentralised administrative framework, the independence of institutions of government such as the central bank and tax authorities, the capacity of governments, and the manner in which power is exercised in the management of public resources for development (World Bank, 1992, 2000a). In the Bank's conception, "bad" governance is understood to mean the absence of "good" governance such as it is defined and operationalised by the Bretton Woods institution at different moments in time. Apart from the questions which arise with regard to the appropriateness of the highly subjective notions of "good" and "bad" in qualifying the state of governance, it is clearly too simplistic to assume that the absence of "good" governance means, ipso facto, the presence or prevalence of "bad" governance. In this connection, and for some of the reasons pointed to in the preceding paragraphs, the terrain of governance is not itself easily open to the kind of binary opposition between the "good" and the "bad" that has been erected by the Bank. For, the record in most countries is always a mixed one that involves a straddling of the "good" and the "bad". Moreover, experiences of governance also fluctuate at different points in time, characterised by a complex dialectic of advances and setbacks that constitute the stuff of every day politics. Furthermore, an understanding of governance in terms of its import for the democratic development of society and, therefore, a comparison between democratic and undemocratic/authoritarian governance, as well as a careful study of processes of democratisation offer a more effective possibility to grasp the complexities of the governance experiences of societies at different stages of its development than a simple and simplistic dichotomisation between "good" and "bad" (Olukoshi, 1998; Olowu et al., 1999; Hyden and al., 2000).

It is the highly problematic notion of "good" and "bad" governance popularised by the World Bank during the 1980s that was largely adopted and carried over into the decision-making processes of the leading donor countries to become a lightening rod for the pursuit of their foreign policy objectives. In many cases, governance concerns were woven into the conditionality clauses of most bilateral donors in their overall dealings with aid-receiving countries and/or pursued in their own right as part of the new political conditionality that was adopted in the wake of the end of the old East-West Cold War. Governance concerns were also integrated into multilateral cooperation agreements such as the Cotonou Accord. In becoming an element of the regime of conditionality, the governance question in general and the quest for "good" governance in particular flowed into the uneven equation of power between donors and recipients, with the latter often adopting governance measures in order (only) to facilitate (continued or resumed) aid flows and the former sometimes being simply content with cosmetic, pro forma reforms that fed into the fulfilment of all righteousness. "Good" governance as conditionality was, clearly, not the effective tool of political re-engineering, economic reform and social transformation that it was purportedly designed to be; as an instrument in the foreign policy arsenal of donor countries, it was very easily coupled to the promotion and advancement of their own national interests, interests which were generally seen to be ultimately paramount in the management of relations with African and other developing countries that were deemed to have a strategic value (Mkandawire, 1992; Mkandawire and Olukoshi, 1996).

Another generalised misconception that has emerged out of the contemporary governance discourse relates to the correlation that may exist between the level of socio-economic development and the quality of governance. In much of the academic and policy discussion on the subject, it seems to be suggested by the logic of distribution of labels of "good" and "bad" governance that the more developed countries of the global North, especially Western Europe and North America, are seen as enjoying "good governance" while the more underdeveloped countries of the global South, including especially those of Africa, seem invariably to wallow in problems of "bad" governance. Yet, there is no automaticity in the correlation between the state of economic development and the type of governance that is in place in a given country. For, even in contexts where the overall level of economic development measured in gross domestic product/gross national product terms, for example, may still be categorised as low, the robustness of the political system may be such that the polity qualifies to be considered as democratic or democratising. Conversely, a country may be considered to be developed by all the conventional measures available and yet experience undemocratic forms of governance. Germany under Hitler, Spain under Franco, Portugal under Salazar, and Italy under Mussolini are a few prominent examples of this situation in recent historical memory. Even within supposedly highly developed economies with an established democratic system, the terrain of governance is not a uniformly and consistently democratic one, as evidenced by the post- September 11 situation in many Western countries, where civil liberties have been or are being abridged in favour of a security logic, and practices such as "water boarding" and "extraordinary rendition" which were once considered to be unthinkable in advanced democracies were freely deployed.

Within the logic of the economic development-democracy nexus, it has also been suggested that the institutionalisation of "good" governance is almost a prerequisite for economic development (World Bank, 2000b). Countries that have "good" governance in place are well positioned to achieve economic success as they are able to attract foreign investments and grow their economies. This perspective was presented as one more argument in favour of the promotion of "good" governance in Africa, a region whose requirements for accelerated economic growth is thought to be one of the highest in the world given the relative state of socio-economic underdevelopment on the continent. Yet, both historically and contemporaneously, there is no basis to assume that "good" governance will necessarily lead to improved economic performance while "bad" governance undermines economic prospects. There is no better example of this than the experience of China which is one of the countries enjoying the highest growth rates in the world but without conforming to the standard, mainstream attributes of "good" governance as defined by the World Bank, including private property rights.

Among African researchers in particular, given the recent history of the continent, the principal governance challenge which they have identified centres on the democratisation of the polity. Indeed, the very first usage of the concept in contemporary African social science discourses goes back to the second half of the 1980s when, in disagreement with the World Bank's suggestion that the only viable solution to Africa's economic problems lay in "getting prices right", leading icons of African social research such as the late Claude Ake, insisted that the solution lies more in getting the politics right (Claude Ake, 1996; 2000). Getting the politics right inevitably means paying much closer attention to the nature of state-society relations, and the mode of organisation of the contestation for power. And it is on these questions of state-society relations and the mode of organisation of power that the conventional governance discussion is at its weakest. For, central to governance questions in any society are concerns about the governability of the inherited national-territorial spaces as much in terms of the integrity of national boundaries and the deepening of national integration and identity as in the enhancement of citizenship, the strengthening of legitimacy and the expansion of the democratic space. In many senses, a legitimate framework of governability is a sine qua non for democratic governance and it speaks directly to processes of state and nation-building so as to be a central determinant of economic, social, political and cultural policy. If governance challenges are integral to the organisation of societal relations and the configuration of the state-society relationship, it follows that they are also a domain of permanent work-in-progress. It is, therefore, a myth to suggest, directly or indirectly, that governance questions have been resolved in or by some societies once and for all and/or for all time. At one level, it bears pointing out that both in theory and in practice, no society can ever succeed in resolving all the challenges of governance with which it is confronted at any given phase of its development. At another level, it should be emphasised that every stage of development of society begets its own governance challenges; the resolution of a set of challenges within a given historical period does not preclude the emergence of a new set of challenges within that same historical context or under a new set of conditions. It is precisely because governance, like democracy, is a permanent work-in-progress that politics becomes a living experience among contending interests for the overall direction in which society should be moving. It is, therefore, an error, frequently committed in the academic literature and policy interventions, to approach the challenges of governance on the basis of a package of standard/standardised technocratic solutions that either do not take social contestations into account or treat them as a problematic nuisance that should be contained.

Governance has been assessed in most contemporary discourses on the basis mainly of an isolated treatment of the political, the economic and the corporate. Although for analytic purposes, it is both possible and useful to distinguish among different domains/elements of governance, sight must never be lost of the essential inter-connections among them. Thus, for example, much of what manifests itself as a problem of political governance often have roots in challenges of economic governance and social inclusion. The repercussions of the problems of political governance are frequently refracted into economic processes in ways which may compound the challenges faced at that level, and vice versa. Effectively, therefore, governance as concept and practice only makes sense to start with as a holistic concept. The treatment of one dimension of the governance challenges confronting a given society should not blind the researcher or policy maker to its inter-connections with other dimensions that may not be under direct or immediate consideration. In maintaining a holistic perspective, solutions proposed for overcoming identified challenges would have a better chance of being more wholesome, complete and effective rather than fragmented, dispersed and ineffective.

In the period since the mid-1980s, policy intellectuals have sought consciously to articulate measures supposedly aimed at improving governance in the developing regions of the world, including Africa, and purportedly building local capacities for "good" governance. But the intervention frames that they have developed have been eminently technocratic in nature, thereby emptying the concept of the politics that gives meaning to it in the first instance. Moreover, there is an assumption which is not fully justified, that governance as a domain is one that is (uniformly) susceptible to capacity building initiatives, with the route to the launching of such initiatives being paved by the spirited efforts at technocratising the theory and practice of governance. And yet, considering that the key concerns of governability and governance require to be played out among contending social forces, it is not obvious what the impact or meaning of such capacity-building initiatives would be in contexts where the key governance challenges posed centre on matters of inclusion, the civility and accountability of the political elite, or the forging of national cohesion, to cite a few examples. The most critical challenges that inform the governance experience are not always the easiest to quantify and measure; in many cases, they also belong to the realm of history, memory and cognition that could be as powerful in the mobilisation of people into action as anything else in a political system.

A considerable element of the contemporary governance discourse has been undertaken without adequate attention to the roots of the issues which are put at its centre and the strategic (policy) objectives they are designed to serve. This is particularly so with the operational definition of governance that came to inform the work of the World Bank in Africa and other regions of the global South during the late 1980s onwards. As noted earlier, this definition was centred around issues of transparency, property rights, and rule of law, concerns that were deemed, in the framework of the objectives of the structural adjustment programme, to be critical for private investors and the Bank's own requirement for accessing economic data. All too often, most commentators ignored this narrow contextual framework of the Bank's governance framework to seek to generalise the issues prioritised by the Bank into general propositions about governance in Africa and elsewhere in the global South. A decomposition of the expenditures registered by the Bank under the rubric of governance reform in adjusting countries would reveal clearly just how particular its interests were in employing the concept to lift what it considered to be the main obstacles to the promotion and protection of private investors, the advancement of its project of neo-liberal market reforms, and its domination of the policy terrain of the adjusting countries through unobstructed access to information and documentation.

Technocracy vs democracy in governance

The narrowing of governance challenges to specific objectives within the overall strategy of the World Bank for securing the structural adjustment programme was but one small element of a bigger project to discipline politics to the requirements of what came to considered as the primary goal of the neo-liberal agenda during the 1990s onwards, namely, the attainment and institutionalisation of a set of measures that were thought to be the key component elements of "sound" macro-economic policy-making. The prevalent thinking at the time, expressed most directly by Lawrence Summers in his capacity as the Chief Economist of the Bank, could be summarised as follows:

> "Sound" macro-economic policy is an indispensable goal which all nations must strive for but for which the existing frames of politics, authoritarian or democratic, may not be suitable (Lawrence Summers, 1994).

The challenge which is posed is to reform political systems so that they can be brought more in conformity with the requirements of "sound" macro-economic policy.

Although the ambitions underpinning the idea of reorganising politics with a view to instrumentalising it for the goal of "sound" macro-economic policy-making may have proved much more difficult to achieve than its authors in the Bank may have imagined, spirited attempts were nevertheless made to shift entire swathes of economic policy-making out of the purview of elected political officials in Africa and elsewhere in the global South. As part of this process, all over Africa, efforts were invested not only in the creation of executive agencies of government that were imbued with autonomy in decision-making but also constituted as technocratic islands of policy formulation. Insofar as monetary policy was concerned, African countries were encouraged during the 1990s to reorganise their central banks to reflect and lock in the shift to the restrictive, deflationary policy measures that were at the heart of the Bank's version of "sound" macro-economic policy. The mandates of the central banks as the guardians of macro-economic stability were reinforced and their independence to perform their duties as narrowly defined without interference from outside was asserted.

Central bank independence was designed in the first instance to achieve specific local policy objectives in the countries of the global South and to help lock in the orthodox macro-economic policy orientation that was the hallmark of the structural adjustment. It was, however, pursued as part of what the World Bank and the International Monetary Fund (IMF) presented as an international "best practice" to which all countries were encouraged to conform. Indeed, central bank independence came to be a key element of the notion of "good" governance which the World Bank promoted as the 1990s wore on. It was argued that there could be no possibility for sustaining "sound" macro-economic policy without "good" governance and a key element/measure of "good" governance is the degree of autonomy of central banks.

Both in theory and practice, central bank independence raises several challenges for democratic governance. In the first instance, arising as it does out of the ambition to subordinate politics to the requirements of a particular kind of economics – in this case orthodox macro-economics – it seeks to overturn what should normally be the key foundational basis of state-society relations and the social contract. For, citizens reserve the right in a political community to define the mode by which they would be governed, that right being one of the kernels of democratic governance. Once they have decided the political framework for their governance, the challenge of policy is to feed into and not subvert the sovereign wish of the citizenry. The appropriate ordering of policy should, therefore, be a striving to ensure that economic, social and cultural policies are in conformity with the broadly-defined aspirations of the citizens who make up the political community. In this regard, within the framework of the quest for stable growth and development, economics should be fashioned to serve the requirements of governability and democratic governance, not vice versa. The idea of the independence of the central bank subverts this basic foundational principle of political communities.

At another level, in the specific context of Africa, not a few commentators have noted that at the same time as countries on the continent were re-establishing a democratic framework for governance in the 1990s, key economic policy making institutions were being taken out of the system of democratic accountability and oversight, none more so than the central banks. It was as if to suggest that (African) democracies could not be trusted to produce robust policies and undertake effective economic management. Elected political officials were effectively faced with a fait accompli regarding the macro-economic policy direction of their countries. This is the situation that Mkandawire (1999) has characterised as 'choicelessness' in the contemporary African democratic experience. It is a 'choicelessness' which erodes the very essence of politics and its democratic content, taking key policy concerns out of the remit of political parties, elected legislative houses, and, in the worst cases, even the council of ministers. Effectively, it means that politics has to be organised according to the macro-economic policy dictates set by the independent central bank, and policy choices on macro-economic issues are no longer open to debate among politicians competing for elective office or can only be debated in futility.

The management of national economic resources is a domain that is at the heart of the state-society relationship and the functioning of the political system. The case for a judicious management of the resources is not in contention and, indeed, constitutes one of the reasons for political competition in a democratic system. What is in dispute is the attempt, through the theory and practice of central bank independence, to prevent or sideline national debates on an on-going basis around questions of policy that ought to be put in the public domain as part and parcel of the democratic governance process. It is little wonder that in several African countries, over the period since the mid-1990s, tensions have recurred between the governors of central banks and elected political office holders, including the legislature, over matters of accountability and the definition of the priorities for domestic monetary policy.

Concluding reflections

The challenges of governance are integral to all political systems and are, therefore, not peculiar to any one region of the world. Governance is also a holistic concept that encompasses the entire spectrum of issues that are necessary for the achievement and reproduction of balanced state-society relations. Viewed from this perspective, the story of governance ought to be less about the misdeeds of elites and more about struggles for the expansion of the frontiers of citizenship in a democratic developmental framework. Furthermore, the idea of the governance agenda in any given country as product of history and context cannot be overemphasised, as is the position that democratic governance is an ideal with the status of permanent work-in-progress. In effect, this implies that specific governance episodes and phases are best understood in terms of their location in a historical flow. Finally, a dialectical understanding of the concept of governance needs to be developed by which governance concerns are seen as being played out not in a unilinear, unproblematic manner, but in a multidimensional way which is replete with contradictions that simultaneously embody advances and setbacks. In other words, governance is not necessarily or always "neat". It is in such a dialectical approach that a useful conceptual foundation can be found for an assessment of the potentialities of governance as democratisation.

Bibliography

Ake, C. (2000). The Feasibility of Democracy in Africa, Dakar, CODESRIA Books.

Ake, C. (1996). Democracy and Development, Washington, D.C, Brookings Institution.

Dia, M. (1996). Africa's Management in the 1990s and Beyond: Reconciling Indigenous and Transplanted Institutions, Washington, DC, World Bank.

Hyden, G. et al (eds.) (2000). African Perspectives on Governance, Trenton, Africa World Press.

Mkandawire, T. (1992). "Adjustment, Political Conditionality and Democratisation in Africa", mimeo, CODESRIA General Assembly, Dakar.

Mkandawire, T. (1999). "Shifting Commitments and National Cohesion in African Countries" in Lennart Wohlgemuth et al, Common Securityand Civil Society in Africa, Uppsala, NAI.

Mkandawire, T. (1996). "Economic Policy-Making and the Consolidation of Democratic Institutions in Africa", mimeo, CODESRIA, Dakar.

Mkandawire, T and A. Olukoshi (1996). The Politics of Structural Adjustment in Africa: Between Liberalisation and Repression, Dakar, CODESRIA Books.

Mkandawire, T. (1999). "Crisis Management and the Making of Choiceless Democracies" in Richard Joseph (ed.), State, Conflict and Democracy in Africa, Boulder, Lynne Rienner Publishers.

Olowu, D., A. Williams and K. Soremekun (eds.) (1999). Governance and Democratisation in West Africa, Dakar, CODESRIA Books.

Olukoshi, A. (1998). The Elusive Prince of Denmark: Structural Adjustment and the Crisis of Governance in Africa, Uppsala, NAI.

Olukoshi, A. (2008). Governance Trends in West Africa, 2006, Dakar, CODESRIA & OSIWA.

Summers, L. (1994). "Foreword" in Stephen Haggard and Steven Webb (eds.), Voting for Reform: Democracy, Political Liberalization and Economic Adjustment, Oxford, Oxford University Press.

World Bank (1992). Governance and Development, Washington, DC.

World Bank (2000). Reforming Public Institutions and Strengthening Governance: A World Bank Strategy, Washington, DC.

World Bank (2000). Governance Impact on Private Investment Washington, DC.

12

Are Human Rights Soluble in Governance?

Ibrahim SALAMA
(Translated from the French)

"The reasoned basis of Human Rights lies in the importance of human freedom and the need for solidarity. That far-reaching recognition demands engagement – both at the local and at the global level. The right to development has to be seen in the context of this much larger challenge."

Amartya SEN[1]

The evolutionary course taken by both bilateral and multilateral development aid recently, highlights the importance of Human Rights as an integral component of "good governance". However, the near total consensus amongst the majority of actors affected regarding such a fundamental requirement has not always resulted in Human Rights being integrated within governance on a coherent, long-term basis – whether that be on a conceptual or practical level, either nationally or internationally.

One of the major difficulties in integrating Human Rights within the development process, including the medium of governance, is due to the fact that the links between these rights and development have not been made sufficiently clear. Beyond the rhetoric, there has also been a

---

1. Sen, A. (2006). Development as a Human Right, Legal, Political and Economic Dimensions, London, Harvard University Press, p. 8.

blurring of these links in practice by fragmented and often inconsistent standards and policies on the part of key national and international actors in several areas affecting development[2].

Over and above all the legal and conceptual difficulties, linking development to Human Rights gives rise to the problem of "conditionality", which is rejected by developing countries. This rejection has been vindicated by the failure of the structural adjustment policies of the eighties. Furthermore, developed nations take a dim view of the South's demand for "national policy space" in the fields of commerce and development, when this is brought up in relation to Human Rights. The Northern countries' scepticism is focused less on the concept itself than on how it might possibly impact these rights.

The lack of a consistent approach between Human Rights and other developmental sectors

As far as institutions are concerned, and without seeking to determine responsibilities in such a complex field, it is undeniable that national and institutional institutions' policies on commerce, finance and development reflect a diverse set of dynamics and defer to governing authorities pursuing varied objectives. The problem we are faced with, of a lack of strategic coherence between Human Rights and the other areas, manifests itself within differing frameworks on the national and international stages.

At a national level: the importance of taking economical, social and cultural rights into account alongside civil and political rights

---

2. Hence the recommendation of the Working Group on the Right to Development on the occasion of its 7th session, which considers that: "States, while adopting agreements and making commitments at international forums, such as in the context of WTO, as well as in the implementation of Goal 8, remain accountable for their human rights obligations. Ensuring policy coherence between a State's international human rights obligations and all its multilateral and bilateral trade and development engagements is, therefore, a central prerequisite of the right to development. In negotiating such engagements, Governments should comply with and ensure respect for their human rights obligations, by applying a coherent and coordinated approach. The Working Group also recognises that states should implement the resolve to integrate the right to development into national policies, including development strategies, at the national and international levels." E/CN.4/2006/26.

Nowadays, the integration of Human Rights within governments' policies by means of civil and political rights is universally accepted. Indeed, progress has incontestably been made here, including within a growing proportion of developing countries. Mechanisms within civil society for promoting and protecting Human Rights together with various national institutions for the promotion of Human Rights, have jointly bolstered the progressive integration of civil and political rights within governance. There is no longer any question as to the primacy of Human Rights and the centrality of the individual as a participant in and beneficiary of the development process. There is now an ongoing consensus that no real, enduring development can be achieved without democratic governance, participation of the people and political freedom.

However, democratic governance is not always a guarantee in itself of equitable, enduring and global development. To achieve long-term human development it is also necessary for economic, social and cultural rights (ESCRs) to be accorded the same degree of institutional and judicial attention and protection as civil and political rights. This is not to imply that there should be any letting up in the safeguarding of civil and political rights – indeed, Human Rights are indivisible and interdependent. And yet the development of ESCRs remains relatively lacklustre, both nationally and internationally. The successful conclusion of the negotiations currently taking place regarding an additional protocol to the covenant on ESCRs could, however, herald a new and positive dawn in this respect[3].

One of the fundamental problems impeding the development of ESCRs at a national level lies in the contradiction, at least in the present economic climate, between requirements to liberalise the economy whilst also providing for the most vulnerable. The discrepancy between the state's shrinking role in the economic life of the country and its growing responsibilities regarding ESCRs is becoming ever more pronounced. When a state undertakes economic reforms, those hardest hit are obviously the poorest and most marginalised members of that society. Supporters of neo-liberal economic reforms have shown their commitment to the path of economic liberalisation by way of the multilateral commercial system. They insist that society as a whole will benefit in the not too distant future from the fruits of these reforms. However, the exacerbation of the problem of global poverty, both a cause and a consequence of various Human Rights violations, shows that

---

3. Ref: document A/HRC/8/WG.4/3, issued by the 5th session of the Working Group on an optional protocol to the International Covenant on Economic, Social and Cultural Rights for more information on the status of these negotiations.

this hope is far from realistic. Indeed, as the UN High Commissioner for Human Rights notes:

> "Technological progress, scientific advances and nations' increasing wealth are of immense benefit to only a very small number of individuals and are thus betraying the ideals of equality and non-discrimination enshrined in the Universal Declaration of Human Rights, ideals which are often supplanted by the principles of competition or merit, which inevitably favour those who write them"[4].

At a multilateral level: the necessity of affirming the right to development as a driver for integrating Human Rights within governance

Inconsistencies between cooperation policies are clearly of a structural and political nature. On account of the specific mandates held by the various international organisations, multilateral cooperation takes place on parallel, vertical planes, with insufficient regard to the horizontal links between the different cooperative sectors. From this point of view, globalisation should stimulate a whole new approach:

> "New thinking about network-like set ups that create, global issue by global issue, a sort of horizontal, cross-border source of legitimacy that complements the traditional vertical representation processes and legitimacy of nation-states"[5].

As regards links between development and Human Rights, the international system's inconsistency is exacerbated by the

> "dissymmetry in internationalisation processes, which seem, in the absence of success in defining and imposing a – still undiscovered – world order, systematically to favour market values. Furthermore, Human Rights' legal enforceability, which is already weakened on the level of the state due to the ineffectiveness of any control mechanisms, remains virtually non-existent in the business arena"[6].

---

4. Speech given on 3rd March 2008 in Geneva on the opening of the Human Rights Council's 7th session.

5. Richard J.-F. (2002). High Noon, Twenty Global Problems, Twenty Years to Solve Them, UK, The Persus Press, p. 200.

6. Delmas-Marty, M. (2003). Globalisation économique et universalisme des droits de l'Homme, University of Montreal, Thémis, p. 17.

This phenomenon is clearly illustrated by the asymmetric development of the right to intellectual property in comparison with the right to benefit from science and technology. These are, nevertheless, two Human Rights, established under the same article – whether that be within the Universal Declaration of Human Rights or the International Covenant on Economic, Social and Cultural Rights. These two faces of the same coin have progressed completely differently along their legal and institutional routes. Economic globalisation does not, in fact, go hand in hand with Human Rights and the two are not easily married. The policy repercussions of this upon democratic governance and international cooperation are clear.

There are no intrinsic contradictions within the international agenda as it appears in writing. The multilateral commercial system, as envisioned by the Marrakech agreement establishing the World Trade Organization, includes sustainable human development among its objectives[7]. However as is often the case, there is a gap between political rhetoric and policies as they are carried out in practical terms. Thus, from the point of view of Human Rights at the very least, the WTO pays insufficient heed to the consequences of the rules it institutes regarding ESCRs. Even though the Doha round of trade negotiations refers to the economic development and interests of developing countries, this objective is being pursued neither in terms of rights nor – even less so – in terms of the right to development. The gap separating the Millennium Development Goals and the ESCRs testifies to the same conceptual gap. These two "formulae" constitute:

> "Ships passing one another in the night, each with little awareness that the other is there, and with little if any sustained engagement with one another"[8].

---

7. The preamble to the Marrakech Agreements stipulates that the Parties recognize that: "their relations in the field of trade and economic endeavour should be conducted with a view to raising standards of living, ensuring full employment and a large and steadily growing volume of real income and effective demand, and expanding the production of and trade in goods and services, while allowing for the optimal use of the world's resources in accordance with the objective of sustainable development, seeking both to protect and preserve the environment and to enhance the means for doing so in a manner consistent with their respective needs and concerns at different levels of economic development" and that "there is need for positive efforts designed to ensure that developing countries, and especially the least developed among them, secure a share in the growth in international trade commensurate with the needs of their economic development".

8. Alston, Ph. (2005). "Ships Passing in the Night: The Current State of Human Rights and Development Debate seen Through the Lens of The Millennium Development Goals", Human Rights Quarterly, Vol. 27, p. 825.

The right to development appears to us to be the most strategic tool for building these "missing bridges" and creating a consistency between the different prescriptive fields, norms and policies which govern international cooperation regarding the interaction of Human Rights and development.

It is unsurprising, therefore, that the right to development is the most controversial human right to date. It is a right whose implementation provokes huge conceptual, legal and political difficulties. Some people, notably in the West, are fearful that the concept of a right to development, formulated as vaguely as it is in the Declaration on the Right to Development (which was adopted in 1986 by the UN's General Assembly in resolution 41/128[9]), might be used to spark off revisions to international mandates or even institutional splits. Any such multilateral challenge to the established order is unacceptable to some and essential to others. Seen in this light, the right to development borders upon a demand for a new international economic order[10]. This 1980s demand by the Third World, which is classed by some as a Cold War episode, is still one of the disruptive factors undermining the right to development's very foundations and content. It should also be stressed that the attitude of a number of developing countries has scarcely helped to dispel the image of a so-called "subversive" right, whose "development" aspect is nothing other than a diplomatic attacking manoeuvre on the international stage. From this perspective, one legitimate question cries out to be asked: how many of the countries demanding the right to development in the international arena have actually tried to implement it on a national level?

Internationally, it is a statement of fact that those countries demanding the right to development have not always managed to flesh out its contents in a way that is intelligible and makes operational sense. This may be due – at least in part – to the climate of politicization which surrounded the right to development in the first two decades of its theoretical existence. Whatever the reason, the right to development is not as revolutionary as it might seem. Indeed, as formulated in the declaration of the 1986 General Assembly of the United Nations, this right is still at

---

9. Article 1 of this declaration states that: "the right to development is an inalienable human right by virtue of which every human person and all peoples are entitled to participate in, contribute to, and enjoy economic, social, cultural and political development, in which all human rights and fundamental freedoms can be fully realized".

10. Abi-Saab, G. (1984). Analytical study on the Principles and Norms of the New International Economic Order, submitted pursuant to para. 2 of GA resolution 38/128 of 13 January 1984, annex II-1 the report of the Secretary-General, Progressive Development of the Principles and Norms of International Law relating to the New International Economic Order, A/39/504/Add.1, 23 October 1984, p. 89.

the embryonic stage of a set of general principles requiring negotiation in order to sketch out its consequences for the various areas of application. As Professor Georges Abi-Saab notes:

> "Unfortunately, the Declaration on the Right to Development, which was adopted in 1986 on the occasion of the 41st session of the General Assembly (Resolution 128/41) has not resolved all the controversies to which this notion gave rise and gives us scant help in further defining its essence and outline. Given the divisions at the time between the various nation groups regarding this, the end result was a text setting out – due to the need for consensus – nothing more than a fragmented and ill-structured set of proposals (designed to satisfy the lowest common denominator) and which, furthermore, focused more on the issue of "respect for Human Rights within the development process" than on the right to development in itself"[11].

This right is, we believe, individual and collective in nature, requiring that all states commit, above all else, to a consistent relationship between their obligations and their respective policies regarding commerce, development and Human Rights both nationally and internationally. The fact that the obligations arising from the right to development are far from perfect does not, in itself, represent an insurmountable barrier to its implementation.

In practical terms, this obligation of conduct requires that those standards and policies of mutual impact within national and international action sectors be periodically reviewed, so as to be sure that what one wishes to achieve on the one hand is not being undermined elsewhere due to the inadequacies or even inconsistencies within the rules and policies in force. What is required internationally as part of this "obligation of conduct"

> "is not any specific externally-given level of assistance, but the need to consider these issues through open public discussion. What is demanded is nothing like an automatic agreement on some pre-determined formula, but a commitment to participate in a process, which includes an exercise of social ethics, within each country and across borders"[12].

The right to development's ambiguity is also due to the issue of links between civil and political rights (true obligations) and economic, social and cultural rights (imperfect obligations). This epitomises the challenge

---

11. Abi-Saab, G. (1996). Droits de l'Homme et Développement: quelques éléments de réflexions, African Yearbook of International Law, p. 5-6.

12. Sen, A. op. cit., p. 7.

posed by the indivisibility of Human Rights, itself a prior condition to their integration within governance. Whatever the ESCRs' relative weakness in comparison with civil and political rights, one must allow, as Sen states, that

> "ambiguity of obligation, however, whether in law or in ethics, does not indicate that there are no obligations at all and that one simply need not bother"[13].

In this respect, the Human Rights Council's current phase of negotiations on implementing the right to development is extremely promising. Indeed, the choice of Goal Number Eight of the Millennium Development Goals (global partnership for development) as the subject of these negotiations is an indication that the right to development could finally be rediscovering its true role as a framework for consistency and detector of protection loopholes regarding the links between development and Human Rights. In the course of its 7th Session, the Working Group on the Right to Development adopted an initial version of the "criteria for periodic evaluation of global development partnerships from the perspective of the right to development". These criteria

> "are primarily to be applied by the parties to a partnership. These criteria would have to be applied on a continuing basis in order to achieve coherence and accountability"[14].

Universality of Human Rights and distinctive cultural features: the challenge of democratic governance

No list of challenges to the integration of Human Rights within governance would be complete without mentioning the principle of their universality. Indeed, the issue of cultures is fundamental to the problem of Human Rights and development.

---

13. Ibid., p. 7.

14. For the text setting out these criteria please refer to paras 67-68 of Document E/CN.4/2006/26.

The cultural legitimacy of Human Rights

The main stumbling block here is the fact that the universality of Human Rights is still sometimes more a piece of legal fiction than actual, socio-cultural reality. Unfortunately, Human Rights are still seen as an essentially western, interventionist and selective concept in certain parts of the world. This has led to many developing countries becoming sceptical and trying

> "to neutralize the weapon they think used against them: the weapon of Human Rights, a weapon of the West against the East during the Cold War and now, in the eyes of developing countries, a weapon of the rich North against the poor South"[15].

For historical reasons linked to the decolonization process, the "Third World" has taken a back seat in formulating the rules for the global Human Rights system. Today, many developing countries' contributions to the debates and to the Human Rights movement continue to be hampered by under-development and a shortage of democratic governance. This is especially the case with regard to the role of civil society within southern nations. The politicisation of Human Rights issues, the lack of cultural sensitivity and the failure to recognize the realities of under-development have all strengthened the perception, in certain parts of the world, of Human Rights as a globally-imposed legacy from the West, or even some form of neo-colonial rule.

Clash of civilisation theories and certain actors' "human rightism" (to use Alain Pellet's expression) have not helped in affirming Human Rights' genuine cultural legitimacy either. Abuses in the fight against terrorism have also had a hugely detrimental effect on the credibility of the international system for promoting and protecting Human Rights. Worse still, these abuses have been amply exploited by fundamentalist movements to gain more ground with all manner of oppressed people.

Over and above terrorism, the clash of civilisation theories have also been fuelled by an intensification in extreme poverty, which continues to sustain waves of migration – both legal and illegal – and whose consequences create a great many challenges, particularly in western countries. The integration of legal immigrants, the fight against illegal immigration, plus new manifestations of racism and all forms of discrimination together represent challenges to Human Rights, which are themselves supposed to form the cornerstone of democratic governance.

---

15. Ramcharan, B. (2000). Human Rights: Universal and Cultural Diversity, Rendering Justice to the Vulnerable, Kluwer Law International, p. 239.

These challenges are further complicated by numerous issues such as the superimposing of national and international factors, the inter-dependence of the problems in question, globalisation, ambiguities in causality and the failure to adapt international cooperative mechanisms to react to such interdisciplinary challenges. In a word, the "multilateral facility" seems incapable of integrating Human Rights into governance.

How should we begin to deal with a situation like this? Nobody can claim to have a perfect answer to this fundamental question. Given that it was virtually impossible to achieve any sort of initial consensus on the definition of the issues involved, what are the chances of resolving these issues? In the current international context is it not imperative to tackle the complexity of the links between Human Rights and governance step by simple step?

Taking into account the cultural paradigm within Human Rights

Democratic governance is, by definition, governance which emanates from the populace and reflects its own value system, history and aspirations. Therefore, for any analysis of the dynamics of democratic governance for a given country, the socio-cultural context is extremely important. The cultural model and thus the acknowledgement of distinctive cultural features therefore have a place within governance as well as falling under the Human Rights remit. This should not, however, serve as a pretext for relativism or for the denial of universally recognised principles. That is the basic condition for enabling cultural diversity to have a positive and enriching effect on an international level.

From the perspective of global aid and cooperation, and development aid in particular, it seems essential that national choices be respected if the impact from any acts of cooperation is to be effective and long-lasting. Democracy's "ingredients" are more important that its "packaging". If democracy, both as a concept and as a political regime, continues – rightly or wrongly – to be the subject of debate, not to mention controversy, the concept of Human Rights is no longer in any doubt, not only as regards its universality, but also its ability to cut across all of the world's cultures and civilisations. Democratic governance therefore seems to us to be the best vehicle for integrating the concepts of a proper management of public affairs and of Human Rights within the context of sustainable human development. However, in order to achieve this integration of Human Rights within governance, it is vital that the cultural legitimacy of Human Rights concepts be re-established within the national framework. At a national level, the role both of the elite and of civil society is critical. Equally essential to the aim of integration is a global Human Rights system operating in tandem with this, which is not seen to be western, dictated by donors, selective, or based upon conditionality.

Self-examination and belief, together with political will on the part of each nation should therefore be the motors driving the development process through democratic governance based above all else on Human Rights. Of course the international factor can and must stimulate a process of this sort, but on condition that this is achieved with due regard for positive diversity and for every nation's legitimate choices. International diplomacy is of fundamental importance here, whilst civil society plays an even more decisive role on a national level.

Strengthening national potential in developing countries and demystifying distinctive cultural features as regards Human Rights are two connected courses of action, both of which are necessary to support democratic governance in developing countries and to neutralise the causes of civilisation clashes. Another priority is the introduction of consistency on a multilateral level through a community of interest based on the right to development. Together, these two levels of priority represent basic starting points for a true integration of Human Rights within national and international governance. What is called for is a collective responsibility on the part of governments and civil society in each and every country.

The Universal Periodic Review mechanism

Seen from this point of view, the new Universal Periodic Review mechanism (UPR), whose modality was defined by Decision 5/1 of the Human Rights Council on 18th June 2007, represents an historic opportunity for integrating Human Rights within governance, both on a national level and also in terms of international aid and cooperation. As Professor Abi-Saab states:

> "when all is said and done, the entire issue of the international protection of Human Rights is only conceivable within the framework of an "international law of cooperation"... Only a common value, established as being in the greater interest in accordance with the assumption of "joint endeavour" underlying the international law of cooperation could justify any such monitoring right...In the absence of any such universally-shared vision, the system will not genuinely function"[16].

---

16. Abi-Saab, G. op. cit., p. 7-8.

This new "peer review" system does indeed appear to have innovative features, which would deal with several of the challenges described by us as obstacles to the integration of Human Rights within governance.

Firstly, it is a global system, covering every country and every right and is therefore tainted neither by partiality nor selectivity. It is also a three-dimensional system in the sense that the assessment of the state of Human Rights within each country is based upon three critical views: a self-assessment by each state, a compilation of United Nations inspections (treaty bodies and special procedures) and a summary of contributions from other relevant stakeholders (NGOs, national Human Rights organisations). And thirdly it has the goal of strengthening national potential through international aid and cooperation in order to implement the recommendations emerging from the UPR. Will the international community's "monitoring right" be accompanied, in fact, by incentives translating a "duty to provide aid and cooperation" into concrete action? This is one of the keys to integrating Human Rights within governance as a concerted, dialogue-based effort, which takes account of levels of development and development needs. The future of the international system for promoting and protecting Human Rights depends on this and the new Council for Human Rights bears this responsibility[17].

---

17. See: Schrijver, N. (2007). "The UN Human Rights Council: A New 'Society of the Committed' or Just Old Wine in New Bottles?", Leiden Journal of International law, 20, p. 809-823.

13

Governance and the Rule of Law[1]

Mireille DELMAS-MARTY
(Translated from the French)

Governing without government and the institution of a rule of law with no state, these are the current globalisation challenges. Interdependencies have evolved to such an extent that most major public debates, from sustainable development to the fight against poverty, not to mention the protection of health, the environment and biodiversity – or on a wider scale, peace and security – call for answers both at a national and international level.

There has therefore been a need in the last fifteen years or so to link global governance with the rule of law. This concept, which has been enshrined in a series of international texts by bodies such as the European Union, the United Nations (UN), the World Trade Organisation (WTO), the World Bank and the International Monetary Fund (IMF), has become a genuine standard, with which every nation shall be expected to comply. Whilst this has clearly had some positive effects, for example, on the progress of law in Europe[2], or even in China[3], its limitations should not be under-estimated. On the one hand there is local political resistance, exacerbated by linguistic differences ("rule of law" can be written in two different ways in Chinese). On the other hand there is the risk that a particular superpower could exploit the concept to further its own ambitions for primacy. Rather than helping to pacify international relationships therefore, the rule of law tends, on the contrary, to legitimize the use of force[4].

1. From the conclusion of the lecture series given at the Collège de France published in 2007 as: La refondation des pouvoirs, Seuil.
2. Carpano E. (2005). État de droit et droits européens, L'Harmattan.
3. (2007). La Chine et la démocratie, Fayard.
4. Chevallier J. (2006). "État de droit et relations internationales", Annuaire français des relations internationales, Vol. VII, Bruylant.

Imposing the rule of law at a national level only actually makes sense if international society itself defers to legal principles which bolt "supra-state" laws onto the existing inter-state legal framework, thus transforming absolute sovereignty into a shared sovereignty. But this division is only acceptable if that every state, together with all the international institutions, is equally bound by it and the subsequent precise reduction of their autonomy in the name of the law. The rule of law is invoked by each and every project for institutional reform, from the Treaty establishing a Constitution for Europe (which in turn became the Simplified Treaty), to the reform of the UN and the global financial institutions, via the debates on the future of the WTO and international criminal justice – yet the term's meaning remains ambiguous.

Far from establishing the famous divide upon which the two pillars of the rule of law are founded, namely, lawfulness and the judicial guarantee, international practice tends instead to confuse the various powers. Legislative power is normally exercised by governments (the executive) and judicial power, stimulated by competition between national and international judges and freed from an internal legislative framework by the direct integration of – often loosely-defined – international law, tends to infringe upon legislative power (judicial governance). As for human rights, so long as they continue to be seen as occupying a niche sector within international law and thus separated from other areas (such as commerce, the environment, labour and health) they will be unable to constitute a founding platform upon which, through adherence to their principles, a third pillar of the rule of law may be built.

In the current framework, which is neither purely national, nor purely international, but rather "internationalized" – i.e. simultaneously national, international and supra-national – subjecting powers to the law (the very raison d'être of the rule of law) would entail a complex structure, capable of functioning at various levels (national, regional and global), of including all the relevant actors (state and non-state) and of organising the various legal sub-sectors.

We need to create, therefore, a sort of "legal monster" which could only come about by hybridizing the methods of governance and the rule of law. From governance we would need to borrow the art of co-ordinating, i.e. organizing the relationships and interactions of those state and non-state participants in the exercise of power. But in order to guarantee its legitimacy and ensure its effectiveness, this monster would also need to draw upon the rule of law's methodology in an attempt to subordinate – and this would doubtless be the greatest challenge – power to principles in law, which could establish a hierarchy of collective preferences and devolve responsibilities to the various actors.

Coordinating relationships between actors

Governance in the absence of a government effectively boils down to coordinating relationships between the various actors. However, any shift in the term's use is controversial when the direction is away from "corporate governance", borrowed from company law, towards national practices imposed by financial institutions in the eighties[5] and described as "good governance", and finally to "global governance", as in: an "instrument for manufacturing standards and public interventions" allowing us to "consider the way the global economy is governed, in a world which continues to be politically divided"[6].

Indeed, the reorganisation of powers required for a move from the economic sphere ("the way the global economy is governed") to the political sphere ("in a world which continues to be politically divided") remains problematic. Thus, whilst the financial crises in Asia and then Argentina have generated calls for a re-think of the Bretton Woods system (IMF and World Bank), none of these projects has yet come to a successful conclusion, doubtless because any such change presupposes a more political reorientation, entailing new competences. On a wider scale, there is the issue of the "unspoken elements of good governance"[7], with criticisms emanating not only from advocates of alter-mondialization and national sovereignty but also from liberal thinkers, on occasion.

Governance seems nevertheless to have become – in spite of these criticisms or perhaps thanks to their showcasing of the term – "a platitude in global political vocabulary"[8]. The use of this term on a global scale dates back to the creation of a United Nations-endorsed Commission on Global Governance, in the aftermath of the fall of the Berlin Wall. Its report, published in 1995[9], tackled the issue of national sovereignty and the reform of the United Nation's institutions in a fairy classic manner, arguing that relationships continue to be international in nature, whether this is in the context of harmonizing functions or assigning competences.

---

5. Cf. Arnaud A.-J. (2002). LGDJ, 2nd edition p. 233, for further discussions on the ambiguities of "good governance".

6. Jacqet P., Pisani-Ferry J and Tubiana L. (2002). Gouvernance mondiale, Conseil d'analyse économique, La documentation française, p. 12.

7. Haut Conseil de la coopération internationale (2001). Les non-dits de la bonne gouvernance, Pour un débat politique sur la pauvreté et la gouvernance, Karthala.

8. Lamy P. (2005). "La gouvernance, utopie ou chimère?", Études. Revue de culture contemporaine, Vol. 402, Issue. 2, p. 153.

9. The report of the Commission on Global Governance (1995). Our Global Neighbourhood, Oxford University Press..

On the other hand and on a European scale, the Commission's white paper entitled European Governance[10] proposes a change in methodology: "the linear model of dispensing policies from above must be replaced by a virtuous circle, based on feedback, networks and involvement from policy creation to implementation at all levels".

Feedback, networks and levels: the method described summons up less a separation of powers and rather more a distribution of competences amongst the various institutional actors (governments, national parliaments and international institutions) as well as the involvement of so-called "civil" society – i.e. non-institutional actors.

The distribution of competences amongst state and inter-state institutions is determined by the status of the various international organisations. This distribution is all the more varied due to the uneven way in which the competences are devolved regionally and globally.

This is apparent in the field of economics, where the effects of market stabilisation and the allocation of resources have been partially transferred onto a global scale while the effects of redistribution remain extremely confined.

But this may also be seen in the legal domain: on the one hand, enforceability continues to be guaranteed, in the main, by states, and yet legislative and judicial competences have been partially transferred – although with dissymmetries, notably between social and economic rights.

And when provision is made for a transfer of competences, the international sphere assumes pre-eminence (exclusive competence) on occasion, whilst at other times accepting subsidiarity (shared competence). Transfer to the international level, on the other hand, is only brought about through a nation state's inaction, either due to a lack of power or of will. The principle of subsidiarity, whose application is clarified and monitored by the judges of the two European courts, will, in the near future, also fall within the remit of the judges of the International Criminal Court (ICC). For, in criminal matters, this globally-sanctioned court can require the active participation of nation states (cooperation on the part of nation states is imposed by the ICC's statutes). But if it wishes to take up a case, it must show that the normally competent nation state neither can nor wishes to pass judgement itself. This issue was also tackled in the 2005 report on the future of the WTO[11].

This having been said, governance is not limited to institutions, for indeed it is often those members of so-called "civil" society, i.e. economic operators (corporations), civic bodies (Non-governmental Organisations – NGOs and unions), and scientists/experts, who are, through their inventiveness, the real architects of globalisation.

---

10. (2001). European Governance, a White Paper, 25th July 2001, 428 final.
11. See Sutherland report (2005). The Future of the WTO.

Organizing civil society participation is therefore one of the issues of global governance, for its dealings with both national and international institutions often remain informal and even confrontational (certain parties going so far as to take illegal or even violent measures), rather than being based in law.

Hence the need to specify conditions for engaging in the exercise of legislative, and occasionally, judiciary power for non-state participants. Whether we are talking about multinational corporations, experts on the Intergovernmental Panel on Climate Change (IPCC), citizens' assemblies – or "citizens' conventions" as they have now become – or NGOs: civil society has begun to take an active and sometimes decisive role in fleshing out measures and pronouncements as varied as, for example, the International Centre for the Settlement of Investment Disputes (ICSID), the Kyoto protocol on climate change, or the Rome Statute creating the International Criminal Court.

On the one hand, it is essential to specify conditions for determining the legitimacy of such a wide range of contributors, given that they represent private interests with no proven link to the public interest. There is also the risk of a conflict of interest in the case of civic or scientific participants such as NGOs or experts, respectively – such risk being particularly manifest where economic operators are involved. Even simple citizens' assembly delegates or online citizen-reporters might be compromised in this way. Hence the importance of conditions such as transparency and pluralism, which can be applied just as well to multinational corporations as they can to the status of experts and NGOs and even the world's future citizens.

On the other hand civil society's various forms of intervention via application to the courts should also be made clear, whether these take the form of intervention by a litigant, by the representative of a group of people directly concerned or as an amicus curiae.

The fact remains that coordination in itself is not sufficient, even within this framework. It might contribute towards a more fluid and democratic arrangement of international society, but the key to the rule of law continues to lie in the subordination of powers to principles of law.

The subordination of powers to principles of law

The transfers in competence arising from globalisation call for a re-think of the concept of a rule of law by transposing to an international level the two principles upon which legal validity is dependent: the principle of coherence, which uses common values as a basis for legitimacy and the principle of responsibility, which ensures that these are effectively implemented. Even if these principles have generally been left out of any institutional discussions so as not to give fright to those nations scarcely inclined to accept any such division in sovereignty, we can try to sketch out an outline, using the fragments of currently-existing positive law as a starting point.

Let us begin with the principle of coherence, which could be a means of resolving conflicts caused by the current compartmentalization of the various sectors of globalisation. What is needed to orient governance is a compass indicating collective preferences so that a hierarchy of value choices may be constructed.

The Universal Declaration of Human rights, clarified by the two UN treaties, seems at first sight to be that compass. It is true that human rights initially found their way onto the UN charter "virtually by forced entry", but texts on the subject have proliferated and their increase in power within the jurisprudence of the International Court of Justice (ICJ)[12] is clear. Particularly worth quoting in this respect are those cases involving the death penalty, where the ICJ has become progressively bolder. There have also been improvements – achieved or currently underway – in the operation of bodies monitoring various UN treaties with respect to human rights (circulation of an individual complaints procedure, rationalization of the procedure for reports by nation states[13]). Finally, there has been a growth in the importance of so-called "subsidiary organs" such as independent experts, and country and thematic special rapporteurs[14].

On the other hand, some nations have ratified treaties in a selective manner and most have tabled reservations limiting the scope of their commitments. Furthermore, the attacks of September 11th 2001, which heralded a new global terrorism have, far from strengthening the universality of human rights, instead triggered a process of re-nationalization symbolized by the slogan of a "war against terror" – a slogan coined initially by the American government and then taken up by numerous countries, both democratic and non-democratic.

This way of legitimizing grave violations of human rights in the name of national security further strengthens resistance to these rights, which are seen as a tool of western dominance. I recall the comment of a Chinese student, who was surprised to discover when visiting the

---

12. Dupuy P.-M. (2006). "Conclusions générales", Les Nations Unies et les droits de l'Homme, Enjeux et défis d'une réforme, E. Decaux (ed), Pedone, p. 311-312.

13. Eudes M. (2006). "Les organes de surveillance des traités", Les Nations Unies et les droits de l'Homme, Enjeux et défis d'une réforme, E. Decaux (ed), Pedone, p. 251-269.

14. Frouville O., general report on "Les organes subsidiaires de la Commission des droits de l'Homme", ibidem, p. 171-200.

European Court of Human Rights that China had never been indicted there (and for good reason!), while the judges took turns in condemning all the European countries. This student told me with a broad grin that when he arrived in Europe, he "hated human rights", as he saw in them an ideological set of views invented to criticise his country. But at Strasburg he came to understand that they could also be the basis in reason upon which a legal argument could be constructed, put before a judge and set against a nation state irrespective of the political colour of that nation's government – and even in such sensitive areas as the fight against terrorism.

At a global level however, the international community, whilst on hold for the brand new Human Rights Council to consolidate its position, continues to operate a two-tier system depending on the power of the countries concerned.

Moreover, we still need to deal with the fact that all the international institutions are working in isolation from one another, whether it be the financial institutions, who do not consider themselves constrained by UN treaties, or international criminal courts of law which quote texts and sometimes case law from regional courts or from the UN committee, but refuse to consider themselves bound by the mechanisms for protecting human rights. The WTO could lead the way here by creating synergies with other organisations such as the International Labour Organization (ILO) for social norms or the World Health Organization (WHO) in the field of health. When it decided, on 1st December 2007 to extend by two years the deadline for ratifying the amendment to the Agreement on Trade-related Aspects of Intellectual Property Rights (TRIPS), which allows patent law to be side-stepped so as to facilitate poor countries' access to medicine, the WTO recognised that the importance of health is truly global. Without waiting for a real human rights-based hierarchy to be established, the principle of coherence could thus act as a prompt for exploring other avenues, such as "global public goods", even if one is then faced with the problem of transposing an already highly-contentious and anthropologically-problematic economic concept into the legal and political domain.

Supposing that we succeed, despite all the difficulties, in legitimizing the construction of a global rule of law, we would still need to guarantee its efficacy. Hence the importance of the second principle of responsibility.

The principle of responsibility is a driver towards recognition that possessing power on a global scale, whether it be political, economical, scientific, media-based, religious or cultural, necessarily entails some global responsibility.

The apparent simplicity of this proposition is deceptive. This is, in fact, one of the most obscure legal questions, as the issue of responsibility is fragmented between various legal branches depending on whether nation states or non-state actors are involved. It is this area which will pose the most problems in any attempt to hybridize governance and the rule of law.

As regards nation states, the international community has tried for years to derive a set of rules for codifying their responsibility (not to be confused with governing bodies' criminal responsibility, which is handled by the international criminal courts). The first attempts at this go back to 1930 and there have been more than twenty reports by the UN's International Law Commission (ILC) since 1963[15]. The most recent draft was finally adopted by the ILC in August 2001 and "recommended" to governments by a resolution of the United Nations General Assembly on 12th December 2001. The resolution still needs to be turned into a convention with the power to bind nation states, but it is already recognized as expressing common law on many points and represents a staging post at least, even if it has not fully resolved the issue of counter measures. By retaining the notion of "serious breaches of obligations arising under peremptory norms of general international law", the resolution actually establishes the existence of a system of responsibility towards the international community as a whole[16]. This is an important advance, as this responsibility is founded on an attack on the interests of international public order as such, hence the resistance on the part of nation states, who prefer to confine themselves to the previously accepted set-up of a strictly bilateral framework limiting responsibility to a case opposing the perpetrator state against the victim state.

In the run-up to an extremely hypothetical agreement, nation states may only be charged with global responsibilities in the field of trade (WTO). As regards human rights, the efficacy of treaties classed as "sectorial" varies from one region to another: high in Europe and Latin America, where human rights courts exercise real control, but low on a global scale. This is due on the one hand to the absence of a global human rights court, and on the other hand, because the ICJ clings to a restricted view of its role by refusing to overstep the limits of its optional jurisdiction even when serious human rights violations are cited, as we have recently seen in the Bosnian genocide case[17].

---

15. See Stern B. (2003). "Les dilemmes de la responsabilité internationale aujourd'hui", Les colloques du Sénat, "Vers de nouvelles normes en droit de la responsabilité publique ?", p. 261-284.

16. Villaoando S. (2005). L'émergence de la communauté internationale dans la responsabilité des États, PUF.

17. ICJ (26th February 2007, §277). Application of the Convention on the Prevention and Punishment of the Crime of Genocide (Bosnia and Herzegovina v. Serbia and Montenegro); Cf. Ascencio H. (2007) "La responsabilité selon la CIJ dans l'affaire du genocide bosniaque". RGDIP, 285.

But the construction of a global rule of law will not be able to be confined to nation states alone. Criminal or civil courts will need simultaneously to acknowledge the responsibility of non-state actors, given their ever-increasing role. And yet this second course, towards a universal (or global) responsibility for non-state actors varies in its impact according to whether the competent judge is a national or international judge.

Proceedings against international crimes before an international judge (ad hoc criminal courts and the International Criminal Court) – regardless of whether the perpetrator is an ordinary individual or a head (or ex-head) of state – are heard in the name of the international community as a whole. In this sense, this criminal responsibility may be understood to be universal, but many of the larger nation states have refused to ratify the convention establishing the ICC.

On the other hand, the so-called "universal" jurisdiction sometimes accorded to national judges remains beset by problems. Universal competence, a notion defended by Grotius in the name of natural law or the law of nations and established from the eighteenth century onwards as regards piracy, did not, at that time, have the authority to safeguard universal values but rather to take charge of common interests. It was only at the end of the twentieth century that the idea of a national judge as protector of universal values was taken up again, as and when issues arose (genocide, torture, breaches of the Geneva Convention, terrorism), but it is the subject of fierce criticism. Poorly framed within vague international law and timorous jurisprudence on the part of the ICC, it is even occasionally decided by national law on a unilateral basis, as demonstrated by the example of the 1789 Alien Tort Claims Act (ATCA). The ATCA, giving American courts jurisdiction for torts committed in violation of international law was recently revived for use against political leaders and corporations and then ratified by the US Supreme Court in 2004[18]. On this occasion, several countries filed amicus curiae briefs, seemingly in an attempt to furnish themselves with the basis for a future universal civic responsibility.

This universal responsibility, which one group of adherents already wishes to broaden into a responsibility for major hazards[19] would actually require a minimum of harmonisation based, for example, on the "principles of responsibility" model currently under development at the UN[20].

---

18. Sosa v. Alvarez Machain, Supreme Court of the United States, 29th June 2004, 124 S. ct. 2739.

19. Thibierge C. (2004). "L'avenir de la responsabilité, responsabilité de l'avenir", Recueil Dalloz, p. 577.

20. Dedaux E. (2005). "La responsabilité des sociétés transnationales en matière de droits de l'Homme", RSC, 789.

In conclusion, practices which have sprung from globalisation show, by their very abundance, that it would be entirely possible to combine the art of coordination – taken from governance – with that of subordination – inspired by the rule of law.

However, there is a risk that global governance will content itself with a minimalist conception of the rule of law, restricting coherence to the protection of a few rights, which are seen as vital for the market economy[21], and devolving responsibilities to the goodwill of the various nation states. We then risk ending up being doubly hamstrung by a legal system which would be opposable neither to nation states nor to economic operators.

Do we need to try to transpose the notion of public authority into a global area without state in order to make this monster viable? Or must we, on a broader scale, look for an answer in the interface between the fields of law, politics and economics? These are the questions still to be explored.

---

21. Flauss J.-F (2001). "Le droit international des droits de l'Homme face à la globalisation économique" in Institut international des droits de l'Homme (ed.), Commerce mondial et protection des droits de l'Homme, Brussels, Bruylant, p. 223.

14

Parliaments and Budgetary Democracy in Latin America

Carlos Santiso
(Translated from the French)

"He who lives beyond his budget, lives in error"
Carlos Fuentes, The Eagle's Throne (2003)

How far can parliaments serve to anchor budgetary democracy in good financial governance? One of the principal challenges for democratic governance in developing countries and emerging economies is the maintenance of the balance of power, subtle and often precarious, between the prerogatives of government and parliamentary oversight of the budget. It is a question of retaining the advantage of a strong central authority while at the same time reinforcing the institutional checks and balances which guarantee democratic legitimacy. As privileged arenas of public scrutiny in a democracy, parliaments have a triple function in budgetary matters: that of representation (as an elected body), legitimation (giving assent to the budget), and oversight (by means of regulatory law). Budgets are not merely a question of arithmetic; they express the aspirations of a society and are the result of fine-tuned political negotiation. The quality of the budgetary process reflects the legitimacy of the exercise of power.

As William Gladstone put it; "The finance of the country is ultimately associated with the liberties of the country... If the House of Commons by any possibility loses the power of control of the grants of public money, depend upon it, your very liberty will be worth very little in comparison" (1891).

A central facet of parliamentary sovereignty is expressed in the budget process. In the context of the social contract which binds the state to its citizens, parliament holds the de jure power to tax and spend.[1] The evolution of parliaments' budgetary powers follows three stages: parliament winning the power to raise taxes and authorise expenditure; the development of governmental procedures to devise and execute the budget; the establishment of routine and regulated parliamentary budget procedures. In practice, these functions remain to be consolidated in the emerging economies. They are often limited as much by deficiencies in the parliaments' management of public finances as by the predominance of executive power. Nevertheless, there are major risks attached to the concentration of budgetary powers often exploited to excess by governments, especially under presidential regimes. The weaker the institutional counterbalances and mechanisms of control are, the greater these risks become. However, the rebalancing of budgetary powers equally demands that parliament play a more effective and responsible role in the management of public finances.

This chapter sets out to underline the benefits of a more balanced relationship between government and parliament in budgetary affairs. To understand the relationship between the executive and the legislature in budgetary matters, it is necessary to uncover the interplay between the powers as well as the interaction between formal institutions and the informal arrangements which mould their relationship. This chapter examines the role of parliaments in the budget process in Latin America, a region which is characterised by presidential regimes and centralised budget systems. An enhanced role for parliaments can reinforce budgetary democracy by making the process more transparent and legitimate, however little these parliaments exercise their budgetary powers in a coherent and responsible manner.

Budget institutions and fiscal responsibility

Can parliaments reinforce political legitimacy in budget management without undermining fiscal discipline? The role of parliaments in budget policy is re-examined in the context of reinforcing legitimacy and probity in public finances. The enhancement of the budgetary role of parliaments forms part of the second wave of structural reforms in governmental

---

1. Schick, Allen (2002). Can national legislatures regain an effective voice in budget policy? OECD Journal on Budgeting, 1 (3).

financial administration. This renewal of interest is based on the belief that a more effective and responsible contribution by parliaments would allow for greater transparency and democratic legitimacy in public finances. However, parliaments usually play a role in budget management which is negligible and at times dysfunctional. Paradoxically, as far as the budgetary role of parliaments is concerned, while they possess a wide range of constitutional powers, they rarely exercise these in an effective and responsible way. This is due not only to the predominance of executive power in budgetary policy, but also to the parliaments' own defects, both as regards to their capacity and to their motivation. In Brazil, for example, parliamentary amendments are driven by considerations of patronage or by concerns which have more to do with increasing their own subsidies. In Argentina the budget is subject to horse-trading and political negotiations, most often conducted outside parliament, over which provincial governors have a decisive influence.

How do we explain this dissonance between the formal powers of parliaments and the role they actually play? We can begin by adopting a neo-institutional perspective. An analysis of how the actors behave, of how the institutions are organised, and of the political framework can shed light on why parliaments have not used the full range of their budgetary powers in the most effective and responsible way. How budget policy is managed institutionally is critical to the understanding of financial governance and budget performance. According to Alberto Alesina et al:

"the nature of budget procedures strongly influences fiscal outcomes".[2]

Parliamentary oversight is in effect hampered by factors which are at once technical and political: parliaments do not always have the institutional competence or technical capacity to intervene in budget matters constructively; political actors often lack sufficient incentives to exercise effective political control and to reinforce parliamentary capacity in budget matters. The lack of parliamentary discipline which has traditionally characterised its role in budget matters has resulted in a conviction by the political classes as well as parliamentary representatives that the centralisation of the budget process within the executive and the limitation of the parliamentary prerogative over the budget is the only guarantee of fiscal discipline.

Thus the consensus of opinion on budget governance warns against

---

2. Alesina, Alberto, Ricardo Hausmann, Rudolf Hommes and Ernesto Stein (1999). Budget Institutions and Fiscal Performance in Latin America. (Washington: IADB OCE Working Paper 394).

budget drift due to the weak structure of parliamentary budget powers. The literature on budgetary institutions emphasises the advantages of concentration of budgetary powers.[3] According to this logic, fiscal discipline and budgetary responsibility is achieved through the concentration of budget authority within the executive, especially the Ministry of Finance and the Treasury, and clear limitations on parliamentary budget prerogatives. These theories of political economy maintain that such institutional arrangements allow the development of fiscal discipline, control of budget deficits and the introduction of any necessary fiscal adjustments, subject to credible budgetary constraints. In France, for example, the Constitution of 1958 and the Ordinance of 1959 limited parliamentary prerogatives to avoid the excesses and abuses of the Fourth Republic.

Centralised budget systems limit parliaments' budget prerogatives by means of, for example, restrictions on the power of amendment, by the reinforcement of the right of veto by the government, or even by conferring budgetary initiative exclusively to the government. Parliaments often themselves renounce certain powers, delegating significant prerogatives to the executive, for example on fiscal affairs or on the control of credit allocation. As Allen Schick observes:

> " the legislature voluntarily yielded budgetary power to the executive because it accepted the view that parliamentarians cannot constrain their political inclination to tax less and spend more. Legislatures entrusted budgetary authority to the government because they could not trust themselves to make responsible financial decisions."[4]

These considerations have influenced the reform of budget systems in numerous emerging economies, notably in Latin America. In the course of the nineteen nineties a number of countries reformed and rationalised their system of managing public finances, significantly in Argentina under Carlos Menem (1989-1999), and in Peru under Alberto Fujimori (1990-2000).The case of Chile illustrates the tensions between discretionary executive power and strong prerogatives of the legislature.[5] The revolution of 1891 was in part the result of a budget impasse between the executive

---

3. See Santiso, Carlos (2005). Budget Institutions and Fiscal Responsibility: Parliaments and the Political economy of the Budget Process. (Washington, World Bank Institute, Working Paper 37253).

4. Schick, (2002) loc. cit., p. 16.

5. Interview by the author with Mario Marcel, former director of the Budget department of the Ministry of Finance of Chile between 2000 and 2006, Santiago, 8 August 2004 (OECD (2004), Budgeting in Chile (Paris: OECD/ GOV/PGC/SBO(2004)7.)

and the legislature during the Liberal Republic (1861-1891) and the parliamentary regime (1891-1925). The role of parliament progressively declined after the adoption of the constitution of 1925 until the Finance Administration Act and the Constitution of 1980 confirmed the primacy of the president. The centralisation of budget governance in Chile is the result of a long historical process. However, there are real risks associated with centralised budget arrangements. They tend to increase the discretionary powers of the government in public finance administration, especially in presidential systems. They inhibit the development of compensatory mechanisms for fiscal transparency and budget accountability, which makes public finances vulnerable to the abuses and corruption which are linked to all discretionary power. Centralised budget systems are generally less transparent, which is particularly problematical when one considers that the executive has a virtual monopoly over financial information. Centralised budget institutions moreover place more emphasis on budget discipline than on objectives which are no less important in budget politics, such as justice, effectiveness and efficiency in public expenditure.

Moreover, unconstrained and uncontrolled executive power undermines the credibility of the budget as an instrument of strategic planning, making it vulnerable. It prevents the consolidation of an established budget process with clear procedures and an adequate structure. Finally public oversight of the budget under parliamentary control helps to correct asymmetries in budgetary information between the state and society, opening the budget to public debate and societal control. For example, it allows for independent evaluation of fiscal projections, for critical analysis of the political choices which underpin the budget, and for an open discussion of budget allocation.

Parliaments and budgetary governance

Arenas and actors

In Latin America, as is often the case in emergent economies, there is a considerable gulf between the formal powers of parliaments and the role they actually play in the budget process. This is a result of the interplay between formal rules and informal procedures, and this interplay varies at different stages in the budget process. It is essential to understand the political and economic aspects of the budget process in order to discern the institutional factors in budget

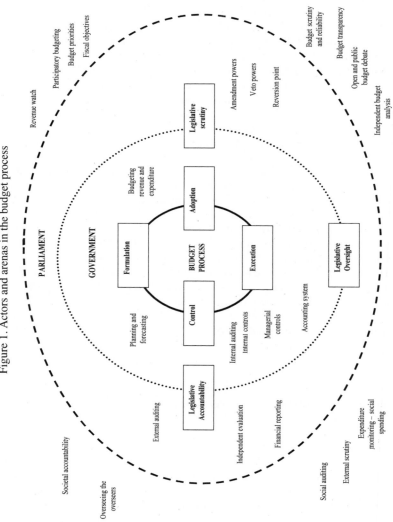

Figure 1. Actors and arenas in the budget process

performance.[6] The budget process is the result of dynamic interplay and delicate balancing performed by actors interacting in multiple arenas according to the shifting rules of the game. According to this analysis, budgetary governance must take into account the interests and political motivations of the actors in the context of institutional constraints imposed by the rules of the budgetary game and the balance of power between those participating in the formulation, approval, execution and oversight of the budget, as illustrated in Figure 1.

The evaluation of the role of parliaments must be placed within a context of parliaments which are weak and often not fully institutionalised. Parliaments are the central actors in the budget process: they adopt the budget, approving allocations and implementation. The budget cycle is completed by another act of the legislature, the discharge of the government. However, the influence of parliaments over the budget is limited by structural constraints, namely the rigidity and inertia of the budget itself. Moreover, the area of public expenditure over which parliaments have the greatest influence, investment, represents a mere fraction of public spending, even though at times this acquires strategic importance in the formation of political alliances for the adoption of specific reforms, as in the case of Brazil. The adoption in recent years of macro fiscal rules and procedural constraints on budget formation has further limited the potential for intervention by the legislature. Largely welcomed by the executive, these initiatives have certainly helped to secure fiscal discipline and to rationalise the budget process; they have also reduced the room for manoeuvre of governments as well as parliaments.

A three step waltz

What are the constraints which govern the role of parliaments in the administration of public finances and the budget process? Three groups of factors influence the role of parliaments in the budget process:
– their legal competence (that is, the formal budget powers of parliaments)
– their technical capacity (their institutional and technical capacity in terms of resources, structures and procedures) and
– their political agenda (the institutional and political context which defines the informal rules of the budget 'game').

---

6. Wildavsky, Aaron and Noemi Caiden. (2000). *The New Politics of the Budgetary Process*. New York, Addison Wesley.

Legal competence

The balance of power over the budget between the executive and the legislature varies with the different phases of the budget process (formulation, adoption, execution and control of the budget).

• *Formulation of the budget*

The first series of factors is linked to the constitutional competence and legislative prerogatives of parliaments in the formulation of the budget. In Latin America the formal, constitutional and legal powers of parliaments in budgetary affairs are limited. The government plays a predominant role in the formulation of the Finance Bill and only they can initiate the budget process and undertake expenditure, while parliaments' powers of amendment are restricted. The government's monopoly over financial information gives it a decisive advantage over parliament. The strategic use of budget information constitutes a significant dimension of the relationship between the powers in budgetary affairs.

• *Adoption of the budget*

Two critical stages in the budget process are parliament's adoption of the budget, followed by characteristic sparring between the executive and legislative powers. As with any other law, the budget must receive parliamentary assent before coming into force. The Finance Bill is submitted to parliament for scrutiny and approval. Four variables constrain the role of parliament and its powers of amendment before approving the budget: the time allowed for scrutiny of the Finance Bill is usually too short, ranging from thirty days in Mexico to one hundred and twenty in Honduras; thus, impelled by such restrictions their powers of amendment, parliaments have recourse to dangerous budgetary subterfuges to increase their influence, compromising the integrity and credibility of the budget;[7] the ability of the government to impose its partial or total veto;[8] and, finally, the mechanisms which apply in the case of budgetary impasse (what happens if the budget is not approved by parliament within the time allowed), which usually favour the government.[9]

---

7. As a general rule, parliaments may not increase public expenditure without identifying corresponding sources of finance. In Bolivia the parliament increases its influence by overestimating revenue projection, while in Nicaragua the government underestimates it in order to maximise its discretionary power to make unbudgeted revenue grants after the budget has come into force.

8. The legislative body cannot overrule the presidential veto unless it is able to muster a qualifying majority, which rarely happens, given that the government often commands a parliamentary majority.

9. In most cases either the previous year's budget remains in force during the interim period, (Argentina, Uruguay, Nicaragua, Venezuela), or the government's budget

• *Budget oversight*

Parliament disposes of significant prerogative powers and responsibilities to ensure that the budget is carried out in accordance with the democratic mandate conferred by the Finance Act. However this role is equally limited, particularly because of political game playing and informal rules. Delegation of parliamentary powers and the systematic resort to the use of decrees have allowed governments to considerably extend their de facto powers in budget matters. In Argentina, for example, Parliament has delegated a considerable portion of its budget powers, which allows the government full discretion to amend the budget during execution. Since 1997, Parliament has authorised the executive to dispense with the restrictions imposed on it by the Finance Administration Act of 1992.

• *Budget control*

Finally, parliaments possess a potentially powerful tool to secure budgetary democracy: the a posteriori supervision of budget execution. The scrutiny of public accounts and the discharge of the government by means of regulatory law allows it, if need be, to undertake the political responsibilities of the government. The certifying of public accounts by autonomous audit agencies under parliamentary scrutiny is part of a political process which serves not only to regulate how public resources are employed, but, more fundamentally, to guarantee democratic legitimacy. In Latin America the certifying of public accounts is marked by numerous dysfunctionalities which undermine the credibility of the process, particularly because of difficulties in the relationship between parliaments and audit agencies.[10] In Argentina these uncertainties have paralysed and distorted the process of certifying public accounts since 1994.[11]

Technical capacity

The role of parliaments in budgetary matters is similarly constrained by the weakness of their capacity as institutions. The organisation of

proposals are automatically adopted, (Bolivia, Chile, Colombia, Peru). These provisions give the government a considerable advantage over the legislative body, since their inaction will not prevent the executive's proposals from being adopted.

10. Santiso, Carlos (2007), Eyes Wide Shut: The Politics of Autonomous Audit Agencies in Emerging Economics, Buenos Aires, CIPPEC.

11. Interview by the author with Oscar Lamberto, President of the Bicameral Commission for Public Accounts of the Argentine government, Buenos Aires, 12 April 2005. See also Santiso, Carlos (2007). "Comme un vieux tango amer? L'économie politique du contrôle des finances publiques en Argentine" Revue française d'administration public, 2007/3, no.123, 337-351

parliamentary committees and the extension of their technical capacity have had a decisive influence on the quality of parliamentary budget functions.

• *Parliamentary Committees*

Although those concerned with the budget and finance are amongst the most influential committees, their structural weakness is a primary constraint. In Latin America the organisation of parliamentary committee work is insufficiently institutionalised in terms of their remit, structure, and internal regulation. Their composition, based on proportionality and therefore predominantly from the majority government, lessens the incentive for representatives to exercise control over the government.[12] Public audit committees are even weaker, especially where they function independently of budgetary and finance committees. The rate of rotation of the committees, most often on an annual basis, as in Peru and Nicaragua, further undermines their ability to effectively intervene in the budgetary process.

A more rational division of responsibilities between committees concerned with the various elements of public finance (fiscal matters, budget, supervision), would enhance coherence and the impact that Parliament makes on the budgetary process. There are exceptions, however, such as Brazil and Mexico, where finance committees have been strengthened considerably. In certain countries, such as Chile, the reduced turnover and the individual expertise of members of the budget and finance committee have compensated the lack of institutional expertise.[13]

• *Consultative capacity*

Another weakness of Latin American parliaments lies in the inadequacy of parliamentary committees' access to advice and assistance in evaluating finance bills. There are few technical consultants on permanent attachment to budget and public accounts committees. In practice, it is parliamentary political advisers sitting on committees who do most of the consultative work, even though they are not always specialists and do not always work exclusively on budget matters. Rarely do Latin American parliaments have enough dedicated personnel who are embedded and sufficiently qualified for rigorous oversight of public

---

12. In many parliamentary systems based on the Anglo-Saxon model, the presidency of the public accounts committee is held by the opposition party, which reinforces the incentive to exercise control over the government.

13. Interview by the author with senators Alejandro Foxley and Edgardo Boeninger, members of the Budget and Finance Committee of the Chilean Senate, Santiago de Chile, 8 and 12 August 2004 respectively.

finances. Their capacity for research and analysis is inadequate for strict scrutiny of finance bills and audit accounts. Parliamentary committees must therefore rely on information from government agencies, which further undermines their capacity for independent analysis.

Parliamentary departments for budget analysis have however emerged or been enhanced, for example in Chile, Costa Rica, Nicaragua, Panama and Venezuela[14], sometimes to a level comparable with those in more advanced democracies. In Brazil a research department composed of thirty-five professionals advises the parliamentary committee for planning, budget and control. In Mexico, budgetary research and advice capacity has been considerably enhanced by the creation of a Centre for the Study of Public Finances within parliament. Argentina and Guatemala are evaluating the feasibility of establishing such a centre. Moreover, a number of countries have parliamentary research units and libraries, (Brazil, Chile, Colombia, Peru).

Political motivations

The influence of political parties and electoral systems is critical to the understanding of the role of parliaments in the budget process. These define the parameters of the rules of the game for the budget and the political context of the budget relations between the government and parliament. In Latin America the extent of political competition is determined by the political configuration of parliament. This swings between two extremes, neither of which favour effective and responsible parliamentary control: the acquiescence of a parliamentary and government majority or the acute fragmentation of parliamentary representation produced by proportional electoral systems.

When the group in power commands a majority and parliamentary discipline, as in parliamentary systems, or in presidential systems with fused majorities, control may be diluted or neutralised.[15] Thus "when the interests of the legislative majority and the executive branch coincide,

---

14. Interview by the author with Francisco Samper, General Directorate of Budget Analysis of the Nicaraguan National Assembly, Managua, 7 February 2006; Alejandro Hormazabal, Budget Scrutiny Unit of the Chilean Senate, Santiago, 25 January 2005.

15. In this regard it is interesting to note that presidential regimes, such as in France, have a tendency to emphasise parliamentary budget powers in terms of control ex ante through voting on taxes and credits, while parliamentary regimes such as that of Great Britain, tend to emphasise scrutiny ex post by means of enhanced scrutinising bodies, such as public accounts committees. Moreover, external control mechanisms are, equally, attached to Parliament, unlike in France, where there is limited contact between the National Assembly and the General Audit Office.

the majority has little incentive to oversee the executive."[16] As with the presidential nature of political systems, so with the nature of party political systems. In numerous countries in the region political parties do not possess sufficient internal cohesion nor the parliamentary discipline to have an effective influence on the budget. These influences affect the role of the players in the budget process.

A second group of factors affecting budget governance is linked to the methods of 'economic governance' which prevail in the region and which similarly reduce parliamentary budgetary prerogative. Governance by expedient along with frequent recourse to emergency decrees severely damage parliamentary control.[17] Parliaments rarely oversee presidential decrees amending the budget or approving supplementary expenditure over the fiscal year. In Peru for example, of the one hundred and forty emergency decrees issued by the government between January 1994 and March 2001, 27% amended the budget directly and 41% had an impact on public finance.

Finally, the efficacy of parliamentary control depends on the degree of political competition present, and more precisely on the strength and cohesiveness of the parliamentary opposition. In Brazil the proportional system fragments parliamentary representation and reduces still further the impact of the opposition on parliamentary oversight. In Chile, in contrast, the influence of the opposition is due to its cohesion and to a majoritarian electoral system which has favoured the emergence of two strong electoral alliances and a bi-partisan political system more inclined to enforce institutional checks and balances. In Mexico, the emergence in recent years of a strong and cohesive opposition since the political changeover in 2000 has led to a re-engagement in the budget process on the part of parliament. This is demonstrated, for example, by the creation of a parliamentary office for budget analysis and the reform of the audit agency, now placed under parliamentary authority.

Conclusion

Parliaments are the key actors in budgetary democracy. Good financial governance requires that the role of parliaments in budgetary matters

---

16. Messick, Richard (2002). Strengthening Legislatures: Implications from Industrial Countries Washington: World Bank, PREM Note 63, p. 2.

17. Carey, John and Matthew Shugart, eds (1998). Executive Decree Authority Cambridge, Cambridge University Press.

should be not only enhanced, but also reformed. Four conclusions emerge from this brief analysis of the role of parliaments in the budget process.

The first concerns the role itself. Although debates about that role tend to concentrate on parliamentary prerogatives during the approval stages of finance bills, more attention should be paid to their contribution at later stages of the budgetary process, notably the a posteriori scrutiny of budget performance.

The second conclusion is that although parliaments possess a broad range of budgetary powers, they do not exercise them effectively unless the balance of power provides a motivation. The existence of a strong, cohesive and credible parliamentary opposition is a key factor here. As underlined by Thomas Carothers:

> "to build effective legislatures body, mobilising political power is more important than increasing technical skill."[18]

The third conclusion is that parliaments cannot gain strength in isolation. They are part of a much wider system of political control, the effectiveness of which depends on the links between the different components of the system. To engage effectively, it is important to understand the complex interdependence which exists between these institutions.

Finally, the fourth conclusion concerns the delicate balance between enhanced parliamentary oversight and the securing of fiscal discipline. In order to achieve qualitative change in the balance of power between the executive and the legislature over the budget, financial governance needs to be adjusted significantly. As emphasised by Allen Schick:

> "The legislature's new role in budgeting cannot come from government's weakness..... The legislature's role must be defined more in terms of policy, accountability and performance and less in terms of control and restriction."[19]

18. Carothers, Thomas (1999). Aiding Democracy Abroad: the Learning Curve (Washington: Carnegie Endowment for International Peace, p. 181.

19. Schick. (2002). loc. cit., p. 17.

15

The Democratic Control of Natural Resources Management

The Example of the Extractive Industries Transparency Initiative

Jean-Pierre VIDON, Olivier LOUBIÈRE and Michel ROY
(Translated from the French)

The Extractive Industries Transparency Initiative (EITI) was set up in an attempt to remedy the curse of the mismanagement of natural resources, which is often a source of fragility or even of conflict.

The initiative brings together countries, corporations and civil society groups wishing to promote better governance in countries rich in hydrocarbons and mineral resources. This initiative, which sets out to ensure transparency through the application of accounting controls upon revenue streams generated by the exploitation of these resources, is intended to act as a brake upon corruption and help populations benefit from a greater proportion of the revenues. In order to render governments and corporations accountable for their activities, and through this, to give indirect encouragement to an allocation of resources which promotes sustainable economic and social development, the public must have access to information on nation states' revenues from natural resources.

The EITI's approach, which consists of combating corruption through greater transparency, is part of a broader process covering all economic and financial information and its dissemination, by exploiting democratic checks and balances and certain civil society actors. In contrast to the past, transparency within governance in all its forms is now seen as a token that democracy is functioning properly. The search for transparency appears, furthermore, to be a goal shared by all stakeholders, whether they are political, economic or social.

We are certainly taking a first step by strictly applying the initiative. But this will only be of full benefit to the countries concerned if it is brought within the mainstream of governance, and more specifically, public finance management reforms. Indeed, whilst the EITI enables actors to consolidate their abilities so as to gain a better understanding of the context and issues surrounding the exploitation of natural resources, in terms of its overall effect the procedure is currently only concerned with one link of this chain, namely, reconciling the information voluntarily provided by these actors. Specifically, the EITI deals neither with the question of transparency in the issuing of licences and exploitation rights, upstream, nor with the thorny issue downstream regarding the proper use of revenues.

The aim of this article is to present the initiative and some of the issues surrounding it as seen from the perspective of different actors in this fledgling and as yet unconsolidated process. They are represented by Ambassador Jean-Pierre Vidon, who has been tasked in particular with representing France in the fight against corruption, Olivier Loubière in his capacity as ethics advisor to a multinational group and finally Michel Roy, coordinator of the French arm of the NGO coalition movement: "Publish what you pay".

An international initiative aiming to establish a prescriptive supervisory framework
Jean-Pierre Vidon

There have been several international initiatives aimed at supervising the management of natural resources, particularly since the turn of the last century. Various measures – each intended to improve governance and each with starkly differing traits – have been put in place. We now have, for example, the Kimberley process, which established a set of certification rules intended to counter diamond trafficking; the International Tropical Timber Organization, with a similar set of objectives in its own particular field and the EU Action Plan for Forest Law Enforcement, Governance and Trade (FLEGT), which is tasked with combating illegal logging and the international trade associated with it. The Extractive Industries Transparency Initiative was announced by the British Prime Minister at the World Summit for Sustainable Development in 2002. The ground gained by this Initiative since then fully justifies its being held up as an example of international action towards a better allocation, in terms of sustainable development, of revenues from raw materials.

Drawing wide inspiration from civil society, Tony Blair proposed creating via the EITI a mechanism, which would bring together governments, companies, civil society groups and investors on a voluntary basis. Their aim would be to improve governance within countries rich in natural resources by guaranteeing transparency in the revenue flows generated from oil, gas and mining. To achieve this, nation states would be required to publish details of this income, with companies conversely publishing details of payments to nation states. A third-party expert would then have to reconcile and report on this data.

Whilst the Initiative's sights are set purely on the publication of these results, its ambition, in the final analysis, is to render nation states accountable to their citizens for the use of the resources they receive from the extractive industries. It may seem a simple premise, but implementing the EITI is more complex.

It is principally targeted on countries that derive at least 25% of their tax revenue or 25% of their exports from the exploitation of natural resources. The reference list, compiled by the IMF, is made up of 53 countries from Africa, South America and Asia Pacific, although the EITI remains open to other candidates. Out of the 47 countries which, as of 31st March 2007, had shown various degrees of interest in the Initiative, 14 are not included on the list.

The coalition of NGOs behind the "Publish what you pay" campaign, which was intimately involved in the EITI's launch, plays a very active role within the civil societies of those countries concerned by the Initiative. A major actor amongst the French NGOs is Secours Catholique. Companies participating in the Initiative have, on the whole, been set up within OECD countries and include, for example, Areva, Gaz de France and Total.

The prescriptive framework for implementation, which was outlined at the first plenary conference at Lancaster House, London in 2003, became the focus of the International Advisory Group (IAG)'s efforts, after its formation at the 2005 London conference. The IAG's recommendations were approved by the third plenary conference, held in Oslo in 2006.

The Initiative now has a structure to drive its implementation, made up of three forums. The EITI Conference, whose operational frameworks have yet to be clarified, will meet every two years specifically to pronounce opinion on proposals by the Board regarding future directions for the Initiative. Representatives from stakeholders in EITI-endorsing countries and also in donor countries may officially attend the Conference. The Board, whose current make-up was approved for two years by the Oslo Conference, equally mirrors its stakeholder base. Its task is to oversee the Initiative's implementation, as guarantor of its credibility, and to provide strategic direction, development and advancement. The

Board is charged with supervising evaluations and acting as arbitrator in any disputes to which these give rise. It also falls to the Board to take any necessary decisions regarding countries that are not making any progress in implementing the Initiative. The President of the Board directs these tasks, leads consultations in between meetings and ensures that there is cohesion amongst the stakeholders. Peter Eigen, founder of "Transparency International" and former director of the International Advisory Group, is the current holder of this position and represents the Initiative at the highest level. The Secretariat, under the President's authority, manages the Initiative on a day-to-day basis. Initially based at and run by the UK Department for International Development, the Secretariat is now established in Oslo, where it is hosted by the Norwegian authorities but operates on an autonomous basis.

A second important advance in 2006 was the finalising of a key procedure for the EITI: that of validating nation states' implementation of the Initiative. Step one in this process is the appointment of a validator by the national stakeholder group from a list of validators accredited by the Board. The validator refers for support to the country work plan, self-validation forms created by companies operating in the country and the EITI's validation grid – an extremely important tool containing twenty indicators for assessing progress achieved. The indicators are divided into four stages: "sign up", "preparation", "disclosure" and "dissemination". "Candidate status" is granted to countries meeting the requirements for the first stage, which entails fulfilling four indicators. They must: issue an unequivocal public statement of their intention to implement the EITI, commit to work with civil society and companies on EITI implementation, appoint a senior individual to lead nationally on EITI implementation and publish a fully costed work plan.

In April 2007, the Board decided to launch the pre-validation procedure so as to be able to draw up an initial list of "candidate countries". Those countries eligible were informed that they would have to fulfil the four initial indicators in order to remain on the list of EITI-endorsing countries. In October, fifteen[1] of these were recognised as having achieved this status and nine[2] others were given an extension to the end of the year to satisfy the requirements. The EITI International Board then went on to accept seven[3] of these as candidate countries on 22nd February 2008. Candidate

---

1. Azerbaijan, Cameroon, Gabon, Ghana, Guinea, Kazakhstan, Kyrgyzstan, Liberia, Mali, Mauritania, Mongolia, Niger, Nigeria, Peru and Yemen.
2. The Republic of Congo, The Democratic Republic of Congo, Equatorial Guinea, Madagascar, Sao Tome and Principe, Sierra Leone , Chad, Timor-Leste and Trinidad and Tobago.
3. The Republic of Congo, The Democratic Republic of Congo, Equatorial Guinea, Madagascar, Sao Tome and Principe, Sierra Leone and Timor-Leste.

countries have two years to become "compliant countries" by attaining the ultimate goal of publishing and making widely available the EITI report reconciling the data provided by nation states and companies, learning lessons from this report and acting on them accordingly. To date, no country has achieved "compliant country" status, although several countries are at an advanced stage in the procedure. Once a country has achieved this status it may retain it for five years, after which time the country has to undergo validation again.

At present, whilst recognising the achievements that have already been made, we must also try to devise solutions for the challenges facing this young initiative. One such challenge, common to all of the international measures to fight corruption, is ensuring that everybody plays by the same rules. This is why we, and others, are calling on economic operators within emerging countries as well as those countries' authorities to also become involved in the EITI. In order for these efforts to succeed, there will need to be close links between the various initiatives attempting to promote transparency and good governance. Provided that this occurs, the EITI should be able to list itself amongst the international standards in these areas.

Companies' expectations
Olivier Loubière

As a sectoral, voluntary initiative, the EITI is perceived by the multinationals, which have endorsed it as occupying a special place. With its ambitious goals, it unites all the elements of a now classic triptych within globalisation, made up of nation states, companies and civil society. The first initiative of its kind in the field of financial transparency, it covers a key sector, bringing together oil, gas and mineral resources. Their influence upon regional conflicts and the functioning of nation states is known, and a barrel price apparently fixed above $80 for the long term is a constant reminder of their strategic nature.

Whether the EITI is successful or becomes bogged down in the future will determine the emergence of a new paradigm in economic development: financial transparency as a basis for development, as a form of governance within countries aiming for economic lift-off, as a rule of corporate governance and as a key to partnership with NGOs, essential constituents of civil society. The early results, subject to universal scrutiny and of much hope, will be used as an indicator for other economic sectors likely to adopt the EITI's philosophy.

With the EITI has come a boost to the NGOs' traditional role of advocacy/alert in the form of a crucial new function: the long term partnership with other stakeholders, under the close scrutiny of the World Bank. Acting, in practice, as a central mediator for the process, the latter deploys its expertise in strengthening the skills and abilities of countries with natural resources. Those countries usually request this themselves by initiating the process locally.

The multinational business world, for its part, is carefully scrutinizing the EITI's ability to get an on-the-ground fix on three concrete issues, which could be analysed as threats to the process, but also as major opportunities if they can be integrated effectively into the initiative's deployment.

• *Adapting the EITI specifically to mining*

Although the oil and gas sectors have appeared to dominate the process to date, mining industries are due to play a crucial role in global development in the coming years because of the growing scarcity of resources. A huge variability in company sizes within this sector justifies it being handled separately within the EITI's framework.

• *No systematic provision for the phase prior to the acquisition of licences and exploitation rights*

This is the crucial phase where stakeholders set their relationships, a phase which stamps its mark on all that follows. If the decision as to whether or not to include this phase in their local procedure is left to the nation states, without its being taken account of in the awarding of the EITI's seal of approval, there is a risk that this will only be incorporated much later, at the production stage. This may be several years down the line, whereas transparency is required from the very offset. This is the moment at which the die is cast, and when positions are taken – both political and economical – sometimes for decades.

• *The delay in extending the EITI's policy scope to include fast growing developing economies, primarily the four "BRIC" countries*

These countries seem to be keeping themselves at a safe distance from the process at present. However their accelerated growth pattern often goes hand in hand with insufficient domestic extractive resources, with the exception, for a few, of coal. The result is that these are precisely the countries searching the hardest for new external exploratory perimeters to support their current and future development. For all businesses, whether multinational or not, but all the more so if they are, the key strategic problem, the major fear, is the risk of an uneven playing field. Such a risk develops swiftly from any potential flaw in the procedures, whether that is geopolitical in terms of the BRIC countries, a timing issue due to the

non-inclusion of the exploration phase, or technical, bearing in mind the
need for a specific accommodation of the mining trade.

One cannot be unaware of the debate when the initiative first
came into being and which has since been much discussed amongst
NGOs, especially "Publish what you pay", as to whether the EITI
should one day take the form of an obligatory international standard,
or whether hard law should prevail over soft law in the field of ethics
and transparency. However, for multinational companies, which have
set an example by adhering to the Initiative, it might – and with good
reason – appear essential to prevent entire states from sidestepping it.
Public enterprises within these countries, whose cumulative population
represents more than half of humanity, have a business culture and set
of practices which differ hugely from ours. Thus, in prospecting regions
where EITI-endorsing businesses are already operating, they are granted
entire operational zones by local and national authorities without having
to observe transparency procedures.

Fortunately, these challenges to the EITI may also be regarded as
remarkable opportunities for the development of this international
initiative. Whether this turns out to be the case or not depends on the
extent to which the international community joins forces. Hesitation
on the part of certain major players to join the EITI or, conversely, the
reluctance of some of its members to integrate specific stages – notably
those upstream of exploitation – clearly show that this instrument of
governance is indeed a fitting tool and ideal framework for striving
towards the financial transparency for which its instigators have hoped
and prayed. Overcoming this resistance constitutes a critical phase for
the EITI.

All ethical subjects, and transparency falls within this category,
necessarily entail some effort to accommodate slow take-up and local
problems in implementation. This is the common fate of fragile regions
prone to instability, where there is a constant struggle for survival,
independence and access to economic lift-off. Transparency, whilst
being met ever more frequently with political goodwill, occasionally
comes up against other short term interests as well as the distrust of
sceptical populations who, more often than not, have good reason to
be sceptical. As regards ethics: whilst it is imperative that the nation
state set the tone, it is even more crucial that it implements what it has
advocated.

It is therefore essential that delays do not build up on the ground.
Thanks to the unambiguously written reminders issued, as of May 2007,
by its president, the Board took the necessary decisions to re-start the
process where it had seized up. In so doing, they reaffirmed the risk

of official expulsion from the Initiative for those who persist in their delays.

Now that it is equipped with the necessary follow-up structures, with the Secretariat based in Oslo and the strong political support of its members and the G8, the EITI undoubtedly has all the ingredients for success.

A critical and constructive review by civil society
Michel Roy

The creation, in 2003, of the Extractive Industries Transparency Initiative responded to one of the proposals of the "Publish What You Pay" (PWYP) campaign, which was launched the year before by a coalition of British NGOs who had observed that those countries rich in natural resources were also those most often ravaged by violence and poverty. The money brought in by oil, gas and certain minerals stimulates greed in many quarters, on the domestic front just as much as abroad, and the siphoning off of this wealth creates dire circumstances for populations deprived of the development which they should rightfully expect. The promotion of total transparency vis-à-vis the revenue streams generated by these resources will enable citizens and their elected representatives to bring governments to account regarding the destination of this revenue.

As well as having a seat on the Board and participating actively in the Initiative's proceedings on a national level, civil society's role within the EITI also consists in ensuring the best possible results, by taking a critical and constructive look at those already achieved. Its attention has fallen upon nine major issues:

1. If EITI's credibility is to be maintained, it must take into account only those rhetorical commitments which are truly followed up with concrete actions within a meaningful timeframe. Half of the member countries, however, have not fulfilled this requirement. The failure to close the gap between rhetoric and reality fuels the impression that these governments are only paying lip service to the principle of transparency embodied in EITI, whilst pursuing other economical and political objectives. The Initiative's Board has, by dint of the "prevalidation" process, the duty of maintaining and strengthening the Initiative's reputation by acknowledging those countries which have made satisfactory progress and removing the rest from the list of candidate countries.

2. Those charged domestically with driving the EITI process need to be given enough time, powers, political influence and functional longevity to be able to take effective action. Shedding light on financial information, previously shrouded in secrecy, can be a laborious and contentious process. The role of the leaders spearheading the initiative is therefore crucial if the necessary resources for the reforms that EITI implementation requires are to be mobilized by their respective governments.

3. It is also essential that civil society representatives be independent of the authorities, free in their engagement, not subject to harassment or intimidation – as, for example, has been the case in the two Congos – and prepared to participate on an equal footing with the other stakeholders. Governments, which clamp down on civil society activists campaigning for transparency are not only committing a human rights violation but are also rendering meaningless the main objectives, criteria and principles of EITI.

4. Legally enacting the EITI, as Nigeria has done, gives it greater force. In many countries, even in those that have made substantial progress towards implementing the initiative, the future commitment of governments would be less dependent on political change if the Initiative didn't simply fall within a regulatory remit.

5. Disaggregating data which is currently consolidated at the national level, by company and payment (type of revenue), will be another real success for EITI, in the long term. Where extractive industry financial flows have previously been completely hidden from public scrutiny, it is a significant step forward for a government to publish the aggregate comparative figures, but it does not allow citizens and their representatives to know about the individual contributions of companies to the national economy. Likewise, they are unable clearly to identify the source of capital outflows and to take action in this respect. In addition, one effect of this aggregation is that one company's poor performance can tarnish the reputation of all the other companies. Finally, it does not foster public confidence in the process.

The disclosure of disaggregated data is of concern to certain companies, who think that this could be harmful to their commercial competitiveness. However in Nigeria, where the reconciled report published in April 2006 corresponded to this requirement, none of the companies mentioned, such as Shell, Exxon and Chevron reported having suffered any negative commercial fallout.

6. The EITI must be able to become a model for transparency and to inspire other mechanisms with the same objective. At present, company reporting relies on resource-dependent governments taking the lead and only occurs in countries where companies are required to report and even then, maybe only for a limited period.

In recognition of the need for a more systematic and sustained transparency, EITI has recommended that its objectives and strategies be mainstreamed into other mechanisms that affect governments and company financial disclosure. These mechanisms include the International Funding Institutions' (IFI) lending criteria, the Export Credit Guarantee requirements, accounting standards and security rating criteria.

7. The promotion of transparency with regard to contracts should be seen as a crucial step in making revenue flows transparent and accountable. Without the disclosure of investment contracts between foreign corporations and host governments, citizens have no means either of knowing what their country's natural resources are being sold for, or of judging whether payments made match the terms of the contracts.

Governments and business often assert that disclosing the contents of contracts will undermine commercial and competitive advantages, but the IMF's Guide on Resource Revenue Transparency notes that: "In practice, however, the contract terms are likely to be widely known within the industry soon after signing. Little by way of strategic advantage thus seems to be lost through publication of contracts."

8. In many countries dependent on natural resources, some proportion of revenues collected at the federal level are then transferred to regional and local authorities. According to a report in 2006 on this aspect of EITI's implementation, seventeen out of fifty-six natural resource-endowed countries have a mechanism governing these transfers.

In some of these countries, companies make direct payments to sub-national entities in accordance with procedures, which the report claims generate, in certain cases, corruption, poverty and conflict. This is the case when such transfers are administered by recipients of patronage or when sub-national authorities have no legally-binding financial reporting requirements.

9. As well as revenue transparency, it appears crucial to encourage and help EITI-endorsing governments in establishing mechanisms that promote transparent and accountable expenditure management.

In several EITI-endorsing countries, such as Azerbaijan, Chad, Timor-Leste, Mauritania and Sao Tome and Principe, there has been more focus on expenditure management, primarily through the creation of oil funds and sometimes through a legal framework to manage them. Such mechanisms are indispensable, even if insufficient in themselves, to ensure the responsible management of oil revenues.

Four years after the launch of EITI, much progress has been made. Several governments have produced, audited and reconciled reports and some have established the institutions necessary for its implementation. The EITI's International Advisory Group, then the Board which succeeded it in 2006 and the Secretariat have worked relentlessly to develop guidelines, criteria and governance structures essential to the Initiative. Many oil, gas and mining companies have offered rhetorical and sometimes practical support to the process. The PWYP coalition has established local civil society coalitions in endorsing countries to support national efforts to implement EITI. This will require a renewed and intensified commitment on the part of all stakeholders. The policies and changes currently in development can help end the "curse" of extractive sector revenues and transform them into a source of development and prosperity for all citizens of resource-rich countries around the world.

Bibliography

Eigen, P. (2007), "Fighting Corruption in a Global Economy Transparency Initiatives in the Oil and Gas Industry", Houston Journal of International Law, University of Houston Law Center, Vol. 29, Issue.2, p. 327-354.

EXTRACTIVE INDUSTRIES TRANSPARENCY INITIATIVE, http://www.eitransparency.org/

IV

GOVERNANCE AND TERRITORIES

16

Towards a System of Governance Serving the Poorest[1]: The role of local governance

Carlos LOPES
(Translated from the French)

Governance has been revealed as the fundamental challenge by the recent and profound change in the local-global relationship. In fact, globalisation – which demands more flexibility and efficiency in the delivery of services at the local level – linked to an increased demand by citizens for a decision making process that is closer to their concerns, has resulted in a new phenomenon often referred to as "glocalisation". The intersection of local and global levels at the heart of "territories" has increased the importance of these echelons as connection points for the distinct interests and the power struggles between political, economic and social actors resulting from multiple levels. New spaces for the analysis of needs, participation and policy formulation – in summary, the building of a totally new type of governance – are now appearing in the limelight: with local administrations, public bodies and different sectors of civil society representing the main actors.

A series of recent phenomena, which has not escaped the notice of development actors, has made the process of governance take on vital importance. Demographic growth has radically changed the world within that, mainly urban one, of homo urbanus; 2008 marks the rupture between the world population's rural past and its resolutely urban future. Whilst

1. My thanks to my colleagues – Philippe Athanassiou, Léontine Kanziemo and Berta Pesti – for their research work and their contribution to the content of this article. I must also thank Charlotte Diez, in particular, for her help with finishing this text. Without her support it would not have been possible to meet the editors' deadlines.

urban growth has considerable potential for the reduction of poverty through the economies of scale that it generates, it also represents a challenge to sustainable and socially equitable development that can only be overcome through "good governance" – which promotes the involvement of all sectors, and in particular that of the poor[2]. At the same time, the erosion of central authority to the benefit of multiple local actors, has allowed the emergence of new forms of leadership, types of collective action and networks. This state of affairs has resulted in an overturning of the methods of access to and sharing of information and know-how which, under the impact of new technologies, now requires totally new knowledge.

Developing countries, and their partners, which have at their disposal a young, highly urbanised population, thirsty for democratic participation and new technologies, and having for the most part reformed their governmental structures towards greater decentralisation, have seen the reduction of the great economic and social gaps boosted within these changes. Whilst the preceding period had put the emphasis on economic reforms, the decade of the 90s saw the appearance of "good governance" as the keyword of a controlled, sustainable economic growth whose results would be equitably shared. Within this context "glocalisation" arises as an opportunity for the acceleration of poverty reduction. The latter is embodied in the Millennium Development Goals (MDG), which now form the road map for all national poverty reduction policies. It is based not only on indispensable economic growth accompanied by development of infrastructures and basic services to the population, but equally on a number of institutions, mechanisms and linking processes and various interests and accountability more commonly grouped together under the name "governance". Some recognise that today, the challenge of development lies not only in the level of available financial resources or technology transfer but even more in the State's level of efficiency and on governance, especially governance at the heart of the "territories" or local governance.

The importance of local governance

It is more and more often at the local level that sustainable solutions to fight inequalities can be found. If it is generally accepted that decentralisation of power at a local level facilitates the implementation of the

---

2. United Nations Population Fund (2007). "Unleashing the Potential of Urban Growth" State of the World's Population p. 67-76.

Millennium Development Goals (MDG) by bringing public authorities closer to those they administer and their preferences, it is also true that as national policy commitments the Goals give citizens the opportunity to make their governors accountable for their actions. Indeed, the achievement of most of the MDGs is linked to efficiency in the provision of basic community facilities at the local level, and it is essentially at the local level that citizens are able to challenge and put pressure on their decision-makers. This is particularly true for the poorest populations[3]. In this sense, the adoption of the MDGs as a global strategy has only underlined the importance of local governance.

Local capacities at the intersection between governance and the fight against poverty.

However, if decentralisation was at one time considered a panacea, it seems that today it is no longer seen as the only means of reducing poverty in a significant way. Studies which try to make the link between decentralisation and poverty reduction show contrasting results in this respect. Beyond administrative, political or fiscal decentralisation, it is exactly this "enabling environment" or "good governance" at the local level which makes the difference: the ability to organise citizen participation in strategic decision making and the monitoring of the implementation of public policies; to build and lead partnerships between actors from different sectors (public, private, civil society) and backgrounds at a local, national and global level; or even the ability to manage the flows of information and knowledge from the global towards the local, from the grassroots towards local and national government, and funders; and, finally to ensure that policies are directed towards the poorest.

That is why we once again find the issue of local capacity at the centre of the debate linking governance to poverty reduction. For new decentralised ways of management in a "glocal" world, there are matching new types of leadership, of types of collective interest regroupings, of multi-actor partnerships, of management of differences, of mobilisation of resources or knowledge sharing. But equally, the totally new processes of appropriation of change and knowledge. New information and communication technologies from now on facilitate exchanges through networks but, at the same time, this turnaround causes a great need for capacities which allow individuals and institutions to absorb and manage the change

---

3. Human Development Report (2003). "Mobilizing grass roots support for the Goals", chapter 7 of, Millennium Development Goals: A Compact Among Nations To End Human Poverty, p. 134-137.

themselves[4]. We are witnessing a knowledge transfer which is no longer vertical and hardware related – of the technology transfer type – but horizontal, through networks, often thematic, which allow a crossing of cultural barriers, the global-local dichotomies, central-peripheral or those between the spheres of government and collective action. Local, city and regional networks are significant examples from this viewpoint. Their enormous growth in recent years only highlighted the need to continually appropriate world or local knowledge in order to reinvent it and adapt it to one's own context.

Indeed, governance and capacity building interact so closely that, as we showed earlier in Ownership, Leadership and Transformation, they are but one and the same structuring factor:

> "The third level of capacity is that of a society as a whole, and especially of a country and its governance. A society brings together all segments of the population through numerous groups and networks. It provides an ethos that largely determines the value system within which move people and the economy function"[5].

Beyond the given financial resources and the administrative or technological conditions, it is very much the ability to listen and dialogue between multiple sectors on the one hand, and the processes which allow the reaching of the participative definition of goals with transparent monitoring of the results, passing through strategic planning, on the other hand, which are at the heart of the debate. These different provisions - associated with leadership, which allows the maintenance or transformation of the values of a given society – are the key aptitudes attributed by numerous researchers to any individual capable of "moulding his own destiny" through the ability he has to manage his environment[6]. Incidentally, these correspond almost exactly to the list established by the United Nations Development Programme (UNDP) as constituting the necessary base which would allow a country, its institutions and its actors to achieve the MDG[7]. In summary, whoever is equipped to manage change and the process of development according to the rules of "good governance" would be capable of coping with poverty and anticipating the great societal phenomena, such as urban demographic growth and its share of political choices which are crucial for the future of the planet.

---

4. Carlos Lopes and Thomas Theisohn (2003). Ownership, Leadership and Transformation: Can we do better for Capacity Development?, London, Earthscan, p. 26.
5. Ibid., p. 24.
6. Ibid., p. 26.
7. Ibid., p. 26.

The construction of new forms of governance at the local level

If the involvement of a multitude of actors in public decision making and networking have become key words, then it must follow that the ability of different development actors who interact at the local level to work together – communities, civil society, private companies, local government, national and devolved governments, international donors – must be strengthened in order to contribute in a more significant manner to poverty reduction. Whatever forms of association or networks are given priority by the different development models based on capacity building – financial institutions/International Organisations/local governments/ companies; national governments/local communities/NGO; International Organisations/universities/North-South city networks, etc.[8] –, the building of new types of governance at the local level requires that a series of parameters are taken into account.

• *Training local managers*
First of all, responding to the needs that arise from decentralisation demands competent and efficient local authorities to plan and manage infrastructure policies and the improvement of basic community service provision on the one hand and, on the other hand to ensure the exercising of the rights and responsibilities of all. The processes of decentralisation take on different characteristics in different regions of the world and local political cultures. Africa, Latin America or Asia are characterised in this regard by different modes of decentralised urban government, whose construction requires totally new knowledge and forms of association. Think for example of the different methods that exist for the administration of a territory and delivery of essential services to the population there – whether these assume the support of central administrative levels, cooperation between municipalities or types of public-private partnerships – and in a general way, of the need to formulate a vision of development that is capable of directing the actions of all the actors whilst at the same time putting itself at the service of the poorest. It is undeniable that the new powers, duties and functions of local governments and cities should have put these protagonists in the position of essential actors for local development in the eyes of international institutions and funders. However, not everywhere has the recognition of these actors been enough to create the conditions for their political and financial autonomy. Very often, the administrative and legislative framework in place, or the lack of specific knowledge, deprives the local political officers of the ability to master

---

8. See the case studies in Carlos Lopes and Thomas Theisohn (2003), *Ownership, Leadership and Transformation: Can we do better for capacity development?*

work and negotiation with funders. Training local managers is therefore a necessary condition for efficient government of territories.

• *Setting up networks and alliances between development actors*

Secondly, the reduction of poverty through the setting up of solid alliances between different development actors – whether they be governmental, from civil society, private companies or development cooperation partners. Leading the actors from these different spheres to act together in order to improve the lives of poor populations and to be accountable represents a complex challenge. Cultures of shared collaboration and collective ownership of local development plans form an important barrier to counter, the potential hostage taking of the benefits of decentralisation by dominant categories or individual interests.

• *Knowledge sharing*

Additionally, in a world where knowledge management seems vital across all sectors for the optimisation of technical, human and financial investments, it is crucial to establish viable mechanisms for learning and the transfer of local knowledge to the national and global level for the replication of good practices and, inversely for solutions developed by global and national networks to be brought to local actors for adaptation to their respective contexts. New methods of "horizontal" knowledge sharing, from community to local government, from Non Governmental Organisations to businesses, from universities to public administrations, etc., and "vertical" between actors at the micro and macro levels (national governments, donors, financial institutions), must replace the classical methods of knowledge transfer in order to adapt to the different ways of networking[9]. National and regional associations of local governments or training institutes for elected officials and local actors can, in this regard be good anchor points for the facilitation of knowledge sharing[10].

• *The role of development partners*

Finally, development cooperation partners, including United Nations Agencies and Programmes, must be led to play a catalytic role in the establishment of institutional schemes which promote the capacity building processes, the setting up of a multi-actor partnership culture and the systematic knowledge sharing mentioned above[11].

---

9. Ibid., p. 97-98.

10. UNDP (2004) Decentralised Governance for Development: A combined practice Note on Decentralisation, Local Governance and Urban/Rural Development, Practice Note, p. 11.

11. Carlos Lopes et Thomas Theisohn (2003), Ownership, Leadership and Transformation: Can we do better for capacity development?, London, Earthscan, p. 97-98.

Seen from this angle, governance appears therefore, finally to be like a network of development actors. It sees itself as a sharing of the local knowledge and technical expertise of each partner, but leaves each one an important share of autonomy in his strategic choices.

Strengthening local capacity for better governance: case studies

Several initiatives could be quoted as examples that illustrate an approach to development based on the progress of governance at the local level. In recent years, the United Nations Institute for Training and Research (UNITAR) has notably invested its efforts in the setting up of appropriate institutional frameworks and capacity building in developing world territorial authorities to implement the MDG. Four examples reflect the complementary processes at work in the building of new forms of governance at the local level: the setting up of an institutional framework which incentivises the intergovernmental level for access to essential services, strengthening local governments' capacity for the management of urban services at grass roots, putting development actors into a durable network through decentralised cooperation, horizontal knowledge sharing and finally, the definition of territorial frameworks of agreed development ensuring the ownership of policies at the local level.

The setting up of an institutional framework at intergovernmental level for access to basic services: the "Access to basic services for all" initiative

The "Access to basic services for all" initiative started by UNITAR, in collaboration with the United Nations Human Settlements Programme (UN-HABITAT), with the support of France and other States, particularly of the South, aimed to influence local, national and international decision makers to adopt policies in favour of the poorest. By setting up an incentivising institutional framework, it encourages partnerships between the different actors of local development and a joint approach for the provision of basic services. The initiative culminated in two resolutions which open the way for a future international Declaration on access to essential services for all.

With this in mind, it was recommended that directive principles be conceived recognising transparency in decision making and governance as the cornerstones of successful local development[12]. To date, UNITAR and UN-HABITAT have, on the basis of a consultative process with the key actors in basic service provision, drafted the first version of these directive principles[13]. This body of principles emphasizes citizen participation in the decision making process, the implementation of mutually advantageous partnerships, the recognition of the rights and responsibilities of the various local development actors as well as the adoption of policies in favour of the poorest. The document essentially aims to promote a true strategy of sustainable and equitable development which would allow the reconciliation of the aspirations of the State, local authorities, civil society, public and private operators, as well as the resources at their disposal to start up a forward looking project and work rationally for its achievement.

The joint initiative also aims to encourage good practice in terms of access to basic services and to exploit the institutional solutions which have already been proven, thus offering a reference framework for the facilitation of decision making where some choices are not compatible. Local and national decision makers should therefore have at their disposal a tool to help with decision making which would allow them to better understand the specific needs of the poorest but which also encourages them to adopt policies that favour the poorest whilst at the same time involving them in the decision making process.

More transparent and efficient decision making, on the delivery of basic services associated with a regulatory framework which increases predictability, will have a clear impact on investments and, as a consequence, the quality and coverage of services. Certainly, the existence of a reference point, guaranteed by an intergovernmental consultation process within the framework of the United Nations, is able to promote public and private investments for the benefit of territories and populations which are likely to generate relatively little profit. Nevertheless, it is equally important to support local governments in such a way that they may master, in practice, the rules of the game, in particular those of contractualisation. The training network for local actors put in place by UNITAR since 2002 completes this institutional approach adopted under the framework of the "Access to basic services for all" initiative.

---

12. Resolution 21/4 (April 2007) of the Administrative Council of UN-HABITAT.
13. It is anticipated that the final version will be presented at the UN-HABITAT Administrative Council (meeting) in April 2009.

Capacity building of local governments for the management of grass roots urban services: international training centres for local actors

The international training Centre for local actors (CIFAL)[14] in Ouagadougou, with the active participation of the municipality, and the support of French decentralised cooperation through Lyon Urban Community, has notably allowed the management of efficient institutional schemes to spread out which promote access to drinking water and sanitation in several municipalities in western and central Africa[15].

In recent times, decentralisation has led local African governments to become more and more involved in the management of basic public services, particularly in water and sanitation services, thus creating demand for new technical knowledge. In a context where resources are limited, the challenge for local government lies in finding adequate methods and institutional mechanisms to ensure access by all to quality public services. Some try to respond by having recourse to formalised agreements with different operators – in the form of contracts – with a view to improving the provision and management of public utility services. UNITAR linked its support project to respond to two good governance challenges in the sector: capacity building for management of the contractual process and the introduction of a dialogue and partnership policy between the actors involved in the provision of drinking water and sanitation services.

The training programme organised by the Ouagadougou CIFAL aims to contribute to the implementation of a local policy for access to drinking water and sanitation services which is not only controlled and transparent but also adapted to local needs. It allows municipal officers in charge of urban services to acquire a better understanding of the phases of contractualisation (assessing the situation, mobilising the stakeholders, drafting and negotiation, then monitoring and evaluation of the contracts), as well as of the potential and limitations of contractualisation within their own context (success factors, interests and risks for the municipality). The approach does not aim to transpose contractual models but to promote ownership of the process by local authorities. Armed with these decision making tools, local governments who are considering, or have already chosen, the contractualisation option are therefore in a position to choose the contrac-

---

14. The International Training Centres for Local Authorities (CIFAL) are platforms for capacity building and sharing of experiences between local and regional authorities, international organisms, the private sector and civil society. These Centres, linked to UNITAR, have the essential aim of improved public services at local level. The CIFAL network has twelve Centres throughout the world, and covers all continents.

15. Benin, Burkina Faso, Mali, the Democratic Republic of Congo.

tual form which suits their contexts. They will also be in a position to clearly define the role and responsibilities of the stakeholders, to monitor the fulfilment of the contractual commitments, to foresee the limitations and the risks of the contract in order to reduce their impact. Controlled thus, contractualisation can be more efficient and contribute to the improvement of access for all to drinking water and sanitation at the local level.

In addition, the initiative, by inviting representatives of the various stakeholders – local authorities, citizen-user associations, public and private operators – to the dialogue has allowed the structuring and strengthening of partnerships and collaboration between those who, on a daily basis, must find agreement to make citizens' demands result favourably in access to better quality and socially equitable essential services. Since relationships between these actors are more often than not conflictual, it was a case of bringing out agreement frameworks and mechanisms for the coordination of action. Based on their experiences, representatives of the three sectors within each territorial authority were able to assess their positions, the limitations and the constraints for each in the contractualisation. The learning and sharing between peers from different local and national contexts has, in return, aided dialogue and resulted in a strengthening of the agreement frameworks between the main actors of the water sector within the local authorities concerned.

Sustainable networking of development actors through decentralised cooperation and horizontal knowledge sharing

Beyond time-limited training programmes, it is important to note that the sustainable networking of development actors on a global and regional level contributes to strengthening ownership and adaptation of knowledge based on local experience. In this way, cooperation established between UNITAR and CITYNET, a network of territorial governments which works on sustainable urban development within the Asia-Pacific region, is exemplary in its approach to reinforcing the capacity of local actors and local democracy through decentralised cooperation.

Since 2002, UNITAR and CITYNET have been collaborating to build the capacities of territorial governments in Asia and the Pacific to plan and manage basic urban services (drinking water, sanitation, transport, town planning). Regular assessments, every three years, carried out by CITYNET on its members – more than one hundred, grouping together the largest cities – allow for the identification of the training and technical cooperation needs of the latter in order to serve them better. For each training workshop, the identification of the participants and the speakers is the subject of a selection process which aims to ensure knowledge sharing between authorities who want to learn and those which have something to share in the area of expertise being considered. Based on case studies submitted by the candidates and information available to CITYNET about the needs of its members, a balanced list of participants is proposed. Selection is made based on a set of criteria, of which the most important are in the achievement of an urban project considered exemplary and of particular interest to other cities, or even on the planning of a project linked to the workshop theme and which needs the expertise of another city in the region.

The selection of the participating towns, in accordance with the criteria mentioned above, allows the preliminary matching of mentor towns and beneficiary towns, facilitating as a consequence the development of decentralised partnerships. As a follow-up to the training workshops, decentralised cooperation projects are facilitated by UNITAR and CITYNET. These projects aim to build on the expertise exchanges started during the workshops and to provide a concrete framework for the monitoring of the training activities. The two protagonists in these projects are the city which has the skills and can demonstrate good practice in a specific field (mentor city) and the city requesting support from its peers (beneficiary city). The mentor city commits to support the beneficiary city in the setting up of a project within a specific field of expertise (sanitation, drinking water, transport, town planning) with the support of the highest political officials (mayor, governor). The beneficiary cities can, in turn, become mentor cities, once the projects have been implemented and experience in the subject has been acquired through decentralised cooperation.

Several elements contribute to the originality of these projects. On the one hand, good practice and experts are identified at the workshops by the cities themselves, thus ensuring strong ownership of the projects by the interested parties and considerable political support. In addition, the projects are generally based on the expertise of cities of the South with similar socio-economic, cultural and climatic contexts. This aids in the duplication of good practices. Finally, the projects are implemented through collaboration between local governments (the cities), and also between local communities. Government participation ensures significant political support, without which the implementation of the project would be compromised, whilst the communities aid involvement by the inhabitants. In addition projects which succeed at the level of local communities are easier to reproduce with the approval of political decision makers. The originality of training provided by CIFAL in Kuala Lumpur has not gone unnoticed by the territorial elected members and civil servants from the most dynamic authorities in the region – the big cities of Mumbai and Manila, for example – which recognise that they no longer need look West to face up to the challenges of urbanisation, since their Asian partners are capable of supporting them efficiently.

This mentoring scheme would not have been possible without CITYNET's active participation. Which is why it is crucial to consider the strengthening of regional networks of territorial governments within development cooperation strategies aiming for better governance. Once consolidated in support networks, these can, by themselves, ensure a peer monitoring mechanism which is self-sufficient, so that external initiative, which catalyses horizontal South-South cooperation, does not become essential in the long term.

The defining of agreed territorial development frameworks ensures ownership of policies at the local level

The final example concerns the case of an initiative which involved just one municipality, Port Gentil in Gabon, but which reached a level of implementation which allowed its replication in other municipalities in the country. This initiative was made possible by UNITAR and received the support of several partners.

Within the context of urbanisation and the decentralisation of Gabon's administration, the local authorities have a vital role to play alongside the State, development partners and the private sector for the implementation at local level of the MDG. In support of the achievement of these goals a project entitled "Multi Partnership Initiative for the development of Port Gentil" was brought to fruition during 2005 and culminated in the establishment of a local economic development Framework for the city of Port Gentil. The local economic development Framework (LDEF) was formulated on the basis of two parallel and complementary approaches, combining a study of the local economic profile and the results of the participatory process of local agreement. This exercise has allowed the start-up of strategic directions and the identification of realistic, specific actions, adapted to the Gabonian context and to the current economic and social climate, taking into account human and financial resources which are available or can be mobilised locally.

Three major concerns, linked to the building of better governance at the local level, guided the design process for the LDEF: capacity building, participation by all the local actors in the territorial projects, the creation of partnerships between the groupings of actors present in the field.

However advanced the level of decentralisation or the financial means available to it, the territorial body cannot guarantee its mission if the human resources are insufficient. Local development must be based on a municipal team which is capable of running and encouraging the participatory process of ownership and transformation of the territory. In addition, the initiative gave the municipality of Port Gentil a methodology and territorial planning toolkit – equipment and software for geographic information systems (GIS) – which allows it to define a strategic vision for its future development, to conceive the local development plan and to coordinate its implementation. In addition, the participatory approach allowed for the involvement of different groups of actors in all the stages of the project – from formulation to implementation, and including planning – ensuring, through this, the durable and reproducible nature of the approach. The involvement of the national authorities notably facilitated the linking of the local development axes identified as priorities in Gabon's national development framework. The multi actor process encouraged the protagonists to make compatible the approaches, the logic and the interests which are sometimes divergent, if not in competition, for the benefit of a joint development project[16]. So, the coordination mechanism set up for the design of the LDEF also prompted the international funders to register their actions within the framework of goals defined in a participatory manner, which in turn, contributed to strengthening the legitimacy of the local governance process at work in the territory.

Finally, from these brief case studies it emerges that governance rests on a certain number of characteristics which are strongly correlated and build on one another. The legal and institutional framework, participation, transparency, information and knowledge sharing, multi partnership approach, consensus seeking, accountability, a strategic development vision, efficiency, which best respond to needs by optimising the allocation of resources, are the bases. So, a stable institutional framework, for example, enhances the confidence factor between partners and favours the design of a consensus. Information sharing and knowledge transfer mean more transparency and efficiency in decision making. In return, enhanced legitimacy in the government system encourages greater participation. Local leaders who opt for a long term development vision can gain legitimacy, with central authorities or funders, which in turn, guarantees them more resources for the implementation of their territorial policies. In summary, each society builds it own vision of "good governance" in accordance with the relative importance attributed to certain factors and on the basis of the best balance between the State, the market and civil society within a given context. The challenge is to start and maintain this virtuous circle as well as this balance between the three sectors, so that it may underlie the development of all to the best of their abilities, and in

---

16. Certain actions written into the LDEF are being carried out: municipal support cell for territorial planning with information technology tools (databases and GIS); opening up of the Port Gentil area; structuring of the river and lake transport in the Ogooue and Fernan Vaz basin.

17

The Role of Decentralisation
in the Governance of African States

Jean-Pierre ELONG MBASSI
(Translated from the French)

In the face of what must be called the governability crisis of contemporary societies, the issue of governance has become unavoidable. This governability crisis is felt everywhere as a crisis of trust of populations in their public institutions. This crisis is worldwide and shows the gap between their needs and the abilities of public authorities to meet them which is increasingly felt by populations. All States are questioned in their relationship with their citizens and their ability to master their integration in the globalised economy. All States are experiencing the difficulty of being close enough to their populations to meet their needs, and distanced enough from the local or even national contexts, to be up to the challenges of the world. The role of the State is questioned in its capacity to take into account the diversity of local situations, and to ensure it listens closely and meets the needs of the different categories in local populations. But it is equally questioned in its ability to bring credible responses to the uncertainties brought about by the integration of national economies into the globalised economy. The State is therefore attacked on two fronts: a demand for grass roots democracy, which puts the need for decentralisation on the agenda; a demand for cooperation between neighbouring countries to lower the constraints that the globalised economy puts on each of them individually, leading to the need for integration in supranational regional groups. This dynamic is at work throughout the world, and Africa is not exempt from it.

Practically all States in a situation of civilian peace have begun reforms of State organisation and public life, by adopting decentralisation policies. The majority of these States have held local elections, which have seen the emergence of local authorities as the new figures of public authority alongside national authorities. In nearly all States in the region, this splitting of the public corporation poses problems, since the majority of national authorities have not yet integrated this major institutional change into their behaviour. Whilst they only represent a small proportion of the inhabitants of the continent, the importance of the local authorities is constantly confirmed in the lives of African populations.

In terms of numbers the situation of local authorities is presented thus in Africa:

Regions	Population	Urbanisation rate	Towns
	(millions)	%	(number)
North Africa	154	62	4,200
West Africa	264	40	3,000
Central Africa	98	47	1,000
East Africa	245	31	1,900
Southern Africa	148	36	1,300
All Africa	909	38	11,400

Source : PDM (2006).

Despite real and sometimes persistent resistance, decentralisation advances in the region, and one can expect even more significant progress with the increase in local authorities and their capacity building. But the paths of decentralisation policies are not identical: policy content is strongly influenced by historic contexts which gave birth to them and by the administrative tradition inherited from the colonial period. The organisation of the authorities and the administration of the new African States have been largely inspired by the colonial legacy which has had a significant impact on both the conception and the management of decentralisation policies of these States. States have been made in a likeness of the colonial State, and there have been attempts to correct them little by little. This mimicry was pursued after the democratisation movement of the 1990s. Many African States had embarked on the dynamic of democratisation, what was then called "the East winds", and many were thrown into confusion and were unable to adapt at the necessary speed. Very often this adaptation was experienced as a strong demand from development partners. One could even say that decentralisation was a condition for receiving support from the international community. Faced with this situation, African States naturally tended to turn to their past colonisers, whose supposedly democratic States acted as a reference point for the adaptation of their institutions to the new international deal.

Nevertheless, we must not exaggerate the impact of these configurations and these relationships. The recent dynamic toward regional integrations contributes a lot to offsetting the influence of colonisation. The fact that the Organization of African Unity (OAU), which was succeeded by the African Union (AU), chose to move towards sub-regional groupings based on geography rather than language, has contributed a great deal to reducing the colonial legacy in the structuring of affiliations of African States. Since then there is more closeness between Anglophone Nigeria and Francophone Ivory Coast, both members of ECOWAS, than between Nigeria which belongs to ECOWAS and Kenya, also Anglophone but which belongs to a different sub-regional group, the East African Community. For its part, the New Partnership for Africa's Development (NEPAD), by giving a truly African perspective on development of the continent's States is another way of reducing the impact of the colonial heritage. Elsewhere, the regional integration dynamic has put on the agenda the need for a grouping of the different States on a continental level at the heart of specialised technical committees of the African Union. Ministers in charge of local authorities have therefore joined forces in the All Africa Ministerial Conference of Decentralization and Local Development (AMCOD), which has become the specialised technical committee of the African Union on the subject of decentralisation, through the decision made at the Heads of State Summit in Addis Ababa in January 2007. Along these lines, since May 2005, African local authorities joined together in the United Cities and Local Governments of Africa organization, which aims to be the High Council for local authorities at the African Union. These continental groupings go beyond the linguistic barriers inherited from colonialisation; they work towards the harmonisation of administrative practices and the building of a truly African intelligence on the challenges of decentralisation. In other words, more and more development and governance issues are dealt with in the African framework, and references to the colonial heritage are tending to lose importance, even though their continued influence on the way different States tackle and implement decentralisation policies cannot be denied.

In general terms, decentralisation is defined as the recognition of a certain degree of responsibility for the management of matters at levels of governance other than the national one. Applied to the management of a country, decentralisation corresponds to the recognition of a certain level of responsibility by local authorities for the management of their affairs. This responsibility can take the form of the transfer of certain remits previously carried out by the central State (delegation) or can be translated as the granting of general jurisdiction to the territorial community (devolution), with the exclusion of a limited number of areas (foreign affairs, public security, macro-economic management). Observers agree that Francophone countries have mostly opted for a delegation of the powers of the central State to decentralised levels, which is formally translated as a significant number of legal and statutory texts (relating to practically every area of sectoral policy in addition to general administration). Anglophone countries, for their part, have above all resorted to the approval of omnicompetence at the decentralised levels, which is translated as an approval of and organisation of local authorities as an autonomous sphere of government, either within the constitution, or in a limited number of legal texts. In its implementation, and whatever the context, decentralisation is tackled either as an administrative technique (bringing the State closer to those administered), or as a power sharing system between the State and its divisions.

There is controversy about the scope to be given to the sphere of intervention in decentralisation policies. For the school of thought influenced by French administrative culture, decentralisation is essentially linked to the public institutional sphere. In this sense, the implementation of decentralisation policies is conceived above all as the introduction of legal frameworks for decentralisation, the organisation of local elections, and the introduction of local authorities and devolved supervising institutions, tasked particularly with the guidance of public local authorities in the execution of their mandate. This is the most common idea in Francophone countries in Africa, where decentralisation often goes hand in hand with devolution of the State. On the other hand, in the Anglo-Saxon idea, decentralisation is seen as a gradual process of power transfer to the populations, which moves from devolution to privatisation, through the delegation and devolution of powers. Seen in this way decentralisation policies do not just involve the public sphere; they can go beyond public local authorities and involve all local actors, including grassroots organisations and associations, NGOs, private sector participants, in short non-state actors. It is this idea which is dominant in the Anglo-Saxon world and which widely pervades the concept of decentralisation policies of Anglophone countries of Africa.

Even in countries where the process is relatively old, decentralisation remains mainly administrative. Political decentralisation has not yet truly become reality (except in South Africa), despite demand and strong social pressure, and certain benevolence by governments, who see the potential for market growth and therefore political clientele. But one feels strongly that the political challenge is becoming more present, as lively debate on laws organising local elections show: the argument pits those who are for the independence of candidatures against those who wish to limit the presentation of candidatures at local elections to political parties only. The challenge of this debate is neither more nor less than the exclusion of national political society from local affairs, for the sake of building a local political society. It is therefore about the building of a transfer of power or, if you like, the opening up of the political class. How this debate will end is uncertain in both Anglophone and Francophone countries. Some countries have opted for independent candidatures (for example Benin, Cape Verde, Ivory Coast, Ghana, Guinea, Mauritania); others have chosen a party list system (for example South Africa, Cameroon, Mali, Senegal); elsewhere the debate is still open. Nevertheless it remains that the political debate on decentralisation puts the issue of relationships between public institutions and African civil societies at centre stage. The organisation of this debate is one of the challenges of the building of a negotiated State of law in Africa. It is here that one can say that decentralisation plays a role in the reform effort of African States.

State institutionalisation on the scale of each country has not involved a transcendent dynamic and a joint framework, which wins the support of all. Many believe that the troubles the continent is experiencing are mainly due to its States. During the first two decades of independence, African States were above all centralizing. The first and natural concern was building the Nation. For this reason, the particularisms, be they regional or local were considered obstacles in the building of the Nation. Very often the dynamic itself of the countries led to focussing of effort on the central State. The political parties united around a single state party; Nation building is the only aim pursued. The problem is that at the same time, States do not manage to keep the promise of access to modernisation for all. The truth is that they could not keep this promise. And, after about a decade, the people realised that the State was not sufficiently powerful and organised to meet the needs of all. It was concerned above all with its own survival in the world of States; for that, it needs to give itself the attributes of a State. So essential resources were concentrated on what could give the State attributes, namely the building and modernisation of the capital, the setting up of infrastructures and major facilities. So little by little state's marginal areas, the most remote regions, were abandoned to the point that these regions questioned their membership as post-colonial States. From that moment on, it was the very foundations of the African State that were the subject of questions. In less than half a century of existence, it runs out of breath, weakens, is moribund, and even disappears. As Antoine Sawadogo rightly says,

> "The State remains stuck in the centralised management of the "sinecures" and does not give rise to any support for transcendent standards of general interest. Whilst monopolising the use of legitimate violence, it does not manage to control all the national territory"[1].

---

1. Raogo Antoine Sawadogo (2001), The African State in the Face of Decentralization. Paris, Karthala.

With the adoption and the implementation of structural adjustment policies over some twenty years, the majority of African States have experienced a "partial abdication of their sovereignty with regards to political decisions between the World Bank and the International Monetary Fund"[2], which has contributed to undermining the political legitimacy which the elites of the State had managed to amass at independence. Towards the end of the 1970s and at the beginning of the 1980s, rebellions or questioning of the State emerged almost everywhere and social pressure for the State to give more scope for action at the infra-state levels and civil society becomes stronger and stronger. The search for true decentralisation of powers in African States dates from this period.

In such a context, many could have thought that decentralisation carried risks of dissipation and fragmentation of the State. It freed centrifugal forces, which could feed and amplify regional or even secessionist instincts. The weakening of the State in the field is surely not a good thing, in the face of the swarming of local players and the challenges of decentralisation and it is regrettable that some of its functions should today be carried out by organizations (NGOs and other clientelist networks) who are not answerable to any other body than those they set up for themselves. In this jumble of players, involved in various capacities in local governance, there is a risk that the building of a State of law may not always be the concern, and that numerous groups organise themselves from endogenous practices at the margins of the State. It is rather implausible that central power could react efficiently against such manoeuvres, especially since it does not have a lot to offer in exchange. The threat of the breach of public order that States were able to handle in the early years of independence no longer has the same efficiency as before. Advances of democracy and the universalization of Human Rights, the fact that information on what happens across the world travels at great speed now, all strongly limit the potential for recourse to brutal force to make those who might not, stick to the injunctions of the national authorities (it still happens, sadly, but happily less and less often).

Why can it nevertheless be said that decentralisation offers a chance to relegitimize the African State? One of the reasons is that the local level is a propitious framework for the negotiation of a new citizenship. Firstly, the district, as a local public institution tasked with guaranteeing the general interest in its territory, starts to be a significant reality in many African countries. If the district manages to show some efficiency, it will be able to ensure better credibility with the local populations

---

2. Michael Bratton, Donald Rotchild (1997). "Institutional Bases of Governance in Africa", in Goren Hyden and Michael Bratton, Governing Africa, Toward Role Sharing, Nouveaux Horizons, p. 377.

and players than the State, which has lost a significant share of its legitimacy due to its inability to take on all its tasks. Secondly, the district also seems the most relevant scale for thinking about and building new socio-political organisational frameworks allowing the State to be reconciled with the populations. Expressed another way, in the face of the challenges of globalisation and the crisis of the African postcolonial State, decentralisation can be the opportunity to "refound the State"[3], starting with local structures which allow for the maintenance of solidarity between people and meeting the demands for material, economic, cultural, moral security, etc. Thirdly, it is clear that decentralisation gives certain credibility to the idea of sanction by popular vote. Political transfers of power, or at least the renewal of local political personnel thanks to local elections, keeps a certain faith in the mechanisms of democracy, contrary to what is observed at the level of States, where changeovers are extremely rare or certain leaders do not hesitate to manipulate the constitution in order to remain in power. Whence the rejection of States globally perceived as illegitimate and, with it, the risk of the rejection of the idea of democracy itself if it does not truly allow the people's will to come into play.

The rejection of the African State is in reality the rejection of a particular type of State and, similarly, a call for another type of State. Rather than externally driven reforms, the African State needs true reform. The decision needs to be taken internally to create, to dialogue on a daily basis, to move the State away from the local scale, where this process is more easily managed. It is on this condition that the legitimacy of the State and public institutions will be real and sustainable. From whence the hypothesis that decentralisation can constitute a factor which allows the renegotiation of commitment of all to state institutions and thus create a citizenship based on the negotiation of a new social contract which takes into account local socio-political reality. The question which will be asked is that of the process. How will States respond to this demand for local democracy? And how will they adapt to the rise in power of the different sources of legitimacy to which people refer in their daily lives, sources of legitimacy whose claims were put on hold during the years of the single party and in which attention was prioritised on Nation building? It is in this response to these questions that there is a divergence between Anglophone and Francophone countries.

In Anglophone countries, the practice of indirect rule prepared the countries in question to permit some autonomy for local bodies. As has been mentioned earlier, this autonomy is interpreted by the governors of these countries in the framework of a broad concept of decentralisation.

3. R.A. Sawadogo The African State Facing Decentralization. op. cit.

The fact that the traditional authorities should have been the depositories of certain legitimacy promoted devolution of power to the levels close to the people. However, this was not so easily done. A number of States also went through regimes of single parties, which tried to eliminate anything that was not in the single party ideology. And traditional leaders have often been perceived by the State, including in Anglophone countries, as obstacles to the modernisation of the country. When the demand for greater decentralisation becomes more pressing, in Anglophone countries, the question arises as to whether reinstating customary authorities undermines the dynamic of State modernisation. If one considers a country like Ghana one realises that successive regimes thought about the opportunity to recognise customary authorities or, symmetrically, about the potential to reduce their significance in local societies. This hesitation still exists today. The only country which has succeeded right from the start in integrating customary powers, depositaries of a legitimacy recognised by populations, in the decentralisation system, is South Africa, and to a lesser extent so has Uganda.

In Francophone countries, decentralisation will be the continuation of the negation of traditional powers. Either this traditional authority is an auxiliary of the administration and then, there are no problems; or this authority has desires for autonomy from the central State authorities, and it is fought, or enlisted and subverted, to the power of the modern State. This subversion mechanism will paradoxically be double-edged. It is true that Francophone States will try everything so that traditional authorities are integrated into the administrative machine as administrative auxiliaries. But it is also true that the traditional authorities will see all the potential benefits of building bridges between the administration and populations through decentralisation, to subvert local institutions in their turn and put them to their service. This has been observable in some countries such as Mauritania, or to a certain extent in Cameroon.

In all cases, with regard to the most suitable attitude towards traditional authorities, decentralisation raises formidable issues at the local level. First of all, at land management level. In the area of property, the sources of legitimacy to which most populations refer are the traditional authorities. Whence frequent situations of conflict between local authorities and customary authorities regarding the management of lands, both in Anglophone and Francophone countries. In the majority of Anglophone countries, due to the fact that traditional leaders continued to have a strong presence in the resolution of conflicts surrounding land management and development, they are taken into account better and there are fewer tensions regarding property management than that which is observed in Francophone countries. It must be said however, that in these countries, the move from traditional land management which gives priority to the community ownership of the land, to modern land management, which gives priority to individual ownership of lands, problems, that are not yet correctly resolved, continue to arise. The superimposition in this field of the heritage of the large colonial estates, or that which results from the policy of apartheid, tends to complicate even further this move, as local authorities bring to mind that decentralisation in the area of property should correspond to a return to the order which prevailed before colonisation or the policy of apartheid. It is known what this type of claim may provoke as can be seen in the current repercussions in a country such as Zimbabwe.

Towards the end of the 1970s, Francophone countries, apart from Togo, where the State gave a great degree of freedom to traditional leaders for land management and where the administration was called on to register and follow up customary land transactions, a law was devised on the national estate in the area of land management. This law states that any unoccupied, undeveloped land belongs to the national estate, and that the State manages it. Yet the majority of Africans know that customarily all land belongs to a village, there are no vacant lands. This law led to property imbroglios which are still unresolved. Decentralisation policy put the issue of the property dispute resolution back on the agenda, because decentralisation was interpreted by local populations as the return of those who are local land management trustees, and therefore as the return of the customary trustees. From the moment that the State claimed this was not the case, a crisis of trust was sparked off, in which the customary leaders got into the habit of selling lands, knowing perfectly well that this would fuel property litigation. Currently, one of the great issues of development is that the property tangle is completely covered up by the fact that when decentralisation occurred in Francophone countries they did not know how to address this problem inherited from another era, when the State claimed to be all powerful and therefore did not know how to manage the people's basic problem. That is to say the problem of land management.

The second case is that of the law. If decentralisation should help to relegitimize the State, law is one of these areas where there are great expectations. The majority of the people believed that States were aware that law, as it is delivered at the level of the modern State, is not relevant to people's lives. Sadly, whilst there are countries where this issue of local law is taken very seriously (South Africa, Ghana, Nigeria), in the majority of Francophone countries this issue is very poorly resolved, because its importance to people is not fully appreciated. This issue is complicated even further as it lies at the heart of major cultural differences between the ideology of the modern State and customary wisdom. What is said in customary law? It is said that the fact of appearing before a customary judge is already in itself a wrong for both parties because they were unable or did not know how to manage their differences between themselves, within their family, their lineage or their clan. Therefore, customary law punishes the two people who come before it, and even if it punishes one more than the other (the one who, in its opinion caused the most wrongs), both parties are punished. Justice is meted out in order to maintain consensus and harmony in the community. There is not, as in the sentencing of modern law, a winner and a loser, but two losers, one of whom loses more than the other. In this way no one loses face and group harmony is protected. This form of justice recognises that for social harmony, all individuals are not equal. This is possibly its main weakness. A leader is not judged like any other person in the society. Hence, sometimes, abuses committed by certain customary authorities remain in relative impunity. But the reality is also that there is a set of social controls whose aim is to limit the risks of abuses in the exercise of power by traditional leaders. The pursuit of consensus as a conflict resolution method, and the promotion of inclusive debate as a tool for the legitimization of decisions (discussions open to all social groups according to previously agreed parameters) make traditional justice decisions seem to have more solidity and to be more acceptable than those of modern justice in the eyes of the people.

Modern justice, which stipulates that everyone is equal before the law, is perhaps fairer from the individual's point of view, but it is much riskier in terms of the harmony of social groups and authorities. Lots of African peoples do not understand it. How can a leader and anybody else in the clan be judged equally? How can a native and non-native be judged equally? How can it be imagined that access to property is the same for everyone? We are at the heart of serious issues and serious contradictions, for which decentralisation should have opened up a debating space. Unfortunately, decentralisation did not provide this debating space, except in a very limited number of countries (South Africa, Ghana, Nigeria, Uganda), and even then in a very imperfect manner. An opportunity was missed, and this is in part the result of support for decentralisation, much of which was imported from countries of the North. They did not cease trying to integrate Africa with full force and urgency into globalisation. The partners' idea was that the sooner Africa adopted the models of democracy and governance tried and tested in countries of the North, the sooner it would achieve its integration in the globalised economy. It is clear that this is a dangerous bet, because on the contrary, Africa for not having resolved a number of fundamental issues cannot positively be part of the world as it currently functions. Returning to the land problems, in the capitalist system, land is at the root of all wealth creation activity. It must have a market value. Many see the weak commercialisation of property in Africa as one of the main reasons for the continent lagging behind the rest of the world. It is one of the places in the world where this issue is still pending, partly because there has not been this fundamental debate about inclusion, dialogue, negotiation of the transfer of customary lands to individual lands, of land as property for use to land as a property for exchange.

Another difficulty in making sure that decentralisation legitimises the State is the issue of representation, a basic issue. This concern is shared by all countries, Anglophone and Francophone. The local level was conceived by leaders as an extension of the political market. Which is why the majority of countries did not plan local authorities as a space for the emergence of local elites, but as places for the positioning of national elites. It can be seen that it is a fierce debate between those who support the idea that, to be eligible on a local level, one needs to appear on a party list, and those who are in favour of independent candidacy. The majority of Francophone countries chose party candidatures. In Anglophone countries, it is often the system of independent candidature which prevails at the local level, with the notable exceptions of South Africa and Zimbabwe. In fact, one can see that the parties have often tended first to follow the play of internal powers, often regulated at the level of national states. The preoccupation with sticking to local political realities often takes second place to finding posts for political friends. From this arise situations where electors do not see themselves reflected in the candidates who request their votes, which leads to a disaffection in the electoral body in relation to local consultations. Faced with this risk to democracy, more and more countries are beginning to allow the presentation of independent candidatures alongside political party candidatures.

The issue of representation is still more difficult in the rural environment. Following decentralisation laws the choice of municipal councillors must be made through a democratic vote according to the one person/one vote formula. Local social reality is sadly far from being that simple. Populations have not traditionally had the same weight. There are in some ways big voters (lineage chiefs, clan chiefs, family heads, religious or caste leaders...) who do not always understand why their voice should have the same weight as that of other community members, without even mentioning those of "strangers", and it is not understood why they can be asked their opinion and even to stand for election. Numerous "by-pass" strategies are implemented so that local elections do not upset previous socio-political balances too much. But it is also noticeable that in some places, local elections are put to good use, especially by young people, to liberate themselves from the weight of traditional clan organisation. In this case local elections tend to introduce political competition between members of the community there where before the systematic pursuit of consensus was the rule. One witnesses then a splitting of the local political arena transforming the sources of legitimacy (traditional and democratic), which singularly complicates the agreement on decisions concerning the community.

The functioning of institutional bodies of local authorities is equally a source of concern in relation to democratic expression. Here too, the colonial influence has left its mark.

In Francophone countries, in principal, by law, each community has at its disposal a deliberative body, the community council which represents the whole of the authority and is the depositary of local authority; and an executive body either elected, or nominated, which is tasked with the implementation of the decisions of the deliberative body, the Mayor or the President of the municipal council and his deputies. The term of local mandates is mostly the same length as that of national institutions (generally 4 to 5 years) and the mandates are renewable. The municipal executive is assisted in this role by the municipal administration which he heads. But this decision making capacity is often limited by the practice of the single fund which brings all public resources together in Treasury funds managed by the ministry in charge of finances. This practice gives the representatives of the Finance ministry at the community (financial controller, municipal receiver) exorbitant powers, which can go so far as the ability to block financial commitments even if they are executed in respect of laws and regulations. This is why the abolition of the single fund appears in the demands made by the national associations of local authorities in Francophone countries in Africa.

In Anglophone countries, local authorities are endowed with both elected deliberative bodies and elected or nominated executive bodies. The deliberative bodies' mandates are of the same length as those in Francophone countries, but the executive body's mandate is generally shorter (1 to 3 years maximum) and in certain cases, it is not renewable. Mayors are generally "ceremonial" and not "executive". True executive power belongs to the Town Clerk or Chief Executive Officer (CEO), generally nominated by the minister in charge of local authorities. It is not surprising, in this context, that prominent among the demands made by national associations of local authorities in Anglophone countries is the establishment of executive mayors instead of ceremonial mayors, and the lengthening of mayor's mandates.

The functioning of local assemblies is a concern everywhere. These assemblies must in principle debate all the problems that the community encounters within the limits of the prerogatives set out for them by laws and regulations. To do this council commissions are set up, which must prepare files submitted for the consideration and decisions of the council. Sadly, the reality of the functioning of deliberative bodies is different that which is written in the texts. The majority of authorities function under the impetus of just the Mayor and the municipal administration. From this viewpoint, local authorities can become spaces that are not very democratic, where one witnesses a form of personalisation of the local community and the presidentialisation of the role of Mayor, which brings into question the balance of power intended by the legislator. The result is that the populations have the impression that the community management is entrusted solely to the Mayor. Effectively, local elections are often reduced to the question of knowing who will be Mayor, leading at the same stroke to making local democracy a fight between individuals, whilst the letter of the law insists that authorities be administered by elected councils.

From all evidence the debate on representation is the heart of governance problems in Africa. We share the idea according to which "to be legitimate, all forms of governance should be inclusive"[4]. Decentralisation offers the opportunity to complete representative democracy, privilege of the modern State, through participatory democracy to which authorities sign up within the framework of the traditional control system.

> "In governance which is meant to be legitimate, all the actors are acknowledged and involved in the organisation and management of the society through public spaces which are frameworks for the evaluation of everyone and the connection point for all. These public spaces are places for the recognition, consecration and valuation of the competence, abilities and aspirations of everyone. Because they are inclusive, they at the same time allow the control of interests and the creation of a visionary community around shared values and collective social projects. [...] The process of reforming governance must therefore be defined with continual thought for the limitation of exclusion phenomena and conflict factors within public spaces. [...] Consensus as a form of management negotiated from the challenges and aspirations should allow each and everyone to recognise themselves in the decisions taken and to feel responsible for their implications"[5].

Certain countries, like Ghana, have tried to introduce an innovative system which attempts to reconcile representative democracy and participatory democracy at the local level, decentralisation of authority and devolution of the central State. This is the experience of the District Assemblies. The District Assembly is made up of 70% locally elected members and 30% nominated important people. The personages are

---

4. Alliance to refound governance in Africa, (2005). Towards a legitimate governance, Acts of the Forum on governance in Africa, Addis Ababa, p. 22.
5. Ibid. p. 24 and 25.

nominated in accordance with their skills. Since traditional authorities are no longer within municipal councils (for some ten years now), the nomination of personages is made following consultation with them. The District Assembly is a hybrid body, both a devolved step and decentralising authority. It sanctions the progressive withdrawal of sectoral ministries in the execution phase of the national sectoral policies. This is expressed through passing to the authority of the District Assembly of devolved services which were held by the sectoral ministries in their territorial jurisdiction. This organization seems to yield good results in the field. This experiment, which is not without critics, deserves to be monitored closely. It represents in any case an attempt to implement an inclusive policy which truly encourages decentralisation.

It can be concluded that decentralisation can be an opportunity for the refoundation and relegitimisation of the State, on the condition that it allows the opening of a space for debate on the role of customary authorities, on the issue of property, on the issue of justice, on the issue of representation, on the functioning of the local authorities and on the problem of cooperation of local actors among themselves and with the State. Yet what has been most lacking in the implementation of decentralisation policies in Africa, is the consideration of the cultural bedrock of societies. Attention is focused on the formal aspect of local democracy, with the organisation of elections, where the pursuit of a majority as the decision making method becomes the priority, to the detriment of negotiation between protagonists in public life. Within this logic, the recourse to mediation and consensus, though rooted in the traditional control methods, accepted and practised on a daily basis by the people, becomes the exception rather than the rule. In this case there is a risk that local authorities should suffer the same fate as national authorities in terms of mistrust and defiance. It is said that one does not develop a country, but that a country develops itself, so one cannot modernise institutions in a country without the autonomous reflection of that country. This calls strongly on cooperation since the timing of cooperation, the method of cooperation, the cooperation industry, sadly make this need to take into account an inevitably long and slow process, inevitably not determinist in the beginning, with the potential for trial and error, all this poses numerous problems for the cooperation industry, and as a result, for Africans. So that African decentralisations truly serve to strengthen the legitimacy of African States, one cannot put off the need for these in-depth debates through which African societies, in the context of the different countries and regions, will discuss their adaptation to the changes taking place and will decide on the minimum consensus for the closer linking of the local populations to the management of local affairs, contributing thus to the reconciliation of public institutions with populations within their ensemble.

18

The Territorial Dimension
of Decentralisation

Mahaman Tɪᴅᴊᴀɴɪ Aʟᴏᴜ
(Translated from the French)

Decentralisation is today at the heart of political debates and controversy in the majority of African countries (Nach Mback, 2001 ; Totté, Dahou and Billaz, 2003). However, with a few notable exceptions, they only made a commitment very late to this institutional reform dynamic. This tardy interest is not unlinked to the strong Jacobinist tradition which shapes public action, particularly in Francophone States (Mabileau, 1994, p. 17). The concept of building national unity remains, in many respects, a strong political axis and a mobilizing ideology in countries, which for a long time were resistant to any decentralizing steps. Today, in nearly all African countries, we are witnessing a change of perspective, encouraged by the fall of the Berlin Wall and the democratisation processes that it sparked off or accelerated. Beyond these dynamics of political liberalisation in their many expressions, decentralisation can be understood as a significant dimension of those changes that are still taking place (Nach Mbach, 2001).

Hence one understands why it remains written into most of the political agendas of African countries that set in motion democratic processes at the beginning of the 1990s. A country like Senegal began it in 1972 (Blundo, 2001). Mali has for several years created municipalities (Kassibo, 1998 and 2006). Benin followed in the same wake from 2003. Niger has been organizing local elections since July 2004, not without fear for that matter, enrolling thus in a dynamic of creating integrated local authorities just like the experience of Mali. So it is now a new phase of the democratisation process which is starting up. Each country, in accordance with the will of its specificities and its interests of the moment, chooses the rhythm and content of its reform. Decentralisation is therefore the subject of significant debate in the majority of Sub-Saharan African countries. The majority of them (but also the least known) take place in political and community arenas. They are devoted to the goals to be set for decentralising reform – which has become unavoidable – and to the awareness raising necessary for the implementation of "good decentralisation".

Many works, which could not all be fully mentioned here[1], exist on the subject. Analysis of the latter shows the following trends: some works point out the democratisation process which is taking place throughout the rural African world (Bierschenk and Olivier de Sardan, 1998). This type of research inevitably leads to interest in the reconfiguration of the local political arenas to the benefit of democratic openness and its consequences in terms of electoral competition – on the actors and their repositioning, and on the challenges of their confrontation. Within this wave is a whole collection of socio-anthropological research, carried out notably within the framework of the Euro-African Association for the Anthropology of Social Change and Development (APAD) (Kassibo, 1998; Bako-Arifari and Laurent, 1998; Blundo and Mongbo, 1998) as well as numerous conferences organised on the subject (Fay, Koné and Quiminal, 2006). Other works tackle the subject from a political and institutional angle. In this respect, the research carried out by Nach Mback is the most enlightening (Nach Mback, 2001 and 2003). This work studies in great detail the genesis and the comparative dynamics of the decentralisation process in sub-Saharan Africa, through case studies drawn from Niger, Benin, Burkina Faso, Mali, Cameroon and Gabon. It is about in depth works which give priority to the juridical method and comparative law. Another type of work is the work of "decentralisation practitioners" who have worked in the field for a long time and who draw lessons from their experiences through various publications. These are equally enlightening works which describe often totally unpublished knowledge and open up new paths for research and action. In that capacity, one could quote the works of Sawadogo (2001) who gives an account of his experiences gained working in the field in the decentralisation process of his country, Burkina Faso. Other works are part of the activities of The Municipal Development Partnership (MDP) – Cotonou. We will refer to the book recently published by this body on the state of decentralisation in Africa (MDP, 2003). This builds a range of decentralisation profiles, both on the regional and national level. It also presents specific information on the juridical and institutional framework of decentralisation in African countries, their administrative organisation,

---

1. It had good reason to comment that in a recent assessment of works dedicated to democratisation in sub-Saharan Africa, decentralisation is not part of the major themes studied (Van Walraven et Thiriot, 2002).

the competence transfer, local finances, local democracy and local development. Finally, it took into account the significant number of studies carried out within the framework of consultations commissioned by international institutions and other development bodies.

This article deals more specifically with the territorial dimension of decentralisation. Such a perspective, of course, returns to the issues linked to territorial integration in the dynamics of nation building. This theme is recurrent in the political speeches of leaders who have often used the pretext of building national unity to sidestep, in discussions on territorial organisation, the issue of decentralisation. From this one understands, at least in part, the long held reticence of African public authorities regarding the subject. There is however a paradox there that shapes decentralisation policies as they have been implemented in the last few years. How do you balance the powers of a centralising State in the face of emerging local institutions within the framework of decentralisation? How do you confine the centrifugal tendency of local political forces to the framework of a decentralised State? How do you contain the state authorities against the assertion of local freedoms? So many questions which are present in the implementation of a decentralised organisation of the State and its management.

This work is based on general facts drawn most often from literature on the subject and which are reinterpreted in light of the issues of territorialisation. In some way, it is a case of recognising that local authorities established for the promotion of decentralisation policies, in the words of Pourtier "do not float in an indeterminate space" (Pourtier, 1987, p. 341). They are permanently anchored in the territories that limit them geographically and which in fact allocate to them natural, human and infrastructural resources. In this perspective two axes should be explored here. First of all, if one admits that the State plays a determining role in the start-up and design of decentralisation policies, these must above all be understood as policies of territorial production. Then, with regards to the need to give it real forms, decentralisation can also be interpreted as a territory building dynamic.

Decentralisation, a territorial production

Decentralisation in its most classic form literally means "self administration". It refers to a transfer of central power allocation to local bodies, legally distinct from the State and endowed with organs elected by the citizens concerned. With the creation of territorial authorities, decentralisation produces institutions, but also territories which, even if they tend to be homogenised by classical legal discourse, are never uniform.

The establishment of territorial authorities

The establishment of territorial authorities constitutes without doubt one of the most real manifestations of decentralisation. As a result it is fitting to define them in order to understand their scope.

The history of territorial authorities is generally confused with that of decentralisation, that is to say the slow movement of recognition of a legal autonomy to local bodies, legally distinct from the State. The autonomy of territorial authorities has the peculiarity of being allocated by the State in its territorial organisation; it is inseparable from it, to the same extent as the related idea of devolution. The latter marks the influence of the State on all of its territory through the intervention of officials nominated by it and acting in its name. Thus,

> "the territorial authority fits within the institutional landscape with the allocation by the State of legal status to an institution representing the collective interests of the inhabitants of the areas previously defined by the State. The institution is all of the inhabitants of the area designated. In this hypothesis, as opposed to the nominated prefect, the community of inhabitants of the area designates its own representatives who administer local affairs and define their own policies" (Galletti, 2004, p. 236).

Over the last few years decentralising reforms taking place in unitary African States (and more or less completed, depending on the case) were replaced by the implementation of territorial authorities. Of course, they existed during the colonial period, but they were rarely democratically based. If one excludes the four Senegalese municipalities (Wesley Johnson, 1991) and the municipalities of full exercise implemented later under the framework of the French Union (Deschamps, 1954, p. 433-436), one could barely call the local bodies, which managed certain colonial territories, territorial authorities. The latter were run by administrators who exercised power without reference to any local democracy. One can thus consider that the territorial authorities, such as one can observe today in African countries, were born with the on-going decentralisation policies. As a result they fit within the new political deal engendered by the democratisation process.

Some territorial authorities are based on old, pre-existing administrative organisations. In other cases, existing bodies were allocated autonomy within new local institutional configurations. Finally, many territorial authorities came about for the promotion of decentralisation within the framework of an administrative redistribution. The case of Niger is a strong illustration because the effective introduction of municipalities was preceded by a territorial redistribution. The municipalities are therefore totally new and are part of the extension of State control of the territory. This distinction between the historic trajectories of the territorial authorities is not anodyne : each situation in fact brings specific problems in terms of territorial ownership.

Territorial authorities based on pre-existing administrative bodies allow for the establishment of an elected body in the State representative. Thus the same territorial space is shared by the State representative dispossessed of his initial resources as head of the authority and a new deliberative body, introduced for local elections and which becomes the central actor of the new decentralized space.

The new territorial authorities, created for the benefit of decentralising reform, fit into a new dynamic which consists of taking ownership of the new territory and managing it within the framework of an electoral mandate. In this case, the transfer of power does not take place between two authorities with different legitimacies and operating within the same space. The context is more one of an authority to be invented in a specific territory, through the institutionalisation of a new elected body. More often than not, the new local configurations make the customary authorities (village head, head of canton) and the elected authorities compete within a renovated administrative context.

In any event, the challenge is that of the assertion, over a defined territory, of an authority attributed by the State to a body it has established.

The diversity of territorial authorities

The territorial authorities created by the State are characterised by their diversity. They do not have the same spatial configuration nor the same resources and are organised according to different methods (imposition or negotiation). Several spatial levels can be distinguished.

The urban territorial authorities are the oldest. They precede the creation of the decentralized institutions and correspond most often to the administrative centres of the arrondissements, departments or municipalities when they exist. The new dynamic puts them from now on under the responsibility of the democratically elected bodies.

The rural territorial authorities are new and participate in the democratisation of the rural world (Aghulon, 1978). In most countries, the rural world has stayed on the margins of political changes brought about by the national conferences that took place at the end of the 1980s. The establishment of the authorities aims for a connection between the administrations and the people they administer and also seeks better participation of the populations both in the choice of local governors and in the control of their activities. The rural territorial authorities are subdivided, in some countries like Niger and Mali, into nomadic and sedentary communities in order to take into account the specificities of the lifestyles of populations.

In addition, whichever they may be, territorial authorities vary in dimension, in terms of surface and population. Some authorities are viable and can function within their own resources (taxes and other duties). Others do not have sufficient available means and depend on external resources to function (private income, patronage). These resources can come from development projects, significant purveyors of investments in villages, or even the State, national traders or from decentralised cooperation, another source of finance that is not insignificant in countries like Burkina Faso and Mali.

So the question arises of the logic which defined the territorial authorities. Some match a relatively homogenous and integrated geographical set, dividing administrative authorities which have existed for a long time and to which the decentralising reform allocates more freedom. Others match fiscal logic completely based on their viability. These organisations are totally new and group together varied village communities, sometimes with different histories, with the sole aim of financial self-sufficiency. The recent institutional reforms integrate them in a new body which needs to be built.

One can also identify the "political" territorial authorities, created under pressure from politicians or by influential "big men", who succeed in "carving out made to measure fiefdoms", or even to give themselves a new legitimacy in their region of origin: "everyone wants his municipality" seems to be the "leitmotiv" of the introduction of this type of territorial authority. In all cases, the electoralist concerns are never absent from these decentralising reforms which allow politicians to consolidate their local position.

Decentralisation, a territorial construction

Until recently, in most African countries, the central State and its representatives were at the heart of the functioning of the local organisations. They still keep a fairly important initiative power within a context of limited, even non-existent, participatory policy. Also, decentralisation poses above all the question of the integration in their territory of new authorities created by it. The challenges of territorial integration are therefore linked to the sustainability of decentralisation, taking into account the fragility of some processes which it encourages.

The dynamic of territorial integration

If one admits that decentralisation institutes new territorial jurisdictions at the local level this raises the question of their construction. This necessarily includes a political dimension characterised by public action implemented by local authorities in relation to competences they are given. Local authorities remain framed by the State which, within the framework of decentralisation, preserves the multiple prerogatives linked to the exercise of their new missions.

Local public action is a significant dimension in territorial authorities building. Since the starting of the decentralisation processes, the oldest authorities have had at their disposal autonomy and the strengthened means to build themselves, whilst the new ones must legitimise their existence within a context where public action is already carried out by other actors present in the local arenas. The decentralising dynamics thus direct public action towards territorial authorities whose inhabitants are, above all, the beneficiaries of implemented policies. In such a context, the action of local elites takes on a particular importance due to the mission that is then devolved to them to build their territory, to attract investment (development projects, decentralised cooperation and the private sector) there to create an attraction pole to the benefit of their citizens and outside all intervention by the State. It falls to them, in summary, to promote development towards their authority. The local space, in its different configurations, thus takes on a true autonomy and becomes a totally separate area where the actors face each other around well identified challenges.

In African countries, local public action goes back to the problematic of local economic development. The previous territorial authority schemes made the State the main actor, often determinant in the conception and construction of the local public action. State policies were in charge of the transformation of the regions and other constituencies in the country. At the local level, the State held real power for the allocation of public resources. But it was held to the demands for equity which forced it to treat the different localities in the same way, running the risk of promoting inequalities of treatment that were highly prejudicial to national unity. In the framework of decentralisation, the State transfers to the territorial authority which it sets up, whole sections of its prerogatives and in a way divides up its territory. This becomes a mosaic of political arenas, of variable size and shape, run by the elected officials, and no longer nominated authorities. The locally elected hold in this logic a new democratic legitimacy within the territories which come under their jurisdiction. These local territories do not necessarily share a common history, but reflect at a given moment the concept that the State has of its own organisation and the projection it built on the national scale (Giraut and Lajarge, 1998).

Local public action assigned to the elected officials is therefore transformational in the sense that it is essentially tasked with territory building, giving it an identity and shaping it in the way its inhabitants want. From this perspective, decentralisation policy takes on a completely different meaning. It is not just limited to the setting up of bodies elected in the territorial authorities created by the State. It also consists of a voluntarist rebalancing of the powers between a State that is too powerful, or in some cases absent, and local societies that are marginalised or not very integrated into the social dynamics of state public action. In fact, it is a case of promoting local initiative in the conception and implementation of public action.

Another aspect, no less important, of the creation of territorial authorities concerns reducing the distance between the administration and those administered. Thus, the allocation of real administrative prerogatives to the decentralised bodies brings public services closer to their users. Elsewhere, the users have easier access to the administrative officials in order to express their expectations, and vice versa.

However, the assertion of local freedoms does not mean a negation of the State. It remains at the local level through its representatives and technical services. But its tasks are redefined within the new context where the State is more often given a power of control of legality over the actions of territorial authorities (Tobin, 1997). This power varies in importance depending on whether it is exercised ex ante or ex post facto. The State technical services, in their different branches, also fulfil substantial missions within the authorities when the need is expressed. There too, it is worth specifying that these technical services are not present at the same level throughout the national territory. The setting up of territorial authorities thus allows for the measurement of populations' access to these public services which are often seen as implementing human rights.

It must be acknowledged that in many African countries, the setting up of decentralised authorities also corresponds to the only significant administrative presence of the State in some regions. These commonly occurring situations reflect the weak establishment of the State in its territory. In this particular dimension, decentralisation presents itself above all as an undertaking of democratisation, but also of the nationalisation of the rural areas which for a long time remained outside these integrational dynamics of the public authorities.

The challenges of territorial integration

These processes run their course, with mixed fortunes which throw light on the challenges of decentralising institutional reform. This directly affects the local authorities but equally the State, within the framework of the new roles that are assigned to it. Through better transparency and more egalitarian and equitable access to resources, decentralisation aims to promote direct participation by citizens in the decision about management of the territorial authority's resources which they carry. Such a perspective anchors this reflection at the heart of the issues of democratic governance.

In fact, within the framework of the competencies defined by the State itself, decentralisation allows the shift of decision making downwards, closer to the local challenges and in accordance with democratic procedures (Fukuyama, 2004, p. 109). In doing so, it brings the administration closer to its users by promoting the emergence of a local democratic arena, clearly differentiated and integrated in the national space. From then on it counts on the existence at its centre of a plurality of territories and local arenas which are largely autonomous. Such dynamics include significant challenges for the anchoring of decentralising reforms. These challenges are linked: to the emergence of a local democracy; to the imperative of management for the economic durability of the local authority; to the building of local citizenship which allows for the integration of populations in the selection of locally elected members and the management of local matters; to the building of a local public space, sine qua non of strengthening local democracy; and to local development which constitutes an element of legitimisation of decentralisation.

Decentralisation faces local democracy

Decentralisations implemented in African countries go hand in hand with the dynamics of the establishment of local democracy. The latter implies that from then on the local authorities shall be elected by universal suffrage and no longer, like in the preceding institutional schemes, nominated by the State (authorities devolved from the State) or elected in accordance with customary rules (customary authorities). The decentralisation schemes bring democratic legitimacy to the local level. This is supposed to supersede the preceding ones, which is not an easy task in a context that is largely managed by the political parties, most often controlled by local worthies, merchants or officials. The entire challenge is then knowing if the authority that emerges from the decentralisation process will not be confiscated. In this regard, one can assert that there are serious risks that the political actors who already held power will keep hold of it within the framework of the new institutions, adding thus to their initial legitimacy the resources of universal suffrage and distorting in this way the representativeness of the elected members. Beyond the choice of governors the question also arises of the responsibility, the obligation to be accountable, which will devolve upon the new authorities. It is therefore this political culture which has to be instituted at the local level to make real the democracy which underlies the decentralisation process.

The imperative of management

The issue of management is important, both because until now the discussions on decentralisation have only tackled this very marginally. Yet, numerous examples, drawn from the experiences of some countries, show that management has not always been at the centre of the concerns of decentralised organisations. It includes its share of avatars: management that is not very transparent results in serious breaches of administrative accountability, the misappropriation of local taxes, a disproportionate payroll intended for the maintenance of a political clientele, extra-billing, etc. (Blundo, 2001). In many situations, the elected officials have little training for local public management. Elsewhere, it is also a case of inventing management methods which did not exist before and which most often put local elected officials in a learning role. The lack of training is generally criticized to explain this state of affairs. But the issue of the management of the new authorities remains completely open and constitutes a new decisive dimension for the durability of the new local institutions. Its treatment will depend on the capacity of the new authorities to survive and make decentralisation effective.

The quest for local citizenship

The issue of local citizenship is raised in all its intensity due to the sometimes heterogeneous character of the divisions which were created. These often create new bodies which include populations of diverse origins who must from then on co-exist. It is not an easy task in a context that is marked by a strong fiscal lack of public spirit and where local authorities depend largely on external resources (State and development aid) to function. It must be said that until now taxation was not seen as a financing tool for the authority, but more as a way of financing power. The colonial power and then the post-colonial power, in their relationship to taxation, were largely seen through this prism. Now because citizens finance the authority they can demand accountability. It is true that, everywhere, there is reliance on community action plans from the World Bank or on decentralised cooperation to finance investment in the municipalities. Few actions are envisaged to promote another concept of taxation which is also and above all an archetypal act of citizenship in the service of the territorial authority.

The local public space

How does one promote the emergence of a local public space in the local authorities? Local public space goes back here to the existence of places for debate about local concerns, where local challenges are discussed and gain the upper hand, where local opposition is formed, far from national challenges, except when they have local impact (Habermas, 1978). It is a crucial challenge of these decentralisation dynamics, marked most often by the prevalence of national concerns brought by the political parties to the contexts where the local populations are most often barely involved in dealing with the treatment of issues which concern them directly and where the local challenges are rarely at the centre of local political life.

Local development

Here, local development is understood as "a new approach to development issues which gives priority to the initiatives of actors in the field, the very same people who are faced daily with the problems and the reality of the needs of the local populations" (Nach Mback, 2001). Such initiatives can be top down, but it is vital that the base takes ownership of them and is encouraged to direct them. This requires an involvement of the populations or their different groupings in the drawing up of development policies at the local level. And this also implies that local authorities have the relevant skills in the subject. Here one comes straight to the point of the problematic of capacity building in local authorities. One knows that they are weak. The human and technical resources are cruelly lacking, as are the financial resources. This is therefore the important challenge to be taken into account if one does not want to limit decentralisation to its strictly political dimensions and to make of it a true method of local development.

Conclusion

Seen thus in this binary dynamic of territory making and building, decentralisation is revealed as a true governance challenge in African countries that are trying it. In fact it is an open bet which will depend a great deal on the ability of the State to direct this reform to its conclusion, but also on the will of the local actors to introduce a viable local governance framework directed at the interests of the authorities they head. It is a major challenge that is a long way from being won in these African political and institutional contexts that are being built, where the States today face the double dynamic of integration in the global field and the inevitable expectations of the local.

Bibliography

Agulhon, M. (1978). La république au village, Paris, Seuil.
Baguenard, J. (2006). La décentralisation, Paris, PUF, coll. "Que sais-je ?".
Bako-Arifari, N. (1997). "Institutions et types de pouvoir en milieu rural : description d'un paysage politico-administratif local au Niger (canton de Gaya)", Documents de travail sur les sociétés africaines, n° 8.
Bako-Arifari, N. and P.-J. Laurent (1998). "Les dimensions sociales et économiques du développement local et la décentralisation en Afrique au Sud du Sahara", Bulletin de l'APAD, n° 15.
Bierschenk, T. and J.-P. Olivier De Sardan (1998). Les pouvoirs au village. Le Bénin rural entre démocratisation et décentralisation, Paris, Karthala.
Blundo, G. (2001). "La corruption comme mode de gouvernance locale : trois décennies de décentralisation au Sénégal", Afrique contemporaine, numéro spécial, 3ᵉ trimestre, p. 115-127.
Blundo, G. and R. Mongbo (1998). "Décentralisation, pouvoirs et réseaux sociaux", Bulletin de l'APAD, n° 16.
Bonnard, M. (ed.) (2002). Les collectivités locales en France. Les notices, Paris, La Documentation française.
Buijtenhuijs, R. and C. Thiriot (1995). Démocratisation en Afrique au sud du Sahara, 1922-1995 : un bilan de la littérature, Leiden-Talence, ASC-CEAN.
Capul, J.-Y. and P. Tronquoy (ed.) (1999). "Les collectivités locales en mutation", Cahiers français, n° 293, octobre-décembre. Deschamps, H. (1954). "Les assemblées locales dans les territoires d'outre-mer", Politique étrangère, vol. 19, n° 4, p. 427-436.

Dimier, V. (2001). "De la décolonisation... à la décentralisation. Histoire des préfets coloniaux", Politix, vol. 14, n° 53.

Direction du développement et de la Coopération, 1999, Décentralisation et développement, Berne, janvier.

Dubresson, A. and Y.-F. Fauré (2005). "Décentralisation et développement local : un lien à repenser", Revue Tiers Monde, n° 181, janvier-mars.

Faure, A. (1989). "Le trousseau des politiques locales", Politix, vol. 2, n° 1, p. 73-79.

Faure, A. (1994). "Les élus locaux à l'épreuve de la décentralisation. De nouveaux chantiers pour la médiation politique locale", Revue française de science politique, vol. 44, n° 3.

Fay, C., Y.F. Kone and C. Quiminal (2006). Décentralisation et pouvoirs locaux en Afrique. En contrepoint, modèles territoriaux français, Paris, Éditions de l'IRD.

Fukuyama, F. (2004). State-Building: Governance and World Order in the 21st Century. New York: Cornell University Press.

Galletti, F. (2004). Les transformations du droit public africain francophone. Entre étatisme et libéralisation, Bruxelles, Bruylant.

Giraut, F. and R. Lajarge (1998). "Fabriquons du pays, il en restera toujours quelque chose", Projet, n° 254, p. 59-68.

Giraut, F. (1999). "L'idéologie du tout territorial et la dérive autochtoniste. Les inquiétudes d'un observateur engagé", in Développement et territoires : chance ou illusion ? Acteurs et chercheurs en forum, CPAU/Hegoa, p. 9-11.

Greffe, X. (2005). La décentralisation, Paris, La Découverte.

Habermas, J. (1978). L'espace public. Archéologie de la publicité comme dimension constitutive de la société bourgeoise, Paris, Payot.

Kassibo, B. (ed.) (1998). "La décentralisation au Mali : état des lieux", Bulletin de l'APAD, n° 14, p. 1-20.

Kassibo, B. (2006). "Mali : une décentralisation à double vitesse ? Kamara la segi so ou le lent et délicat retour du pouvoir à la maison", in C. Fay, Y.F. Koné et C. Quiminal, Décentralisation et pouvoirs locaux en Afrique. En contrepoint, modèles territoriaux français, Paris, Éditions de l'IRD.

Laurent, P.-J.(1995). "Les pouvoirs politiques locaux et la décentralisation au Burkina Faso", Cahiers du CIDEP, n° 26, septembre.

Laurent P.-J., A. et al. (2004). Décentralisation et citoyenneté au Burkina Faso. Le cas de Ziniaré, Paris-Louvain-la-Neuve, L'Harmattan-Académia-Bruylant.

Loada, A. (2003). "La décentralisation en Afrique francophone, où en est-on ?", Marchés tropicaux, n° 3000.

Mabileau, A. (1985). "Les institutions locales et les relations centre périphérie" in Grawitz, M. and J. Leca. Traité de science politique, Paris, PUF, volume 2.

Mabileau, A. (1994). Le système local en France, Paris, Montchrestien.

Mabileau, A. (1997). "Les génies invisibles du local, faux semblables et dynamiques de la décentralisation", Revue française de science politique, vol. 47, n° 3-4, juin-août, p. 340-376.

Nach Mbach, C. (2001). "La décentralisation en Afrique : enjeux et perspectives", Afrique contemporaine, numéro spécial, 3e trimestre, p. 95-114.

Nach Mback, C. (2003). Démocratisation et décentralisation, Paris, Karthala.

Partenariat pour le développement municipal (PDM) (2003). État de la décentralisation en Afrique, Paris-Cotonou, Karthala-PDM.

Pourtier, R. (1987). "Encadrement territorial et production de la nation", in E. Terray, L'État contemporain en Afrique, Paris, L'Harmattan, p. 341-358.

Richard, P. (2003). Les citoyens au cœur de la décentralisation, La Tour d'Aigues, Éditions de l'Aube.

Sawadogo, A. (2001). L'État africain face à la décentralisation, Paris, Karthala.

Tobin, I. (1997). Le préfet dans la décentralisation, Paris, L'Harmattan

Totté, M., T. Dahou and R. Billaz (ed.) (2003). La décentralisation en Afrique de l'Ouest. Entre politique et développement, Paris-Dakar, COTA-Karthala-Enda Graf.

Van Walraven, K. and C. Thiriot (2002). Démocratisation en Afrique au sud du Sahara. Transition et virage. Un bilan de la littérature (1995-1996), Leyde-Bordeaux, Centre d'études africaines-Centre d'études d'Afrique noire.

Verpeaux, M. (2006). Les collectivités territoriales en France, Paris, Dalloz, 3e édition.

Wesley Johnson, G. (1991). Naissance du Sénégal contemporain. Aux origines de la vie politique moderne : 1900-1920, Paris, Karthala.

19

Urban Governance
and International Cooperation

Charles GOLDBLUM and Annik OSMONT
(Translated from the French)

Urban governance, as it is understood in this text, concerns a sphere of action linking urban management and urban development in the context of international cooperation. It refers to situations marked by economic globalisation, in which urbanisation is proposed as the source and driving force of development, and the city – in particular large cities – is now no longer considered as the site where "bad development" and reliance on external interests crystallise, but rather as a vector that helps national development. To continue in the same vein, the corrective lens of urban policies seeking to control the urbanisation process tends to give way to an institutional approach responding to the demands of management involved in adapting to the global economy, as the reform or rationalisation of urban institutions goes together with the idea of easing the urbanisation process.

Ascher (1995, p. 269) defines urban governance as:

> "a system of government which articulates and associates political institutions, social actors and private organisations, in development and implementation processes of collective choices able to inspire the active support of city dwellers."

Apart from the fact that these arrangements – even if the powers that be are somewhat inflexible in this respect – presuppose, in the author's opinion, the existence of a democratic state and institutions and of a reactive urban civil society. On the other hand, in the context of the developing world which we are discussing here, it is the task of urban governance to develop the idea of citadinité alongside a "local" citizenship within regional management bodies and the bodies responsible for the implementation of urban projects, which are the framework for democratic cooperation. However, in the context of international aid, the promotion of such arrangements raises questions as to the role of the state – facilitator or regulator? – especially in the case of large agglomerations, economic and technical centres which often function as political capitals identified, on the same count, as "driving forces of development".

Logic of actors and logic of projects

The concept of governance today goes beyond the context of the countries of the Southern hemisphere and international aid, and has re-entered the domain of the institutions and organisations of the industrialised countries from whence it came. At the same time, however, its modern entry onto the stage of public policy is occurring precisely in the context of development aid, with the support of powerful international investors who are aware of the need to reconcile the efficiency of the actions financed in the framework of international cooperation and the ideal of democratic development, without infringing, in principle at least, on the sovereignty of the states concerned.

According to the definition given by the United Nations Development Programme (UNDP) in 1997, urban governance is:

> "the sum of the many ways individuals and institutions, public and private, plan and manage the common affairs of the city. It is a continuing process through which the conflicting or divers interests may be accommodated and cooperative action taken. It includes formal institutions as well as informal arrangements and the social capital of citizens." (cited in UNCHS, 2001, p. 68, note 2.)

Action in the context of urban-related development, where multilateral and bilateral cooperation come together, and which is generally classed as municipal management, infrastructure, urban poverty reduction, skills development, etc., has two characteristics:

– on the one hand, the mobilisation of multiple actors – often in the same operation or project – whose different status and strategies, or even interests, raise the question of coordinating cooperative action as well as its implementation;

– on the other hand, the idea of an all-encompassing project, involving the entire spectrum of actions by segment (by sector, by donor) – whether these are concerned with the running of cities, development planning or implementation of urban projects (stricto sensu), public intervention in the urban sphere relying on outside financing because of the cost or level of technical know-how or expertise.

Sources of urban governance: the World Bank's views on urban issues

Among the countless contributors to international urban cooperation, it is worth singling out the strategic role of the World Bank, which promotes the concept of urban governance in relation to development. This international institution believes that urban governance has a special place in the general sphere of governance; the latter in fact being defined as:

> "the manner in which power is exercised in the management of a country's economic and social resources for development" (World Bank, 1991 – cited in Osmont, 2002).

This particularity stems first of all from the conditions in which governance, as a key instrument for structural adjustment, is, under the aegis of the World Bank, entering onto the stage of international cooperation in relation to cities (Osmont, 1995). In this light, cities appear to be both the object of the adjustment and the stage where its social impacts are dealt with.[1] The initial intention – in the context of necessity and rationality – of making cities more efficient and more productive thus results in compensatory arrangements to combat urban poverty and in the implementation of public works and employment agencies (AGETIP).[2] Setting up these safety nets, in particular in

---

1. The "Washington Consensus" gives us a better understanding of what the social compensation reforms and structural adjustment mechanisms, as they are known, are and what their objective is. The implementation of the consensus in 1987 was left to the Social Dimension of Adjustment (SDA) unit, which in 1991 became the Social Policy and Poverty Reduction Division, which primarily intervenes in cities, these being considered particularly vulnerable to the social effects of structural reforms, which give rise to new categories of poverty, and are particularly responsive to its effects, as shown by the urban riots in the 1980s in Caracas, Tunis and Casablanca.

2. These agencies, initially intended to implement public works (sanitation in particular) together with local governments, primarily urban ones, quickly became, in Senegal, agencies supporting the control of urban work, the social engineering function being to some degree delegated to non-governmental organisations.

the poorer neighbourhoods of large cities, makes this type of social mobilisation (social networks) the popular face of the participation of "urban actors".

The concept of urban governance brings together in a single concept various aspects of urban intervention implemented in earlier phases by the main actors of international urban cooperation such as the World Bank, UNDP and the United Nations Human Settlements Programme (UN-Habitat). This was also eventually the case for the integration of social or environmental programmes, such as those related to the "Inclusive City" and to Agenda 21, notably in the context of the Global Campaign on Urban Governance (UN-Habitat, 2002). This systemisation was accompanied, starting in the early 1990s, by a remarkable effort to create theories based on operations which were considered exemplary; a "conceptual strategy" (Crowley, 2003) to which academic research contributed, in particular, by the Centre for Urban and Community Studies of the University of Toronto, in the context of the programme called the Global Urban Research Initiative (GURI), that brought together the Centre and the Ford Foundation.[3]

Urban governance, thus promoted, is characterised both by the way in which it approaches urban development, with the idea of controlling urban development using institutional control, leaving to market forces the means and methods of urban development, and by the particular status conferred upon projects (stricto sensu) in urban management and development.

As a result, two types of intervention began in the 1980s, one related to project management, the other to the regionalisation of management, both of which found other intermediaries, in particular in bilateral cooperation. This logic of institutional action led to a smaller role for the state and a larger one for local regional institutions, to the privatisation of services and to a greater role for private initiatives, in accordance with the neo-liberal management model.

As far as projects are concerned, there was a shift from the management of cities and their development, based on development actions depending on their physical and social space, to urban management, based on municipal development, and an institutional approach seeking to improve the use of local resources (improving

---

3. An example of this analytical approach linking economic (including taxation), politico-institutional and social aspects, a collective work on the challenge of governance in India, edited by Om Prakash Mathur (1999), also shows how important the Indian context is in studies on this topic (see also Sivaramakrishnan and Green, 1992). Also noteworthy are the works that bring together, under the heading of urban governance, case studies related to various geographical cases, such as the April 2000 issue of Environment & Urbanization entitled "Poverty reduction and urban governance".

tax and duty collection, creating charts of accounts and increasing productivity of technical services). These measures were generally complemented by the creation of a national institution for loans to local authorities. This helped to set up, at the national level, instruments designed to ensure the efficiency of urban administration and management according to general principles of government, which generally take no account of the specific forms and principles of local power or of the local balance of power.

This singular shift in the political sphere – in the sense of its technification in terms of institutional engineering – clearly manifests itself in, what is known as, decentralisation programmes, whose objective to make management less concentrated is, in fact, accompanied by a redistribution of powers between the central level and the regional level. These arrangements affect municipal institutions inasmuch as they involve the devolution of new responsibilities to existing local governments, or even the creation of new entities in charge of managing and developing urban areas. This is notably the case in Dakar (Senegal), where the decentralisation project required a new regional organisation plan (dividing the agglomeration into municipalities, creating arrondissements in each municipality, setting up an urban community that brings all of these together), intended to become part of the hierarchy in the regional system set up in 1997. These outside institutional bodies are still, however, fragile, as shown when the urban community in Dakar in 2000 was removed and the old authorities returned, thanks to a change in the presidential majority (Osmont, 2002).

Whatever the case, even though for the World Bank this type of intervention is classed under the heading of urban projects, the fact that, in the countries concerned, these interventions are most often the responsibility of ministries in charge of local government (and no longer that of ministries in charge of urban planning, except in cases where, as in Thailand, the two areas are the responsibility of the same ministry – the Ministry of the Interior in this case) is a perfect example of the shift, from the point of view of controlling urban development, from the operational sphere of urban planning, to that of the structural reform of state institutions.

Project governance and democratic governance

The arrangements supported by the World Bank clearly belong to the domain of international cooperation and development assistance; a multifaceted domain and the multiplicity of partnerships which makes implementing public policies and defining decision-making powers and responsibilities all the more complex, and often more problematic. The arrangements thus made strongly impact the landscape of international cooperation, including at the bilateral level – cooperation between states or involving regional organisations (in the supranational sense) – which often serves as an intermediary. In addition, the principles and models which underlie them generally inspire the modus operandi in the world of cooperation and serve as a reference model for these, to the detriment of their own logic or thinking, in short, depriving states, developing countries and also bilateral partners – states, regional associations and local authorities – of their independence in this area. World Bank officials do not hesitate to reaffirm the important position this international institution plays in the urban sphere, regarding it as the "primary provider of assistance in the urban sphere and [...] the only international agency with a perspective that is both global and operational in relation to urban issues" (Wolfensohn, 1999), and to express their preference for supra- or infra-state organisations and for non-governmental organisations as the best intermediaries for the Bank's principles of action.

In its relation to governance in general, the "urban sector" is not always identified as such by actors of international cooperation.[4] However, interventions linked to regional development are on the front line of development aid, if only because of the role of the infrastructure sector in development aid. The importance of the funds raised by these sectoral actions, the socio-economic impact of development choices, the issues of administrative responsibilities and technical expertise make it an excellent way to test the ideas of "good governance" in an urban context. In addition, the development of local government's responsibilities in the current context of decentralisation, as promoted in the name of international, multilateral and bilateral cooperation, with intermediaries in decentralised cooperation (as is the case for the local government development programme in sub-Saharan Africa – later called the Municipal Development Partnership or MDP – and in its coordination with urban management programmes or UMP) is to be considered as a way for regional governments to come to terms with, at their hierarchical level (redefined for this purpose if needed), general urbanisation trends at a global level, which are now accepted as irreversible.

We find here that, as well as the issues of "projects" governance (lato

---

4. Unlike major sources of international funding and some other donor countries, the French Development Agency (AFD) has only recently introduced an urban department; as for the European Union, it addresses this aspect through programmes such as Asia Urbs or Urbal.

GOVERNANCE AND TERRITORIES   293

sensu) between the sectoral and global levels (in the sense of comprehensive planning, but also of comprehensive municipal management), are questions raised about the validity of the premise connecting efficiency and democracy, or even – in terms of the process – rationalisation and democratisation.[5]

In its theoretical form, the principle of urban governance does not lend itself to being a retrospective source for the participatory strategies and the advocacy planning of the 1960s. However, it is worth noting that the specific nature of the conditions and contexts of international cooperation (multiplicity of actors, reliance on aid, etc.) in which the notion of urban governance has been propagated, not forgetting that it was initially promoted in these contexts by supra-state organisations. This last point affects the way in which urban governance is conceived at the local level, which raises questions regarding sectoral urban policies (land policies, housing policies, environmental policies, etc.) and large-scale national projects (major facilities such as an international airport or sporting complex for example, but also development efforts such as the preservation of a historic centre), particularly in terms of their potential conflicts with local interests, and more generally on the question of public works. From this point of view, the increased importance of environmental issues illustrates the ambivalence of views that, on the one hand, take into account the impact of actions in certain sectors at a local level and, on the other, keep in mind the broader picture of public interest that underlies the concept of sustainable (urban) development.

Trends in town-planning of the time of urban governance: "metropolisation" issues

It is clear that the strategies related to urban governance tend to direct cooperation action towards urban management models and thus highlight the institutional systems which are thought to be consistent with these idealities that lay claim to universal rationality. This of course does not mean that all fear concerning physical space is left aside, but rather it determines and orients the way interventions are set up in an ad hoc institutional framework where the goals of rational management and (no

---

5. Here rationalisation is understood in the sense of rational action towards an end (Zweckrationalität) as defined by Max Weber (1922/1980); the performance of development action is generally evaluated on the basis of completed "projects" rather than on the contribution to the process of democratisation.

less rational) planning are intended to come together. The example of Vientiane is rather informative on this subject, where we start with a holistic approach to a blueprint and move on to the basis of setting up, under the aegis the Asian Development Bank (ADB), an ad hoc regional and administrative entity – the Vientiane Urban Development and Administration Authority (VUDAA) – despite the fact that there is no elected government for the corresponding area (Goldblum, 2008).

All these approaches converge towards a more global outlook that is more closely integrated in urban development. One only needs to refer to Wolfensohn's speech (1999) in which he defines the scope of this new urban strategy for the World Bank:

> "If one considers the sixty megacities of more than ten million people expected to be established in developing countries by the year 2025, with growth in all urban concentrations, and with our existing experience from Jakarta to Mumbai (Bombay), we have ample illustration of the special problems of urban management. It is clear that governments must have an urban strategy which differs from an overall national strategy to the extent that concentration of population causes special and unique problems. Urban planning and appropriate action will be crucial in the next millennium."

Part of this approach, as put forward by the World Bank in 1999, is to encourage the implementation of development strategies for (large) cities ("City Development Strategies" – CDS) with the aim of fostering local economic development and reducing urban poverty. It is based on the principle of increased citizen participation as a way of improving the balance in economic and social development of agglomerations. This approach, which is included in the Cities Alliance programme[6], can be seen as an attempt to resize to a local scale the urban problems of large agglomerations and the way these are dealt with and managed. As a backdrop to all this, it is easy to see one of the paradoxes of urban governance. That is to say, the fact that the socio-spatial configurations – adopted by large agglomerations because of the combined effects of globalisation and of the adjustments and projects seeking to attract foreign direct investment – are far from leading to the balance expected from market forces; they generally result in social inequalities becoming bigger and these being shown through spatial fragmentation, where the real estate sector is an extremely sensitive issue and access to transportation and urban services is a factor in discrimination.

---

6. Coalition of bilateral and multilateral investors set up in a joint initiative by the World Bank and UN-Habitat.

This strategy, and its inclusion in the framework of various cooperative actions, is explained at two different levels, which are now linked by the same demand for technical rationality, for "technification" (which makes bringing back democratic policies and views all the more important), in this case linking urban governance (notably in the form of the public-private partnership in the development of urban infrastructures, the privatisation of urban services, decentralisation, and skills training in municipal management) and strategic planning (inspired by the approach in Barcelona, albeit without the democratic legitimacy of the actors in the Catalan capital necessarily being successfully reproduced elsewhere) (Borja, 1998).

Top-down or bottom-up governance?

The partnership between actors, which urban governance, in principle, requires (in much the same way, it is worth noting, as "strategic planning"), seeks to make distinct, and potentially contradictory, interests compatible, in order to reconcile efficiency when executing projects (possibly assessed) and the dialogue required because of the intervention of outside financing and external experts (as well as the ambiguous position of project leader, seeking a solution by creating partnerships), sometimes in the form of a democratic exercise. It is, however, necessary to distinguish between cooperative actions in urban management and development that mobilise major national actors and localised actions for which international aid is often obtained through non-governmental organisations.

In the context of the rapid urbanisation that many countries of the South are experiencing, urban development should not only be seen from the point of view of demographic pressures; it is also produced by major infrastructure projects and industrial, tourist and residential areas. These projects do not all rely on international cooperation in the sense of public development aid; they nonetheless define not only the physical space of urban interventions (characterised by a change in the scale of the projects and areas concerned, and by the effects of the specialisation and determination of property prices), but also the institutional context and the configuration of urban powers and interest groups.

At this level there are a range of urban management and intermediation structures between external actors of urban cooperation (public or private) and internal public actors allowing for the adjustment of economic arguments, and even the political references and the principles of action that underlie them, notably in the case of countries with transitional governments. This is the case in Laos for VUDAA, which is an instrument of urban management and support for development operations in Vientiane with financing from international aid (multi- and bilateral). It is also the case in Vietnam for the Project Management Units (PMU), notably in the context of projects that receive international aid (Goldblum, 2008).

Partnerships with private foreign companies involving foreign direct investment (including in the context of joint ventures), in particular in equipment, infrastructure and urban services, also contribute to the shift "upward" of decision-making bodies for the development and governance of cities. The result is that the forces and challenges for urban governance become more complex, and the compatibility of urban governance with the principles of participatory democracy, as set out in the "urban development strategies" (UDS) by developing the "shared diagnostics", becomes questionable (Villes en devenir, 2007, p. 32-37). Indeed, since they cannot themselves take charge of the investment and maintenance costs required by large infrastructure networks – which are essential for urban life and activities and for creating attractive conditions for foreign investments with the aim of opening up the market for urban services in line with the principles promoted by international investors, local governments or public bodies in charge of managing large cities – they are driven to involve private international operators in the running of urban services. They are also driven to resort to various forms of partnership, ranging from the complete privatisation of services to various forms of distributing public services and concessions (as in the Anglo-Saxon system known as BOT – build-operate-transfer –, in which the concessionaire is in charge of implementing and operating the service).

Other than the fact that these means of intervention contribute to shifting responsibility away from the local authorities rather than strengthening them, the argument that they operate according to their own idea of efficiency and profitability nonetheless affects local populations (village society in urban development areas or groups of people in poorly integrated neighbourhoods), in particular in the form of eviction or forced displacement, including when actions are for the common good (environmental protection, protection of cultural heritage and social housing operations), and also affects the way their participation is sought. In terms of the issues related to eviction and forced displacement, the principle of urban governance has to face its limitations in relation to the public authorities' negotiation capacity, but also the limitations of the involvement of international cooperation (except to set targets for urban governance, at the risk of infringing on national sovereignty, regarding the sensitive subject of real estate and the conditions for receiving aid).

Localised approaches related to community development, upgrading (the restructuring of poorly integrated areas), construction of sewage systems and public drinking fountains or paved access roads require the population's participation in different ways (including when these projects involve property redistribution or even the arrangements for land sharing). The contributions of local government then address actions which concern it, including in terms of the maintenance of equipment and technical installations, waste collection, etc. Such actions may indeed be the subject of discussion and consensus, and may encourage mutual support networks, whether they are institutionalised or not. In this regard, it has become common practice, in the specialised literature, to refer to the participatory budget of Porto Alegre as proof of the relevance of participatory approaches in urban governance. It must be said that this approach remains unique. It was prepared in a particular political context: Brazil's return to a representative democracy and the exercise of local government responsibility by the Workers' Party in 1988, giving rise to the idea of a local citizenship; in other words, this arrangement was not reached under external pressure.

As soon as local participatory actions are the result of external initiatives adopted in the context of international cooperation, they depend on complex arrangements, however valid, and how these are financed is revealing, even if the non-governmental organisations, who are so often the mediators or even instigators of this, tend to gloss over that fact. This, however, does not in any way mean that the actions carried out at the most basic level and which contribute to building and reassuring civil society at the local level are invalid. However, it is impossible to ignore the complexity of the social dimension resulting from – precisely because of it is a question of cooperation – the expert positions which are linked to it, even if it is only because of the coordination problems (together with those of urban governance) raised by these new configurations of actors. The participatory democracy put forward by these approaches aimed at local development and the improvement of living conditions raises questions concerning representation, legitimacy and continuity, in particular relating to the starting point of the initiative and the method of action. In this respect, we can see that the actor referred to when we speak of urban governance, whether he is specialised or not, institutional or not, only becomes an actor (or is recognised as such) if he enters the sphere of governance; in other words, if he is asked to implement projects in the general sense. Obviously, the rules of the game are not set in stone, but this observation also leads to the question of how permanent governance arrangements are beyond the timeframe of the project financing that sets them in motion. The question is related to what will become of the problems which the projects were intended to resolve once the project is over, but also what will happen to the systems of powers, regulations and forms of solidarity which existed prior to the appearance of the projects and logics of governance.[7]

Considering urban cooperation with governance

Whether urban cooperation relates to institutional arrangements of national scope and major structural projects involving primary cooperation partners or to infra-institutional or local sectoral actions, the question remains regarding the nature of the actors required and the nature of the participation needed, the reference to democratic ideals, which have to be examined in the context of the modus operandi.

While international organisations and NGOs have in common that they draw upon an ideal abstraction of (good) urban governance – made up of general principles, charters, participatory democracy –, the actors of bilateral cooperation (state-to-state or decentralised) tend to draw on political reference points, on institutional legal frameworks and specific methods for dispute settlement, and on tried and tested management in terms of planning or overseeing.

However, despite the picture being different, it is still the same notion which prevails today. Urban governance seems therefore to belong to the list of "elusive concepts" (Osmont, 1998), along with urban management, for which Richard Stren (1993) came up with this pertinent formulation. This shows, in its own way, the need for relatively vague terminology to enable the implementation, in different areas and involving actors with different reference points and interests, of arrangements in some way connected to and stemming from shared logic. In the area of urban cooperation that we are concerned with, it is the notion of the "project" – broadly speaking action supported by external financing – which is the main word that brings all of these ideas together; it is the factor which makes the arrangements of urban governance necessary, at the same time as being its vector in various forms according to the idealities required by the main donors. In this particular sense, there is reason to admit that urban governance only exists in the context of "projects", which

---

7. In the same way as the reappearance of traditional authorities, especially in the management of real estate issues, such as the "circle councils" in Mali, helps to set up municipal councils and elected mayors.

8. This aspect of political neutralisation led John Crowley (2003) to introduce a distinction between governance and Michel Foucault's concept of "governmentality".

themselves relate to the field of the technical engineering of development or, to use Tania Murray Li's (2007) appropriate term, the "the will to improve".

Does this mean that the idea of urban governance, promoted in the context of international cooperation, is politically neutral[8], showing, on the scale of large cities or even metropolitan areas, the somewhat peaceful image of a conciliation of acknowledged interests in the efficiency of public aid and the profitability of foreign direct investment, all the while seeking, at smaller regional levels and, if needed, with the mediation of non-governmental organisations or international solidarity, the direct and active participation of populations with few resources through local-interest programmes? Basically, steered from the top (or even the supranational level) and regulated at the local level. Could the disappearance, as is apparent in the recent work of researchers published by the World Bank (Freire and Stren, 2001), of the expression "urban governance" to be replaced by "urban government", be the sign of the end of the concept, the root of which can be found in putting politics on hold – including in its goals of democratisation – and in politics being saturated by best practices? Whatever the case may be, if bilateral cooperation partners want to make it theirs, they urgently need to attach to the notion of urban governance a political dimension, from which international cooperation itself draws meaning and value.

Bibliography

Ascher, F. (1995). Métapolis ou l'avenir des villes, Paris, Odile Jacob.

Borja, J. (1998). "Las ciudades y el planeamiento estrategico. Una reflexion europea y latinoamericana", Urbama, n° 22.

Crowley, J. (2003). "Usages de la gouvernance et de la gouvernementalité", Critique internationale, n° 21, p. 52-61.

Freire, M. and R. Stren, (eds) (2001). The Challenges of Urban Government. Policies and Practices, Washington D.C., World Bank Institute (WBI Development Studies).

Goldblum, Ch. (2008). "Métropolisation et transition urbaine – à partir des exemples du Sud-Est asiatique", in Osmont A., Ch. Goldblum (ed.) et al., La gouvernance urbaine dans tous ses états. Analyses et propositions du groupe de réflexion sur la gouvernance urbaine, Paris, Ministère des Affaires étrangères et européennes – DgCiD (Études), p. 26-29.

Mathur, O. P. (ed.) (1999). India: The Challenge of Urban Governance, New Delhi, National Institute of Public Finance and Policy.

Murray, Li T. (2007). The Will to Improve. Governmentality, Development, and the Practice of Politics, Durham and London, Duke University Press.

Osmont, A. (1995). La Banque mondiale et les villes. Du développement à l'ajustement, Paris, Karthala.

Osmont, A. (1998). "La 'governance', concept mou, politique ferme", Les Annales de la recherche urbaine, n° 80-81 ("Gouvernances"), p. 19-26.

Osmont, A. (2002). "La citta efficiente", in Balbo M. (ed.), La Citta inclusiva, Milan, Franco Angeli, p. 13-29.

"Poverty Reduction and Urban Governance" (2000). Environment & Urbanization, vol. 11, n° 2.

Sivaramakrishnan, K.C. and L. Green (1992). Urban Governance in India, New Delhi, Centre for Policy Research.

Stren, R. (1993). "Urban Management in Development Assistance. An Elusive Concept", Cities, n° 10-12, p. 125-138.

UNCHS – United Nations Centre for Human Settlements, (2001). Cities in a Globalizing World: Global Report on Human Settlements, London, Sterling, Earthscan.

UN-Habitat, (2002). The Global Campaign on Urban Governance, Nairobi, Concept Paper, 2nd edition.

Villes en devenir (2007). Montpellier, MEDAD, MAEE, AFD, ISTED.

Weber, M. (1922/1980). Wirtschaft und Gesellschaft, 5, Auflage, Tübingen, Mohr-Siebeck.

Wolfensohn, J.D. (1999). Proposition pour un cadre de développement intégré, Washington D.C., World Bank, Draft Paper (French version).

20

Local Economic Governance in Africa

François YATTA
(Translated from the French)

Governance can be defined as the set of formal and informal regulations that a society adopts to manage their living together. Governance generally applies to groups of people living in a given territory. In this paper, local economic governance refers to the body of regulations of sub-national territories aimed at generating jobs and income, essentially focusing on the competitiveness of local economies and the improvement of living conditions of populations. Only fifteen years ago, local officials had a wait-and-see attitude towards local economic governance. For many national and local actors, economic development was a national matter, determined by the ministry in charge of the economy. It is true that most African countries were emerging from several decades of one-party rule, which were characterised by centralised development planning where the spatial dimension was barely taken into consideration. The development objectives were national and were meant to help sub-national territories share inputs and benefits. This was followed by decentralisation, which brought with it new responsibilities for local authorities. Among these was local economic development, which had, until then, been an almost or completely unfamiliar concept to them. From then on, local economic governance became one of the responsibilities of local authorities in Africa. Far from being a simple transfer of responsibilities, local economic governance confirms a truly territorial approach that highlights the reality of the new functions of the territories (Sauquet, M., Vielajus, M.).

This renewed interest in local economic governance is reinforced by two other factors in the African context.

The first factor is population. All the studies show that all of Africa is in the middle of a rapid demographic transition, and is shifting from being mainly rural to mainly urban (WALTPS, World Urbanization

Prospects The 2007 Revision Population Database). In most African countries, natural population growth and high urban growth rates have combined to produce an urbanisation rate that is constantly increasing. From 1960 to 1980, the growth rate of the most dynamic cities frequently reached or surpassed 10%, i.e. nearly triple the growth of European cities at the height of the Industrial Revolution. In the next thirty years, the total urban population, as well as the urban area, will probably triple again. This likely development shows that, even though the population growth rate is expected to decrease in the coming years, the urban population will probably continue to grow, although at a lower rate because of the relative decrease in the "pool" of rural dwellers.

This growing urbanisation – produced by the urban population's growth rate, which has been on average more than four times higher than that of the rural population – has not only affected capital cities. It is true that capital cities have absorbed a large part of the region's demographic growth (about two-thirds), but medium-sized cities have absorbed three out of four urban dwellers. Urbanisation is therefore characterised by the emergence of many medium-sized urban centres, which have gradually come to make up the bulk of the urban population, while helping to strengthen the urban framework.

The second factor is globalisation. It is one of the reasons local economic management has grown in importance. There are two reasons for this. The first is linked to the new context of economic development on a national scale. While the post-independence years saw positive and sustained economic growth, regions were a passive element of national development. The region was where activities took place within the framework of a national strategy for decentralising economic activity, but it was in no way a factor in development. With the increased competition brought about by globalisation, regions became a place for competition. Hence territories started to become increasingly important in national strategies. From then on, the characteristics, comparative advantages and competitiveness of territories, to name but a few aspects, became the focus of attention for national decision-makers. The second reason is linked to company strategies at the global level, and the logic behind the location of production systems. New trends in the organisation of production systems and the way these are related to space show that choosing a location put the territory and its comparative advantages centre stage (Savy, M. and Veltz, P.). Paradoxically, globalisation means that regions have become a concrete reference point in virtual space that now belongs to multinational companies and globalised society. This trend gives local authorities a prominent role to play in reconciling economic forces with social change, and in searching for a better balance between the collective will, the public authorities and private initiatives and interests.

Thus, urbanisation, globalisation and decentralisation have given rise to regions, putting local economic governance centre stage. The national territory is now managed as if it was a combination of different types of local economy. It is at the local economic level that Africa has gained a foothold in globalisation, and where the development challenges for most of the countries occur, especially in terms of their contribution to the globalised economy and their capacity to minimise the negative effects of globalisation, and all this despite the diminishing opportunities and capacities of states to confront this trend.

Subsequently, national governance is gradually being replaced by governance that is based on local concerns and is better adapted to sub-national regions. In order to do this, it was necessary to overcome several obstacles. The first was to get rid of the predominant "centralist" approach of national and international actors. The second was to get rid of the defensive approach of local management, with its slogans on the fight against AIDS, unemployment, insecurity, poverty, etc. These slogans, which are more widely used than any in favour of local economic development, leave local officials and actors with a wait-and-see attitude that is harmful to decentralisation. Local economic governance as a positive approach to local management, therefore, seems to be at odds with widespread beliefs. Only ten years ago, we would almost have apologised for promoting local economic development in African local authorities, since the local management's "defensive" approaches were so common.

Support tools for local economic governance

The approach to local economic management is different depending on whether it is traditionally an English-speaking or French-speaking country. In countries that are traditionally French-speaking, the local authorities are primarily responsible for providing basic local public services. In these countries, local economic management is approached in an indirect way: local economic development will depend on the provision of adequate local public services. Local economic management is perceived as a complement to national strategies for economic development, partly supported by the tradition of centralisation in these countries. In English-speaking countries, the local authorities are more directly in charge of economic development and the fight against poverty at the local level. Providing local public services is considered to be the basis for local economic development, which is the ultimate goal. In these

English-speaking countries, the approach to local economic development in the activities of local authorities is broader and more inclusive.

However, the first constraint that the local officers encounter in local economic management is the availability of tools to "capture" the local economy, allowing them to identify those levers they can ultimately use in order to improve conditions and quality of life for the population, as well as the competitiveness of local businesses. What is the local population (the city and its area of influence), what are the demographic and migratory processes at work, and what are the growth prospects? What is the role and significance of the local economy within the national and regional economy? What are the key components of this economy and the actors' strategies? In a local authority, what is the relative weight of different revenue streams and what role do they play, according to their provenance (i.e. public and private salaries, margins of the modern and informal sector, transfers by non-residents)? Where does the money circulating in the city and local economy come from, and where is it going? What would be the immediate knock-on and fiscal effects of public investment in a particular sector of the local economy? What would be the advantages and constraints of the different sectors in the local economy? Who are the project initiators, and what are their demands and proposals? What are the long-term challenges? What infrastructure is required and what return will it give? What might be the effects of these investments on, for example, the local, regional and national economies, or on tax revenue?

To overcome these obstacles several support tools for local economic governance are used by local African officials and elected representatives, so that they can understand their local economies. These tools have generally been developed with the help of international cooperation. The most widespread are the World Bank's Local Economic Development (LED) programme, the International Labour Organization's (ILO) programme, the ECOLOC programme, the PACA programme, and the UN-Habitat programme.[1]

---

1. The World Bank's LED programme is implemented in five stages. The first stage is organising the effort for the process; the second is conducting the local economy assessment; the third is developing the local economy development strategy; the fourth is implementing the LED strategies; and the fifth is reviewing the LED strategy. This tool is set up within the framework of World Bank projects and aims to identify which projects should be funded. The LED programme is usually carried out by closely working together with local governments and the private sector, and it is based on an assessment of the local economy's role in a regional and national context. Following the example of Africa, this tool has been implemented in other parts of the world.

The ECOLOC programme, developed by the Municipal Development Partnership (MDP) and the Sahel West Africa Club (SWAC), has three phases: the first is a study phase, the second is a policy dialogue and consultation phase, and the third is the

Although the levels of capture of the local economy differ, these tools show that local economic governance is part of the economic picture in Africa and that it aims to include decentralisation as part of a new approach to kick-start national development. The proponents of local economic governance argue that regional authorities should be recognised as economic actors in the same way as states or private businesses. In other words, it is possible to build another national development model by using local economic policies as a basis.

However, is the question here the decentralisation of national tools for capturing the economy? Or are we seeing tools being developed to truly take into consideration the particularities of local economic management? Practice is closer to the former than the latter, which could be extremely damaging to local economic management. Indeed, national accounting procedures – which have the same limitations as its parent discipline, macroeconomics –focus only on the general state of the economy, which includes local authorities, and do not take into account sub-national regions. Will this requirement be taken into account when considering

---

implementation of local development and economic revitalisation strategies, which begins after the consultation phase. Local economies set out in the ECOLOC programme organise regions around urban centres, providing a structure for the identifiable rural hinterland. Thus the local economy is both urban and rural. It covers an area with an estimated population of between 50,000 and 500,000 inhabitants and where the main urban centre represents between a third and a half of the total population. The ECOLOC programme provides institutional support for local authorities. The programme aims to help local officers and actors identify the levers they should use to help shape the future of their local authorities. The programme also helps mobilise local resources and strengthen the institutional capacity of local authorities, mainly concerning economic and financial issues.

The International Labour Organization (ILO) programme also contains five stages although they are not necessarily sequential: territorial diagnosis, consensus-building, promoting the local economic development forum, developing local economic development strategies and implementing LED strategies. What is unique about this programme is that local economic development agencies have been set up, whose role is, on the one hand, to ensure inclusive dialogue based on the broad participation of populations in the process, and, on the other hand, to put make financial or other services available to micro-businesses and small businesses in particular.

The GTZ programme, called PACA (Participatory Appraisal of Local Competitive Advantage) comprises several phases: preparing, carrying out the PACA exercise and implementing it. The PACA exercise has about seven stages and lasts no longer than three weeks. What sets this programme apart is that it supports small and medium-sized enterprises, especially by developing and implementing action plans for local economic development.

The UN-Habitat programme is based on four questions. Where are we today? Where do we want to go? How do we want to get there? How do we know when we are there? Compared to the other programmes, this one places the emphasis on creating a favourable environment for business (both in terms of infrastructure and legislation) and endeavours to take into consideration the categories generally forgotten in other programmes, such as young people, women and children.

local economic governance tools? If so, what does this mean regarding the tools for economic governance at the national level?

Of course, the issues of coordinating the various levels of economic governance (local and national), and developing the corresponding tools still need to be addressed. The problem here is making the economic governance systems, in place at every level of governance, compatible with each other. This is one of the next challenges for governance in Africa.

Instruments for local economic governance

Establishing local economic governance depends on the effective use of instruments whose importance varies depending on the local or national context. This is why local officials and elected representatives stress three main instruments: local taxation, local public spending and borrowing. Another institutional instrument that is often used is "inter-communality".

In most countries, local taxation is the result of two complementary strategies: the first is to define the pool of resources exclusively for the local authorities and the second is to identify the pool of resources to be shared between the State and local authorities. Local public finance will then ensure that the local environment and minimum conditions required for economic activity are managed efficiently. In order to do this, an adequate level of taxation of the local economy is needed, to enable local authorities to play a significant economic role with the aim of promoting the local economy. However, one of the most important constraints mentioned is, without doubt, the weak contributory capacity of populations. Indeed, the many micro-activities in the formal sector have a common denominator: low productivity and low wages. This situation does not favour the mobilisation of local resources.

Local authorities in French-speaking countries have very little leeway in terms of public financing. In French-speaking African countries, the local tax rate, basis and base are decided by the National Assembly. The local authorities are therefore not at all involved in the decisions concerning this aspect of their financial autonomy. Establishing a tax base, allocating roles and collecting are carried out by the services of the Ministry of Finance, who show few signs of urgency. The English-speaking countries have set up a system of real local taxation, which is determined by the local authorities themselves, often in agreement with central government. In addition, collecting these duties and local taxes is generally left to the local authorities, who thus have the opportunity to invest in the tax chain and make it more productive.[2] But whatever the context, English-speaking or French-speaking, and despite the innovations that take place here and there, we are forced to recognise the fact that, in general, local tax collection is still a major obstacle to the mobilisation of local resources.

Property tax is a special case, as the private residential capital stock is rarely used by local public management. Thus according to the estimates of the ECOLOC programme, the ratio between property tax and the value of private capital stock is close to 0%. This situation is all the more harmful because property tax is the local tax, par excellence, since it cannot be delocalised. But it is also and especially harmful because residential private capital strongly internalises positive external factors of the urban environment – external factors that are created by transport systems, the proximity of facilities, and work to improve the urban environment. Strengthening local budgets inevitably involves a better mobilisation of land resources.

Local public expenditure is an important instrument to revive the local economy (Cour, 2000). Local authorities are "economic agents". Their spending affects the local economy in the same way as the expenditure of other economic actors, such as businesses or households. This expenditure, regardless of type or purpose, is income for those service providers who offer goods or services to the authorities, or who benefit from the authority's support.

The third instrument of local economic governance is borrowing (Arnaud, 1999). Although local authorities represent a way for lending institutions to diversify, the latter remain very conservative. There are a number of reasons for this wariness towards the financial capacities of local authorities.[3] But the absence of specialised banks is also explained

---

2. What is striking in some English-speaking countries, especially South Africa, is the fact that local authorities are responsible for sectors such as water and electricity. This allows them to make the most of their resources.

3. There are several reasons for this:

– Local authority risk. Here we are generally able to note that savings (operating revenues-operating expenditure) are weak, even negative, often because there is a lack of local management, but also because local authorities rely on the central State in terms of revenues.

– State risk. A local authority can show positive savings even without owning liquid assets. This situation is especially true for French-speaking African countries, where the "single treasury principle" (unicité de caisse) (the maladministration of authorities' resources by the State within the context of central public finance crises) can put a local authority in a position where it is impossible for it to pay back the loan.

– Project risk. Regarding "sunk cost" investments (roads, gutters, education, etc.), when there are no procedures to recover the costs, the only option is to rely on the savings of local authorities. In the case of "cost recovery" investments, the local authorities do not have the technical and financial capacity to analyse the project.

by the fact that in African countries the market is restricted. Indeed, the number of cases dealt with per year and by country is linked to the number of authorities likely to start projects, i.e. no more than ten a year. This situation means that it is not very profitable to establish proper lending chanels for public authorities with specialist staff.

Lastly, the fourth instrument of local economic governance is inter-communality. Local officials, particularly those in medium-sized and large cities, know that working on the future of their towns definitely does not mean restricting work to inside the city limits. Urban prosperity largely depends on what is happening in its hinterland, both close by and further afield, and especially on the fundamental issue of improving the general inter-accessibility of urban and rural markets. Similarly, local authorities also know that towns make up "the market" and that any local economic development strategy should be coordinated with it. Most of the urban activities take place in nearby rural areas or are explained by the "primary complex". Thus, if the city is the motor driving development in the local economy, the primary sector is the fuel. But although expenditure in the hinterland can generate considerable returns for cities (often more than if the expenditure had been carried out in the cities themselves), the legal and regulatory provisions in force do not allow a mayor to spend budgetary resources outside his jurisdiction. Establishing inter-communality between urban and rural local authorities helps ensure that the spatial dimension of local economic development is taken into account. In most countries, decentralisation laws provide for inter-communal bodies to be set up. Establishing inter-communality takes into account this geographic economic continuity and enables more robust economic development strategies to be developed and implemented.

However, there are many constraints, most of them institutional, on the use of local economic governance instruments. This raises two big questions.

The first is linked to government contracting. More than two-thirds of government contracts in a local authority are secured by outside businesses, generally from the country's political or economic capital. This fact does not strengthen the impact of local public spending on the local economy, as these businesses tend to import both the labour and the goods that are needed to implement these government contracts. The greater the amount of imported goods in public spending is the less public spending benefits the local economy.

Can decentralisation and government contracting be better coordinated to improve local economic governance? In other words, should government contracting remain a minor aspect of government reform in general, and decentralisation in particular? Admittedly, equality of access of businesses to government contracts in a country is one of the foundations of economic life, but shouldn't a little more emphasis be placed on the idea of equity? As things stand, national businesses have comparative advantages that allow them greater access to local government contracts. Decentralising government contracts should be an essential component of local economic governance.

The second question is linked to the use of borrowing, taxation and spending instruments in local economic governance. Indeed, national political leaders, notably from finance ministries, monitor the use of these instruments very closely. In the context of structural adjustments, it is thought that the use of borrowing, expenditure and taxation by local authorities may weaken national macroeconomic management. Is there a contradiction between the economic activity of local authorities and the effectiveness of national macroeconomic policy instruments? Is it possible to create a different national macroeconomic approach that is more focused on the economic activities of local authorities within the framework of decentralisation? Can a combination of these instruments at both levels of governance be used to improve living conditions for the population? Does the fact that economic decision-making is becoming more and more territorialized, and that local space is becoming a strategic space that drives the economy, not suggest a need to refound national macroeconomic management instruments?

Conclusion

Decentralisation, on an economic level, will more and more often result in the differentiated management of the national territory. There are as many local authorities as there are economic development strategies, even if the national macroeconomic framework that covers local authorities is set at the national level. In this way, the economic health of local authorities is a decisive factor in national macroeconomic performance. In some countries, the State has signed performance contracts that set a number of national economic development goals for local authorities. State subsidies or certain incentives encourage local authorities to help achieve some of the national development goals. But decentralisation is also a competition between local authorities. The rapid increase in spatial disparities can have a negative impact on macroeconomic performance and often on national unity too. Decentralisation and the emergence of different types of bodies highlight the need to evaluate the impact of public policies at the national level. This is because all economic policy has a spatial dimension through its impacts, which very often vary depending on the area. In some areas, general measures can even bring about results contrary to those sought by official policy. Coordination between local economic governance and national governance is more important than ever for a better outcome for the population.

Even if local economic governance is run by local authorities, officials and actors, problems persist. The first is linked to information. Local economic governance is based on local economic information. And yet, at the moment, the information needed to identify and assess the measures to be taken at a local level is, on the whole, insufficient or even non-existent.

The decentralisation of economic and social information has not kept pace with political and administrative decentralisation. It is imperative to take into account the spatial dimension in national information systems, for two reasons. The first is that, since local authorities are responsible for local development, local elected representatives and actors must have local economic and social information at their disposal, enabling them to develop, implement and assess local economic development strategies. The second is that the State, in its mission to achieve national stability and redistribution, must have local development indicators, especially since the differences in the structures and development of sub-national regions are going to become more and more pronounced. Approaches, such as the ECOLOC programme, have worked towards developing economic dashboards in order to allow an informed dialogue between actors to take place. One of the roles of the ECOLOC programme is to measure local wealth (output, private and public capital stock) and the activities that generate it. Another is to identify and understand the dynamics of structural changes (economic, social and spatial), which will serve as a platform for development strategies and a sustainable economic upturn. The programme results in a body of coherent information (reviews and forecasts) on the local economy, the actors, the stakes and dynamics. All of these are expressed in quantitative, qualitative and spatial terms, and summed up in a reference framework called the "Local economic dashboard".

Permanently reducing this lack of local information will involve adding a spatial dimension to economic and social information systems in countries. This will also require a thorough restructuring of the information systems set up at the time when national economic management was centralised. Starting at the local level has two advantages: to combine the level of governance and the information systems; and to highlight the shortcomings of existing information systems in order to build new systems that are able to deal with the challenges faced by African countries.

The second problem is linked to State support and international cooperation to increase the spending capacity of local authorities. Local expenditure is a factor in local economic development. At the same time, efforts to mobilise local resources have to be increased, and taxation levels raised. In order to do this, local authorities need to educate citizens about local public spending. Money paid in taxes is not "lost"; through local authority expenditure, money is injected into the local economy, which allows whole sectors of the local economy to function. Through public spending, taxes become an important instrument to boost the local economy. Educating citizens about taxes should be at the centre of strategies to mobilise local resources in order to reduce the impact of the lack of tax civicism, which all too often undermines the financial autonomy of local authorities.

Not only local resources but also resources from international cooperation and the state need to be directed at only one objective: increasing the spending capacity of local authorities. A local authority that levies taxes, spends those taxes to improve the quality of its public infrastructures, develops its economy and thus collects even more in taxes. The inability of local authorities to spend is the starting point for a vicious circle where a poor environment leads to stagnation, and even a relative decline, in the local economy. The less a local authority taxes and spends, the poorer the people become.

The third problem is to get people involved in managing local public affairs. This participation process leads not only to the development of strategies but also to their implementation. Indeed, how many strategies have been drawn up but have never seen the light of day because of reluctance on the part of people who were not involved in the initial stages? Organising and holding a constant dialogue between different local actors should be done within the framework of a permanent consultation forum set up for this purpose with the goal of creating a local coalition. The establishment of such a local forum to provide a framework for dialogue, allow local actors to reach consensus, and help monitor the implementation of the local economic development plan, will help create local economic governance.

In terms of local economic governance, local leaders have realised that elective democracy and participatory democracy are not mutually exclusive. Even though they are elected, local leaders consult with the local people on matters relating to local public services and local economic development strategies. In Africa, there are now many examples of local economic development strategies being developed and implemented with the participation of the people.

Finally, the constraints on capacity development faced by local authorities mean that local economic governance takes longer to take root. The low level of institutional development of local authorities is a huge challenge to be taken up in the context of decentralisation. Taking on communal ownership for local economic development programmes is a prerequisite for successful local economic governance.

Bibliography

Arnaud, M. (1999). Programme d'action en faveur du financement de l'investissement communal par emprunt, Ministère des Affaires étrangères – Coopération et Francophonie.

Cour, J.-M. (2002). Quelques éléments de réflexion sur la lutte contre la pauvreté issus du programme ECOLOC, Séminaire de restitution du programme ECOLOC, Paris, juin.

Kessides, Ch. (2006). The Urban Transition in Sub-Saharan Africa: Implications for Economic Growth and Poverty Reduction, Cities Alliance, World Bank.

Mbassi, J.P.E. (May, 2004). "Les politiques de déconcentration et de decentralization", Organisation internationale de la francophonie (OIF), Symposium on access to international financing, Paris.

Mbassi, J.P.E. (1998). "Quand les villes s'émancipent", Alternatives économiques, n° 035, Hors série, january.

Partenariat pour le développement municipal, (2003). Observatoire de la décentralisation: État de la décentralisation en Afrique, Paris, Karthala.

Partenariat pour le développement municipal (2000). "Financer les collectivités locales pour renforcer la démocratie et le développement local", Sommet Africités 2000, summit held in Windhoek (Namibia).

Partenariat pour le développement municipal (2000). "Accès des collectivités locales à l'emprunt et aux marchés financiers", Sommet Africités 2000, summit held in Windhoek (Namibia).

Partenariat pour le développement municipal (2000). "Politiques économiques et développement local durable", Sommet Africités 2000, summit held in Windhoek (Namibia).

Partenariat pour le développement municipal, (2001). "Regard sur les économies locales, une approche renouvelée sur les stratégies de développement en Afrique de l'Ouest".

Yatta, F.P. (2003). "Les enseignements des études de cas sur les villes ouest africaines et les économies locales (ECOLOC)", Région et développement, n° 17.

Yatta, F.P. (2006). Villes et développement économique en Afrique: une approche par les comptes économiques locaux, Economica.

Yatta, F.P. (2007). La gouvernance financière locale, United Nations 7th Global Forum on Reinventing government, Vienna (Austria).

21

The Implementation of Local Solidary Governance in Porto Alegre, Brazil

Strategies for Social Inclusion Promotion

José Alberto FOGAÇA DE MEDEIROS[1]

Local Solidary Governance Program (PGSL): its philosophy and what is at stake

The principal objective is to promote a reformulation of the relationship between public authorities and society and the municipal-administration model itself.

The program is not focused on one single social practice, but rather upon a change of culture and the way of considering citizens and political agencies. As can be seen from the background history of the PGSL, this fits with objectives of the current application, as it is raising public awareness of the challenges of the urban era and identifying solutions, together with disseminating a new concept based on the solidary management of public affairs and innovative changes in the ways of thinking about the relations and responsibilities of the inhabitants of the city.

Institutionally, PGSL is seen to be innovative by basing public administration on the following principles: plurality (recognizing that society consists of multiple differences), dialogue (contributing towards society becoming a system of connections that are always open and respectful) and consensus (forming a community of projects and pacts for social responsibility for sustainable development).

---

1. Mayor of Porto Alegre

With implementation of the PGSL, the administration of Porto Alegre is changing the way of thinking of the city, promoting a real revolution of concepts, which is most difficult to achieve, since both political agencies and citizens have to be open to these challenges. The success of the Program is already being seen, making Porto Alegre into an inter-sectoral multidisciplinary network that is being territorially organized to promote living spaces that can strengthen the culture of solidarity and cooperation between government and local society. This new form of governance is founded on the premise that citizenship is not just exercised by demands, but mainly as a way of adding value, with rights and responsibilities shared between all participants.

This new focus on the policy of sustainable development enables expansion of the social capital of each region, district and city as a whole for better quality of life and advancing social indicators, together with improving peaceful coexistence between people and qualifying municipal public services. The municipal administration's priority strategies are being worked on to these ends: attention to and protection of children and teenagers; improving access and quality of healthcare services; improving the population's safety; and fighting poverty through citizen self-sustainability and emancipation. The principal player in all this is the citizen, not the public administration. It is citizens who determine the needs of their neighbourhoods, their districts, identifying the main requirements and preparing a plan for the medium- and long-term future of the places they live in. After this identification of its proposals, the citizens, together with all the other sectors of society, prepare the necessary strategies for the success of the future plan, the measures required, and start to carry out these actions. Transversality is a term that better describes these steps, as public policies and governmental actions alike will be founded on the plan developed by society.

As a new and innovative technology, implementation of the PGSL is not a straight road but more of a difficult path, because putting into practice what many have written about "social capital", "cooperative spirit" and "transversality" is not an easy task, but it is certainly challenging and is being operated in Porto Alegre as a way of creating a climate of reciprocal trust between all the different social players of government and society (the private sector, all forms of civil organization and the citizen).

It is also important to underline the value of replicating and disseminating the PGSL in other regions. As it involves a change of paradigms, the concept of Local Solidary Governance is an individual project within a broad spectrum of good practices and projects aimed at sustainable urban development, recognized by UNESCO, since it is a way of rethinking the city and not just a single link in its chain. The

PGSL has the potential to be disseminated and replicated throughout the world, as it deals with universal concepts, such as cooperation, social capital, plurality, dialogue, partnership and many others. The idea of promoting an inter-sectoral and multidisciplinary network which is territorially organized for promoting spaces of coexistence between government and local society can and should be disseminated and replicated, simply adapting the principal points of restructuring according the needs identified by the players in their own regions. The PGSL's methodological structure is a flexible tool which can be adjusted to the particular requirements of each region, without losing its conceptual value and theoretical foundations.

Finally, implementation of the PGSL and effective internalization of its concepts by the players, mean that Porto Alegre is collaborating in the city becoming a real Network-City, a huge municipal web interlinking citizens connected to local networks, engaged in the sustainable development of its communities and the city as a whole, guided end to end by common objectives, and working to achieve, although experimentally, the Millennium Development Goals.

Economy and the background of PGSL

The PGSL was devised based on the latest published theses by important writers of our times and in the history of Porto Alegre itself, seeking to serve the needs of the city, which is a key player and setting for several social changes, especially the Participative Budget, with the aim of consolidating the idea of advancing concepts of democracy and seeking to publicize the concept of social capital so that each citizen is aware of his or her rights and responsibilities as a participant in the Network-City being formed through this Program. A brief background history of how the Local Solidary Governance Program came about, its objectives, results and perspectives, follows: the intense activities of the social network in the state capital, the emergence of the Participative Budget (OP) and implementation of advances brought about by the 1988 Constitution, brought progress and improvement to this history of struggle and success, while presenting shortcomings in the city of Porto Alegre's effective construction of other alternatives for local sustainable development.

We can see progress in terms of the organization of portions of the population of Porto Alegre in the struggle for public services; advances in the fights against prejudice, domestic violence, and child abuse; and advances in guaranteeing rights and raising citizen awareness. But there are also shortcomings in sensitizing huge contingents of unorganized, scattered social players indifferent to the value of the democratic process; shortcomings in social development achieving greater recruitment, as a result of low involvement in the participative process – Councils, OP, Congresses, social networks – Union and Business organizations, Associations, NGOs –, and the various spheres of Federal, State and Municipal Public Authorities.

It is also important to underline the role of decentralized cooperation in this process. It is because of this that Porto Alegre has shared its experience with a large number of cities across numerous continents, especially Latin America and Europe, with the European Union's Urb-Al programme. This exchange of experiences has enabled Porto Alegre to "export" its experience of democratic participation and equally to improve this experience based on the analysis of the lessons learnt by other cities.

There are also shortcomings in diagnosis (social, economic maps of citizen initiatives); in an essential compass of indicators for assessing the appropriateness, efficiency and effectiveness of each action, project and program in all phases of planning, monitoring and execution. And as important as the related shortcomings is the lack of transparency, or the absence of a Municipal Social Balance Sheet which gives an account of each party involved in the City Council's actions, transparency and performance – Public Authorities, Private Initiatives, Non-governmental Organizations – in fulfilling previously established and agreed Goals, through an effective Contract of Social Responsibility.

The challenge we face with Local Solidary Governance is to demonstrate that the city is ready to create alternatives that remove the boundaries imposed by internal inequalities, bringing a leap forward in the quality of the city's social management, with its sights on the Sustainable development of its districts, territories and neighbourhoods.

To respond better to this challenge we can start by asking the following questions:

– How can local communities be empowered?

– How can more cooperation be generated between the city and the community?

– How can more people become involved in achieving targets for social improvement and developing a common project for sustainable development?

– How can the efficiency of Executive actions be increased through integration of public policies and services?

– How can social inclusion, quality of life and the peaceful coexistence of citizens be promoted?

– How can social inequality be reduced in the city?
– How can a new level of social-environmental welfare be achieved?
– How can the democratic process be strengthened?

The guiding principles for finding solutions to these problems are transparency, plurality, dialogue, access to information, transformality and territoriality. That is why we are working with a new concept of government – Local Solidary Governance – and have also adopted a specific program for implementing local solidary governance, made possible through technical cooperation established with UNESCO.

The need for the program has arisen because, while the concepts of governance, solidarity and territoriality are not so new in themselves, they have yet to be applied jointly to Brazilian municipal public administration. This requires Porto Alegre City Council to increase their efforts in group learning and diffusing this new practice.

That is why we have established a cooperation protocol with UNESCO that is enabling qualified production of educational material and training of governmental agencies, which we will now expand into schools, telecenters and communities, union and business organizations. This partnership ensures the necessary support for forming agencies of governance, training public-sector workers and management and social leaders alike in the development and stimulus of social capital.

By December 2008, we hope to have 13,000 voluntary agents connected and linked in a great network of local solidary governance working in the city's 82 neighbourhoods and 478 settlements. By the end of the following year we also hope to have at least 700 civil-society organizations trained in project management and attracting funding – all based on a view that it is no longer possible to think that responsibility for solving social problems lies solely with public authorities.

From the point of view of our strategic map, Local Solidary Governance is supported on the pillars of transparency, (promoting a culture of social and financial responsibility and ensuring access to information and dialogue with society); democracy (planning and carrying out our actions territorially and mobilizing local social capital); and the modernization of public administration (encouraging inter-sector relations, seeking excellence in administrative and operational processes, training public-sector workers and modernizing and integrating information technologies).

People have been found in each region of the city willing to work voluntarily with government agencies. Networks have been formed without worrying about adding names to more names. The objective is for the voluntary involvement of people who see they can offer something to their locale. At the meetings – not assemblies for voting on this or that - people are starting to relearn how to dream. They imagine a better future for the place where they live, identifying its vocations, mapping the needs and potential of each region, starting to seek out possibilities for alliances and partnerships, and in particular coming to see that everyone has to help in building that dreamed-of future.

Dissemination of material about the proposal for Local Solidary Governance requires permanent training. We are producing handbooks, video-lessons, multimedia products – educational material used in meetings for raising awareness and energizing networks. Seminars, lectures and courses have also been organized. Six editions of Jornal do Region have been produced to date, which is a monthly publication directed towards each of the 17 regions of the city for publicizing the actions being carried out in the spirit of governance. At the same time the Governance Blog[2] has been created, which is a contemporary tool for integrating, updating and creating links between all those willing to assist in confronting local problems. Equally, the first stage of the Project Development and Attracting Resources Course (Capacitapoa) has trained 261 people from 188 civil-society organizations in all regions of the city in project management, attracting resources and governance, providing knowledge for their emancipation and qualifications for democratic participation.

This construction, also described step by step below, especially in step n°1, aims to involve communities in constructing agendas for development and agreements for carrying them out.

City Budget – Local Solidary Governance generates a new budget by operating government and community resources in favour of local development and the social inclusion of the regions. It was therefore firstly necessary not to restrict citizen participation simply to discussions of governmental priorities for the particular interests of one group, sector or locale. The huge potential of communities and individuals must no longer be squandered by being directed or channelled simply towards demanding this or that key action from government, disconnected from a dream of the future, and from participative analysis and planning. This generates dispersal of effort, transforming participation into confrontational situations that result in low-intensity experiences of democracy and a high degree of antagonism. Local Solidary Governance is being constructed based on the contemporary belief that citizenship is both a right and a responsibility. For each right demanded of the state, a corresponding responsibility should be taken up by society and the citizen.

Instead of restricting the forms of people's participation to requesting the state to carry out this or that action, focusing just on the governmental budget, it is also necessary to incorporate the potential of society for discovering and developing its own assets and energizing its potential.

---

2. www.governancalocal.com.br

Not just requesting, but also suggesting. Not just demanding, but also doing. Instead of just asking for funding, mobilizing and attracting new resources that cannot be obtained as or from revenue income, but can be found at the base of society. Instead of being centred just on combative demands for extracting a particular action or public service from the state, it should make the public a social (not statal) sphere of initiatives, accepting responsibilities and gathering new skills. Alongside the participative budget, we seek participative planning, local players, collective entrepreneurship, and partnerships between the various forms of negotiation (state, private enterprise and civil society) for solidary governance. The sum of the Council budget added to this new budget of mobilizing the resources of society (not necessarily financial), and governed by a dream of the future, is materialized in the real City Budget.

Current status and the lessons learnt by the implemention of PGSL

Porto Alegre's administration is dynamic and innovative with distinctive accumulated social capital and a developed network of people's participation. This is a favourable climate, founded on citizen participation for putting into practice a new stage of sustainable development of the city, synthesized in the Local Solidary Governance Program, for undertaking work that is still lacking in Porto Alegre: social inclusion and improvements to people's lives and coexistence. Being a Program that radically transforms concepts and seeks continuous adaptation to real conditions, the PGSL is already yielding visible results and is always working towards further social advancement. It is not a Project with a beginning, middle and end, but has a defined beginning and current continuity until, together with its theoretical premises; it becomes something seeded in the collective subconscious of the network-city.

Key features of PGSL

Listed below are some of the results achieved, although partially, as mentioned above, from the management process, and hoped to be achieved through the PGSL, from which a socially responsible administration can be formed and which can be disseminated and replicated elsewhere.

Sustainable Development and Social Capital

For a long time the idea prevailed in Brazil that it was firstly necessary to "allow the cake to rise before distributing it". This understanding guided the economics of various governments, for which accumulation of capital would generate enough wealth to provide Brazilians with access to education, healthcare, housing, sanitation, and cultural assets, allowing them to benefit from their individual capacities. It has been sufficiently shown that economic capital does not accumulate and reproduce sustainably in climates with an insufficient supply of social capital. This can be defined, although only partially, as mobilization within a territory or a community of material, psychological, cultural, environmental, moral, ethical, and civic factors that systematically feed back through horizontal connections.

Nevertheless, it is necessary to point out one important aspect. We often run the risk of inverting the factors of the simple proposition of "letting the cake rise". It is as if we were thinking, "the cake of social capital first needs to rise before the accumulated human abilities can share the wealth." In conjecture, we have to ask: What wealth? When an economic authority says, "The social sphere is nothing to do with me," it is reproducing the old paradigm. Obviously, if the social field understands economics in the same way, fragmentation will be the rule for any government.

That is why we yearn for a form of development that will be both economic and social at the same time. A Sustainable Development.

Transversality and Integration

Public Authorities are expected to break with the classic paradigm of being structured as a closed system. Increasing permeability enables updating the knowledge base of its public agents, its skills, nurturing communication and dialogue, burying the practice of secrecy as a source of power and generating new leaderships. Stimulus for coexistence between its internal Departments and/or Secretariats and the living fabric of society, and also permanently training and enabling its frameworks of public-sector workers, will bring about action practices integrated internally and externally and with other public, municipal, state and federal spheres.

Promotion and organization

The Public Authorities take up their social responsibility, becoming the promoter, the sector which, through its own characteristic relations with the local and the global, "carries forward" the common capacities and projects of society; organizing initiatives; providing its physical structure, human capital and democratizing decision-making power, putting it at the service of the public good and especially for those most in need of it.

Empowerment of social and human capital in the area of territoriality

The Public Authorities are expected to promote the accumulation of social capital and empower human capital, stimulating cooperation in the Municipality, involving the social participation network in decentralized planning, monitoring, execution and assessment of projects, programs and actions, facilitating network connections and enabling the formation of citizen-administrators. Public investments should also take account of valuing the local economy and society, pointing out to the territories, neighbourhoods and regions, that enterprise is good business. The Public Authorities should pursue Sustainable Local Development.

Diagnostic maps and citizen initiatives

It is expected that diagnostic maps will be produced to meet the specific requirements and identities in the smallest territorial unit, accompanied by considered indicators of the focus of the project, which can assess the process, impact and participation: Who are the poor? What is economic increment? What is environmental conservation?

The Public Authorities should also produce maps for diagnosing the social capital in its smallest territorial unit: How does social organization and participation work? How many and which organizations and non-state public participation bodies are there, and in which fields do they operate? How many volunteers and social players are there, and who are they? What human resources and materials are available? What is the framework of installed public equipment? What public social programs are being developed, what human resources are available and in which spheres: State, Municipal, Federal? What external, human, environmental factors have or could have a positive or negative impact on the accumulation of social capital? How many individuals have access to the Internet? How many bookshops, newsstands, cinemas, theatres, and museums are there?

Goals and assessment systems

Based on the maps and in partnership with society, the Public Authorities have developed a strategic plan, defining projects, programs and actions and annual, and multi-year goals for improving social indicators – global and territorial – and an efficient and effective assessment system (integration, suitability and adaptability, engagement with the target public) and anticipated results: How much does it cost (efficiency)? What impact does it have (effectiveness)? Whom does it impact upon (focus)?

Partnerships and co-responsibility

The Public Authorities should promote a culture of partnerships, connecting public, private and Third-Sector investment, defining joint priorities and rationalizing the joint efforts of the human, social and material resources involved. Co-responsibility commitments for achieving the social results should be agreed between all the partners involved in each project.

Transparency and the Social Balance Sheet

The Public Authorities are developing the Social Balance Sheet, presenting annual accounts containing a detailed report of the social results achieved, based on the goals established in partnership with the social-participation network, for carrying out programs, projects and actions and demonstrating the effective involvement of each responsible party.

In pursuit of these results the Local Social Governance Program indicates a collection of actions which provide an institutional climate favourable to implementing and consolidating the spirit of Local Governance, within the perspective of promoting social inclusion and the fight against poverty, being committed to:
– training professionals, community leaders and public agencies to carry forward the practice of developing Local Solidary Governance territorially, multi-sectorally, transdisciplinarily and transversally;
– encouraging actions that ensure the technical, scientific and technological support necessary for carrying out the activities promoted by both the Council's Social and Environmental Policy Management Committee and the administrative committees and organizers of Local Solidary Governance;
– monitoring the changes seen in the Local Solidary Governance model by systematic assessment methodologies;
– offering and qualifying geo-processed information (within the local and global aspect of the city), through tele-centers, to Local Solidary Governance and to professionals in the social support network, managers and other players in the local community.

Some results from the first twenty-four months

Implementation of Local Solidary Governance in the 17 regions of the Participatory Budget (OP), with an effective impact on promoting the social inclusion of the most vulnerable sectors of the population;

Training of technical teams, social organizers of the Local Solidary Governances, Participative Budget delegates and advisors by investing in the development of human resources and improving information systems;

Implementing the Local Solidary Governance Information System which, linked with other assessment tools, enables regular monitoring of indicators of social participation, social capital, human development and sustainable development, bringing greater agility and quality to the management process of governance within the logic of the Program;

Strengthening the OP, expanding and quantifying citizen participation with other social and solidary-support networks in pursuit of co-responsibility for Sustainable Local Development.

Lessons learnt from the introduction of the programme and the implementation of PGSL

Important Innovation

The Management Committees in each region are new democratic spaces which link to the OP as a Forum of the GSL, formed by the Organization and Organization Networks Team and the Management Committees themselves, generating another opportunity for an organized civil society and private enterprise, with the government enabling actions that are played out by the community itself, without passing through all the administrative stages for materializing their visions of the future.

The steps described can be exemplified by looking at the Construction Project for the Professional Training Centre in the Cruzeiro Region, with 200,000 inhabitants, mostly living in socially and environmentally vulnerable conditions, which had long been planned by the region without ever being realized: the Local Management Committee, together with the community in the region, formed an organizing team, defined a Vision of the Future of the Region and identified its assets and needs, prepared Plans and Goals and their Priority Agenda, finally agreeing their Pact for Local Solidary Governance. From this Agenda and their Vision of the Future, the inhabitants of the Cruzeiro region organized themselves with the rest of Porto Alegre society and succeeded in completely building the Professional Training Centre.

This project will provide a space for training and acquiring skills in the Cruzeiro region, bringing technical and professional qualifications to all, promoting actions for income generation and social inclusion through various activities requested by the community, which will be developed in the Cruzeiro Professional Training Centre.

Allied to this process, the community is taking up the project for a Cultural Centre to complement the efforts begun with the Training Centre. Porto Alegre City Council, through the Political Coordination and Local Governance Secretariat, and implementation of the Local Solidary Governance Program, has made viable the mobilization that already existed among local players and made this action possible through the technical consultancy and participation of socio-economic players directly linked to the local development process.

The effectiveness of the program

The first display of the effectiveness of the PGSL can be seen in the Municipal Management of Porto Alegre itself: while there has been no question of adapting the global vision of government in other administrations, Porto Alegre City Council has used the concept of Local Solidary Governance to form its Government Programs, taking into account the need to act transversally. It is constructed based on three axes: Social, Environmental, Financial, (Economic and Management). These axes lead to the projects in the governmental sphere, all being transversal, and in the sphere of partnership with the private and public sectors. (www.portoalegre.rs.gov.br):

All these programs are operated transversally in the public sphere, always organizing partnerships with various private and community bodies. Each program above is being organized and put into practice by society.

The 'outer fruit' is already visible. A good example is that the advent of the PGSL has enabled united efforts between the Municipality and the Federal University of Rio Grande do Sul, the Participative Budget Council, Pocempa, the Economy and Statistics Foundation, the Inter-syndicate Department of Statistics and Socioeconomic Studies (DIEESE), Pontifícia Universidade Católica do RS and the Urb-Al Network (European Commission) to construct an important instrument for accessing information about the city:

Another united effort through the PGSL which is radically changing the lives of inhabitants of Porto Alegre is moving the inhabitants from the "Vila do Chocolatão" settlement to a location worthy of human habitation, without argument or alteration but, on the contrary, with a transparency constructed with the community directly involved and other necessary partners, which is not only bringing benefits to all participants but also to the city in general. The inhabitants of the settlement will move to houses with facilities, basic sanitation, the availability of public services such as refuse collection, running water, all the duties that the public administration should fulfil, which will later be reflected in the health of the direct beneficiaries, generating personal growth, increased self-esteem, the feeling of citizenship and engagement for the common good: beneficiaries of the project will feel part of a larger body and will tend to continue collaborating for the city's further improvement. This is the cycle that Local Solidary Governance intends, and is already managing, to put into practice in Porto Alegre, to be a program broadly used as a compass for public administration and spreading throughout the whole society of Porto Alegre.

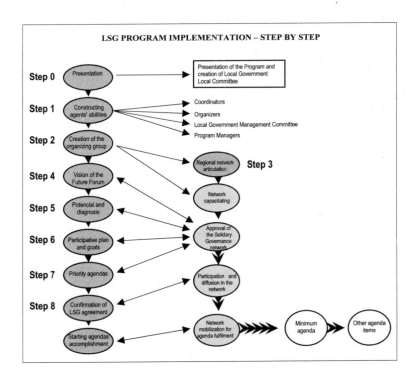

Bibliography

Barros, R.P. de, R. Henriques and Mendoçar (2000). Desigualdade e Pobreza no Brasil: Retrato de uma Estabilidade Inaceitável, Rio de Janeiro, IPEA.

Busatto, C. (2001). Responsabilidade Social, Revolução do Nosso Tempo, Porto Alegre, Editora Corag, Edição Esgotada.

Busatto, C. and J. Feijò (2006). A Era dos Vagalumes – o Florescer de uma Nova Cultura Política, Canoas, Editora da Ulbra.

Capra, F. (1997). A Teia da Vida: Uma Nova Compreensão Científica dos Sistemas Vivos, São Paulo, Cultrix.

Castells, M. and J. Borja (1999). Local y Global: La gestion de las ciudades em Ia era de Ia información, Madrid, Grupo Santillana de Ediciones.

Araujo, M.C. d', (2003). Capital Social, Rio de Janeiro, Jorge Zahar Editores (Coleção Passo a Passo).

Franco, A. de (2003). Terceiro Setor: A Nova Sociedade Civil e seu Papel Estratégico para o Desenvolvimento, Brasília, Agência de Educação para o Desenvolvimento (AED).

Geertz C. (1978). A Interpretação das Culturas, Rio de Janeiro, Jorge Zahar Editores.

Gladwell, M. (2002). O Ponto de Desequilíbrio: Como Pequenas Coisas Podem Fazer uma Grande Diferença, Rio de Janeiro, Editora Rocco.

Gleick, J. (1989). Caos: A Criação de uma Nova Ciência, Rio de Janeiro, Editora Campus.

Johnson, S. (2003). Emergência: A Vida Integrada de Formigas, Cérebros, Cidades e Softwares, Rio de Janeiro, Jorge Zahar Editores.

Landes, D. (1998). A Riqueza e a Pobreza das Nações: Porque São Algumas Tão Ricas e Outras Tão Pobres, Rio de Janeiro, Editora Campus.

Levy, P. (1998). A Inteligência Coletiva: Por uma antropologia do ciberespaço, São Paulo, Loyola.

Lewontin, R. (2002). A Tripla Hélice, São Paulo, Companhia das Letras.

Maturana H. and F. Varella (1997) De Máquinas e Seres Vivos: Autopoiesis: A Organização do Vivo, Porto Alegre, Artes Médicas.

Maturana, H. and G. Verden-Zöller (1997). Amor y Juego: Fundamentos Olvidados de lo Humano: desde el Patriarcado a la Democracia, Santiago du Chili, Instituto de Terapia Cognitiva.

22

Urban Mediation

A Practice at the Service of Local Democracy

Pierre LAYE
(Translated from the French)

The world is urbanising: in 2007 half of the world's population lives in cities, though urbanisation rates can vary greatly, depending on the country. Although the vast majority of developing countries are experiencing growth, poverty continues to spread, especially in African cities; inequalities are becoming greater between those who benefit from the fruits of growth and those who do not.

Rapid urbanisation, internal and external migration, developments in communications and openness to the world all "shake up" the organisation of civil societies. As local governments from the decentralisation process gain ground, increased cooperation between the state, elected local representatives and civil society is taking place in an effort to keep a modicum of social cohesion while at the same attempting to better meet the demands of populations, notably regarding access to basic services.

Such multiple partnership strategies do not, as a general rule, come about spontaneously and are, more often than not, the work of representatives of institutions or groups, or leader figures. The debate on this subject over the years produced a whole generation of social welfare and development professionals, known as "facilitators" or "mediators", at the local level.

A close look at their work reveals how politically sensitive their actions were, as well as all the technicalities they entailed. Furthermore, it seems, now more than ever, that it is necessary to try to define the "job description" for these urban mediation activities and to invest in training, in order to help create a real pool of professionals in this field in countries of the South.

Approach and aims

Urban mediation

There are always a number of actors involved in any goal intended to lead to a project or public policy. These actors include public authorities – especially local ones – decentralised services, and authorities elected in a decentralised system. They also include the population, grouped in various ways, comprising a civil society with different levels of organisation, at times more apparent than at others, and developing complementary, competing or opposing strategies. The actors also include grass-root organisations, development NGOs, and local development technicians. It is in the interests of these three groups of actors, whose aim is development, to come together in a participative strategy.

But spontaneous cooperation between all these actors is not automatic, either in the North or South. It can be seen in the North, for example, in the policies for difficult neighbourhoods; it can be seen in the South in urban local development. It is often necessary for a third party to act so that the actors involved start to work together in a participative way. Urban mediation, as a catalyst for this participative action, encompasses a number of strategies and measures, all of which are aimed at making the urban resident more of a "citizen" of his or her city, and therefore collectively more involved, together with different local institutions, especially municipalities, in developing their environment.

To date, the mediation process, which is also called facilitation or intermediation, is not part of a clearly established methodology. As with all matters relating to the social sphere, this is a sector that is constantly changing, and strategies need to be continuously adapted to the changing issues. It is also a good idea, and this is the aim of this article, to help pave the way for mediation practice.

Urban mediation: aims and intervention

Local authorities, operating democratically, need a space for dialogue and the exchange of ideas so that they are able to meet the demands for urban services with which they are faced, while at the same time helping to improve the living conditions of the population. It is the local authorities' responsibility to organise this local dialogue and it is specifically up to them to make it possible for all actors to participate by setting up this dialogue. Local development initiatives have, already, for several decades, been facilitating the establishment and running of spaces for this dialogue. What is new, in the context of decentralisation, is the arrival of a new key actor, the municipality, and the key role that it is called on to play. The 1990s saw support strategies deployed in this way.[1] Recognising the existence of this space requires work to be done on the conditions that will allow social organisations to establish their own aims, to coordinate, and to set up a dialogue with representatives of local or decentralised authorities. However, involving civil society in the participative management of cities also requires awareness-raising, training and communication activities. Therefore one of the top priorities we should set for ourselves is undoubtedly to enable actors on the ground to implement and manage urban management projects in a participative way, while ensuring the municipality retains its responsibilities.

The role of mediation

To strengthen local democracy is to strengthen relations between the local authorities and the associations that are present in all areas of life, for cultural, religious and social activities, as long as this is in accordance with the legal and political conditions, and also taking into account whether the historical context slowed down or encouraged the emergence of a more or less dynamic civil society. In France, for example, some writers believe that participative democracy dates back to 1901 with the right of association, in the period that followed the legalising of trade unions (1884). The emergence of associations may have come about following the difficulty of the local public authorities had in meeting the demand for urban services. This movement thus became the means through which to raise questions, put forward proposals and act.

The local political challenge is to create the best conditions for the dialogue between local institutions and the representatives of civil society. These optimum conditions usually require the "deficit in relations" to be reduced. The deficit in relations between public authorities and local associations, between public authorities and local groups, and between public authorities and grass-root organisations, may be linked to political reasons, one partner's lack of credibility in the eyes of the other, or a desire to steer clear of potential competition.

---

1. Many French cooperation projects that aid decentralisation have had a three-pronged approach: fostering decentralisation, supporting municipalities and supporting civil society in its relations with the municipality. The project "Urban Integration and Neighbourhood Cooperation", developed between 1996 and 2002 in Togo, is an example of this.

The mediator's action is, de facto, aimed at reducing these "deficits", endeavouring to get the actors to change their approach to the development of a project, strategy or local public policy. The mediator's sphere of action is within the central state or local institutions, which must be sufficiently strong both to be able to develop a strategic vision for the city and to provide urban services. The mediator's role is also to facilitate a space for dialogue for the participative strategy, which furthermore would enable civil society actors to contribute to the creation of "neighbourhood" urban services. We also find here a strategy that illustrates these ideas and produces positive changes that are perceptible in programmes agreed by multiple actors, which have been developed with French aid and implemented by local actors in a number of countries.[2]

Thus it is a question of mobilising grass-root organisations, the population and public authorities on a participative project. It is no longer a question of a top-down relationship between public authorities and the population, but a question of mutually respecting each group's scope for initiatives.

Requirements for establishing a mediation strategy

Social analysis

A "mediation" strategy may contain several stages that overlap or occur at the same time. At the start, mediation always relies on observing and on making a social analysis, which is not simply a monograph, but something that will make it possible to identify the social challenges and the groups of actors in a specific urban territory. Defining the scope of such observation raises itself raises a number of problems; by defining the boundaries, certain elements will inevitably be excluded, which could, at a later stage, turn out to be harmful to the participative strategy. This work and observation, which is not neutral vis-à-vis society and which, to some extent, puts society "on the alert", must very quickly lead to concrete proposals – often worth being preceded by trial runs – which make the actors and the participative strategy credible through their operational reality. It is in the crucial stage when practicalities materialise and society is involved that the integration of a participative

---

2. Morocco, Algeria, Democratic Republic of the Congo, Cameroon and Romania.

course of action in the municipal strategy, as well as in the decentralised administrations' strategies, has been shown to be truly effective.

Taking account of the concept of the neighbourhood

Urban management relies on a vision, that is, on a project that a municipal team must be able to develop for its city. It is at the neighbourhood level that many public policies fail. Choosing a neighbourhood to intervene in is a strong political choice, which also indicates the choice of social targets and of social segregation. The idea of neighbourhoods is linked to the historical development of cities, traditional social structures, and a collective feeling of belonging to a group. The mediator's analysis, beyond its socio-technical content, must therefore carefully take into account this political responsibility, and it is clear that the choices that are to be made at this level are no longer technical, or even technocratic, choices. They are political choices that, as such, decentralised local authorities are accountable for. These political choices provide answers to matters relating to social development. They are the product of a strategic vision for urban development, and the studies should be all the more relevant since they will provide a basis and direction for these choices.

Choice of actions and the representation of groups

A public policy involves choices of localisation at various stages, but it also leads to the process of deciding what action to take. A social demand can be met with services, equipment and infrastructure; there is a big gap to be bridged between making a demand and deciding on a solution. The response to a social experience is often expressed as a demand in a familiar area, such as, a demand for infrastructure. However, great care needs to be taken regarding this approach to social requests, which will take into account the fact that the strength with which a demand is made might say more about a group's organisational ability, than about how representative it is.

It is always, by definition, impossible to be exhaustive when defining a system of representation of a group in society, if only because commitment strategies are different depending on the possible interests, individually assessed, in relation to setting up a project, programme or public policy, but also in relation to the individual capacities of each member of the group concerned. The participation process can therefore quite easily result in the over representation of certain groups, especially the middle classes. Indeed, the poorest, who are mostly concerned with earning the minimum to survive, are more difficult to mobilise in participative strategies. A financial contribution by members of a group that benefits from a public policy is one of the key elements in many participative policies, and the sum of the contribution can be, from this point of view, a factor in social discrimination.

Organising citizen representation is a sensitive matter. And it is further complicated because it is difficult to establish representation of all the actors in a forum for dialogue and in the different committees that could be set up. This results in some discrepancy between the discourse on participation and the actual practices. The members of grass-roots associations may not be effective representatives of the people living in a given neighbourhood; the decisions taken in a committee, because they lack real legitimacy, therefore concern only a minority of the population.

The role of institutions

Of course, any participative approach on a local scale, which is one of the key functions of mediation, only makes sense if local institutions are involved. It is primarily the municipality, as a political institution, that has a role to play. Decentralised services also play an important role as, genuine technical expertise aside, they are the ones who generally bring coherence to a project or public policy by having a broader, rather than a local, picture. Naturally, their presence is therefore essential in any sort of steering committee that brings together institutions and representatives of civil society.

Indeed, successful mediation, which leads to effective participative approaches, cannot fail to have an effect on institutions. The emergence of new spaces for dialogue, regulation, and local public policy naturally leads to some institutional adjustment and this will lead to the emergence, beyond the confines of the municipal council and its various technical, economic and financial commissions, of new prerequisites for dialogue between institutions and population groups: that is how neighbourhood committees and councils emerge.

The importance of time and the issue of costs

Whatever institutional adjustments are caused by urban mediation and the technical solutions adopted in response to the expectations of civil society, keeping the local dynamic depends on the level of investment by local institutions in local management, but equally on permanently changing the political attitude of local officials from being focused exclusively "upwards" to a more "downwards" approach. To maintain the local dynamic, a lasting approach to dialogue, research and the consolidation of alliances between actors is required in order to continue to integrate actions that have already been started. This search for long-term alliances is necessary, as conflict is one of the dimensions in social relationships. Mediation also results in resolving conflict situations. The lasting implementation of open local governance on civil society therefore has to involve a learning phase regarding the participative approach as well as establishing a monitoring process. Any review – and at this stage it is not yet an evaluation – of public policy requires the monitoring of both the methods and the results obtained through partnerships of institutions and local organisations. Mediation therefore cannot be conceived as a limited action; it is, in fact, an integral part of a mechanism for establishing local governance – as a perennial and democratic mode of operation for local institutions – because it is based on citizen participation. Therefore, the undertaking, the success and the continuation of these approaches can only be developed over time.

As well as its duration, taking the cost of mediation interventions into account constitutes a determining factor in the success of the mediation process in itself.

The mediator becomes a participant who needs to be paid, but other participants in this process for the implementation of public participative political practices can also demand that their contribution be recognised as professional, by means of payment. Various means of contracting projects, managing the projects, technical monitoring, and carrying out the projects can be found. At each stage, expertise is necessary. This can be found internally; for example, the leading of operations involved in project contracting might be undertaken internally, if the expertise is there, by a municipal official. However, in other cases it is necessary to rely on external expertise, particularly for activities relating to project management. There have been cases where the contribution of expertise from someone in the community has been acknowledged as a contribution by the people to the participatory approach. How is it possible to accept this expert will ultimately be working for free and will bring a significantly greater contribution than what can be reasonably expected? It is very important to acknowledge all contributions which cannot be fairly divided up as participatory elements of an involved group of people, without endangering the participatory approach. The remuneration of various participants can also be set, taking into account their degree of involvement in the various steering and management committees. It is true that in the context of low levels of monetization and standards of living, time devoted to civic life is far from representing a marginal cost. This cost is also the reason for the under-representation of the poorest strata of the population. Grass-roots organisations are most often made up of unpaid workers and volunteers, and the limits of their involvement are quickly reached.

The importance of training and of an appropriated administrative organisation

As participative approaches are often "firsts" in a given context, the training of committees or project managers on their roles and those of other actors, on the type of services expected of them by the other actors involved in the execution of a project when drawing up and implementing a public policy must always be done transparently from the start of the process. It is essential that the way of carrying out a project is clear, so that the people do not see the participatory organisation as an unfair system of distributing benefits. It is not immediately obvious what the tasks and responsibilities are of an on-site manager, a project manager, a monitoring body or a contractor, or who pays for their services. There is a significant risk of causing the participative approach to fail if these are misunderstood, and mediation has an important role to play in avoiding this. More generally, training the leaders of local associations to better identify, carry out, monitor and support actions, as well as the coordination and education of the people, still require the mobilisation of considerable financial resources. Those on the receiving end do not always see the usefulness and importance of training, which must be innovative and adapted to their real needs.

Nevertheless, it must be possible for the mobilisation of financial resources to be coordinated with commitments to carry out the project. This goes without saying, but the complexity and the lack of efficiency, indeed of professionalism, when managing processes linked to public spending all too often show the inability of the administrative process to keep pace with the processes of carrying out projects and implementing public policies. It must be possible for the structuring of financial resources for major infrastructure or public policy projects to eventually be carried out using funds which, while allowing transparency and efficient operation, must facilitate bringing together the means of intervention in a given area. Of course, decisions relating to the use of these funds, in a decentralised system, are made by local authorities. There are currently some initiatives that are heading in this direction, notably in the Niger and Mauritania: these demonstrate the validity of the approach. It is nevertheless advisable to remain aware of the potential risks of distorting the process of creating demand by using supply-side logic through introducing such funds.

Which method?

While the prerequisites for mediation have been discussed above, the question of method remains unanswered, quite probably because it is a positive approach which must be developed, without considering the "mediator" as a simple "executive agency" and thus being allowed to benefit from his or her own experiences, initiatives and innovations. It should also be left to the "mediation" organisations and actors to suggest their methods of intermediation. Mediation comprises several tasks, whether they relate to knowledge of the actors and the city, knowledge of the neighbourhoods and their dynamics, or knowledge of the living conditions of the population. In general, mediation requires flexibility and dialogue between partners; it also includes leadership, methodological monitoring and training support. Mediation is in itself a job.

The intermediation approach is often entrusted to a participant from outside the local actors' system. Although in such cases the expertise is real, long-term recruitment is difficult. So, building skills in intermediation within the structures of local governments, in order to have an effect on these local authorities, as well as between local authorities and decentralised services and between these two categories of actors and the population groups, can represent an interesting alternative. An experiment run in recent years in Mauritania, which involved as much bilateral cooperation as decentralised cooperation, seems promising in this respect.[3]

The fabric of communities is the basic material for the action of the mediator, who makes full use of its richness, emphasises its importance and puts it in the position of an effective actor. Beyond surveying community organisations and identifying initiatives, it is necessary to envisage in-depth work with them and depend on them – whatever their nature and objectives – to carry out analysis and involve them in setting up participatory structures. The federation of structures and approaches may be an underlying recommendation for confronting the tendency towards a fragmentation of civil society and of its representations.

It should also be reminded that structuring takes place in several ways, beyond associations and the traditional geographic limits of the neighbourhood. Such is the case, for example, with tontines. A good mediation exercise always includes sharing in the daily life of the neighbourhoods' inhabitants – it is necessary to get to know each

---

3. Decentralised cooperation in Mauritania of the Sénart Association of New Towns with a group of ten town councils and the French Embassy in Mauritania's "Social Development Project" in Nouakchott.

other and therefore to share moments of daily life – and any method of initiating dialogue that allows educational barriers to be overcome is worth using: life stories, stories about the neighbourhood and what life is like in the neighbourhood as seen in children's drawings all constitute means of understanding local society that should not be ignored.

Mediation is essentially an act of communication, which must support and reinforce exchange-based relationships between different actors. Beyond the physical problems of communication linked to problems of transport, which are a reality, and the time needed for communication at the level of neighbourhoods and the city, as well as between municipalities and the structures of civil society, between the actors of a common project and similar external references, communication is insufficient and increasingly necessary in ensuring the success of undertakings. The establishment of experience exchange networks, including visits and debates, is always an asset for training in participatory methods for all actors involved.

Conclusion

For some fifteen years, governance has been at the heart of development issues. It is worth emphasising that, on the basis of the governance strategy which France adopted in 2006 and which reveals all the space opened to mediation by democratic practice, if public policies are important, their content and legitimacy will gain proportionally greater recognition as a result of having been drawn up and put into practice in a participative way. Therefore "the approach of governance goes beyond the question of institutions or forms of government"[4] and covers the mechanisms of social coordination and the decision-making processes that contribute to political action. Local governance requires support and participation on the part of the actors involved resulting from negotiated processes.

Therein lies the challenge for mediation.

---

4. Minister for Foreign and European Affairs (2006). Stratégie gouvernance de la coopération française, December 2006, p. 4.

Bibliography

Arcens, M.-T. "La participation communautaire dans les projets d'eau potable et d'assainissement en milieu urbain et périurbain", Info CREPA, n° 17.

Attolou, A. and P. Langley (1995). "Postface", in Attolou A., Société civile et développement au Bénin. L'évolution des associations locales de développement, Cotonou, CEDA.

Bierschenk, T. and J.-P. Olivier de Sardan (n.d.). ECRIS : Enquête collective rapide d'identification des conflits et des groupes stratégiques.

CEDA, (1997). Espace de négociation en milieu urbain au Cameroun, Douala, CADE for GRET.

CEDA (ed.) (1997). Vers un développement urbain participatif, Cotonou, CEDA for GRET.

DRAS, (October 2000). Développement social des quartiers "Sigidi Kura", Bamako, DRAS-SCAC.

Elong-Mbassi, J.-P. (ed.) (1995). Communes et développement local dans les pays du Sahel, Cotonou, CEDA for PDM.

ENDA, (1998). Agir aujourd'hui pour le 21e siècle, Dakar, ENDAECOPOP.

ENDA, (March 1998). "Projet de ville de Pikine. Gérer ensemble la ville", Courrier du développement local, n° 4.

ENDA-TM, (January-March). "Une initiative populaire au Sénégal. Alimentation en eau potable en milieu périurbain à Dakar", Info CREPA, n° 19, p. 8-9.

GRET, (1997). Développement urbain participatif au Bénin : une etude pour agir, Paris, GRET-Ministère de la Coopération.

Guene, O. "Dynamique du cadre institutionnel de la gestion des ordures ménagères en Afrique subsaharienne", Info CREPA, n° 24, p. 4-6.

Guibbert, J.-J. (1998). Des équipements et des hommes : pour une approche communautaire des équipements en milieu urbain, Dakar, ENDA-TM.

Langley, Ph. (1994). "La participation communautaire à la gestion municipale", in J.-P. Elong-Mbassi (ed.), La participation communautaire à la gestion municipale, Cotonou, CEDA for PDM.

Olivier de Sardan, J.-P. and A. Souley (1999). Enquête collective de Niamey (15-22 February 1999), Niamey, UNICEF-Coop. française-IRD (Volet socio-anthropologique du programme de recherche sur l'équité et l'accès aux soins dans 5 villes africaines).

Seddoh, A.K. (n.d.). Concept de capital urbain socio-communautaire – CURSOC. Approche communautaire dans le développement urbain, Lomé, BCCT.

SNV, (October 1999). Plan de développement de Dogbo 2000-2004. Fil conducteur pour la bonne gouvernance, Dogbo, SNV.

Toure, F. (January–March 1997). "Des outils SARAR pour la promotion de l'assainissement autonome à Ouagadougou", Info CREPA, n°15, p. 3-4.

V

**DEVELOPMENT POLICIES
AND
DEMOCRATIC GOVERNANCE**

23

Governance at a Crossroads

Jean Bossuyt
(Translated from the French)

A finger points to the moon.
Too bad for those who see only the finger.
Zen saying.

Governance at the core of development policies

In less than a decade governance has become a central pivot of the cooperation policies of development partners. The notion first appeared in the early 1990s, in the continuation of the new wave of democratisation that crossed the world following the fall of the Berlin wall. The initial definition of the term was rather narrow and technocratic, placing the emphasis on the transparent, responsible management of public resources. Gradually the governance agenda expanded to become a "holistic" concept encompassing the various political and economic dimensions of development[1].

Over time governance was brought into all the regional cooperation agreements of the European Union through a panoply of political declarations and communications[2]. The political priority given to governance is manifest in a growing use of political dialogue with third countries, which can lead to sanctions such as the suspension of

---

1. The European Commission includes six issues under the heading of political governance: human rights; democratisation and elections; the rule of law and justice; public sector reform and management of the public finances; support for civil society; decentralisation and local governance.

2. Africa Caribbean and Pacific (ACP); Asia and Latin America (ALA), Mediterranean non-member countries (MEDA), Eastern Europe and Central Asia (TACIS).

co-operation. The issue of governance is increasingly at the heart of EC programming processes and is reflected in a growing mobilisation of resources. A similar evolution can be seen among the other bilateral and multilateral development partners, reflecting a general trend towards the "politicisation" of aid. Above and beyond variations in the definitions used and approaches followed, governance has become a political objective shared by donors. The European Consensus on Development (2006) establishes the dominant place of governance in the European Union's development policies.

Several factors helped bring the concept of governance to the fore. The mixed results of international aid have fostered an awareness of the limitations of the model of financial and technical cooperation that long prevailed. Experience has shown that the injection of money, programmes and technical assistance into political systems that are unreceptive to democracy and respect for human rights does not generally bring sustainable effects in terms of development. In some cases this type of aid has had the perverse effect of prolonging the life of authoritarian political regimes or postponing necessary reforms. This has led to a recognition of the crucial importance of the political context and "rights" in the processes of development. The existence of legitimate, efficient systems of governance is now seen as a necessary condition for the realisation of key development objectives such as poverty reduction, peace and security, or the Millennium Development Goals. Governance is also at the core of the new modes of implementing aid. The transition towards budget support critically depends on a set of conditions for the management of public finances, which must be respected by the beneficiary countries. Similarly the substantial growth in the volume of aid expected in coming years will not provide the hoped-for results without major progress in terms of governance.

Governance is no longer the exclusive concern of development partners. The great majority of African governments have formally adopted the governance approach, for example by including it in their strategies to combat poverty and drawing up national good governance programmes. At the continental level, the African Union is developing numerous initiatives, some within the context of its New Partnership for Africa's Development (NEPAD) and the African Peer Review Mechanism (APRM). Throughout Africa civil societies are emerging. African citizens are becoming more vocal in their demands for new modes of governance based on principles of participation, transparency and accountability.

Should we welcome this evolution? The international community's emphasis on governance clearly answers a growing societal demand in many countries and is a necessity if aid is to be effective. Such an approach could prove particularly useful where dialogue on governance becomes a tool for the establishment of a partnership based on national ownership and mutual accountability (rather than a new set of imposed conditions).

Searching for the appropriate response strategies

The transition from a primarily financial and technical form of co-operation to a more highly politicised approach represents a "Copernican revolution" in the international aid system. The traditional aid agencies are invited to change roles (leaving technocratic approaches behind) and to become "political animals" (with the tools and capacities necessary to provide appropriate support in the complex, sensitive domain of governance).

In response to this challenge, most development partners have set about reviewing their political and institutional arrangements, at different speeds and levels of intensity. European co-operation offers an illustration of this search for appropriate strategies to meet the many challenges posed by the rapid rise of governance as a priority goal in relations with other countries.

Since 2000 the Commission has striven to clarify its approach and means of action.

Governance as long-term societies transformation process

This principle is systematically adopted in all the political documents of the EC. The Communication on Governance and Development (2003) notes that governance is intimately connected with notions of "power", "interests" and the "management of resources". It concerns the organisation of the social contract between the state and its citizens. Improved governance implies a fundamental change in the way power is exercised and in relations between the different public and private actors. This in turn means governance must be seen as a process by which societies are transformed in the long term, following different paths in different countries. Development partners who propose to support this type of process are invited to follow its logic and to avoid trying to implement "off-the-peg" models of governance.

Ownership, dialogue and assessing the progress made

Governance cannot be decreed in grand political statements or through externally imposed conditions. It must be built up day by day through real processes, linked to development issues (such as access to basic material services, the management of natural resources, the efficiency of public institutions and the functioning of the justice system). In this light the Commission does not see governance as just another condition, but as a shared goal based on common values. It advocates systematic political dialogue with partner countries on the best way to move domestic governance agendas forward and assessing progress made, based on jointly agreed indicators.

Need for a broad approach

The European Commission defines governance as a multidimensional concept encompassing different areas; it calls for principles of good governance to be mainstreamed in all programmes, areas of intervention (such as food safety) and tools (such as budgetary aid); it requires support for different groups of actors (central government, local government, civil society) and calls for consistency of action at different levels of governance (local, national, regional and Pan-African).

A panoply of tools to support governance

The European Commission proposes to use all available tools to provide relevant support for governance. In particular it aims to adopt approaches based on dialogue and requests from other countries (programme-based approach/Sector Wide Approach, general or sector-based budgetary aid), considering that these offer additional incentives to implement reforms. According to the Communication on Governance and Development mentioned above, budgetary support can act as a lever to encourage better management of public finances, multi-player dialogue on the content of public policy, stronger involvement in national democratic institutions such as the parliament and national audit office, and an enhanced role for civil society in monitoring the action of the state.

Capacity strengthening

Several measures have been taken to enhance the Commission's institutional capacity in the field of governance, including increasing the number of governance experts within Delegations, creating a specialised team in Brussels, increasing the involvement of geographical and sector teams in questions of governance, and expanding the numbers of groups and training initiatives.

The governance of aid

The European Commission recognises that governance is not only an issue for non-member countries. The obligation of "good governance" should also apply to external players and be reflected in the appropriate, transparent and consistent governance of aid. This implies respect for the Paris Declaration on Aid Effectiveness, which calls for the alignment, harmonisation and predictability of external aid, greater policy consistency in key fields such as agriculture, trade and the environment and greater effort by the European Union to redress the deficit in global governance.

Comparative analysis of the response strategies of other development partners – notably the member states of the European Union – shows a great similarity of approaches and logics of action. Above and beyond the remaining differences in how the concept of governance is defined, the same keywords recur across the various political documents: governance as a "process" of political and social change, the need for "ownership" and "multi-actor partnerships" to draw up and implement national governance agendas and the need for "realistic, pragmatic" support strategies.

These principles are supposed to guide the action of development partners in support of governance. However this is not a static field. On the contrary everything about it is work in progress and constantly changing. This dynamic specific to governance can be illustrated by two examples. The first concerns local governance. This is an issue was long left slightly to one side, the main debates on governance tending to take place at the national, regional and global levels. However, in the wake of decentralisation, the local level of governance has become very important. On the ground we are witnessing a proliferation of new practices in terms of local power, relations between actors and management of territories. This evolution means that development partners face the double challenge of connecting with these potentially promising local dynamics and adapting their intervention strategies to incorporate the local dimension more successfully.

The second example is linked to the new Africa-Europe joint strategy, drawn up during the recent Lisbon summit (December 2007). The Action Plan provides for the establishment of eight partnerships on particular issues, including a forum on governance. This new mechanism offers real opportunities to establish a structured, participative dialogue on governance issues and modes of practical co-operation. However, a lot will depend on how the forum is set up. It will take institutional creativity to ensure true, multi-actors dialogue that steps outside the traditional frameworks of consultation on governance, which are usually highly formalised and unproductive.

Governance support in practice

How have development partners given practical support to governance? To what extent have they respected the guiding principles set out in their political documents? What lessons can be learned from the support given in the different domains of governance? What results have been obtained? What are the main constraints encountered in support for governance?

It is no easy matter to evaluate the impact of external support where governance is concerned. Several conceptual and methodological difficulties arise when we try to "measure" or "attribute" the effects of support programmes in a complex process of transformation such as governance. The fact that the process unfolds over time makes things even more complicated; tangible progress cannot be expected in the short term.

A growing number of studies and evaluations of governance are now available. These contain a wealth of information, reflecting the many experiments and innovative approaches being implemented on the ground. Where the impact of programmes to support governance is concerned, one fundamental message emerges clearly from the different documents: the many initiatives supported by development partners in the different areas of governance have generally facilitated the launch or consolidation of positive dynamics in the countries targeted. On the other hand, at this stage there are few indications that these positive effects have been translated into "systemic" changes (in other words profound, lasting modification of the prevailing governance culture).

How should we explain this difficulty in obtaining systemic impact with real changes in the norms, processes and behaviours linked to governance? A brief analysis of the approaches followed by donors in various fields of intervention could help identify elements of explanation.

Support for judicial reform in Africa has increased considerably over the last decade. During this period the development partners have tested a variety of approaches. One important lesson from this experience relates to the limitations of the "project approaches" targeting individual judicial institutions. It became apparent that justice functions as a "sector" with a great many organisations emanating from the state or civil society. The challenge is to strengthen links between these actors and improve institutional coordination.

This lesson encouraged the emergence of sector-based approaches in support of justice systems. But the adoption of sector-based approaches is not in itself enough to guarantee effective, appropriate support. According to Laure-Hélène Piron[3], too often development partners still adopt "technical" solutions to deal with judicial dysfunction that is primarily a matter of politics. Programme development generally excludes the political context, or does not integrate it sufficiently. Piron advances the provocative thesis that it is rather "naive" to talk about national ownership in an environment where the justice system functions within a logic of corruption and clientism.

Improved management of public finances is a central pillar of governance. Its importance is heightened by donors' current enthusiasm for budgetary support. It is also linked to the struggle against corruption. Recent studies indicate that the results obtained by programmes in this area are disappointing overall. Despite considerable outlay, notably for training and the strengthening of institutions, it is hard to identify any real changes in the management of public finances in the organisations involved. For example, a comparative study of corruption in the tax authorities of Tanzania and Uganda[4] criticises the "technocratic" approaches of development partners. The reform of fiscal authorities tends to be regarded as an "organisational" problem that can be improved by providing the personnel with training, technical assistance and financial incentives. The authors of the study identify a lack of attention paid to political factors affecting reform, such as the existence of a real demand for change in the tax system and the negative impact of clientist networks involving political, bureaucratic and economic actors. As a result support programmes have only limited or temporary effects.

---

3. Piron, L.-H. (2005). Donor Assistance to Justice Sector Reform: Living Up to the New Agenda?, Open Society Justice Initiative.

4. Fieldstad, O.-H., I. Kolstad and S. Lange (2003). Autonomy, Incentives and Patronage. A Study of Corruption in the Tanzania and Uganda Revenue Authorities, Chr. Michelsen Institute.

Support for the process of democratisation offers another well documented example. The lessons of experience reveal the limitations of a normative approach based on western institutional models, which translates into support for formal democratic structures (the parliament, the national audit office and electoral commissions). But investment in the hardware of democracy is not enough. The crucial thing is to influence the software, in other words the values, norms and behaviours linked to democratic management. In most of the countries targeted, there are many informal obstacles to the emergence of a real culture of democracy. Development partners have great difficulty in grasping these informal constraints and integrating them into the development and implementation of support programmes. The result is a gap between the stated objectives and practices on the ground. One concrete illustration is provided by the European Initiative for Democracy and Human Rights, one of the European Commission's programmes, which aims to provide direct finance to civil society activity in difficult contexts. Practice shows that it is precisely in authoritarian countries that implementing this programme is often very hard, not to say dangerous, for the local organisations involved. The global evaluation of community support for voter education[5] indicates that the European Commission is continuing to focus support on formal electoral institutions and election observation. It pays comparatively little attention to voter education, although this is an "essential precondition" for holding meaningful elections where citizens are well informed of their rights and able to exercise them to the full. The evaluation also shows that the support provided tends to be focused on quantitative aspects (such as the number of voters who voted) to the detriment of aspects linked to the quality of participation (well-informed voters capable of casting a vote).

The European Union is allocating increasing funds to the strengthening of civil society, notably in its role of advocacy and monitoring public action. A recent evaluation[6] suggests that overall interventions by development partners have had positive "intermediate effects". Support has, for example, helped improve access to information, strengthen the individual organisations of civil society and give a voice to marginalised communities and other vulnerable groups, such as women. However, the evaluation observes that to obtain broader effects at the systemic level of governance, it is vital to implement "integrated approaches" that go beyond individual "projects" in support of specific organisations. The

---

5. European Commission (2001). Evaluation of Voter Education in the Context of EU Electoral Support, Particip.

6. O'Neil, T., M. Foresti and A. Hudson (2007). Evaluation of Citizen's Voice and Accountability: Review of the Literature and Donor Approaches, London, ODI.

challenge is to promote multi-actor "processes" seeking to influence both formal and informal institutions. The evaluation also stresses the importance of the "political factor" in programmes to support civil society. In reality the organisations and actors involved are not "neutral". Their social action is motivated by specific norms, interests and incentives. It is crucial for donors to have a good understanding of the logics of action, dynamics and internal functioning of civil society organisations. Too much institutional support is still based on a normative or instrumental vision of civil society. These approaches are unlikely to attain the expected objectives[7] or to make a significant impact.

The issue of accountability is fundamental to governance. However, donors still need to come to grips with the concept of accountability as it manifests itself in the field. Recent research emphasises the need to avoid purely "legalistic" and "bureaucratic" approaches to the concept. Accountability is primarily a matter of establishing democratic processes that enable citizens to question state institutions on concrete development issues (such as access to water), to demand rights or make the private sector more responsible[8]. To progress towards real impact, development partners are invited to concentrate on issues of power and the political processes that can lead to greater accountability. Experience in many countries shows that accountability functions better when it is demanded "from the bottom up" (rather than simply given "from the top down").

What lessons should be drawn from these mixed results?

We could make a similar examination of many other fields of governance, such as support for decentralisation and local governance, the strengthening of parliaments and political parties, the promotion of a culture of human rights and so on. But our observations concerning the challenges and difficulties faced by donors seeking to have lasting and systemic impacts would be broadly the same.

Four key lessons can be drawn from the experience accumulated through the first generation of programmes in support of governance.

Lesson 1: Where the political nature of governance processes and support programmes is concerned, words are not the same as deeds. In their strategy documents the donors state loudly and clearly that

---

7. In relation to normative approaches to civil society, see the critical analysis by Chandhoke, N. (2007). "Civil Society", Development in Practice, vol. 17, no 4-5, p. 607-614.
8. IDS (2006). Making Accountability Count, Policy Briefing 33.

governance is an endogenous, long-term process of political and social transformation, seeking to establish new relations between the state and society. Each country must follow its own evolutionary path towards more appropriate modes of governance, in accordance with its own history, culture, values and norms. However, in practice it is clear that development partners are still too often adopting normative, technocratic and short-term approaches, contrary to the principles set out in their own strategic documents.

Lesson 2: Donors lack the capacity for political analysis in order to act in the field of governance. The European Commission's Communication on Governance and Development (2003) is clear: governance is fundamentally a matter of power, interests and resources. These elements form the hard core of governance and the nub of the problem. External support that skirts around or leaves out these issues of power cannot produce real change in the functioning of formal institutions. It is also necessary to deal with informal aspects linked to the norms of the exercise of power, to cultural references and the issue of interests and incentives. In practice the integration of these "political factors" into programmes to support governance is generally superficial. There is rarely any in-depth diagnosis of either the underlying reasons for "bad governance" in the country, the difficulty of sustaining political commitment to reform or the type of political process that might assist the development of more legitimate and effective systems of governance. The increased importance of governance has brought a proliferation of analytical tools and indicators intended to measure, evaluate and analyse it in all its aspects. The number of donors who have developed their own analytical tools has grown spectacularly. For the most part these tools are designed, developed and used by and for the donor (to the extent that they are linked to the cycle of scheduling or providing aid). Where content is concerned, comparatively few analyses or tools go beyond the "visible". They do not generally consider aspects crucial to perspectives for change, including power relations, the informal structures of governance and the motivations and interests of the main actors.

Lesson 3: This relates to the principles of ownership and dialogue. In their strategic documents the donors categorically state that there must be national ownership of governance programmes and dialogue with all relevant actors in order to develop shared governance agendas. However, it proves particularly difficult to put these entirely reasonable guidelines into practice. In many countries the definition of "good governance" itself is not accepted. On the contrary it is a matter of major debate within the society, a subject of disagreement between the different stakeholders. For example, who defines the type of reforms the country needs? The competence of central government to make unilateral decisions is increasingly being challenged. Other groups of actors (civil society, local government, private sector, trade unions) are demanding to be fully involved in elaborating governance agendas. In such contexts, the call for "national ownership" rings very hollow and has limited practical application[9]. How and in what circumstances can this concept be applied in a country with a myriad heterogeneous perspectives of governance priorities, or in a country where the government's legitimacy is challenged by its own population? Donors often find it hard to position themselves in such an unpredictable context of antagonism and even conflict. In such a situation they tend to "rush blindly on", taking formal criteria (such as the existence of a national policy of good governance) as the basis for an assumed national ownership. Multi-actor dialogue on governance remains relatively under-used, despite its potential to generate governance agendas rooted in local realities.

Lesson 4: the donors intervening in governance are not neutral. They must be regarded as full actors, with the potential to be "agents for change". In practice however, there is a great deal of confusion about the role that donors can play in governance processes. The case of the European Commission can serve as an illustration. The evaluation of Community support for governance (2006) revealed a lack of consistency in the response strategies of the European Commission. In some countries the Commission is proactively, directly and visibly engaged in governance processes, playing an active role as agent for change. In other countries it toes the line of government-backed governance agendas, without asking too many questions or trying to bring other actors into the process. There are also countries where the Commission adopts a timid, even passive position, despite the existence of serious governance problems. This diversity of approaches can also be seen in the application of sanctions against recipient countries (for example in the context of article 96 of the Cotonou Agreement) and in the use of budgetary aid (sometimes granted to countries with very low governance capacities). On this point the evaluation concludes that the European Commission should clarify its roles and responsibilities when it intervenes in governance processes. Many questions are left with no clear answers: how can the Commission encourage the adoption of reforms without compromising the principles of ownership and partnership? How can governance be promoted in countries where the regime in power is opposed to any reform? How can strategic alliances be made with agents of change at the national level in order to enhance governance?

---

9. Buiter, W.H. (2007). "Country Ownership': A term whose time has gone", Development in Practice, vol. 17, no. 4-5, p. 647-655.

Need for a paradigm shift

All these lessons from experience suggest that the donor community is at a crossroads where support strategies for governance are concerned. The time seems ripe for a major qualitative leap. In the first phase the development partners gave an enthusiastic welcome to the new thinking on governance and were keen to support a whole series of political and institutional reforms in a wide variety of countries. Over time they realised that promoting governance in environments hostile to such formulas is a very complicated, high-risk business, for which the aid agencies were insufficiently prepared. Gradually the idea is gaining ground that the thinking and action in support of governance requires fundamental revision. A paradigm shift seems necessary to enable more effective action in this complex arena which at once is so vital for development.

What would such a paradigm shift mean in practice? Four areas seem particularly important.

Changing the way to look at governance

This is the first priority and a precondition for more appropriate operational strategies. The new generation of governance support programmes should go beyond normative, technocratic approaches based on the institutional models of the rich countries. Instead of analysing a country's governance through the prism of what should ideally exist – and then measuring the distance to be covered – it seems more useful to start with an analysis of where the country currently is, to try to understand the forces and factors underlying the establishment of observable systems of governance and to identify what is politically feasible. The challenge is to try to look below the top of the iceberg to gain a better understanding of the fundamental governance drivers, including issues of power, interests, resources and incentives for change. Some donors have recently set off on this path by trying to analyse drivers of change.

More realistic and courageous engagement strategies

When donors are willing to focus their support more precisely on the "hard core" of governance (the informal rules of the game), they are led to a fundamental revision of their modes of action. The abandonment of technocratic solutions in favour of a more political approach invites development partners to enhance their credibility and their capacity to act as political agents. This requires greater determination to play the role of agent for change, engaging in dialogue that is respectful, but also frank and robust, with the various public and private players on the priority issues of governance, and enhancing capacities for political analysis with the aim of identifying realistic support programmes for "good enough governance"[10].

Investing in "demand" for new modes of governance

The new paradigm requires a change in the role of the donors, who should no longer be concerned primarily with the content of governance reforms and imposing agendas. Their task is now to play an indirect role in supporting long-term processes for change carried through by local actors. This gives rise to a need to invest strategically in the creation of a stronger societal "demand" for better governance, by supporting the emergence of citizenship, promoting multi-actors dialogue on governance at the national level and enhancing the capacity of institutions responsible for producing new norms for governance (such as the African Union).

Change of institutional culture for donors

To become more credible and effective, donors are invited to review in depth certain key aspects of their own institutional culture. Firstly they need to change the aid agencies' incentives systems in order to enable more appropriate action to be taken in the field of governance. The pressure to spend is an example of a bureaucratic incentive that can have perverse effects, since it tends to reduce opportunities to support the long-term processes that are so necessary to governance. The second challenge is to identify more precisely the appropriate roles and responsibilities of donors in promoting governance. The notions of "governance of aid", "mutual accountability" and "policy coherence" need to be given far more precise and practically effective content. In addition the aid system needs to be decompartmentalised. The evaluation of the European Commission's support for governance, cited above, concludes that effective action by the European Commission/European Union requires close collaboration between the political actors (general management of external relations), actors involved in development (general management of development, the EuropeAid Co-operation Office) and the administrative side. At the moment these links are not very strong, making it hard to carry out coherent, effective action in the field.

---

10. Grindle, M. (2002). Good Enough Governance: Poverty Reduction and Reform in Developing Countries, World Bank Discussion Paper.

24

Democratic Governance
Central to the External Action
of the European Union

From Conditionality to Dialogue between Partners

Philippe DARMUZEY
(Translated from the French)

The current situation: a deep crisis of governance

From the bankruptcy of the postcolonial state...

The developing countries, particularly those in Africa, are facing the two challenges of becoming "modern" states and adapting to globalisation at a time when they have not yet travelled the distance down the road to governance that the European countries took centuries to cover. We should remember, for example, that long before the colonial period Africa had its own "institutions" and organisation for managing societies, notably with its own arrangements for the handover of power and conflict resolution. For decades relations between the different communities were organised over large territories on the basis on these precolonial institutions.

There is no denying that the nation states established since the colonial period are now facing structural crisis. Many of these post-colonial nation states are suffering from a two-fold crisis of legitimacy linked to the weakness, indeed absence, of any real social contract between state and citizen and to their ineffectiveness, in other words their limited capacity to provide elementary social services. The result is a growing disconnection between the legality of the state apparatus and its legitimacy in the eyes of citizens.

In many developing countries the legitimacy of power – linchpin of a stable state accepted by all, making democratic progress possible – is today in question. Traditional arrangements for the handover of power in developing countries cannot always be reconciled with the ideal of "universal" democracy. The choice of leaders and transition from one government to the next thus raise questions for the external partners, who would like their strategies to last over the long term.

Many – particularly African – countries have responded to this crisis of state legitimacy by engaging in a process of decentralisation. In some, such as Mali and Rwanda, decentralisation has strengthened democracy by enabling a more equitable share of receipts to remain in the regions rather than being absorbed by central government, and allowing cities and rural communities be part of conflict prevention by turning military demands into political demands. In other countries reforms in favour of decentralisation and local development, much favoured by donors, have had difficulty establishing legitimate local governance. Often the models and processes of decentralisation are copies of external models and local institutions sometimes lack substance.

... to the failure of Western formulas

It must be admitted that it is in the area of "good governance" that the multilateral and bilateral partners have proved most demanding, setting new conditions according to which aid is given in exchange for tangible progress on democracy and human rights, or in the fight against corruption. These conditions, addressed to all partner countries, have exasperated some, whose intentions to move down the path to democracy were real. These countries have felt isolated and suspect in the eyes of the international community in the same way as countries whose leaders had no intention whatever of implementing reforms.

Governance must be more than a fashion used either to explain difficulties faced by the aid-givers, or to impose new conditions. It is regrettable that governance has sometimes been reduced to a list of formulas modelled on a universal idea of the state, which the developing countries must implement in order to be recognised, accepted and assisted by the international community.

In order to avoid these difficulties, partner countries are now advised to take ownership of their own governance reforms. In reality, in a period that has seen more and more countries, particularly in Africa, rejecting colonial discourse and all that flows from it, such as the western model of governance, it is no longer possible to implement governance formulas copied from external models to bring about the development of societies in partner countries.

The answer: a new European approach

Neither good students nor bad: a broad, transparent and objective approach

Starting from the fact that without decisive progress on governance the Millennium Development Goals cannot be reached and the additional aid promised will not bear fruit, the European Union has sought to place democratic governance at the centre of its development agenda.

Given the weakness of post-colonial states, consolidation of the sovereign state is often the only effective response to problems of governance. The notion of governance thus appears linked to the ability of the state to provide the population with services in an impartial way.

From this point of view the governance situation is often described as "good", "poor", "bad" and so on. Such descriptions can introduce confusion, particularly when used by donors to describe the situation in partner countries. They can sound like an attempt to impose a model of governance that is perhaps not adapted to the specific context of the country. These descriptions may also appear rather static and ill-suited to reflect the trend, process or movement particular to each country.

The notion of "democratic governance" clearly expresses the dynamic, evolutionary, multidimensional and political nature of governance. It reveals the need to approach the political, economic, environmental, cultural and social components in a global, balanced way, in order to gain a better understanding of the processes at the local, national and regional level and to maximise the impact of political action by the various actors and development partners.

The European Union has adopted a broad approach to governance, involving all its dimensions (political, economic, social, cultural, environmental and so on). This multidimensional perspective reflects both values shared by all, including respect for human rights and fundamental freedoms and for the rule of law, and also other concerns shared by societies, such as human security, the harmonious management of migration, effective institutions, access to basic social services, the sustainable management of natural resources, energy and the environment and the promotion of sustainable economic growth and social cohesion in a climate favourable to private investment.

So attention is no longer paid solely to the institutional or sovereign aspects of governance, but extends to all the activities of society. This multidimensional approach makes it possible to move away from the focus on a list of formulas for the implementation of "state" governance towards a new understanding, sense of responsibility and dialogue between the partners at either end of the co-operation relationship.

Incentives rather than conditions, dialogue rather than sanctions

The other innovation Europe has sought in facing the difficulties mentioned above has been to abandon policies of conditionality linked to good governance in favour of a so-called incentives policy. This approach is based primarily on political dialogue with the partner country, which acknowledges certain weaknesses of democratic governance and embarks on a plan of reform in the medium term.

These policy principles were implemented in the context of the partnership between the African, Caribbean and Pacific countries and the European Union (ACP-EU), when spending for the 10th European Development Fund was scheduled for 2008-2013. When the partner country's government presents a sufficiently ambitious and credible action plan, the European Commission allocates supplementary funds in addition to the money awarded through the National Indicative Programme in order to encourage the country to implement the reforms.

This approach of dialogue and incentives has seen the creation of a new tool in the form of the governance incentive tranche. Governance is an integral part of the funding dialogue, including the delicate and often controversial matters of respect for human rights, democratic principles and the rule of law, economic and financial matters, the management of natural resources and questions linked to social governance. Each state is free to decide whether or not to embark on reform. Additional finance is then made available to those countries whose leaders do opt for reform. The 10th EDF's incentive tranche for governance totals three billion euros.

Where practical implementation is concerned, Europe has not developed indicators permitting the evaluation of a country's governance, analogous to those developed by the World Bank for example. Many indicators already exist and to create still more would simply add to the confusion. Europe focuses on the governance situation in a country at a given moment in order to engage in more successful dialogue with the partner on the weaknesses the latter would like to deal with. The governance profiles developed for this purpose analyse the situation solely from a qualitative point of view, in terms of nine main areas. These profiles are important only for an understanding of the main obstacles to the application of democratic governance principles. The rest of the process relies on trust placed in a particular government to bring about the reforms transparently and with the participation of the other national and local actors.

The allocation of the incentive tranche has a second objective of updating and strengthening political dialogue. Governance has always been a sensitive subject. From now on the dialogue that the European

Union is developing to support the processes of democratic government should rely more on an approach based on partnership. Ousmane Sy, former Malian minister and coordinator of the Alliance to Refound Governance in Africa, believes what is needed is a "permanent movement between African tradition and the best inventions of the world". This idea of regarding modes of governance across the world as a wealth of experience that can inform and assist developing societies to invent their own governance is a line of thinking that the European Union and Africa will follow in this partnership, particularly in the context of the new Joint EU-Africa strategy and its first action plan for 2008–2010.

As has been explained earlier, the importance given to democratic governance in the wide sense requires Europe to adopt new methods and practices based on the notion of mutual commitments and changes in the "governance of aid". The new partnership approach should give partner countries better ownership of reforms by avoiding the imposition of a western vision of democratic governance. The Union's approach is then based on the political will of governments to implement reforms they have decided on themselves. Rather than waiting for the partner to come round to the European vision of governance, the reform process is launched through frank, open dialogue, in which the Union's expertise is placed at the service of governments to help the strengthen their institutional capacity.

Lastly we should say something about harmonisation and coordination across the European Union. Where governance is concerned harmonisation becomes even more important, since partner governments are increasingly being asked by donors to embark on reforms (International Monetary Fund, United Nations Development Programme, World Bank, bilateral partners, Non-Governmental Organisations and so on). Most of the time these reforms are set in motion without consultation and governments find it very hard to own them as they are fragmented and do not reflect any global strategy. So the international community needs to agree to review its own aid governance by jointly establishing a long-germ, global process that will lay down solid foundations for building governance in a particular country.

Partnership: an updated and uninhibited alliance

In late 2007, during the second – long awaited – summit between Europe and Africa, a new stage was reached in the development of a shared governance agenda for Europe and Africa. The Partnership on

Governance and Human Rights marks a break with reflexes of bygone days – on both the European and African sides. For, as explained above, we now know that moralising, paternalistic language is inappropriate and that the imposition of conditions involving sanctions is rarely the right method.

We also know that corruption is merely the symptom, the result of a system failure; we need a broad approach to governance. The idea of the "just state", a state that guarantees democracy and citizens' rights, is gaining ground in Africa. In practice, development, poverty reduction, security for all and stability are very largely dependent on states being capable of carrying out all their functions. It is the primary responsibility of African states and leaders to adopt this exemplary state governance.

Africa has shown us that it understands this responsibility and is ready to take it on. The coups d'état that were once the norm are now giving way to democratic regimes that, though certainly often fragile and imperfect, indisputably reflect a positive development. A pan-African governance framework has gradually been established, whose centrepieces are the African Charter on Democracy, Elections and Governance and the African Peer Review Mechanism (APRM).

This African governance agenda now permits a more uninhibited, sustained political dialogue between the European Union and Africa on governance and human rights. Above and beyond bilateral dialogue with African countries, we still have difficulty entering into continent-to-continent dialogue on these subjects. However, it is important that we should be able to debate fundamental issues such as our co-operation with the International Criminal Court and the limits of sovereignty in relation to the responsibility to protect, when populations are victims of their own leaders with no internal means of redress.

This is why the Partnership on Governance and Human Rights provides for a forum on governance. This forum will be a platform for global, open and structured dialogue between Europe and Africa on all questions of governance.

Global: in accordance with the broad conception of governance pursued by the European Union, this forum will cover both thematic policies, such as decentralisation and corruption, and the situations in particular countries, as well as the analytic tools themselves. It will also be an arena in for tackling difficult issues, since this too is part of the partnership. The important thing is to refrain from making definitive, moralistic, ideological judgments. No one has the monopoly of virtue.

Open: this forum must not be restricted solely to governments and civil servants. All the forces that give life to a society – the parliament, civil society in Europe and Africa, trades unions and the private sector – will be involved in the forum to make it a real driving force for change.

Structured: the forum must make regular, concrete contributions to the political dialogue at the local, national, regional and pan-African levels. The Africa Governance Institute in Dakar can play a key facilitating role, supported by the United Nations Development Programme. "Seminars" and "public consultation" could also be organised around discussion documents on specific themes.

Conclusion: a revised vision and shared responsibility for democratic governance

So the European Union has a realistic vision of the processes and practical approaches for encouraging partner countries to embark on reform, while insisting on rigorous respect for the principles of governance. The reform processes are by definition slow and complex, since they impact on the organisational heart of a state and a society. So the European Union advocates a long-term engagement in which respect for ownership is crucial. Having learned the lessons of its past mistakes, the European Union intends to support reforms but knows that it cannot make them for the partner countries. In this respect interesting developments are occurring for example on the African continent, where the African Peer Review Mechanism (APRM) should enable greater ownership of reforms and give them greater legitimacy among the population. The European Union has undertaken to support partner countries on this path.

To take things further, the new strategic partnership proposes to recreate the Europe-Africa relationship as one of partners with equal rights and fully-accepted responsibilities. As the European Commissioner Louis Michel writes, "We must put behind us the outdated, threadbare relationship of 'donor' and 'beneficiary', which merely encourages sermonising and hand-wringing."

This partnership should make it possible to engage in frank, open and respectful political dialogue, in which both sides accept their responsibilities.

25

Democratic Governance for Human Development

Reflections from the United Nations
Development Programme[1]

Over the last decade, UNDP has gradually shifted its approach to the provision of technical cooperation in governance from a traditional emphasis on public administration reform to a broader agenda of democratic governance. Growing demand for democratic governance cooperation from all regions has placed the organization in a central role in this area.

During 2006, 134 UNDP Country Offices engaged in promoting democratic governance. UNDP's comparative advantage in the provision of support for democratic governance cooperation is due to the organization being viewed as a neutral but committed partner working to apply appropriately internationally agreed norms and standards rather than seeking to impose arbitrary conditionality through its cooperation. Therefore, UNDP is often invited to play an important coordination and resource mobilization role on sensitive democratic governance issues.[2]

---

1. This article would not have been possible without the core contributions of a number of individuals. In particular, the Democratic Governance Group in UNDP's Bureau for Development Policy wants to acknowledge the role of Clara Brandi in drafting and bringing this article together. Special thanks also go to the following colleagues who provided insights and extensive comments: Pasipau Chirwa, Daniel Esser, Aleida Ferreyra, Bjoern Foerde, Terence D. Jones, Lenni Montiel, Joachim Nahem, Elissar Sarrouh, Anga Timilsina, Patrick Van Weerelt, and Raul Zambrano.

2. To further strengthen UNDP's niche, in 2001, the Democratic Governance Thematic Trust Fund (DGTTF) was established as a new instrument to address UNDP's development priorities. The democratic governance work of UNDP is further supported by the Democratic Governance Practice network and the Oslo Governance Centre.

This chapter seeks to illustrate both UNDP's theoretical and practical approach to democratic governance for human development. The first part establishes the conceptual and argumentative basis by setting out the relevant definitions and interpretations regarding democratic governance and human development. The second describes the set of UNDP services available to countries at their request, with illustrations from concrete examples.

Democratic Governance and Human Development

UNDP has been at the forefront of the growing international consensus that argues that governance and human development are indivisible.[3] But it is of course important to specify what the exact links are between democratic governance and human development. This section therefore outlines the relevant definitions regarding these two concepts, before presenting the argument that democratic governance is part of human development in two ways, both as a development goal in its own right and as a means for advancing human development.

Democratizing Good Governance for Human Development

All societies have to meet the challenge of creating a system of governance that promotes, supports and sustains human development – especially human development for the poor, the vulnerable, the marginalized. For UNDP, human development is about expanding capabilities and enlarging the choices people have in fulfilling their lives. From the evidence of a practice established by UNDP for over a decade, governance is defined as comprising the mechanisms, processes and institutions that determine how power is exercised, how decisions are made on issues of public concern, and how citizens articulate their interests, exercise their legal rights, meet their obligations and mediate their differences.[4]

What does it mean to promote good governance for human development? There is no single or simple answer. But much of the

---

3. For a recent discussion, see Dervis, K. "Governance and Development," Journal of Democracy 17, no. 4.

4. UNDP (1997). Governance for Sustainable Human Development: A UNDP Policy Document, New York, UNDP.

recent discussion about the definition of good governance has centred on what makes institutions and rules more effective and efficient, in order to achieve equity, transparency, participation, responsiveness, accountability, and the rule of law.[5] These aspects are crucial for human development, particularly since ineffective institutions usually result in the greatest harm to those who are poor and vulnerable.

Yet, in order to achieve and sustain human development, both the ends and means of good governance should be 'democratized.'[6] Democratic governance requires efficient institutions and an economic and political environment that renders public services effective and that makes economic growth possible; at the same time, democratic governance for human development must also be concerned with whether institutions and rules are fair and accountable, whether they protect human rights and political freedoms, and whether all people have a say in how they operate. So from the human development perspective, good governance is democratic governance.[7]

Hence, the notion of democratic governance employed in this chapter is people-centred: it epitomizes the most fundamental principle of democracy—that people should govern themselves through the systems they choose through open and transparent participatory processes. Democratic governance means that people have a say in the decisions that affect their lives and that they can hold decision-makers accountable. It further entails that the rules, institutions and practices that govern social interactions are inclusive and fair, that women are equal partners with men in private and public spheres of life, that people are free from discrimination based on race, ethnicity, class, gender or any other attribute, and that the needs of future generations are reflected in current policies. It also means that economic and social policies are responsive to people's needs and their aspirations, that these policies aim at eradicating poverty and expanding the choices that all people have in their lives, and that human rights and fundamental freedoms are respected.[8]

The relevance and importance of human rights in democratic governance has led to its integration into development cooperation by adopting a conceptual framework for the process of realizing human development that is normatively based on international human rights standards and treaties and operationally directed to promoting the rights

5. — — , Human Development Report 2002. Deepening Democracy in a Fragmented World, New York, UNDP, p. 51.

6. UNDP and UN-OHRLLS (2006). Governance for the Future: Democracy and Development in the Least Developed Countries, New York, UNDP, p. 36. 7. UNDP (2006).

7. UNDP, Democratic Governance Thematic Trust Fund Annual Report 2006, New York, UNDP, pp. 19ff.

8. — — — , Human Development Report 2002, p. 51.

possessed by all persons, by virtue of their common humanity, to live a life of freedom and dignity.[9] One of the main advantages of using a human rights based approach [HRBA] to development is that it emphasizes that the plans, policies and processes of development are anchored in a system of rights and corresponding obligations established by international law.

The human rights based approach to development espouses, among others, the principles of inclusiveness, participation and transparency and is an important implementation tool of UNDP to achieve these principles, which also form a key part of the concept of democratic governance. Such an approach is also a vital instrument in the context of governance issues as it brings vulnerable and marginalized groups into the development process through the identification of their needs from the community perspective – promoting ownership – and by enhancing their participation throughout the varied phases from designing to implementing projects.[10]

The Dual Notion of Democratic Governance

Democratic governance and its focus on participation and accountability is a development goal that is intrinsically valuable in its own right. Enjoying both political freedom and the ability to participate in the decisions that shape one's life are fundamental human rights: they are capabilities that are as significant for human development – for expanding people's choices – as being able to read and being in good health. People who lack political freedom and who are therefore not able to join associations, form an opinion and express their point of view, have a far more narrow range of choices in life. Democracy is the political process that secures political and civil freedoms and assures the right to participate, making democratic governance an intrinsically desirable goal in itself.[11]

But democratic governance is part of human development not only as a goal in itself but also as a means for advancing human development. The literature suggests a variety of theories about how democratic governance can promote human development. One suggested linkage refers to democratic regimes as being most successful at promoting

---

9. UNHCR (2006). Frequently Asked Questions on a Human Rights-Based Approach to Development Cooperation, New York and Geneva, United Nations.

10. Furthermore, the approach clarifies development priorities of governments; for instance, in the Philippines, the human rights based approach to development was a national initiative instigated by the government to re-profile governance projects from the perspective of human rights.

11. For a more detailed discussion of the classic normative principles of democracy, see Dahl, R. (1999) On Democracy New Haven, Yale University Press.

economic growth. However, in recent decades there have been a number of cases in which high levels of economic growth occurred under very different circumstances. It is therefore useful to look into what empirical studies say about the relationship between democracy and economic performance.

A large body of research demonstrates that wealth helps sustain democratic regimes.[12] One of the most prominent studies of this phenomenon, conducted by Adam Przeworski et al. confirms that wealthier countries are more likely to maintain democracy.[13] At the same time, their study emphasizes that the reverse relationship does not hold and that democracies were no better (and no worse for that matter) than dictatorships at generating long-term economic growth, at least in the period under consideration.[14]

A review of the literature therefore supports the propositions that greater wealth helps sustain democracy and that democratic regimes do not necessarily display a better (or a worse) aggregated, long-term economic performance.[15] But although empirical evidence of a positive effect of democratic governance on long-term economic performance in the aggregate is weak or inconclusive, recent research provides evidence that democracy influences productivity growth in different sectors differently, and that this differential effect may be one of the reasons for the ambiguity of the aggregate results.[16]

Other studies suggest that democratization undermines growth in countries with poor rule of law, while it stimulates economic growth

---

12. The basis for this body of research is the work by Seymour Martin Lipset, "Some Social Requisites of Democracy: Economic Development and Political Legitimacy," American Political Science Review, no. 53 (1959).

13. See Przeworski, A. et al. (2000). Democracy and Development: Political Institutions and Well-Being in the World, 1950–1990 New York, Cambridge University Press.

14. Feng (2003) confirms similar results. Feng, Y. (2003). Democracy, Governance and Economic Growth: Theory and Evidence, Cambridge, Mass., MIT Press. See also Barro, R. J. (1997). Determinants of Economic Growth: A Cross-Country Empirical Study Cambridge, Mass., MIT Press.

15. Historically speaking it is the sequence of institutions that mattered: democracy almost never preceded economic growth whereas the reverse has been an often-observed trajectory. Therefore, the contemporary take on democratic governance and development, namely co-evolution, is a strongly normative approach. At the same time, there is no conflict in acknowledging this, as the foundation for this normativity remains solid both in terms of international law (HR) and regarding international political commitments (e.g., MDGs).

16. Aghion, Alesina and Trebbi (2007) provide evidence that political rights are conducive to growth in more advanced sectors of the economy, possibly because of the beneficial effects of democracy and political rights on the freedom of entry in markets. See Aghion, P. Alesina, A. and Trebbi, F. (2007). "Democracy, Technology and Growth," NBER Working Paper 13180.

where the rule of law is strong.[17] Moreover, several empirical studies suggest that democratic regimes have smaller variance in the rate of growth than autocracies.[18] For example, according to Rodrik, a range of evidence indicates that participatory democracies yield long-run growth rates that are more predictable, produce greater short-term stability, handle adverse shocks much better, and deliver better distributional outcomes.[19]

Empirical studies generally support the thesis, therefore, that democratic states promote human development, welfare spending, and social equality more effectively than other types of regime.[20] In Africa, for instance, democratization, particularly multiparty competition, has been found to be associated with greater state provision of primary education.[21] Thus, the conclusion that can be derived from the literature is that democratic governance is associated with stronger social welfare policies.

However, despite the positive links established between democratic governance and human development, severe challenges persist. One such challenge being highlighted in recent years is the fact that many societies which have held democratic elections for several decades continue to display high inequalities in income distributions, discrimination against minorities, and taxation and spending policies that favour the interests of the rich.

It is therefore being argued that competitive elections are not enough to promote and sustain human development in all of its dimensions. If people

---

17. Polterovich V. and Popov, V. (2006). "Democratization, Quality of Institutions and Economic Growth," Working Paper 2006, no. 56. Rodrik and Rigobon find that democracy and the rule of law are both good for economic performance and that, while the latter has a much stronger impact on incomes, rule of law and democracy tend to be mutually reinforcing. See Rigobon, R. and Rodrik, D. "Rule of Law, Democracy, Openness, and Income: Estimating the Interrelationships," Economics of Transition 13, no. 3.

18. Przeworski et al., Democracy and Development, Sen, A. (2000). Development as Freedom, New York, Random House, Acemoglu D. et al. (2005). Income and Democracy, Boston, MIT,, Rodrik, D. "Democracy and Economic Performance" Cambridge, Mass., Harvard University.

19. Rodrik, D. (2000). "Institutions for High-Quality Growth: What They Are and How to Acquire Them," CEPR Discussion Paper 2370.

20. For example, see Halperin, M., Siegle, J. T. and Weinstein, M. (2005). The Democracy Advantage, New York, Routledge, Halperin, M., Siegle, J. T. and Weinstein, M., "Why Democracies Excel," Foreign Affairs 83, no. 5. Other studies usually confirm such patterns. See Nel, P. "Democratization and the Dynamics of Income Distribution in Low- and Middle-Income Countries," Politikon 32, no. 1, Mulligan, C. B., Gil, R. and Sala-i-Martin, X. "Do Democracies Have Different Public Policies Than Non-Democracies?" Journal of Economic Perspectives 18, no. 1.

21. Stasavage, D. "Democracy and Education Spending in Africa," American Journal of Political Science 49, no. 2.

make use of their voting-rights in elections, but feel no improvement in their day-to-day lives, their trust in democratic processes is likely to erode, and this seems to be the case according to surveys in recent years in both Africa and Latin America. If, on the other hand, government capacity increases, but this capacity is not being used to respond to public concerns and needs, capacity-development processes are unlikely to generate benefits for all members of society, including the poorest of the poor.

Therefore, efforts to promote democratic governance for development have to focus both on fostering inclusive participation and on strengthening responsive state capacity, and this combined approach is now at the core of the democratic governance thinking of UNDP:

First, free and fair elections must be accompanied by efforts to ensure that all people have full opportunities to participate in the decisions affecting their lives, so that traditionally under-represented groups are free to choose how they are governed.

Second, the state needs capacity to respond effectively to public demands: local and national governing institutions must have the capacity and resources to deliver effective economic and social policies.

Third, human rights, gender equality and anti-corruption principles are to be protected and promoted.

How UNDP goes about strengthening these three main elements of its democratic governance approach is set out in the remainder of this chapter.

UNDP Support for Human Development

To support a pro-poor, gender-sensitive, and human-rights based approach to development, UNDP organizes its democratic governance agenda around the fostering of inclusive participation and strengthening of accountable and responsive governing capacity in the context of well-established international standards and principles of human rights, gender equality and anti-corruption.

Fostering Inclusive Participation

To foster inclusive participation, democracies need effective channels to allow every citizen to cast a vote in free and fair elections, to participate in the public sphere, and to promote their interests through political parties, civil society organizations, and volunteerism. Through these numerous channels, people can articulate their demands, pressure public officials and hold elected representatives and governments accountable for their actions, and contribute directly themselves, to better development policies and social outcomes.

UNDP interacts directly with key stakeholders to foster inclusive participation and civic engagement at the local and national levels—with a spotlight on under-represented segments of society such as the poor, women, and minorities.[22] Mechanisms and opportunities to deepen inclusive participation include focusing on electoral laws, institutions, and processes, mobilization channels such as political parties and civil society organizations, and communication channels in relation to access to information, e-governance, and independent media.

Well-functioning Electoral Systems and Processes

To secure opportunities for participation through free and fair elections, UNDP supports the reform and management of electoral systems. On average, UNDP is engaged in supporting an election somewhere in the world every two weeks. Yet, UNDP does not only concentrate on particular election events but embraces an integrated, long-term election-cycle approach to electoral assistance, which encompasses supporting independent and permanent electoral management bodies; developing effective electoral system designs and legal reforms; election planning, monitoring and budgeting to ensure credible elections and more cost-effective electoral processes over time.

Strengthening the Capacity of Political Parties and Civil Society

As outlined above, inclusive participation does not only require opportunities for participation in free and fair elections but also calls for increasing electoral turnout among marginalized and under-represented members of society as a key basis for fostering their voice and participation in the policymaking process, for instance, by strengthening the capacity of political parties and civil society organizations or by conducting civic and voter education programmes.[23]

Direct channels of social accountability, illustrated by community

---

22. These interventions contribute to democratic governance but also fundamentally improve local governance since they have a strong impact at local and community levels.

23. See also, for example, UNDP and Oslo Governance Centre (2005). UNDP's Engagement with Political Parties, New York: UNDP.

boards, social audits, and participatory processes of local decision-making, are other essential mechanisms to help foster inclusive participation, above all in states where the formal institutions of representative democracy are weak.

Expanding Access to Information and e-Governance

Accessible and relevant information and the means and ability to communicate are important for enabling people to participate in policy making processes and the decisions that affect their lives. Accordingly, UNDP engages with governments, a variety of civil society organisations and the private sector to further the accessibility, relevance, and quality of information and communication mechanisms for poor people and vulnerable groups of society. UNDP's initiatives in this context include enhancing the legal and regulatory environment for freedom and pluralism of information, increasing government–citizen dialogue and interaction, expanding the opportunities for the poor and marginalized to voice their concerns through 'communication for empowerment,'[24] and supporting the capacity of independent and pluralistic media.[25]

This is complemented by the work UNDP undertakes, since the late 1990s, under the aegis of e-governance policies and initiatives. The focus here is on increasing basic service and information delivery to the poor via Information and Communications Technology (ICT) and fostering citizens and stakeholder participation in decision-making process via ICT networks that can promote collective action. Access to both the ICT networks (not only Internet based) and public information via ICTs are fundamental underpinnings to accomplish such goals. Finally, in the context of the MDGs, UNDP is collaborating with a non-profit foundation to deploy affordable learning technologies for poor children that attend public schools in developing countries as part of overall national e-governance plans and strategies.

---

24. The Oslo Governance Centre has developed a Practical Guidance Note on "Communication for Empowerment: Developing Media Strategies in Support of Vulnerable Groups". This approach is presently being piloted in Mozambique, Madagascar and Malawi as part of a UN Democracy Fund funded project in cooperation with the 'Communication for Social Change Consortium.'

25. In Lao PDR, for example, a community radio project was implemented in remote and poor districts, where lack of access to information is an impediment to socio-economic development. — — —, DGTTF Annual Report 2006, p. 19.

Strengthening Accountable and Responsive Governing Capacity

The combination of inclusive participation with the expansion of accountable and responsive state capacity can be regarded as necessary for promoting democratic governance and sustainable human development, ultimately helping to achieve the MDGs. UNDP's work in the context of governing capacity concentrates on the areas of strengthening public administration reforms, fostering local governing institutions, assisting parliamentary development, and improving access to justice and the rule of law.

Supporting public administration reform is a crucial aspect of strengthening governing institutions that are accountable and responsive to public concerns and social needs. UNDP provides assistance for improving efficiency and equity in the delivery of public services and helps countries develop professional, exemplary civil services through performance-based management. This, in turn, promotes equal opportunity for women and minority groups. UNDP also offers assistance in developing anti-corruption legislation and codes of conduct and training of civil servants.[26]

To increase access to public services for the poor and nurture democratic culture at the local level, UNDP assists in strengthening countries' local governance. Where appropriate, UNDP also helps design and implement national strategies for decentralizing authority and responsibility, emphasizing the rights of women and the poor. UNDP assists countries in improving coordination among key ministries as well, to make sure that sectoral decentralization is integrated with local planning and appropriate budgetary mechanisms.

In a democratic polity, parliaments are crucial for channelling public participation in policy making by linking voter's concerns with elected representatives and the delivery of public services, for example, regarding social welfare policies. Moreover, support to parliamentary development reinforces the role of the parliament in holding government accountable for policy commitments and the use of budget resources, for instance, for poverty reduction goals. By watching over government action, legislatures also play a key role in enhancing transparent governance.[27]

UNDP supports one in four parliaments globally. Initiatives in this context encompass training parliamentary members and staff; supporting constitutional reforms that guarantee basic rights, freedom of association,

---

26. For further details on public administration reform, see Ibid., pp. 28f. See also UNDP, Democratic Governance Group Annual Report 2005 (New York: UNDP, 2005), pp. 26ff.

27. See also — — —, Engaging Parliaments in the Millennium Development Goals: A Key Part of National MDG Strategies (New York: UNDP, 2006). For a discussion of UNDP initiatives regarding parliamentary development, see also UNDP, Democratic Governance Group Annual Report 2005.

expression and participation; promoting sustainable human development in legislative deliberations through support for committees related to poverty issues, gender mainstreaming and budget allocations.

Supporting well-functioning, responsive and efficient justice and security institutions and organizations are key preconditions for the observance and enforcement of fundamental human rights, reducing corruption, and assisting the formation of a stable societal basis for human development and the achievement of the MDGs. Moreover, promoting the effective use of public interest litigation and legal aid for the poor helps create precedent, empowerment and knowledge where the poor and disempowered can successfully use the formal legal system to ensure that corporations and governments deliver on commitments and actually pay redress for violations of the same to poor citizens.

Grounding Governance in International Principles

To strengthen human rights, foster gender-sensitive human development, and reduce the development-hampering effects of corruption, UNDP grounds its democratic governance work in the well-established international standards and principles of human rights, gender equality, and anti-corruption. In addition, UNDP is engaged in the development of governance assessments methodology as a means of developing the capacity of governments to benchmark their governance reform efforts based on national ownership.

UNDP strengthens the capacity of requesting programme countries to promote and protect human rights through support to human rights policy development, advocacy, and training; through the promotion of national human rights action plans; and through the creation and support of human rights institutions at national and sub-national levels. Moreover, UNDP strengthens the international human rights system at the global, regional and national levels through support to the ratification and dissemination of international human rights instruments.

Advancing gender equality and enhancing women's empowerment cut across various democratic governance issues, whether through elections and parliamentary development projects aiming at greater avenues for women to gain access to legislative deliberations, participate in political processes at the national and local levels and help them reach positions of political leadership, or through legal mechanisms in justice and human right interventions.[28]

---

28. Work in this area also includes gender-sensitive budgeting and reducing the access to justice gap between men and women. For projects that aim at reducing the gender gap in access to justice, see UNDP, Democratic Governance Group Annual Report 2006, pp. 8ff.

Efforts to increase women's political participation have focused on capacity-building for women candidates and women who have been elected to office. But since the ability of women to share information, processes and techniques through networking is also critical to their successful participation in public life, UNDP and its partners developed iKNOW Politics,[29] an online network for women in politics worldwide in order to increase their participation and effectiveness in political life by utilizing a technology-enabled, one-stop access to relevant resources and expertise, stimulate dialogue, create knowledge and share experiences on women's political participation.[30]

Corruption corrodes democratic institutions and the rule of law and hampers economic development by distorting markets and undermining the integrity of the private sector. It can damage trust in political leadership and, ultimately, in the fundamental principles of democratic governance. UNDP therefore supports initiatives that are directed at reducing corruption and emphasizing the importance of public accountability and transparency for democratic governance and poverty reduction.[31] UNDP's approach links anti-corruption to other democratic governance programmes such as gender equality, electoral assistance, human rights, e-governance, and access to information. New communication technologies and e-governance applications have a significant potential for helping to curb corruption by increasing the dissemination of information, revealing governmental malfeasance and encouraging the creation of independent media.

An increasing number of organisations are giving greater priority to the need to assess democracy, governance and human rights as part of their development assistance programmes. Assessment tools, frameworks and global datasets enable comparisons over time and across countries and regions. However, while this data is a rich source of information for a range of analyses, it does not necessarily point to particular institutions or institutional arrangements as the cause of governance challenges, nor does it help identify appropriate operational solutions and performance improvement processes. It can thus be of only limited help

---

29. The International Knowledge Network of Women in Politics (iKNOW Politics) is an online workspace designed to serve the needs of elected officials, candidates, political party leaders and members, researchers, students, and other practitioners interested in advancing women in politics. It is a joint project of the United Nations Development Programme (UNDP), the United Nations Development Fund for Women (UNIFEM), the National Democratic Institute for International Affairs (NDI), the Inter-Parliamentary Union (IPU) and the International Institute for Democracy and Electoral Assistance (International IDEA).

30. UNDP, Democratic Governance Group Annual Report 2006, pp. 5.

31. Ibid., pp. 23ff.

in policy-making processes. Furthermore, such tools often lack national ownership and engagement in the assessment process and rarely include the necessary disaggregation to capture the impact, experiences and perceptions of marginalized groups in society, especially the poor and women. Such assessment tools also do not address the capacity deficits that exist to ensure an effective monitoring system.

For UNDP, the value of a nationally owned governance indicator system is that it serves as a critical accountability mechanism for local stakeholders, especially the citizens of a country and non-state actors rather than donors. A nationally owned system provides upward internal rather than external pressure for reform. And through the transparency of information stemming from it, it also provides a catalyst for greater citizen engagement in democracy processes and for demanding greater effectiveness of government.

Some conclusions

While there are considerable opportunities for expanding democratic governance, serious challenges remain. To consolidate democratic governance, free and fair elections must be complemented by efforts to assure that all people have full opportunities to participate in the processes and decisions affecting their lives, both directly through community engagement and indirectly through elections. Moreover, governing institutions at local and national levels need the capacity and resources to deliver effective economic and social policies that promote human development and respond to public needs and demands, whether in terms of wider access to schools and health care, a cleaner and less hazardous environment, or redistributive social and economic policies to alleviate poverty.

Without inclusive democratic participation, accountability and strengthened institutional capacity, it is unlikely that governments will be able to deliver on their commitments to achieve the Millennium Declaration, including the MDGs. Given these challenges, UNDP will continue to promote and facilitate democratic governance as one of its core focus areas.

26

Strengthening Governance and Anticorruption for Poverty Reduction

The World Bank Group's Strategic Approach

Anupama DOKENIYA, Colum GARRITY,
Sanjay PRADHAN[1]

Both empirical research, and decades of development experience, have demonstrated the value of good governance – good policies, a workable regulatory framework for markets, and reasonably efficient and effective provision of public services – in helping to reduce poverty and strengthen aid effectiveness. On a daily basis, poor people around the world are unable to access health clinics, schools or other essential services because their public systems are unresponsive or because they themselves cannot, or will not, pay bribes. Corruption and weak governance often mean that resources that could help create opportunities for poor people instead enrich corrupt elites. Where transparency and accountability mechanisms are weak or lacking, poor people's needs are often marginalized and development outcomes are weak. Consequently, a focus on improving governance in the World Bank's client countries, including by fighting corruption, has become an important component of the Bank's assistance agenda over the last decade.

In March 2007, the Board of Executive Directors of the World Bank Group approved a landmark governance and anticorruption strategy, building on more than a decade of sustained engagement in this area,

---

1. Sanjay Pradhan is Director, Colum Garrity is a Public Sector Specialist, and Anupama Dokeniya is a Consultant, all in the Public Sector Governance unit of The World Bank. The views expressed in this article are those of the authors, and do not necessarily reflect the views of the management or Executive Directors of The World Bank or member governments.

triggered by a recognition that improved institutions   are part of what needs to be done to achieve long term growth and poverty reduction. The strategy sets new frontiers for the Bank's engagement in this area: systematically integrating and mainstreaming work on governance and anticorruption into the Bank's country and sector-specific programs and projects; engaging with a range of stakeholders, including strengthening the demand side of governance; scaling up measures to combat corruption in Bank-financed projects; and building support for global coalitions and partnerships to collectively further the goal of better governance as a critical precondition for effective development and service delivery.[2]

Governance and development: Long-term relationship and country-specific trajectories

An extensive body of academic research – based on large cross-country analyses of countries – has shown a positive correlation between many aspects of 'good' governance – such as rule of law, greater transparency, independent judiciary, checks on executive power and discretion, and accountability – and critical development and welfare outcomes – such as higher income levels, lower child mortality and illiteracy; improved country competitiveness and investment climate; and greater resilience of the financial sector. These studies show that over the long run, the quality of governance, including control of corruption, has a significant positive correlation with income levels and poverty reduction.

Complementing this body of research on the long-term relationship between governance and development levels, is a parallel stream of research that emphasizes that the specificities of country contexts, historical legacies, and institutional endowments are critical to determine both what kinds of governance reforms are desirable, and what specific institutional change trajectories are feasible. For instance, recent research by North et al (2007) shows that although countries with high levels of development demonstrate openness in their social systems ("open access orders"), in other countries, where more closed social systems provide stability, interventions need to be framed within the possibilities afforded by these systems.

---

2. Note: This paper does not discuss the World Bank's work in combating corruption in Bank-financed projects. For additional information on this area, see: http://www.worldbank.org/integrity.

Empirical research by Meisel and Ould Aoudia (2007) shows that while the level of income is positively correlated with governance, countries with diverse institutional and governance structures can accomplish growth and 'economic take-off'. Levy and Fukuyama (2008) also point to the diversity of development strategies depending upon country-specific realities: for instance, some countries in East Asia emphasized state building for economic growth before democracy and social mobilization, while some middle-income countries in Latin America focused on increasing the quality of democracy. Social mobilization was the entry point for governance reform in "blocked cases" (such as Ukraine's Orange Revolution), while some countries such as Bangladesh capitalized on "just enough governance" for incremental growth accelerations, anticipating that stronger institutional reform will occur at higher levels of income. Collier's (2007) work has been important in demonstrating that improving governance is crucial for certain types of countries among 'the bottom billion', for instance, those facing the resource trap. Other significant research in this area – for instance, by Grindle (2007) – points to the importance of selectivity in assessing what kinds of institutional and governance reforms might be feasible in the short run, and designing more modest and successful interventions strategies, based on this principle, rather than attempting large-scale and comprehensive governance reform all at once.

To summarize, this research points to the diversity of institutional growth paths, and hence, entry points, necessary, given the institutional endowments of a country. The Bank's work has also been based on a recognition of this specificity of context. Indeed, a key principle of the Bank's governance and anticorruption strategy is to identify the appropriate interventions given specific country contexts and governance challenges, and tailor strategies based on local knowledge, innovation on the ground, and extensive consultation and collaboration with local constituencies.

The world bank group's increasing focus on governance and anticorruption

For many decades, the Bank was constrained in its work on governance issues. There was even a de facto taboo on the use of the 'C' word ('corruption') in Bank work. In 1996, the former President of the Bank, James Wolfensohn, made a speech at the 1996 WBG-IMF Annual Meetings on the 'cancer of corruption' as a key constraint to achieving

Box 1. Guiding Principles for Strengthening World Bank Group Engagement on Governance and Anticorruption

Guiding Principles. The process of preparing the strategy—including guidance from the Bank's Board, the Development Committee, and global multi-stakeholder consultations—helped crystallize seven guiding principles for GAC work by the WBG going forward:

1. The World Bank Group (WBG's) focus on governance and anticorruption (GAC) follows from its mandate to reduce poverty—a capable and accountable state creates opportunities for poor people, provides better services, and improves development outcomes.

2. The country has primary responsibility for improving governance—country ownership and leadership are key to successful implementation, and the WBG is committed to supporting a country's own priorities. A country's government remains the principal counterpart for the WBG.

3. The WBG is committed to remaining engaged in the fight against poverty, and seeking creative ways of providing support, even in poorly-governed countries—"don't make the poor pay twice".

4. The form of WBG engagement on GAC will vary from country to country, depending on specific circumstances—while there is no 'one-size-fits-all', the WBG will adopt a consistent approach towards operational decisions across countries, systematically anchored in national strategies, supported by WBG Country Assistance Strategies, with no change in the performance-based allocation system for IDA countries or IBRD resource allocation system.

5. Engaging systematically with a broad range of government, business, and civil society stakeholders is key to GAC reform and development outcomes—so, consistent with its mandate, the WBG will scale up existing good practice in engaging with multiple stakeholders in its operational work, including by strengthening transparency, participation, and third-party monitoring in its own operations.

6. The WBG will strive to strengthen, rather than bypass, country systems—better national institutions are the more effective and long term solution to governance and corruption challenges and to mitigating fiduciary risk for all public money, including that from the Bank.

7. The WBG will work with donors, international institutions, and other actors at the country and global levels to ensure a harmonized approach an d coordination based on respective mandates and comparative advantage—"the WBG should not act in isolation".

the Bank's mission and objectives. Subsequently, key policy and strategy documents made work on governance integral to the Bank's development assistance – these documents included the 1997 Helping Countries Combat Corruption: The Role of the World Bank; the 1997 World Development Report and The State in a Changing World; and the 2000 strategy paper, Reforming Public Institutions and Strengthening Governance. Since then, the focus on governance, and especially on anticorruption, has been integral to the World Bank Group's agenda — including through policy dialogue, technical assistance, lending, and research.

In 2006, in response to a mandate from the Development Committee and the Board of Executive Directors, the World Bank prepared a new Governance and Anticorruption (GAC) strategy, Strengthening World Bank Group Engagement on Governance and Anticorruption, which was approved the Board of Executive Directors in March 2007. Subsequently, an Implementation Plan for the strategy was endorsed by the Board in October 2007.

The strategy was prepared with wide-ranging consultations with representatives from governments, donors, civil society, parliaments, private sector, academia, and other stakeholders in 35 developing countries and 12 donor countries through face-to-face meetings and videoconferencing, and several consultations with global audiences. An estimated 3,200 individuals participated in the consultations around the globe. From the consultations emerged key principles to guide the Bank's work in this area (See Box 1).

Complementing wide-ranging consultations with external stakeholders was an intensive process of internal consultations, with groups across sectors and countries in both the headquarters of the Bank and from field offices. This intensive participatory process has generated ownership, commitment, and leadership of the strategy throughout the Bank Group, essential to the strategy's central element of mainstreaming governance across the Bank's sectoral and country interventions. The implementation of the strategy is overseen by a high-level Governance Council, with representation from top management from all the operating units across the Bank Group, including the IFC and MIGA, and chaired by the Managing Directors on a rotating basis.

Frontiers of the Bank's new governance and anticorruption agenda

The strategy seeks to systematically scale up the Bank's support to strengthening governance and anticorruption for better development outcomes, by pushing the frontiers of Bank work in seven key areas:

– Systematically addressing challenges posed by weak governance to a country's development priorities and systematically integrating support for strengthening governance and fighting corruption in the Bank's Country Assistance Strategies (CASs).

– Supporting cross-cutting public management systems, such as public financial management and administrative and civil service reform, and independent oversight intuitions, such as State Audit Institutions, Parliamentary Committees, and the judiciary.

– Mainstreaming governance engagement as part of the Bank's support to enhancing services and performance in various sectors, such as delivery of public services (health, education etc.), infrastructure development, natural resource management, and extractive industries.

– Supporting enabling frameworks and capacity on the "demand-side" of governance (civil society organizations, media, community and local governance).

– Enhancing partnerships with the private sector such as business associations and chambers of commerce, especially to address the private sector's role in corruption.

– Supporting Global Collective Action for better governance through such initiatives as the Stolen Assets Recovery Initiative (StAR), United Nations Convention Against Corruption (UNCAC), and the Governance network of OECD.

– Monitoring progress on the impact of the Bank's efforts on actual improvements in the governance environments in countries through strengthening governance indicators.

Mainstreaming Governance and Anticorruption in Country Programs

The Bank's governance and anticorruption (GAC) strategy proposes that governance dimensions will be systematically integrated across the Bank's country assistance programs. The Country Assistance Strategy (CAS) is the basic plan that guides the Bank's activities in a partner country, identifying key areas in which the Bank Group's support can best assist the country to achieve sustainable development and poverty reduction. It sets a country's vision for growth and development priorities, the Bank's diagnosis of the country's development situation, and a selective program of support tailored to the country's needs.

Tailoring the scope, sequencing, and speed of governance reforms to country contexts has emerged as an increasingly important principle. Since countries are at different levels of institutional development, with a diverse range of institutional configurations, no one formula for improving governance can fit all and the GAC strategy does not propose to rigidly classify or rank countries in terms of their governance. Rather, it posits that strategies for country level governance and anticorruption work will be designed depending on both the initial political context and the longer-term historical processes that shape and constrain institutional reform.

This more diversified and context-specific approach implies different entry points to improve governance in different country contexts. For instance, in some countries, Bank support might principally take the form of supporting improvements in public administration and expenditure management capacity. In other countries, the focus might be more directly on helping strengthen formal institutions of executive oversight and civil society efforts for better governance. Where opportunities for governance reform at the national level are limited, there may be 'entry points' at the local level. In some settings, the 'entry point' might be bottom-up participatory reform, such as community-driven development, especially when it also supports the local government transparency, capacity, and accountability.

Identifying and engaging the most promising entry points and modes of engagement requires a deep understanding of the political economy realities, governance configurations, and ways in which governance can be integrated into the development priorities of a country. Country-level Governance and Anticorruption processes have been launched in 27 countries as a first step in this effort. A country-level governance and anticorruption or 'CGAC' process is a 'systematic and disciplined' stock-taking of the country's GAC environment and its impact on the Bank's projects, growth, and poverty reduction, and assesses GAC impediments to country development goals, and 'entry points' for Bank support for GAC reforms. The conclusions and insights from the process are expected to inform Country Assistance Strategies, and yield a clear plan for how country programs and strategies will address governance and corruption barriers to and country's development goals.

Strengthening Public Management

The Bank has been involved in public sector reform operations in many countries, historically with a strong focus on core public management reforms. In Fiscal Year 2006, over 20 per cent of new Bank-supported operations and almost 20 percent of new financing commitments tackled public sector governance issues broadly defined.

Helping countries improve public finance management systems has been the core pillar of the Bank's traditional governance work. A notable achievement has been the development of specific monitorable indicators – the Public Expenditure and Financial Accountability (PEFA) indicators

– that benchmark and track improvements in PFM systems. PEFA was developed through a multi-donor initiative and the PEFA assessment tool is now being applied in over 70 countries.[3] The frontier issues within PFM are to: match institutional reform to country capacity (e.g., doing the basics first, as in Cambodia's platform approach), and identifying and tackling political economy of reforms.

By contrast with PFM, public administration and civil service reforms have proven more challenging. Experience across countries shows that earlier reforms sought comprehensive, across-the-board reforms (e.g., through massive retrenchments) that require strong political commitment and that have often proven not to have traction. In most countries, more incremental reforms are likely to yield better outcomes, such as in Albania, where reforms are seeking to promote meritocracy among the top 1000 civil servants. The GAC strategy provides for scaling up the Bank's work in this area as a necessary element of building capacity in public administration and public financial management systems.

Strengthening Governance at the Sector Level

The Bank has recognized that governance and anticorruption is fundamentally about health services being delivered properly, teachers showing up to school, roads being built without pot-holes, and a predictable investment climate – in short, it is about accountability in the use of public resources in sectors. A large proportion of the Bank's lending is dedicated to strengthening the effectiveness of services and performance in key sectors – such as health and education, building critical infrastructure such as road and rail transport, electricity, water systems, and communications, and supporting the management of natural resources such as forests, fisheries, and extractive industries.

During the past decade, governance reforms in these sectors has primarily focused on experimenting with more efficient means of delivering services, including through restructuring, contracting out to private sector firms, and privatization – and with rising attention to the new ways of incorporating social accountability into operational design. More recently, attention has also been given to addressing vulnerabilities of sectors to illegal practices, including corruption and fraud, with some evidence of success. Some sectors, such as forestry, roads, extractive industries, fisheries, water, and agriculture, have begun to develop risk assessment tools, specialized databases, and monitoring systems.

---

3. See http://www.pefa.org

Box 2. Tackling Vulnerabilities at the Sector Level

The Many Faces of Corruption: Tracking Vulnerabilities at the Sector Level, a World Bank Group publication, sets out an approach to combating corruption that is being piloted in many sectors in the Bank: preparing a detailed "road map" at the beginning of a program with indicators along the way to signal possible corruption risks that might arise at various points in the program cycle. Two examples:

- In public procurement, corruption risks could arise during procurement planning, product design, advertising/invitation to bid, prequalification, bid evaluation (technical and financial evaluation), post-qualification, contract award, and contract implementation.
- In the delivery of essential drugs in the primary health sector, corruption risks could arise in the manufacturing of the drugs, drug registration, drug selection, procurement, distribution, and dispensation/prescription (see figure).

A road map approach provides a structured and detailed picture of a problem area and can help identify remedial measures. In the transport/ roads sector, for example, the capture of resource allocations by vested interests during budget formulation can underpin bid rigging during the procurement stage (when the budget is executed), which in turn can trigger so-called "change orders" during contract implementation. Similarly, in the forestry sector, high rents are reaped (and large-scale corruption takes place) during the stage when illegal lumber is laundered into legal products such as furniture; and any serious attempt to address corruption in the sector would have to focus on this particular link in the chain. The road map also offers a tool for developing measurable indicators for tracking the incidence of corruption. In procurement, for example, if bidders systematically drop out from the initial expression of intent through the financial evaluation of bids, it may signal some form of collusion among participating firms.

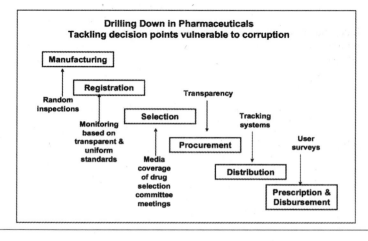

Drilling Down in Pharmaceuticals
Tackling decision points vulnerable to corruption

Scaling up approaches to improve governance and identify and address points of vulnerability to corruption in specific sectors – through a value-chain or process flow methodology – is a key frontier area of the GAC strategy. The Bank is building a comprehensive assessment of governance and corruption issues in its sector work, from pharmaceuticals, to forestry, to education, roads and extractive industries as illustrated in the recent publication The Many Faces of Corruption: Tracking Vulnerabilities at the Sector Level (see Box 2). Experience has shown that addressing governance weaknesses and corruption vulnerabilities in only a few points in a sectoral value chain is not adequate as the points of vulnerability vary in different countries, and more comprehensive, sector-wide strategies are needed. Sector-level governance diagnostics are useful tools for this.

Other new approaches to addressing these issues have emerged. One of the more effective ones has been multi-stakeholder collaborative networks and coalitions based on the principles of mutual accountability and transparent monitoring. One emerging success in this area is the Extractive Industries Transparency Initiative (EITI, Box 3), a coalition between resource-rich countries and extractive industry multinationals, supported by donors, and monitored by civil society, targeted to ensuring transparency in resource revenues. There are now more recent and important efforts to expand this transparency both upstream to awards of contracts and licenses and downstream to expenditure management.

Box 3. Innovative Approaches to Improving Governance in the Sectors – The EITI Case

- Independent review of payments made to the government by oil, gas and mining companies and of revenues received by government from those companies by a reputable third party (i.e. audit firm)
- Publication in a readily accessible form of payments made by the companies and of revenues received by government
- Extension of all of the above to companies including state owned enterprises
- Active engagement of all stakeholders in the design, monitoring, and implementation process
- Several countries implementing EITI, but risk of free-rider problem and tokenism in weaker settings

Engaging Stakeholders to Strengthen the Demand Side of Governance

Greater participation and oversight by citizens and media that have broad access to information on the operation of state institutions is important to foster accountability in state institutions. Strengthening accountability requires a variety of mechanisms, broadly referred to as the 'demand side of governance,' and including:

– Creating concrete opportunities for participation and oversight, for example, through participatory development of policies and public spending priorities (the poverty reduction strategy process has provided a major impetus in this area in IDA-eligible countries), social accountability in the delivery of services, community-driven development, civil society and media oversight over public procurement;

– Supporting the development of an enabling environment and of capacity so that that civil society organizations can effectively take advantage of these opportunities;

– Improving transparency of government functions and public officials through reforms in the policy, regulatory, and operational environment for greater transparency, freedom of information, and income and asset disclosure; and

– Enabling the development of independent and competitive media that can investigate, monitor and provide feedback on government performance, including corruption.

Over the past decade the Bank has engaged increasingly with civil society groups, and Bank capacity and sophistication in this work have expanded. Initiatives in this area have included: enabling citizens to access information and participate in the development of policies, spending priorities, and service provision; promoting community participation to improve local governance; strengthening the enabling environment and capacity of civil society and the media to monitor public policymaking and implementation; and encouraging greater oversight over public procurement, asset declarations, and other important dimensions of government performance.

While working with the government as its principal counterpart, the GAC strategy proposes that the Bank scale up existing good practice in working with a broad range of stakeholders, consistent with its mandate, anchored in the country context, in collaboration with other multilateral and bilateral organizations. The Bank will focus its work with groups that are with groups that are competent and accountable, and consistent with the Bank's legal mandate. The Bank is also revising its disclosure policy to improve the Bank's own transparency, and enhancing guidance to staff to apply best practices on consultation and participation in Bank-financed operations.

Engaging the Private Sector to Improve Governance

The private sector is an intrinsic partner in growth strategies and in fighting corruption. A better governance environment is necessary for competitive and productivity-enhancing private sector — and a thriving, open, and competitive private sector can be a strong source of support for better governance. But private businesses, including those from developed countries, can also fuel the supply-side of corruption by engaging in corrupt practices.

The Bank Group's new strategy proposes to strengthen the governance-private sector links in two ways: on the one hand, the Bank Group will continue to deepen its support for improving the enabling environment for the development of competitive private and financial sectors and increased private investment, benchmarked internationally, through indicators such as Doing Business database, Investment Climate Assessments, and enterprise surveys. These indicators monitor corporate practices by domestic and multinational firms at the country level, including measures of bribery and firm influence.

On the other hand, partnering with the private sector to root out corruption and create good governance environments is key. Consultations undertaken for the GAC strategy have shown a strong momentum from within the private sector in both developing countries and globally, to lend support to efforts to improve governance and combat corruption. Various instruments of effective engagement with the private sector, and working directly with the private sector to strengthen ethical corporate practices, have emerged. For instance, showcasing examples and evidence that 'avoiding corruption is good for business', can be very useful for improving corporate governance.

Other mechanisms include: supporting initiatives to promote business ethics and voluntary codes of conduct – such as the International Chamber of Commerce's Rules of Conduct and Recommendations for Combating Extortion and Bribery, Transparency International's Business Principles, the World Economic Forum's Partnering Against Corruption Initiative (PACI), or the UN Global Compact's 10 Principles, all underpinned by effective, verifiable internal programs of implementation and compliance, building coalitions of businesses and other stakeholders for anticorruption, and encouraging businesses to join public-private coalitions for reform, such as the Extractive Industries Transparency Initiative (EITI) and Publish What You Pay coalition.

IFC and MIGA are the key institutions within the Bank Group that interface with the private sector – the IFC through providing financing to private sector operations in developing countries, and the MIGA through providing political risk guarantees. These two agencies are critical to building this focus. The Bank is also using public disclosure to raise the cost to businesses of continuing to engage in corruption.

Harmonizing and Coordinating Globally

Working with multiple global actors – multilateral institutions, civil society, private sector, and global initiatives – is crucial to leverage synergies, harmonize approaches and make assistance more effective. The strategy aims to strengthen the Bank Group's bilateral and multilateral partnerships in accordance with the Paris Declaration:
• Harmonization and coordination: The strategy proposes to promote coordinated action with the IMF, United Nations, regional development banks, and other donors, including in public financial management, procurement, and judicial reform. Recognizing the limitations of the Bank's legal framework, the Bank will also work with partners on the principle of a division of labor among donors with others taking a lead in areas that are outside the Bank's mandate or comparative advantage. A process of joint sanctions reform by the multilateral development banks (MDBs), is also making investigative rules and procedures more consistent, strengthening information sharing, and establishing mechanisms to recognize each other's sanctions decisions.
• International Conventions: The Bank is supporting implementation of key international conventions such as the OECD Anti-Bribery Convention, the UN Convention Against Corruption, and regional initiatives.
• Transnational Corruption: The Bank is proposing to work with developed countries, the OECD, and the private sector to provide assistance on anti-money laundering, and greater cooperation to address tax havens and asset restitution. An important initiative, the Stolen Assets Recovery Initiative (StAR), is under way to helping countries enhance ability to track, freeze, and recover the proceeds of corrupt behavior. Ongoing activities of the StAR Initiative include (see Box 4):

– Persuading all jurisdictions to ratify & implement the UNCAC;
– Helping developing countries build capacity for requesting mutual legal assistance for asset recovery;
– Advocating with financial centers to lower barriers to recovery;
– Developing partnerships to share information & experience; and
– On a voluntary basis, offering expertise to monitor the use of recovered assets for development (e.g., Nigeria).

Box 4. Stolen Asset Recovery (StAR) Initiative

The World Bank Group, in partnership with the United Nations Office on Drugs and Crime (UNODC), launched the Stolen Asset Recovery Initiative (StAR) on September 17, 2007 in New York City with UN Secretary General Ban Ki-Moon, UNOCD Executive Director Antonio Maria Costa and Bank Group President Robert B. Zoellick. The primary purpose of StAR is to help developing countries track, freeze, and recover the proceeds of corruption as well as preventing it from being stolen again. StAR focuses on practical activities including building capacity to request mutual legal assistance necessary for asset recovery, advocating with financial centers to lower barriers that retard recovery, developing partnerships to share information and experience, and on a voluntary basis, offering expertise to make transparent the use of recovered assets for development. The foundation for this work is the United Nations Convention Against Corruption (UNCAC) and for that reason StAR focuses on persuading nations to ratify and implement this important treaty. Following the launch, StAR established a joint Secretariat located at the World Bank headquarters in Washington, D.C., which is responsible for the implementation of the StAR work program.

Measuring Results

Monitoring progress and tracking results is key to assessing the success of the Bank's interventions, and adjusting programs, based on success and lessons. There are two broad categories of governance indicators:

– Broad and Aggregated: Broad measures to measure governance at more aggregated levels. Help reveal systematic patterns – and basis for monitoring trends over time; and

– Specific and Disaggregated: Specific measures of quality of key governance subsystems, including using "actionable indicators" to benchmark and track reforms.

The Development Committee and the Bank Group's Board of Executive Directors have asked for the development and greater application of disaggregated and 'actionable' indicators, to both inform the CPIA[4] and to help track progress in specific reforms implemented by governments.

---

4. The Country Policy and Institutional Assessment (CPIA) is a World Bank tool to rate countries against a set of 16 criteria grouped in four clusters: a) economic management; b) structural policies; c) policies for social inclusion and equity; and d) public sector management and institutions. For the 2006 Questionnaire, see: http://siteresources.worldbank.org/IDA/Resources/CPIA2006Questionnaire.pdf.

Table 1. A Typology of Governance Indicators

	Measuring Quality of Processes/Rules	Measuring Outcomes
Specific Measures	• PEFA indicators* • CPIA sub-indicators* • Global Integrity Index (GII) sub-indicators* • Open Budget Index (OBI) sub-indicators* • OECD Procurement Index* • Doing Business	• Investment Climate Assessments** • Business Environment & Enterprise Surveys (BEEPS)** • Worldwide Governance Indicators (WGI) - selected sub-indicators)***
Broad Measures	• Overall CPIA* • Overall GII* • Overall OBI* • Overall DB Index*	• Transparency International*** • WGI*** • Freedom House* • Polity IV (executive constraints)*

Sources: *Expert assessments **Surveys ***Combination

There has been significant progress in the development and use of disaggregated and actionable indicators, such as the public financial management indicators developed by the multi-donor Public Expenditure and Financial Accountability (PEFA) initiative.[5]

During the recent consultations on the Bank's governance and anticorruption strategy, the majority of stakeholders endorsed an approach of using a mix of indicators – aggregate governance indicators, country monitoring and evaluation systems, specific disaggregated indicators, and outcome indicators – judiciously and with care, keeping in mind their strengths and limitations for particular purposes.

Conclusion

While the World Bank is moving rapidly forward in implementation of its governance and anticorruption strategy, challenges of effective implementation will undoubtedly arise. These include: making sure that the Bank's country and sector teams integrate governance dimensions

---

5. For additional information on the multi-donor Public Expenditure and Financial Accountability program, see: http://www.pefa.org (in English and French).

more systematically into their work; finding creative ways of working in difficult settings, where governance is a major constraint, but the government is not committed to reform; catalyzing change from both initiatives at the top and the frontlines; and ensuring that the Bank has access to the appropriate skills base and talent to effectively deliver the strategy. As the Bank moves to undertake necessary internal changes to tackle these issues more effectively, the main, sustainable solution will clearly come from reformers within developing countries themselves. They hold the key to success – external agents can only play a facilitating and supporting role.

Bibliography

Collier, Paul. 2007. The bottom billion: why the poorest countries are failing and what can be done about it? Oxford and New York: Oxford University Press.

Campos, Edgardo and Sanjay Pradhan, eds. 2007. The Many Faces of Corruption: Tracking the Vulnerabilities at the Sector Level. Washington, DC: World Bank.

Grindle, Merilee. 2007. Good enough governance Revisited. Development Policy Review 25 (5), 553-574.

Levy, Brian and Francis Fukuyama. 2008. Development strategies: integrating governance and growth. World Bank Discussion Paper. Washington, DC: World Bank.

Miesel, Nicolas and Jacques Auld-Oudia. 2008. Is 'good governance' a good development strategy? Working Paper 58. Paris, France: French Development Agency.

North, Douglass, John Wallis, Steve Webb and Barry Weingast. 2007. Limited access order in the developing world: a new approach to the problems of development. Policy Research Working Paper 4359. Washington, DC: World Bank.

World Bank.1997. Helping countries combat corruption: the role of the World Bank. Washington, DC: World Bank.

World Bank.1997. The state in a changing world. World Development Report. New York: Oxford University Press.

World Bank. 2000. Reforming public institutions and strengthening governance: a World Bank strategy. Washington, DC: World Bank.

World Bank. 2007. Strengthening World Bank Group engagement on governance and anticorruption. Washington, DC: World Bank.

27

The State in Development Policies[*]

The Challenge of the Democratic Governance Approach

Séverine BELLINA and Hervé MAGRO
(Translated from the French)

> "Politics is a creative activity [...] it is responsible for
> the reorganisation of relations between the groups that
> make up society and a redefinition of our vision of the world".
> Goran Hyden[1].

There are many questions about the real, long-term outcomes of development policies. The debate is regularly rekindled by leaders in donor countries, public opinion in the North and more and more also in the South, and among development practitioners.

Although the extent to which perceptions reflect reality is debatable, it remains the case that overall the results of development policies are unsatisfactory. Since the late-1990s governance has been at the centre of the debate on these policies effectiveness. From the Millennium Declaration to the New Partnership for Africa's Development, effective fight against poverty is linked to respect for the fundamental principles of governance. Encouraged by the World Bank, followed by other development partners, the effectiveness of aid is closely correlated to "good governance". Specific programmes are then developed, supposedly to create the necessary conditions for the optimal use of aid in the countries concerned.

---

1. Hyden, G. and M. Bratton (eds.) (1992). "Gouvernance et étude de la politique", in Gouverner l'Afrique, vers un partage des rôles, translated from English by B. Delorme, Paris, Nouveaux Horizons, p. 6.

There is no denying that this approach has not provided all the results expected by its promoters. This has led them to look for new directions and to modify their own definition of governance from a primarily managerial to a more political conception. This orientation was confirmed at the G8 meeting of June 2002 in Kananaskis, where the political dimension of governance was established. One of the most striking aspects of this evolution has been the new attention paid to the role of the state by the very people who, just a few years ago, were denying its relevance on the grounds that the state was at best useless and more often predatory.

Dominique Darbon's article explains the evolution of the debate on the role of the state. This was almost certainly accelerated by the attacks of 11 September 2001 and the international community's realisation that the state should no longer be ignored as an actor. Ultimately states do exist for a reason, even though this may be perceived as primarily a matter of security (contributing to international security), economics (favouring market mechanisms) and/or utility (satisfying the immediate needs of the population). Consideration of the state has direct implications for the type and aims of development policies implemented around governance and well illustrates the challenges posed to the "development world".

In this respect the example of the state in Africa is revealing[2].

Governance oscillates between an instrumental, technicist approach and one that is more political. The former works by transfer and external pressure. Its aim is effective institutional development for growth. The latter is more dynamic. It looks at what underlies the institutionalisation of state power and legitimacy, in other words processes that are eminently political, socio-cultural and historical. Its aim is well-rooted, sustainable human development.

Revisiting the state in Africa

A form of Western ethnocentrism has long confined studies on Africa to monist interpretations that look at African societies through the lens of a truncated comparativism, taking the modern, Western state as reference. The primary objective seems to be to incorporate African societies into the Western model, notably in terms of law and the economy. Challenges

---

2. "The state in Africa" is an expression used generically in the present paper. The authors are aware that a descriptive analysis would oblige them to adopt the precautionary terms "states" in "the Africas".

to this evolutionist approach began in the 1980s. The real functioning of African states, the context of globalisation and developments in the social sciences (particularly anthropology) imposed changes, leading the disciplinary fields to open up and become more international.

The state in Africa as a subject of research

The structuring of societies and institutions has meaning only in relation to the imaginary universe in which they exist, which carries their vision of the world. Official truth represents only a part of reality. Above and beyond its regulatory role, power reveals discords between social practices and official structures[3]. Power is grasped in its realities and specificities through the reintegration of its historical and political dimensions.

Difference can no longer be assimilated to backwardness in relation to the Western model. On the contrary, it supposes a reading of the otherness of each society. This has encouraged the development of innovative concepts and interdisciplinary approaches that have enabled the state in Africa to acquire the status of a subject of research. In the late-1960s legal anthropologists set about dethroning positivism with legal anthropology, highlighting the existence of legal frameworks other than those of the state. This revealed the limitations of the unifying mechanisms of state law (enculturation, deculturation and codification) and of its privileged role in instilling social change. In the late 1980s Africanist politologists started looking at the anthropological origins of social change, opening new directions for research, including politics from below[4], the enunciation of the political[5] and the invention of the political[6].

---

3. Rivière, C. (2007). Introduction à l'anthropologie, Paris, Hachette, p. 40.

4. Formulated on the basis of Bayart, J.-F. (1979). L'État au Cameroun, Paris, Presses de la FNSP, and several authors (1981). "La politique en Afrique noire : le haut et la bas", Paris, Karthala.

5. Sociological viewpoint introduced in the 1980s making it possible to go beyond dichotomic arguments contrasting the state with civil society. Bayart, J.-F. (1985). "L'énonciation du politique", Revue française de science politique, vol. 35, no 3, p. 947-949.

6. This aims to understand both the common substance of the political in African societies and its specific historical consistency. Bayart, J.-F. (1989). "Avant-propos sur l'invention politique", Revue française de science politique, no 6, p. 789.

The state in Africa as an object of development policies

Despite these theoretical developments, a paradox continues to inform development policies: there is a real mismatch between the diversity of analyses available and those underlying development policies. This is because the international context (colonisation, postcolonisation, gobalisation) establishes development at the core of international relations and market mechanisms, in other words of influence. The analyses and practices underlying development policies then target these objectives and remain fundamentally rooted in approaches that generate models, with economics as the primary matrix and dominant discipline[7].

Thus the international community keeps on trying to find a paradigm (developmental state, failed state, fragile state, and so on) that will offer a better model of an effective state with its corresponding toolkit (good governance, externalisation, and so on). There are as many descriptions and formulas as there are supposed representations of the state, all compared to the theoretical model of a modern state. In this perspective the African state exists only in negative form, as the lack of what it is not and compared to what it should be. Every day the disjuncture between the state and its populations increases. There is less and less interaction between legality and legitimacy. So the issue becomes one of the (re) construction, even "internationalisation"[8], of the state. Being part of a dogmatic and positivist frame of reference, this quest for a model, and the formulas following from it, rarely allow for a paradigm shift around interdisciplinarity that would bring to light the real expressions of power and enable new kinds of development policies to emerge.

A different "diagnosis" of the state in Africa

Conclusions differ depending on whether the state in Africa is examined through the prism of classical institutional analysis or through that of dynamic institutional analysis. Between the two, a paradigm shift takes place: we move from the search for the ideal model to an understanding of social change which the state both expresses and helps to produce.

---

7. Delpeuch, T. (2006). "La coopération internationale au prisme du courant de recherche 'droit et développement'", Revue Droit et société, no 62, p. 139
8. Vircoulon, T. (2007). "L'État internationalisé: nouvelle figure de la mondialisation en Afrique", Études, no 4061, p. 9-20.

Classical institutional analysis, based on European positivist legal traditions[9], and the "formal legalism[10]" of the American political scientists, regards the institution, a power structure, as a reproducible[11] model[12]. The state as a political institution is then confused with the idea of a stable framework for political life, thought to be embodied in the form of the modern Western state. So the elements of comparison are contained in the reference to an ideal model. Any nuance is then interpreted as a dysfunction in relation to the "typical ideal", to be remedied by means of techniques intended to transfer constitutive elements of the ideal model, leading to normative mimetism and institutional transfer.

The inclusion of the satisfaction of social needs as a criterion for evaluating the effectiveness of the state and the necessary consideration of the actor's point of view open up a new direction of institutional analysis[13]. Furthermore, in the political model culture is integrated as a variable and regarded as a primary factor. Moreover a systemic conception of politics is developed, in which the political system is assumed to form a strategic framework for action by the actors.

It is when the analyses (new-institutionalism in political science and the dynamic conception of the institution in law) turn their attention to the structuring of actor choice in the context generated by the institution, and thus of the choice of a viable institutional option, that a paradigm shift appears. The institution is then seen as an actor and not just as a context for action. The institution influences the forms and content of the actors' action in terms of both choices and duties. It guides the definition and articulation of interests underlying the actions of political actors. So it influences the definition of legitimacy. What must then be understood are the interactions between the actors and the institutions, between the state and the society in terms of institutionalisation. In this perspective the focus is on institutional change, on processes rather than simply the formal framework of the institution itself.

---

9. In France the institution was abandoned by sociology in the 1970s in favour of concepts of organisation, system and structure, and by politologists until the 1980s, being considered almost exclusively in the context of the legal sciences and analysed in dogmatic, positivist terms. J. Chevallier, Institution politique, Paris, LGDJ, 1996, p. 14-15.

10. Until the late 1950s. See Stone, A. (1992). "Le néo-institutionnalisme", Politix, no 20, p. 157.

11. All other approaches are ignored. Thus a large part of M. Hauriou's book on (pluralist) institutions is ignored in favour of "generic" institutions. See Mazères, J.-A. (1998). "La théorie de l'institution de Maurice Hauriou ou l'oscillation entre l'instituant et l'institué", in Pouvoir et liberté Brussels, Bruylant, p. 257.

12. Mazères, J.-A., op. cit., p. 269.

13. French approaches never entirely abandon the institutional point of view.

The institution is understood as a permanent dialectical process between the instituter (instituant) and the instituted. And if the institution loses its dynamics, if the instituted becomes disconnected from the instituter, it falls into formalism: legitimacy, supposedly driven by the commitment of the actors to the collective enterprise that reveals social meaning, crystallises into legality. The state is understood not as a particular entity but as a relation to society. It is defined dynamically as an outcome of the balances realised within the society. To grasp the nature of the state it is thus necessary to understand it "where it has its source and roots, in other words in the nation itself and in all the multiple components that make it up[14]".

This approach simultaneously considers the three levels of social reality: the individual, the group and society. Institutions are not reduced to their official functions alone, but incorporate the symbolic and imaginary dimensions that shape both the language and actions of the actors. Analysing the state through the prism of institutionalisation thus leads to an understanding of it as necessarily resulting from a permanent, positive interaction between actors and political structures.

The state in Africa: the whole instituted

From this perspective it appears that the institutionalisation of power established in Africa by transfer of the state model is, in most cases, essentially inverted: the power structure of the state has been (im)posed as a model or "typical ideal" towards which African societies, reputed to be instituters, have to move. In reality not only does the imported state not translate the social dynamic it is intended to regulate but it is also expected to generate this social dynamic by transforming the sociocultural logics of the societies involved. So it is hardly surprising that there is a disjuncture between this type of state and African societies; indeed it is fairly logical.

In this context in Africa the state is often primarily a matter of form, an expression of legality, it is completely "frozen" in the instituted. The state institution has neither its origins nor its dynamism in the society it organises. Similarly the institutionalisation of its power is restricted to formalism and materialised in a constitutional and institutional mimetism. Political problems are reduced to technical problems. Sociological grounding has often been replaced by constraint (colonial and post-colonial states with authoritarian one-party states) and international injunctions (the most extreme example being the structural adjustment plan).

To overcome this disconnection, the countries involved and their development partners try to (re)construct the institution by giving it content

---

14. J.-A. Mazères, op. cit., p. 257-258.

on the basis of the fixed variable of the state. But, as Dominique Darbon and Adebayo Olukoshi show, while institutional reorganisation, in other words a technical change, can be established by decree, it is not possible to decree its socialisation, still less its institutionalisation.

Refounding the state: breathing new life into the institutionalisation of power

As soon as it is established, the state in Africa poses the problem of its own legitimacy. The analytical force of the concept of governance[15] lies in its ability to look at power through the issue of its legitimacy. Governance studies the origins of political authority and understands power as the process of interaction between actors and structures. At the institutional, normative level governance represents the evolution of legitimacy, which cannot be approached from a purely legal point of view but must also be regarded from a pragmatic, sociocultural perspective.

Re-establishing the link between power and legitimacy

By breaking the link between belief and authority, in other words eliminating the local symbolic dimension of power, "modern" power has blocked its own legitimacy and effectiveness. Institutional development policies based on model transfer and normative mimetism have contributed to this phenomenon. Over a very long period "modern" power could have recreated a form of legitimacy, but by strongly questioning the state during the 1980s-1990s, the donors themselves, particularly in the English speaking world, increased this legitimacy deficit. Things were further complicated by decentralisation policies. Today several levels of power co-exist, all of them de facto pertinent to a degree, but none ever filling the gap.

In addition traditional and religious forms of legitimacy, those that are experienced and most firmly etched in the popular unconscious, have little direct, official power to take decisions in the major strategic orientations of the state. The legitimacy of state power remains fundamentally exogenous in nature and affects only a minority of the population. In this context

---

15. Since 1989 when it began to spread through international relations, governance has primarily been used for normative ends, notably with "good governance" as institutional matrix of the modern state.

Western legitimacy is appropriated essentially as a tool: it is used but not incorporated[16].

Thus the state is unstable because it is no longer in line with the relays of legitimate power. Legitimate power[17] is that which integrates real political authority, in other words the one felt by social actors as an asymmetrical reciprocal relationship.

Legitimate political space

Governance makes it possible to go beyond the dichotomy of state and civil society and to define the public and private spheres. The public sphere corresponds to the space of potential co-operation between the state and society. It represents the framework for the expression of legal and administrative pluralism which "constitutes the organising principle from the system of norms and mechanisms of regulation to the period of governance[18]". The "civic public sphere" is an open, legitimate political space. It is understood as the context of legal pluralism and social relations, hence of the expression of the creative freedom of actors whose desire to act is orientated towards the realisation of a collective interest.

This requires the existence of spaces of reconciliation between the political (power) and social (the civic public spheres), whose paths have diverged strongly since colonialisation and, consequently, of spaces for the re-emergence of the dialectics of "instituter" and "institued" that is the driving force of institutionalisation.

Individuals and power

The state in Africa produces a management that only rarely touches the everyday depths of the social. The sidelined populations function in terms of "a social regulation of survival[19]" through pragmatic, inter-individual management which, while it may enable the satisfaction of immediate material needs, does not reinforce or build a collective objective that can

---

16. According to M. Hauriou the instituting phenomenon assumes the internalisation and incorporation of the idea, thereby enabling subjects to support the institution voluntarily.

17. Hyden, G. and M. Bratton. op. cit., p. 1-37.

18. Gleizal, J.-J. (2000). Coopération décentralisée, action culturelle et francophonie, Agence internationale de la francophonie, p. 8.

19. Bellina, S. (2001). Droit public et institutionnalisation en situation de pluralisme normatif le cas de l'État malien, doctoral thesis: administration publique, Grenoble II, p. 364-369.

represent social meaning. While reflecting the courage and extraordinary will of populations, the "social survival regulation" contributes only slightly to the durability of social practices and the objectification of social phenomena into rules, which M. Hauriou calls the passage from the "rule of fact" to the "rule of law", and to the reinforcement of the civic public space.

The reconciliation of the individual with power[20] requires the population to reinvest the political, individually and/or collectively. This leads to the emergence of political actors, in other words individuals who are capable of differentiating between "what I am through my membership of a culture, of a community, and what I am through my political action[21]", a fundamental factor in the institutionalisation of the state.

Here and elsewhere, in both North and South, the issues linked to the institutionalisation of a state that is sociologically effective because it is legitimate, are eminently political, directly questioning the way that communities want to live together.

> "Understanding the public space of a living together as a democratic requirement involves the self-constitution of politics in an independent space open to the Other and to free public discussion [...][22]."

As Etienne Le Roy states, one of the great problems that societies face, the complexity of which has been studied, is how to combine institutional responses arising out of different social arrangements[23].

Rethinking development policies in order to transform them

For donors this perspective raises very complicated problems. Donors are used to working within well-defined institutional, financial, technical and time frameworks. For a long time there have been well identified governance programmes, institutional co-operation that has developed habits, reflexes and even dependencies (in both directions) that are hard to

---

20. Redor, M.-J. (1992). De l'État légal à l'État de droit. L'évolution de la doctrine publiciste française 1789-1914, Paris-Aix-en-Provence, Economica-Presses universitaires d'Aix-Marseille, p. 313.
21. Tassin, E. (1999). Le trésor perdu. Hannah Arendt l'intelligence de l'action politique, Paris, Payot & Rivages, p. 444
22. M. Tshiyembe, "Des guerres à la crise sociale. L'Afrique face au défi de l'État multinational", Le Monde diplomatique, September 2000, p. 14-15.
23. Le Roy, E. (1999). Le jeu des lois. Une anthropologie "dynamique" du Droit, Paris, LGDJ/Montchrestien, p. 157.

challenge. While no one today denies the need to develop new approaches to work on what has hitherto been missing, notably state legitimacy, which alone can reinforce the legitimacy, and hence the effectiveness and efficiency, of processes for developing public policies, the formulas are not easy to apply.

On the logic of project and process

Current tools of development co-operation are not appropriate to supporting processes. Support for processes requires the definition of more complex tools that are hard to implement because their logic conflicts in many respects with that underlying current tools. It is easier to develop a project with measurable objectives (number of magistrates or police officers to be trained, wells or roads be built and so on). In these cases the tools and skills exist and the context is known, as is the time-frame (usually 3–5 years, followed by an evaluation). The whole has an air of coherence and offers the illusion of providing answers to questions from political decision-makers, in both North and South, who are looking for immediate results because they deal in short term actions, punctuated by elections.

It is more complex to adopt a perspective of processes support and, moreover, to define the dynamics that should be implemented to support them. In practice moving away from the exclusive dialectics of projects and their toolkits to move towards the dynamics of support for processes implies thinking in depth about the actors and how to help them. This in turn supposes sitting round a table to build a shared project in a context often characterised by great mistrust (or worse) and a lack of financial and above all human resources. A project scheduled for three or four years, with essentially quantitative realisation indicators does not permit the assement of changes, which sometimes require several generations to become concrete or which perhaps may not even be realised, since no one can guarantee that a process will ultimately have the expected outcomes. This is one of the major cultural (r)evolutions that development partners must take on board: some positive or negative outcomes are neither quantifiable nor predictable.

While the two terms are increasingly used indiscriminately, "good governance" and "democratic governance" are fundamentally different in method. The former is primarily based on external pressure for change through model transfer, while the latter works to help identify factors for change within societies in order to support their emergence and expression in a collective project. Furthermore the former is more attached to economic development goals, although both aim to support the emergence of more democratic societies founded on universally recognised values and contributing to the overall sustainable and global human development. There is a big difference depending on whether the ultimate goal is regarded as economic development or sustainable human development (of which economic development is a fundamental pillar).

The institutional dimension of development assistance remains crucial: it remains vital to support the strengthening of Justice Ministries and the police and to develop human rights. Similarly it is vital to improve public finance systems. The challenge lies in not implementing these programmes from a normative perspective of transfer. The appropriate approach is more global, taking account of the political aspects of institutional reform and looking to the long term, with a parallel effort to develop processes and spaces for dialogue so that these actions become part of a real development dynamic driven by local actors. The "democratic governance" approach thus goes beyond that of "good governance" by including a qualitative dimension, rather than remaining simply quantitative. The application of turnkey technical solutions, however appropriate to local ownership, cannot facilitate responses to political dynamics. Promoting governance means agreeing to work on "a social process of societies transformation in the long term, following different paths in different countries[24]". For donors this means a change of profession. From being prescriptive technical experts they must become political actors and partners.

In this respect it might be suggested that part of the increased development aid planned for coming years (if the donors fulfil their commitments) should be used to support processes that enable the state to reconnect with dynamics. Indeed many experts are saying that often the major problem of development assistance is not the lack of resources (aside from certain countries described as aid orphans) so much as how they are used. And it is only by changing the understanding of governance that this can be achieved.

So the real problem is not whether to work with the state or to bypass it by working at the decentralised level (when it exists) or with civil society, which each development partner moreover defines in their own way. It is the development of "process projects" encompassing all these dimensions and actors. These can be developed only by those directly concerned, with the support of the international community.

---

24. See, in the present work, Bossuyt, J., "Governance at the crossroads".

On ownership...

This need to draw on local dynamics is not new. It is supposed to be reflected in the notion of ownership, which is part of the development assistance vocabulary (along with partnership, donor alignment, predictability and coherence of aid and so on). All donors, in their language at least, have adopted it along with the requirement to make recepient countries "responsible". The Paris Declaration on Aid Effectiveness is one of the most complete examples of this awareness that the country concerned should be given control of the exercise. In the same order of ideas, the strategic frameworks for the fight against poverty and other strategy papers for poverty reduction were created, on the initiative of the World Bank, to serve as frameworks for the concrete implementation of this ownership. The problem is that both the Paris Declaration and the strategic frameworks are products of the Northern countries. Ownership then risks having a restrictive meaning of adaptation to an external framework. The "artificial" legitimacy brought by participation in drawing up such documents soon gives way to instrumentalisation. We are a long way from negotiated processes for developing public policies, a factor in the latter's legitimacy and effectiveness.

As a result, while there is no denying that the stated intentions are good, the reality is quite different: the donors' frames of reference remain primarily their own and they find it hard to understand why their formulas, often backed up by major finance, have so little result. Though they may say the opposite, donors each have their own vision of the world, their own history and culture, which they necessarily incorporate into their approach to development. These cognitive and socio-cultural references need to be factors in dialogue rather than conflict, enriching the shared frame of reference rather than remaining implicit elements of imposed models.

Here we should make it clear that we are not pleading for inaction in the name of respect for local particularities. Certainly, as Ibrahim Salama and Ousmane Sy show in their articles, the application of principles common to humanity should take account of the socio-cultural context of each society. Cultural diversity is a fundamental issue, but there is no denying that it has its limits when it becomes synonymous with culturalism, and it cannot justify the abandonment of universal values (understood as the common values, not yet "frozen" to be developed), which are our common frame of reference.

Conditionality or contracts?

The limitations of the purely managerial approach to "good governance" are no longer in dispute. All donors recognise that it lacks a crucial ingredient which is political in nature and relates to the willingness of the states concerned to respond in real terms to their citizens' aspirations in the general interest. The (central and decentralised) state must be the real regulator of social dynamics in order to uphold the general interest, support development and actively promote respect for common universal norms.

But instead of challenging the conceptualisation and functioning of development assistance, this observation often leads to impatience with the paucity of results obtained by co-operation, despite "good governance" programmes, and to doubts about the political will of the states involved, their corruption being presented as the main cause of failure and consequently as the main problem to be dealt with. This puts the issue of conditions for publicly funded aid back on the agenda, with the accompanying threat of reduced amounts of aid for the country concerned.

This approach emphases as a panacea institutional reform of the state, under external pressure, to impose change. The state's legitimacy is still judged in the light of the donors' criteria and not those of the populations. In this purely external logic of accountability, the gap between the state and its population is accentuated still further. Change has to be initiated externally since internal forces cannot be counted on to do it or because that would take too long. In recent months some statements from development administrators in France have suggested that this is now the favored approach in Paris, which would represent a striking shift from previous positions, which were rather more reticent where conditionality and sanctions were concerned.

The external imposition of change can even involve the takeover of the states concerned (as in Sierra Leone, Iraq, even Afghanistan). In 2006, in the context of the OECD, the United States proposed a variant in which the recipient state would itself place entire areas of its administration under the supervision of international experts (private sector included) for a given amount of time in exchange for financial and technical support from the international community[25].

Of course approaches of this kind raise a number of questions. They require fair treatment of all the countries concerned, and hence an evaluation based on recognised, credible criteria. They also require

---

25. This initiative has now been taken up by the OECD as the Partnership for Democratic Governance.

international consensus, since in our globalised world it is hard to see how effective measures could be applied if the donors did not all agree and some refused to play the game. Of course conditionality provides donors with a clearer framework, since it is based on a mechanism that is apparently coherent and comprehensible to all. On the other hand, and perhaps contrary to what its promoters think, it does not remove the need for a long term engagement on the ground. As we have seen on many occasions, a too-rapid withdrawal may have fatal consequences. So time remains an unavoidable element, welcome or not.

The democratic governance approach does not offer the same apparently immediate answer to the problems facing the decision-makers. It seeks to integrate the paradigm shift described in the first part of this paper. It requires time, will and consistent action and, above all, it requires partners to be regarded as full actors of their own destiny. In this regard reform of the state that is not part of the evolution of the society itself would seem to have little chance of success. But this does not mean that the states concerned should not be accountable to the international community for their actions. It is legitimate for donors to make certain demands regarding the usage of the money they give in development aid.

In this context it is surely possible to explore the idea of a contract as an appropriate legal basis for trust, shared responsibility and a fair relationship between donors and recipients. In this contract the receiving country would give a commitment, to both the donors and, more importantly, its own population, to take a certain number of measures. There would be a clause setting a date for a meeting at which developments and delays would be presented. In exchange the international community would undertake to provide financial and technical support for the country's efforts over time. The action plan would be developed in processes of real dialogue between all the parties concerned, and the indicators would be jointly drawn up, involving as much of the population as possible. The European Union, the foremost donor of development aid, could launch an approach of this kind in the context of its governance strategy adopted in 2006.

Conclusion

The state refoundation problematic illuminates the state in Africa from a new operational angle. Where ideas on democratic governance are concerned, it reintroduces a dimension that was sorely lacking hitherto and does much to explain why co-operation policies have been inappropriate to realities on the ground.

In the South it represents a unique opportunity for African societies to take back "the initiative of which they have been deprived by the 'modern' period [...]. By being immediately located in transmodernity, these societies would avoid the difficulties associated with the end of modernity, which the societies of the North will inevitably experience. This gives them a comparative advantage[26]".

For the donors it involves a major challenge and a culture shift: they must adopt a partnership approach based on knowledge and recognition of the Other. From this perspective, governance means getting to know others and sharing their experiences because the challenges they face are identical to their.

The violent manifestations of fragility and crisis in states should not lead us to forget that fundamentally, here as elsewhere,

> "what is in crisis today is the Idea of common or public good. Reconstructing this as a notion assumes that there is what Aristotle called friendship, in other words free and peaceful communication between people. [...] It is in this space of intersubjectivity that the democratic tradition can take root and erect the poles of civility and solidarity[27]."

The goal of human fulfilment pushes old habits aside. It requires bold political courage, in both donor and recipient countries, since development policies must be built on governance not in order to transfer and (re)construct the model elsewhere, but to "give back its creative autonomy to each human group[28]".

26. Le Roy, E. op. cit., p. 379.

27. Diaw, A. (1998). "Repenser la société civile", Globalisation et sciences sociales en Afrique, Dakar, CODESRIA, p. 12.

28. Person, Y. (1983). Samori la renaissance de l'Empire mandingue, Dakar, NEA, p. 18.

28

Governance in Turmoil

The Political Economy of an Endogenous Process

Nicolas MEISEL and Jacques OULD AOUDIA
(Translated from the French)

Today, we are experiencing the end of absolute global domination by a handful of European countries and their North American descendants. For the first time in 400 years, these countries are seeing the world escape their hegemony with the emergence of new and powerful actors and the already palpable effects of this emergence on the other developing countries. This is the end of the post-colonial era that contrasted a developed core with a developing periphery. This movement is massive in terms of its repercussions on the new ways of functioning in the world. And its full scale has yet to be seen.

How do the Northern countries perceive the emergence of these new actors? The analytical tools developed and promoted by the developed countries and the multilateral and bilateral agencies have so far accounted for neither the economic rise of certain developing countries in Asia nor the barriers to growth that hinder the vast majority of the other developing countries. The East Asian economies that have taken off in the last 50 years have developed and applied strategies that differ from the standard analytic framework of liberalisation and "good governance". In the meantime, the countries that have conformed the most to this framework – especially in Latin America, Africa and the Arab world – have remained trapped in low, halting growth rates. This has put the effects of 50 years of prescriptions and projected aid out to the "developing countries" largely into question.

Yet is the most important factor in the rise of the Asian countries the content of the policies implemented or the fact that these policies have been developed, discussed and weighed up within the societies themselves? Four centuries of Western hegemony have probably made this kind of question a blind spot in the Western understanding of the world. This is borne out by the current "blind rush" to prescribe economic liberalisation and then "good governance", it is now the turn of democracy to be projected onto the rest of the world.

Firstly, it should be noted that, in today's world of globalised information the Southern countries now view these prescriptions in terms of the difference between words and deeds. Gone are the days when a Batavian merchant, an active supporter of one of the world's most open and democratic societies in Amsterdam, could coolly order the enslavement of peoples in Indonesia and the deportation of Chinese workers in atrocious conditions. Today, the sermonising on economic liberalisation, "good governance" and democracy is too often blatantly contradicted by the commercial, financial and political practices of the Northern and Southern elites to be totally credible.

Secondly, this battery of prescriptions from the West disregards the experiences of the countries that have wrenched themselves free from underdevelopment. These experiences could be briefly summed up as a combination of strategic vision drawing on a collective imagination, economic diversification into new income-generating activities with growing returns, and a political organisation guaranteeing the convergence of the elite and society's interests around the attainment of a "common good". The societies in question, of which Singapore is possibly the most consummate model, have therefore been able to advance at their own speed towards a rule of law (efficient and uncorrupt administration and justice system, protected property rights, etc.) without this progress necessarily including democracy.

In the relationship between politics and economy in the development process, what really matters is the legitimacy of the leaders rather than compliance with the formal rules of democracy, and particularly the holding of elections, which is increasingly used as an indicator of democratic functioning. Although developed countries regard the legitimacy of leaders as broadly equivalent to compliance with the electoral rules, it is not based on the same mechanisms in hierarchical societies where defence of the nation, achievement of national ambitions and shared economic successes can unite the people around their leaders.

The democratic governance discussed in this book is based on the recognition of the necessarily endogenous nature of development processes, which itself stems from the eminently political nature of human government. Yet there are ambiguities in this attitude, which bears the marks of the prescriptive approaches of the past. The command to be free, to take charge of yourself and make your own decisions is nevertheless still an order.

This paper looks at how the question of institutions has been introduced into the field of development policies and economics, to provide a more detailed analysis of economic development in its close relationship with forms of political organisation. It finds that the institutional transition, which includes governance, only prompts economic and political development if it is based on a process endogenous to the societies. This process does not rule out borrowings from the outside, but borrowings that are recontextualised and reappropriated by the societies: although the institutions cannot be exported, they can be imported. So where does all this leave development assistance?

Development economics rediscovers institutions

The first factor in the renewed interest in institutions is the repeated failure of growth models to satisfactorily account for economic development successes and failures worldwide. Growth accounting may well identify the contributions of the traditional factors (physical, financial, human and labour capital), but it is unable to clearly explain a "residual" that often accounts for over half of the growth in gross domestic product (GDP). Although economists have given this residual the clever name of "total factor productivity", supposedly reflecting the performance of the combined factors, the residual itself remains poorly explained and, more importantly, points up the shortcomings of a purely economic appreciation of growth.

The second factor is a positive one. It concerns the progress made in the field of economic analysis by the advocates of endogenous growth, information economics, institutional economics, and the sociology of collective action.

The growth models that dominated through to the end of the 1980s (based on R. Solow's work) posited that long-run growth was a function of demographics and technical progress. These two factors were assumed to be exogenous, i.e. independent of the will of the economic players. Such a view made government intervention superfluous, liable merely to hold back the economy's "natural" rate of growth. In the late 1980s, the endogenous growth theorists posited that technical progress was the result of deliberate investment by players. In so doing, they reopened the way for public intervention in research and development (P. Romer), education (R. Lucas) and infrastructures (R. Barro) so as to boost this progress and the synergies between investments.

At the same time, information economics (G. Akerlof and J. Stiglitz) revealed the limits of the assumptions of neoclassical theory: markets are rarely "perfect", but present strong power and information asymmetries. These imperfections and their repercussions justify government intervention.

In accordance with a long-standing institutionalist tradition in the United States (T. Veblen and J. Commons) and transaction cost economics studies (R. Coase and O. Williamson) combining historical methods with economic approaches, "new institutional economics" (R. Fogel, D. North, A. Greif and M. Aoki) has adopted a view almost totally opposed to the other growth theories since the 1970s. It suggested that innovation, technical progress and investment should be seen more as manifestations of development than as its causes. Various studies by this school revealed the central role of "institutions" upstream of technical progress.

Lastly, there are the contributions made by the microeconomics and microsociology of collective action, underpinned by advances in game theory. These advances have revealed and considered the problems inherent in all collective actions, especially resistance to change and the phenomenon of free-riding. Strategic games between interest groups and inequalities in the distribution of power and resources can help or hinder institutional change, even if such change is wanted by all (M. Olson, P. Bardhan and A. Dixit).

What do we mean by institutions? The definition is far from fixed. However, Douglas North's definition carries the most weight in economics. He describes them as the rules of the economic, social and political game, which may be formal (written, explicit) or informal (tacit, implicit). These rules define the incentive structure that guides human behaviour, in a way that is more or less conducive to individual and collective efficiency.

The link between institutions and growth is forged by the fact that their stability reduces uncertainty in social interactions in general and in transactions in particular. This reduction in uncertainty may take a static form, with the reduction in transaction costs (the costs of information, contract specification and enforcement), or a dynamic form, with the stabilisation of expectations. For example, the role of the French Planning Office in the 1950s and 1960s was to set optimistic (but credible) growth standards that, being immediately incorporated into actors' expectations, raised consumption and investment decisions in a self-fulfilling loop.

In the 1990s, and especially with D. North's Nobel Prize in 1993, reference to institutions became more and more important amongst competing explanations of growth (by investment, culture, geography, etc.).

Institutions burst onto the scene of development policy

Alongside this shift in ideas came a change in practice and development policies, reflected in increasingly explicit incursions by bilateral, and particularly multilateral aid organisations into the field of institutions.

Policies from the 1950s to the 1970s were dominated by an insistence on capital investment (infrastructures) and the creation and protection of national capitalists in the nations concerned, who were supposed to trigger a process of strong growth in their country. With the exception of a few Asian countries, most of the developing countries went through a phase of extensive growth artificially boosted by aid from the first and second worlds, only to end these three decades dangerously in debt with infant industries so well protected that they refused to grow, a firm tendency towards unprocessed and semi-processed export commodities, and political elites generally set up as dictatorships in league with the economic elites.

When the debt crisis exploded at the turn of the 1970s-1980s, the Bretton Woods Institutions (BWIs) were quick to point the finger at the State and all its associated structures, which were behind the increase in unproductive "rents" that had taken place under the wing of public protection. The stock remedy was to reduce the size of the state system by all means possible: liberalising the different economic sectors (notably the financial systems), tackling all forms of subsidies, privatising everything that could be privatised, and obviously curbing all deficits and inflation to foster a return to solvency for the failed states. Although these measures fell behind schedule in their implementation, their results were more often than not extremely disappointing: in the countries that followed this prescription, inflation may have come down, but per capita incomes did not grow.

The BWIs' impatience drove a redoubling of efforts in the following decade (1990s) leading to a consolidation of stabilisation and liberalisation which is still underway. In the mid-1990s this agenda, now known as the Washington Consensus, was given more emphasis as it turned to institutional matters. Governments were advised to refocus on their core functions as service providers and to "own" the principles of "good governance" (anticorruption, efficient and transparent administration, freedom of operation and regulation of the markets, protection of private property rights, and democracy). This placing of institutions higher on the international agenda can be found in the World Bank's World Development Reports, the 1993 report on the Asian Miracle, the 1997 report on the State, and the 2002 report on institutions. "Good" institutions, in this case, are not perceived so much in terms of social cohesion or even economic growth, but in terms of their resemblance to the developed countries' models and their observance of market expectations. It has to be said that the markets had their fingers badly burnt by the string of financial crises that began to hit the emerging countries in 1997, which they put down to a lack of transparency, corruption and crony capitalism – in short, to poor governance by the countries concerned, their financial institutions, businesses and regulatory bodies.

Whole arrays of codes of good conduct and indicators quickly sprang up to measure progress. Among the most well-known and utilised are those of the World Bank itself (Country Profiles and Institutional Analysis, Worldwide Governance Indicators, Doing Business).

So did this new emphasis on setting up "good institutions" yield better results than the previous recipes?

With hindsight, other studies have shown that the supposedly given relationship between "good governance" and growth had not been established: countries with identical (poor) governance scores are capable of posting totally opposite economic performances (M. Khan, N. Meisel and J. Ould Aoudia). For example, China and Zimbabwe have similar governance scores. Yet, over the last 15 years, one has posted average growth of 10% per year while the other has experienced recession averaging at 4% per year. In fact, the only relation that holds is the very strong correlation between "good governance" and development level (per capita GDP level). However, this relation gives no clue as to what might be the appropriate reforms to raise the economic growth rate in poor countries. It simply shows that "good governance" corresponds to the major functions of the complex institutional systems built by the rich countries over centuries, regulatory systems which the poor countries lack, by definition, since they would otherwise already be developed. The relationship between "good governance" and development level is therefore a tautology. And the relationship between "good governance" and pace of development (per capita GDP growth over 10 to 15 years) does not hold.

While, in most of the poor countries, rent-seeking behaviour, far from declining as was expected by the Washington reformers, adjusted to cope with the new development assistance conditionalities and economic liberalisation measures (privatisations, trade opening, financial opening, etc.), the countries that have exhibited the best performance scores in recent decades, mainly in Asia, have not really complied with these principles.

These disconcerting observations raise a major question: has the reform menu concocted by the West once again overlooked an important element? And what about the very way in which "institutions" have turned up in the field of development policies, which has, to a remarkable degree, avoided the question of the role of the State in the history of the Western countries and of the symbolic and ritual function of institutions, proposing a "technology" of human government (good governance) from which the political factor is carefully eliminated and which is supposed to be universally valid whatever the local institutional configurations?

The institutional heart of development processes

All the theoretical and empirical economic, sociological and anthropological analyses confirm that the core substance of long-term institutional change is the transformation of the regulation structures governing human societies, from systems based on social ties and interpersonal interactions, to systems based on formalised, impersonal regulations.

In the first case, the regulation systems are based essentially on the relationships between individuals, operating in keeping with generally unwritten rules dictated by the characteristics and choices of the group's members and hence valid on this small scale. These rules are enforced by means of often informal, implicit institutions (keeping your word, a sense of honour, standing guarantor, reputation, etc.), with the main rule enforcement mechanism being the threat of expulsion from the group for breaching the rules.

In the case of much more formalised regulatory systems, the rules become general in scope in that they are produced and observed on a systemic scale (society or country). They apply to everyone across the board in an indiscriminate, impersonal and hence universal manner. This institutional infrastructure is found at the heart of the two products of Western development: the rule of law and the capitalist economy. "Good governance" means none other than an advanced state of depersonalisation and formalisation of the rules.

This theory is borne out empirically: as mentioned above, when the institutional databases are analysed, the extent to which rules are formalised in a society is found to be closely correlated with its level of development (per capita GDP). The relationship is circular: the formalisation of economic and political rules creates an environment conducive to the expansion of trade (itself driven by demographic growth, urban development and the search for new markets).

The increase in wealth that results from the broader market base supports the financing of this anonymous institutional infrastructure, now better able to ensure the security of transactions, with a centralised administrative and tax system, a unified judicial system attached to the State, a banking system and debt guarantees. The late 17th century saw the emergence of stock exchanges, first in Holland and then in England, to support trade in securities, etc. Administration, justice and market supervision were the foundations of the rule of law and the capitalist, market infrastructure that had begun to develop in the West in the Middle Ages. The longstanding rise in the share of market and non-market services in GDP reflects this huge change in governance systems.

Where this institutional infrastructure is actually implemented and respected, i.e. in rich countries, it raises stakeholder confidence by taking collective responsibility for a growing number of factors of uncertainty (security, disputes, information, as well as health, old age, unemployment, etc.). This, in turn, reduces the level of risk and costs borne at individual level, thereby enabling actors to extend their time horizons and take riskier, but also more profitable gambles. The marginal cost of transactions between unknown parties at the point of trade is drastically reduced.

Yet this institutional infrastructure is extremely expensive to implement and enforce. This is why its introduction is necessarily accompanied by higher taxes and, ultimately, an increase in the role of the State as the capitalist sphere expands. The State also serves as collateral and insurer of last resort for the risks taken by this sphere, which is constantly threatened by its excesses, as shown by the succession of systemic crises it has experienced since the Renaissance. Higher taxes are themselves made possible by the productivity gains made by the economic players who benefit from economies of scale and synergies. While capitalist entrepreneurs, bolstered by the institutional handling of risks at a systemic level, can launch into ever-riskier dealings in search of maximal gain, the increase in wage-earners in the 19th century created middle classes whose fate was bound up with that of the system of capitalist production and trade. We see at work here the mutually sustained cycle of the parallel extension of the State and capitalism.

By contrast, the regulation system characteristic of developing countries remains based on interpersonal relations. This system is adapted to a world in which most of the population lives at the level of what Fernand Braudel and Karl Polanyi termed "the subsistence economy". As they accumulate no surpluses, they are always vulnerable to the effects of life's ups and downs (climate, health, conflicts, etc.). The poor countries, by definition, cannot afford the institutional infrastructure described above, so that the populations turn to "traditional" systems of informal financing and insurance. The risks borne by the individual are so high (premature death, eradicated from the rich societies, is ever-present and life expectancy is short) that the rational response to this level of risk is to constantly "diversify" to the utmost, mainly through social networking (a Malian proverb defines a poor person as "he who has no friends"). The Washington reformers believe that such a hedonistic and risk-averse attitude should be fought head-on, since "breaking out of the cycle of poverty" (monetary poverty) necessitates the adoption of behaviour in keeping with long-run risk taking.

"What the West does not see of the West" (P. Legendre)

Contrary to the BWIs' linear vision of institutional progress, the real way in which societies have evolved unfortunately shows that the transition from one regulation system to another is neither automatic nor linear nor simultaneous in all sectors of society.

Moreover, this period of transition actually increases the factors of uncertainty: it is marked by a weakening of respect for word given orally at a time when the force of the written word has not yet been established, since it implies literacy, the enforcement of rules, efficient legal proceedings, and so on. The societies find themselves faced with periods of heightened uncertainty and hazy standards. This in-between state also perturbs individual and collective identities, formerly clearly defined but now destabilised since they are no longer "given". What we are too quick to term "ethnic" violence could well be much more the product of deculturation and a clouding of norms than an assertion of ethnicity in the strict sense of the term.

Now what do the rich countries say to the developing countries? Put our institutional infrastructure in place and you will develop. They ignore a number of facts: firstly, these institutions were born of a specific historical context; secondly, it was centuries before they were running more or less smoothly at nation state level in the North; thirdly, they are extremely expensive to set up and manage; lastly, they do not exist in the abstract and are only "effective" as part of an institutional whole that is greater than the sum of its parts.

This is why transplanting formal rules and institutions into the least prepared environments can prove counterproductive and give rise to a blurring of the boundary between legal and illegal, an increase in corruption, a distrust of the administration born of the disparity between formal rules and actual practices, and a feeling of arbitrariness – in short, a form of normative chaos leading to social malfunctions. However, any transplantation is possible provided it is wanted by a society (as was the case with Japan's Meiji Restoration in the late 19th century). The mechanisms of development are endogenous.

The path from the informal to the formal is therefore uncertain and does not always bring progress. It can lead to periods of loss of confidence, instability, criminalisation and a drop in total productivity. This explains why the link between "good governance" and growth is so tenuous, however ethically desirable it may be to fight corruption and establish democracy.

What does the example of the countries that have successfully made this transformation show, from the European countries of the Renaissance to the Asian countries from the 1950s onwards?

It shows that confidence is needed for a society to change. It also shows that such change is not necessarily in the interests of the main interest groups in power, since it could threaten the privileged access to certain economic and political rents that makes them the elite groups they are. Last but by no means least, their example shows that the capacity of the political leaders to provide a vision of this change, to propose a strategy, and to rally and co-ordinate the stakeholders to carry it out is vital. Such institutional capacities are disregarded by the standard agenda of "good governance", indeed the remedies imposed on the poor countries over the last 25 years have in practice tended to destroy them.

The institutional reforms recommended today may well display a welcome recognition of the importance of institutions. Yet they do seek to impose a single, abstract, idealised model via all sorts of quick-fix reforms, with no regard for the age-old local structures. Insodoing they contradict the experience of the rich countries, which are governed by a wide variety of institutional configurations that took centuries to reach maturity. Does the State mean the same thing to the Americans, the Italians, the Chinese and the French? Were their respective states planned in a standardised way? Why should things be any different "in the tropics"?

Most importantly, these reforms are designed in a technical, apolitical manner, as if separate from the rest of society. Symptomatically, they do not incorporate the manœuvres of such institutions fundamental to capitalism as the State, the world of big business and the interest groups acting through them. Consequently, these reforms do not link the societies' institutional change to capitalist transformation.

The BWIs' standard economic analysis and recommendations disregard the question of the development of economic activities with increasing returns, employment-rich and internationally competitive, the industrialisation of essentially agricultural countries and the nature of the – more or less protectionist, more or less temporary – rents granted to capitalists to encourage them to develop productive activities. They overlook all of these eminently economic and institutional issues that have been at the heart of the successful capitalist transformations in recent centuries.

With today's institutional reforms and "good governance", now an international standardized product, the West is once again merely imposing its norms. We have to ask whether it is possible even to formulate this basic institutional question of the West's relations with the non-West and with itself, with its subconscious constructions, a problem explored by anthropologist and jurist Pierre Legendre. Perhaps this impossible question explains why the "good" institutions that the West tirelessly devises to "assist" the poor countries seem so often buckled and little effective.

Despite the good intentions behind them, doesn't the projection of these "good" institutions onto the developing countries, and especially the poorest among them, paradoxically act to undermine the capacity, will and even the need for the Southern elites to devise their own development strategies?

This exploration of institutions leads us to conclude that development is fundamentally a never-ending process of projection and learning, in which the economic and the political are inextricably interlinked, and that the life of a society cannot be invented or controlled on its behalf, any more than can that of an individual.

Whatever happened to the principle of reciprocity?

If societies are sole masters of their own development, then the bases of aid as it has been managed for the last fifty years start to crumble. This is probably because the relationship between the West and the rest of the world, which is based on development assistance has avoided taking into account the universal scope of the principle of reciprocity, which states that any favour or benefit granted should be returned in kind, without which the relationship is distorted.

Yet for all this, international solidarity continues to mean something in areas where both parties have shared interests and common policies can be developed jointly. One such area is that of the global and regional public good: global environmental issues such as combating climate change; regional environmental issues such as the conservation of the Mediterranean sea and combating water stress and desertification; health issues, including the purchase of patents for drugs to combat "globalised" diseases; action to combat instability and financial crime; international cooperation on law enforcement, etc.

Where the global and regional public good is concerned, it is possible to find common ground for consensus. Moreover, action in these areas would be regarded as highly legitmate in the rich countries (common interests) and would not be regarded as charity, high-handedness, condescension, etc.

The effects of the global ecological crises and new international balances of power are combining to increasingly undermine the credibility of current attitudes to "North-South" relations. However, they are also opening up new perspectives based on more balanced relations.

29

Capacity Building, Governance and Development

The Concepts, their Links and their Limits

Floribert NGARUKO and Soumana SAKO

In recent decades the concept of governance has been very popular as an approach to development. However, despite – or because of – this success, advocates of development through governance cannot agree on how to define the concept. Thus definitions of governance cover a broad spectrum: at one extreme are those that focus on the way power is exerted in the socio-economic management of a society, at the other those that insist on the sharing of responsibilities between the state and non-state actors (Olowu, 2002). Where the former insist on leadership qualities, in other words the way that political leaders manage, use or abuse their authority to promote socio-economic development or to pursue aims that put that development at risk, the latter regard "good governance" as resulting from the state's efforts to promote partnership with groups of non-state actors in the formulation and implementation of development policies. Between the two extremes are mixed definitions, such as that of the French Ministry of Foreign and European Affairs, which regards governance as the

> "Art of governing, articulating the management of public affairs at various level of territories, regulating relationships within society and coordinating interaction of the varioust actors[1]".

---

1. Comité interministériel de la coopération internationale et du développement (2006). Stratégie française de gouvernance.

In parallel to this growing importance of governance, three other approaches to development also became remarkably popular. The first is that of "sustainable development", understood as a model for a balanced response to the needs of today's generations that does not compromise the abilities of future generations to meet their own needs (World Commission on Environment and Development, 1987). The second is that of capacity building, in other words the process by which individuals, organisations and communities acquire the knowledge, skills, resources and institutions, and also the necessary attitudes, values and behaviours, to define and carry through specific tasks and missions intended to reduce poverty (African Capacity Building Foundation 2007). The third approach meanwhile is that of public policy decision-making; where traditionally the ownership of public policies was assessed in terms of their nature and the problem they were intended to deal with, the recent evolution sees the validity of public policies as equally related to the process by which they were chosen.

The concomitant rise in importance of these three approaches on the one hand, and of that of governance on the other, raises the question of the relationship between capacity building, public policy decision-making and sustainable development on the one hand and governance on the other.

This article seeks to explore the relationship between these aspects of development. For the authors, the last two decades have seen each of the three approaches moving towards the integration of dimensions of development that are central to governance. This essay also takes a critical look at the operationalisation of the concept of governance. It describes the limitations of the first generation of governance reforms that have prevailed hitherto and gives a few signposts for the second generation of reforms, which might have more chance of triggering a process of real development, particularly in Africa.

This paper aims to consider the convergence of visions of sustainable development, public policy decision-making and capacity building with that of governance, before focusing on divergences in the operationalisation of the concept of governance and the questions that this concept still leaves unanswered.

Convergence of vision(s)

Capacity building and governance

Until the late-1970s the availability of financial resources and technical skills was broadly regarded as sufficient to ensure a country's development. Capacity building was then understood in terms of human knowledge and skills, and efforts to promote it centred around education, primarily of a formal kind. The emphasis placed on education in Africa reflects this belief. Thus, for example, from 1970 to the early 1980s, the average number of teachers in primary schools more than doubled across the African continent, while the number of teachers in secondary schools quadrupled. Where higher education is concerned, while in 1960 only eighteen African countries had a university or institute of higher education, around ten years later there was at least one in almost every country. Meanwhile the number of graduates from higher education passed from 1,200 in 1960 to 70,000 in the early 1980s (World Bank, 1991).

At the very time that development practice was investing heavily in physical capital and formal education, economists quickly understood that growth – at the time still widely regarded as equivalent to development – was the result not only of the volume of investment and technical knowledge and skills, but also, and more importantly, of their effectiveness and productivity. Thus the 1980s saw the development of a consensus accepting that the effectiveness of investment was a greater key to the success of development efforts than its volume (Levy, 2004). The effectiveness of investment depends not only on the technical skills of human resources and the performance of equipment, but also and more importantly on whether or not the institutional framework in which those human and technical resources function provides an incentive. At this point policy reform became a central concern for development actors, in the form of structural adjustment programmes inspired, or indeed imposed, by the Bretton Woods institutions.

Thus, where technical assistance tended to focus on deficits in technical skills, the emphasis gradually shifted to organisational and institutional capacity. In practice this change, which occurred in the 1980s, heralded another upheaval, leading to the emergence of institutions as a central issue for development, at a time when it was gradually becoming accepted that institutional variables were the most important factor in destabilising reforms. Based largely on the observation that development had too long been regarded as essentially a matter of technical and financial resources, the new approach took the view that capacity building and development were more than simply a technical challenge. The emphasis thus gradually shifted to the institutional aspect. This effort to update approaches to development was initiated not only by practitioners on the ground, but also by researchers, who contributed to the groundswell that brought the issue of governance to the fore among today's approaches to development.

Until the late-1980s the notion of organisation tended to be confused with that of institution. But since the early 1990s a clear distinction between the two has been established. Douglas North defines institutions as "a society's rules of the game". As such institutions are thus different from organisations, regarded by North as "players" or "actors" (North, 1993). In his view, organisations include public service bodies and structures whose nature may be economic (firms, trade unions co-operatives), social (churches, clubs, associations) or educational (schools, universities, training centres). Institutions on the other hand consist of rules that may be formal (laws and regulations) or informal (conventions, value systems, unwritten standards of behaviour) and systems of incentives and positive or negative sanctions.

Thus, in addition to its human and organisational dimensions, capacity building must pay attention to institutional capacities, which reflect the existence (or lack) of a coherent system of incentives within which individuals and organisations operate (Ngaruko, 2005). Here a degree of convergence can be seen between the issue of capacity building and that of governance, whose agenda was based on "pivotal" themes, notably institutions, leadership, transparency and participation.

Governance and public policy decision-making

In essence the approach of the structural adjustment policies was that all the countries facing economic problems in the 1980s should follow the same course of treatment with no notable distinctions. Taking little account of the socio-economic specificities of the countries, this treatment, known as the "Washington consensus", was translated into programmes that had no need to involve national actors closely in their formulation. The questioning of structural adjustment policies triggered by the emergence of the concept of governance was simultaneously a questioning of the process by which development policies were formulated. In its relation to development policies the notion of "good governance" had main three categories of objective.

Firstly, the improvement of the institutional framework of the decision-making process, notably through the involvement of citizens and groups in the making of public decisions, the promotion of the rule of law and the independence of the justice system, the existence of contradictory sources of information, the duties of accountability and transparency, the promotion of forces of opposition and a dynamic, engaged civil society, an independent, professional press and a multiplicity of sources for the analysis and evaluation of public policies.

Secondly, the concept of "good governance" emphasised the need for values and standards of behaviour – notably in the government and public service – to be well rooted in a culture of transparency and accountability.

Thirdly the notion of "good governance" aimed to improve the capacity for independent action and for dialogue between actors in the public and private sectors and in civil society.

This resulted in convergence between the approach of public policy decision-making and that of governance. After a period dominated by the belief that it was enough for all countries to apply the same formula, it became apparent that the intrinsic quality of public policies had to be improved by making them part of a process based on the values advocated by the governance approach to development.

Sustainable human development and governance

In parallel to the evolution described above, another major change was taking place. In the 1970s, particularly after the first oil crisis of 1973, some academic researchers began asking questions about the meaning, goals and sustainability of growth and development. The idea that development was simply a cumulative, infinite process, measurable against economic aggregates such as per capita gross national product, began to be questioned in favour of a new vision favouring research into truly sustainable development – in other words a kind that respected the natural environment and preserved opportunities for future generations. Defined in this way, development had to be centred around human individuals, expanding their range of choices, and around the protection and promotion of resources and ecological values.

The World Summit on Sustainable Development of 2002 defined the process of sustainable development as involving many mechanisms and fields of action in which political and institutional factors have primordial importance. At the minimum, sustainable human development was seen as including solid institutions, economic, social and environmental policies centring on the human individual, the rule of law, equality of the sexes and a favourable investment climate (World Summit on Sustainable Development, 2003). These factors all lie at the heart of the notion of governance.

Thus the notion of governance lay at the convergence of three approaches: capacity building, the improvement of public policy decision-making processes and sustainable human development. It is this position at the intersection of three major themes in the language and policies of development that goes some way to explaining the rise in importance of the concept of governance.

Operational divergences and unanswered questions

Operational divergences and mixed results on the ground

While governance seems to have come to dominate political language, for both donors and governments, there still remains no consensus as to its real content. Each of the actors involved seem driven by their own "agenda" and calculations of the benefits to be had from promoting the concept of governance.

For the World Bank for example, governance is:

> "the norms, traditions and institutions through which a country exercises authority for the common good. It includes the processes for selecting, monitoring, and replacing those in authority; the capacity of government to manage its resources and to implement sound policies; and the respect that citizens and the state have for the institutions that govern economic and social interactions among them. (Kaufmann, 2005)."

However, from an operational point of view, the strategy of the World Bank is essentially limited to reform of the public service and state finances with the main aim of fighting against corruption, although recently there have been signs that this field of action is expanding (Kaufmann, 2005).

Meanwhile the International Monetary Fund, in its actions on the ground, regards "good governance" as primarily a matter of liberalising systems of exchange, trade and pricing, limiting ad hoc decision-making and the preferential treatment of certain individuals and organisations and eliminating budgetary subsidies as sources of price distortion, economic inefficiency and interference with the rules of the market economy (International Monetary Fund, 2003).

Similarly the United Nations Development Programme (UNDP) links governance to sustainable human development, whereas the Organisation for Economic Co-operation and Development (OECD) links it to the duties of accountability, transparency, efficiency, effectiveness and the primacy of law.

Thus a comparison of the mandates of the different development actors and their interpretations of "good governance" reveals that each actor was guided by the same motivations and objectives in defining what it thought governance should cover. Unsurprisingly, the concept of governance thus defined has been used by its promoters as a tool to apply pressure. In this regard Africa is a particularly illuminating case.

The issue of "good governance" emerged at a time of growing doubt about the effectiveness of the first generation of structural adjustment policies (1980s and early 1990s). In some respects the emphasis placed on governance often came down to blaming African governments for the continent's economic failure, while concealing the failure of development aid and co-operation policies and the responsibility of the economic, trade and strategic policies of the developed countries in Africa's political, economic, financial, social and ecological crisis.

Furthermore, the values of "good governance" were often used as conditions for aid, when it might have been better to promote them as the natural and inalienable rights of peoples and citizens or, at the very least, as elements in a wider system of positive incentives, rather than punishments or negative incentives tending to undermine the national ownership of development policies.

Thus, while the developing countries were brought to heel by these conditions, governance within the international organisations and countries of the North remained outside the field of critical examination, when a real will to root out bad governance would have required the demand for improvement in the countries of the South be accompanied by concomitant efforts to improve governance and fairness at the international level[40].

From this point of view the governance reforms did not really change the asymmetrical power relations between the "partners" of North and South. On the contrary, these reforms often tended to infantilise the governments of the South. They thus served as a springboard for various forms of interference, supervision, not to say management of states manifesting "bad governance" and even vague attempts at externally-led "regime change", in accordance with an old paternalist tradition going back to the "civilising mission" of colonisation[3].

---

2. On the failures of governance throughout the world and the need to strengthen it, see, in the present work, Salama, I., Delmas-Marty, M., Severino, J.-M., Olukoshi A. and Darbon, D.

3. On this subject see, in the present work, Sauquet, M. and M. Vielajus.

As for results on the ground, these do not seem to have matched the ideas and hopes generated by the rise of the concept of governance. The World Bank, for example, in its Annual Review of Development Effectiveness for 2006, says that governance is still not perceived as showing any significant improvement following the substantial reforms undertaken by the institution (World Bank, 2006). This observation is moreover confirmed by studies on the evolution of governance over the last ten years, notably including a recent study by the World Bank Institute team specialising in governance and corruption, which concludes that there is no clear indication of any improvement in governance across the world in the period 1996-2006 (Kaufmann et al, 2007).

Many questions remain unanswered

The divergences arising out of the operationalisation of the concept of governance and the paucity of results from the reforms to which it gave rise raise many questions. In relation to Africa in particular, the questions left unanswered by the implementation of governance are many and varied. These questions concern the role of the public sector, the promotion of democracy and human rights, the underlying ideological framework and also the contradictions between that framework and African socio-cultural and economic contexts[4].

Thus, where the public sector is concerned, how can the need to have effective professional public services free of political interference be reconciled with the requirement for these services to be accountable to the political authority in accordance with the elementary principles of democracy? What systems of incentives, performance measurement and recruitment policies should be established in order to obtain this kind of public service? How can the need for broad public participation in the development and evaluation of public policies be reconciled with the technical requirements for research and analysis in relation to economic policies in contexts where illiteracy is widespread?

These questions are supplemented by others raised by capacity building in a context of growing globalisation. How can the need to build and use national capacity to improve national ownership of the development process be reconciled with the demand for African public institutions to be open to external input in a context of growing globalisation?

---

4. On this subject see the illuminating, though not exhaustive list proposed by Sako (2003).

There are also many questions related to economic governance and the dominant neo-liberal ideological framework: what is the optimal balance between the role of the state and that of the market?

The unanswered questions are equally numerous and complex in relation to the promotion of democratic governance in a context marked by massive illiteracy and by informal public institutions that are becoming increasingly patrimonial in nature.

Conclusion

The aim of this essay was to explore the relationship between the concept of governance and three approaches to development, through capacity building, sustainable human development and the improvement of public policy decision-making. It has shown that the notion of governance has become a point of convergence.

Firstly there is convergence with the approach of capacity building in development policy management which, having previously regarded technical knowledge and financial resources as sufficient to make development happen, realised that economic reforms and structural adjustment were the real path to development before discovering, in the 1990s, that the effective reform of development policies required focusing attention on institutions and their reform.

Secondly, there is convergence with the approach of public policy decision-making which, after considering for some time that it was enough for all countries to apply the same formula, realised that it was necessary to improve the intrinsic quality of public policies, notably through a more participative decision-making process.

Lastly there is convergence with the vision which, having long seen development as a matter of economic well-being that could be measured according to simple criteria such as per capita gross domestic product, discovered that real development had to be sustainable, fair, centred on the individual and respectful of societies. This implied growth that was not only sustained, but also respectful of the environment, the existence of a healthy, inclusive institutional framework and far-sighted, committed leadership. All these elements were already central to the notion of governance.

However, this essay has argued that the limitations of the operationalisation of the concept of governance require the concept to be refined. More precisely, one of the major issues for the translation of the concept of governance into changes that can significantly advance the cause of development seem to lie in the emergence of second generation governance reforms, at both the national and international levels. These reforms should seek to compensate for the gaps in the reforms implemented until now.

At least two conditions seem necessary for the success of these second generation reforms. Governance needs to be promoted as the set of natural, inalienable rights of peoples and citizens or, at the very least, as a set of elements in a system of positive incentives, rather than negative sanctions or measures tending to undermine the national ownership of indispensable political, economic and social reforms, which Africa cannot avoid, but which Africans must own if they are to have sustainable effects. It is also imperative that such reforms in the countries of the South be accompanied by changes in the North to avoid some policies of countries in the North undermining these reforms.

Bibliography

African Capacity Building Foundation (2007). Developing a Performance Measurement Framework and Performance Indicators for Capacity Building, GOV/AN 16/6-A, Harare, ACBF.

Barclay A., (2004). The Political Economy of Sustainable Development: The Governance Perspective, Working Paper No. 1, Harare, ACBF.

Department for International Development (2005). Why We Need to Work More Effectively in Fragile States, London, DFID.

Favereau, O. (1989). "Marchés internes, marchés externes", Revue économique, n° 2. International Monetary Fund (2007). Annual Report. Independent Evaluation Office of the International Monetary Fund, Washington, D.C., IMF.

International Monetary Fund (2003). Good Governance: The IMF Role, Washington, D.C., IMF.

Kaufmann, D. (2005). "Myths and Realities of Governance and Corruption", Global Competitiveness Report, World Economic Forum, p. 81-98.

Kaufmann, D., A. Kraay and M. Mastruzzi (2007). Governance Matters VI: Aggregate and Individual Governance Indicators 1996–2006. Policy Research Working Paper 4280, Washington, D.C., World Bank.

Levy, B. (2004). "Governance and Economic Development in Africa: Meeting the Challenge of Capacity Building", in B. Levy, and S. Kpundeh (eds.), Building State Capacity in Africa. New Approaches, Emerging Lessons, Washington, D.C., World Bank.

Ministère Français des Affaires Étrangères et Européennes, Direction

Générale de la Coopération Internationale et du Développement (2006). L'approche française: la governance démocratique, http:// www.diplomatie.gouv.fr/fr/actions-france_830/ governance_ 1053/ index.html.

Moharir, V. (2002). "Governance and Policy Analysis", in D. Olowu and S. Sako (eds.), Better Governance and Public Policy, Bloomfield, Kumarian Press, p. 107-123.

Ngaruko, F. (2005). The Evaluation of the World Bank's Support for Capacity Building in Mali, Washington, D.C., World Bank. http://lnweb90.worldbank.org/oed/oeddoclib.nsf/ DocUNIDViewForJavaSearch/D96AD079D0D4390985256FE10067F B4E/$file/mali_africa_capacity_dev.pdf.pdf

Ngaruko, F. (2007). Capacity Development and Governance in War-Prone Countries with Fragile States. Paper presented at the Conference on Capacity Development and Governance in Fragile States, Addis Abeba (Ethiopia), 23-25 July.

North, D. (1993). The New Institutional Economics and Development, mimeo, St. Louis, Washington University.

Olowu, D. (2002). "Governance and Policy Management Capacity in Africa", in D. Olowu and S. Sako (eds.) op. cit., p. 1-10.

Sako, S. (2003). The New Partnership for Africa's Development: Building Economic and Corporate Governance Institutions for Sustainable Development, ACBF Occasional Paper No. 2, Harare, ACBF.

World Bank (2006). Annual Review of Development Effectiveness 2006: getting results, Washington D.C., World Bank.

World Bank (1991). The African Capacity Building Initiative: Toward Improved Policy Analysis and Development Management, Washington, D.C., World Bank.

World Bank (1989). Sub-Saharan Africa: From Crisis to Sustainable Growth, Washington D.C., World Bank.

World Commission on Environment and Development (1987). Our Common Future, Oxford, Oxford University Press.

World Summit on Sustainable Development (2003). Plan of Implementation, Advance unedited copy, September.

30

Water

Responsible Governance
for a Dream Accessible to All

Pierre VICTORIA
(Translated from the French)

Water, our first mirror, you also reflect what we do.
Jacques Lacarrière.

The challenges of water policy

Water is life. A lack of water for drinking and sanitation means death;
it is the primary cause of mortality and morbidity in the world, with
800 millions people[1] having no access to drinking water and 2.5 billion
having no water for sanitation. This is something no one can regard
as acceptable. In 2002, in the context of the Millennium Development
Goals, the world's Heads of State undertook to reduce the numbers of
people without access to water or sanitation by a half by 2015. These
commitments have been undertaken without any implementation strategy.

Since that undertaking was made, access to water and sanitation has
been confirmed as the focus of the Development Goals. As Kofi Annan,
Secretary-General of the United Nations, noted in 2004, in his speech
launching the work of the Commission on Sustainable Development,
access to water is a precondition for the realisation of all the international
community's other undertakings to combat poverty:

---

1. "Joint Monitoring Programme 2008".

Water is intimately linked with education and gender equality. Girls who have to spend time gathering water for the family tend not to be in school. And where schools have sanitation, attendance is higher, especially for girls. Water is connected to health, since millions of children get sick and die every year from water-borne diseases and from lack of basic sanitation and hygiene. [...] It is linked to environmental protection, since poor water management degrades and squanders a precious resource. It is linked to the urbanization of poverty, since rural impoverishment rooted in water and land-tenures issues drives people to migrate to already crowded cities – and most often to their growing slums.

This view is so widely shared that the United Nations Development Programme, in its excellent report of December 2006 Beyond Scarcity: Power, Poverty and the World Water Crisis, quantifies the benefits of realising the Millennium Goals as a million lives saved in ten years, 272 million schooling days gained over the same period and 38 million dollars a year in economic benefits for communities in which women are released from the chore of fetching water and the population is in good health.

So water poses many, diverse and serious challenges.

The first challenge is that of sanitation. Pasteur used to say, "We drink 90% of diseases." Lack of water for drinking and sanitation is one of the main causes of disease throughout the world: every year, 3 million children under five die from diarrhoea, typhoid and cholera because they have no access to drinking water.

It is also a social challenge, because poor shanty-town dwellers who are not connected to the public water supply generally have to pay ten or twenty times more for water, with additional costs and worse service (poorer quality water than from the public water supply).

Then there is the challenge of the urban crisis: population growth and higher living standards increase water needs. These are expected to grow by 25% in the next 25 years. Resources are limited, needs increasing and there is more and more competition between different uses of water. The urban population is growing at a rate of 70 million new inhabitants per year, or a city the size of Madrid every month. Most new city-dwellers live in the countries of the South. Expressed in terms of essential services, urban growth presents gigantic challenges.

The challenge also relates to food. Water used in agriculture represents between 70 and 90% of the water collected in developing countries, and is used for irrigation. Today agriculture is the world's greatest consumer of water and also its greatest waster: in many irrigation systems up to 60% of water is wasted before it can be used. Increased agricultural production cannot continue unless water is used in a less wasteful way.

The challenge is also environmental, since in many developing countries 90% of waste water is dumped untreated in rivers, lakes or oceans. Half the world's rivers and lakes are polluted by waste water. Sanitation remains the poor relation of water management.

Lastly, a balance must be found between urban and rural areas. It is imperative to develop essential services in both the countryside and secondary cities if the flow of populations towards tentacular, unmanageable megalopolises is to be avoided.

Eight years before 2015, how close is this possible dream?

In its Global Human Development Report the UNDP provides an intermediate overview of the Millennium Goals. This shows that, give or take a year, the world is likely to meet its drinking water goal – notably because of progress made in the two population giants, China and India. However, this overall observation hides great discrepancies: if the pace of drinking water provision does not increase, 55 countries will miss the Millennium Development Goals and we will be below the target in 2015, with 235 million people without supply.

Meanwhile sanitation is seriously lagging behind drinking water in most developing countries. Seventy-four countries are way behind and failure to meet the goal will mean 430 million people miss out. So while, overall, the Millennium Development Goals for drinking water will be almost reached in 2015, it will be a different matter for sanitation.

Where drinking water is concerned Sub-Saharan Africa is some way behind: it is expected to reach its goal one generation or 27 years late and, where sanitation is concerned, not until 2076, in other words over two generations after the deadline. The Arab states are expected to be a generation late where drinking water is concerned. South Asia will miss its sanitation target by four years.

It is all the more important to note these delays because, as millions of individuals are left out of the statistics, the data do not reveal the full extent of the deficit.

Lastly the Millennium Development Goals should be regarded as a minimum threshold and not as a ceiling. Even if they were realised, the world deficit would remain huge: 800 million human beings would remain without water and 1.8 billion without sanitation.

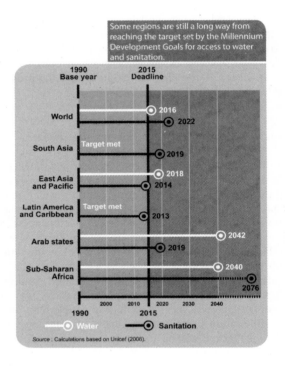

To make up for lost time, Sub-Saharan Africa will have to double its speed from 10 million people a year connected to a drinking water supply to 23 million; it will have to quadruple its rate of sanitation provision, connecting 28 million people a year between now and 2015 instead of the current 7 million, while South Asia will have to provide sanitation to 43 million people a year instead of the 25 million covered annually over the last decade.

Though these goals are ambitious, they are not beyond the reach of an international community that decides that it is really going to eradicate poverty. But has it done so?

A global priority that has not been fully adopted

Aid provision does not match the financial needs of nations, particularly in Africa. Water, and still more sanitation, are marginalised in poverty reduction programmes and government budgets. According to the UNDP, governments should allocate at least 1% of GDP to spending on water and sanitation; in fact they commit less than half.

Meanwhile development aid is ungenerous: donors allocate less than 5% to water. Only four countries rise above this threshold in bilateral aid and deserve to be named. They are Luxembourg, Denmark, Germany and Japan. Total development aid even fell between 2000 and 2002, the first years of the period in which the Millennium Development Goals were supposed to be met. This was an odd way to set about reaching them. The additional investments necessary to reach the Millennium Development Goals for water and sanitation came to 10–30 billion USD per year, the lower figure reflecting the most elementary technology possible. The funding challenge can be met if all financial resources (and not just some of them) are doubled. But will we go down this path, given that a growing proportion of public funds are being put towards dealing with exceptional disasters, such as once-in-a-lifetime floods, turning away from the treatment of ordinary, boring ills such as the lack of drinking water that still kills ten times more people than war?

The markets and financial institutions compete to see who can be more creative – every day we read about the consequences of this in the press – but they do not apply their imagination to the issue of water. A few rare but welcome initiatives have emerged however, including the Oudin-Santini Law passed in France. This made it possible to collect 17 million euros in 2007 for decentralised cooperation on water, but ten times more could be mobilised per year if all the French actors played the game.

The 10 billion USD a year needed to meet the Millennium Development Goals represents less than half annual spending on mineral water in the rich countries and less than five days of global military spending. Ten billion USD is 1/30,000th of stock market capitalisation world wide. Ten billion dollars a year is only 10% of public development aid; objectively speaking it is a sum equivalent to a "planetary gratuity?", but one that never reaches the table.

More worryingly still, as the times change so do planetary priorities. Climate change has given the political community something new to think and talk about, to the point of sweeping aside the torrent of commitments made and never met. Doubt settles, reflecting the weakness of an aleatory world governance that unoriginally defines its priorities according to

2. Orsenna, E. (2007). *Un monde de ressources rares*, Paris, Perrin.

their media impact. It encourages the management of uncertainty through adaptation to climate change and refuses to mobilise actors around an agreed priority and facts generally accepted as obvious.

The UNDP report most opportunely reminds us that the sources of the paucity of drinking water have far more to do with power, poverty and inequality than physical availability. The crisis in water and sanitation is highly discriminatory. It affects the poor of poor countries and spares the rich of all countries.

The real scarcity is that of national governance

The fourth World Water Forum, held in Mexico in March 2006, brought all the water actors together around the two major objectives of ensuring that the right to water remains a priority and strengthening the role of local authorities in the management of water and sanitation services. Given the general pessimism on the low priority given to water by many leaders, it is widely agreed that this local resource would be far better managed if it were given to decentralised authorities. Local governance would then replace state failures. However, this observation covers only part of the reality.

In practice the countries that are likely to succeed in providing access to water have all established it as a priority of national policy.

– In Uganda, in the last ten years, over 5 million people have gained access to clean water, most living in rural areas. The country has increased its public spending on water and sanitation from 0.5% to 2.8% of GDP. It is not insignificant that in Uganda legislation requires women to be represented within associations of water users.

– In South Africa 10 million more people have gained access to clean water since 1994. This is one of the few countries where government spending on water and sanitation outstrips the military budget.

– In Morocco ten years ago, fewer than two in ten people had access to drinking water in the countryside, compared to nine out of ten in towns and cities. Over the last decade 4 million more people have gained access to clean water in the countryside, taking rural coverage to 50%. The attendance of girls at rural primary schools has leaped from 30% to over 50%.

There are successes too in sanitation. West Bengal has made spectacular progress. In 1990, when the government of this Indian state launched its rural sanitation offensive in the Midnapur district – the largest district in India – the rate of rural coverage was no more than 5%. It is now 100%. Across the whole of the state of Bengal 2 million toilets have been built in the last five years. Sanitation service levels have now passed the 40% mark.

Governance priorities must be to declare a national policy for water and sanitation and to clarify responsibilities at the central and local levels. This is a precondition for the necessary and desirable goal of decentralising responsibility for water and sanitation to the authorities at the most local level, with, as a corollary, the devolution of the financial and human resources needed to manage a local service. It is this that gives meaning to Michel Camdessus's message to the financial institutions at the third World Water Forum in 2003 in Kyoto: "donors must be ready to direct aid to the local authorities that need loans at preferential rates for projects in the water sector".

Unlocking the gates[3]

To prevent the fulfilment of the Millennium Goals becoming a vain chimera, the paper elephant referred to by two experts in government aid for development[4], it is necessary to unlock the gates to water and sanitation. In the light of the experience of those working on the ground, there seem to be five major barriers.

• *Firstly the prohibitive cost of connection*
The average price of connection for poor families is equivalent to three months' salary in Manila, a period rising to six months in Kenya and more than a year in Uganda. What is the point of charging a socially acceptable price for water supply if the price of connection remains beyond reach within that society?
Drinking water consumption is very often priced at a subsidised, social rate, but connection to the supply is not. In other words, inhabitants who are connected benefit from subsidies, but those without a connection, who are usually also the poorest, do not. So aid is not targeted towards those who need it most.

• *The difficulty of connecting populations with no formal property rights*
Many public services deliver water only to households with official property deeds. However, over a billion people live in urban and peri-urban areas that are not officially recognised. Abidjan, one of West Africa's most prosperous cities, has over 80 non-authorised residential neighbourhoods.
Who is going to invest and build water infrastructure in peri-urban neighbourhoods whose inhabitants are regarded as illegal and can be

---

3. This section borrows elements from Nicolas Renard's paper at the resources seminar, Niamey, 29 November 2007.
4. Egil, F. (2005). "Les éléphants de papier", Politique africaine no 99, p. 97-115.

moved by the authorities to distant suburbs at any moment? Not many people, if the truth be told. So essential services seldom go there.

Yet developments are emerging. In Morocco legislation did not allow public service operators to serve areas of unofficial habitation. With the launch of the National Initiative for Human Development in 2005, the government lifted this restriction.

• *The lack of a maintenance culture*

In many cities, including some in developed countries, lack of maintenance has turned drinking water networks into sieves. Infrastructure provision is a three-beat waltz of construction – neglect – reconstruction.

Things are not much better in rural areas. In Burkina Faso, Mali, Niger, Malawi, Rwanda, Ethiopia and South Asia, a third of water outlets are unusable due to lack of maintenance. This maintenance failure eliminates all the benefits supposedly brought by the infrastructure that governments, local authorities, NGOs and operators have taken the trouble to build.

• *Unrealistic technical standards*

Our dream is inaccessible because the standards dreamed up by others are just too lofty. There is a very strong "ideal" where standards are concerned, but the more demanding the norms, the more removed from the reality of everyday functioning in peri-urban and rural areas. Slapping on international standards that are in fact defined by OECD nations and are often inappropriate to developing countries means that informal arrangements remain illegal and the poor are excluded from the public service. What really is the point of burying pipes 1.20 metres underground in small towns with almost no road traffic?

• *Adapting to the diversity of expectations*

Private operators of water and sanitation services, have learned to understand consumers better in the diversity of their living conditions and expectations, the better to adapt the service that they provide to them. This is reflected in satisfaction surveys among our subscribers, which do not of course replace dialogue, but do encourage it, and by giving them flexible structures that simplify procedures, such as the "Mobile Offices" created by the Moroccan team of Veolia. These buses fitted out as offices go out to the associations and inhabitants in their neighbourhoods, both on the urban periphery and in the countryside. People can pay their bills there and ask for information about water prices and quality without having to travel to the city centre.

Another lesson is the need to strengthen the educational aspect of these activities. In some places the scarcity of water resources has led to increase educational work with subscribers, to make every individual an agent of their own consumption and a protector of their environment. This involves making them understand the need to save water and to move from a culture of water supply to one of water demand management.

The place of the private sector: a modest but sometimes vital actor

Unlike other public services, such as telecommunications, private water service operators are a marginal phenomenon on the global scale, since they serve less than 10% of the world's population lucky enough to benefit from a public water distribution service. Yet in recent years protest against their presence has become emblematic for a section of the anti-globalisation movement and radical activists, to the point where the real debates and analysis of the conditions for success and reasons for failure have been obscured. On this subject too, the UNDP dares to speak the truth:

> Many public provision services neglect the poor, combining inefficiency and the refusal of management responsibilities with iniquity in relation to finance and pricing. The criteria for policy evaluation should consider not whether a service is public or private but the progress or lack of it made to benefit the poorest.

The debate is thus not about a juxtaposition of the public and private sectors, but the emergence of real professionals capable of responding to the division in access to water which sees the poorest people paying the most for a degraded service.

Once the ideological debate is set aside, the private-public partnership becomes one possible response to the issue. Within this contractual framework Veolia has helped give 1.5 million people in developing countries access to water in recent years, notably in Morocco, Gabon and Niger.

The public-private partnership combines a public service mission with the efficiency of a professional operator. Such partnerships enable the authorities to gain access to the high level expertise provided by a professional operator, while retaining control of water policy and pricing and ownership of the infrastructure. At a time when the need for governance to evolve is strongly felt, the flexibility of public-private partnerships, which have developed across the world, adapting to the specific expectations of each locality, is a major advantage.

In public-private partnerships the division of roles between public authority and water service manager is clearly defined in a contract. It is one of the intrinsic virtues of these partnerships that they require a healthy clarification of roles, a precise definition of expected results and a concentration on performance. The operators have to use all their skills and knowledge in order to optimise performance as far as possible, to improve the water service at every level, from technical aspects to the human, organisational, financial, environmental and so on. This "all-out" optimisation can improve the quality of the service provided and release recurrent funds for new infrastructure.

While public-private partnerships can provide rapid results, they need time to bear all their fruit. Efforts to improve a service require perseverance. The public-private partnership offers local authorities an opportunity to take a long term view. Its time-frame is not that of neoclassical economics or elected terms of office. It is much longer. In a world obsessed by the short term, this is sufficiently rare to be worthy of mention.

Indispensable consultation

We have learned more in recent years from our work on the ground and from dialogue with the populations concerned and their representatives than from all the summits, counter-summits and conferences where access to water and sanitation has been considered and discussed. Not that the latter were not useful. They made it possible to identify false debates and real convergences and to compare points of view, particularly on the right to water and the clarification of levels of responsibility.

What have we learned on the ground? In essence that without consultation with the populations involved nothing lasting or fair is possible. The historical form of dialogue between a public authority and a public service manager is inadequate if it is exclusive. It becomes a source of incomprehension if the conditions in which an operator is acting, particularly a foreign, private operator, are not transparent. Is it right that Ghanaian associations should learn in Paris, from a company tendering for a contract, that the privatisation they are fighting represents five years of service provision to the benefit of the public company?

So often an operator's intervention is presented by the politicians in charge as an immediate response to the lack of drinking water, without the time-frame for the work of connection to the local supply being made known or clear to the population. And how can works be managed in areas of temporary habitation without creating new inequalities between those for whom connection is technically feasible and those for whom it is not and who will have to buy water from the lucky beneficiaries?

Faced with a lack of interest from the politicians, the only response is to consult the populations involved. This alone makes it possible to grasp the priority needs and improvements expected in order to propose a service that meets the expectations of a community. Mediation becomes indispensable; it can be internal or external to the enterprise, or even both. Without the involvement of the neighbourhood associations that relay the consultation, without a dedicated internal team, the programme of social connection in Morocco would never have been carried through so widely, nor would the mobile offices have been set up for the inhabitants of neighbourhoods a long way from the city centres.

By explicitly undertaking not to respond to invitations to tender whose content it judged incompatible with the interests or subscription capacities of the populations involved, and encouraging the optimum involvement of populations in the management of water and sanitation services, Veolia has made the support of local populations for service levels and pricing one of the conditions for long-term success in managing a local public service. Recognition of the importance of this element can contribute to the emergence of a local civil society in Africa. Thus in October last year more than 40 people representing different components of Nigerian civil society responded positively to Veolia's invitation to take part in a day of discussions marking the mid-term report on the contract between the Nigerian state and the Société d'exploitation des eaux du Niger.

It is to be hoped that such multi-player dialogue will help promote a new culture of responsibility and put an end to the ideology, opacity, demagogy and populism that are the "infantile" evils of water governance.

By way of conclusion

The water sector lacks two crucial elements: the political will and the trust between actors that would see our collective commitments respected and, beyond that, make water and sanitation accessible to all. The two are closely linked. Without trust no policy can emerge or last, no finance can be raised, no partnership agreed. One of the issues for a governance system appropriate to the sector is to establish stable relationships focused on action and to create the conditions for mutual trust between all the actors dealing with water, from the managing authorities to operators (be they public or private, formal or informal), donors, NGOs and populations.

This trust requires that all actors agree to respect four principles: efficiency, accountability, transparency and integrity.

With these we can turn our collective dream into reality.

Bibliography

Camdessus, M. et al. (2004). Eau, Paris, Robert Laffont.

Frerot, A. (2006) "Proclamer le droit à l'eau ne suffit pas", Le Monde, 17 March.

Frerot, A. (2008). "Avec l'eau, pas de confiance sans transparence", Le Figaro, 4 January.

United Nations Development Programme (2006). Beyond scarcity: Power, poverty and the global water crisis.

Victoria, P. (ed.) (2005). L'accès à l'eau et à l'énergie: de la vision à l'action, Paris, Hermès-Lavoisier.

The Mini Drinking Water Network programme in Cambodia: an example of successful partnership

In Cambodia the countryside remains the poor relation in terms of connection to drinking water supplies. Less than 25% of the rural population has access to water and only 11% has running water at home. Since 2001, thanks to an innovative partnership between the private and public sectors involving GRET and the Cambodian company Kosan Engineering, villages in the provinces of Takeo, Kandal and Kampot have been connected. This programme known as MIREP (Mini-Réseau d'eau potable or Mini Drinking Water Network) was financed by the Syndicat des Eaux d'Île-de-France, Fondation Veolia Environnement, the French Ministry of Foreign Affairs and UNICEF. In all fourteen supply systems, each serving between 200 and 900 families, were built in rural villages, twelve within the concession and two on the basis of a lease.

For its part Veolia subsidised units in two of the fourteen villages (the water treatment station, the distribution network, the Prey Phkoam pumping station, the treatment facility at Angkor Borey) and facilitated technical assistance for the small Cambodian operators relating to both the production of drinking water and institutional and financial aspects and client management. However, all the units were locally designed and built, an approach which fosters replication. The MIREP projects translated into growth in capacity for initiative and organisation and the consolidation of local project management.

The results reveal the worth of such an approach:
– 90%–100% of bills are paid. Unpaid bills are extremely rare;
– the price of water is half that of water sold by the jar, barrel or jerrycan;
– connections (15–25 USD) are five times cheaper than those in a provincial city and ten times cheaper than those in Phnom Penh. This is due, among other things, to cheaper materials, shallower burial of pipes and the participation of the inhabitants in the connection works.

The entrepreneurs were able raise the finance necessary to make investments (30–60,000 USD) and the operators have demonstrated their capacity to maintain and manage the operation. Moreover the investing operators took on almost all the risks and have a 25-year commitment, as in Angkor Borey. Overall, for every 1 USD in subsidy, the private entrepreneur has contributed 2 USD. Thus the mode of finance has made it possible to lighten the financial commitment of the local authorities and to solve the problem of insolvency.

This new kind of operators have proved that they are as able as anyone to be part of the creation of drinking water networks and now plan to come together to protect themselves against corruption and exchange ideas on technical matters.

VI

WHICH DEVELOPMENT COOPERATION TOOLS FOR DEMOCRATIC GOVERNANCE?

31

Which Toolkit
for Democratic Governance?

Jean-Marc CHÂTAIGNER[1]
(Translated from the French)

Defined in the beginning of the 1990s by international financial institutions as the "sound management of public affairs", "good governance" has become a constantly mentioned priority of the donor community. The contents of "good governance" have nonetheless varied considerably over time. Early on, it allowed the International Monetary Fund (IMF) and the World Bank to recommend very liberal economic policies, combining the processes of privatisation, deregulation and the lowering of fiscal and customs taxes in line with the recommendations of the "Washington Consensus". Next, good governance was recommended in order to obtain better results in the implementation of policies in the fight against poverty and in the definition of ambitious strategies in the domains of education and health (one can observe, not without irony, that the years of structural adjustment largely contributed to diminishing the funds dedicated to these social issues and to dismantling human and administrative management capacities in these sectors). "Good governance" was presented as one of the natural compensations of the financing effort expected of donors and their commitments to increase aid made in 2002 during the Monterrey Conference of Finance and Development. The objectives of the New Partnership for Africa's Development (NEPAD), launched in 2001 by South Africa, Algeria and Senegal, notably follows this rationale.

---

1. The views expressed in this article are purely personal and can only be attributed to the author. The author would like to thank Maylis Labusquière for the assistance given in the preparation and bibliographic research linked to the writing of the article.

Donors generally emphasise the economic dimension of "good governance", which is the easiest to measure, by reducing it to the simple format of a single managerial fig leaf (defined as the capacity to manage donor-driven indicators and objectives). They do not dwell overly on the conditions of the practice of this "good governance" and do not appear particularly concerned about the authoritarian functioning of certain regimes—as long as they implement policies that conform to the recommendations of the international consensus and obtain expected results in terms of growth and integration into international trading division. Under the presidency of Paul Wolfowitz, which was, thankfully, ephemeral, the World Bank was even tempted to use a particularly limited interpretation of "good governance" by restricting it to efforts to fight corruption.

In an interesting effort aimed at ending the practice of qualifying governance as "good" or "bad", the CICID[2] endorsed for France in December 2006 a governance strategy based on the concept of "democratic governance" that avoids the trap of a definition of a level of performance (an assessment that would necessarily be relative or tarnished with misplaced culturalism). This French strategy adopts a broad definition covering two principle issues: governance is defined as a decisional process, beyond the form of government and institutional mechanisms alone; its objective is to favour the participation of different societal actors at different levels in the definition and establishment of public policies. In this perspective, the term "democratic" does not therefore designate the institutional finality of governance, but underlines its nature as a process of association in decision-making around a legitimate state. It is, in fact, an inclusive definition, considering a large number of determinants of governance that arise from the particular history of each country: legitimacy of the state as a guarantor of the general interest, reinforcement of the implicated actors' capacities of interaction, participation in the decision-making process and articulation on different levels. This approach of "democratic governance" is not to be confused therefore with the much more limited stance of Stephen Krasner[3], who promotes a regime of shared sovereignty for fragile States, which, with the support of the American government, was at the origin of the Organisation for Economic Cooperation and Development (OECD) initiative aiming to externalise and outsource the principal sovereign functions to private structures.

---

2. Interministerial Committee for International Cooperation and Development (Comité interministériel pour la coopération internationale et le développement) presided over by the Prime Minister, coordinates the actions of different administrations that are involved in the domain of development.

3. Krasner, S. (2004). "Sharing Sovereignty. New Institutions for Collapsed and Fragile States" International Security, vol. 29, n° 2, pp. 85-120.

The French approach of "democratic governance" applied to cooperation modalities goes far beyond the paradoxical injunction for "ownership" that figures in the slogans of donors, whose Paris Declaration[4] is the best illustration. The contradiction here is double: it is the donors who assign the task of directing and coordinating aid to those countries receiving it while their own practices contrast entirely with this discourse—to the point of chasing away national administrations from their own offices in order to install expatriate experts (as witnessed with real-life examples observed in Kosovo and Afghanistan). In contrast with a colonial philosophy, which is one of the inspirations of the "civilising" method of development[5], a call for democratic governance is a plead for renewing our vision of development cooperation—so that it may be used to allow a society to rethink its own modalities of public action. Directly questioning our approach to partnerships, this strategy questions in fine, the roles that development institutions grant, more or less generously, to its country partners: co-financer, project manager, client, evaluator, beneficiary, forced consumer or even "beggar" (one can only be struck by the opposition between the politically correct character of the "newspeak" in use among lenders and the expression much more raw and severe of their local representatives in the judgement of local realities, including in countries considered as good students of aid.) We should be led to wonder about the expectations of the in-country partners, not to "put them in the driver's seat", as is often suggested in the discourse of donors, but to allow them to freely choose the entire car, without imposing the cylinder, the colour of the body, the accessories and the need to go to one dealer or another.

This democratic governance approach does not, in itself, provide procedures to follow. Like any approach, it can be decreed, but will not put itself into place on its own. This is particularly true if, under the gloss of fancy language, local representatives remain responsible for completely contradictory objectives (such as goals of gaining influence, defence of short-term French interests, meeting business targets, etc.) Which instruments should then be used? They are numerous and can be of quite different types, since the principle of democratic governance is applied to all domains of aid. In a sense, it is fanciful to want to conceptualise and propose one sole model of public aid management with instruments for

---

4. "Ownership" is the first engagement of the Paris Declaration on Aid Effectiveness, adopted in 2005. It is defined here as follows: "Partner countries exercise effective leadership over their development policies, and strategies and co-ordinate development actions." (p. 3)

5. Bayard, J.-F. B. Romain, G. Thornike, B. Hibou and F. Mengin (2006). (FASOPO – Fonds d'analyse des sociétés politiques), "Legs colonial et gouvernance contemporaine", Agence Française de Développement, Working Paper n° 13, www.afd.fr.

universal use, since the principle of democratic governance proposes the establishment of consultative committees so that actors can choose their own development path for themselves. Certain tools can, of course, create favourable conditions for such systems, but they cannot define them.

This reflection will nevertheless attempt to clarify a major issue of the application of the notion of democratic governance to our programmes of international development assistance. If the instruments must integrate the particularities of beneficiary nations, they are supposed to call on the active participation of the development stakeholders from the full range of diverse actors in the same country. A dose of imagination is therefore required to not only find the mechanisms to bring together very diverse actors, from the local to international levels, but also for these programmes to be as efficient as they are open. The challenge of "democratic governance" is as simple as it is formidable: How is it possible to find the tools of public aid management while governance is only an approach and an ensemble of mechanisms that create the conditions for a long-term process of "nationalisation" of their own modalities of public action by the States and their populations? Democratic governance does not create a result but a process.

The quest for the Holy Grail of effectiveness

Donor countries placed the question of governance at the centre of their theories in order to improve the efficiency of their international development aid as well as, over the long run, the development of recipient countries. The first programmes, established through institutional support at the French Ministries of Finance, Justice and the Interior, aimed at transposing a certain number of technical formulas for the management of public affairs. However having taken into account the political realities of the recipient societies, nor the cultural and power relationships, social or ethnic relations these programmes led, for the most part, to failure. An example experienced by the author of this article was the attempt to restructure the Chadian armed forces at the beginning of the 1990s in order to create a truly national army along with the demobilisation and disarmament of a certain number of ex-servicemen. The unforeseen results of this process were very quickly evident; the reinforcement of the position of the ethnic groups closest to President Idress Deby in the army, chasing out the most upstanding and democratic actors and creating new economic networks for the recycling of out-of-date and unusable arms.

Today, governance theorists should no longer be able to ignore the question of the nature of political regimes and the particularities of each country (the use of the conditional remains essential here, because the systematic temptation of the donor and specialist of aid is to not understand local realities and thus to "imagine" or "impose" a problem that corresponds to the technical solutions they are able to propose). From this deduction is born a form of consensus for the recipient countries to not only take hold of their own development strategy and programme implementation, but they must also implicate the different actors of their society to ensure its sustainability. The call for ownership, already mentioned, leads to a demand for the definition of development projects by the actors concerned or, in other words, in conformity with the principle of participation. This step, with less than clear practical details, is today considered necessary to respect the second principle of the Paris Declaration, which recommends the alignment of national development strategies, including in the majority of developing countries where governance is considered weak.

It is worthwhile to take the time to come back to this absolute principle of a shared definition of development strategies between the concerned populations and donors, because history reserves many surprises. If one gives credence to the generally accepted idea according to which democratic institutions were determinant for economic development in the West, the most recent examples of strong economic growth in China and Vietnam contradict the universality of this principle. There is no denying that these are countries with strong regimes that do not have characteristics of Western democratic institutions and, on the contrary, have political authorities in power over a long period of time. The authorities were thus apt at leading development policies in an interventionist, if not outright authoritarian manner, that was revealed to be effective – in spite of nepotism and corruption that would be considered insurmountable in Africa. These countries demonstrated their capacity to use international aid in a way that was favourable to them. This is the case with China, now the fourth world economic power, or even India that has the presumption to regularly choose donors that correspond with their interests. In itself, the development of democracy is not a spring for development. On the contrary, it can create instabilities or even a growing gap between expectations and actual results[6] whereas, as Nancy Birdsall reminds us, impatience is indeed one of the seven deadly sins of donors[7].

---

6. Châtaigner, J.-M. and L. Ouarzazi, (2007). Fragile States and the New International Disorder, FRIDE, Working paper, www.fride.org.

7. Birdsall, N. (2004). Seven Deadly Sins: Reflections on Donors Failing, Washington, Center for Global Development, Working paper n° 50, www.cgdev.org.

The common characteristic of countries who have succeeded their development resides in their capacity to define and then to put into practice a development strategy in a broad sense that is political, economic and social, perhaps even having to impose it by force on donors. This is what Nicolas Meisel and Jacques Ould Aoudia in a recent study call "the State's capability to bring about convergence of interests and secure their strategic anticipations",[8] an essential capacity that distinguishes, at the same levels of governance, countries that have stagnant economic growth and those who realise their economic take-off. Two other factors characterise the latter countries, according to the base of criteria used in this study: a high level of education and basic healthcare as well as securing property rights to begin a more global formalisation of the rules of exchange. These objectives go in the direction of an integration of different actors of society in a progressive "depersonalisation of regulation systems".

Would theories of democratic governance therefore summon these countries without these three capacities for reinforcing their institutions in a democratic and participatory way to insure the effectiveness of their development strategy, even though their strategy is not yet truly defined? It is a simple question of sequencing and prioritisation. It is, indeed, easier to establish milestones of democratic governance for support in the long-term in a country having acquired the capacities cited above allowing to reduce uncertainties and to establish a feeling of trust. It remains to elaborate the rules of management of a country: on the one hand, by "rule formalisation" concerning the administration, economic exchanges solidarity systems; and on the other, by "the openness of systems of social regulation in the political, economic and social domains", or, in other words, the establishment of liberties, regulations of competition, decentralisation, social mobility[9] etc. These objectives go in the direction of an integration of different actors of the society at the price of a progressive "depersonalisation of the regulatory systems".

On the illusion of the double compact principle or the aid cartel's ambitions of control

One could then think that a "national development strategy" is the first presupposition in economic development. Would it be the first instrument

---

8. Meisel, N. and J. Ould Aoudia (2007). "A New Institutional Database: Institutional Profiles 2006", AFD, Working Paper, n° 46, www.afd.fr.

9. Meisel, N. and J. Ould Aoudia, op. cit.

of our governance be it democratic or not? Yes, to the extent that all strategy allows to bring together different actors at different levels around a common project.

It is rather significant that it was in the countries where the States are weakest, the rules of national governance the most unstructured and the societies that are in the most conflict that the most well developed forms of coordination were tried and planned.[10] The international community considers the reestablishment or the establishment, of a "national development strategy" as a priority in these so-called "Fragile States". In the urgency of reconstruction, the donors want to create a political platform around which the national authorities, different sections of the population and donors can come together. Ashraf Ghani, former Minister of Finance in Afghanistan and President of the Institute for State Effectiveness (ISE) theorised this idea in a double contract, double compact passed by the national authorities as much with the donors as with the population. It is the Afghan compact, the compact in Burundi, issuing from the work of consultations and negotiations of the Peace Building Commission—in addition there is also that of Sierra Leone where the same process recently took place. Different analyses agree on the weak impact of the objectives documents that resulted, due to the consensual definition of development objectives, which were broad but vague. A second critique is addressed at the weak monitoring mechanisms, as much at the level of public authorities as of civil society. Mechanisms that are in fact penalised by the overly broad representation of decision-making bodies erected to this effect and by the conflicts of interest that are at play.[11] The disconnect of this type of national strategy with reality and any possibility of operationalisation stem certainly from the will to establish consensual decisions shared by an overly large number of actors, but also to the fact that the countries concerned do not have a state structure capable of the orchestration of such a multi-sectoral policy of development.

An older instrument also corresponds to the objective of reinforcement of national strategies as stipulated in the Paris Declaration: the Poverty Reduction Strategy Papers (PRSP), introduced in 1999 in the framework of the mechanisms aiming at the reduction of debt voted on by the G8[12].

---

10. Brachet (De Catheu), J. (2007). "La coordination des acteurs en faveur des États fragiles", in Jean-Marc Châtaigner et H. Magro (dir.), États et sociétés fragiles: entre conflits, reconstruction et développement, Paris, Karthala.

11. International Crisis Group (ICG) (2007). "Afghanistan's Endangered Compact", Asia Briefing, n° 59.

12. Châtaigner, J.-M. and F. Bonet (2002). "Les enjeux pour la France d'une mise en œuvre réussie de l'initiative PPTE et de son volet additionnel bilateral", L'écho des CSLP, n° 5, October-December, www.diplomatie.gouv.fr

The PRSP has the aim of encouraging donor coordination, including at the forefront the international financial institutions and also improving relationship through consultation between these lenders and national authorities on the one hand and between national administrations and their populations on the other hand. The formulation of the PRSP in practice became more of a passport for loans and grants from international financial institutions than a dialog process leading to realistic and quantifiable engagements in poverty reduction. If the PRSP places the State in the role of coordinator of development projects, the tools can be reproached for a lightweight diagnostic of the actual levers to reduce poverty, as well as a poor understanding of the limits of human and budgetary resources of the State.

Three conclusions are called for about the reform of the PRSP. First, this type of document founded on the consensual decision-making of a large number of actors offers an analysis that is too superficial in terms of the development needs and objectives of the country. Secondly, this national strategic document, produced in coordination with the different lenders, does not replace documents that state objectives accompanying each donor's aid and include allocation criteria and specific evaluations. We know, besides, that these documents from donors are the fruit of intense and at times confrontational debates and interministerial coordination between different actors from the same national aid agency. Finally and above all, the elaboration of these national documents of objectives, realised in coordination with the lenders, conditions the granting of international aid: the national strategy therefore becomes a pretext for the granting of funds rather than a national resource management tool.

Regarding the failure of these coordination tools for the elaboration of a "national development strategy" upon which they can be in agreement, two questions must be resolved to define adapted instruments or to create new ones: the reinforcement of State capacities in the role of coordinator of a national project and the imposition of exogenous norms for the same national development project.

Towards an endogenous definition of the "national development strategy"

The imposition of exogenous norms on a complex and unique reality is recognised as a principal cause of failure of development policies. Henceforth, how is it possible to meet, in an endogenous manner, this objective of reinforcing "national development strategies" advocated by the Paris Declaration? A strategy that proves to be, for the donors, an instrument upon which to base their efforts in order to improve the effectiveness of their aid in a consultative manner. The role of the State is essential in the definition of this national project. However, are there not greater chances that country particularities and diversity be taken into account in this project if a participatory process is led by the public authorities? The concept of participation can be questioned under many angles. Who represents whom? And even, what participation are we demanding abroad that has truly been instituted in France? As pertinent as these questions are, they correspond in fact to the differences in terms of political participation peculiar to each country. The cooperation of a lender can encourage the establishment of systems allowing different categories of the population to progressively become involved as citizens. The interest of the donor's intervention resides, a priori, in the possibility it gives to these systems to exist through their funding, but also through the mediating function that this intervention can have by bringing people who do not generally meet with one another, to have discussions at the heart of such occasions.

These participatory apparatuses for the elaboration of a development project can play out on several levels, while enriching the project throughout the process. This is, for example, the principle of the National Solidarity Project funded by the Afghan State that aims for the establishment at the village level (in 5000 participating villages) of an inclusive elected entity in charge of defining and implementing community projects with the participation of the population. These community entities have the responsibility of passing up, through a subtle play of hierarchy, information about the needs met at the local level in order to better define the State sectoral policies. Currently, the main difficulties of the project, which is in constant evolution, are the State's disbursements for community projects. In addition, the creation of this type of mechanism can, through the contribution of financing, reinforce local conflicts of interest or incite new ones by the establishment of new illegitimate authorities. Just as Juana Brachet has correctly pointed out, in spite of its limits, participatory development has the advantage of making mechanisms of local governance emerge in countries that have had none whatsoever.[13]

The local scale effectively seems the most appropriate for the participatory definition of development needs, the elaboration of projects and their monitoring and evaluation, according to endogenous criteria. That is, indeed, the principle that founds local democracy projects, notably

---

13. Brachet (De Catheu), J. (2007). "Le développement par les communautés : l'ambition de transformer les États fragiles", in J.-M. Châtaigner and H. Magro (eds.), États et sociétés fragiles: entre conflits, reconstruction et développement, op. cit.

with the establishment of "participatory budgets" in certain municipalities of Latin America. It is more than likely that these processes would benefit from an external consideration. Not only that of the evaluating donor, but also the regard of an actor of the same nature through an exchange of experiences. This idea is the basis for a development fund for African cities, presented by the Charles Léopold Mayer Foundation for the Progress of Man. The cities meet with a seal of approval guaranteeing respect for the "Six principles of Yaoundé"[14] regarding the delivery of basic services. The cities defining the objectives and criteria of their programmes are no longer subject to donor's conditions. The respect of these criteria is assured by a double evaluation: that of the local population and that of their peers, the latter allowing for the creation of a bank of successful experiences for this standard. Much more than just ownership, these assessing processes, if rigorous, allow the involvement of different parties in a change strategy over the long term.

If the local level necessarily connects with the national level and is able to enrich national development policies with its observations; at the regional level, an exchange of experiences can also participate in the endogenous definition of a national development strategy. A regional African NEPAD project, the African Peer Review Mechanism (APRM), seems to have shown its value on this issue (but is regrettably attracting relatively little interest within the French aid system). This programme, even if expensive, bureaucratic and lacking flexibility (to succeed, it relies on the strong adhesion of the country partner) is largely based on a logic of shared experiences. The analyses of the APRM lead to the publication of a report, based on an annual evaluation, which contains a plan of action that the State commits to respect. The State is thereby established and reinforced in its role as the leader of the "national development strategy" as much in the eyes of peers as in those of society.

The State becomes legitimate, above all, through its capacity to exert its authority and to assure the management of public policies in the general interest. Which instruments of reinforcement of state capacities demand an adaptation to move in the direction of democratic governance?

---

14. The Africités 3 Summit defined urban governance quality in terms of delivering basic services, six principles from Yaoundé, broken down into 23 criteria that can be used in an evaluation grid. P. Calame (2006). Les termes de référence de l'étude de faisabilité du fonds de développement fondé sur les critères de Yaoundé, Methodological Working Paper (bip 3251).

Technical assistance or the risks of the poisoned remedy

The founding principles of the democratic governance approach are alignment with national strategies and ownership by local actors. These two principles presume real capacities exist as much in the heart of the state as in civil society organisations in the recipient countries. This fact places the question of capacity building at the heart of governance strategy.

Capacity-building tools are numerous and technical assistance is one that seems symptomatic of the contradictions of the donor community concerning the application of the governance doctrine. It is, in any case, an important subject, since technical assistance represents a quarter of spending on official development assistance (ODA) at the global level.[15] And it is also one of the most controversial points in recent debates on international aid. Such is the case for rehabilitation that Paul Collier makes, according to which technical assistance has a decisive role in making true reform processes see the light of day in States of weak governance. The reason for technical assistance is, in fact, simple: if the country does not have local competencies to put into place its reforms, the donor must see to it to provide them. However the reality is much more complex and technical assistance often lends itself much more to being assistance as substitution than assistance that leads to autonomy. The expatriation of foreigners at the heart of Southern countries' administrations can lead, in fact, to a distortion between admitted practices and an unconscious imitation or a transfer of a model that does not benefit the administration if the monitoring mechanisms do not assure its continuation. There is also distortion in the level of salaries at the heart of the same administration and important consequences, finally, on management and the valuing of local or regional elites.

The failures of the system of technical cooperation are particularly well known.[16] Beyond the questions of institutional organisation and of reactivity and flexibility of the technical cooperation systems that continue to be based on the permanent expatriation of personnel, two structural questions remain. First of all, technical cooperation is determined more on the basis of the available instruments than by the measure of an overall strategic vision of the country's needs. Secondly, technical cooperation never ceases to maintain the ambiguity between direct aid and a policy of influence,

---

15. Collier, P. (2007). The Bottom Billion. Why the Poorest Countries are failing and what can be done about it, Oxford University Press.

16. For a detailed analysis of the strengths and weaknesses of the French system see the report of the Haut Conseil pour la coopération internationale (HCCI) (2002). Quelles ressources humaines pour quelle coopération?

because the donor plays the different roles of funder, project manager and client. The substitution can even extend (in cases that are not all that rare) to the formulation of demands in the place of the country partner. And thirdly, technical assistance remains too often detached from administrations and local bureaucracies. The accompaniment of the State can be pertinent as much in reinforcing administration capacities as in the reinforcement of civil society capacities, in order that the latter play the role both of a balancing power and a partner with political authorities in the framework of a dialog. This ambition demands open recruitment for all socio-professional categories for the technical experts and a radical procedure of untying of technical assistance (the only way to reinforce legitimacy and to make an undisputable process). The diversity of recruitment would definitively confirm the already urgent need of common training between the technical assistance of different donors, in order to give them the tools of analysis and comprehension of shared situations.

All of the problems evoked above bring up the key question of the mobilisation of local competencies. Local elites often work in the diaspora or in the parallel networks of international NGOs, multinational enterprises or in consultancies. Their presence in such networks allows, at times, to legitimate foreign projects by their association with one part of the project. International aid would gain in the long-term from finding systems of integration of local competencies at the heart of national institutions through technical cooperation; this would resolve not only the problems of substitution and of legitimacy of technical cooperation, but also that of the drain of local elites. Some international cooperation actors have given themselves the objective of reinforcing local competencies at the heart of their own structures, such as through decentralised development programmes or those of certain NGOs. A contrario, most actors attract these elites to their organisations, thus creating a social gap with the attribution of high salaries, a phenomenon that can be proven irreversible regarding the reintegration of these elites into national structures. Technical cooperation could give itself the opposite objective of encouraging the mobility of local elites by co-financing incentive measures with the country partner to encourage integration into national institutions, by identifying in the immigrant community of the donor country a workforce capable of moving to reinforce the structures of the country of origin. For greater legitimacy, these aid experts could come from neighbouring countries, in the framework of South-South cooperation as has already been done in South Africa and Brazil and elsewhere.

Such a widening of the field of technical cooperation actors to include people of many origins would imply the development of international call for bids for technical experts, whose selection criteria, mission monitoring and evaluation would be guaranteed by a standard or a system of certification that would be not only national, but also regional or even international. This ambitious system would demand the asking country to provide a systematic definition of the terms of reference of the mission, as well as implication in the monitoring, allowing the country to break the contract if the objectives are not met. This solution is only foreseeable in the case that the asking country takes upon itself the financial charge of the expert, either exclusively or at least with a majority stake.

The country partner asking for the expert goes therefore from the status of being just the client to being the project manager as well. Such a framework for technical cooperation would allow, in addition, to escape from all political accusations, to place greater value on competencies from the South, all the while reorienting them towards local hiring circuits and, above all, reintroducing a dose of flexibility that is necessary to face the current challenges. The issues of opening the field of intervention of technical assistance demonstrate today that the accompaniment of the State can be fulfilled in the reinforcement not only of its institutional capacities but also those of society at different levels.

The Support of the State at all levels

All actions of State reinforcement that are today concerned with questions of governance must work on the creation of systems of legitimisation and their integration with international, regional and local levels. The local level favours endogenous resolution of development problems and it is for this reason that donors have been investing for several years in the process of decentralisation. By encouraging the development of local institutions adapted to local realities, one favours the emergence, over time, of negotiated processes between different actors in the local area. This level is decisive in the settlement, for example, of property disputes, thanks to renewed interest in informal management practices, at times based on customs, with a perspective of normative pluralism.

The issue then is how to reinforce elected bodies in their role of animators of local development, all the while reinforcing the different social components of their area. It is with this dual objective that projects of the United Nations Capital Development Fund (UNCDF)[17] in Mauritania and Niger (projects including bi- and multi-lateral funding from the French and

---

17. Fund associated with the United Nation Development Programme of which voluntary bilateral financing and donor financing have not ceased to decrease, while studies, evaluations and audits conducted have always, over the years, confirmed results obtained and real effectiveness in the field.

European Ministries of Foreign Affairs). These two projects bring together four components: institutional support, capacity building, establishment of community development funds and funds for local initiatives and capitalisation. While the project takes care to work in parallel with the reinforcement of community leaders, including those of civil society, confusions exist between the two, notably in relation to the interchangeable use of the two funds. This observation at the mid-point of the project is revelatory of the time investment necessary for the constitution of a multi-actor political process in which roles are defined and bundled. On the other hand, the capitalisation component destined to support national policies is, for the moment, used to improve systems already in place.

Another example of a multilateral programme[18], the Pericles Programme in Mauritania, shows the strategic importance of the implication of national structures in this kind of decentralisation programme. The Mauritanian State is involved from the first phase to encourage a network of four resource centres with national mission. Aiming for the reinforcement of territorial authorities, this four-year programme shows the will to coordinate donors, as well as the State, with local authorities, in order to put into place an integrated approach of decentralisation based on a common vision. Such programmes aiming for complementarity between policies of de-concentration and decentralisation favour a coherent policy of territorial development, likely to guarantee the respect of diversity and national cohesion. It is thanks to the democratisation and reinforcement of local decision-making processes that the national governance policy is reinforced.

Conversely, with the same interest in guaranteeing coherent policies of territorial management, the State can reinforce itself with the sharing of experiences at the regional level. Such is the positive outcome of the AFRISTAT programme (Economic and Statistical Observatory of Sub-Saharan Africa)[19], actively supported by French cooperation since its founding (in the logic of intelligent disengagement from aid of substitution run by INSEE, which had prevailed before) which aims at the reinforcement of national statistical services.

Today, the AFRISTAT project receives the majority of its financing from African members states and their experts are primarily African.

---

18. This programme, started in 2008, is co-financed and implemented by Germany French, Spanish and European Commission development funds.

19. The AFRISTAT treaty was signed between fourteen states in the Franc zone in 1991. This project played an important role in the harmonisation of prices at the interior of the UEMOA (West African Economic and Monetary Union) and encouraged the training of national agents in the national accounting method ERESTES. It also works toward the homogenisation of concepts and means of measuring the informal sector, on the updating of agricultural statistics, as well as the harmonisation of monitoring methods of economic conditions, of macro-economic modelling and of short-term forecasting.

It is a part of numerous efforts necessary to the reinforcement of the State's capacity to absorb international aid and to assure the management according to its own criteria. It is not sufficient to advocate budgetary aid free from lending conditions, it is also necessary to assist the State in the development of its capacities for ownership, in defining criteria for the use of aid and in assuring aid management in terms of public finance. This African project has an essential impact in the improvement of governance in the countries concerned, because it reinforces the capacities of States, in a perspective of regional harmonisation, while making quality information available to citizens; a necessary condition for their involvement in political processes of consultation.

The State can also delegate its sovereignty to regional organisations for the sake of coherence. The Organisation for the Harmonisation of Business Law (OHADA)[20] created, in a decade, unified legal norms at the regional level to improve the governance of States in the domain of economic exchanges. This African organisation established several areas of competence in the region, through a training centre and a high court, that diffuse this culture of legal security with the aim of instituting a climate more favourable to trade and investment in the region.

These examples of interstate consultation systems reinforce legislation and national capacities and encourage new modes of governance by the interaction of different actors at the centre of the same network that stimulates the sharing of experiences and competencies South-South and North-South. The two examples cited are also examples of interstate African organisations that define their own criteria of governance. One must also mention that these initiatives are based on a significant investment in research, investment that can be public but also private. That is the case of the Mo Ibrahim Foundation, which, in an independent manner and with exclusively private funds, not only carries out a monitoring function, but also incites change in the functioning of States through the definition of African criteria for the assessment of State governance.

All organisations, no matter their position as decentralised, devolved or independent, national, local or regional, can play its role in reinforcing the State in its capacities or in commissioning the State to be a legitimate representative in the management of public affairs.

---

20. Created by the Port-Louis Treaty in 1993, OHADA today includes sixteen State members from Western and Central Africa.

Opening up other perspectives?

This reflection has been deliberately focused on the State in its role as coordinator of development issues and on questions of capacity building in development. This is because, as we have demonstrated, the State is the required point of passage of decisive reforms in the first place, then of harmonious coordination at different levels on the same territory for sustainable human development. This is a position that France has always defended in spite of the ever-changing theoretical fashions in the development field. However there must also be a series of actors to put into a network to support or control this State in its management of public affairs, to make it consultative and shared in order to create sustainable human development.

The notion of democratic governance implies the establishment, as rapidly as possible, of a form of subsidiarity in the activity of donor cooperation for the establishment of programmes, based on the competencies and the difference stances of each actor: international organisations, NGOs, foundations, decentralised cooperation, networks of research and action and even private enterprises. In parallel, the major difficulty for partner countries consists in acquiring the capacity to harmoniously orchestrate these different types of networks in order to create multi-actor decision-making systems that would be respectful of the particularities of each territory, but also competent, effective and complementary in their development actions at different levels.

We should, with a certain audacity and without bounds, rethink our national development aid with respect to democratic governance. This does not mean to destroy what already exists, but rather to establish new modes of relating with renewed instruments in order to definitively break with the normative theses developed by certain donors. Assessment and capitalisation could be at the heart of this process, because, by establishing inclusive and participatory networks and organisms (North-South or South-South), they oblige us to be consistent with the directive for ownership. They converge on the support of a process of long-term learning that allows each society to reinvent, to reinforce and to develop their own methods of public action, nourished at the same time by their history and international experience. This is a major undertaking to define refined governance indicators that respect the diversity and particularities of each society, based on a game of exchanging glances from the outside to the inside.

Such an ambition already requires a thorough reflection on behalf of donors on their modes of cooperation to give preference to:

– Predictable aid instead of a short-term investment in programmes;
– Working in an inclusive network instead of tied aid controlled at every step; and
– Long-term work on quality, capable of being assessed in a subjective manner, instead of investments demanding a rapid and quantifiable return.

32

Reinventing Governance to achieve the Millennium Development Goals in Africa

New Approaches and Tools

Gilbert HOUNGBO

In 2007 the world passed the midway point between the adoption of the Millennium Development Goals (MDGs) in 2000 and the 2015 target date for their achievement[1]. Although there has been significant progress on some of the goals by a number of countries, Sub-Saharan Africa as a whole is not on track to achieve the goals. This outcome is in spite of improved political and economic governance that has been witnessed across much of the continent during this decade. Human poverty, in its many forms, remains pervasive, and even the best-governed countries are yet to sufficiently tackle the interlocking challenges of poverty and underdevelopment. Whilst the proportion of people living on one dollar a day or less has declined from 46 to 41% since 1999, reaching the MDG target of halving extreme poverty by 2015 requires a near doubling in the current pace of progress. Despite the recent progress that shows a levelling off in new rates of infection in many countries, HIV/AIDS and its devastating impact on human capacity and service delivery remain a major challenge.

African countries will need significant increases in public and private investments in order to reach the MDGs. In recent years, UNDP has stepped up support to the countries in the region to conduct comprehensive assessments of the financial, capacity and infrastructure investment requirements for meeting the MDGs by 2015. These costings

---

1. The Millennium Development Goals Report. New York, United Nations, 2006.

have to be translated into medium-term budgetary frameworks and appropriately supporting macroeconomic frameworks put in place. In many cases, the financings have to be frontloaded and more predictability of ODA inflows ensured. The countries also need to be supported to put in place more robust and accountable implementation and monitoring arrangements.

However, even if secured, in most cases such scaled-up investment programmes will fall short of the desired impacts unless accompanied by comprehensive governance reforms, on the supply side, and a deepening of democracy, on the demand side, to enhance accountability in all its dimensions. This is because at the heart of the challenge to meet the MDGs is success in addressing structural governance deficits and enhancing the ability of the states to deliver effectively essential regulation and public services to their citizens.

As Blaise Compaore, President of Burkina Faso stated at the opening ceremony of the Seventh (7th) Africa Governance Forum (AGF) in October 2007,

> "building the capacities of the state is the missing link for development and democratization in Africa. Development requires solid, high-performing institutions, among which the first in line is the State, an essential in a functioning economy and society."[2]

Reaching the MDGs requires political will, resources and capacities. But achieving the goals by 2015 depends on much more than merely technical choices. Crucially, it also depends on the capacity of the poor to exercise citizenship and have political power and voice in the political decisions that affect them.

This paper discusses the linkages between governance, deepening democracy, creation of developmental States and their centrality in meeting the MDGs in Africa. It highlights new approaches and tools, and examples of how UNDP and its partners are repositioning support to governance programmes in Africa with a greater emphasis on understanding and addressing structural governance deficits, supporting transformational leadership networks and developing tools for making economic growth and service delivery pro-poor.

---

2. UNDP, Better Governance Tops Africa's Development Agenda. Press release 24 October 2007 http://content.undp.org/go/newsroom/2007/october/africa-governance-forum-20071024.en

Deepening democracy to meet the Millennium Development Goals

UNDP support for democracy in Africa is grounded in principles that reflect the core values of human development, which are to expand people's choices and capabilities. It also embeds in the argument that democratic regimes are better able to promote overall levels of economic growth and national prosperity, although empirical evidence for the claim is inconclusive. Furthermore, the support for democracy upholds the belief that States are less likely to go war with each other when both are democracies; hence, the more Africa becomes democratic the less would be the possibilities of conflicts and war and the more peaceful the continent would be.

Attributing the conditions of abject poverty in Africa mostly to the absence of democratic governance, UNDP resolved to support democratization processes and good governance practice and the introduction of the MDGs reinforced this resolve. Indeed, as far back as the mid-1990s, the UNDP defined good governance[3] and contended that sustainable development was difficult outside that framework and introduced democratic governance as one of its core program areas. Since then, democratic governance has emerged as UNDP's largest development focus area in terms of program coverage and expenditure. Countries have been "supported to develop and share national solutions to the challenges of democratic governance, focusing on inclusive participation, responsive institutions and the internationally agreed principles of human rights, gender equality and anticorruption."

The achievement of these democratic imperatives requires a state capable of delivering development. The lack of capacity of state institutions, civil society and the private sector and other non-state actors are the greatest constraint to governance and development delivery in Africa. Where institutions are weak, a capable State remains indispensable for effective service delivery, good governance and development oversight. State capacity needs strengthening for the state to respond effectively to public demands. Strengthened institutions, including the civil society and the private sector as well as controlling corruption are some of the key requirements that enable the state to deliver its obligations to citizens.

---

3. According to the UNDP, "Governance can be seen as the exercise of economic, political and administrative authority to manage a country's affairs at all levels. It comprises the mechanisms processes and institutions through which citizens and groups articulate their interests, exercise their legal rights, meet their obligations and mediate their differences." See Governance for Sustainable development, a UNDP policy paper January 1997.

To make democracy deliver and to achieve the MDGs, democratic structures, institutions and values must be consolidated and deepened. Deepening democracy is to strengthen and entrench the human and material elements of existing democratic institutions and processes, making them more responsive, effective and efficient in their service delivery. It is also to intensify official and private respect for and function of democratic principles, values and culture. To deepen democracy, therefore, is to add momentum, through programmed activities, to the political processes where certain freedoms and movements towards more democratic regimes are already present, albeit to a limited degree, but where the power-holders and citizens show a commitment to democratic consolidation. The principal aim of deepening democracy, therefore, is to introduce interventions that would entrench the practice of democracy and good governance.

Since the wave of democratization that swept across Africa at the beginning of the 1990s, a number of countries in the region have introduced innovative approaches to democratic governance that hold considerable promise for deepening democracy and strengthening the foundations for human development, human rights, civic engagement and gender equity. At the centre of this is the conduct of regular and broadly credible elections, given the fact that genuine democratization begins with good and legitimate elections and that they remain critical for indirect forms of social accountability in representative democracy. All over the continent, UNDP, working with other development partners, has provided significant financial, technical, political and development management support to these elections. Notable recent examples are in Tanzania, the Democratic Republic of Congo, Benin, Senegal, Mauritania, Zambia and Togo. The nature and type of support has ranged from building the institutional and systems capacities of the election management bodies, support for voter registration, building the capacity of political parties and that of civil society for more effective electoral oversight, to supporting the development of a code of conduct on basic ethical principles and enhanced participation of women in the electoral process.

Besides elections, democratic institutions in several countries, including Parliaments, the Judiciary, human rights commissions, civil society organizations and integrity bodies are given technical and financial support to strengthen their capacity and deepen their role in the democratic processes. In essence, UNDP is assisting in the political transformation of African countries as part of what Samuel Huntington called the 'third wave' of democratization[4]. In Tanzania, UNDP is the anchor and coordinator for a four-year multi-million dollar program

---

4. Huntington, S. P. (1993) The ThirdWave. Oklahoma, The University of Oklahoma Press.

introduced in 2006 by development partners to deepen democracy, focusing on the legislature, electoral management bodies, political parties and civic education.

New tools and approaches: examples from UNDP cooperation

Over the years, the UNDP has adopted several innovative approaches and tools to support the reinvention of governance and deepening democracy in Africa. These have included strategic support for continental initiatives and the creation of specialized forums and institutions to research, discuss and strategize for enhancing the democratization processes and good governance. Among them are the following.

African Peer Review Mechanism

Perhaps the most innovative approach to reinventing governance, the Africa Peer Review Mechanism (APRM) was endorsed in 2003 by African leaders in Abuja, Nigeria to complement the New Partnership for Africa's Development (NEPAD) that was adopted earlier in 2001 in South Africa to herald what was termed the "African renaissance." With the long-term objective to "eradicate poverty" and place African countries on "the path of sustainable growth and development," NEPAD's adoption included the pledge to promote democracy and transparent and accountable governance. This pledge no doubt was informed by the lessons from the painful experiences of bad governance and the debilitating impact it had on human development. Hence, the recognition of good and responsible governance as being key to addressing the African development conundrum and the governments looked to a new development paradigm that subscribed to best practices.

An instrument for periodic peer review and self-monitoring of states, the APRM was introduced to actualize the NEPAD objectives by ensuring the adherence of African States to the values, codes and standards of democracy, political, economic and corporate governance so as to provide the governance framework conducive for reducing poverty. Essentially, it requires the State to undertake an independent, comprehensive and all-inclusive assessment along the lines of SWOT[5] analysis of those four key areas of governance in order to establish the baseline for achieving

---

5. Strengths, Weaknesses, Opportunities and Threats.

conformity. Should the reviewed state resolve to rectify the identified deficits, corrective measures are instituted, including the abrogation or amendment of existing laws found to be incongruous with democratic practice, enactment of new laws and policies to enhance or introduce good governance, institutional development, capacity building, skills training, improvement in education, health, etc. When such measures are designed and pursued diligently they innovate governance, create political stability, stimulate economic growth and strengthen the State's capacity to deliver effectively and efficiently the obligations for socioeconomic development and the well being of citizens.

The new vision for Africa's development concurred with UNDP's longstanding recognition of good governance practices as the basis for building capable States, enabling the organization to readily embrace the APRM and becoming one of three key strategic partners. The others are the UN Economic Commission for Africa and African Development Bank. Since then UNDP has endeavoured to support the process in countries where the APRM has been adopted. It has also supported regional and continental workshops to review and strengthen the process.

While the APRM offers immense opportunities to reinvent governance, particularly in promoting good political leadership, re-engineering the State and public institutions for efficiency and effectiveness, and strengthening a culture of political dialogue and popular participation, several challenges must be addressed to ensure its success. First is the political will and unremitting commitment of States. The utility of the APRM dissipates once the interest of the political leadership or commitment to its independence wanes. Second is the effectiveness and dedication of the process managers, i.e., the Governing Council and executive leadership of the APRM Secretariat. They are the key drivers and their competence, dynamism and commitment to the process are crucial in determining success. The process suffers when the managers assume, rightly or wrongly, to be gatekeepers for government, seeking to "protect" it from what might be embarrassing exposures. Third is the competence of the Technical Review Teams and the thoroughness with which the assessment is carried out. Finally, the challenge is to harmonize the Plan of Action with existing development frameworks in order to avoid parallel strategies and duplications. In a nutshell, governance could be reinvented in Africa by means of the APRM with good governance and economic growth as the consequences. Thus, the objectives of the MDGs to reduce poverty are more likely to be achieved should the APRM be implemented diligently by acceding states.

Africa Governance Forum

Initially a partnership between UNDP, the Economic Commission for Africa (ECA) and the UN Special Initiative on Africa (UNISA), the Africa Governance Forum was crafted and instituted as one of the innovative responses to the continent's governance challenges, with the express objective to a) strengthen partnerships among African governments, its civil society and development partners for improved governance b) facilitate knowledge sharing on best practices in governance c) develop concrete and bankable programmes for joint action and d) create an environment supportive of resource mobilisation for governance-related interventions. The AGF has since provided a unique opportunity for a structured dialogue among African countries, its state and non-state actors, and its development partners on the continent's overarching governance challenges, helped define priority challenges and spurred the institutionalisation of good governance practices at country levels.

Since the AGF's establishment in 1997, seven forums have been organised on the following crucial themes:
- Governance in Africa
- Accountability and transparency
- Conflict management for durable peace and sustainable development
- Parliaments as an instrument for Good Governance
- Local Governance for poverty eradication
- Implementing APRM: challenges and opportunities
- Building the capable State in Africa

The utility and qualitative impact of the AGF series lie in the fact that it has provided a practical platform for policy discourse on common governance challenges, strengthened cross-fertilisation of ideas, promoted a better sharing of experiences and facilitated consensus building on governance standards and norms. In some respects, it has become a vehicle for defining an 'African Consensus on Governance', and by virtue of its inclusive character brought the perspectives of non-state actors - principally civil society, academia and the private sector - to fully bear on the norm and agenda setting, as well as on the governance response and actions. The AGF preparatory processes at national levels, which typically involve broad-based national level consultations has contributed to fostering shared national perspectives, and a shared agenda for informing domestic policy formulation and programmatic actions. And the AGF has proven to be an effective vehicle for mobilising partnerships behind the Africa governance policy agenda. The seventh AGF recently concluded in Ouagadougou saw a partnership between the Government of Burkina Faso, ECA, the Africa Development Bank, UN DESA, UNCDF, the Office of the Special Advisor for Africa at the UN Secretariat, and UNDP.

UNDP's role in the AGF is largely catalytic. At the regional level, UNDP plays a lead role in organising the forums, facilitates the codification and sharing of the knowledge generated, and advocates for the mainstreaming of the AGF outcomes into national governance processes and programmes. At the country level, UNDP Country Offices have provided policy and organisational support to the national level consultations and national level programming of the outputs of the forums. Going forward, the AGF will continue to be an important platform for governance discourse in Africa. Key challenges that remain are to succeed in scaling up bankable programmes derived from the forums, and their integration into the national governance agenda, as well as to mobilise the requisite domestic resources and, where required, development assistance to support their implementation.

UNDP Global Programme for Parliamentary Strengthening

An important missing element in the governance framework for the MDGs is the lack of a robust parliamentary engagement and oversight of the executive arm of the governments in most of the African countries. There is increasing consensus that parliamentarians and local level authorities have a vital role in ensuring the accountability of governments at both national and sub-national levels to their commitment to the attainment of MDGs by 2015. Apart from engaging governments on strategy and policy processes with respect to the MDGs, parliamentarians could also exert pressure on the governments to allocate adequate resources for meeting the financing requirements of the MDGs.

The UNDP Global Programme for Parliamentary Strengthening (GPPS), financially supported by the Government of Belgium, and most of whose beneficiaries are in Africa, is a very instrumental initiative in this connection. The current GPPS constitutes the third phase of the initiative, with the previous phases having been implemented in 1999 – 2003 for GPPS I, and 2003 – 2008 for GPPS II. The evaluation of the first two phases explicitly indicates that the GPPS III could be used even more instrumentally for strengthening parliamentary involvement with MDGs, and the new instruments being promoted by the programme could be used to support that process as well. This could also be related to increasing the focus on parliamentary engagement in economic governance and budget review and control. In a bid to maximize the impact of this GPPS III, synergies are to be fostered between it and UNDP Africa's related regional initiatives for supporting MDG advocacy and social mobilization in African countries as well as the Millennium Campaign's initiatives.

Africa Governance Institute

The contemporary acceptance of the primacy of good governance and its direct linkage with human development has generated a plethora of research and policy work in the governance domain all over Africa and beyond. In Africa, the outputs of these have helped shape policy formulation in some cases, but it has also highlighted crucial and urgent challenges that remain, as well as opportunities for scaling up recent gains in governance. This growing number of research centres, policy think thanks and civil society organisations that have emerged to do research, training and advocacy on governance is a welcome development for the Africa region, but at the continental level there has been no real anchor to foster greater intellectual cohesion on regional governance issues. The absence of an independent Pan-African policy and research institution to support the work of the African Union and sub-regional organisations in the promotion of democracy, good governance and human rights has been seen as a major weakness.

With the support of UNDP, the African Union and other partners, notably the Government of France, the Africa Governance Institute is being established to address this gap. The AGI has been conceptualised as a centre of excellence on governance and democratisation in Africa, and a broker and repository of ideas, information and knowledge. The Institute will focus on four overarching objectives as follows:

– To fill gaps in existing knowledge, training and networking in the promotion of good governance on the continent.

– Act as the anchor for coordinating and harmonising governance research and policy work all over Africa, and play a leadership and catalytic role in the codification and dissemination of lessons learnt and best practices in governance on the continent.

– To promote a common vision on good governance in Africa. Whilst the concept and principles of good governance are universal, their practical applications must be contextualised in the sociological and cultural realities in order to enhance ownership and maximise its relevance to the national and regional context

– To promote a better understanding of governance by facilitating collaborative research through networking governance-related institutions, and the development and dissemination of cutting-edge knowledge products, appropriately packaged to enhance their policy usefulness.

In essence, the AGI will serve as a coordinating anchor for fostering a community of governance practice on the continent. It will help to promote a deeper understanding of structural and emerging governance challenges and through its policy work, advocacy and sensitisation, assist in engendering stronger and a more broad-based ownership of the governance agenda.

As with the Africa Governance Forum, UNDP's role on the AGI has been catalytic. It has been a key champion of the idea of the Institute, and importantly provided human and technical resources to conceptualise the framework and nurture its progress. But it has not done this alone. It has worked with African partners and promoted extensive partnerships in support of the initiative. The Africa Union, the ECA, the African Training and Research Centre in Administration and Development (CAFRAD), CODESRIA, the African Development Bank and the Government of France have been key partners, and so has an eminent group of African Policy makers and intellectuals who have guided the evolution of the process through their work as the AGI Steering Committee.

Southern Africa Capacity Initiative

Healthy democracies require fair and efficient public administrations. A capable state needs institutions that work, such as a civil service that pays a decent wage; a justice system that operates independently; a parliament that stands up when those in power step out of line; power, water and other utilities that deliver services efficiently to all and a free media that gives citizens the information they need to decide how to cast their next vote. Such institutions cannot be developed overnight and need to be built into each country's development strategy. Most countries in southern Africa have been facing constrained institutional capacity for decades for several reasons including inadequate financial, human and technological resources as well as economically induced emigration of professionals ("brain drain").

With an average of 20 percent HIV prevalence among adults in the mainland SADC countries, AIDS-related illness and death exacerbate these existing problems, severely compromising the ability of governments to govern, deliver basic services and sustain its administration. The Southern Africa Capacity Initiative (SACI) project was formulated in response to the capacity challenges resulting from increasing HIV and AIDS, food insecurity and deepening poverty (a triple threat) in the Southern Africa sub-region. A 2004 preliminary review of the public service in the region showed that most institutions were operating on "pre-HIV and AIDS period" norms and procedures and many governments in southern Africa, which has the highest HIV infection rates in the world, had last reviewed the number of employees in public service in 1974.

SACI promotes best business practices used in the private sector to help identify bottlenecks in service delivery, and designs interventions to produce better time management and eliminate duplication. SACI also uses volunteers to fill in skills shortages. Previously hospitals in Botswana had to wait four months for the delivery of emergency medicines, but with the help of the SACI team of policy and managements specialists this has now been slashed to just six days. In Namibia SACI has helped slash the time for issuing passports from 24 months to three days without the Ministry of Home Affairs needing to employ any additional staff.[6]

Support for public sector reform goes beyond southern Africa. In Liberia, for example, UNDP helped shepherd a peaceful election in 2005, following 14 years of war, and is now assisting with the rebuilding of its shattered public institutions. With UNDP support, the Government is revising the mandates of its 20 ministries. It is revamping its civil service regulations, creating a code of conduct for public servants and overhauling financial management procedures. An assessment of local governments, which are often on the frontline of public social service delivery, has produced recommendations geared toward defining their role in Liberia's recovery and re-development.

Conclusion

Despite monumental challenges that Africa still faces, over the past half-decade, the continent as a whole has witnessed strong positive economic growth, enhanced democratic practices and more effective governance, and that conflicts that have been the bane of the continent are generally on the decline. The combination of improved economic and political governance is laying an irreversible foundation for enhancing Africa's competitive base and its better participation in the globalised economy. With support of its development partners, Africa is getting its act together, and turning a corner in its development.

Most African countries are ready to replicate and scale-up the successes from around the continent, but they require more and better-quality official development assistance to finance public investments to achieve the MDGs. While aid to sub-Saharan Africa increased during the first few years of the Millennium, it has remained virtually unchanged since 2004, if one excludes one-off debt relief and humanitarian assistance. Donors need to accelerate their plans to scale up assistance, to maintain the credibility of the 2005 pledge to double aid to Africa

---

6. UN initiative speeds up service delivery, IRIN News 9 October 2006, http://www.irinnews.org/report.aspx?reportid=61282.

by 2010 in order to ensure that the MDGs are achieved by 2015. On their part, African countries need to sustain the present trends towards more democratic regimes as well as strengthen accountable and effective implementation and monitoring mechanisms for development programmes. Above all, it is of utmost importance that current and emerging governance initiatives be better connected to the energies of the people, to make the people the real driving force in the on-going positive change. These are cardinal preconditions for the attainment of the MDGs. The recent gains need to be consolidated, and it must done there is a sense of urgency.

33

The Security Sector Reform in Fragile States

Beyond Capacity Building, the Example of Transitional Justice

Serge RUMIN
(Translated from the French)

After an introductory clarification of the notions of "security sector" and "transitional justice", as well as their interconnections, we will examine, in light of diverse experiences, the challenges presented by security sector reform (SSR) in states called "fragile"[1]. The source of fragility in these States, as it is meant here, is to be found in the legacy of a more or less open, armed conflict that plays out, very often, on the ashes of an authoritarian regime. We will first discuss the traditional responses to this state fragility in the SSR framework and will next explore another approach of institutional reform, basing ourselves on the example of transitional justice, which opens the door to other, complementary, actions.

Security Sector Reform and transitional justice: a global approach defined by the stakes

The notion of a security sector has for some time been limited to the military and paramilitary field and been thought of exclusively in terms of

---

1. Afghanistan, Bosnia-Herzegovina, Burundi, Liberia, Haiti, Kosovo, Mali, Uganda, Chad and the Democratic Republic of the Congo.

its state dimension, in opposition to a societal dimension. This notion has now evolved with, on the one hand, the theme of security which imposes itself as a first step before the reestablishment or the establishment of rule of law and human development and on the other hand, the growing implication of an international community mobilising a large variety of actors (states, non-governmental organisations, multilateral organisations, regional organisations, etc.) in the consolidation of peace. Over the last few years, the combined efforts of the OECD, the European Union, diverse agencies of the United Nations, States as well as civil society have provided a global dimension of the notion of the security sector.[2] The OECD definition, recognised as an international reference, introduced the term of "security system"[3].

Concerning transitional justice, the definition diverges in Francophone and Anglophone circles. The notion of "justice" in English integrates a social dimension while in French it is more restrictive, assimilated to an institutional function or the judiciary system. Thus the notion of transitional justice in Anglophone literature covers an ensemble of measures put into place to allow societies in transition—post-authoritarian or post-conflict—to face needs for justice arising from massive violations of human rights during a conflict or an authoritarian regime. The Francophone literature has the tendency to restrain transitional justice to a type of measure; such as the truth commissions put in place in South

---

2. Thus notes the "Declaration on the Policy of Poverty and the Reform of the Security Sector" in 2000 of the Department for International Development (DFID), the 2002 conceptual framework of the UNDP "Governance of the Security Sector", the 2004 guidelines of the OECD Development Aid Committee (DAC) "Reform of the Security Sector" and the 2005 political framework of the European Union on RSS as well as the 2007 debate on the reform of the security system of the UN Security Council.

3. The OECD-DAC define the security and justice system as including all those institutions, groups, organisations and individuals — both state and non-state — that have a stake in security and justice provision. In the guidelines of the DAC on RSS and governance, a security system includes: "core security actors (armed forces; police service; gendarmeries; paramilitary forces; presidential guards; intelligence and security services, both military and civilian; coast guards; border guards; customs authorities; and reserve or local security units – civil defence forces, national guards, militias), management and oversight bodies (the executive, national security advisory bodies, legislative and legislative select committees; ministries of defence, internal affairs, foreign affairs; customary and traditional authorities; financial management bodies (finance ministries, budget officers, financial audit and planning units) ; and civil society organisations (civilian review boards and public complaints commissions), justice and the rule of law (judiciary and justice ministries; prisons; criminal investigation and prosecution services; human rights commissions and ombudsmen; and customary and traditional justice systems), and non-statutory security forces (liberation armies, guerrilla armies, private security companies, political party militias)." OECD DAC Handbook on Security System Reform 2007.

Africa. The definition in the Anglo-Saxon world of transitional justice is much broader, covering at the same time criminal prosecutions (national or hybrid tribunals), victim's reparations, truth efforts or institutional reform, as ad hoc and complementary measures to the classical judiciary system whose capacity to deliver justice is all too often at its lowest when the need for justice is at the highest[4].

From this perspective, the institutions that massively participated in the violations of human rights must be reformed in order to prevent the recurrence of such abuses[5]. Several types of measures that we will discuss allow taking into account the need for justice in the reform of institutions. Clearly, institutions, of which it is question here, are part of the security sector as described previously. However, transitional justice does not identify institutions to reform as a function of their sectorial positioning, which would make them de facto targets of reform, but rather in function of their role in massive violations in the past. This approach of security sector reform, by targeting institutions for their role in massive abuses while they are in charge of the security of populations, works in harmony with, or can even be at odds with guaranteeing stability, another challenge of the transition. Stability can be difficult to guarantee if the violations in the security system continue and if the feeling of injustice and impunity nourish social fracture (harmony). But supplanting or reducing the power of certain leaders in the security sector can also harm stability (tension). We are here at the heart of the "peace versus justice" debate well known by actors in transitional justice.

The Traditional Approach to Reform of Security System Institutions

An immense and complex challenge

In general, a country coming out of a period of conflict much face this immense challenge at the moment when their resources are at their lowest. Although the assistance of the international community is in constant

---

4. For complete background and information on the notion of "transitional justice" see the site of the International Center for Transitional Justice www.ictj.org and the article: "Qu'est-ce que la justice transitionnelle?" by Mark Freeman and Dorothée Marotine, 19 November 2007, http://www.ictj.org/images/content/7/5/752.pdf

5. The principal of non-recurrence was explained in the Progress report on the question of the impunity of perpetrators of violations of human rights (civil and political rights), prepared by Louis Joinet, pursuant to Subcommission resolution 1994/34, Commission on Human Rights, Economic and Social Council, 28 June 1995, E/CN.4/Sub.2/1995/18.

increase, it is always insufficient. If one determines a typical diagnostic of the situation of institutions of the security sector in the post-conflict context, one identifies that the institutions are, in general, too numerous[6], their mandates are not always clear, one notices redundancies or vacuums in the missions of institutions. Democratic control mechanisms are inexistent or show significant dysfunction. Financial resources are very low, infrastructure is deteriorated or destroyed, weaponry was pillaged and what remains is insufficient, poorly maintained or obsolete. In terms of information (i.e. archives, management systems) they are partially or totally destroyed, making the knowledge of the real situation of certain institutions difficult or impossible. In terms of the organisation itself, chains of command are unclear, the formal organisation is in conflict with informal structures inherited from the conflict, the heterogeneous ranks (civil and military) with inappropriate ratios of officers to non-commissioned officers and agents. A mixed level of staffing in the police and the army are poorly controlled and swollen by integration programmes of former military groups with varied levels of education and training. Members of armed groups and demobilised military stand up to the personnel of these institutions who, in spite of efforts of reintegration financed by the international community, are found without resources. Bathed in a culture of violence and corruption, they take back their arms and resort to criminal acts.

The heritage of conflict is often doubled by the authoritarian and repressive legacy that is no stranger to the causes of the conflict. This is the case for Afghanistan, Bosnia-Herzegovina, Haiti, Iraq, Kosovo, Liberia, Democratic Republic of Congo, Sierra Leone and East Timor whose authoritarian past imposed an overhaul of political institutions and a tutorial in democracy. Concerning the security sector more specifically, that translates, in certain cases, into the inheritance of repressive organisms directly linked to the former power and beyond all democratic control, with mandates and powers out of scale with organs of security (for example the presidential guard or intelligence services). The normative body is incompatible with the notion of the rule of law. At the personnel level, the competencies acquired were at the service of a repressive state and not the population. There exists a culture of impunity, nepotism and corruption. The institutions are under the domination of one social group. At times, networks organised in the shadows and at the service of the ruling power, which dissolved at the fall of the regime, become criminalised. This observation, although empirical and simplified,

---

6. In Liberia at the end of the conflict in 2003, there were fifteen active "institutions" with police powers attached to the State services or State enterprises (mines port, etc.) of which at least eight had a national mandate, the others having restricted mandates.

nonetheless illustrates the complexity and uncertainty that characterise these contexts.

The responses[7] to the challenge and their limits: programmes aiming to reinforce the organisational capacities of institutions

In the face of such challenges, the actors of the international community establish programmes structured around a state institution (the army, police, customs, etc.) or, at times, around one component of the institution (unities of the law enforcement services, officers etc.). The large majority of these programmes aim at capacity building. We can cite, as one example, the development of strategic plans, the training of personnel (initial, specialised, retraining, etc.) the rehabilitation or the construction of infrastructure or the supply of equipment. Certain programmes target the normative framework by supporting the elaboration or review of the body of rules.

The perpetual lack of coordination of international assistance at the heart of the security sector

One cannot avoid noting the parcelling of assistance that results from the lack of coordination between the different actors of aid working on the security sector. It is necessary to also note that the security sector is characterised by a strong presence of bilateral cooperation on one hand and by the growing involvement of the private sector (for example with American and South African companies[8]) on the other hand; two factors that do not facilitate the establishment of coordination mechanisms. One can say that, while the global and systematic nature of the problems is generally admitted, the answers remain, alas, particular and partial.

The illusion of "institutional capacity development"

Consider the training programmes of police personnel, a "classic" of

---

7. On the action of the international community, also read the chapter: entitled "State-Building or Refounding the State? Theoretical and Political Issues" by M. Leclerc-Olive in this publication.

8. For example, one can cite the case of the Dyncorp an American company which was charged with the selection and training of members of the Liberian army or Face technology, the company in charge of the census of the police in the Democratic Republic of Congo.

bilateral and multilateral cooperation programmes. The individuals who make up the personnel of an institution are not exogenous to society. They come from it and bring along its dynamics. Conflict, if one believes Georg Simmel, is above all a type of link that unites, through tension, and participates in the production of the social.[9] The Rwandan example helps us to see the relationship between conflict and the social dimension of the institutional challenge:

> "How are we going to rebuild the police for this country with half of our new policemen having lost a family member during the genocide and the other half having a family member in prison for having committed the genocide?"[10]

Another example is Kosovo, where social structures are very violent and where it was necessary to reconstruct the police ex nihilo after the province was placed under international guardianship. We can follow in the steps of a young Albanian Kosovar of twenty-three years of age who, after weeks of training in the new police academy, is deployed and assigned in his native region to finish his training and obtain his diploma[11]. If the members of his clan are implicated in acts of persecution of an ethnic character against the Serb minority, where would the loyalty of the young policeman lie? With the police or his clan? We face what Edgar Morin described as the "hologrammatic" principle, that is to say "the whole is in the part who is in the whole".[12] The entirety of the major questions that structure the society are, through its members, at the very core of the institutions that are supposed to regulate individual relations. We are at the heart of the problem of security sector reform and at the limit of the action of strengthening capacities. Police training, as good as it may be, cannot resolve the dilemma of the young Kosovar policeman, nor soothe the worries of the Rwandan police chief.

The paradigm of the State institution

If we again consider the example of the young Kosovar policeman, the conflict of interest concerns societal values, those of "public order" and of the clan — which translate as values of "belonging". Family, clan or ethnic

---

9. Georg Simmel, Conflict & The Web of Group-Affiliations, Free Press, (1918) 1964.
10. Jean de Dieu Mucyo, Chief of the Rwandan national police, Kigali, interview conducted summer 1997.
11. See (2003). A Case for Change: A Review of Peace Operations, King's College of London.
12. Edgar Morin (2005). Introduction à la pensée complexe, Paris, Seuil.

belonging structures social relations. Also in the Balkans, following the Dayton Accords (1995), Bosnia-Herzegovina became organised around three major ethnic groups in addition to the major conventional functions of the State. A Commission to restructure the police[13] was established by the High representative in Bosnia Herzegovina in 2004, with the mandate of proposing a single structure for the police[14] who would operate under the control of the national level. This Commission worked on the assessment of structural deficiency and operational limits arising from the parcelling of competencies in terms of police and fifteen totally independent forces.[15] These competencies, at least for the cantons, the entities and district of Brcko[16], correspond to the territorial division of the Dayton Accords.[17] The guidelines for the work of the Commission were to propose a way to carve out the territorial division into coherent operational zones based on objective parameters (number of inhabitants, rates of criminality, distance and access, etc.) by freeing them from the lines of ethnic division and allowing them to share resources through management at the national level. It was an outright failure.[18]

---

13. The Commission on restructuring the police was put into place by the High Representative, Paddy Ashdown. It was presided over by Wilfried Marteens, former Belgian Prime Minister and composed of 15 elected members and members of local governments (district, cantons and entities) the national government, police officers, magistrates and members of the international community. The author was a technical advisor to the Commission. Final Report of the Work of the Police Restructuring Commission of Bosnia and Herzegovina, Brussels, 28 October 2004. Document available at www.ohr.int/ohr-dept/presso/pressr/doc/final-prc-report-7feb05.pdf (consulted 4 January 2008).

14. "The Police Restructuring Commission of Bosnia and Herzegovina (hereinafter "the Commission"), which is hereby established, shall be responsible, as directed by the Chairman of the said Commission, for proposing a single structure of policing for Bosnia and Herzegovina under the overall political oversight of a ministry or ministries in the Council of Ministers." Decision of the High Representative 5 July 2004.

15. Two entities, the Serbian Republic of Bosnia and The Federation of Bosnia Herzegovinia, which contains ten cantons each possessing a government and police force, the district of Brcko, the border police and the national agency of investigation and protection (organised crime).

16. The district of Brcko, following an arbitrage, is an independent territory with a different legal status than cantons and entities.

17. The border police and the agency for the fight against organised crime, which have national mandates, were created a posteriori under the pressure of the international community.

18. The works of the Commission were concluded by a report by its president, and not by the Commission itself, which noted that the Serbian Republic of Bosnia did not endorse the principal recommendations. "Final Report of the Work of the Police Restructuring Commission of Bosnia and Herzegovina", Brussels, 28 October 2004, p. 4. As of 21 January 2008, the recommendations were still not implemented.

This example illustrates a dominant paradigm in the approach of institutional reform, that is to say a conception of institutions as organs of the State, abstracting them from their original foundation.[19] Although a consensus definition of the institution remains a continual quest in social science and while divergences remain regarding this notion, all theories that are proposed see a grounding in social realities or in individuals.[20] Maurice Hauriou[21], known for his theory of the institution, speaks of a "nation organised in State regime". "To grasp the true nature of the State", it is necessary to "comprehend it there where it has its origins and roots, in other words in the nation itself and in the ensemble of multiple components that constitute it"[22]. Society produces and transforms the values that it needs. Thus, justice, security, respect or order are values that exist in each society with different contents and they regulate economic and social exchanges. Individuals supply the resources necessary for the State, guarantor of these values, in order that it may share and organise resources in service to the society, through institutions such as the army, justice, police, prisons etc. To look again at the example of Bosia-Herzegovina, Bosnian society established a hierarchy of values at the end of the conflict. The value of "belonging" dominates and structures the values of justice, order and security. The Serbian Republic of Bosnia organises a judiciary system that it desires to be fair a police that must be professional – but only between Serbs. As Célestin Bouglé remarks:

---

19. For an analysis of the State-society relationship in fragile States read also: "État, pouvoir et société dans la gouvernance des sociétés projetées" by D. Darbon. 20. According to Durkheim, "one can [...] call institutions, all beliefs and modes of conduct instituted by the collectivity" (E. Durkheim, [1895], 1982, Rules of Sociological Method, New York, The Free Press, 1982. For Talcott Parsons, an institution is "a complex of institutionalised roles...which is of strategic structural significance in the social system in question." (T. Parsons, 1951, The Social System, New York, The Free Press). On a different level, Mary Douglas tells us that to acquire legitimacy "every kind of institution needs a formula that founds its rightness in reason and nature." (M. Douglas, 1999, Comment pensent les institutions, Paris, La Découverte). One can complete this evocation of the social basis of institutions by this quote: "Social phenomena are divided into two major orders. On the one hand there are groups and their structures [...] this is social morphology; On the other hand, there are social phenomenon which occur in these groups — institutions or collective representations. (Marcel Mauss and Paul Fauconnet "Sociology", in M. Mauss, M. Gane, W. Jeffrey, (tr. William Jeffrey) (2005) The Nature Of Sociology: Two Essays, Oxford, England, Berghahn Books, p. 29.

21. Hauriou, M. (1925). "La théorie de l'institution et de la fondation. Essai de vitalisme social", in Aux sources du droit: le pouvoir, l'ordre et la liberté, Cahiers de la Nouvelle Journée, n° 23.

22. Millard, E. (1995). "Hauriou et la théorie de l'institution", Droit & Société, n° 30-31.

"If we want to completely renew institutions, it would be best to act beforehand on the hierarchy of sentiments. The world of values is like the invisible work under construction where changes of decor in the visible world are prepared."[23]

An approach that accepts the complex and societal dimension of the challenge of security sector reform

International coordination of beneficiary-led diagnosis and assistance

All actors in the field are familiar with the futile complaints about the lack of coordination in international cooperation. However, each of these actors is a principal part of the problem, none wishing to be coordinated. The only point that unites them all in a given time and place is the beneficiary. The OECD DAC Handbook on Security System Reform, endorsed by member states, provides a first conceptual and operational framework which could, in time, improve this lack of coordination. One condition must always be fulfilled: the recipients of the assistance, here the State, with the participation of civil society[24], must themselves be trained about these conceptual and operational models and be able to affirm their role in this coordination by having the donors comply to their own engagements on evaluation and the conception of the solutions on the one hand[25], and on effectiveness and complementarity of financing mechanisms on the other hand.[26]

Acting amidst complexity and uncertainty: strategies versus programmes

SSR is very complex and dominated by uncertainty. The sources of complexity must be sought out not only in the "hologrammatic" dimension, as we have already stated, but also in the quantity and

---

23. Célestin, B. (1926). The Evolution of Values, translated by Helen S. Sellars, New York, Henry Holt and Company.
24. Also read the article in this publication "The State in Politics of Development: the challenge of the democratic governance approach" by S. Bellina and Hervé Magro, which explores the notion of a contract as an alternative to conditionality.
25. DAC-OECD, Handbook, op. cit., Chapters 3 and 4.
26. Ibid., Chapter 8.

diversity of and the interactions between different stakeholders.[27] Uncertainty is expressed about the future, within this global dynamic of transition spurred on from the fundamental change that has dominated the core of the community during the conflict; change that presents a new framework for social and political forces that are established without anyone being able to predict their effects. But uncertainty is also expressed about the past and the present, since the systematic tools of information, interpretation and understanding of society have been partially or even totally destroyed or made unusable during the conflict (archives, medias, research centres, etc.). One part of the past and present therefore escapes the actors of SSR. This complexity and uncertainty fit poorly with the programmatic logic of donors that functions on cycles of certainty with well determined timing and objectives. If we believe, once again, Edgar Morin, the complexity and the logic of programmes are barely compatible.[28] It would be preferable to substitute strategic logic for programme logic, leaving a margin for the definition of operational action and the flexibility necessary to reorient it. It is evident, however, that today the trend remains towards the opposite, an increase in control and predictability of results.

Going beyond the paradigm of the state institution for the diversification of competencies

The paradigm of the state institution has pernicious side effects. Among them is the belief among donors that providing technical assistance in the domain of SSR, according to which magistrates are the most well placed to accompany reform of the judiciary system, police officers to reform the police etc. The example of missions of the police from the Europe Union speaks for itself, since it was quasi-exclusively composed of seconded police officers.[29] Even so, can we mention one individual who joined the police force or the judiciary to work for the reform of post-conflict and post-socialist institutional reform and who, in their training programme, was trained for this type of challenge? The challenge goes beyond the technical competencies of police and judiciary.

---

27. M. Liu "Traiter la complexité dans l'approche classique et par la démarche holistique", Masters course 2001, Dynamique des organisations et des transformations sociales, Université Paris-Dauphine, unpublished.

28. Ibid.

29. Cf. The European Union police missions to Bosnia-Herzegovina, in Macedonia, the Democratic Republic of Congo, in Afghanistan, or the Palestinian Territories. See www.consilium.europa.eu.

This multi-dimensional and therefore complex challenge requires a combination of several competencies (political, legal, sociological etc.). Such is the teaching of the systemic approach: an organisation that evolves in a complex and unpredictable environment has no other choice but to become more complex itself.[30] Furthermore, a response focused on technical competencies of each sector favours the state approach of institutions, eclipsing the social dimension of the challenge.

Going beyond institutional capacity development, an example from transitional justice

Presenting the challenge of SSR based on societal issues—such as the need for justice in the society and the necessity to give justice as a condition for a durable peace—drives one to emphasise an approach reintroducing the societal dimension of institutions on the formal one of the institution. As an example, we will consider the International Center for Transitional Justice that, in its institutional reform approach, identifies four properties of institutions that limit risks of recurrence of massive violations of human rights. The first property that has already been mentioned and cannot be ignored is that of capacity. It is a fundamental property, since the lack or weakness of institutional capacity (lack of training, lack of suitable resources, etc.) is a factor that generates violations. For all that, capacity building must work with social realities. Imposing, for example, the requirement that each policeman must be able to read and write was a factor that proved to be discriminatory and that caused some tension in creating a new police force in East Timor. Indeed, members of the rebellion whose activities had not allowed them to attend school and who were consequently illiterate were not eligible to join the new police force put into place by the UN mission[31], while members of the former Indonesian police force were able to join[32].

This having been said, capacity alone is not sufficient to prevent violations – as is shown in the special police units of Milosevic that

30. Emery, F. and E. Trist, (1965). "The Causal Texture of Organizational Environments" Human Relations, vol. 18, p. 21-32.

31. The United Nations Transitional Administration in East Timor (UNTAET), 25 October 1999 to 20 May 2002 (Date of independence of East Timor), had a very broad mandate and, among others, the mission of establishing the East Timor Police Service (ETPS).

32. After strong pressure from veterans of Falintil, the United Nations finally accepted to include a group of ex-combatants in the new national police.

DEMOCRATIC GOVERNANCE

did not lack capacity. The institution must also have integrity and that is a second property. The institution must operate conscientiously, according to the principles of morality and only in the service of the founding values. This integrity can be sought out by an action on the individuals that compose its personnel. The non-recurrence of violations of an institution of the security system cannot guarantee if it is directed by individuals having a past linked with these violations. It is possible to have recourse to vetting a process aiming, through a minute examination of the past actions of an individual, to determine his aptitude to occupy (or to continue to occupy) a position in an institution. The establishment of a procedure of vetting should nonetheless work within the social reality that the individuals come from.[33] Can one exclude the leaders of a violent group and include the combatants that they directed without a risk of instability? It goes without saying that this measure is conditioned by a firm political will and the power to act on behalf of the political .authorities; this is at the core of the dilemma of "peace vs. justice". The integrity of an institution can also be sought in terms of work on its rules. For example, by introducing principles and rules of transparent management relating to merit promotions, budget development, disciplinary codes, the management of weaponry etc.

The question of institutional integrity brings us to that of legitimacy. In order to complete its societal mission, an institution should be recognised as legitimate by members of society. It must therefore have members constituting it who are representative of society. But it is not a question here of justifying a recourse to quotas. The case of Liberia offers an interesting illustration. It is unthinkable, in the Liberian context, that each of the numerous ethnic groups be proportionally represented in the police. Indeed, if we consider the history of the country, the groups with a tradition of being merchants never participated in the life of public institutions. Instead, one sees to it that no group, among those represented, can be dominant. But, speaking of social representativeness, it would also be inappropriate to reason only in terms of ethnic or gender

---

33. For more information on vetting, see the study International Center for Transitional Justice (ICTJ) has just published: A. Mayer-Rieckh and P. De Greiff (2007) Justice As Prevention: Vetting Public Employees in Societies in Transition, Social Science Research Council. Also available in PDF on: www.ssrc.org.

34. The audit was conducted in December 1998, A team of 16 police officers and international professional civilians conducted 46 interviews with local police officers, inspected buildings, archives and police equipment. The audit concluded that the police station of Stolac was under nationalist political influence and ethnically unintegrated. United Nations Mission in Bosnia-Herzegovina, Building Civilian Law Enforcement in Stolac and throughout the Herzegovina-Neretva Canton, HRO 2/99 External, December 1998-May 1999.

35. Op. cit., par. 29.

groups. Taking into account other groups, such as victims, also proves to be necessary. It is important that these questions of representativeness be evoked in the framework of a transparent debate to which diverse social groups have access. But the legitimacy of institutions cannot pass only by the composition of its members. Of equal importance is the use of symbols that are accepted by all, such as insignia, uniforms, motto, etc. An example comes from an audit, by the Human Rights Department of the United Nations Mission in the city of Stolac, in the predominantly Croat[34] canton of Mostar of Bosnia-Herzegovina three years after the Dayton Accords. One of the reasons for the audit was the inactivity of the police station in the face of multiple violent incidents regarding the Muslim minority. This audit brought out the fact that inappropriate symbols were being used, such as the hanging of a flag of the "Croatian Republic of Herceg-Bosna" in the office of the station's chief. The operation also showed that Croat policemen had their custom of going to a bar across from the police station, where an Ustaša flag was hung above the entryway[35]. One imagines just how difficult it would be for a victim of ethnic violence to come and present a complaint in such a context. This illustration reminds us how important it is to assure ties between individuals and the institution with cultural references – symbols being one example.

Another important property that an institution must revere is that of the power of control it leaves to citizens. Admitting that an institution is founded on societal values and that it mobilises resources placed at its disposition by the nation, organised as a state regime, is also to admit that it must be accountable to citizens. Any kind of institution of the security sector must establish practices of this type: examples include the obligation for members of the police force to carry certain identifying service cards, or the publication of an annual activity report or other information and communication campaigns.

This approach, which is based on the need for justice and the non-recurrence of violations does not pretend to place an exhaustive framework on the challenge of institutional reform. What is important, as we have tried to demonstrate here, is the social dimension of SSR. Beyond the state apparatus, is it not a system of values that is in crisis and that the wounded society must reconstruct? SSR proceeds as much from a social reconstruction, or rather a new construction, as there can be no return to the status quo ante, as from a restructuring of rules and means of the institutions of the State.

---

35. Op. cit., par. 29. * This article is inspired from Christiane Arndt and Charles Oman, Uses and Abuses of Governance Indicators, Paris, Development Centre, OECD, 2006. The authors thank Séverine Bellina and William Oman for their comments.

34

Governance Assessment

Charles OMAN and Christiane ARNDT
(Translated from the French)

The growing interest in the quality of governance in developing countries witnessed over the last fifteen years has given rise to a spectacular development of the use of governance indicators. Faithful to the principle that one can control or manage only what one can quantify, numerous national and multilateral development aid agencies attempt to measure the quality of governance in developing countries.

The most frequently used indicators, among the hundreds that have appeared in response to this growing demand, are composite indicators founded on perceptions. These indicators reduce to a number (by country and by year) the data that is supplied by diverse and often numerous information sources—data about the comparative perceptions of individuals on the quality of governance or of certain aspects of governance in diverse countries. These individuals are in general "experts" and managers in private companies but also, for certain indicators, other individuals interviewed through household surveys.

One observes that even the most carefully constructed composite indicators suffer from limits of which their users seem often to be unaware. Among the most important limits are: the lack of transparency of their content; the invisible nature of their partiality; their lack of utility as an instrument to guide concrete actions for those interested in improving the quality of governance in a country; and their weakness in their statistical bases as instruments of comparison of governance quality between countries or over time.

This article attempts to clarify the limits confronting the users of these indicators, from development cooperation agencies to international investors or development researchers. The article aims at a double objective: on the one hand, to contribute to the reduction of problematic or erroneous use of these indicators and, on the other hand, to participate in the improvement of their quality. If it is true that the perfect indicator will never exist, it seems nevertheless essential to improve the transparency of governance indicators as much in their construction and publication as in their use.

Why is there so much interest in governance?

It will be useful, first of all, to revisit the causes of the recent interest for the assessment of governance quality in developing countries.

Four major factors explain the significant growth in interest that has been evident, for a dozen years, for governance quality and its measurement in developing countries. The first of these factors is the spectacular growth in international financial flows to the "emerging markets". Foreign direct investments in these economies thus went from an annual average of 10 billion US dollars at the beginning of the 1980s to more than 67 billion from 1992 -1994 and to 150 billion since 1997. Portfolio investments, whose annual net flows did not reach 2 million dollars at the end of the 1980s, came in at more than 50 billion dollars in the 1990s (acquisition of stakes and stock purchases take together). Following this increase, developing countries received 650 billion dollars in investments in 2006 (compared to 70 billion in official aid, almost 10 times more).

The spectacular growth in the interest of international investors for the quality of governance in developing countries therefore comes first from the spectacular increase in the value of their assets exposed to risk in these countries. Nonetheless, this interest equally reflects the major reversal of the principal economic and monetary polices that the developing world had known since the 1970s, a period that witnessed the introduction of much more liberal policies, more favourable to international investors. The intensification of competition between public powers to attract investors to their country not only served to consolidate and accentuate this change of policy orientation, it also brought about a strong convergence, a genuine homogenisation of economic and monetary policies, during the last fifteen years. The orientation of these policies thus ceased to constitute, in the eyes of an increasing number of investors, the most important factor in their choice of a developing country in which to carry out their operations. Instead, international investors perceive differences in terms of local governance quality as the determining factor with which to judge the credibility of economic and monetary policies of an "emerging economy."[1]

---

1. This is all the more true since the financial crises in emerging markets at the end of the 1990s, investors were wary of indicators of "country risk".

The second factor that explains the strong increase in interest for governance quality in developing countries is linked to the ending of the Cold War. Until the end of the 1980s, the countries of the OECD, their national aid agencies and multilateral development organisations, sought to promote economic and social development in developing countries not only to fight poverty and improve quality of life in these countries, but also to stifle their vague desire to choose communism. Becoming interested in governance quality in a non-democratic but pro-Western country could have been proven counterproductive. It was only after the collapse of the Soviet Union that these attitudes and behaviours truly evolved, especially since 1996, when the then-president of the World Bank, James Wolfensohn, openly recognised that corruption constituted a major obstacle for development. Although problems of a political nature were excluded from the official mandate of this organisation since its creation in 1944, the World Bank, according to its president, could no longer ignore the problems of corruption and bad governance in its borrowing countries.[2]

The third factor lies in the general perception that reforms actively promoted through conditional loans of multilateral financial organisations and largely undertaken by developing countries in the 1980s and 1990s were a relative failure. These reforms, at the origin of a change in policy direction evoked above, were grouped together by certain authors under the name of the "Washington Consensus". Beyond the debate on the cause of this relative failure, blamed on an insufficient or, on the contrary, excessive application of recommended reforms, arose the idea, today widely shared, of the necessity of public governance capable of assuring the functioning of a market economy. Poor governance in numerous developing countries that were beneficiaries of conditional loans, was therefore perceived as a probable cause of the relative failure of reforms in the 1980s and 1990s.[3] It was also perceived as a potential obstacle to the effectiveness of political reforms and of future international cooperation efforts.

The fourth factor, whose importance is significant, although difficult to quantify, resides in the influence of the analyses of New Institutional Economics (NIE). These have demonstrated in a convincing manner since the 1990s the importance of a system of governance in a country for its success in terms of long-term growth, improvement of well being and the development of society—its formal and informal institutions, including

---

2. According to the World Bank Annual Report 2004, for example, loans granted by the Bank for improvement of local governance increased by 11% per year between 2000 and 2004, while those for economic reform fell 14% per year in the same period. According to this same report, one quarter of the loans undertaken by the Bank in 2004 were attributed to judiciary and public administrations in borrowing countries.

3. Principal or sole cause for some, complementary cause for others.

culture and implicit values and their interactions with the behaviour of entrepreneurs and political and economic organisations.

Indicators analysis

As we previously mentioned, the most commonly used governance indicators are composite indicators based on perceptions. Among these are the Corruption Perceptions Index (CPI) of Transparency International and the six Worldwide Governance Indicators (WGI) developed by Daniel Kaufmann, Aart Kraay and their team at the World Bank Institute. One of the essential qualities of both the CPI and WGI indicators is that they associate the individual score of each country (point score) with an estimation of the probable margin of error (confidence range of 90% probability). The authors also emphasise the fact that differences that separate the scores whose confidence ranges overlap should be interpreted, statistically speaking, as negligible or insignificant.

The central quality of the composite indicators therefore resides in their capacity to reduce the complex realities of governance in each country to a number – a number that is paired with, in the best cases, an estimation of its degree of imprecision. The indicators thus offer a quantified estimation of the quality of governance in a country or an aspect of such (as, for example, the quality of regulation, the efficiency of public powers or the mastery of corruption) and allow comparisons between countries or over time.

Many users seem nonetheless to overestimate the precision of national scores provided by these indicators and to ignore the very meaning of the estimations of margins of error associated with these scores. The fact that the creators of the indicators probably underestimate margins of error – as we will see below – is less serious than their weak appreciation by users.

Pyramidal Construction

To better understand the causes and consequences of the problem, it is useful to imagine each indicator WGI or CPI as an ensemble of pyramids where each pyramid represents the score of a country. This score, for a given year, therefore corresponds to the summit of the pyramid, illustrated by the point "s" in the figure below.

The indicators and the sources of information used directly for calculating this score consist of primary sources and correspond to the level "1" of the figure. But each one of the primary sources constitutes in itself the aggregation of other, sometimes numerous, sources, which are secondary sources or the composite indicator and which correspond to the level "2" of the figure.

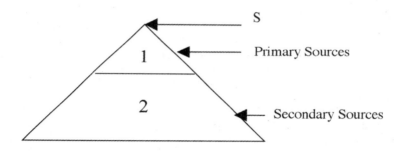

This mode of construction implies two other characteristics that should be emphasised. The first is that the score of each country has its own pyramid and that each pyramid is different from the others: indeed, secondary sources and even primary sources differ from one country to another for a given indicator and year. The second characteristic is that the content of each pyramid (that is to say the sources of information from which the score of a country is calculated for a given indicator) change continually, even if the reality of governance in the country does not change.

This means that the score of a country changes year to year independently of the reality of governance that this score is intended to reflect and this for two reasons. First of all, the primary and secondary sources of information used to calculate the score of a country are in constant evolution and this evolution takes place without the knowledge of the indicator's creators, at least as it concerns the secondary sources; indeed new sources are included while others are excluded, disappear or are modified each year. The second reason is that the perception of governance quality can easily change in the absence of or independently from all change in the objective reality of governance. This implies that no one, neither the users, nor even the creators of an indicator based on perceptions — can know all the modifications operated at the heart of a pyramid and likely to be at the origin of change of a country score from one year to the next.

A Concrete Example

We can take the concrete example of Bangladesh scores in 1998 and 2005 of the WGI indicator "regulatory quality".[4] First of all, we should note that each year all the scores of some 200 countries covered by a WGI indicator are standardised so that all scores are between -2.5 and +2.5. In 1998, the score for Bangladesh was 0.13[5], which places it in the 39th percentile in relation to some 200 national scores. Bangladesh's score was based on four primary sources that year and the confidence range of 90% went from the 19th to the 66th percentile. The degree of precision of this score was therefore very weak, as the confidence range was very large. This weakness was due, at least in part, to the reduced number of primary sources used to calculate the score.

In 2005, the score of Bangladesh was -1.07, which placed it in the fifteenth percentile of countries covered by this indicator that year. This score was based on ten primary sources and the confidence range estimated at 90% went from the 8th to the 22nd percentile. The degree of precision estimated of the score was therefore higher in 2005 than in 1998, and this, thanks, at least in part, to the larger number of primary sources used to calculate it.

This apparent decline in the regulatory quality of Bangladesh between 1998 and 2005 –if we judge by the decline the WGI score from -0.13 to -1.07 (in an interval between -2.5 and +2.5) which is equal to a fall from the 39th to the 15th percentile can be explained by one or several of the four following causes:

– Regulatory quality really declined in Bangladesh between 1998 and 2005. It is nevertheless interesting to note that, over this same period, the country had relatively strong economic growth;

– Perceptions of regulatory quality deteriorated (independently of all real evolution of regulatory quality in Bangladesh during this period;

– Perceptions of regulatory quality in other countries covered by this indicator improved (independently of all evolution or absence of evolution of the regulatory quality in Bangladesh) between 1998 and 2005.

– The change in the score of Bangladesh between 1998 and 2005 is a statistical artifice caused by the modification of the sources of information at the heart of the pyramid between these two years.

---

4. We have only chosen this example because we prepared it to participate in a seminar in Bangladesh on this subject in 2006. In the rest of the article we continue to concentrate on the WGI to illustrate our arguments because they are the most widely used and influential composite indicators of governance, while the CPI concerns only one particular dimension of governance.

5. See Kaufmann, D. (2006) et al., Governance Matters V.

This example allows us to recall that, according to the creators of the WGI indicators, the overlapping of confidence intervals estimated for the two years forbids the interpretation of a drop in Bangladesh's score as a decline of the real regulatory quality in this country between 1998 and 2005. The rule according to which all apparent difference between two scores must be interpreted as statistically insignificant seems to us all the more essential to underline as it is too often ignored by the users of these indicators.

Warning for users – four problems to avoid

Four major interlinked problems are associated with the very nature of composite governance indicators based on perceptions.

The paradox of transparency

The first of these problems, which contributes to aggravating the three others, relates to the relative lack of transparency of the indicator content. This problem is all the more significant and paradoxical in that these indicators are used by aid agencies precisely to bring more transparency and objectivity to their decisions relating to fund allocation.

Three principal factors combine to explain this relative lack of transparency of indicators.

The reduction of a large quantity of subjective information to one number, which is inherent to the very nature of composite indicators, constitutes a first important case in the lack of transparency. This problem is all the more serious as the weight attributed to the different sources of information by the method of aggregation varies not only by indicator but also according to the country and over time for a same indicator. The fact of omitting the publication of the weights assigned to each source reinforces the problem.

Secondly, since the information used to calculate indicators is not fully published, it is, in practice, impossible to replicate the construction of the indicators.[6]

---

6. In spite of the recent decision to publish a large majority of primary sources for the WGI indicators, which constitutes an important advancement, these indicators remain impossible to replicate or reproduce by other actors, in the absence of the availability of all primary and secondary sources.

Finally, the absence of a theory of "good" (or of "bad") governance to guide the selection and interpretation of data[7] constitutes, without a doubt, at the same time the most important cause of a lack of transparency of the indicators and the most difficult problem to overcome. Indeed, all systems of comparative evaluation between countries, whether they relate to quality of their governance or any of the criteria, necessarily imply a normative judgement. The construction of indicators should therefore be based on a concept of "good" or "bad" governance, or on a normative definition of governance. And yet, this is not the case.

The definition that the WGI indicators imply is simply based on the "traditions and institutions through which authority is exercised in a country" – these traditions and institutions being later disaggregated into institutional, political and economic components. The authors do not provide any criteria for judging or evaluating the quality of these "traditions and institutions". They do not provide any normative definition of governance, no concept of good or bad governance, no explicit criteria to judge or evaluate the quality of these traditions and institutions through which authority is exercised in a country.

In reality, the authors of the WGI indicators draw on quantified perceptions that constitute the secondary sources aggregated by the primary sources and then they re-aggregated them to produce a final score. The normative de facto definition of what constitutes good or bad governance, implicit in the WGI indicators therefore depends on the information about the perceptions themselves and on the manner in which these are aggregated in the process of calculating the score. This is subjective information inside of each pyramid and the technique employed for aggregating it, which gives a "direction" or the "real content" of the concept of good or bad governance, implicit in the facts but invisible in these indicators.

Neither the users nor even the creators of these indicators can know the true normative definition of governance that is used and that determines, concretely, the scores of the evaluated countries.

---

7. The problem does not have to do with the subjective character of the information used for the indicators. Indeed, as Kaufmann, Kaay and others have observed, the indicators developed on the basis of objective data suffer as much, if not more, from subjective interpretations than indicators based on perceptions. These are subjective interpretations of objective data by the creators of indicators that introduce an important element of subjectivity in the indicators based on the facts. One observes, for example, that countries which have regulations of protection of worker's rights and or of the environment see themselves attributed with low scores in the domain of "regulatory quality: than those who do not have them. This reflects the subjective interpretation among the creators of the indicators based on objective data, according to which such regulations interfere with the proper functioning of the market.

Invisible Partialities

The second problem relates to the existence, at the heart of these indicators, partialities or biases of which the users are unaware. Every system of normative evaluation necessarily incorporates partialities that can please some and displease others. The problem therefore does not reside in the existence of bias or partialities, but in their relatively invisible or hidden nature. Consequently, numerous users use these indicators without being aware of the biases.

One observes, for example, that the regulations that aim at protecting the environment or the rights of workers are interpreted as factors reducing the regulatory quality of a country. The problem does not lie in the negative interpretation of these regulations as such—one can be for or against this interpretation—but in the relatively obscure, or even invisible nature of this interpretation.

Another good example of this problem is that information issued from household surveys has a relatively weak weight in relation to the perceptions provided by the "experts" and corporate managers. However, these surveys offer a privileged access to the experiences and perspectives of relatively poor segments of the population that would otherwise not be taken into account. These sources of information have little weight in the calculation of the country scores. Their presence in the list of sources used in the construction of the indicators—as is the case for the WGI indicators but not for that of CPI of Transparency International— nonetheless leads users to overestimate the importance that the indicators grant to poor populations.

Two factors explain the marginal position that the WGI indicators grant to the perceptions of the poorest populations. The first is the relatively high cost of surveys conducted with households. This explains why very few household surveys are realised a fortiori for studies concerning more than one country and which offer results to be used for the construction of the indicators. On the other hand, international studies with enterprises and "experts" have the advantage of being less costly or, at least, better financed and therefore much more numerous.

The second factor that explains the lack of weight accorded to the voices of the poor in the WGI indicators relates to the method chosen by their authors to aggregate the primary information sources in the calculation of the country score. The method used gives priority to the sources whose evaluations tend to agree amongst each other to the detriment of those evaluations that diverge from the dominant majority. As we have emphasised, the studies conducted with households are few in number and therefore in the minority compared with those coming from experts and company managers. Their voice, if it goes against the experts and company managers, appears in the end negligible in the calculation of the country score.

The problem, again, does not lie in the bias actually incorporated into the WGI indicators vis-à-vis the perceptions issuing from the household surveys, and therefore from the poor in relation to the "experts" and enterprises. The true problem lies in the lack of visibility of this type of bias. Many users are unaware of it because they are much more visible than the list of information sources allows one to believe.

The lack of usefulness to guide concrete action

The third problem concerns the relatively little amount of useful information that the indicators provide for those who wish to engage in concrete action to improve the quality of governance in a country.

As an example, the country score of the WGI indicator "Rule of law" provides information on the degree of security that company managers feel regarding their property, which can, in itself, constitute useful information for diverse potential users of these indicators. These scores however provide no information on the concrete reasons that motivate these feelings neither on the measures to take to improve these conditions and act therefore on the rule of law of the country.

In this same vein, the CPI of Transparency International provides information on the degree of perceived corruption in a country by numerous "experts" and company managers, but does not provide any concrete indication likely to serve as a guide to those who would like to act to reduce the level of corruption in the country.

Composite indicators are therefore, above all, useful as evaluation or decision-making tools, by users external to the evaluated countries but do little for the needs of national actors. Even if this limitation is practically inherent to the nature of composite indicators based on perceptions, it is very important for the potential users, particularly aid agencies, to be aware of.

Comparison is not a reason

The fourth problem relates to the overestimation, by many users, of the degree of precision and of reliability of the scores provided by these indicators. The users therefore overestimate the usefulness of the indicators to compare scores between different countries, especially when the scores are relatively close and, even more so, to measure the evolution of one or several countries over time. They seem to be unaware of the importance of the rule of caution stated by the authors themselves, according to which all apparent difference between two scores whose confidence intervals overlap is statistically insignificant.

It is important to note that these problems of imprecision affect all composite indicators. Only the best include confidence intervals. Nonetheless, in the case of the WGI indicators, these intervals are probably underestimated. Indeed, the elaborators of the WGI indicators consider that errors contained in the different primary sources are independent of each other, a greater number of sources therefore guaranteeing greater precision of the score. And yet numerous empirical elements suggest that the margins of error of different sources are not totally independent of one another. Consequently, the confidence intervals tend to be underestimated and the degree of precision of scores overestimated.[8]

The problems associated with between-country comparisons and over time are therefore even greater than we have indicated previously and these comparisons are even less founded in statistical terms. However, if users were to take the recommended usage of the 90% confidence intervals into account, this would already constitute significant progress, even if the size of these intervals or the degree of imprecision of the scores, remains underestimated.

Conclusion

The governance assessment remains problematic. The absence of a more or less credible theory that could provide the analytical framework necessary for the definition of objective indicators of governance quality to explain the relation of cause and effect between the specific qualities of governance in a given country and the development process in that country explains, in part, the very widespread use of composite indicators based on perceptions.

The principal problem lies not in the subjective nature of the information used to construct the indicators. The absence of a theory capable of serving as a frame of reference for the definition of indicators based on objective information makes the indicators based on perceptions very useful and, in the end, not less objective than indicators constructed

---

8. We find, in other words, that the size of the 90% confidence ranges to be underestimated. See Chapter 4 of C. Arndt and C. Oman, (2006) Uses and Abuses of Governance Indicators, op. cit., for a detailed explanation of our criticisms about these estimations and the suppositions upon which they are based.

from objective data. This is all the more true because of the importance of the subjective interpretations inherent in the construction of indicators based on objective information and the very weak degrees of availability and reliability of such information in many developing countries.

The main problem lies in the underestimation or the lack of awareness about the limits of the precision of these indicators. This underestimation or lack of awareness is visible and very widespread in the use of these indicators by aid agencies, as with other users.

A first practical conclusion consists therefore in strongly emphasising the importance for the users to take careful consideration of the meaning of confidence intervals. They must not forget that all difference between two or more scores of overlapping confidence ranges must be considered insignificant. In other words, that the users must use the intervals in place of the precise scores in their decision-making or calculations from the indicators to avoid the very widespread overestimation of the precision of the scores.

A second practical conclusion consists in encouraging users, including aid agencies, to minimise the use of composite indicators that are not sufficiently precise, such as the WGI, and to increase the use of more precise indicators whose information sources and weights attributed to different sources are transparent and theoretically well founded. A good example is the PEFA (Public Expenditure and Financial Accountability Programme).

This conclusion applies with even greater importance to those users who seek to use the indicators to create concrete improvements in the quality of governance in developing countries, whether these users be internal or external to these countries.

With a rapidly evolving "supply" of governance indicators, we suggest that users consult one or several of the better guides to familiarise themselves with what is available. Among these guides we can recommend for example:

– Inter-American Development Bank (IADB) Datagob: Governance Indicator Database;[9]

– United Nations Development Programme, Governance Indicators: A User's Guide;[10]

– Metagora (OECD), Inventory of Initiatives Aimed at Measuring Human Rights and Democratic Governance;[11]

– World Bank Institute, Governance Data: Web-Interactive Inventory of Datasets and Empirical Tools.[12]

---

9. Available on-line at: www.iadb.org/datagob/
10. Available on-line at: www.undp.org/oslocentre/docs07/ undp_users_guide_online_version.pdf
11. Available on-line at: www.metagora.org/html/aboutus_inventory.html
12. Available on-line at: www.worldbank.org/wbi/governance/goodatasets/index.html

35

The African Peer Review Mechanism

The Promotion of Governance in Africa

Marie-Angélique Savané
(Translated from the French)

In this Africa, about which one speaks only in the negative, today there is some good news: The African Peer Review Mechanism (APRM)! Twenty-eight African countries adhere to this mechanism voluntarily. And we can assert that it is one of the flagship programs of the African Union in the domain of governance.

Indeed, as of 2000, Heads of State and Government launched initiatives that led to the creation of the New Partnership for Africa's Development (NEPAD) in 2001. The NEPAD was the result of a general consensus on the strategies and policies to put into place to confront new challenges—economic challenges linked to competitiveness and growth but also that of political integration to fight poverty and promote human development and good governance. To reach such objectives, it became imperative to encourage the mobilisation of material and human resources made available thanks to different types of partnerships and aid as much on the international as on the national level, between governments and with civil society, the private sector and development partners.

In this same vein, the APRM was introduced to create the best conditions to reach these major NEPAD objectives. During the inaugural summit of the African Union held in Durban, South Africa, 8 July 2002, the founding committee of NEPAD adopted the "Declaration on Democracy, Political, Economic and Corporate Governance"[1] which engages States to respects the rule of law and to adopt transparent,

---

1. 38th Ordinary Session of the Assembly of Heads of State and Government of the OAU: African Peer Review Mechanism, Durban, AHG/235(XXXVIII) Annex II.

responsible and participatory public affairs management. It recommends the creation of an "African Peer Review Mechanism" in order to encourage the adhesion and respect of these engagements in each country. This idea was formalised during the Sixth Summit of NEPAD Heads of State and Government Implementation Committee (HSGIC) held in Abuja, Nigeria, in March 2003 with the adoption of a Memorandum of Understanding (MOU) on the APRM. Afterwards, the Heads of State also adopted the principal documents exposing the basic principles, processes and objectives of the APRM, including: the Base Document of the APRM; the Organisation and Processes document (O & P document); and the Objectives, Standards, Criteria and Indicators (document OSCI).

The aim of this article is to present the APRM, still relatively unknown in its entirety, its principles, organs, functioning, processes of ownership and participation, indicators and norms, all that make it unique and a major contribution to the consolidation of governance in Africa.

The principles and pledges of effectiveness of the APRM

Widely proclaimed as the jewel of the NEPAD, the APRM is a unique exercise that allows the exchange of information and best practices between peers, based on the mutual confidence of States and their shared faith in the process. It is also an engagement to the norms of governance in Africa. Because of this, its ultimate goal is to encourage participating countries to proceed to the adoption of polices, norms and practices leading to political stability, high economic growth, sustainable development and accelerated sub-regional and continental economic integration through the exchange of experiences and the reinforcement of best practices. It thus promotes the identification of weaknesses and the evaluation of needs in capacity building.

The principles of the establishment of the mechanism are the following:

– Voluntary adherence: The member States of the AU adhere freely to the mechanism that cannot therefore be perceived as an instrument of control that would violate state sovereignty. Although the concept of intervention is established in international relations, the liberty of adhesion to the mechanism offers a pledge of total collaboration of the authorities, all throughout the exercise, and ownership of its findings.

– Ownership and steering by the participating countries constitute the essential factors of effectiveness of the APRM process. All during the progression of the review, the APRM requires leadership capacities at the level of the national authorities and with other stakeholders of the evaluated country. This means leadership as it is practiced in other existing national processes, That is to say: the processes of the Poverty Reduction Strategy Paper (PRSP), Medium-Term Expenditure Framework (MTEF) , the National Human Rights Plans of Action, and the Strategy for the Millennium Development Goals (MDGs), the institutional reforms under way, other strategies of poverty reduction, governance, socio-economic development and the related programmes and projects.

– The non-exclusive aspect: All the member States of the AU, without exception, can participate in the process. This principle postulates equality in the treatment of countries. At the start, there is no difference between post-crisis States and those with a long experience in terms of stability and democratic processes. To participate, the country has only one obligation, to notify the Committee of Participating Heads of State and Government of the APRM (APR Forum) of their wish to adhere. On this basis, the State commits to collaborating openly and totally with the team to which it will afford every opportunity for conducting the exercise.

– The APRM process is open (or inclusive) and participatory. The process involves citizens and civil society organisations through the use of self-assessment questionnaires and consultations organised by the evaluation team. The advantage of the APRM is therefore to open the political space to non-state actors as laid out in the 2006 report of the Secretariat "...the participation of diverse stakeholders in the APRM is in itself a central element in the improvement of the level of governance and socio-economic development of the participating country." Although planned in the base texts, this participation remains a challenge for the majority of countries and often demands capacity building. Efforts must therefore be deployed in the direction of actors with a view to encourage mobilisation around the process and its ownership. The group of key actors, such as the government, the parliament, the judiciary power, the private sector, youth, women's organisations, civil society organisations, media, universities, political parties, unions, agricultural workers' associations etc. must be engaged and mobilised for the APRM process. Targeted efforts must be undertaken with the aim of associating the main actors, marginalised groups, as well as poor from urban and rural areas.

– The principle of confidence and peer pressure or emulation: the report issued from the evaluation measures the progress made, indicates weaknesses and makes recommendations. The APRM, it should be noted, does not have the aim of excluding or punishing countries. The mechanism does not come with any conditionality, nor does it have any legally constraining sanctions, because the fundamental objective of the mechanism is to help countries improve their governance practices. In fact its effectiveness depends on peer pressure, which comes through formal recommendations in the report, the public character of the debates during the evaluation team visit, the examination by the Committee of Heads of State and Government that allows comparisons between evaluated countries and good practices.

– The APRM is also guided by the principles of transparency, reporting obligations, technical competency, and credibility and it must be free of all manipulation.

– The quality of the evaluation: the process can be seen as credible because it is based on criteria and standards, defined from the outset, and a quality evaluation conducted with rigor and competence. The criteria are the same for all countries.

APRM domains and governance indicators

The four domains of governance (political, economic, corporate and socio-economic) retained in the Durban declaration (2002) allow coverage of a large spectrum of problems identified on the Continent, notably by the NEPAD.

– Political governance measures the legitimacy of elected officials who help to bring about the credibility of institutions and the adherence of the population to policies and therefore their acceptance of corresponding measures. Political governance assures the respect of principles according to which all the positions of powers are acquired, in a republican spirit, through a competition that is free and open to all citizens. This practice allows for "smooth" political transitions.

– The economic aspect of governance takes into account macro-economic policies and their impacts.

– Corporate governance assures that, inside each enterprise, employers and employees establish and respect the norms of human and financial resources management conform to the interest of the business and its environment.

– Socio-economic development takes account of the living conditions of the populations. The indicators, standards and criteria defined by the APRM are conceived in such a way that each aspect of governance be apprehended as a prerequisite to the success of development policies.

Democracy and political governance

The evaluation of democracy takes place through a certain number of indicators founded on the effectiveness of electoral process management structures, the existence of rule of law, the protection of human rights and the effectiveness of the fight against corruption and misappropriation. The regularity of the electoral process is a crucial question of governance in Africa. The refusal to accept political transition is at the origin of several major crises. Following the example of the four other evaluation domains, other criteria were retained for this review, such as the level of ratification of international instruments that demonstrate the capacity of the State to integrate international engagements into national legislation.

The prevention, management and resolution of conflicts, at the national and regional levels are also part of the criteria that are closely studied—the links between actors in conflict.

Governance and economic management

The criteria for economic governance lead to a study of the norms of economic management, the quality of tools for policies and economic programmes, the potential of growth and the quality of key indicators of monitoring and evaluation. For example, the independence of the Central Bank is a criteria of choice to appreciate the quality of development institutions. This is also the case for the reliability and transparency of the budgetary process.

Rules of competition must also be respected to guarantee competition and a healthy competitiveness between economic actors. The fight against money laundering, which constitutes one of the parameters studied by the APRM, is included in this framework. Several initiatives are under way: the Eastern and Southern Africa Anti-Money Laundering Group (ESAAMLG) and the Intergovernmental Anti-Money Laundering Group in Africa (GIABA). Initiatives that the NEPAD and African countries can appropriate to make them into instruments to fight against money laundering and illegal financial transactions.

Corporate governance

The criteria of corporate governance aim to take stock of management best practices linked to transparency, financial information and business responsibility. Corporate governance is also linked to the legal and judiciary framework of business, the protection of its material and intellectual property rights, sources of financing, ways of settling lawsuits and its relations with the State. The corporation thus has the rights and obligations, vis-à-vis the State and other economic operators, that one can analyse under the angle of regulation of the private sector, of the legal framework of business, of property rights and debt rights. Legal texts relative to commercial law on corporations and for-profit organisations are largely based on uniform acts of the Organization for the Harmonization of Business Law in Africa (OHADA) whose application is thus being evaluated.

Another aspect of private sector governance concerns the quality of dispute settlements between companies that guarantees the security of transactions, the decontamination of the environment and the attraction of foreign investment. This form of legal security presupposes the existence of impartial and credible legal institutions.

Socio-economic development

Socio-economic criteria, considered as performance indicators of socio-economic and human development, include the domains of food security, health, education, progress realised towards the Millennium Development Goals, inclusion of gender issues, the Human Development Index and the percentage of the budget used for social development.

Examining different African countries using these criteria in the four domains of governance allows one to reach a complete diagnostic of the socio-economic situation in Africa. This wide panorama reveals itself to be all the more useful in that it imposes the development of a harmonised system of inter-country comparison where the lack of reliable and up-to-date information is a persistent problem.

Management components and partners

Management components

The three management components of the APRM are the Forum, the Panel of Eminent Persons and the Secretariat.

The responsibility of general supervision of the organisation and processes of the APRM has been granted to the Committee of Heads of State and Government of the member states of the AU (called the Forum) who voluntarily acceded to the APRM. Among other issues, the APRM

Forum is charged with:

– Naming the Panel of eminent personalities of the APRM, examining the country evaluation reports, making appropriate recommendations to the countries that are the object of evaluation and conducting a constructive exercise of dialog and persuasion of peers;

– Assuring that the APRM process is fully funded;

– Convincing development partners to provide technical and financial assistance necessary for the establishment of work programmes for countries having been the object of an evaluation.

– To discuss the reports presented by the Panel and to follow the implementation of action plans with annual reports.

The Panel of Eminent Persons, named by the Heads of State, is charged with the supervision of the conduct of the APRM processes and to guarantee the integrity of the APRM. More specifically, the Panel directs the Secretariat and the field missions and writes the evaluation report. It also controls the establishment of the action plan.

The Secretariat provides the coordination services and technical and administrative support for the establishment of the APRM.

APRM partners

Three categories of partner institutions were admitted in order to support the APRM: strategic partners[2] and regional and international resource institutions.

Concerning the budget, African countries finance the majority of the mechanism and certain development partners also contribute. In 2006, the central budget of the APRM was self-financed by the participating countries to the level of 62%, the rest being financed by partners. From the start, the 35th session of the conference of ministers of finance, planning and development held in 2003, took cognisance of the fact that the mechanism would be established "with resources coming principally from Africa". The contributions of the partners are nonetheless welcome as long as, in their terms, they respect African ownership of the APRM, its principles and processes.

---

2. The following institutions were designated strategic partners of the APRM: Agencies of the African Union, The African Development Bank; the United Nations Economic Commission for Africa (UNECA); and the Africa Bureau of the United Nations Development Programme (UNDP)

The processes

The APRM process includes five successive phases that are defined in the Base Document. They are briefly described below.

Phase One is a preparatory phase, as much at the Secretariat level of the APRM as at the national level. Under the direction of the Panel of the APRM, the Secretariat submits a questionnaire to the country to be evaluated that covers the four domains of interest to the APRM. The country then leads an exercise in self-assessment based on the questionnaire and, if necessary, with the help of the Secretariat of the APRM and/or partner institutions of the APRM. Once the self-assessment is completed, the country prepares a preliminary programme of action based on existing policies, programmes and projects, with the aim of responding to the identified issues, challenges and problems of governance. The Country Self-Assessment Report and the preliminary Programme of Action are next submitted to the APRM Secretariat. Over the course of the same period, the APRM Secretariat develops a contextual document about the country. This document is based on documentary research and the collection of pertinent and up-to-date information about the state of governance and development in the country in the four domains of the evaluation.

Phase Two includes the evaluation visit to the country. Under the supervision of the APRM Panel, the Country Review Team visits the country in question. Its priority is to undertake, beyond the country self-assessment report, as many consultations as possible with the government, officials, political parties, parliamentarians and representatives of civil society organisations, including the media, university professors, unions, businessmen and professional organisms. Its principal objectives are the following:

– To find out about the perspectives of different stakeholders in terms of governance in the country;

– To clarify the challenges identified in the documents relating to the questions that are not taken into account in the preliminary action plan; and

– To establish a consensus on the way in which these can be approached.

It is important to note that the country plays a role of facilitator during the visit to assure that the Country Review Team can successfully complete its evaluation. The Review Visit has access to all sources of information and to stakeholders as stipulated in the Memorandum of Understanding on the Technical Evaluation and Review Visit in the country signed between the country and the APRM.

During Phase Three, the report of the Review Visit is developed, based on the Country Self-Assessment Report, the contextual documents and the questions prepared by the Secretariat of the APRM, as well as the information taken from official and unofficial sources during the broad consultations with stakeholders during the evaluation mission.

The draft country review report:

– Examine the applicable engagements relative to political, economic and socio-economic development taken in the Preliminary Programme of Action;

– Identifies the remaining weaknesses; and

– Recommend the insertion of supplementary actions in the final Programme of Action.

The Panel, officially the author, first of all, examines the draft country review report. It must clearly explain the actions to undertake in case important issues are identified. The draft report is first debated with the Government with the goal of verifying the accuracy of the information contained therein.

Phase Four begins when the final report of the Country Review Visit and the final Programme of Action of the country are sent to the Secretariat of the APRM and to the Panel of the APRM for consideration. The Panel then sends them to the APRM Forum of Heads of State and Government participating in the Mechanism to examine and formulate the actions judged necessary and enter into the framework of the Forum's mandate. If the country demonstrates a will to rectify weaknesses identified, it will be incumbent upon participating governments to provide all assistance that is in their power, and to exhort governments and donor institutions to assist the country.

Phase Five is the final phase of the APRM process. Six months after the Heads of State and Government of the participating countries examined the report, the report is officially and publicly examined by the principal regional and sub-regional structures. These structures include the Regional Economic Commission to which the country belongs, the Pan African Parliament, the African Commission on Human and People's Rights, the Council on Peace and Security and the Economic, Social and Cultural Council (ECOSOCC) of the African Union.

The schedule of the process can vary considerably according to the country, as a function of the particularities of each country. The duration planned for each peer review from the beginning of Phase One to the end of Phase Four is between six and nine months.

The reviewed State: responsibility and active cooperation

The country that is a candidate for review does not have a passive role. Accession implies an engagement of the country concerned to submit to periodic reviews, to facilitate them and to carry out the programme of action that results. The Agreement protocol of APRM[3] that the countries sign at the moment of accession clearly defines their responsibilities. This includes to:

– sign the agreement protocol relative to the technical reviews and the country review visit[4];

– contribute to the financing of the APRM[5];

– drive the process of self-assessment by using the APRM questionnaire;

– develop a national Programme of Action;[6] and

– guarantee the participation of all the actors in the process.[7]

It is incumbent upon the participating countries to be involved in the establishment of management structures at the national level. In this regard, several activities must be considered:

• The organisation of a national participatory and transparent process: each participating country must designate a focal point for the process who must have ministerial rank, or a person who reports directly to the Head of State or Government. One of the roles of this focal point is to assure that the principal actors participate in the self-assessment and in the development of the national Programme of Action. In addition, a national commission must be formed to include the representatives of all stakeholders. The size of this commission can vary from one country to another.

• The definition, with the collaboration of the stakeholders, of a roadmap on participation in the APRM, which must be broadly disseminated and which should provide information on national coordination structures, the steps of the APRM process, the roles and responsibilities of actors of government, non-governmental organisations, the private sector and international development partners.

• The establishment of a communication mechanism between the different levels of administration and the actors who are not part of the administration.

• The placing of annual activity reports with the Secretariat of the

---

3. NEPAD/HSGIC/03-2003/APRM/MOU, 09 March 2003.
4. Paragraph 23.
5. Paragraph 20.
6. Paragraph 21.
7. Paragraph 22.

APRM on the implementation of the action plan: the States are in effect engaged in a process of monitoring the reforms contained in the national Programme of Action.

• Finally, in a more global manner, one can consider the APRM as a factor of "responsibilisation" of the State. The mechanism constrains decision-making authorities to report not only to the national population, but also to the community of African peers and, more generally, to the international community. The originality of the APRM is indeed to mobilise political will of high-level government authorities but also the participation of all development stakeholders (unions, the media, associations and NGOs, opposition parties, private sector, etc.), all under the control of the public opinion. All of these conditions are indispensable to its effectiveness.

In conclusion, everything in the approach and process of internalisation show that the APRM is well adapted to African realities to help with the promotion of governance. It can all the better play the role of catalyst for governance as it presents itself not as an external censor but as a facilitator. Its role is to help each participating country to undertake its self-assessment on the basis of AU and NEPAD objectives in the "Democracy and Good Governance" domain, directives from the APRM questionnaire and international and African norms, standards and criteria. The process of self-assessment is an essential phase of citizen participation; it must be shared with all the social actors — given the fact that they are the ultimate beneficiaries of an improvement in the quality of governance. The interactive and inclusive nature of the APRM has already brought about or reinforced a culture of political dialog in the evaluated countries. This potential for improvement in the processes of democratic governance, thanks to the participation of actors in the elaboration of public policies, their implementation and their evaluation, must be recognised and encouraged. Today, after nine countries have been evaluated as of the end of June 2008, the APRM offers itself as an alternative, civilised social dialogue to construct or reinforce the institutional base and the democratic cultures that will facilitate the emergence of sustainable human development.

Acronyms

ACP	Africa Caribbean and Pacific (Group)
AFD	Agence Française de Développement (French Development Agency-FDA)
AfDB	African Development Bank
AFRISTAT	Economic and Statistical Observatory of sub-Saharan Committee
ANC	African National Congress
APAD	Association euro-africaine pour l'anthropologie du changement social et du développement
APRM	African Peer Review Mechanism
AsDB	Asian Development Bank
ASEAN	Association of Southeast Asian Nations
AU	African Union
BDP	Bureau for Development Policies
CADDEL	Conférence africaine de la décentralisation et du développement local (African Conference of Decentralization and Local Development-AMCOD)
CEAN	Centre d'étude d'Afrique noire (African Studies Centre)
CFSP	Common Foreign and Security Policy
CICID	Comité Interministériel de la Coopération Internationale et du Développement (inter ministerial Committee for International Cooperation and Development)
CIFAL	International Training Centre for Local Authorities and Actors
DAC	Development Assistance Committee
DDR	Disarmament, Demobilization, Reintegration

DFID	Department for International Development
DGTPE	Direction générale du trésor et de la politique économique (ministry of Finance, France)
DSRP	Document of Strategies to Reduce Poverty
EC	European Commission
ECA	Economic Assistance Committee
ECLAC	Economic Commission of Latin America and the Caribbean
ECOMOG	Economic Community of West African States Ceasefire monitoring Group
ECOWAS	Economic Community of West African states
EDF	European development Fund
EHESS	Ecole des Hautes études en sciences sociales
EITI	Extractive Industries Transparency initiative
ESCR	Economic, Social and Cultural Rights
EU	European Union
FAG	Forum Africain sur la Gouvernance
FAO	Food and Agriculture Organization of the United Nations
G8	Group of Eight
GEMDEV	Groupe pour l'étude de la mondialisation et du développement
ICC	International Criminal Court
ICISS	International Commission on Intervention and State Sovereignty
ICJ	International Court of Justice
ICSD	International Centre for Settlement of Investment Disputes
ICTJ	International Centre for Transitional Justice
IDHEAP	Institut des Hautes Etudes en Adminsitration Publique (Swiss Graduate School of Public Administration)
IEP	Institut d'études politiques
ILC	International Law Commission
ILO	International Labour Organization
IMF	International Monetary Fund
IPCC	Intergovernmental Panel on Climate Change
LAIPT	Legal Aspects of intellectual Property relating to trade
MDG	Millennium Development Goals

MDP	Municipal Development Partnership
NATO	North Atlantic Treaty Organization
NGO	Non-Governmental Organizations
OAU	Organisation of African Unity
ODA	Official Development Assistance
OECD	Organisation for Economic Cooperation Development
OHADA	Organisation pour l'Harmonisation en Afrique du Droit des Affaires
OIF	Organisation internationale de la Francophonie
ONU-Habitat	United Nations Agency For Human Settlements
OSCE	Organization for Security and Co-operation in Europe
PRSP	Poverty reduction Strategy Papers
SADC	Southern Africa Development Community
SSR	Security System Reform
SWAC	Sahel and West Africa Club
UCLG	United Cities and Local Governments
UCLGA	United Cities and Local Governments of Africa
UNCDF	United Nations Capital Development Fund
UNDP	United Nations Development Programme
UNESCO	United Nations Educational, Scientific and Cultural Organization
UNFPA	United Nations Population Fund
UNICEF	United Nations Children's Fund
UNITAID	International facility for the purchase of drugs against HIV/AIDS, Malaria and Tuberculosis
UNITAR	United Nations Institute for Training and Research
UNO	United Nations Organisation
WHO	World Health organisation
WTO	World Trade Organisation

Abstracts

I

CROSS PERSPECTIVES ON GOVERNANCE

Governance Reform and International Cooperation for Development? The Point of View of a Former Head of State
Henrique PEREIRA ROSA

The author explores the theme of "democratic governance as a (new) paradigm for development" by analysing the historic realities. We need to heed the lessons of the past, correct mistakes and improve instruments, to conceive – why not? – new models at internal level or in the framework of international cooperation; this is essential for the economic development and social progress of our so "fragile countries". This critical perspective establishes democratic governance as a strategic condition or variable to achieve development. However, the threats to the efficiency of democratic governance for development are a major concern. Indeed, political pressure of a populist and ethnic nature – which claims to incarnate democracy as it betrays –, the plague of corruption – that eats away at our public institutions – and the poverty spiral – that has not yet been inverted – constitute real threats for a truly democratic governance. We know that such governance cannot be achieved through the mere ritual of regularly organised democratic elections. It is necessary to establish a democratic order that empowers the practice of active citizenship, enabling an integrated, participative, development-oriented democracy, where all individuals share the conviction that they are, and will continue to be, the fundamental components of a whole.

Governance, a Global Question that Calls for Specific Responses in Africa
Ousmane SY

In recent years, "good governance" has become a fashionable theme that all development agencies try to include in their agendas or cooperation programmes with developing countries, especially Africa. It is frequently limited to a list of formulae to respect if the countries wish to secure the favours of the "international community". But, to be legitimate, the governance mode should refer to the assets and expectations of the society or nation concerned. Democratic governance – which cannot be democratic unless it is legitimate – is built on the principles and values that every society should come together according to its specific cultural references. Quality of governance reflects the manner in which certain universal principles, common to all humanity, are respected. However, such principles cannot be implemented according to one standard model. The questions raised by democratic governance in relation to the respect of these principles are undoubtedly common to all societies on our planet, but the nature of the response must remain specific to each society and draw on its references, values, etc. It is evidenced by the great challenge faced today by African States: to achieve legitimate governance, they must establish a true correspondence between societies, institutions and values that give true meaning to public administration. According to the author, the decentralisation of public administration is one step in that direction.

Governance: The Asian Counterexample?
Pierre CALAME

What is the link between governance and development? For the past twenty years, Global development has been driven by Asian development – and more precisely, Chinese development. If a link exists between governance and development, that is where we must look. The article examines such questions within four sections: (1) "Did you said counterexample?", where the author rejects the pre-conceived notions laid down by the international institutions; (2) "The ingredients of Chinese development", where the factors that led to China's unprecedented development in thirty years are outlined; (3) "Chinese development and the theory of governance", where the author confronts Chinese governance with the general principles of governance; (4) "Will the economic efficiency of Chinese governance foster sustainable human development?", where it is demonstrated that China, like the West, must prepare for a governance revolution which holds, for Europe and China, the prospect of a particularly rich cooperation.

Governance for Equality in Latin America
Jaime ROJAS ELGUETA

Economic growth in Latin America goes hand in hand with fierce inequality. On account of today's exceptional political context, governance is at the heart of political action in the region. Social cohesion is a key governance element to fight inequality. Various experiments in this area reveal that governance and social cohesion, far from being univocal concepts, are empirical notions. A new strategic alliance between Europe and Latin America is possible in the future. Certain aspects such as identity and affinities favour such an alliance, common values make it possible, like the importance granted to small and medium-sized firms to promote sustainable and fair development. An essential factor of fair development rests with the excellence of the product or the service, which combines respect for the environment and working conditions with continuous innovation.

Global Governance: The Illusory Quest for the Leviathan?
Jean-Michel SEVERINO and Olivier RAY

At the dawn of the 21ˢᵗ century, the new challenges faced by the community of nations urge on us the elaboration of a world policy based on solidarity and regulations. Combining these two elements, Public Development Aid reflects our longing for improved governance at global level. Its deficiencies and inconsistencies illustrate by contrast the structural difficulties that undermine collective action at international level. Where do they originate? To answer this question, the paper explores the deep divergence, at global level, over the notion of "Common Good" and the collective processes that would help define it. Such divergence is unlikely to fade in the near future. Only by realistically recognising these deep, but legitimate differences, and by accepting that the field of international collective action is complex can we hope to figure the range of possibilities. For their realisation the battle for more powerful and effective global governance deserves to be waged.

II
POWERS, INSTITUTIONS, LEGITIMACY:
AT THE HEART OF DEMOCRATIC GOVERNANCE

Legitimacies, Actors and Territories:
Rooting Governance in the Diversity of Cultures
Michel SAUQUET and Martin VIELAJUS
The Institute for Research and Debate on Governance

Reaching beyond the concept of governance as an institutional mechanism drafted upon western models of democracy, this paper draws attention to a notion of "governance" that identifies a set of processes enabling
the implementation of economic, social and political regulations adapted
to the realities of societies. International cooperation actions need to
move beyond the overly normative approach of "good governance" to
take into account, in their strategic decisions, three key questions running
through all different societies: the legitimacy and "rootedness" of the
body of power, the role of non-state actors, the local level's role and how
it articulates with the other levels of governance.

Legitimacy and Legality: Words and Realities
Sophia MAPPA

The historical, comparative and philosophical analysis of legitimacy
and legality issues helps clarify the specificity of such notions viewed
as theoretical construction and through the exercise of political power
in Europe since the 17th century. Traditional development policies were
until now shaped by the belief that international cooperation could only
be founded on western values. Are democratic governance policies an
attempt to move beyond the stalemate of such convictions, against the
background of a shifting democratic paradigm in Europe, and more
widely in the West?

State, Power and Society in the Governance of Projected Societies
Dominique DARBON

Governance or state-building in fragile societies and states, particularly in "projected societies", implies re-visiting the classical debates
about the production process of institutions. Theoretical analyses, like
empirical studies, reveal that States' capacities, and reliability are directly

affected by the level of "embeddedness" established between these forms of power organisation and the societies over which they assert their control. Opposing State and society within fragile contexts is doomed to failure. In contrast, it is the organisation of autonomous and "embedded" relations between the two social poles that provides solid foundations for a stable, and accepted, power. This means capitalising on the social practices to which state injunctions give rise and redefining them, by trial and error ("muddling through approach") according to local appropriations, whilst maintaining, in the long term, the great principles and objectives that establish and structure social initiatives.

State-building or Refounding the State? Theoretical and Political Issues
Michèle LECLERC-OLIVE

Ever since the end of the Cold War, and especially after the "9/11 attacks", rebuilding the weak states has become a priority for the international community. The "state-building" and "nation-building" frames of reference supporting these institutional engineering operations advocate a political system modeled on a purely instrumental idea of democracy. The intervening authorities, generally supported by military forces, take the risk of delegitimizing the country's authorities by substituting themselves in executive legislative, legal, and even administrative missions in the country. Conversely, the "Cultural Refounding" frame of reference recommends relying on indigenous modes of organisation to rebuild the weaker states and risks ethnic or religious fragmentation and the "naturalisation" of inequalities and exclusions operating at local level. Another path, aiming to re-establish the State's legitimacy on a truly political basis, can draw on institutional reforms (decentralisation, for instance) that preserve or promote the experience of plurality when managing the affairs of the nation.

A Sustainable Response to Crises: The role of Democratic Governance Lessons Learnt from the West-African Context
Massaër DIALLO

This paper emphasizes the value of contextualising approach and response, the fundamental aspect of prevention and the major role of democratic governance in the emergence of sustainable solutions to crises. It reviews the foundations, issues, forms and modes of response to current crises at international level, in a context of pre-eminent multilateralism in

528 DEMOCRATIC GOVERNANCE

terms of intervention. Drawing on the West-African example, the author emphasizes existing correlations between history, sociology, states' fragility and conflicts, and establishes the fundamental role of prevention as a response to crisis. With this in mind, he examines the dedicated mechanisms and strategies of the Economic Community Of West African States (ECOWAS).

III
RULE OF LAW, DEMOCRACY AND HUMAN RIGHTS:
THE CORNERSTONES OF DEMOCRATIC GOVERNANCE

Demystifying Governance and Improving its Democratic Content
Adebayo OLUKOSHI

For the past twenty years, governance has been central to debates about the problems and prospects of economic development and political reforms in southern countries in general, and Africa in particular. While such analyses have clarified certain aspects, they have also spread all sorts of ideas and myths that require qualification. A more global approach is necessary to reconfigure the concept of governance itself and rethink the prevailing governance-related practices that have multiplied in the last two decades. The author pleads for the abandonment of the notion of governance as it is so frequently used – the a-historical, all-purpose and unidimensional view – and draws attention to a more dialectic approach, regarding governance in terms of contradictory proposals and constant reconstruction. The paper defends the notion that while the ideal form of governance is democratic in definition and operation, governance and democracy should not be confused. A national territory's capacity to be governed by legitimate means is a prerequisite to the implementation and sustainability of democratic governance. Understanding that governance is intrinsically about power helps us put into perspective the solutions of a technocratic nature that have flourished over the years. This is particularly important on account of the inherent risks attached to technocratic deficits; they may prove, in the long-term, as counter-productive as they are subversive, for democracy and legitimacy.

Are Human Rights Soluble in Governance?
Ibrahim SALAMA

The issue of incorporating Human rights in governance is fundamentally linked to the principles of indivisibility and universality of Human rights. Indivisibility of Human rights implies, among other things, that the right to development be met and the Additional Protocol to the International Covenant on Economic, Social and Cultural Rights be elaborated. As for the universality of Human rights, it demands that we demystify the concept of cultural particularities, stimulate its positive potential and distinguish it from relativism. The periodical universal review of the Human rights situation in all countries is a promising institutional novelty with regards to the integration of Human rights in governance at national and international levels.

Governance and the Rule of Law
Mireille DELMAS-MARTY

The interdependencies produced by globalisation call for both national and international solutions to the dilemma created by the necessity of associating global governance and rule of law. Such an association proves even more complex when the rule of law concept, that tends to impose itself at national level, may be double-edged and is blocked, in the absence of a State or a global government, by some confusion of powers at international level. On the basis of this observation, the link between the two concepts should be perceived in terms of a "hybridisation" of governance and rule of law methods. The author suggests combining the art – borrowed from governance – of "co/ordinating" relations between the actors, both by allocating competences between instituted actors and organising civil society's participation, and "sub/ordinating" powers to principles of law, inspired by national rule of law, thus linking the principles of coherence and accountability.

Parliaments and Budgetary Democracy in Latin America
Carlos SANTISO

To what extent do parliaments contribute to establishing budgetary democracy and sound financial governance? Can they strengthen the political legitimacy of budget management while preserving fiscal discipline? This paper evaluates the conditions and constraints presiding over the involvement of parliaments in the budgetary process, in Latin American presidential regimes with centralised budgetary systems. It emphasizes the importance, for good financial governance, of preserving the often delicate and precarious balance between political legitimacy and fiscal discipline when managing public finances. Effective budgetary governance consists in combining the advantages of a strong executive power, capable of enforcing fiscal discipline, and the existence of institutional checks and balances guaranteeing democratic legitimacy, sanctioning the balance of powers between governmental prerogatives and parliamentary control.

The Democratic Control of Natural Resources Management. The Example of the Extractive Industries Transparency Initiative
Jean-Pierre VIDON, Olivier LOUBIÈRE, Michel ROY

The Extractive Industries Transparency Initiative (EITI) gathers countries, companies and civil society organisations aiming to strengthen governance by improving transparency and accountability in the extractive sector. The States are encouraged to publish the revenue gained through exploitation of natural resources and the Companies to disclose what they pay to the States. The multinationals affiliated to the EITI count on the international community's support to encourage emerging powers and their companies to participate in the initiative, thus helping to reduce the distortions of competition. EITI affiliates call for greater attention to the mining sector and better management of the phase preceding extraction. "Publish What you Pay" is a civil society coalition, created in 2002; its target is to fight the opacity of payments made by extracting companies to governments for the extraction of natural resources. Nine questions outline how its involvement in EITI, will contribute to making it as effective as possible.

IV
GOVERNANCE AND TERRITORIES

Towards a System of Governance Serving the Poorest: The Role of Local Governance
Carlos LOPES

The active trends in our societies – globalisation of networks and knowledge, on the one hand, localisation of interests and democratic forms of expression on the other – flag up local governance as the only governmental system capable of regulating these seemingly contradictory mutations. Such transformations, centered on complex territories vulnerable to change where intensified urban growth may be source of inequalities, trigger an enormous need of mostly new capacities. Several case studies highlight the fact that reducing inequality requires strengthening local capacities in favour of participative and multi-partners development initiatives, based on South-South knowledge transfer.

The Role of Decentralisation in the Governance of African States
Jean-Pierre ELONG MBASSI

Pressed by their own populations or the international community, African countries face an urgent obligation to improve their governance. One method for achieving this appears to be the decentralisation of public affairs management, whereby the State concedes additional powers to local authorities and non-state actors. Implementing decentralisation policies has barely begun in most African countries. The core issues to which it gives rise require serious debate if we want decentralisation to advance the refounding of democratic and legitimate rule-of-law states in Africa.

The Territorial Dimension of Decentralisation
Mahaman TIDJANI ALOU

Drawing from the broad literature regarding decentralisation, this article analyses its territorial aspect. Local authorities established thanks to decentralisation policies are well rooted in territories where they have geographical boundaries that provide them, de facto, with natural, human resources and infrastructures. Within this perspective, the paper explores two axes: decentralisation as the vector of territorial policy – conceding that the role of the State is crucial in terms of initiating and devising decentralisation policies – and decentralisation as a driver for territorial construction because decentralisation must take on concrete forms.

Urban Governance and International Cooperation
Charles GOLDBLUM and Annik OSMONT

This paper aims to divorce the notion of urban governance from its inception, under the aegis of the World Bank. It sets the stakes of the democratisation of urban governance against project drives and institutional reform. Central to this reflection is the confrontation of urban development with urban management for cities in developing countries coping with the multiplication of international cooperation actors. What are the impacts of official development assistance programs in the field of urban development: is the search for technical and economic efficiency, in terms of urban adjustment to global economic constraints, compatible with the principles of local participative democracy? The effects of international cooperation on the government of cities in developing countries may go some way towards answering this question.

Local Economic Governance in Africa
François YATTA

Three elements of the African context determine local economic governance. Urbanisation and globalisation, that tests – in more structural terms – the relationship between territory and economic growth. Decentralisation, that provides an adequate institutional framework for local economic development. Current policy allegedly promotes national growth by encouraging the self-development capacities of infra-national areas according to their comparative assets. With globalisation, we see competition flourishing between regions, metropolitan areas and local authorities, not only countries. The abundant constraints restricting local economic governance raise many crucial questions with regards to national governance. Finally, while decentralised management sometimes alarms national politicians who worry that the multiplication of decision centres will ultimately harm the efficiency of national economic measures local authorities consider national economic policies "restrictive" for the development of local initiatives. Local economic governance and national economic governance must mutually strengthen each other to achieve the Millennium Development Goals.

Local Solidary Governance Implementation in Porto Alegre, Brazil: Strategies for Social Inclusion Promotion
José Alberto FOGAÇA DE MEDEIROS

This paper describes the creation and implementation of the Local Solidarity Governance Programme (PGSL) in Porto Alegre, Brazil. It explains the programme's origin, concepts and methodology. The programme's context – current status and achieved results – is examined along with its prospects. In parallel, the author reflects upon the possibilities of implementing the Porto Alegre model in other cities.

Urban Mediation: A Practice at the Service of Local Democracy
Pierre LAYE

In the context of local governments rising to power through the decentralisation process, partnerships between the State, locally elected officials and civil society are on the increase. Mediation is gradually gaining recognition within this new democratic space. A social and technical function, with high political sensitivity, mediation has yet to possess its own guidelines, whether drafted externally, by a professional structure, or internally, by a local administration. Mediation appears fundamental to the process of building exchange and debate centres filling the relationship gap between the various actors and launching participative approaches. Based on observation and social diagnosis, mediation integrates facilitation, methodological watch and training to achieve concrete proposals. It represents a sustainable approach with a representation system involving the local institutions – city hall, the State's decentralized services, Civil Society representatives. And mediation has a cost that must be taken into account like that of other actors' expertise.

V
DEVELOPMENT POLICIES AND DEMOCRATIC GOVERNANCE

Governance at a Crossroads
Jean BOSSUYT

The theme of governance in the international discourse has become glaringly important and support for governance (in its broadest sense) currently constitutes a major political priority for the European Union. Increasing funds are invested in a wide array of political and economic governance areas. However, promoting governance "from the outside" has proved exceptionally difficult. Despite the elaboration of an arsenal of policies, guidelines and instruments, partners in development struggle to provide pertinent, effective and sustainable support. Beyond the inherent complexity related to promoting governance in diverse, and often hostile, contexts, the donors' methods are also called into question. Drawing on lessons from the past decade, this paper pleads for a change of paradigm in governance-related thinking and support models. This implies, among other elements, deeply reassessing the work culture of development partners.

Democratic Governance Central to the External Action of the European Union: From Conditionality to Dialogue between Partners
Philippe DARMUZEY

From the painful land reform in Zimbabwe to the reppression of grass-roots demonstrations in Myanmar and the difficult post-electoral transition of power in Kenya, governance has become a controversial topic in both developed and developing countries. Democratic governance is sometimes seen as the be-all and end-all for development, so that governance and development are often indissolubly linked, without asserting its capacity to solve all the problems. The European Union launched the debate approximately ten years ago by conducting in-depth research about the position of governance in its development policy. In 2006, based on various conclusions and analyses, a pragmatic though unoriginal approach to democratic governance was adopted, better suited to the challenges faced by developing countries. This paper covers the main lines of the approach and observes how democratic governance, one of the pillars of the Joint EU-Africa Strategy, is addressed in the Action Plan 2008-2010 set out at the Lisbon Summit of December 2007.

Democratic Governance for Human Development
Bureau For Development Policy, United Nations Development Programme (UNDP)

UNDP capacity-building support is firmly rooted in the belief that nations, aiming to promote the human development of all their inhabitants, must implement governance systems that foster inclusive participation and fulfill the notion of accountability. The participation of citizens in the decisions making process, policies and institutions concerning their daily environment is not only a fundamental human right it is also inherent to human development and a development goal in itself. Indeed, democratic governance is a prerequisite for human development. On one hand, it must enable inclusive participation; on the other, it implies the existence of reactive, accountable States, capable of meeting their citizens' needs efficiently, of supporting social progress and of guaranteeing sustainable livelihoods. The UNDP advocates recognition of this democratic governance perspective to achieve the Millennium Development Goals. This paper examines the democratic governance approach approved by the UNDP and its priorities of action in this area.

Strengthening Governance and Anticorruption for Poverty Reduction: The World Bank Group's Strategic Approach

Anupama DOKENIYA, Colum GARRITY and Sanjay PRADHAN

Anupama Dokeniya, Colum Garrity and Sanjay Pradhan show how "good governance" helps poverty reduction and aid effectiveness. The improvement of governance, especially through the fight against corruption, has been over the past 10 years a major strategic axe for the World Bank. In 2007, the new governance and anticorruption strategy stressed the institutions' positive impact on long-term growth and poverty reduction. It focuses on adjusting the scope, the timeframe and the pace of reforms to the situation of each country according to the level of their institutional development. No "one size fits all" formula has been found to improve governance: national programmes are designed according to the existing political background and the long-term historical processes which prescribe the modalities and the limits of institutional reform. In order to improve governance, advance genuine development and an efficient service provision, the "demand side" of governance must be strengthened and multi-actor partnerships and networks developed which are based on mutual responsibility and a transparent monitoring.

The State in Development Policies: The Challenge of the Democratic Governance Approach

Séverine BELLINA and Hervé MAGRO

From the managerial approach, and its purely technical implementation, to a holistic approach heedful of political aspects, governance is at the heart of debates about the efficiency of development aid. From "good governance" to "democratic governance", it is the role of the State that is reasserted. However, as this paper demonstrates by analysing the State in Africa, such rehabilitation can follow the normative logic evolved from the "good governance" toolbox and/or conditionality, or a dynamic approach, reflecting on the State's legitimacy and institutionalisation process. Drawing attention to this second option, the authors show how the democratic governance approach offers a different diagnosis of the State in Africa, thus opening ways to establish new effective cooperation policies for sustainable human development.

Governance in Turmoil: The Political Economy of an Endogenous Process
Nicolas MEISEL and Jacques OULD AOUDIA

The present period, witnessing the end of Western hegemony over the rest of the world, is ushering a complete overhaul of the planet's North-South relations. The reliability of rich countries' development precepts has been shaken: their analyses account for neither the movements which, before our eyes, are creating powerful new actors, nor for the persistence of poverty in most countries of the South. Liberalization, "good governance" and democracy, which characterize the institutions of developed countries, remain at the core of aid policies directed at developing countries. From an analysis of the institutional transition processes and the tools of political economy, it can nonetheless be shown that development processes, particularly governance reforms, pertain to mechanisms that are inherently political and endogenous to societies. That does not exclude borrowing from the outside when this is undertaken by the societies themselves. All in all, these considerations question the very foundations of aid itself.

Capacity-building, Governance and Development: The Concepts, their Links and their Limits
Soumana SAKO and Floribert NGARUKO

The concept of governance has taken more and more importance since the 1990s. This paper shows that the concept's success is mainly due to the convergence of three elements. Firstly, the public policy decision making process which led to a participative approach compatible with key principles of good governance. Secondly, the capacity-building approach, which has progressively adopted institutional aspects, considered central to the governance issue. And thirdly, the development concept, which, by becoming sustainable development, has integrated aspects connecting it to governance. However, noting the limitations in the implementation of the governance concept, this paper makes a case for second-generation governance reforms that minimize the failings of reforms which have prevailed to date.

Water: A Responsible Governance for a Dream Accessible to All
Pierre VICTORIA

Apparently the world is about to reach the Millennium Goal on Drinking Water, focal point of the United Nations' Year 2000 commitments. In reality, this is a statistical smokescreen. Asia's gigantic progress hides deep disparities with regards to sustainable access to water. Among other elements, sanitation – intrinsically linked to water – has been forgotten by the Millennium Development Goals. The dream of "water and sanitation for all" is still possible but to make it happen we must take on this global priority, including its financial aspects (public aid for development). On the other hand, financial input is not the core issue; the real emergency is that of governance. Successful developing countries are those that have established a national policy where the national and local actors and the private operators have clearly defined responsibilities. Solutions exist: reduce connection costs, strengthen maintenance, adjust techniques to the country involved, empower sustainable human development by giving formal rights to populations long denied rights. Private operators are no stranger to this gigantic human challenge; they can become essential allies where political will and trust between actors are realities.

VI
WHICH DEVELOPMENT COOPERATION TOOLS FOR DEMOCRATIC GOVERNANCE?

Which Toolkit for Democratic Governance?

Jean-Marc CHÂTAIGNER

The emergence of democratic governance calls for a reassessment of our vision of cooperation so that societies, themselves, rethink their own modalities of public action. By directly questioning our approach to partnership, we probe, in fine, the space granted by development institutions to partner countries. Yet while this forces us to examine the partners' expectations, it cannot suffice to determine the procedures to follow. This paper seeks to clarify the major stake attached to applying the notion of democratic governance to international cooperation instruments. While such instruments should incorporate the specificities of beneficiary countries, they also need to engage the active participation of the various development actors in that same country. A great deal of imagination is therefore necessary to devise the mechanisms associating local and international actors, and to ensure that the instruments are effective and "open". The challenge of "democratic governance" is as simple as it is awesome: how do we find official assistance management tools when governance is both an approach and a set of mechanisms, creating the conditions for their long-term "nationalization" process by the States and the populations to their own public action modalities? Such ambition calls for deep reflection from the donors regarding cooperation methods favouring the predictability of assistance over short-term investment on programmes, inclusive networking over conditional, closely monitored assistance, over investments demanding rapid and quantifiable return.

Reinventing Governance to Achieve the Millennium Development Goals in Africa: New Approaches and Tools
Gilbert HOUNGBO

Despite the significant economic and political progress made since the beginning of the decade, it has now become obvious that Africa, as a whole, is not on the right track to achieving the Millennium Development Goals (MDGs) in 2015. To achieve the long coveted MDGs, beyond robust macroeconomic growth, African countries must strengthen all measures compensating structural governance deficits: social services must be improved, democracy strengthened and, especially, the poor must have the possibility of exercising their citizenship and demanding account-ability. Some innovative initiatives are attempting to reinvent governance on the African continent. Let us mention, among others, the African Peer Review Mechanism (APRM) and the Africa Governance Forum (AGF). Such initiatives deserve encouragement. However, to maximise the expected results, they must stay deeply rooted in population dynamics and be part of the national political process. The paper presents the role of these new governance approaches towards democracy and achieving the MDGs. It describes the work conducted by the UNDP, in partnership with the countries involved and other development agencies, to readjust the support given to governance programmes in Africa. This approach focuses on ways to manage governance's structural gaps.

The Security Sector Reform in Fragile States: Beyond Capacity Building, the Example of Transitional Justice
Serge RUMIN

Emerging from conflicts that frequently developed with the collapse of authoritarian regimes, States are weakened by poorly controlled and unstructured security systems, often unable to deliver the personal secu-rity needed for stabilizing a complex and uncertain environment. Most international efforts to reform post-conflict security systems focus on building the human and physical capacity of these institutions. This response, of an almost systematic nature, is guided by a paradigmatic conception of the challenge; the institutions are seen as organs executing State functions, with no relation to their social base. Yet institutions grow from the social arena. Not only do they symbolise and serve values regulating social interactions and guaranteeing social cohesion within society (e.g. order, justice, security), but they also operate thanks to the resources stemming from that same society (money, individuals, information, etc.). Post-conflict societies' profoundly transformed system of values failed to maintain the social cohesion. A coherent security system reform shall integrate the social consequences of the conflict. When the classical justice system cannot serve its purpose, transitional justice seeks to undertake the management of litigation caused by massive human rights violation and aims to prevent future abuses, thus offering an example of holistic approach where the social dimension of the institutional challenge is part of the solution.

Governance Assessment
Charles OMAN and Christiane ARNDT

Many aid agencies use governance indicators as funding criteria and as a way of encouraging improved quality of governance in developing countries. However, assessing governance remains problematical. Aid agencies, like other users, have a tendency to over-estimate the intrinsic validity of the most commonly used indicators to compare results between countries and over time. Instead of focusing on indicator results, these agencies should consider the confidence margins of such indicators. Most importantly, they should use more specific indicators, based on varied, transparent and scientifically-proven information sources.

The African Peer Review Mechanism: The Promotion of Governance in Africa
Marie-Angélique SAVANÉ

Both in concept and process, the African Peer Review Mechanism – APRM is unique worldwide. As an evaluation tool designed by Africans for African people, it is open to every willing state of the African Union and firmly rooted in state sovereignty. This self-evaluation exercise aims to build a Plan of Action reached by consensus in order to foster a governance environment following the principles of the NEPAD Declaration: the mandate of the APRM is to ensure that the policies and practices of participating states conform to the agreed political, economic and corporate governance values, codes and standards contained in the Declaration on Democracy, Political, Economic and Corporate Governance[1]. It is an instrument voluntarily acceded to by member states of the African Union (AU) as a self-monitoring mechanism for African states. 29 states have now signed up for membership since 2003 (Togo was the last one), representing roughly 80% of the African continent population. During the last African Union summit, the APRM has been declared the operational tool of the African Charter on democracy, elections, and governance. It is indeed a major vehicle for African integration in governance matters, and more widely in politics.

---

1. APRM Base Document, AHG/235 (XXXVII), Annex II, Durban 8 July 2002, Paragraph 1.

Authors

Christiane **ARNDT** has worked with the Organisation for Economic Development and Cooperation until 2006. She wrote, with Charles Oman, a book entitled "Uses and Abuses of Governance indicators" published in 2006. She graduated from the Institut d'Etudes Politiques de Paris (Sciences Po Paris) and she also holds a Master in International Business Studies from the University of Maastricht. She currently completes her doctoral thesis in economics at the Maastrich Graduate School of Governance.

Séverine **BELLINA** holds a PhD in Public Administration, and is a specialist of governance issues, power institutionalisation and normative pluralism in Africa. She currently is Head of External Relations and Program Coordinator at the Institute for Research and Debate on Governance. From 2004 to 2008, she was in charge of democratic governance issues at the Directorate for Development Policy of the French Ministry of Foreign and European Affairs. She actively contributed to the drafting of Governance strategy for French development assistance. She was also an associate UNDP expert for the Bureau for Development Policy-Democratic Governance Group, worked for the regional office in Dakar and with the Oslo Governance Centre. Séverine Bellina has been consultant notably for the European Commission. She is a lecturer at Sciences Po Paris.

Jean **BOSSUYT** has worked for the European Centre for Development Policy Management (ECDPM) since 1990. He is currently Head of Strategy. Before, he was Programme Coordinator in the Actors of Partnership Programme. He is a specialist of cooperation between African, Caribbean and Pacific Stats (ACP) and European Union and his areas of interest are the political dimensions of EU-ACP cooperation (e.g. democratisation, governance), aid relations with conflict countries, private sector development, decentralised cooperation and relations with NGOs and the current reform of the EU external assistance. He has published widely on a variety of EU-ACP cooperation topics. Prior to joining ECDPM, he worked at the Third World Centre of the University of Ghent, at the UNHCR Brussels Delegation and as a civil servant in the Belgian Parliament.

Bureau for Development Policy – United Nations Development Program

The Democratic Governance Group consists of thirty political advisers, analysts, programs managers, and knowledge management professionals. They are dispatched between the New-York headquarters, the Oslo Governance Centre and seven UNDP regional centres and sub regional centres. The DGG depends on the Bureau for Development Policy and leads the UNDP most important community of practice on governance issues.

Through the promotion of democratic governance, the DGG plays a central role in creating an adequate environment to enable countries to achieve the Millennium Development Goals and fulfil the Millennium Declaration commitments. The main goal of this community of practice is to encourage institution building and the implementation of accountable democratic governance, which could be a response to the citizen expectations, specially the poor and marginalized ones. The electronic network includes about 1800 people, from all over the world and offers democratic governance program in more than one hundred and thirty countries where UNDP works.

Pierre CALAME graduated from the Ecole Polytechnique. He worked for twenty years for the French administration as a town and country development senior officer and served in different positions. Since then, he has devoted himself to the Charles Leopold Mayer Foundation for Human Progress (FPH). He has been at the head of the organisation since 1987. The foundation is dedicated to financing, through donations or loans, research and actions that contribute in a significant and innovative manner to human progress thanks to science and social development. In this context, Pierre Calame contributed to many debates, in particular to those related to governance issues. He is the founder of the China-Europe Forum (www.china-europa-forum.net), which is a new attempt to build a global dialogue between the Chinese society and the European one. He is also the author of several books: Les travailleurs étrangers en France (1969); Un modèle de développement urbain en Algérie (1971); Les déterminants sociaux et culturels des retards scolaires (1973); Projet de réforme foncière (1983); Le semi-échec des accords sectoriels entre la France et l'Algérie (1985) ; Le dialogue des entreprises et du territoire (1987) ; Mission possible (1993) ; Un territoire pour l'homme (1994) ; L'État au cœur

(1996) ; L'Évolution de la coopération européenne (1999) ; La démocratie en miettes (2003).

Jean-Marc CHÂTAIGNER graduated from the Institut d'Etudes politiques of Bordeaux and is an ENA alumnus, Diplomat, was between June 2007 and January 2009 the Head of the Secretary of State's office for French ministry of Foreign and European Affairs. Prior to that, he acted, from 2004, as Director of the department of piloting and strategic relations at the French Development Agency (AFD). From 1995 to 2001, as a member of the French Permanent Mission to the United Nations (UN) in New York, he was involved in development issues and followed several African conflicts resolution at the Security Council. Jean-Marc Châtaigner is author of several articles and books about UN reform and questions of security and development, including, The UN in Sierra Leone: the twists and turns of negotiation (Paris, Karthala, 2005). He co-edited the book Fragile states and societies: between conflicts, reconstruction and development (Paris, Karthala, 2007).

Dominique DARBON is professor of political science at the Institut d'Etudes Politiques (IEP) of the Université de Bordeaux and a researcher at the African Study Center of Bordeaux (CEAN). He is the director of the graduate school in political science of the Université de Bordeaux. His areas of studies are government and public administrations in Africa, reform process, and regulation process. His upcoming book is entitled La tyrannie des modèles: diffusion, mimétisme et dépolitisation de l'ingénierie institutionnelle en Afrique (Paris, Karthala-MSH-A, 2008).

Philippe DARMUZEY has been working for more than thirty years for the external relations/actions of the European construction. He is a specialist of international relations, policy development and relations between Europe and Africa. Philippe Darmuzey mainly worked for the Directorate-General for Development and Relations with African, Caribbean and Pacific States at the European Commission. He held the positions of economic advisor for five African delegations, then the position of head of Delegation in the Caribbean Islands, and finally head of geographic then political unit. He is currently the director of the "Unit -Panafrican issues and institutions, governance and migration". He therefore was the chief negotiator of the European Commission within the European Union troika when was developed the strategic partnership and the Africa Action Plan, decided by eighty-four head of States from both continents, in Lisbon, on 8-9 December 2007.

Mireille DELMAS-MARTY is professor at the Collège de France since 2002. She is in charge of the chair of Comparative Legal Studies and globalisation of Law. She was part, as an expert, to various works on the European criminal law harmonization, in particular by leading the Corpus Juris project. She has published about twenty reference books about criminal law, human rights and globalisation of Law, including: Le flou du droit (Paris, PUF, 2004); Les grands systèmes de politique criminelle (Paris, PUF, 1992); Pour un droit commun (Paris, Seuil, 1994); Vers un droit commun de l'humanité, (Paris, Textuel, 2005); Trois défis pour un droit mondial (Paris, Seuil, 1998) ; Les forces imaginantes du droit : (I) Le relatif et l'universel, (II) Le pluralisme ordonné, (III) La refondation des pouvoirs (Paris, Seuil, 2004-2007) ; La Chine et la démocratie (with P.E Will) (Paris, Fayard, 2007).

Massaër DIALLO is a political scientist (he graduated from Université Paris I Panthéon-Sorbonne) and is a professor of philosophy. He was a researcher at the Centre d'étude des civilisations in Dakar and at the Maison des Sciences de l'Homme in Paris. He then held a professorship at the Université Cheikh Anta Diop in Dakar. He was the Director of the Université des Mutants (Senegal) from 2001 to 2004 and of its Institute for political and strategic studies. He was also a consultant for the World Bank and contributed to the development of networks and think tanks in Western Africa, including WANSED (West African Network for Security and Democratic Governance), located in Abuja (Nigeria). He is also the coordinator of WANSED. Massaër Diallo is since 2004 Principal Administrator at OECD Head of Governance, Conflict Dynamics, Peace & Security unit at the Sahel and West Africa Club, which works in eighteen countries. He is co-writer of the book "Un regard noir" (Paris, Autrement, 1984) and contribute to other books about governance and democracy, the relationship between Africa and Europe, post-conflicts challenges and socio-cultural changes in Western Africa.

Anupama DOKENIYA is an expert in governance issues. She is a member of the Public Sector Governance Group at the World Bank and contributed to the implementation of the new strategy of the World Bank on Governance and fight against corruption.

She previously worked on media and right to information. Her work also focused on liberalization and telecommunication reform: she took part to numerous seminars and conferences.

Jean-Pierre ELONG MBASSI is an urban planner by training. From 1992 to January 2007, he was the coordinator of the Municipal Development Program, then the general secretary of this same organisation, under the new name of Municipal Development Partnership (MDP). Right from March 2005, he held the position of general secretary of United Cities and Local Governments of Africa (UGCLA). Prior to this, he successively held the following positions: from 1996 to 1998 he was Secretary-General of the World Associations of Cities and Local Authorities Coordination (WACLAC); from 1981 to 1991 he directed the first urban project in Cameroon (co financed by the World Bank); from 1973 to 1980, he worked with the Cooperation and Development Agency of Paris. Since March 2007 he has been working for the secretariat of the United Cities and Local Governments of Africa. Jean-Pierre Elong Mbassi is the co writer of several books and plays an important role within numerous associations and scientific communities.

José Alberto FOGAÇA DE MEDEIROS is the Mayor of the city of Porto Alegre and is also the vice-chairman for the southern area of the National Committee of Mayors (Frente Nacional de Prefeiros – FNP, Brazil). He also presides over the Municipal Association of the Metropolitan region of Porto Alegre (Associaçao dos Municipios da grande Porto Alegre – Grandpal). Prior to this, M. Fogaça de Medeiros was a Member of Parliament and Senator, representing Rio Grand do Sul; he has been a parlamentarian for more that twenty four years in Brazil.

Colum GARRITY joined the World Bank in 1998 as a consultant to the Mozambique and Zambia country team in the African Region. He has worked for the last five years in the Public Sector Group, where he assists the coordination of issues of governance and anticorruption, and co-manages the Bank's internal Advisory Services and Knowledge in Public Sector Governance ("AskGov").

Charles GOLDBLUM is a professor at the Institut Français d'Urbanisme (Université Paris 8) and former director of this institute. Vice-president of the scientific organization for the study of globalization and development (GIS GEMDEV – France) and member of its executive committee, he was the chairman of the scientific committee of the Urban Development Research Program (UDRP), an international research program initiated by the French Ministry of Foreign and European Affairs and implemented by GEMDEV. He and Annik Osmont, previously in charge with this program, are now leading a working group on urban governance issue in the framework of GEMDEV, also supported by the French Ministry of Foreign and European Affairs.

Gilbert HOUNGBO is a United Nations Assistant Secretary General, Assistant Administrator of the UNDP, and director of UNDP's Regional Bureau for Africa since December 2005. He covers forty-five African countries and heads the biggest PNUD regional programme, representing about a half of the all organization's ressources. Prior to his appointment as Chief of Staff, Mr. Houngbo served on UNDP's Strategic Management Team and as the organization's Director of Finance and Administration. Mr. Houngbo also has extensive private sector experience, having worked at Price Waterhouse Canada, where he specialized in results-focused management of governmental and parastatal entities, as well as medium- and large-scale private companies, in both North America and Africa. He holds a Maîtrise en Gestion d'Entreprises from the Université de Lomé (Togo), a B.A and DESS (Diplôme d'Etudes Supérieures Specialisées) in Accounting and Finance. He is a member of the Canadian Institute of Chartered Accountants.

Pierre LAYE is a regional senior technical director and served both in France and in African countries. He is currently program officer in charge of decentralization at the Direction of Development Policies (French Ministry of Foreign and European Affairs). He is the chief editor of the Villes en développement magazine. He is also a member at the high-level Group of Experts on Decentralization (AGRED) – UN-Habitat and the author of La coopération décentralisée des collectivités territoriales published in éditions Territorial, on September 2005.

Michèle LECLERC-OLIVE holds post graduate qualifications in mathematics and is a doctor in sociology, is a researcher for the Centre National de Recherche Scientifique (CNRS), France and member of the Centre d'étude des mouvements sociaux (Institut Marcel Mauss) at the Ecole des Hautes Etudes en Sciences Sociales (EHESS). Her works focus on local political practices and migrations. She published les villes: laboratories de démocraties? (2004), Urban Issues and Local Powers: Who can speak for the Community? (2005) and Affaires locales. De l'espace social communautaire à l'espace public politique (2006).

Carlos LOPES was appointed Executive Director of the United Nations Institute for Training and Research (UNITAR) in Geneva on 1st March 2007. In addition, the UN Secretary-General has appointed Carlos Lopes as Director a.i. of the United Nations System Staff College (UNSSC), since November 2007. Dr. Lopes was previously UN Assistant-Secretary-General and Political Director in the Executive Office of the UN Secretary-General, in New York. Carlos Lopes holds a PhD in history from the University of Paris 1 Panthéon-Sorbonne and several degrees in development studies from the Geneva Graduate Institute of International and Development Studies. Dr. Lopes has actively contributed to research on development issues. Specialized in development and strategic planning, he has authored or edited 20 books and taught at Universities and academic institutions in Lisbon, Coimbra, Zurich, Uppsala, Mexico, São Paulo and Rio de Janeiro. He is affiliated with a number of academic networks, and has helped establish various non-governmental organizations and centres for social research, in particular in Africa. In August 2008, Carlos Lopes was elected to the Lisbon Academy of Sciences, Portugal.

Olivier LOUBIÈRE, an alumnus of HEC School of Management and a graduate in economics he is in charge of ethics in a multinational firm. He is head of a multisector- ethics council based in New York, which includes around thirty multinationals, essentially American companies. He is member of the executive board for the Extractive Industries Transparency Initiative in the mining industries (EITI) as representative of mining companies.

Hervé MAGRO is a diplomat graduate from the Sorbonne. Before working for Groupama, where he is currently special assistant to the CEO, he worked between 2002 and 2007, at the General Direction for International Cooperation and Development of the Ministry of Foreign and European Affairs, as head of democratic governance unit. He coordinated the interministerial process of elaboration of the Governance strategy for French development assistance. Previously, he served in Ankara, in Washington and in the Permanent Mission of France at the United Nations Office in Geneva. Besides, he also co-edited the book États et sociétés fragiles. Entre conflit, reconstruction et développement, (Paris, Karthala, 2007).

Sophia MAPPA holds a PhD in history. She leads the Forum de Delphes, a think tank dealing with international cooperation issues. She is Professor (Université Paris 12) and researcher at the LARGOTEC (research center for public governance: territories and communication). She works on international relations, especially development cooperation policies. She currently leads an international project on governance policies, and her main research area is knowledge and power structure in Europe and in Africa. She lectures in numerous universities in Europe, Africa, and Latin America. She chairs the education, higher education and training committee of the French speaking, INGO conference and scientific advisor on HIV/AIDS for the Fondation de France.

Nicolas MEISEL worked for six years as a development economist at the OECD Development Centre before joining AFD in late
2005. His research topics include institutions and governance, the functioning of financial systems, macroeconomics and development strategies in Sub-Saharan Africa. He published in 2004 Governance Culture
and Development: A Different Perspective on Corporate Governance
(Development Centre Studies, OECD), a book of economic history,
which proposes an analysis based on relations between state governance
and corporate governance in the Twentieth Century in France. Basing his
work on Institutional Profile database, he published in 2007, with Jacques
Ould Aoudia, "Is 'Good Governance' a Good Development Strategy?",
Working Paper 58, Agence Française de Développement.

Floribert NGARUKO works for the African Capacity Building
Foundation (ACBF). He is economist, graduated from the University
of Burundi, the Catholic University of Louvain (Belgium) and the
University of Nice-Sophia-Antipolis (France). Before joining ACBF,
he worked as World Bank international expert (Washington, USA) and
taught economics at the Institut universitaire professionnel d'Antibes
(France) and at the University of Burundi. He is member of the research
centre on macroeconomics and international finance (CEMAFI, Nie,
France). He is the author of numerous publications on various topics such
as economics growth, governance, gender and conflict.

Adebayo OLUKOSHI is the current executive secretary of the
Council for the Development of Social Science Research in Africa
(CODESRIA). After graduating at the Ahmadu Bello University
(Nigeria), he postgraduated at the University of Leeds (United Kingdom).
He worked as a teacher, a head of research at the Nigerian Institute for
International Affairs in Lagos, a research program coordinator at the
Nordic Africa Institute in Uppsala (Sweden) and as a senior program
manager at the South Center in Geneva.

Charles OMAN is responsible for the strategy of the Development
Center of the OECD. He is also in charge of the programme on
Corporate Governance. He has previously led research on Globalisation
and Regionalisation, and on New Forms of Investment in Developing
Countries. Charles Oman holds a Ph.D. in Economics from the University
of California at Berkeley, has taught economics there and, for four years,
at the Graduate School of Administration in Lima, Peru, and has worked
for the Ford Foundation. He wrote, with Christine Arndt, Uses and Abuses
of Governance Indicators, edited in 2006 (OECD). He is also the author
of: Corporate governance: A Development Challenge; Policy competi-

tion for Foreign Direct Investment: A study of Competition among Governments to attract FDI; The Policy Challenges of Globalization and Regionalisation; The Postwar Evolution of Development Thinking.

Annik OSMONT is socio-anthropologist, a senior lecturer and a member of the executive committee of the scientific organization for the study of globalization and development (GIS GEMDEV – France). She led from 2001 to 2005 the Urban Development Research Program (UDRP), initiated by the French Ministry of Foreign and European Affairs and implemented by GEMDEV and the Institut des Sciences et des Techniques de l'Equipement et de l'Environnement pour le Développement (ISTED – France). She leads, together with Charles Goldblum, a working group supported by the French Ministry of Foreign and European Affairs on urban governance.

Jacques OULD AOUDIA is specialized in development economics, working at the Ministry of Economy (Treasury and Economic Policy Directorate General). He works on the articulation between institutions and development and on the development of institutional indicators (Institutional Profile database). He published, with Nicolas Meisel, "Governance culture and development" (DGTPE and AFD Working Paper). Moreover, he is a specialist in southern and eastern Mediterranean economies and has just edited Croissance et réformes dans les pays arabes méditerranéens (co-edited by Karthala and the French Development Agency, 2008). He is the president of a transnational NGO "Migrations and Development", created in 1986 by Moroccan migrants, which leads an integrated rural development program in the Moroccan Atlas through migrant financial transfers (http://www.migdev.org/). The ideas, he develops in this present book, are his entire responsibility and the institutions to which he is linked cannot be held responsible for them.

Henrique PEREIRA ROSA is a company manager in varied lines of business. He is a well known and active member of civil society. As such, he agreed in 1994 to be the executive director of the elections national committee for the first general and presidential election which took place in Guinea-Bissau. In 2003, after a military coup against President Koumba Yala, he became, after agreement between the military, the political parties and civil society, President of the Republic with the task of restoring democratic order in the country. He held the post for 2 years and left after holding parliamentary and presidential elections. In 1998, he set up and was the coordinator of a movement called CAPAZ – Civil Society Committee for Peace. He is an honorary member of the Human Rights League in Guinea-Bissau, a founding member of the Guinea-

Bissau Rotary Club, board member of Caritas in Guinea-Bissau, founding member of Forum Afrique and President of the board of the Alliance to refound governance in Africa.

Sanjay PRADHAN assumed the position of Director of the World Bank's Public Sector Group in September 2002. As Director of the Public Sector Group, he chairs the Public Sector Board and oversees network functions (including strategy, staffing and professional development, knowledge management, quality assurance, and partnerships) for staff across the Bank who work in core areas of public sector management, public finance, and governance. Among the themes covered by this Group are administrative and civil service reform, tax policy and administration, public expenditure analysis and management, decentralization, legal and judicial reform, institutional analysis and assessment, and governance and anti-corruption. Mr. Pradhan joined the Bank in 1986 as a Young Professional in the Industry Department. Since then he has held various positions in the Bank, the most recent being Sector Manager, Poverty Reduction and Public Sector, in the South Asia Region. Mr. Pradhan was a principal author of the World Development Report 1997, The State in a Changing World. Mr. Pradhan completed his PhD and Bachelor's degrees at Harvard University.

Olivier RAY has been program officer for the director general of AFD since January 2007. After studying international relations and public affairs at the London School of Economics, Sciences Po and Columbia, he worked at the UN Peacekeeping Department Operations and the Security Council report organization.

Jaime ROJAS ELGUETA is a consultant in international cooperation and organisations development. From 2001 to 2006, he was Secretary General for socio-economics affairs in the italo-latino-american institute (IILA) in Rome. He holds a PhD from the Ecole des Hautes Etudes en Sciences Sociales (EHESS) in Paris, he was a freelance consultant and director of several large companies both in Europe and Latin America, for the Italian Presidency of the Council and European commission. He also gave lessons and was involved in European masters, in the Institute for Management Development (IMD) in Lausanne (Switzerland) and in Luiss Guido Carli University, Rome (Italy). He is member of the core group of the Institute for Human and Organizational Development (IMO).

Michel ROY, economist and linguist, is the director of international advocacy for the Secours Catholique-Caritas France, one of the 162 organisations fighting against Poverty and Promoting Social Justice, which make up Caritas Internationalis Network. Coordinator of the French Platform "Publish what you pay" since 2003, he is a member of the board of the Extractive industries Transparency initiative, as a civil society activist.

Serge RUMIN is expert on system analysis and change management, including Security System Reform in post-conflict situations. He works with civil society, national institutions and international organizations. He worked on these issues for the European Union (on the Euro-Mediterranean MEDA Area, Albania, Tanzania) but also with numerous African governments, with many international and local NGOs (Rwanda, Burundi, Burkina Faso, Kenya Uganda, Zambia, etc.) and various agencies and missions with the United Nations (headquarters of the department of Peacekeeping operation In New York, UNDP, Afghanistan, Bosnia-Herzegovina, Haiti, Kosovo, Liberia, Democratic Republic of Congo, East Timor). He holds a master's degree in Sociology of Organisation (Université Paris-Dauphine), a master's degree in international law and political Science. He is currently professor at the Université Paul Cézanne (Aix-Marseille) and at the Ecole de Management Euromed-Marseille.

Soumana SAKO, former executive secretary of the African Capacity Building Foundation (ACBF), economist, holds a master's degree in public administration, a master's degree and PhD in Project management and planning from the university of Pittsburgh (USA). He has an academics experience in development management, community services and as consultant, both nationally and internationally. He was Prime Minister and Head of the transitional Government of Mali as well as Minister of Finance and Commerce. He was also senior economist for UNDP, professor at the University of Mali and visiting professor and lecturer at the University of California, Los Angeles (UCLA).

Ibrahim SALAMA has served as Ambassador of the Arab Republic of Egypt in Lisbon, from October 2003 to August 2007. He was chair of the United Nations working group on the Right to Development and member of the United Nations sub-commission for the promotion and the protection of Human Rights from 2004 to August 2007. He is currently head of treaties and Human Rights Council in the High Commission for Human Rights in Geneva.

Carlos SANTISO, doctor in comparative political economy and specialist of Latin America, he leads the governance division of African Development Bank since June 2007. He previously held numerous positions within the DFID- United Kingdom, Institute for Democracy and

Electoral Assistance (IDEA) and the French Prime minister's office. He was consultant and advisor in numerous international organisations and governmental agencies such as the World Bank, the European Commission and the United Nations and has worked in many countries (Argentine, Benin, Brazil, Burkina, Faso, Chile, Guatemala, Haiti, Mali, Mexico, Nicaragua, Peru, Tunisia).

Michel SAUQUET et Martin VIELAJUS are respectively director and deputy director of IRG (Institute for Research and Debate on Governance). Created by the Charles Leopold Mayer Foundation (FPH), the institute is a space for debate, data gathering and academic production with a website (www.institut-gouvernance.org) and an annual review, Chroniques de la gouvernance. IRG is based in Paris and is working worldwide in partnership with numerous North and South American, European and Asian universities as well as institutions such as the French Ministry of Foreign and European Affairs, the Swiss cooperation, the Ford Foundation and UNDP. Mr. Sauquet and Mr Vielajus are lecturers at Sciences po Paris. They are also authors of numerous articles and books; the latest one is L'intelligence de l'autre. Prendre en compte les différences culturelles dans un monde à gérer en commun (Paris, Editions Charles Leopold Mayer, 2007).

Marie-Angélique SAVANÉ is a sociologist. She was the first president of the panel of Eminent Personalities in the African Peer Review Mechanism She has worked with various United Nation agencies such as UNRISD, HCR and UNFPA in Africa, Geneva and New York, where she has served as Head of Research, Team Manager and Director for Africa. During this period, she participated in many international debates on issues such as: North-South relations, South-South cooperation, Development Challenges, Women, Population Problems, etc. She has also published articles and edited books. She was also involved in research networks like CODESRIA. Ms. Savané served as a Member of various independent commissions, such as the South Commission; the Global Governance Commission, and the UNESCO Commission on Education in the 21st century. Ms. Savané was the founder of the Association of African Women for Research and Development in 1977 and a Founding Member of the Forum of African Voluntary Organisations in 1986.

Jean-Michel SEVERINO is, since 2001, Chief Executive Officer of the Agence Française du Développement (AFD). After graduating from the Ecole Nationale d'Administration (ENA – France), He became Inspector of Finance. Jean Michel Séverino was previously director in charge of international development in the French Ministry of Cooperation. He worked at the World Bank as director for Central Europe, then as Vice president for Asia. He was a member of the senior expert group on UN system-wide coherence in development, humanitarian assistance and the environment issues, and contributed to the White paper Commission on the France's European and foreign policy. J-M Séverino was associate professor at the Centre d'Etudes et de Recherche sur le Developpement International (CERDI) from 2000 to 2005, where he taught theory and political economy on Global Public Goods. He publishes regularly in the French and international press, and on the blog: www.ideespourledeveloppement.org.

Mahaman TIDJANI ALOU, Professor in political science (admitted to the professoral body by the Université de Bordeaux IV), is currently professor at the Université of Niamey (Niger) and researched at the research centre on local development and dynamics (LASDEL), which he previously headed. His research topics focus mainly on the African State. He works in particular on State building and its evolution in Africa, on political elites and local authorities, before and since the decentralisation policy reform implementation. He is the author of several articles on these various issues and has also contributed to several books.

Ousmane SY, graduate in agroeconomics and development, holding a doctorate in economic and social development, from the University of Paris 1, was researcher in rural areas before working at the UNDP in Mali. He led the Mission for Decentralisation and Institutionnal Reform and conducted out the decentralisation process and state reform. In 2000, he joined the government as minister of Territorial Administration and Local Government, in charge of for the Malian 2002 presidential election. Ousmane Sy is one of the initiators of the "dialogue sur la gouvernance en Afrique », currently the Alliance to refound governance in Africa (Alliance pour refonder la gouvernance en Afrique) which involves fourteen West and central African countries. He chairs since 2007, the director's board of the Institut Africain de la Gouvernance. Ousmane Sy has also established in Mali a Centre for Political and Institutional Expertise in Africa (CEPIA, Centre d'expertises politiques et institutionnelles en Afrique).

Pierre VICTORIA is in charge of international relations, Veolia Water. He is managing director of the Cercle français de l'Eau. Governor of the World Water Forum, as a member of the political process committee of the 5th World Water Forum, hosted in Istanbul in March 2009 he is involved in the design and implementation of the international water policy agenda. Local and regional representative for twelve years, he was a member of the french parliament of Morbihan (FRANCE) from 1991 to 1993, replacing Jean-Yves Le Drian, appointed to the government. Special Rapporteur of Cooperation and Development Budget, Aid and development Fund member, he is the author of a bill on French cooperation policy reform.

Jean-Pierre VIDON, private lawyer, started his career in 1975 at the French ministry of Foreign and European Affairs. He worked mainly in Africa. He was, moreover, French ambassador to Fiji and six other states in the South pacific and has, since 2004, served as Ambassador dealing with the fight against organized crime. He is the French representative in the Extractive Industries Transparent Initiative (EITI) Board.

François Paul YATTA has a doctorate in urban and regional economy (Université Paris 12). Member of the research Centre – Observatoire de l'économie et des institutions locales (ŒIL, Université Paris 12) from 1993 to 1998, he participated in several research projects. Mr. Yatta has also worked as a consultant for the European Commission and the Sahel and West African Club (OCDE); he was a west and central Africa regional adviser in the Municipal Development Partnership in charge of local finance, local economic development and fiscal decentralisation. He is a member of the International Institute of Public Finance (IIPF) and of the association de science régionale de langue française (ASRDLF).